The Soap Opera Book

WHO'S WHO IN DAYTIME DRAMA

Edited by Nancy E. Rout, Ellen Buckley
and Barney M. Rout

THE SOAP OPERA BOOK
Who's Who in Daytime Drama

Copyright © 1992

TODD PUBLICATIONS
P.O. Box 301
West Nyack, NY 10994
(914) 358-6213

All Rights Reserved
No part of this book may be reproduced in any form
without permission in writing from the publisher

Library of Congress - National Serials Data Program
ISSN 1065-402X

ISBN 0-915344-23-8 (trade edition)
ISBN 0-915344-36-X (library edition)

front cover design by NDV Graphic Art

Contents

Introduction i

Biographies - Alphabetical 1

Network Addresses 305

Fan Clubs 305

Actors Index 307

Introduction

The Soap Opera Book: Who's Who in Daytime Drama, is your complete guide to the actors and actresses who light up your screen every afternoon - including some no longer seen on daytime. Go behind the scenes and read the personal side of the stars. Find out if they are married, divorced, do they have any children...a love life? Discover where your favorite personalities grew up and went to school. It might be the same place as you! Read about their other professional credits and what they did before, or since the soaps.

The Soap Opera Book also includes two indexes. The first lists fan clubs, studios and other places you can write to your favorite stars. The second lists each person in the book and every soap in which they have appeared...some have been in more than nine shows.

We have strived for accuracy, researching data from reputable publications, soap opera show publicists, the actors' agents, managers, public relations firms, and most importantly, the stars themselves. As with all publications, many things change from the day the book is sent to the printers to the day it reaches the reader. We tried to be as up-to-date as possible on marriages, births, career credits, and other details.

This book would not have been possible without the help of many people. We owe a great deal of thanks to the following: Rochelle Epsenhart of AFTRA, Doras Buckley, Adam Dworski, Ann Ferrell, Kimberly Joy Ferrin, Jill Hobart, Barry Klein, Nancy Liebowitz, Mark Lizotte, Peter Murray, Charles Riley, Karen Reynolds, Glen Roebuck, Rodi Rosensweig-Hall, Charles Sherman, Janet Storm, Kathy Straining, Frank Tobin, Richard Tomaiko, Jill Yager, and of course, all the stars of daytime - past and present.

We are sure you will enjoy the book. If there are people, or information you would like to see included in future editions, please write to us at Todd Publications, P.O. Box 301, West Nyack, NY 10994.

THE SOAP OPERA BOOK
WHO'S WHO IN DAYTIME DRAMA

MARLA ADAMS

Born: August 28 in Ocean City, New Jersey
Marital Status: divorced, two children, Trip and Pam
Height: 5'4" **Eyes:** blue **Hair:** blond
Education: New York Academy of Dramatic Arts
Interests: tennis, swimming

Daytime Dramas: "The Secret Storm," Belle Clemens, 1968-1974; **"Capitol,"** Maria Clegg, 1982; **"The Bold and the Beautiful,"** Beth Logan; **"The Young and the Restless,"** Dina Abbott Mergeron, 1983-1986, 1991-

A Broadway actress and daytime veteran, Marla Adams recently returned to "The Young and the Restless" after a five year absence. Born on August 28 in Ocean City, New Jersey, Marla was a fan of the theater from an early age, and after attending the New York Academy of Dramatic Arts, she began her impressive stage career. She made her Broadway debut in 1958, at the Lunt-Fontaine Theater, co-starring in "The Visit." She has also appeared in numerous off-Broadway and regional productions such as "The Mikado," "The Devil's A Stranger," "The Odd Couple," with Lee Merriwether, "Deathtrap," "Last of the Red Hot Lovers," with Don Knotts, "Inherit the Wind," with Ed Begley, "Roger the Sixth," with Dorothy Lamour, and "The Max Factor," with Caesar Romero. Ms. Adam's most recent venture on to the stage was in the musical comedy, "La Miz," presented at the Odessey Theatre in Los Angeles. On the big screen she has been seen in the 1961 classic "Splendor in the Grass," as well as co-starring in "Special Delivery" and "Gotcha." A daytime player for over twenty years, Marla made her debut in 1968 as Belle Clemens on "The Secret Storm." Following this show's cancellation in 1974, the actress relocated to Los Angeles, continuing her soap work on several shows, including "Capitol," "Generations," "Bold and the Beautiful," "General Hospital," and "The Young and the Restless." Her additional t.v. credits include "Barnaby Jones," "The Love Boat," "Happy Days," "Starsky and Hutch," "Hill Street Blues," "Hart to Hart," "Beauty and the Beast," "Who's the Boss," "Empty Nest," "The Golden Girls," "Matlock," and "Perfect Strangers." Marla also made ten guest appearances on "Marcus Welby, M.D.," and in 1991 played a recurring role on "Baywatch." A divorced mother of two grown children, Trip and Pam, Marla now lives in Santa Monica, California. Away from the set of "The Young and the Restless," she is active with the Los Angeles Children's Hospital, and relaxes by swimming and playing tennis.

WESLEY ADDY

Born: August 4 in Omaha, Nebraska
Marital Status: married to actress Celeste Holm
Height: 6'1" **Eyes:** blue **Hair:** white
Education: University of California in Los Angeles, B.A.
Interests: bee keeping

Daytime Dramas: "Edge of Night," Dr. Hugh Campbell, 1958-1959; **"Ryan's Hope,"** Bill Woodward, 1977-1978; **"Loving,"** Cabot Alden, 1983-1989

A popular daytime presence for over thirty five years, Wesley Addy has enjoyed tremendous success in the theater and on the big screen. A native of Omaha, Nebraska, Mr. Addy attended UCLA, where he majored in economics but dreamed of being an actor. Not one to waste time, the young economist/actor missed his own graduation in order to head East in search of theater work. His first stop was Martha's Vineyard, just off Cape Cod, where Addy performed proved considerably less gregarious to a young actor looking for a break. After a year of unemployment, Wesley landed his first role, a walk on part in "How Beautiful With Shoes," for which was rewarded the mighty sum of eight dollars per week. His next role, in Leslie Howard's "Hamlet," proved to be the big break he was waiting for, and Addy has since embarked on a career of theatrical triumphs, working along side of some of the legends of the modern stage. His credits include "Henry IV," "Twelfth Night," with Helen Hayes, "Romeo and Juliet," with Laurence Olivier and Janet Leigh, "Another Part of the Forest," "The Traitor," "Antigone," "King Lear," with Louis Calhern and "A Month in the Country," with his wife, Celeste Holm. This phenomenal run was interrupted for a five year stint in the armed forces during World War II, where Addy earned the rank of Major before being discharged. At home on screen as well as on the stage, Addy's film credits are equally impressive, with roles in "First Legion," with Charles Boyer, "Whatever Happened to Baby Jane," with Bette Davis and Joan Crawford," "Hush, Hush, Sweet Charlotte," with Olivia de Havilland, "Tora, Tora, Tora," "The Europeans," "Network," "The Verdict," with Paul Newman, and "The Bostonians." Mr. Addy has worked on several daytime dramas, including "Edge of Night," "Ryan's Hope," "Days of Our Lives," and most recently "Loving." He has also been seen on "The Fugitive," "The Defenders," "12 O'Clock High," "The FBI," and "Ironside." Wesley and his wife, Celeste Holm, presently divide their time between New York City and a farm in Morris County, New Jersey. The couple devotes much of their free time to bee keeping and making apple honey.

GRANT ALEKSANDER

Born: August 6 in Baltimore, Maryland
Marital Status: single
Height: 6'1"   **Eyes:** blue   **Hair:** blond
Education: Washington and Lee University, New York University
Interests: traveling, sports

Daytime Dramas: **"Guiding Light,"** Philip Spaulding, 1982-1984; **"Capital,"** 1986; **"Guiding Light,"** Philip Spaulding, 1986-1991

Born August 6 in Baltimore Maryland, one of three boys, Grant Aleksander grew up wanting to be a professional athlete. It wasn't until a high school drama teacher encouraged him to to try out for a school play did Grant think seriously about a career in acting. While at Washington and Lee University, Grant became very involved in the theater department, winning the title roles in the productions o f "The Owl and the Pussycat," "The Glass Menagerie," "The Crucible" and "Hamlet." Prior to moving to New York, Grant appeared on the Baltimore stage in "The Prime of Miss Jean Brodie" and "Cat on a Hot Tin Roof." Once in New York, he attended the prestigious Circle in the Square school as well as New York University. Grant's t.v. credits include, "The Fall Guy," "Hardcastle and McCormack" and "Who's the Boss?" He also appeared in the afternoon special, "A Very Delicate Matter," and the t.v. movie, "Dark Mansions." Before acting, he worked as a model. Although not a professional athlete, Grant is still a sports enthusiast.

MARILYN ALEX

MARILYN ALEX

Born: in Los Angeles, California
Marital Status: divorced, one daughter, Georgeanne,
one son, Danny
Height: 5'4" **Eyes:** brown **Hair:** blond
Education: Associate's Degree
Interests: travelling, reading, dancing

Daytime Dramas: "General Hospital," Mrs. Dawson;
"As the World Turns," Nurse Doris, 1990; **"The Young
and the Restless,"** Molly Carter, 1991-1992

Whoever said that a picture is worth a thousand words would probably be quite impressed with Marilyn Alex's performance on "The Young and the Restless," as Molly Carter, a stroke victim. Ms. Alex has managed to anchor an entire story line without saying a word. Due to her character's condition, this talented actress must emote using only a minor range of facial expressions and garbled speech, yet she has succeeded magnificently in this task. Known to daytime audiences for several small, but memorable roles, such as Mrs. Dawson on "General Hospital" and Nurse Doris on "As the World Turns," Marilyn is quickly becoming a daytime fixture. Born in Los Angeles, where her family ran an electrical appliance store, Marilyn actually made her daytime debut twenty years ago, with a small role on "Days of Our Lives." Shortly thereafter, the actress made her way to New York, where she has understudied for Broadway leads in such productions as "Deathtrap" and "Agnes of God." Taking over these roles, Ms. Alex accompanied the productions on national bus and truck tours. Most recently, she portrayed the title character in a New Jersey production of "Driving Miss Daisy." Marilyn, who is now divorced, has two children, Danny and Georganne, and one grandson, Nicholas. Danny is an American Airlines pilot, while Georganne works as a Santa Barbara based fashion designer, and is co-owner of the Alex and Noble Firm. Away from "The Young and the Restless," Marilyn is a PTA president, as well as being active with the United Crusade. In her spare time she enjoys reading, baking, drawing, travelling, and dancing.

Terry Alexander

TERRY ALEXANDER

Born: March 23 in Detroit, Michigan
Marital Status: divorced, one son, Christopher
Height: 6' **Eyes:** brown **Hair:** black
Education: Wayne State University, B.A. in theater
Interests: martial arts

Daytime Dramas: "Another World," Zach Richards,
1972-1974 **"One Life to Live,"** Troy Nichols, 1990-

Born and raised in Detroit, Michigan, Terry Alexander has enjoyed great success as an actor of both stage and screen. Initially, Alexander planned on becoming a dentist, but his focus shifted during his years at Wayne State University, where he graduated with a B.A. in theater. Alexander began his career in the sixties, working with a black theater group earning fifteen dollars per performance. He spent the next several years working in both theater and television, shuttling back and forth between New York and Los Angeles. Since those early years, Alexander has established an impressive list of stage credits, including roles on Broadway in "Streamer" and "No Place to be Somebody." Off-Broadway and regional production credits include "Julius Cesar," "The Jones Boys," "Some Sweet Day," and "Fences." Among the feature films in which Alexander has appeared: "All That Jazz," "Deathwish," "Flashpoint," and "Day of the Dead." Daytime audiences first came to know Alexander in 1972 when he joined the cast of "Another World," playing the part of Zach Richards. After playing this role for two years, Alexander was absent from daytime television until May of 1990, when he returned as Troy Nichols on "One Life to Live." Originally the role was supposed to last only four weeks, but the producers decided to expand the part and make Alexander a full time player. Away from daytime Alexander has guest starred on a wide array of prime time series, among them: "Hill Street Blues," Leg Work," "Fame," "Behind the Screen," "Hometown," and "Benson." He also co-starred in the mini-series "King" with Cicely Tyson. Alexander, who is divorced, presently lives in Connecticut, where he spends as much time as possible with his teenage son, Christopher. Both he and his son share an intense interest in the martial arts, particularly kung fu, which the actor feels provides balance and harmony to his life. In his spare time, Alexander lends support to the Juvenile Diabetes Foundation.

JED ALLAN

Born: March 1 in New York, New York
Marital Status: married to wife Toby, three sons, Dean, Rick and Mitch
Hair: salt & pepper
Interests: jazz music, listening to his grand player piano
Awards: 1978 Soap Opera Award, Favorite Actor ("Days of Our Lives"); 1979 Soap Opera Award, Favorite Actor ("Days of Our Lives"); Emmy nomination for "Adam 12"

Daytime Dramas: **"Love of Life,"** Ace Hubbard, 1964; **"Secret Storm,"** Paul Britton, 1964-1965; **"Days of Our Lives,"** Don Craig, 1975-1985; **Santa Barbara**, C.C. Capwell, 1986-

Jed Allan has played opposite some of television's most popular women.. and the most popular dog. For two years he was a regular on the hit series, "Lassie." Born March 1 in New York, Jed Allan's career has spanned three decades and covered every facet of the entertainment industry. He's performed in six Broadway shows, including "Oliver," where he played Bill Sykes. On the west coast he was Sky Masterson opposite Milton Berle in the Los Angles Music Center production of "Guys and Dolls." Allan has been involved with daytime since 1964 when he first appeared as Ace Hubbard in "Love of Life." He then went on to "Secret Storm," and ten years later was back for a ten year run as Don Craig on "Days of Our Lives," earning two Soap Opera Awards along the way. He has also received an Emmy nomination for his work on the primetime series, "Adam 12." Other primetime guest appearances include: "Alice," "Crazy Like a Fox," " The Mary Tyler Moore Show," "McMillian" and "The Street of San Francisco." Jed has also been featured in numerous t.v. movies, among them are: "Brenda Starr," with Jill St. John, " Dangerous Women," with Barbara Eden, "Fast Friends," "Married" and "The Man from Clover Street." A native New Yorker, Jed and his wife Toby, an interior designer, have three sons, Dean, Rick and Mitch and one granddaughter, Alexis Lauren (daughter of Dean). The Allan's recently sold their Malibu home, once owned by Clark Gable and Carol Lombard and are now living in a beachfront in Ventura where they enjoy listening to jazz and their player grand piano.

RACHEL AMES

Born: November 2 in Los Angeles, California
Marital Status: married to actor Barry Cahill, two daughters, Christine and Susan
Height: 5'6" **Eyes:** blue **Hair:** blond
Education: UCLA
Interests: tennis, gardening
Awards: nominated for two Daytime Emmys, Best Actress, 1974, 1975; Best Supporting Actress, 1978

Daytime Dramas: "General Hospital," Audrey March, 1964-

One of the longest running performers in the history of daytime television, Rachel Ames debuted on "General Hospital" in 1964. For her portrayal of Audrey March, Ames has twice been nominated for Daytime Emmys, as well as earning legions of fans. Born in Portland, Oregon Rachel's first acting experience was in the 1949 annual Pilgrimage Play. She later performed in a production of "One Foot in Heaven" at the Pasadena Playhouse, alongside her parents, Byron Foulger and Dorothy Adams, both popular actors of their day. After attending University High School in Los Angeles and studying at UCLA, Rachel decided to follow in her parent's footsteps and pursue acting, eventually becoming a contract player for Paramount Pictures and becoming a member of the Golden Circle of talented young performers. Her motion picture debut was in the film, "When Worlds Collide." Other stage credits include: "Broadway Jones," "The Circle" and "King of Hearts," (all at the Pasadena Playhouse) "The Immortalist," "Mary Rose," "Golden Boy" and more. Rachel and her father appeared together in "Cradle Song." Ms. Ames first came to the attention of t.v. audiences when she starred as Policewoman Sandy McAllister on the prime time series "Line Up." In addition, the actress has appeared in various productions at the Hollywood Little Theater and the Pasadena Playhouse. Away from the bustling world of Port Charles, Rachel is married to actor Barry Cahill, with whom she has two daughters, Christine and Susan, and two grandchildren, Jocelyn and Mark. In her spare time, Rachel who lives in Ventura enjoys tennis and gardening.

JOHN ANISTON

Born: July 24 in Crete, Greece
Marital Status: to actress Sherry Rooney, two children, Jennifer and Alexander
Height: 6'3" **Eyes:** brown **Hair:** graying
Education: Penn State University, B.A.; University of California at Northridge, B.S.
Interests: film, skiing, tennis, cabinet making
Awards: 1986 Soap Opera Award, Outstanding Lead Actor and Outstanding Villain

Daytime Dramas: "Days of Our Lives," Eric Richards, 1970; **"Love of Life,"** Edouard Aleata, 1975-1979; **"Search for Tomorrow,"** Martin Tourneur, 1979-1984; **"Days of Our Lives,"** Victor Kiriakis, 1985-

Chances are if you turned on a television recently you saw some member of the Aniston family. First you could see John Aniston every weekday, playing the powerful, yet troubled, Victor Kiriakis on "Days of Our Lives." His wife, Sherry Rooney, has guest starred on "Parker Lewis Can't Lose" and "Doogie Howser, M.D.," while his twenty two year old daughter (from a previous marriage) Jennifer, was one of the stars of the NBC series "Ferris Bueller." The patriarch of this potential acting dynasty was born July 24 in Crete, Greece, where his father worked as an entrepreneur and his mother was a homemaker, taking care of John and his two older sisters. Moving to the United States, Aniston received his B.A. in theater arts from Penn State University and his B.S. in biology from the University of California at Northridge, before serving as a Lieutenant Major in U.S. Navy Intelligence. Since beginning his acting career, Aniston has enjoyed success in several mediums, starring in such feature films as "Love With a Proper Stranger" and "What A Way To Go," as well as in over fifty stage productions, ranging from Broadway to summer stock. Equally at home on television, the talented actor has guest starred on numerous prime time series, including "Kojak," "That Girl," and "Tomma," but has achieved his greatest success with a string of memorable daytime characters. Aniston debuted on "Days of Our Lives" in 1970, following which he also appeared on "Love of Life" and "Search for Tomorrow," before returning to "Days of Our Lives" in 1985. For his work, he was recognized as Outstanding Lead Actor and Outstanding Villain at the third annual Soap Opera Awards. John met his wife, Sherry, when the two were a featured couple on "Love of Life." Married in 1984, they now live happily in Los Angeles and recently adopted a son, Alexander. To relax, Aniston enjoys tennis, skiing, going to the movies, and cabinet making.

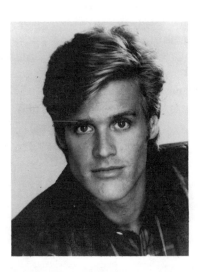

TERRELL ANTHONY

Born: March 24
Marital Status: single
Height: 6'   **Eyes:** blue   **Hair:** blond
Education: B.A. University of Missouri, University of California at Berkeley, Master's credits
Interests: theater, writing

Daytime Dramas: "Another World," Joseph Barron; **"Guiding Light,"** Rusty Shayne, 1986-1989; **"All My Children,"** Tad Martin (one month emergency service)

An actor and a playwright, Terrell Anthony enjoyed a three year run as Rusty Shayne on "Guiding Light." Daytime fans may also recognize the actor for his brief stint as Joseph Barron on "Another World." Born on March 24, Anthony received his B.A. in journalism from the University of Missouri, following which he worked toward his Masters in theology and philosophy at the University of California at Berkeley. A successful playwright, Terrell's most recent work, "Quiet on the Set," which starred daytime favorites Cady McClain and Kate Collins was seen on the off-Broadway stage. Currently appearing in regional theater, Anthony makes his home in New York City.

JOHN APREA

Born: March 4 in Englewood, New Jersey
Marital Status: married to Ninon Zenovich, one daughter, Nicole
Height: 6' **Eyes:** brown **Hair:** brown
Education: Shippensburg State Teachers College
Interests: reading, working out, fishing
Awards: nominated by Soap Opera Digest as Outstanding Villain (Knots Landing)

Daytime Dramas: "Days of Our Lives," Lucas, 1990-1992

With credits such as "The Godfather II," "Knots Landing," and now "Another World," John Aprea is at last able to enjoy the success he worked so hard to attain. A native of Englewood, New Jersey, Aprea was born on March 4th to immigrant Italian parents. A shy child, he divided his youth between football (John was an All County tackle and linebacker) and working in his parents produce store. Upon completing high school, Aprea enrolled as a business major at Pennsylvania's Shippensburg State Teachers College, but soon left the institution when the dean of the school refused to allow him to change his major to political science. Discouraged with this situation, Aprea left college and embarked on a series of truck driving and gas station jobs, all the while harboring a secret desire to pursue acting. When John told his sister of this dream she introduced him to Saul Turtletaub, a television writer who later created such popular series as "That Girl" and "Sanford and Son." Mr. Turtletaub recognized the young actor's potential and enrolled him in acting classes with Joshua Shelley, a renowned acting coach whose students have included Jon Voight, Mia Farrow, and Michael J. Pollard. Spending his days honing his craft, Aprea worked various nighttime jobs to pay the bills. Among these was a stint as the doorman at Schrafft's and as the premiere bartender at the Pub Room at Arthur. This club, managed by Richard Burton's first wife, Sybil, was the favored hot spot of Manhattan's elite during the late 1960's, and Aprea spent his nights serving the likes of the Kennedy's and the Rockefeller's. While this may have proved an intoxicating position, Aprea felt as if he were losing sight of his acting dream, and thus packed up his belongings and headed to California to refocus his ambitions. Continuing his training, John again tended bar to pay the bills, first at the Factory, then the Green Cafe, and finally Robert's. It was while working at this last establishment that Aprea first flirted with film stardom when Francis Ford Coppola tested him for the lead role in "The Godfather." The part eventually went to Al Pacino, but Coppola was impressed with Aprea and later cast him as Tessio in "Godfather II." Aprea's would be film debut, in "Bullitt," with Steve McQueen, was edited from the final version, but he rebounded from this disappointment and went on to appear in such films as "The Idolmaker," "American Anthem," "A Savage Beach," "Stepford Wives," "Crazy Momma," "Caged Heat," "Sweet Kill," "Picasso Trigger," and most recently, "New Jack City." On television, Aprea starred, with "Another World's" Linda Dano, in the short lived series, "The Montefuscos." Seven more failed pilots followed before Aprea landed the role of Vince Novelli on "Matt Houston," which the actor followed with co-starring roles on "Falcon Crest," "Full House," "Knots Landing," and in the television films "Blood Vows: The Story of a Mafia Wife," "Stingray," "Crazy Times," "Guide for the Married Woman," and "Getting Physical." For his work on "Knots Landing," portraying Manny Vasquez, Aprea was nominated by Soap Opera Digest as Best Villain. John's daytime debut on "Another World" came courtesy of his former "Montefusco" co-star, Linda Dano, who informed him of the role of Lucas, which Aprea has played since 1990. He enjoys the thrill of being a working New York actor, and recently exercised his talents in the off-Broadway show "Stealing Souls: Bring Your Camera." Away from stage and screen, Aprea is married to actress Ninon Zenovich, with whom he has one daughter, Nicole born in August 1989. Along with spending time with his child, John also enjoys reading, fishing, and working out.

TICHINA ARNOLD

Born: June 28th in Queens, New York
Marital Status: single
Height: 5'5"   **Eyes:** brown   **Hair:** brown
Interests: roller skating, movies, hair styling, manicures
Awards: Daytime Emmy Nomination, Ingenue Category,
 for "Ryan's Hope," "NAACP Image Award" nomination,
Best Supporting Actress for "How I Got Into College"

Daytime Dramas: "Ryan's Hope," Zena Brown, 1987-1988;
"All My Children," Sharla Valentine, 1989-1991

This accomplished actress has experience in all facets of the entertainment industry. Born and raised in Queens, New York, it was at the age of eleven and with the persuasion of her uncle that Tichina began her professional career. From an early age she sang in her church choir and at eleven, auditioned for the Billie Holiday Theater. Her career took off and as a result she has performed on Broadway, television, as well as in feature films. On Broadway, Tichina appeared in "The Me Nobody Knows" and "Little Shop of Horrors." Other stage credits include "Hair" which played at the Hirschfield Theater in Miami, Florida. Television credits include HBO's, "The Brass Ring" with Sylvia Sidney, PBS's "The House of Dies" with Harold Rollins, "The Cosby Show" with Bill Cosby and Felicia Rashad. Tichina made her motion picture debut in 1985 as Crystal in the film version of "Little Shop of Horrors." She also appeared in "How I got into College" which earned her a nomination for the NAACP Image Award, Best Supporting Actress. Tichina joined the cast of "All My Children" in 1989 remaining with the show until 1991. Prior to "All My Children" she had appeared on "Ryan's Hope" as the young streetwise girl, Zena. During her spare time, Tichina enjoys going to the movies, and roller skating. She is an experienced manicurist as well as hairstylist. She remains active in her church. Currently Tichina is single and resides in New York.

NINA ARVESEN

Born: May 16th in White Plains, New York
Marital Status: single
Eyes: blue   **Hair:** blond
Education: High School
Interests: biking, swimming, tennis

Daytime Dramas: "The Young and the Restless,"
Cassandra, 1988-1990; **"Santa Barbara,"** Angela, 1991-

Named by Soap Opera Digest as one of television's most beautiful women, Nina Arveson has lit up the screen with two sizzling daytime roles. The first of these was Cassandra on "The Young and the Restless," a character Ms. Arvesen played for three years before switching over to "Santa Barbara," and the far more worldly, but equally glamorous, Angela. Born on her mother's birthday in White Plains, New York, the daughter of a Norwegian Ambassador, Nina and the rest of the Arvesen family relocated frequently, living in Cairo, Rio de Janeiro, Norway, and the United States. Always an artistic child, and encouraged by her mother, Nina began to cultivate her creative talents during her early teens. Today her brother Jannik is an investment advisor and her brother Christian is a weapons/special effects film expert; he recently worked on the film, JFK. Living in Scarsdale, New York during this time, she studied dance and piano, as well as enrolling in her school's drama club. Returning to Norway at the age of fourteen, Nina continued her performing, appearing in high school productions, as well as with Chat Noir, the premiere theater of the nation. For Arvesen, the next decade was spent establishing herself in various facets of the Norwegian entertainment industry, not only continuing her theater work but also compiling an impressive list of film and television roles. It was during this period that American audiences, specifically those with extensive cable hook ups, first came to know Nina as the host of "Scandinavian Weekly," a live talk show. Also active behind the scenes, she managed RCA/Motown records in Norway and managed a local television station. In 1985, a visit to a friend in Los Angeles, convinced Nina that she should try to brave the bright lights of Hollywood. She officially relocated shortly after that and began taking acting classes, landing her first big role as Tom Hanks' girlfriend in the popular film "Dragnet." Besides her daytime work, Nina also co-starred in the made for television movie, "Who Gets the Friends?" Away from the set, the busy actress donates much of her time to the American Diabetes Foundation, the Make-A-Wish Foundation, and serves as co-host for television fundraisers benefitting the St. Judes Children's Hospital. To relax, Nina, who is single, enjoys biking, swimming, scuba diving, and tennis.

MATTHEW ASHFORD

Born: January 29 in Davenport, Iowa
Marital Status: married to Christina Saffran, June 6, 1987, one daughter, Grace
Eyes: brown **Hair:** brown
Education: North Carolina School of Arts
Interests: music, theater
Awards: 1989 Annual Soap Opera Award, Outstanding Villain ("Days of Our Lives")

Daytime Dramas: "One Life to Live," Drew Ralston, 1982-1983; **"Search for Tomorrow,"** Cagney McClearly, 1984-1986; **"Days of Our Lives,"** Jack Deveraux

A popular daytime star, Matthew Ashford created memorable characters on "One Life to Live" and "Search for Tomorrow," and is now earning raves for his work on "Days of Our Lives." For his efforts Ashford was named Outstanding Villain at the Fifth annual Soap Opera Awards. Born in Davenport, Iowa, Ashford, with the rest of his family, relocated to Fairfax, Virginia, when he was thirteen years old. A natural ham, Matthew eventually decided to commit himself to acting, enrolling at the North Carolina School of Arts in Winston-Salem. Before beginning his daytime work, Ashford performed with the Ragamuffin Magic and Mime Company of Myrtle Beach, South Carolina, and later performed on stage with Esther Rolle in the touring company of "The Member of the Wedding." In addition Ashford recently took a break from being a daytime actor to portray a daytime actor on the popular series "Quantum Leap." Moving from the east coast in 1987, Ashford now lives in Los Angeles with his wife of five years, Christina Saffran. The couple met in 1985, when the actor auditioned for The World Peace Festival, a production choreographed by Ms. Saffran. Now seven years later on June 15, 1992, their first child, Grace Saffran was born. Recently Ashford assisted his wife with the production of "Sensible Shoes," a promotional video. In his spare time Matthew enjoys going to the theater and listening to music. He is also deeply interested in Buddhist philosophy and has practiced many of its traditions since 1984.

RICHARD BACKUS

Born: 1945 in Goffstown, New Hampshire
Marital Status: married
Height: 5'9 1/2"   **Eyes:** brown   **Hair:** brown
Education: Harvard College, B.A.
Interests: theater, writing
Awards: Variety Critic's Poll Award, Theatre World Award, Clarence Derwent Award ("Promenade All!"), Daytime Emmy Nomination, Best Supporting Actor ("Ryan's Hope")

Daytime Dramas: "Lovers and Friends," Jason Saxton, 1977; **"For Richer, For Poorer,"** Jason Saxton, 1977-1978; **"Another World,"** Ted Bancroft, 1979; **"Ryan's Hope,"** Barry Ryan, 1980-1981; **"As the World Turns,"** Dr. Russ Elliot, 1984-1985; **"As the World Turns,"** Carl Eldridge, 1991-1992

An actor and a writer, Richard Backus has been involved with daytime drama since making his debut on "Lovers and Friends" in 1977. He most recently was seen as Carl Eldridge on "As the World Turns," a show for which he additionally has served as an associate writer for the past four years. Born in Goffstown, New Hampshire, in 1945, Backus after attending Harvard College, he began his professional acting career, which has included extensive work in television and theater. On Broadway, Mr. Backus has appeared in "Camelot," with Richard Harris, "Ah, Wilderness!," "You Can Never Tell," and "Promenade, All!," which earned the actor a Theatre World Award, a Clarence Derwent Award, and a Variety Critic's Poll Award. Richard's additional stage credits include: "The Cocktail Hour," "Talley and Son/ Tomorrow's Monday," "The Dining Room," "Sorrow of Stephen," "Gimme Shelter," "Finishing Touches," "Rhymes With Evil," "The Importance of Being Earnest," "Our Town," "Romeo and Juliet," "Macbeth," "King Lear," "Measure for Measure," "Hobson's Choice," "Scenes from American Life," and "The Heiress," among others. Also a film actor, Backus has co-starred on the big screen in "Secret of My Success," with Michael J. Fox, and "Deathdream," as well as appearing in the television films "Flight 90: Disaster on the Potomac," "Why Me?," "Judge Horton and the Scottsboro Boys," "Mothers Against Drunk Drivers," and in PBS productions of "Camelot" and "Soldier's Home." Among the prime time shows on which he has guest starred: "Law and Order," "Spenser: For Hire," "Kaye O'Brien," "Remington Steele," and as a co-star on "Bare Essence." Over the years the actor has worked regularly in daytime dramas, co starring in "Lovers and Friends," which eventually was renamed "For Richer, For Poorer," "Another World," "Ryan's Hope," for which he earned a 1981 Best Supporting Actor Daytime Emmy nomination, and "As the World Turns," first as Dr. Russ Elliot in 1984, and most recently as Carl Eldridge. Richard, who is married, also flexes his writing skills on "As the World Turns."

JANE BADLER

Born: December 31, 1953 in Brooklyn, New York
Marital Status: married, one son, Samuel
Height: 5'6" **Eyes:** blue **Hair:** auburn
Education: Northwestern University, B.F.A.
Interests: tennis, swimming, film, theater

Daytime Dramas: "One Life to Live," Melinda Kramer,
1977-1981; "The Doctors," Natalie Bell, 1981-1982

Presently living in Melbourne, Australia, where most of her attention is focused on her new baby, Samuel, Jane Badler is taking a break from her successful television career. Born on December 31 in Brooklyn, New York, Jane's family consists of two sisters and one brother, her father, a lawyer, and her mother, who now owns a health spa in Key West. After receiving her B.F.A. from Northwestern University, Jane embarked on a string of popular television roles. She was featured in the mini-series "V," as well as co-starring on "The New Mission Impossible" and as Meredith Braxton on "Falcon Crest." Daytime fans saw Ms. Badler in two prominent roles, first as Melinda Kramer on "One Life to Live," following which she appeared as Natalie Bell on the final season of "The Doctors." Jane, living in Melbourne with her husband and new baby, enjoys tennis, swimming, movies, theater, and reading.

SCOTT THOMPSON BAKER

Born: September 15 in Golden Valley, Minnesota
Marital Status: married to Leilani Soares, January 27, 1990
one son, Thane
Height: 6'4 **Eyes:** blue **Hair:** brown
Education: Oral Roberts University, two years; University of Minnesota, one year
Interests: writing, biking
Awards: "Star Search" Acting Category, Grand First Prize;
1989 Soap Opera Awards, Outstanding Male Newcomer

Daytime Dramas: "General Hospital," Colton Shore,
1988-1990; "All My Children," Craig Lawson, 1991-1992

Scott Thompson Baker got his first big break when Ed McMahon handed him a check for $100,000. This may bear a striking resemblance to a publisher's clearinghouse commercial, but this was not the result of a random, nationwide mailing, but the conclusion to Baker's phenomenally successful run in the acting category of the syndicated variety show "Star Search." Before reaching this milestone, Baker, a native of Golden Valley, Minnesota, had intended on following his father and brother into the insurance business. However after going from Eden Prairie High School to Oral Roberts University, Baker began to give more serious consideration to acting. The clincher came at college when he was cast as Captain Von Trapp in the campus production of "The Sound of Music"; Baker was committed to becoming an actor. After completing his sophomore year, he transferred to the University of Minnesota, where besides working with the school theater, Baker also appeared at the Guthrie Theater in "Peer Gynt" and "A Christmas Carol,'82." It was shortly after this that a talent scout spotted Scott and he was invited to compete on "Star Search." For his first acting assignment, he wrote a brief sketch about the difficulty of auditioning; this routine proved to be a hit with the judges and audience alike, and Baker went on to fifteen more victories before receiving his grand prize check. With this exposure he decided it was time to move to Los Angeles, and although the roles did not come as fast as he had expected, Baker was able to support himself with work in commercials. He continued his study of acting at the Stella Adler Conservatory, working with the acting coach Arthur Mendoza. Since then Baker has appeared in the film "Multiple Listings" and "A Thousand Ways to Die," with Dorothy Malone. On the small screen the actor has been featured in the pilot "War of the Worlds" and made a guest appearance on "Falcon Crest." Before landing the role of Craig on "All My Children," Baker spent time in Port Charles as Colton Shore on "General Hospital." A devoutly religious man, (something he credits to his mother and the evangelist, Billy Graham) Scott is a strong believer in family, spending as much time as possible with his wife Leilani Soares and their son Thane. The family lives in Connecticut,but plan on moving back to California soon. Baker relaxes by bike riding and writing.

LAURA BALER

Born: May 12 in Boston, Massachusetts
Marital Status: single
Height: 5'5" **Eyes:** brown **Hair:** brown
Education: Northwestern University/Eastern Michigan University, B.S.
Interests: environment, hiking, skiing, theater, billiards
Awards: 1991 Best Actress, New York University Student Film Festival

Daytime Dramas: "As the World Turns," Jade Sullivan, 1990-

Like many performers, Laura Baler spent much of her youth daydreaming. Describing this time she writes: "...spent many hours on my own during pre-teen years, climbing trees and hanging out in the woods-creating my own one person plays and dramas." Now years later, Laura is able to display her creative talents to millions as Jade Sullivan on "As the World Turns." Born on May 12 in Boston, Massachusetts, Laura, along with her two siblings, were raised by her father, a professor of Public Health, and her mother, a psychiatrist. Today, her brother is a surgeon, her sister a financial consultant. Her early years were spent in New Hampshire, where Laura has fond memories of family outings to Cape Cod and picturesque New England towns. Definitely the outdoors type, Laura enjoyed exploring the woods, on her own and as a Camp Fire girl. After relocating to Ann Arbor, Michigan, Laura began to nurture her performing talents, appearing in school productions, community theater, and singing in choral concerts. Living in such close proximity to the University of Michigan also meant exciting football games and a plethora of cultural events, all of which added change and excitement to Laura's childhood. After studying at Northwestern University and Eastern Michigan University, Baler began her professional acting career, getting early exposure as one of the girls from the Cindy Lauper video "Girls Just Want to Have Fun." In addition to her work on "As the World Turns," Baler appeared in "Scenes from a Mall." with Woody Allen and Bette Midler, and has starred in numerous student films, winning the Best Actress Award at the New York University Student Film Festival in 1991. Now living in New York City, Laura, who is single, donates her free time to an AIDS hospice, as well as working for environmental causes. Although she has been a regular on daytime for over two years, Baler continues to do occasional temporary secretarial work, pulling in some extra money and keeping her typing skills at peak level. Away from the set and the steno pool, Baler enjoys hiking, cave exploring, travelling, fine restaurants, film, theater, ballet, skiing, and photography.

JACK BANNON

Born: June 14, 1940
Marital Status: single
Height: 6'3" **Eyes:** brown **Hair:** brown

Daytime Dramas: "Santa Barbara," 1991-

A former "Knots Landing" star, Jack Bannon joined the cast of "Santa Barbara" in November, 1991. Although this is his first venture into daytime television, Bannon has appeared on dozens of prime time series. Along with his work as Scott Easton on "Knots Landing," the man behind the kidnapping of Valene Ewing's twins, Bannon has also been a regular cast member on "Lou Grant," playing assistant city editor, Art Donovan, "Trauma Center," and "A Class Affair," as well as making guest appearances on such shows as "Charles in Charge," "Empty Nest," "Teech," "Night Court," "Dynasty," "Falcon Crest," "Murder, She Wrote," "St. Elsewhere," "Father Dowling," "MacGyver," "We Got It Made," "Trapper John M.D.," "Moonlighting," "Quincy," "Cagney and Lacey," "Hunter," "The Fall Guy," "Newhart," and "Simon and Simon." Jack has also been featured in several television movies, including "Boystown," "Matlock," "Street Killing," "Tail Gunner Joe," "Amelia Earhart," and "Take Your Best Shot," while he has been seen in the feature films "Death Warrant" and "The Hungarian Rhapsody." Equally at home on stage, his theater credits include roles in such productions as "Oh Coward," "Mister Roberts," "Waiting for Godot," "Lion in Winter," "Cloud Nine," "Steambath," and "Three Sisters."

HAYLEY BARR

Born: April 27, 1971 in Salzburg, Austria
Marital Status: single
Height: 5" **Eyes:** green **Hair:** brown
Education: New York University, working towards degree
Interest: swimming, reading, movies
Awards: Nominated for 1992 Soap Opera Award, Outstanding Younger Leading Actress

Daytime Dramas: "As the World Turns," Courtney Baxter, 1990-

Born in 1971 in Salzburg, Austria, the second of four children, Hayley Barr has been performing professionally since the age of 11. After spending her early years in Salzburg, Hayley and her family moved to Portland, Oregon, where at five years old she began to study ballet at the insistence of her parents. Hayley's first break came when she played the role of Pepper in the Portland Civic Center production of "Annie," and she continued this success over the next several years, modelling and appearing in Ballet West's production of "The Nutcracker." Along with her community theater work, Hayley also attended Beaverton's Sunset High School, where she worked in the theater department, as well as winning awards for competitive speaking. The summer before her senior year she was selected to attend Northwestern University's five week National High School Institute where she studied with Peter Hedges. After graduating from high school, Hayley moved to New York City, where she enrolled at New York University, as well as continuing her theater training as a Trustee Scholar at the Circle in the Square Professional Workshop. Among her numerous stage credits are roles in "Jesus Christ Superstar," "Addict," "Peter Pan," and "West Side Story." After the first semester, Hayley found that she didn't have the tuition money to continue college, so she moved to Los Angeles in the hopes of landing a role on a television series. As fate would have it the part she ended up getting, was back in New York, playing Courtney on "As the World Turns." Several months earlier, Hayley had auditioned for the role of Lily, and although she didn't get the part, she clearly made an impression on the producers who called her in to play Courtney. Hayley then moved back to New York and in March 1990 joined the cast of "As the World Turns." She is completing her college education through night school. Away from the set, Hayley enjoys swimming, dancing, reading, and going to the movies. Although she moved from Austria at an early age, she retains a dual American/Austrian citizenship.

JULIA BARR

Born: February 8th in Fort Wayne, Indiana
Marital Status: married to Dr. Richard Hirschlag, 1981, one daughter, Allison Jane, born July 8, 1984
Height: 5'1" **Eyes:** blue **Hair:** blond
Education: Purdue University
Interests: theater, movies
Awards: Daytime Emmy for Outstanding Supporting Actress, 1991; Nominated for 1992 Soap Opera Award, Outstanding Lead Actress

Daytime Dramas: "Ryan's Hope," Reenie Szabo, 1976; **"All My Children,"** Brooke English, 1976-1981, 1982-

A fifteen year soap opera veteran, Julia Barr has always been an actress with a strong dedication to her craft. While growing up in Indiana, the future Emmy winner willingly sacrificed a great deal of her high school social life in favor of sharpening her acting skills with the Fort Wayne Community Theater. This commitment to excellence carried Julia to Purdue University where she appeared in such theatrical productions as "Our Town," "A Streetcar Named Desire," and "Endgame." Upon graduation the actress got her first professional acting credit, as well as her Actors Equity card, when she performed with Van Johnson in a Buffalo production of "Girl in My Soup." The next move was to New York City, where Julia supported herself by working for an answering service before landing a role on the NBC drama "Gathering of One." This was followed by a variety of acting jobs, among them a role in the Buffalo production of "Scapino," a Montgomery, Alabama production of "Never to Late," and a return to television as Charles Adam's daughter in "The Adams Chronicles" on PBS. In 1976 Julia made her first appearances on daytime drama in the role of Reenie Szabo on "Ryan's Hope," and later that same year her debut as Brooke English on "All My Children." The role fit Julia perfectly, and she has remained with the show for over fifteen years, receiving a daytime Emmy for Outstanding Supporting Actress in 1991, and garnering four other nominations along the way. In addition Julia has continued her stage work as well, appearing off-Broadway in "Kerouac," as well as touring in the production of "Absurd Person Singular," which featured several daytime performers. Julia's one extended leave of absence from "All My Children" in 1981 proved to be a complete success, both professionally and personally. On the professional front she appeared in the play "West Side Waltz," which starred Katherine Hepburn and Dorothy Louden, as well as in the film "I, the Jury." On the personal front Julia married Dr. Richard Hirschlag, an oral surgeon, with whom she now has one child, Allison Jane, born on July 8, 1984. For Julia this was the second marriage, the first ending in divorce several years earlier. The couple met when Richard enrolled in a musical comedy class with his friend, Rob. More inclined to root canal than song and dance, Richard joined the class in the hopes of getting to know Julia, a gamble which finally paid off when she, much to his surprise, asked him out on a date. He was able to get over the initial shock, and today the couple lives happily in suburban New Jersey. They enjoy going to the theater, collecting snow domes, and are both extremely active in their daughter's school.

BERNARD BARROW

Born: December 30 in New York, New York
Marital Status: married to Joan Kaye
Height: 6' **Eyes:** brown **Hair:** graying
Education: Syracuse University, B.A.; Columbia University, M.B.A.; Yale University, Ph.D.
Interests: theater
Awards: nominated for Daytime Emmy, Best Supporting Actor, 1979, 1988 ("Ryan's Hope"), 1992 ("Loving"); Daytime Emmy for Best Supporting Actor, 1991 ("Loving")

Daytime Dramas: "Where the Heart Is," Earl Dana, 1969-1970; **"The Secret Storm,"** Dan Kincaid, 1970-1974; **"Ryan's Hope,"** Johnny Ryan, 1975-1989; **"Loving,"** Louie Slavinsky, 1989-

Since the start of his career, as a child radio actor of the 1940's, Bernard Barrow has enjoyed great success on stage, screen, and in the classroom. A college professor and a soap opera star, Barrow earned his first daytime Emmy in 1991 for his work on "Loving." The son of Russian immigrants, Barrow was born and raised in the Yorkville section of New York City, where his parent ran a laundry. Although he began working at an early age, Barrow never saw this as a substitute for a formal education. After graduating Syracuse University ar the age of nineteen, Barrow moved on to Columbia University, where he earned an M.B.A. in business administration. During the course of his acting career he has also found the time to pick up a Ph.D in theater history from Yale University. By the time he was twenty two years old Barrow found himself on the other side of the classroom when he became one of Brooklyn College's youngest faculty members; he maintained this status for over thirty years, retiring only recently but still holding the title of Professor Emeritus. Over the years Barrow has taught acting and drama to many distinguished alumni, including t.v. director Joel Zwick and "L.A. Law's" Jimmy Smits. Amazingly enough, Barrow also managed to cultivate an acting career, along with his educational pursuits. He has starred in numerous stage productions, including "Uncle Vanya," "Scuba Duba," "Molly's Dream," "The Play of Daniel," and "Hamlet," with Rip Torn. In 1992 he starred with fellow daytimers Marilyn Chris, Cady McClain and Walt Willey in the Valley Forge and Westbury Music Fairs production of "Barefoot in the Park." On the big screen Barrow has been seen in such films as "Serpico," "Rachel, Rachel," directed by fellow Yale student Paul Newman, "Glass Houses," and "The Survivors." Along with his prominent daytime work, which has included roles on "Ryan's Hope," "Edge of Night," "The Secret Storm," and now "Loving," Barrow has been seen on prime time episodes of "Law and Order," "Kojak," "The Waltons," "The Rookies," "On Our Own," "Rhoda," and "Maude." For each of these last two shows, Barrow had the opportunity to portray a judge, and in the process got to preside over the marriage ceremony of two of television's most popular couples, Valarie Harper and David Groh on "Rhoda" and Bea Arthur and Bill Macy on "Maude." For the past twenty seven years Barrow has been married to actress Joan Kaye, who, along with her husband, has two children from a previous marriage. The couple divide their time between their New York City apartment and their weekend home in Pennsylvania.

PETER BARTON

Born: July 19 in Valley Stream, New York
Marital Status: single
Height: 5'10" **Eyes:** hazel **Hair:** brown
Education: Nassau Community College
Interests: weightlifting, jogging, aerobics, basketball

Daytime Dramas: "The Young and the Restless,"
Dr. Scott Grainger

After taking an eighteen month break from show business, during which time he got his real estate licence, Peter Barton resumed his successful television career with the role of Dr. Scott Grainger on "The Young and the Restless." Born on July 19 in Valley Stream, New York, Barton's initial career plans were to be a doctor. After taking a year off from school, during which time he worked a number of jobs, including stints at a gas station, boat yard, disco, and for his father's concrete business, Peter began his pre-med studies at Nassau Community College. Barton was then set to enroll at St. John's University, when he opted to pursue an acting career instead. This decision made, he took the money he had made modelling and moved out to Hollywood. After spending a short time honing his acting skills, Barton landed his first t.v. role in the 1979 series, "Shirley," starring Shirley Jones, which was soon followed by another series, "The Powers of Matthew Star," in which Barton played the title character opposite Louis Gossett, Jr.. Since then, the actor has additionally starred in two pilots, "Three Eyes" and "Nu Deli," made guest appearances on such shows as "The Fall Guy," "Rags to Riches," and "Scene of the Crime," and co-starred with Jennifer Jason Leigh in the t.v. movie "The First Time." Barton's film credits include "Friday the 13th Part IV- The Final Chapter" and "Hell Night." In his spare time, he works closely with both The American Cancer Society and the Save the Earth Foundation. Barton lists amongst his hobbies, weightlifting, basketball, softball, aerobics, and jogging.

SUSAN BATTEN

Born: in Clayton, North Carolina
Marital Status: single
Eyes: brown **Hair:** brown
Interests: cooking, theater
Awards: Favorite New Character, "Episodes" Magazine, January/February 1992

Daytime Dramas: "All My Children," Deborah;
"One Life to Live," Luna Moody, 1991-

One of daytime's freshest faces, Susan Batten reflects the adventurous new spirit of "One Life to Live." Her character,

Luna Moody, a spiritual, Southern eccentric, who parachuted her way into Llanview in September of 1991, was created specifically for the off-beat Batten. Clearly succeeding in her new role, the actress was voted favorite new character in a recent issue of Episodes Magazine. Ms. Batten was born and raised in Clayton, North Carolina, where she held a variety of interesting jobs. The most unusual of these found Batten donning scuba equipment and fishing for golf balls out of a golf course's pond, receiving five cents for each one found. She eventually put this career aside, moving to New York to pursue her acting dream. Susan has appeared briefly on "All My Children," as well as on stage in "Come Blow Your Horn," "Scooter Cycle," "Birdsend," "Hamlet," "The Cherry Orchard," and "Night Mother." While Batten misses her Southern home, she is happily adjusting to life up North, and away from the set can often be found preparing southern style meals for her friends.

JOHN BECK

Marital Status: married to Tina Beck, four children
Hair: brown
Interests: gardening, landscaping

Daytime Dramas: "Santa Barbara," David Raymond, 1991-1992

A key player in the most elaborate dream in the history of television, John Beck saw his character's entire marriage to Pamela Ewing on "Dallas" dissolve when it all turned out to be a season long dream for Victoria Principal. Fortunately for this Illinois native, his work as Mark Graison was not as easily discarded, and the actor recently made his daytime debut as Judge David Raymond on "Santa Barbara." While growing up in the mid-west, Beck first stepped out onto the stage to overcome his innate shyness. The experiment proved successful, and a few years later, in the late sixties, he moved out to California to pursue an acting career. Entering the business at the same time as such notables as Tom Selleck and Farrah Fawcett, Beck quickly found work in commercials, before getting his first big break with a starring role in the 1971 series "Nichols," with James Garner. This was followed by a starring role in another series, "Dirty Dan," and since then Beck has appeared on several other prime time programs, including "Flamingo Road," "Murder, She Wrote," "Jake and the Fatman," and "Hotel." John's first venture into feature films was alongside Burt Lancaster in "The Lawman." During the filming he not only gained a great deal of experience but also met his future wife, Tina, with whom he has now been married for more than twenty years. Beck's additional film credits include "Pat Garrett and Billy the Kid," "Sleeper," "Deadly Honeymoon," "Audrey Rose," "Rollerball," "The Big Bus," "Other Side of Midnight," "Paperback Hero," and most recently "A Row of Crows," which received several awards from various film festivals. The actor has also flexed his talent on the stage, starring over the years in such productions as "Mister Roberts," "The Glass Menagerie," "The Rainmaker," and "The Importance of Being Ernest." Like his daytime character, Beck, who is the father of four, lives in Santa Barbara, California, where he enjoys gardening and landscaping. He also donates his time to increasing local AIDS education.

NOELLE BECK

Born: December 14 in Baltimore, Maryland
Marital Status: married to Eric Patterson, two daughters,
Forrest and Spencer
Height: 5'6"   **Eyes:** hazel   **Hair:** light brown
Education: Baltimore School for the Arts
Interests: jogging, travelling, reading, cooking, horseback
riding, theater, films

Daytime Dramas: "Loving," Trisha Alden Sowolsky Hartman
McKenzie, 1984-

This woman's success story is one that many aspiring actors only dream about. Noelle Beck launched her career during a trip to New York. Originally the trip was intended to research colleges but it was after meeting a casting agent and auditioning for "Loving" that Noelle landed her first television role. Born on December 14 in Baltimore, Maryland, Noelle has an older sister, a half brother, and four stepbrothers. Still in high school, Noelle landed the role of Trisha Alden on her seventeenth birthday. She made her debut in December of 1984 and still managed to continue her school work at the Baltimore School for the Arts through correspondence courses, graduating in June of the following year. Since that lucky trip, Noelle has become one of daytime's most popular stars, as well as appearing in the Chevy Chase film "Fletch Lives," portraying Betty Dilworth, a newspaper columnist. During a fantasy sequence in this film she also played Scarlet O'Hara opposite Chase's Rhett Butler. Today Noelle's most important role is that of mother to her two daughters, Forrest Lee born in January of 1991 and Spencer Lynn born February 14, 1992. (Noelle went into labor the same day her Loving character gave birth to a son) She is married to Eric Patterson, owner of the New York restaurant, Live Bait. The couple divide their time between New York City and their old country mill house in Pennsylvania. Noelle is presently at work on a children's book. Along with this she enjoys reading, horseback riding, travelling, jogging, film and theater going. She also likes experimenting in the kitchen, especially gourmet Italian recipes which she makes for fellow cast members.

LAURALEE BELL

Born: December 22, 1968 in Chicago, Illinois
Marital Status: single
Height: 5'6"   **Eyes:** blue   **Hair:** blond
Education: The Latin School
Interests: tennis, shopping
Awards: TEEN Magazine national poll: Favorite Soap Opera
Actress

Daytime Dramas: "The Young and the Restless,"
Cricket Blair Romalotti, 1983 -

Nepotism may have provided Lauralee Bell with an opportunity, but it is talent and charm that have enabled her to run with it. It was at the age of nine that Lauralee's father, William Bell, the creator of "The Young and the Restless," allowed his daughter to work as a non-speaking extra on his show. Lauralee enjoyed this and over the next several years made several more appearances before speaking her first line at the age of thirteen. The role gradually evolved, and with each performance came more and more fan mail. Viewers seemed to take an instant liking to the character, a sweet, shy, and very real teenager, and have since enjoyed watching the character of Cricket grow from a young student, to a married woman. While William Bell may have been the catalyst, all the credit should go to Lauralee. A native of Chicago, Lauralee, from an early age, shared the drive and determination to succeed that seems to define the Bell family. William Bell co-created "Another World," and with his wife, Lee Phillip Bell, developed "The Young and the Restless" and "The Bold and the Beautiful." Mrs. Bell also spent years as a popular host of a Chicago television show, which during it's run amassed an impressive number of Emmys and established it's host as a favorite Windy City personality. Lauralee, who has two older brothers, was a typically successful Bell child. At the age of seven she invited neighbors in, at one cent per person, to see a display of some of her artwork; that same year she also ran a popular rush hour lemonade stand. Although the family lived in Chicago, there were frequent trips to Los Angeles, where Lauralee got her first taste of daytime television. From her first cameo she was convinced that this was her calling, and upon returning to Chicago, she divided her time between her studies at The Latin School, and taking classes in acting, dance, and voice. After spending an entire summer working on "The Young and the Restless," during which she received an increasing number of fan letters, Lauralee decided to work full time on the show. In 1986 the Bell family moved to Los Angeles, where Lauralee finished high school and spent her first year as a full fledged cast member. Worried that the other actors would treat her differently because of her familial ties, Lauralee requests that her father not be on the set when she is working. Recently the young actress moved out of her family's house (which once belonged to Howard Hughes) and got her own place. She still, however, spends a great deal of time with her parents and brothers, and the Bell family regularly plays tennis together. But Lauralee is now enjoying life on her own, and recently became the proud owner of a new dog. Along with tennis and shopping, one of her favorite hobbies is to needlepoint Christmas ornaments, which she does year round. She is also an aspiring writer, and hopes to one day be active behind the camera as well. Aware of her position as a role model, (Lauralee was voted Favorite Soap Opera Actress by a TEEN Magazine national poll) Lauralee strives to deal with important issues on "The Young and the Restless," including date rape, teen pregnancy, drug abuse and sexual harassment. In her own life Lauralee is involved in ChildHelp USA .

MEG BENNETT

Born: October 4 in Pasadena, California
Marital Status: single
Height: 5'8" **Eyes:** brown **Hair:** brown
Education: Northwestern University, Bachelor's in Theatre Arts
Interests: theater
Awards: 1986 Daytime Emmy for Outstanding Writing
("The Young and the Restless")

Daytime Dramas: "Search for Tomorrow," Liza Walton Sentell, 1974-1977; **"The Young and the Restless,"** Julia Newman, 1980-1987; **"Santa Barbara,"** Megan Richardson, 1989-1990

A success both in front of the camera, as well as behind the scenes, Meg Bennett has been involved with daytime drama as an actress and a writer for more than fifteen years. Born on October 4, Meg was raised in Pasadena, California, the oldest of four children. After earning her degree in theater from Northwestern University, Meg concentrated chiefly on stage work. She was part of the original Broadway cast of "Grease," (she played Marty) as well as performing in the first off-Broadway production of "Godspell." Other theater credits include: "Barefoot in the Park," "The Wizard of Oz," "Romeo and Juliet," "Hamlet," and "The Twelfth Night." Along with the feature film "Loving Couples," Meg has been seen on the small screen in such shows as "The Paper Chase," "The New Love American Style," and several daytime dramas, including "Search for Tomorrow," "The Young and the Restless," and most recently "Santa Barbara." Not currently performing, Meg now serves as one of "Santa Barbara's" writers, a position she has also enjoyed on "The Young and the Restless," "Generations," "Family Medical Center," and "The Bold and the Beautiful." In addition, Ms. Bennett has written two television movies, "You are the Jury" and "Love Letters from the Grave," (an Aaron Spelling Production shown on NBC in 1991). In 1986 her work on "The Young and the Restless" earned Meg a Daytime Emmy for Outstanding Writing. A resident of Los Angeles, Meg, who is single, is involved with numerous charities. She serves as Co-Director of the Mentor Program, which seeks to aid homeless children, as well as being an active member of the West Coast Creative Coalition and the Los Angeles Coalition for Choice.

JOHN BERADINO

Born: May 1 in Los Angeles, California
Marital Status: married to Marjorie Binder, two children, Katherine and John
Height: 5'11"   **Eyes:** brown   **Hair:** brown
Education: University of Southern California
Interests: tennis, writing
Awards: nominated for three Daytime Emmys, 1974,'75,'76; 1937 MVP (baseball) University of Southern California

Daytime Dramas: "General Hospital," Dr. Steve Hardy, 1963-

In the history of daytime drama, few performers can match the durable appeal of John Beradino. Since April 1, 1963, the day of "General Hospital's" debut, Beradino has played Dr. Steve Hardy, earning three Emmy nominations and the admiration of millions of fans along the way. However, Beradino was in the public eye long before he ever roamed the halls of Port Charles' favorite hospital. His first turn in the spotlight came through his appearances in the "Our Gang" movies, which was followed, amazingly enough, by a career as a major league baseball player. This began at the age of nine when Beradino's parents gave him some baseball equipment. Clearly not one to waste any time, Beradino was playing semi-pro ball on the weekends by the time he was fifteen, as well as playing high school football during the week. It was his football abilities which eventually earned him a scholarship to the University of Southern California in 1936. Beradino played football during his first year, but then switched to baseball the following year, winning the Most Valuable Player Award. In 1939 he was signed by the St. Louis Browns, but with the outbreak of World War II Beradino left the game to serve four years in the Navy. He resumed his baseball career in 1948 with the Cleveland Indians, and with Beradino at second base, the team went on to win the World Series. He continued to play until 1953 when a leg injury ended his baseball career. With his playing days behind him, Beradino decided to return to the world of show business, starring in two ABC series, "The New Breed," and "I Led Three Lives." Along with these he also guest starred on countless others, including "The Untouchables," "The Love Boat," "Cheyenne," and "Laramine." Beradino has also appeared in a number of made for television movies, among them "Do Not Fold, Spindle, or Mutilate," "Don't Look Back," and "Moon of the Wolf." On the big screen Beradino made a cameo appearance in the soap opera satire "Young Doctors in Love." Since he created the role in 1963, Beradino has been known to millions as Dr. Steve Hardy, and to this day no other actor has appeared on as many episodes of a daytime drama. Away from the public eye, Beradino is married to the former Marjorie Binder, with whom he has two children, Katherine and John. The actor lives in Beverly Hills, and in his spare time he enjoys tennis and writing.

PETER BERGMAN

Born: June 11 in Guantanamo, Cuba
Marital Status: married to Mariellen Bergman in 1985, two children, Connor and Clare Elizabeth
Height: 6'1" **Eyes:** blue **Hair:** brown
Education: American Academy of Dramatic Arts
Interests: piano, construction
Awards: 1980 "Most Promising Young Actor in Daytime Television," Soap Opera Digest and Daytime T.V. Magazine; nominated for two Best Actor Daytime Emmys, 1983, 1990 ("All My Children"); 1991 & 1992 Daytime Emmys for Best Actor ("The Young and the Restless")

Daytime Dramas: "All My Children," Dr. Cliff Warner, 1980-1990; **"The Young and the Restless,"** Jack Abbott, 1991-

Peter Bergman has been one of daytime's hottest actors since bursting on the scene over ten years ago as Dr. Cliff Warner on "All My Children." Voted "the most promising young actor in daytime television" in 1980, by both Soap Opera Digest and Daytime T.V. Magazine, Bergman has more than lived up to his reputation, earning two Best Actor daytime Emmy nominations for his work on "All My Children," and bringing home the prize in 1991 and 1992 for his work as Jack Abbott on "The Young and the Restless." A native of Guantanamo, Cuba, Bergman came from a military family, and as a result relocated nine times before he was in the eighth grade. Deciding on an acting career while in college, he worked on a construction crew for a year, using the money he earned to pay his tuition at the American Academy of Dramatic Arts in New York. While at school he starred in such productions as "The Royal Family" and "Henry IV Part IV," as well as working off-Broadway and in commercials. Although Bergman has concentrated chiefly on daytime television, he has also been seen in prime time in several movies of the week, including "Fantasies," "Money, Power, Murder," and a two hour "Kojak" film. In addition, the actor starred in "Pity The Poor Soldier," a PBS production. He can also be seen in the NBC film, "Palomino," based on the novel by Danielle Steele. Away from the set, Bergman is a music lover and piano player. He also enjoys putting his construction skills to work on his own house, executing various plumbing, electrical, and structural adjustments. Peter, who was married to actress Christine Ebersole, shares his Los Angeles home with his second wife, Mariellen and their two children, Connor and Clare Elizabeth. The couple, who have been happily married since 1985, were introduced by Mike Minor. (ex-Brandon, "All My Children")

ROBYN BERNARD

Born: May 26th in Gladewater, Texas
Height: 5'4" **Eyes:** green/gray **Hair:** brown
Marital Status: single
Education: Baylor University
Interests: music, tennis, billiards

Daytime Dramas: "General Hospital", Terry Brock

An accomplished singer, as well as an actress, Robyn Bernard's role as Terry Brock on "General Hospital," afforded her the opportunity to showcase both of these talents. Born in Gladewater, Texas, the daughter of an evangelist, Robyn spent much of her early years travelling and performing with her devoutly religious family. During the school year they would reside in Houston, the summers however were spent on the road, where Robyn first performed on stage at the age of three. Often she would harmonize with her sister, Crystal, who co-stars on the situation comedy "Wings." Robyn proved to be as adept at academics as she was at performing, earning top grades and enrolling in Baylor University at the age of seventeen, where she majored in journalism. Yet music remained her true passion, and when her singing and songwriting abilities began to gain a good deal of attention, Robyn decided to move to Nashville where she could pursue this full time. Clearly not a woman lacking spontaneity or ambition, she decided one day while watching her favorite show, "General Hospital," that she had the talent to be a leading lady on a daytime drama, So with a great deal of confidence in herself, Robyn left Nashville, moved to Los Angeles, enrolled in acting classes, and within a year she landed a role on her favorite show. Robyn remains active in the music business, and has formed her own musical publishing company. She hopes to further cultivate her career both as an actress and a singer. To relax Robyn enjoys tennis, billiards and swimming.

KEVIN BEST

Born: February 26, in New York, New York
Marital Status: married to Karen, one child, Julian Josef
Height: 5'11" **Eyes:** brown **Hair:** black
Education: American Academy of Dramatic Arts
Interests: writing song lyrics, reading

Daytime Dramas: "General Hospital," Dr. Harrison Davis, 1988-1990

Always knowing he wanted to be an actor, it wasn't until after high school and three years in the military that Kevin Best began to pursue his ambition. Born February 26, in New York City, Best moved to New Jersey, and attended Piscataway High School. Upon graduation he began his military service in the United States Marine Corps, stationed at Camp Johnson, North Carolina. After his stint in the Marines, Best began to realize his dream of acting when he enrolled in the American Academy of Dramatic Arts in his native Manhattan. In 1985, Kevin left for Los Angeles to further his professional career. He began his career on stage, appearing in "Three by Bomberg" at the Fly By Night Theater and "Monsoon Christmas" at the Lexington Theater. Kevin also began to appear on television working in commercials as well as the syndicated series "The Judge," as well as a guest starring role on the popular prime-time series "Hunter." In November of 1988 Best landed his first major role, portraying Dr. Harrison Davis on "General Hospital," a role that lasted through 1990. Kevin and his wife, Karen, share a home in the San Fernando Valley area of Los Angeles. Together they have a son, Julian Josef, born March 23,1990. In addition to acting, Kevin also writes song lyrics. In his spare time, he enjoys reading.

LAURA BRYAN BIRN

Born: April 3 in Chicago, Illinois
Marital Status: single
Hair: brown
Education: University of Southern California, B.F.A.
Interests: tennis, horseback riding, aerobics

Daytime Dramas: "The Young and the Restless,"
Lynne Bassett

A Chicago native, Laura Bryan Birn is best known to daytime fans as Lynne Bassett on "The Young and the Restless." Born on April 3, Birn moved to Darien, Connecticut at the age of three, living there for the next eight years before her family returned to Chicago. From an early age, Laura was interested in show business, this largely due to the influence of her mother, Betty Birn, a local singer on radio and television. Along with studying dance and voice, Laura was also an accomplished young athlete, playing field hockey, softball, and tennis, frequently competing alongside her sister in Southern New England and Fairfield County Doubles Tournaments. Returning to Chicago, Birn attended New Trier High School, while spending her summers honing her dramatic skills at the summer theater program at Northwestern University. She eventually enrolled at USC, and after receiving her B.F.A. in drama, began appearing on stage in such productions as "A Chorus Line," "Evita," and "E/R." Ms. Birn landed her "The Young and the Restless" role just one year out of college, after being discovered waiting tables at the Cheesecake Factory in Marina Del Rey. Although her career is going strong, this dedicated actress continues to study drama with Darryl Hickman. Following in Laura's footsteps, the rest of the Birn family has also relocated to Los Angeles, where Mr. Birn is now on the writing staff of "The Young and the Restless." In her spare time, Laura, who is single, enjoys tennis, horseback riding, and aerobics.

TERESA BLAKE

Born: December 12 in Tuscaloosa, Alabama
Marital Status: single
Height: 5'6 1/2" **Eyes:** blue **Hair:** blond
Education: high school
Interests: music, dancing, karate
Awards: Hawaiian Tropic Bikini Modelling Contest,
international level

Daytime Dramas: "All My Children," Gloria Marsh, 1991-

The producers of "All My Children" hit pay dirt when they hired Teresa Blake. Since joining the cast in October of 1991, her portrayal of the vindictive, yet vulnerable, Gloria Marsh, has proven her to be as talented as she is beautiful. A native of Tuscaloosa, Alabama, Teresa got her professional start when she entered a local Hawaiian Tropic Bikini/

Modelling Contest. She wound up winning the contest, and going on to compete on the state, national, and eventually international level. With this impressive start, Teresa launched a modelling career, and after graduation from high school she moved to Miami, where she began acting as well. Among her television credits are guest appearances on "Miami Vice" (she played Don Johnson's girlfriend) and "B.L. Stryker," with Burt Reynolds. Ms. Blake has also co-starred in the television film "Prize Pulitzer," and in the feature films "Revenge of the Nerds," "Payback," "Had to Be You," and the James Bond thriller, "License to Kill." She has also appeared in Billy Idol and Julio Iglesias videos. After living in Los Angeles for a few years, Teresa relocated to New York City in 1991 when she landed her role on "All My Children." Recently her character was the victim of date rape, and the actress has earned raves for her sensitive portrayal. Away from the set, Teresa enjoys karate, dancing, and music. She has also recently begun to learn sign language, and hope to utilize this skill in the future working with the hearing impaired.

YASMINE BLEETH

Born: June 14 in New York, New York
Marital Status: single
Height: 5'5 1/2"   **Eyes:** blue   **hair:** brown
Education: United Nations International School
Interests: cooking, rollerblading, waterskiing, spending time with family

Daytime Dramas: "Ryan's Hope," Ryan Fenelli, 1985-1989; **"One Life to Live,"** Lee Ann Demerest, 1991-

A native of New York City, Yasmine Amanda Bleeth began her successful modeling career at the age of six months, opting not to completely squander her infancy the way so many kids do. It was in fact Yasmine's mother, a model herself, who introduced her daughter to the world of modeling, and the younger Bleeth continued with this career for many years afterward. Her modeling assignments took her all over the world, including extensive periods in Paris and Brazil, and as a result Yasmine is now fluent in French, Spanish, and Portuguese. Turning towards acting, she made her film debut at the age of twelve in "Hey Babe," with Buddy Hackett, as well as appearing in numerous commercials. Daytime fans first came to know Yasmine as Ryan Fenelli on "Ryan's Hope," a role she played for four years. It was while on "Ryan's Hope" that she seriously dated fellow co-star, Luke Perry, now one of the stars of "Beverly Hills 90210." Their relationship ended after three years. Today she is romantically linked with "Another World's" Ricky Paull Goldin whom she met when they performed together in the off-Broadway play "Welcome to My Life." Before moving on to her latest role on "One Life to Live," Yasmine took some time to deal with the death of her mother, spending a year living with her family on the island of St. Barths, as well as with her grandmother in Paris. During this difficult period she forged a special relationship with Tristan (age seven), her mother's son from her second marriage, and the two remain close. She is also close with her other half brother Miles Bleeth (age four). Now living in New York City, Yasmine enjoys cooking, rollerblading, waterskiing and spending time with her family.

LAURA BONARRIGO

Born: October 29 in Brookline, Massachusetts
Marital Status: single
Height: 5'5" **Eyes:** brown **Hair:** brown
Education: Rutgers University, B.A.
Interests: rollerblading, exercising
Awards: 1982 1st Place in National Teenager Pageant

Daytime Dramas: "Another World," Lindsay, 1991;
"One Life to Live," Cassie Callison, 1991-

Clearly, ambition has never been a problem for Laura Bonarrigo. From the time she was in second grade, when she appeared in a school play, she knew that she would be an actress. A scant four years later she decided to expand her field of expertise when she not only starred in, but wrote and directed a school production of "Winnie the Pooh." Now as Cassie Callison on "One Life to Live," she is getting the opportunity to display her talents to a much wider audience. Born on October 29, in Brookline, Massachusetts, Laura and her family (which includes three brothers and three sisters) relocated to a large farm in Thomaston, Maine when the young actress was still in high school. Laura spent the next several years dividing her time between her school work, acting in community theater, and tending to the responsibilities that come with a family farm. Unlike most aspiring actresses, Laura rarely went to the movies, and since her parents, both of whom were teachers, realized the importance of a good education, she only seldom got a glimpse of the medium in which she would soon be working. In 1981, Laura entered the National Teenager Pageant, placing second and earning honors for congeniality. The following year proved more successful as Laura won the state title, as well as being named most photogenic. Upon graduating from high school, Bonarrigo enrolled at the School of Fine Arts at Rutgers University, where she studied acting, voice, and movement; her sophmore year she transferred to the Douglas College Division of Rutgers, which enabled her to broaden her field of study to include English and history. Following commencement, Laura set off for Europe, travelling extensively before settling down in Greece for several months. Returning to the states she officially embarked on her professional acting career, working as a model and in commercials while taking classes at the International Film and Television Workshop and at the School of Performance Studies in Maine. After this initiation Laura took the big step and moved to New York City. With acting assignments scarce, she paid the bills by working as a mother's helper, and although her career is now progressing well, she remains extremely close to the family for whom she worked. Along with "One Life to Live," Laura's other t.v. credits include a three month stint as Lindsay on "Another World" and a role in the t.v. pilot "Against the Law." Away from the set Laura is a serious athlete, and lists among her hobbies horseback riding, swimming, and rollerblading. Recently she competed in a triathalon, along with others from "One Life to Live." Although she is adjusting to life in the big city, Laura misses the tranquility of farm life, and visits her Maine home as often as possible.

STEVE BOND

Born: April 22 in Haifa, Israel
Marital Status: married to golfer/model Cindy Cox,
one daughter, Ashlee, and one son, Dylan
Height: 5'9"   **Eyes:** blue   **Hair:** brown
Interests: running, weightlifting, raising horses, polo
Awards: 1983 Soap Opera Digest, Newcomer of the Year
Award

Daytime Dramas: "General Hospital," Jimmy Lee Holt,
1983-1986; **"Santa Barbara,"** Mack Blake

Born in Haifa, Israel, Bond's family moved to the states when he was a child and settled in Los Angeles. Steve Bond first became interested in acting when his neighbors, whom he thought were perpetually at each others throats, turned out to be actors rehearsing a scene. They were so impressed by Bond that they encouraged him to audition for some juvenile roles, which lead to parts in "Tarzan and the Jungle Boy," "Don't Just Stand There," and "The Arrangement," with Kirk Douglas. While this was an extremely promising start, Bond put his acting career on hold during his late teens so he could join the professional rodeo circuit. He stayed with this until he somehow wound up cushioning the fall of a rather large bull, injuring himself and ending his rodeo career. After travelling through Europe, Bond decided to return to his acting career, landing roles in "Massacre at Central High," "Cat Merkil and Silks," "Magdalene," and "Prey." Other feature film credits include "To Die For," "To Die For II: The Son of Darkness," "The Silver Fox," and "Picasso Trigger" an action/adventure film in which Bond performs his own equestrian stunts. His television work includes appearances on "The Incredible Hulk," "McCloud," "Matlock," You, The Jury," and "Full House." He also appeared in the television movie "Miracle on Ice." On stage Bond held the lead role in "Heaven Can Wait," at the Waldo Astoria Playhouse in Kansas City, MO. No stranger to daytime dramas, he played the role of Jimmy Lee Holt on "General Hospital," for which he won a Soap Opera Award in 1983 as Newcomer of the Year. He also portrayed Mack Blake on "Santa Barbara." Bond continues to study both acting and singing and is a serious runner and weightlifter. Bond is married to Cindy Cox, a golfer/model, together they have daughter Ashlee and a son Dylan. He lists among his interests, horses and polo. He raises horses on his property and is involved with various polo related charities around the country.

JAMES EVAN BONIFANT

Born: August 19, 1985 in Virginia
Marital Status: single
Height: 4'   **Eyes:** brown   **Hair:** light brown
Education: elementary school
Interests: swimming, dancing, skiing, wiggling his ears

Daytime Dramas: "Guiding Light," Timmy;
"One Life to Live," Little Al, 1991-

THE SOAP OPERA BOOK

Generally, it would be unwise for a daytime actor to proclaim: "I love to wiggle my ears for people," but considering the actor in question, James Evan Bonifant, is seven years old and forty three inches tall, it seems appropriate. Known to millions as Little Al on "One Life to Live," Evan (as he likes to be called) has been on the program since 1991, and before that appeared briefly as Timmy on "Guiding Light." The young actor was born on August 19, 1985 in Virginia, where his father works as a surveyor/engineer, and his mother owns a cleaning service. He has two older brothers, Todd and Adam. During his brief career, Evan has appeared in scores of national commercials, including advertisements for Campbell's Soup, Isuzu Trooper, K-Mart, Burger King, Colgate Jr. Toothpaste, and Pillsbury. Along with daytime, he has also tested the prime time waters, co-starring in the t.v. pilot, "Graham," with Griffin Dunn and Allison Porter, and in the television film "Warren Marcus," in which Evan played the title character at five years old. Moving beyond prime time, he also has been seen on "Late Night with David Letterman." Just ending the first grade, where he served as a class monitor, Evan is an excellent student, and writes: "I have the best teacher in the world." Away from school and the set, he lists amongst his many hobbies: dancing, swimming, skiing, biking, reading, putting together puzzles, horseback riding, kite flying, and roasting marshmallows. Evan now calls New York City his home.

BRONWEN BOOTH

Born: February 21 in London, England
Marital Status: single
Height: 5'4" **Eyes:** brown   **Hair:** dark brown
Education: Boston University
Interests: horseback riding, swimming

Daytime Dramas: **"One Life to Live,"** Andy Harrison

Bronwen Booth, who's name means "pure of heart" in Welsh, was born February 21, in London, England. She spent most of her childhood in New York City, before moving to Los Angeles at the age of thirteen. After attending Beverly Hills High School, Bronwen moved back east where she enrolled as a theater major at Boston University. It was during her years in college that she landed her first professional roles in the films "Love Streams," with John Cassavetes, and "Eternal Evil," with Karen Black. In addition, Bronwen had day parts on numerous daytime dramas. Very much like Andy Harrison, her character on "One Life to Live," the actress, who lives alone, is independent and strong willed. When not working, Bronwen makes frequent trips to California to visit her mother, a film producer, as well as spending time riding horses on her father's upstate New York ranch. Her other hobbies include tennis, swimming, and playing with her basset hound, Emmett.

MATT BORLENGHI

Born: May 25, 1967 in Los Angeles, California
Marital Status: single
Height: 5'11"   **Eyes:** brown   **Hair:** brown
Education: high school
Interest: motorcycles, music

Daytime Dramas: "All My Children," Brian Bodine, 1991-

Born in Los Angeles, California, Matt Borlenghi almost became a professional actor at a much younger age. The oldest of three boys, and godson of singer Jerry Vale, Matt was slated to star in a western at the age of seven. Unfortunately the project never materialized and the young actor was forced to wait a few more years before landing his first professional job. While in school, Borlenghi was active in football, tennis, and soccer, earning an MVP award for his goaltending abilities. However, acting remained his passion, and eventually he began to pursue this full time. His first break came with a commercial for Le Tigre clothing line which Matt followed with a starring role in the film "The American Scream." In addition, Borlenghi has appeared in the film "Nightmare on Elm Street 5," as well as on the small screen in "Family Medical Center" and "T.V. 101." However, in terms of career advancement, his most important role was only a 30 second cameo on the NBC series, "Hunter." Borlenghi's performance had such an impact on All My Children executive producer, Felicia Minei Behr, that she recruited him personally for the crucial role of Brian Bodine. Since joining the cast in January of 1991, he has become a favorite among daytime fans. Away from the set, Matt who lives with his girlfriend in New York City, enjoys sports, music and riding his motorcycle.

ROSCOE BORN

Marital Status: separated from actress Randall Edwards
Education: Boston University, School of Fine Arts
Interests: theater, writing
Awards: Dramalogue Award for "A Life in the Theater,"
Emmy nomination for Santa Barbara

Daytime Dramas: "Ryan's Hope," Joe Novak, 1981-1983;
"One Life to Live," Mitchell Laurence, 1985-1987;
"Santa Barbara," Robert Barr

An actor and an author, Roscoe Born's career has included television, film, and theater. He is presently seen as Robert Barr on "Santa Barbara," and has additionally played roles on "Ryan's Hope" and "One Life to Live." Born first became interested in acting during a cross country hitchhiking trip, in which he began to enjoy "reinventing" himself for each car that picked him up. After studying acting at Boston University's School of Fine Arts, as well as training under Robert

Prosky at the Arena Stage Improvisational Workshop, Roscoe began his professional career concentrating on stage work. He appeared in such productions as "The Glass Menagerie," "Fun," and " A Life in the Theater," for which he was awarded a Dramalogue Award. On television, in addition to daytime, Born co-starred in the series, "Paper Dolls," as well as appearing in the television films "Lady Mobster," with Susan Lucci, and "The Haunting of Sarah Hardy." On the big screen, Born has been seen in "End of the World," "Jailbait Babysitter," and opposite his "Santa Barbara" co-star A Martinez in "Powwow Highway." Taking after his father, who worked as a journalist for such publications as The Wall Street Journal, Barrons, and The National Observer, Roscoe published a book of his own, "The Suspended Sentence." Born, who lives in Los Angeles, is now separated from his wife, Randall Edwards, an actress previously seen on "Ryan's Hope."

PETER BOYNTON

Born: November 4, 1955 in Danaiscotta, Maine
Marital Status: married to actress Susan Marie Snyder on October 7, 1989, one daughter, Logan Mae
Height: 6'1 1/2" **Eyes:** brown **Hair:** brown
Education: University of Massachusetts at Amherst, Bachelor's Degree
Interests: aviation

Daytime Dramas: "One Life to Live," Brent Cameron; **"The Catlins,"** Beau Catlin, 1984; **"As the World Turns,"** Tonio Reyes, 1986-1991

Presently taking time away from daytime television, Peter Boynton will not be easily forgotten, having spent five years as the villainous Tonio Reyes on "As the World Turns." Born on November 4, 1955, in Danaiscotta, Maine, Boynton attended the University of Massachusetts at Amherst, where he received his degree in music, specializing in theory and composition. Along with "As the World Turns," Peter has also been seen by daytime audiences as Brent Cameron on "One Life to Live," and as Beau Catlin on "The Catlins." Throughout his career, the actor has worked steadily in regional theater, and recently co-starred in the feature film, "Hellraiser III." Boynton, who lists aviation as one of his interests, lives in a 200 year old home in Rockland County with his wife, actress Susan Marie Snyder. The couple met, before she joined the "As The World Turns" cast, at the shows annual Christmas party. They were married less than one year later. Their first child, Logan Mae, was born in September, 1991.

ERIC BRAEDEN

Born: April 3 in Kiel, Germany
Marital Status: married to Dale Braeden, one son, Christian
Height: 6'1" **Eyes:** brown **Hair:** brown
Education: Santa Monica College
Interests: tennis, soccer, German/American Cultural Society
Awards: 1992 "People's Choice Award" for Favorite Male
Daytime Performer; Soap Opera Award for Best Actor; 1991
Federal Medal of Honor; German/American of the Year;
1991 Soap Opera Award nomination, Outstanding Leading
Actor; 1991 MVP Award, Soap Opera Update

Daytime Dramas: "The Young and the Restless,"
Victor Newman, 1980-

The winner of the 1992 People's Choice Award for favorite male performer on daytime television, Eric Braeden is a man as accomplished and worldly as his character on "The Young and the Restless." Born Hans Gudegast, the third of four sons, in Kiel, Germany, Braeden was a high school track and field star, leading his team to the National German Youth Championship. In 1959, after graduating high school, Braeden set out for the United States, arriving in New York City where he ate his first meal at the Empire State Building. After only a short time he left New York for Galveston, Texas, meeting a cousin who had arranged a translator job for Braeden. This only lasted a few months, and in keeping with his adventurous style, Braeden then moved to Montana to work on his ranch. He remained there for a spell, but after being awarded a partial track scholarship, Braeden enrolled in Montana State University, where he not only ran track but also worked nights at a lumber mill and trained with the R.O.T.C.. His life took another unexpected turn when a friend asked Braeden to join him on a boat trip up Idaho's Salmon River. Unaware that this particular river was known as "the river of no return," Braeden and his friend became the first men to survive the trip up and down the river. They filmed their expedition, naming the film "The Riverbusters," which they brought to Los Angeles in the hopes of finding a distributor. Enjoying the atmosphere of California, Braeden decided to remain, enrolling in political science and economics courses at Santa Monica College. His plans came into focus, however, when he found out that German actors were in high demand. Braeden quickly acquired an agent and began receiving offers. One concession he eventually made was to change his name to something more accessible to the American public. (Eric is his family name and Braeden is the village he comes from in Germany). His first role was in the film "Operation Eichman," which Braeden followed with an appearance on "Kraft Suspense Theater." Also getting his feet wet on stage, Braeden co-starred in the production of "Kean," at the opening of the Santa Monica Theater, and has also been seen on stage in the Broadway production of "The Great Indoors," with Curt Jurgens and Geraldine Page. On the big screen, Braeden's additional credits include "Colossus: The Forbidden Project," "The Ultimate Chase," "Honeymoon with a Stranger," "A Hundred Rifles," and "Escape from the Planet of the Apes." On television, Braeden has achieved great success for his work on "The Young and the Restless" and "Rat Patrol." His role as Victor Newman has gained him tremendous popularity, but initially he only intended the role to last for three months. Fortunately, Braeden grew to like the day to day challenge of serial television. In addition he has guest starred on over 120 t.v. programs, as well as in several t.v. films, including "The Judge and Mrs. Wyler," "Happily Ever After," "Cry of the Rooster," and the mini-series "Lucky." As one of the first German actors to gain American popularity, Braeden has become an important diplomatic figure. In 1991 he was awarded for being a positive representative of Germany with the Federal Medal of Honor, which was presented by Germany's president. Braeden is also the co-founder of the German/American Cultural Society which helps to establish German/Jewish dialogue, and is the only actor on the German-American Advisory board, which includes such distinguished members as Dr. Henry Kissinger, Katherine Graham, Alexander Haig, and Paul Volcker. Braeden and his wife, Dale, whom he met while at Santa Monica College, have been married for over 25 years. The couple lives in Los Angeles and has one son, Christian. Still active athletically, Braeden plays soccer regularly, (his team, The Maccabees, won the 1972 National Soccer Championship) and enjoys boxing, tennis, skiing, and running.

MICHAEL BRAINARD

Born: November 23, 1965 in Hollywood, California
Marital Status: single
Height: 6'   **Eyes:** blue   **Hair:** light brown
Education: Laguna Hills High School, Pacific Christian College, Cal State Fullerton, School of Performing Arts in Costa Mesa, Lee Strasberg Institute in Los Angeles
Interests: volleyball, surfing, theater, movies, videos, camping, hiking, traveling the United States
Awards: 1992 Soap Opera Award Nomination, Younger Leading Actor ("All My Children")

Daytime Dramas: "All My Children," Joey Martin, 1988-1991; **"Santa Barbara,"** 1991-

This young talented actor made his daytime debut in December of 1988, joining the cast of "All My Children." As his character, Joey Martin, headed off to California, so did Michael Brainard return to the west coast. Never really getting into the hustle and bustle of New York, he is happy about the move back to his native state and equally happy about joining the cast of "Santa Barbara." Born Michael Scott Brainard in Los Angeles on November 23, he and his older sister Dawn were raised in Laguna Hills where his father was a Los Angeles firefighter and his mother an accountant. A graduate of Laguna Hills High School, Brainard enrolled at Cal State in Fullerton, and also studied acting at Pacific Christian College, the School of Performing Arts in Costa Mesa, and also at the Lee Strasberg Institute in Los Angeles. Some of the productions he performed in during this time include: "Mister Roberts," "Fiddler on the Roof," "Front Page," "Flowers for Algernon," and "One Flew Over the Cuckoo's Nest." His professional debut was on the syndicated television series "Divorce Court." Brainard originally auditioned for the part of David Rampal on "All My Children," but was cast as the youngest member of the Martin family, Joey. Brainard feels strongly about education and is involved in reading programs such as RIF (Reading Is Fundamental). He also gives his time to the Alison Ann Ruch Burn Foundation in Los Angeles. A true Californian, Michael lists among his hobbies, volleyball and surfing. Other interests include theatre, movies, videos, camping hiking and traveling through out the United States.

JOSEPH BREEN

Born: July 5 in Mt. Kisco, New York
Marital Status: divorced, three daughters, Caitlin, Meghan and Devon
Height: 6'1"   **Eyes:** hazel   **Hair:** brown
Education: American Academy of Dramatic Arts, Julliard School
Interests: opera, boating, gardening, carpentry

Daytime Dramas: "Guiding Light," Dr. Will Jeffries, 1987-1988; **"Loving,"** Paul Slavinsky 1989-1992; **"As The World Turns,"** Scott Eldridge, 1992-

During his years in daytime drama Joseph Breen has created some of the most memorable characters on television. Just ending his run as the scheming Paul Slavinsky on "Loving," he is best known for his years as Dr. Will Jeffries on "Guiding Light." Breen was born in Mt. Kisco, New York, one of six children, his sister, Carolyn Breen, is a highly acclaimed author of books on Ireland. He first discovered his love of performing at the age of 14, when his neighbor Broadway actor Robert Rounseville, realized that Joe had an excellent singing voice, and encouraged him to develop this talent. By the time Joe reached high school he divided his time between athletics and starring in school plays, a pattern he planned on continuing at Oberlin College in Ohio. In this instance, however, Joe's rebellious streak got the better of him and he was kicked out of school. He then decided to return to New York, where he enrolled in the American Academy of Dramatic Arts, finding work in off-Broadway and regional productions of such classics as "The Glass Menagerie," "Playboy of the Western World," "The Taming of the Shrew," and "Cat on a Hot Tin Roof." With this impressive list of credits behind him Joe then landed the role as the son, Jean-Michael, in the Broadway production of "La Cage Aux Folles," a part he continued to play throughout a national tour. When the tour eventually concluded in Los Angeles, Joe considered staying out west, but at the advice of his agent he returned to New York to further hone his acting and singing skills at the Julliard School. Since then Joe has become a fixture on daytime television, for his work on "Guiding Light," "Loving" and now on "As The World Turns." Yet it is clear that Joe is not one to rest on his laurels, for while he enjoys his work on daytime dramas, Joe has definite plans for the future. Most significantly he would like to pursue a professional opera career, a dream he has had since his days at Julliard. Along with this he is an aspiring playwright, and has even started his own construction company, which he recently established during his hiatus from daytime television. In his spare time Joe enjoys boating, gardening, and carpentry. He presently resides in Connecticut, where he enjoys spending time with his three daughters, Caitlin, Meghan, and Devon.

TRACEY BREGMAN-RECHT

Born: May 29 in Munich, Germany
Marital Status: married to Ron Recht, one son, Austin Alexander
Height: 5'3" **Eyes:** hazel **Hair:** auburn
Education: Westlake School, Lee Strasberg Theatre Institute
Interests: music, charity
Awards: "Best Actress in Daytime TV" from Youth in Film Magazine, two time winner; Daytime TV's "Most Popular Newcomer;" Canadian Peoples Poll for "Most Exciting New Actress in Daytime TV" and "Favorite New Actress;" 1979 Soap Opera Award, "Favorite Female Newcomer," (all for "Days of Our Lives") 1985 Daytime Emmy, "Outstanding Ingenue," 1985 Daytime Emmy nomination, "Outstanding Ingenue" ("The Young and the Restless")

Daytime Dramas: "Days of Our Lives," Donna Temple Craig, 1978-1980; **"The Young and the Restless,"** Lauren Fenmore, 1984-

A winner of numerous daytime awards, Tracey Bregman-Recht has been a favorite of soap fan's for almost fifteen years. In 1978, on the first day of her school's Easter vacation, Tracey received her first professional acting assignment; a three day stint on "Days of Our Lives." However, she became such a favorite of the fans and the producers, that the three days have turned into fourteen years of daytime and counting. Born in Munich, Germany, Tracey lived in London until the age of eleven, when her family moved to southern California. Once in America, Tracey attended the Westlake School for Girls. It was during this time that she also began her formal acting training, working with Francis Lederer at A.N.T.A., as well as studying at the renowned Lee Strasberg Theatre Institute. While still in school, Tracey got her big break with the role of Donna on "Days of Our Lives." During her years on the show Tracey received several awards, including Most Popular Newcomer (Daytime TV), "Most Exciting New Actress in Daytime TV" and "Favorite New Actress" (Canadian Peoples Poll), and was twice named "Best Actress in Daytime T.V." by Youth in Film Magazine. Although best known for her work on daytime, Tracey has also appeared on such programs as "The Fall Guy," "The Love Boat," "Gavilan," and "Fame." She starred in the afterschool special "The Girl with E.S.P." and in the television motion pictures "Three on a Date," and "Fair Weather Friend," with Olivia-Newton John, and "The Littlest Hobo." Her big screen credits include, "Happy Birthday to Me" and "The Funny Farm," both also afforded her the opportunity to display her musical, as well as dramatic abilities. An accomplished singer and songwriter, Tracey, whose great uncle is renowned pianist Jule Styne, wrote and performed the theme songs for both her films. It is, however, her role as Lauren Fenmore, the conniving, and sometimes singing siren on "The Young and the Restless," that has established Tracey as one of daytime's leading vixens. Like her earlier role on "Days of Our Lives," her work on "The Young and the Restless" has earned her several important awards, including two daytime Emmy nominations as Outstanding Ingenue, an award she took home in 1985. A dual citizen of Canada and the United States, Tracey is married to real estate developer Ron Recht. The couple's first child, Austin Alexander, was born on March 18, 1991. She also has two step daughters, Emily and Lindsay, from her husbands previous marriage. A strict vegetarian, Tracey stays in shape by attending daily dance classes. In addition, she serves as the chairperson for "The Young Persons Committee," an organization that helps the underprivileged. Tracey is also active with the SPCA and The Young Musicians Music Foundation.

MARK BRETTSCHNEIDER

Born: September 2, 1969 in Cincinnati, Ohio
Marital Status: single
Height: 6'2" **Eyes:** blue/green **Hair:** blond
Education: Carnegie Mellon University, B.F.A.
Interests: basketball, movies

Daytime Dramas: "One Life to Live," Jason Webb, 1991-

Two months after Mark Brettschneider finished college and was on the brink of life as a struggling actor he landed the much sought after role of Jason Webb on "One Life to Live." He was slated to begin work as a doorman at a New York's Morgan Hotel, (in the midnight to 7 A.M. shift) when he found out he had landed a soap opera role. Now a year later he has become one of daytime's most popular newcomers. Born in Cincinnati, Ohio, where his father worked as an accountant and his mother a doctor of pharmacology, Mark was committed to acting from an early age. At thirteen he enrolled in the Cincinnati School of Performing Arts and divided the next several years between school, appearing in local commercials, and occasional stage work, including touring the nation in a production of "Oliver." Brettschneider then went on to receive his B.F.A. in theater from Carnegie Mellon University. The actor has performed on stage, both at school and in regional theaters, in such works as "As Is," "Jesus Christ Superstar," "A Chorus Line," and "Antigone." Following graduation, he moved to New York, where he quickly caught the attention of Linda Gotlieb, the executive producer of "One Life to Live," who cast him as the rebellious, illiterate, Jason. He began growing his trademark long blond locks after an unsuccessful attempt several years earlier to cut his own hair. Disgusted with the results, Brettschneider swore he would not cut his hair again, and thus far has lived up to this vow. The actor's other distinguishing trademark, a scar under his left eye, came courtesy of the surgical removal of a beauty mark. Lately,

Mark has been dedicating a great deal of time to environmental issues, and even took the challenge of going door to door in an attempt to raise funds for a research group. In his spare time, Brettschneider is a sports enthusiast, and particularly enjoys basketball and playing on the "One Life to Live" softball team. His other hobbies include going to the movies, exploring his new home (New York City), and spending time with his dalmatian puppy, Sebastian.

BRENDA BROCK

Born: March 29 in Beaumount, Texas
Marital Status: married to restaurant owner, Paul Barclay de Tolly
Height: 5'7"   **Hair:** blond   **Eyes:** green
Education: University of Texas
Interests: cooking, running

Daytime Dramas: "One Life to Live," Brenda McGillis

Suppose one day on the set a crew member is injured and needs some quick first aid. Who should he see? Why not Brenda Brock, she spent years studying to be a nurse. And suppose one day on the set the producers decide to cook a special dinner for everyone. Who should they see about dinner? Why not Brenda Brock, she is an accomplished chef who often practices her craft in New York and Rhode Island restaurants. Now as it turns out, during dinner every single writer on the show mysteriously disappears and there is still a scene to be completed; hey what about Brenda; she recently wrote and produced a play for the New York stage. Oh yeah, she's also an actress. A native of Beaumont, Texas, Brenda was raised outside Dallas, dividing her time between her mother's home in South Texas, and her father's cotton ranch in the central part of the state. Although she was involved in community theater from an early age, Brenda's original career goal was nursing, which she pursued at the University of Texas at Austin. With one more semester to go, she was offered a scholarship to study acting, and was forced to make a choice. Heeding the advice of her father, Brenda decided to follow her heart and she began studying drama. After college she relocated to Denver where she spent two years with the Denver Center Theater Company, appearing in such productions as "Taming of the Shrew," "The Rise and Rise of Daniel Rocket," "Arms and the Man," and "The Hostage." With a strong record of stage performances, Brenda moved to New York City to find acting work. She spent the next year learning the ins and outs of the acting world, supporting herself through an array of odd jobs. It was during this stretch that she penned "Summer at Pilares," which was recently produced at New York's Michael Howard Studio Theater, and is most likely going to be appearing in various regional theaters. In addition Brenda is a member of The Harrier Group, a production company who's members include Paul Newman, Tony Curtis, and Jamie Lee Curtis. Away from acting, the real life Brenda spends much of her spare time in Rhode Island, renovating her Victorian home. While there she can often be found practicing her culinary skills at a local restaurant; and recently Brenda was invited to serve as quest chef in a New York City restaurant as well. No stranger to cooking for a lot of people, the actress spent a semester of college near the Mexican border, working as a cook for a geological team in search of uranium. An owner of two cats, (Maurice and Odet) Brenda keeps in shape through running and a proper diet, and keeps her skin clean and clear by drinking her own formula of beet juice and apple-cider vinegar. Since leaving "One Life to Live," Brenda's plans included a sailing vacation that would take her to Los Angeles in time to explore the primetime possibilities.

RANDY BROOKS

Born: January 30 in New York, New York
Marital Status: single, two sons
Height: 6' **Eyes:** brown **Hair:** black
Education: The Lee Strasberg Institute
Interests: football, cooking, music, writing

Daytime Dramas: "Generations," Eric Royal;
"The Young and the Restless," Nathan Hastings, 1991-

Last seen by daytime audiences as Eric Royal on the now defunct "Generations," Randy Brooks has returned to serial television as Nathan Hastings on "The Young and the Restless." Born on January 30, Brooks lived in New York City until the age of twelve, when his parents decided to relocate the family to the safer world of South Carolina. Always interested in acting, Randy appeared in numerous high school productions, as well as establishing himself as a tennis and football star. Following his high school graduation, Brooks decided to ignore his many athletic scholarship offers and head back to New York to pursue his acting ambitions. He landed his first role, in the chorus of "Hair," just two weeks after arriving. Brooks spent the next year working with the musical and attending acting classes at the prestigious Lee Strasberg Institute. When the production of "Hair" began it's national tour, Brooks remained with the company, and by the time it reached Los Angeles he had secured himself a starring role. In 1971, looking for a change of pace, Randy moved to Hawaii, where he spent the subsequent five years singing with the Honolulu Symphony Orchestra at the Honolulu International Center. Returning to L.A. in 1976, Brooks continued his acting training with John LeBue and Walter Lott, eventually landing roles on the NBC series "Brothers and Sisters," and alongside Patrick Swayze in "The Renegades." Additionally, Brooks has starred in the series "Hardesty House," as well as making guest appearances on "Murder, She Wrote," "Tour of Duty," "In the Heat of the Night," and in pilot episodes of "Nightingales," "Sirens," and "Dark House." He also co-starred in the mini-series "Rituals" and in the made for television films "Forbidden Love" and "Scared Straight: Another Story." On the big screen, Brooks has been seen in "Halls of Anger," "Assassination," "Defenseless," with Barbara Hershey," "Colors," with Sean Penn, "Eight Million Ways to Die," with Jeff Bridges and Andy Garcia, and most recently "Reservoir Dogs," with Harvey Keitel. The busy actor also wrote a screenplay, "Snow Angels," which was recently optioned by a production company. Now living in Los Angeles, Brooks, who is the father of two boys, relaxes by playing the piano and violin, and also enjoys cooking, football, and racquetball.

KIMBERLIN BROWN

Born: June 29 in Hayward, California
Marital Status: married to Gary Pelzer
Height: 5'6" **Eyes:** hazel **Hair:** brown
Education: Grossmont College
Interests: travelling, skiing, scuba diving
Awards: Miss La Mesa and Miss California

Daytime Dramas: "Santa Barbara," Danielle Steele;
"The Young and the Restless," Sheila Carter, 1989-1992;
"The Bold and the Beautiful," Sheila Carter, 1992-

A model and an actress, Kimberlin Brown began her career at the age of nine, and is today best known as the psychotic Sheila Carter on "The Young and the Restless." Creator Bill Bell was so impressed by Kimberlin, that when her "The Young and the Restless" storyline was ending, he brought her character over to his other show, "The Bold and the Beautiful." Born on June 29 in Hayward, California, Kimberlin's career took off after being discovered at the age of nine by Nina Blanchard helping the young model to eventually take home the titles of Miss La Mesa and Miss California. Putting her studies at Grossmont College on hold, Kimberlin modelled in Europe for a year, followed by a six month stint in the Orient. While certainly attaining a fair amount of success as a model, Kimberlin decided to focus on acting upon her return to the United States, enrolling in drama classes, and soon landing guest roles on such show as "Matt Houston," "T.J. Hooker," "Hawaiian Heat," "Dragnet," and "The New Adam-12." In addition, Ms. Brown appeared in the feature films "Who's that Girl?," "Eye of the Tiger," and "18 Again." Prior to "The Young and the Restless," the actress had small roles on "Capitol," and as Danielle Steele on "Santa Barbara." Away from the set, Kimberlin is active with two charitable organizations, The Free Arts Clinic and The City of Hope. An avid traveller, she also enjoys scuba diving, skiing, mountain climbing, and golf. She was the only woman invited to play at the celebrity pro-am Greater Greensboro Open in 1991. Brown recently married Gary Pelzer, and the couple will soon be featured on an episode of "Runaway with the Rich and Famous."

LISA BROWN

Born: August 2 in Kansas City, Missouri
Marital Status: divorced, two children
Height: 5'3" **Eyes:** brown **Hair:** brownish-red
Education: high school
Interests: theater, dance, music, antiques
Awards: nominated for two Daytime Emmys, Outstanding Supporting Actress, 1987, 1988 ("As the World Turns")

Daytime Dramas: "Guiding Light," Nola Reardon Chamberlain, 1980-1985; **"As the World Turns,"** Iva Snyder, 1985-

A star of both the Broadway stage and daytime television, Lisa Brown has risen to the top of each of these divergent mediums. She made her television debut as Nola Reardon Chamberlain on "Guiding Light" in 1980, and remained on the show for the next five years, during which time she also starred in the popular Broadway musical, "42nd Street." Lisa has continued this pattern since joining the cast of "As the World Turns" in 1985. Along with being nominated for an Outstanding Supporting Actress daytime Emmy for her work on the show, she has also played the lead in the regional theatre production of "Sweet Charity." Born on August 2, in Kansas City, Missouri, Ms. Brown first came to appreciate performing from her grandmother, an actress of the early 1900's, who regaled Lisa with stories of the Empire Theater in New York City. Committed from an early age, Lisa began taking dance classes at the age of three, and by the time she was thirteen she had become a member of the dance and drill team for the Kansas City Chiefs. Immediately after graduating high school, she moved to New York City in search of theater work, landing her first role as a dancer in a bus and truck tour of "Seesaw." She followed this with a national touring company production of "Hello Dolly," with Pearl Bailey, that eventually reached the Broadway stage. Lisa's next Broadway appearance was in the chorus of "Pal Joey," which was followed by her first dramatic role in "Hit the Deck," at the Goodspeed Opera House. Since then, the talented actress has starred on Broadway in "The Best Little Whorehouse in Texas," "42nd St.," and in a Los Angeles based production of "Furnace Park," which saw Lisa serving as both producer and star. At the present time, she is putting together her own cabaret act, as well as preparing a possible role in the sequel to "Best Little Whorehouse in Texas." For MTV fans, Brown can be seen blowing bubbles in the Aretha Franklin video, "Everyday People." Lisa now lives in New Jersey with her two children.

PETER BROWN

Born: October 5, 1945 in New York, New York
Marital Status: married to Mary Brown, 1986
Height: 6' **Eyes:** hazel **Hair:** brown
Education: UCLA
Interests: rodeo, tennis, golf, mountain biking
Awards: Theater Owners of America- Most Outstanding Newcomer

Daytime Dramas: "Days of Our Lives," Greg Peters, 1972-1979; **"The Young and the Restless,"** Robert Lawrence, 1981-1982; **"Loving,"** Roger Forbes, 1983-1984; **"One Life to Live,"** Charles Sanders, 1986-1987; **"The Bold and the Beautiful,"** Blake Hayes, 1990-

A television favorite for many years, Peter Brown has played popular roles on "Days of Our Lives," "The Young and the Restless," "One Life to Live," "Loving," and most recently as Blake Hayes on "The Bold and the Beautiful." Born on October 5, 1945 in New York, New City, where his mother worked as a radio and t.v. actress, Peter spent most of his early years living on a California ranch, where he first developed his life long love of horses and rodeos. His first foray into acting came during his stint in the army. Stationed in Alaska, Brown decided to organize a theater group, and the experience proved so rewarding, that upon leaving the service he enrolled as a theatre arts major at UCLA. He has since gone on to enjoy a successful career on both the big and small screens, appearing in such feature films as "Eagles Attack at Dawn," "Summer Magic," "Darby's Rangers," "Merrill's Marauders," "A Tiger Walks," "Ride the Wild Surf," "Piranha, Piranha," "The Aurora Encounter," "The Gentle Savage," and "Demonstone." His box office appeal earned him the Most Outstanding Newcomer Award from the Theater Owners of America, a prize presented to Brown by John Wayne. Equally prolific on television, Brown has been a series regular on several shows, including "Lawman," "Laredo," and "Car Care Central," while he has guest starred on "Magnum P.I.," "Hunter," "Knightrider,"

"Dallas," "Fantasy Island," "Crazy Like A Fox," "Hart to Hart," "Ohara," "Airwolf," "Wagon Train," "Baywatch," "The A Team," "Riptide," "T.J. Hooker," "Fall Guy," "Bob Newhart Show," and "Simon and Simon." In addition his t.v. film credits include "The Girl, The Gold Watch & Everything," "Top of the Hill," "Cover Up," and "Hunters Are for Killing." Throughout his career, Brown has simultaneously developed his equestrian skills, appearing at rodeos and state fairs, often with Phil Carey of "One Life to Live." He has also organized charity rodeos and even put together an instructional penning video, through his production company, Handshake Films. Now living in Hermosa Beach, Brown, who is the father of two sons, Matthew and Joshua, has been married since 1986 to his fifth wife, Mary, whom he met in 1984 at a Michael Landon Tennis Tournament. In his spare time the actor lists amongst his hobbies, tennis, golf, mountain biking, movies, and rodeo, where he excels as a cutting horse rider and team penner (which means to remove certain cattle from a rushing herd in a beat the clock competition). Peter also spends as much time as possible enjoying the outdoors and his family.

PATRICIA BRUDER

Born: April 14 in Brooklyn, New York
Marital Status: married in June 1959 to Dr. Charles Debrovner, two daughters, Diane and Carolyn
Height: 5' 2" **Eyes:** blue **Hair:** blond
Education: Columbia University
Interests: theater

Daytime Dramas: "As the World Turns," Ellen Lowell Stewart, 1960-1975, 1976-

A native of Brooklyn, New York, Patricia Bruder is one of daytime dramas enduring favorites. During her schooling years at James Madison High School and later Columbia University, Patricia also managed to cultivate a performing career as well. She first gained attention at the age of nine, as a singer on the radio show, "Rainbow House," following which she joined the cast of another radio show, "Juvenile Jury." When this program made the transition to television, she remained on this show in the new medium. An accomplished stage actress as well, Ms. Bruder first appeared on Broadway as Flora in "The Innocents," and since then has tallied up an impressive list of theater credits, including roles in "Gypsy," "Lace on Her Petticoat," "The Sap of Life," and "The King and the Duke." Active behind the scenes as well, in 1977, Patricia produced and starred (with her two daughters) in a New York City production of "The Miracle Worker," and most recently headlined a production of "The Effects of Gamma Rays on Man-in-the-Moon Marigolds" at the Theater in the Park in Queens, New York. It was her performance in "Gypsy" which first caught the eye of the producers of "As the World Turns," and in 1960 she made her debut as Ellen Lowell Cole, a role in which she remained for over 30 years. Among her other television works are guest appearances on "Studio One," "Kraft Television Theater," "Suspense," and "Robert Montgomery Presents." Off screen, Patricia is married to Dr. Charles Debrovner, a gynecologist whom she met when both were in high school. They were married in June of 1959 and have two daughters, Diane, born in 1965, and Carolyn Joy, born in 1968.

LEE BRYANT

Born: August 31, 1945 in New York, New York
Marital Status: married to Norman Schwartz, three children, Elizabeth, Teddy, Andy
Height: 5'4" **Eyes:** blue **Hair:** blond
Education: Endicott College, Wayne State University
Interests: theater, hiking, skiing, reading
Awards: two Emmy nominations for "This is the Life"

Daytime Dramas: "Another World," Rose 1989;
"As the World Turns," Hannah Cafferty, 1991-

A familiar face on the Broadway stage, feature films, and prime time television, Lee Bryant joined the cast of "As the World Turns" in February, 1991. Born on August 31, 1945 in New York City, Lee grew up, along with her two younger sisters, in Grosse Point, Michigan, where her father owned amusement parks and developed real estate. Reflecting on her childhood, Lee says she had "a happy, athletically active growing up with two terrific younger sisters, who are still my best friends." Completing high school, Lee went on to attend Endicott College and Wayne State University, following which she began her acting career, appearing on Broadway in "End of the World," and in off-Broadway productions of "Powder" and "The Saving Grace." Ms. Bryant's film credits include "Airplane," "Airplane II," "Deathmask," with Danny Aiello, "Capricorn One," "The Main Event," as well as the television films "How the West was Won," "Lassie: A New Beginning," and "The Mysterious Two." Along with her current role as Hannah Cafferty on "As the World Turns," Lee has been seen as a regular on "T.J. Hooker," "The Lucie Arnaz Show, "Another World," and as a guest star on dozens of prime time series. Since 1988, the actress has been on the Board of Directors of the Screen Actor's Guild. A New York City resident, Ms. Bryant is married to Norman Schwartz, and has three children, Elizabeth, Teddy, and Andy. Extremely active with her children's school, Lee also donates her time as a Red Cross volunteer. In her spare time she enjoys skiing, reading, scuba diving, and going to the theater.

LARRY BRYGGMAN

Born: December 21 in Concord, California
Marital Status: divorced, three children, Michael, Jeffrey and Heidi
Height: 6' **Hair:** blond
Education: City College of San Francisco, Bachelor's Degree
Interests: sports, reading, music
Awards: Daytime Emmy for Outstanding Lead Actor, 1984, 1987; nominated for Daytime Emmy for Outstanding Lead Actor, 1990

Daytime Dramas: "As the World Turns," Dr. John Dixon, 1969-

Since he joined the cast of "As the World Turns" in 1969, Larry Bryggman has set the standard for acting excellence in daytime drama. And his role was originally slated as a day part. He has brought to the role of Dr. John Dixon an intensity and complexity which has made the character one of daytime's most fascinating. Born in Concord, California, Bryggman began to study acting at the City College of San Francisco, and upon graduation he embarked on an outstanding theatrical career. He made his professional debut in "Death of a Salesman," and with the exception of his stint in the army, has enjoyed a consistent string of memorable stage roles. His Broadway performances include "Ulysses in Nighttown," with Zero Mostel, "The Lincoln Mask," "Checking Out," "The Basic Training of Pavlo Hummel" and "Richard III," both with Al Pacino. His most recent role was in the critically acclaimed Broadway production of "Prelude to a Kiss." Bryggman has also been involved with countless off-Broadway and regional theater productions, among them "Marco Polo Sings a Solo," "Waiting for Godot," "Bodies, Rest and Motion," "Coriolanus," "Whose Afraid of Virginia Woolf," and as the title character in "Henry IV, Part I and II," which was presented at The Public Theater in New York. Bryggman has also starred on the big screen, opposite Al Pacino in "...And Justice for All," and in "Hanky Panky" with Gene Wilder and Gilda Radner. Bryggman first came to daytime drama in "Love is a Many Splendor Thing," and along with his work in "As the World Turns," he has also been featured in such television productions as "Trial of Panther 13," "The Witches of Salem," "A Celebration for Wm. Jennings Bryan" and "Strike Force." For his work on "As the World Turns," Bryggman has received two daytime Emmy awards for Outstanding Lead Actor, and was nominated an additional time. Bryggman has two children by his former wife, actress Jacqueline Schultz (whom he met on the set of As The World Turns) Michael, born in May, 1966 and Jeffrey, born February, 1970. He also has a daughter, Heidi, a screenwriter. Bryggman lists among his hobbies sports, music, and reading.

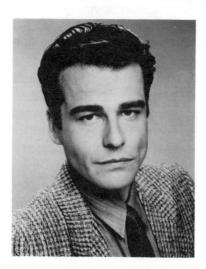

IAN BUCHANAN

Born: June 16 in E. Kilbride, Scotland
Marital Status: single
Height: 6' **Eyes:** green **Hair:** black
Education: Strasberg Theatre Institute
Interests: classical music, reading, antiques
Awards: 1987 Soap Opera Award, Outstanding Male Newcomer

Daytime Dramas: "General Hospital," Duke Lavery 1986-1989

A descendent of poet Robert Burns, Ian Buchanan was born the second of six children. He left home at fifteen and by his early twenties Buchanan began a successful modeling career. Making his home in London, he was known throughout Japan as "Mr. Walkman" in television commercials which first introduced the portable stereo to the orient. Interested in an acting career, Buchanan moved abroad to New York and began to study acting at the Lee Strasberg Theatre Institute. He has since enjoyed success in all facets of the entertainment industry. His stage credits include workshop productions of Jean Genet's "The Maids" and Edward Albee's "Zoo Story." He also appeared in the Los Angeles production of "Losing Venice," which co-starred "General Hospital" wife, Finola Hughes and a London stage production of "The Heiress. His television credits include a guest starring role on "The Equalizer" Daytime audiences know Buchanan for his three year stint on "General Hospital," where he portrayed Duke Lavery. Making the transition from daytime to night time seems to have been easy for Buchanan. Since leaving "General Hospital," television audiences have seen him co-starring on many prime time shows, including a two year run as "Ian" on "It's Gary Shandling's Show," "Columbo," and the cult show "Twin Peaks," portraying Richard Tremayne. It was a Calvin Klein "Obsession" commercial, with "Twin Peaks" co-star Lara Flynn Boyle and directed by Twin Peaks creator, David Lynch which led to his work on that show. Most recently, Buchanan starred in another David Lynch television show, "On the Air." Buchanan's feature film credits include "The Seventh Sign" which starred Demi Moore. Currently residing in New York, Buchanan spends his free time enjoying plays, reading, antiquing and listening to classical music.

JENSEN BUCHANAN

Born: July 18 in Montgomery, Alabama
Marital Status: married to Gray O'Brien on
December 28, 1991
Height: 5'4" **Eyes:** blue **Hair:** blond
Education: Boston University, B.F.A.
Interests: singing, sports

Daytime Dramas: "All My Children;" "One Life to Live,"
Sarah Gordon; **"Another World,"** Victoria Love/Marley Hudson,
1991-

Replacing an Emmy winning actress in a popular daytime role is certainly a difficult task, but for Jensen Buchanan this was only half the problem. When joining the cast of "Another World," Ms. Buchanan took over two roles, Victoria Love and Marley Hudson, both of which had previously been played by Anne Heche. Yet just as Heche successfully succeeded Ellen Wheeler, an Emmy winner as well, Jensen has smoothly assumed the role for herself. Hailing from Montgomery, Alabama, and raised in Neenah, Wisconsin, Jensen's family also included her father, William, now deceased, who ran the family paper business, Jensen's mother, Mary, who wrote for the local paper, Mary's second husband, a veterinarian, and Jensen's half-sister, Amy, a student at the University of Wisconsin at Milwaukee. Growing up amidst all of this, Jensen was always interested in singing and theater, performing in various high school and community productions, as well as studying with such notables as Seizi Ozawa, Aaron Copeland, and Leonard Bernstein at the Young Vocalists Program at Tanglewood. After graduating from Boston University, where she majored in music with a concentration in opera, Ms. Buchanan divided the next few years between summer stock and children's theater, performing in such shows as "The Gondoliers," "The Sound of Music," "They're Playing Our Song," "Pippin," and "Babes in Toyland," at the Loom Theatre in New York. After moving to New York, Jensen was accepted into the ABC Talent and Development Program, during which time she continued her training at the Circle in the Square Professional Workshop. In addition, the actress has also studied at the Boston University Theatre Institute. Her first foray into daytime television was as Sarah Gordon on "One Life to Live," and she also appeared briefly on "All My Children." Putting her voice training to work, Jensen has performed with the Light Opera of Manhattan and in various cabarets. Currently residing in Brooklyn, New York, she enjoys playing the piano, discovering new restaurants, and all sports, particularly tennis. Jensen was married in December of 1991 to Gray O'Brien, a high school classmate she ran into at their ten year reunion.

BRYAN BUFFINTON

Born: April 1, 1980 in Ridgewood, New Jersey
Marital Status: single
Height: 4'8" **Eyes:** blue **Hair:** sandy
Education: Currently in grade school
Interests: soccer, baseball, basketball
Awards: Two Daytime Emmy nominations for Outstanding Younger Actor, 1989, 1990

Daytime Dramas: "Guiding Light," Little Billy Lewis, 1989-

Bryan Buffinton, who joined the cast of "Guiding Light" in September of 1989, has quickly established himself as one of the premiere child actors on daytime television. In fact, Bryan has already been nominated for two daytime Emmys for Outstanding Younger Actor in a Drama Series. Not one to limit himself strictly to one medium, Bryan has also appeared in numerous commercials and print ads, as well as making his motion picture debut in "Mr. Destiny," a Disney film starring Jim Belushi and Michael Caine. Bryan was born on April 1, 1980 in Ridgewood, New Jersey, and lists among his hobbies music and bicycling. He also was selected as sweeper for his soccer team, the Hot Spurs, who went on to win the prestigious Minolta Cup. Bryan currently lives outside New York City with his parents, his father is a sports director, and his two brothers, Kyle and Brett.

GREGORY BURKE

Born: September 8 in Staten Island, New York
Marital Status: single
Height: 4'6" **Eyes:** green **Hair:** light brown
Education: elementary school
Interests: bike riding, baseball, football, bowling, collecting comic books and baseball cards

Daytime Dramas: "Guiding Light," Ben Reade

Although Gregory Burke is only ten years old, he has more experience before the camera than many actors twice his age. Gregory's professional career started when he began modelling at the tender age of three, and is still going strong. Gregory's first taste of acting came when his first grade teacher told his parents about an open audition for a Wagner College production of "Annie Get Your Gun." He auditioned and won the part of Annie's brother Jake, which was the beginning of Gregory's love for acting. Shortly after his stage debut, Gregory began making commercials and quickly was in great demand. Some of his most memorable commercials are for Reese's Peanut Butter Cups, Kodak Film, Toyota, Banquet Kid Cuisine, Nabisco's Sprinkled Chips Ahoy, Fleishman's Light, Friendly's Restaurant, Burger King, Duncan Hines and many more, too numerous to mention. Gregory has also been seen on primetime in "Law and Order." In addition, he has also been featured in many "Late Night with David Letterman" and "Saturday Night Live" skits. Other television credits include the pilot for "Toonces the Driving Cat." Daytime audiences know Gregory for his fine portrayal of Ben Reade on "Guiding Light." When not performing, Gregory likes to ride his bike, play wiffle ball with his friends, and enjoys playing both basketball and football. A fine athlete, Gregory plays little league baseball, pitching as well as catching, and also belongs to a bowling team. In what little spare time this busy actor has, he likes to collect comic books and baseball cards. Gregory is a student in public school and tells us his favorite foods are pepperoni pizza, grilled cheese sandwiches, and bacon.

MAGGIE BURKE

MAGGIE BURKE

Born: May 2 in Long Island, New York
Marital Status: married to Dr. Arthur Snyder, two children, Eric and Nancy
Height: 5' 4 1/2" **Eyes:** dark brown **Hair:** brown
Education: Sarah Lawrence College
Interests: theater, cooking, travelling, swimming, animals, ballet, walking
Awards: 1988 Guttman Institute Award for Special Courage; 1989 New Jersey Best Actress Award for "Brighton Beach Memoirs" and "Broadway Bound"

Daytime Dramas: "Edge of Night," "Guiding Light," "Another World," "One Life to Live" all variety of roles ranging from one to six months; **"As the World Turns,"** Dr. Audrey Samuels, 1985-

A stage and television actress, as well as a best selling author, Maggie Burke is a woman of great accomplishments. Her 1990 book, "An Informed Decision," written under the pen name Marilyn Snyder, chronicled the actress's brave struggle with breast cancer, and offered advice to others. Endorsed by the Sloan Kettering Cancer Institute, Ms. Burke's book provided the author with an opportunity to vent her feelings about her illness, and at the same time help the millions of women similarly afflicted. It has earned legions of fans who's lives were deeply affected by her writing. In recognition, the Guttman Institute presented Ms. Burke with an award for special courage. Born on May 2, on Long Island, New York, Maggie was interested in acting from an early age, and after attending Sarah Lawrence College, she embarked on her professional career. Along with many guest appearances on prime time television, Burke has also co-starred in the feature film "Lemon Sisters," with Diane Keaton, and is slated to appear in Woody Allen's next screen project. Her stage credits include roles on Broadway in "Brighton Beach Memoirs," "Cafe Crown," and "Driving Miss Daisy," as well as scores of off-Broadway and regional productions. In 1989 she was awarded the New Jersey Best Actress Award for her performances in "Brighton Beach Memoirs" and "Broadway Bound." Now a mainstay on "As the World Turns," Maggie has also played a variety of minor roles on "Edge of Night," "Guiding Light," "Another World," and "One Life to Live." The actress is married to Dr. Arthur Snyder, with who she has two children, Eric and Nancy. Maggie devotes much of her spare time to organizations such as "Common Cents," which benefits the homeless, and at both the Guttman Breast Institute and Sloan Kettering Institute, where she frequently lectures and provides support for cancer patients. To relax, Maggie enjoys cooking, travelling, theater going, swimming, and walking.

ANTHONY CALL

Born: August 31 in Los Angeles, California
Marital Status: married to Margo Husin, one daughter Abigail
Height: 5'10" **Eyes:** green **Hair:** brown
Education: University of Pennsylvania
Interests: theatre
Awards: nominated for Daytime Emmy for Best Supporting Actor, 1983, 1985, 1987; nominated for Drama Desk and Tony Award for "The Trip Back Down."

Daytime Dramas: "Edge of Night," Sen. Colin Whitney, 1970-1971; **"Guiding Light,"** Dr. Joe Werner, 1972-1976; **"One Life to Live,"** Herb Callison," 1978-1992

Considering that he grew up a matter of blocks from the New York City theatre district, it seems only fitting that Anthony Call should pursue a career as an actor. Entertaining seems to run in his family; his father, Abner Biberman, was a prominent character actor, his mother, Helen Churchill Dalby, an opera and concert singer, and his stepfather, John Call, was a New York stage actor. Anthony left New York to attend the University of Pennsylvania, where he played football (quarterback) and aspired to be a classical pianist. However, during a trip to Los Angeles to visit his father, Call auditioned for a part in the series "Route 66." He wound up getting the part and never returned to school. Taking his stepfather's name, Tony pursued a career in acting, against his family's wishes. He moved back to New York to study with Lee Strasberg, and since then has enjoyed a wide range of show business success. He made his Broadway debut in "You Know I Can't Hear You When the Water's Running," and has also appeared on stage in such productions as "Crown Matrimonial," "The Taming of the Shrew," "The Rivals," "Cactus Flower," and "The Trip Back Down," for which he received nominations for a Tony Award and a Drama Desk Award. His numerous off-Broadway credits include the two-character play, "Suspenders," which was directed by Al Freeman Jr., who worked with Call on "One Life to Live." Call has also worked extensively in daytime drama, appearing in "For Richer, For Poorer," "Edge of Night," "Guiding Light," and "One Life to Live." For his work on "One Life to Live," he has been nominated for three Emmys. Call recently decided to leave "One Life to Live" when his status changed to recurring from a contract player. His other television work includes appearances on "Star Trek," (he is still recognized for his role) "Gunsmoke," and "The Virginian." Call has also been active behind the scenes, particularly in the Los Angeles Art Theatre. He also helped form the Los Angeles Repertory Company and the American Renaissance Theatre in New York. He is married to Margo Husin, Director of Research and Continuity for "One Life to Live" and together they have a daughter Abigail.

JOHN CALLAHAN

Born: December 23 in Brooklyn, New York
Marital Status: married, two sons
Hair: light brown
Education: University of California at Berkeley
Interests: reading, travelling, theater, softball

Daytime Dramas: "General Hospital," Leo Russel, 1984-1985;
"Santa Barbara," Craig Hunt; **"All My Children,"** Edmund
Gray 1992-

Originally intent on becoming a lawyer, John Callahan changed his career plans after a stint as a nightclub manager, a job which introduced him to the world of show business. A Brooklyn native, Callahan moved to California when he was accepted into the pre-law program of the University of California at Berkeley. While he did eventually work at the Oakland Legal Aid Center, Callahan found his job as a nightclub manager far more stimulating, and the possibility of an acting career far more intriguing. Deciding to pursue his dream, John began auditioning for stage work, quickly landing roles in many California productions, including "The Madwoman of Chaillot," "The Taming of the Shrew," "The Rainmaker," and the world premiere of "Tequila," presented at San Francisco's Eureka Theater. During a performance, Callahan was spotted by a talent scout for Universal Pictures, who recruited the young actor for a role in the television film "M.A.D.D.." This was quickly followed by a guest appearance on the t.v. series, "Seven Brides for Seven Brothers" and another t.v. film, "When She Says No," with Kathleen Quinlan. Since then, Callahan has been a regular cast member on two primetime series, "Our Family Honor," and as Eric Stavros on "Falcon Crest," and has additionally appeared on "Murder, She Wrote," "Days of Our Lives," and "General Hospital," where he played Leo Russel, a health club masseur. Callahan returned to daytime television as Craig Hunt on "Santa Barbara" and now can be seen as Edmund Gray on "All My Children." As for the future, he hopes to continue performing on stage, and perhaps try his hand at directing. In his spare time, the actor is involved with several charities. He serves as a spokesman for the Olive Crest Foundation, an organization devoted to finding and building homes for homeless children, as well as tutoring for Project Literacy. In addition, he frequently speaks about drug abuse and AIDS on behalf of the Entertainment Industry Council. John and his wife of eight years have raised two sons, hers from a previous marriage. In his spare time, Callahan enjoys softball, travelling, and reading.

DAVID CANARY

Born: August 25 in Elwood, Indiana
Marital Status: married to Maureen in 1982, two children,
Chris and Katie; daughter Lisa from a previous marriage
Height: 5'11" **Eyes:** blue **Hair:** gray
Education: University of Cincinnati, Bachelor's Degree
Interests: playwriting, theater
Awards: Daytime Emmy Outstanding Lead Actor, 1986, 1988,
1989, 1991; nominated for 1992 Daytime Emmy; 1992 Soap
Opera Award, Outstanding Lead Actor; 1990 Soap Opera
Award, Outstanding Villain

Daytime Dramas: "Another World," Steve Frame, 1981-1983;
"All My Children," Adam/Stuart Chandler, 1983-

Ruthless/sweet, powerful/childlike, flamboyant/soft spoken, David Canary's dual role as Adam/Stuart Chandler affords the actor the opportunity to run the gamut of emotions. Clearly capable of handling this assignment, his efforts have earned him four daytime Emmys as outstanding lead actor. A native of Elwood, Indiana, Canary spent most of his youth in Masillon, Ohio, where he was a high school football star. He parlayed his abilities into a scholarship to the University of Cincinnati. While at college, Canary continued his football career, as well as majoring in music with a particular emphasis on voice training. This enabled him to enroll in a special University program which combined study with the Cincinnati Conservatory of Music. Initially Canary intended college to be a stepping stone towards a career in medicine, but it was his father who convinced him to follow his heart rather than his head and look towards a career as an entertainer. Not surprisingly the elder Canary became a die hard "All My Children" fan. And for a while he saw two of his sons on the show, when David's brother, John portrayed the womanizing, Dr. Voight. Upon graduation David moved to New York City, making his Broadway debut alongside Colleen Dewhurst in Jose Quintero's production of "Great Day in the Morning." However, this stage of his career proved to be short lived, due largely to the efforts of Canary's local draft board. During his years in the service he continued his performing, and was even named best popular singer in an All Army Entertainment Contest. Upon his release Canary moved to San Francisco, reviving his stage career with a role in "The Fantasticks." To this day the actor continues his theater work, and has appeared on Broadway in "Clothes for a Summer Hotel," with Geraldine Page, "The Happiest Girl in the World," and "Blood Moon." His additional stage credits include "The Beggar's Opera," "The Sea Gull," and "Man of La Mancha." Over the years he has also developed an interest in playwriting, and currently works with Robert Lupone's Manhattan Class Company. While Canary has certainly made a name for himself in the theater, he is best known for his television work. Before "All My Children," he co-starred in two of the most popular television series of all time: "Bonanza" and "Peyton Place." As Candy and Russ Gehring respectively, Canary's popularity soared during the sixties. Along with numerous guest appearances on other programs, he also starred in the made for television movie "The Drain Curse," with Jean Simmons, and in the feature films "Hombre," "The St. Valentine's Day Massacre," "End of a Dark Street," and "In a Pig's Eye." Despite his success on "Bonanza" and "Peyton Place," Canary found Hollywood life to be ultimately unfulfilling. He moved back east, and in 1982 made his debut as Adam Chandler on "All My Children." His work on daytime has earned Canary tremendous praise as well as allowing him the time to occasionally return to the stage. Preferring a quiet home life, the actor currently lives in a small Connecticut town with his wife, Maureen, and their two children, Chris and Katie. Canary also has an older daughter, Lisa, from an earlier marriage. An intensely private man, Canary believes strongly in the importance of keeping one's professional and personal lives separate.

MacDONALD CAREY

Born: March 15, 1913 in Sioux City, Iowa
Marital Status: divorced, six children
Hair: gray
Education: University of Iowa, Master's Degree
Interests: poetry, swimming, karate
Awards: Daytime Emmy, Best Actor, 1974, 1976; nominated Best Actor, 1968, 1973, 1975; Soap Opera Award, Outstanding Actor in a Mature Role, 1978, 1979, 1984, 1985; United States Karate Association, Longevity Award

Daytime Dramas: "Days of Our Lives," Dr. Tom Horton, 1965-

Unquestionably the most quoted daytime actor of all time. Macdonald Carey can be heard every day, reminding faithful viewers that "Like sands through the hourglass, so are the days of our lives." From the first episode of "Days of Our Lives," back in 1965, Carey has played Dr. Tom Horton, a role that has earned him four daytime Emmy nominations, a prize he took home in 1972 and again in 1975. Additionally, he has four times been named Outstanding Actor in a Mature Role at the Soap Opera Awards. Born on March 15, 1913, in Sioux City, Iowa, Carey was raised by father, Charles, a banker, and mother, Elizabeth, a violin teacher. Macdonald's first acting experience was at the age of six, when he played Simple Simon in a Mother Goose Play. After receiving his M.A. from the University of Iowa, Carey moved to New York City in 1938 to begin his acting career. He quickly found work on Broadway and in many radio plays. On stage he received tremendous praise for his work in "Lady in the Dark," and was heard over the air waves in such radio soap operas as "Stella Dallas," "John's Other Wife," "Just Plain Bill," "Ellen Randolph," "Woman in White," and "Young Hickory." After a stint in the Marine Corps during World War II, Carey returned to the U.S. where he signed as a contract player for Paramount Pictures. He went on to star in over fifty feature films, including "Dr. Broadway," "Wake Island," "Excuse My Dust," "Stranger At My Door," "John Paul Jones," and the Alfred Hitchcock film, "Shadow of a Doubt." Along the way he co-starred with such legendary performers as Marilyn Monroe and Hedy Lamar. During the fifties, Carey began working on television, both as a regular, on "Dr. Christian" and "Lock Up," and as a guest star on "G.E. Theatre," "U.S. Steel Hour," "Mr. Novak," "Police Story," "Burke's Law," "Outer Limits," "Ben Casey," and "Lassie." Away from the camera, Carey was married to Betty Hecksher, with whom he had six children. The marriage ended in divorce in 1969, after twenty six years, a break up due largely to Carey's increasing dependence on alcohol. Sober now for over a decade, Macdonald documented his bout with addiction in his autobiography, "The Days of My Life." Although the actor doubts he will ever marry again, he has been involved with the same woman, Lois Kraines, for over eighteen years. Carey is also a published poet, having completed three volumes of verse, "A Day in the Life," "That Further Hill," and a third, still untitled work. He also was the first movie star to be featured in "Black Belt Magazine" and has been a brown belt in Karate for over forty years. Currently living in Los Angeles, where he swims laps every day, Macdonald is at work on another set of poems, and still enjoys the day to day challenge of portraying Dr. Tom Horton.

PHILIP CAREY

Born: July 15 in Hackensack, New Jersey
Marital Status: single
Height: 6'4" **Eyes:** blue **Hair:** brown
Education: University of Miami
Interests: golf, horseback riding

Daytime Dramas: "One Life to Live," Asa Buchanan, 1979-

Looking at the extensive list of Philip Carey's career credits, it is obvious this man has left no stone unturned. His motion picture debut was in the film, "Operation Pacific" with John Wayne. He has also appeared with Henry Fonda in "Mr. Roberts," "Springfield Rifle" with Gary Cooper, and "Fighting Mad" with Peter Fonda. Always wanting to be an actor, Carey was born in Hackensack, New Jersey and raised in Rosedale and Malvern, New York. After high school Carey studied drama at the University of Miami. A former marine, Philip was active overseas in both World War II and the Korean War. His illustrious career began when a Warner Brother's representative saw him in a Sayville, New York stock theater presentation of "Over 21." Impressed by what he saw, the representative asked Carey to take a screen test. For several years he was under contract with both, Warner Brothers and Columbia Pictures. During this time, Philip worked with director John Ford in "The Long Grey Line" with Tyrone Power as well as "Mr. Roberts." He also starred in "Pushover" with Fred McMurray and Kim Novak. (in her first leading role) No stranger to television, he has starred in several prime time series including, "Laredo," "The Untamed World," "Philip Marlowe," and "Bengal Lancers." He has also guest starred on many shows, among them are: "The Bionic Woman," "Police Woman," "Gunsmoke," "Little House on the Prairie," and "All in the Family." Carey's impressive stage credits include, Arthur Miller's "Cyrano de Bergerac" and "All My Sons." His current role as the Texas tycoon, Asa Buchanan on "One Life to Live" marks his first ongoing appearance on daytime television. When he does get time to relax, Philip loves to play golf. He is also an accomplished equestrian, as evidenced by the many westerns he has acted and ridden in. Carey also enjoys participating in rodeos, sometimes he can be seen with fellow daytime star & equestrian, Peter Brown.

JEAN CAROL

Born: April 13 in New Jersey
Marital Status: divorced
Eyes: blue **Hair:** blond
Education: Florida State University, M.S., Phi Beta Kappa
Interests: skiing, writing
Awards: Ms. Teenage Miami; Ms. Miami; Emmy Award for "P.M. Magazine" 1990 Annual Soap Opera Award, Outstanding Female Newcomer; 1992 Annual Soap Opera Award, Outstanding Comic Performance

Daytime Dramas: "Guiding Light," Nadine Cooper Lewis, 1989-

Born on April 13, in New Jersey, Jean Carol began her professional acting career at the age of three, as the youngest member of the Junior Repertory Company. The group performed at New York's Carnegie Hall, and Jean remained with the cast for seven straight years before her family moved to Florida. Jean has since kept active in theater, appearing in such works as "Crimes of the Heart," "The Unsinkable Molly Brown," "Oliver," and "Cat on A Hot Tin Roof." After completing high school, Jean attended Florida State University from which she graduated Phi Beta Kappa, receiving both her B.A. and M.S. in theater arts and broadcasting respectively. While studying at Florida State, Jean was named Ms. Miami, and began her television career hosting a show with fellow graduate student Robert Urich. For her efforts she was honored in "Who's Who," as well twice being featured in the yearly book "Outstanding Young Women in America." In 1979, Jean continued her television success as host and producer of the Group W nationally syndicated program "P.M. Magazine" for which she was awarded an Emmy for her producing, writing, and performing. During her six year stint with "P.M. Magazine" she was nominated for an additional four Emmys, as well as being awarded by Group W as producer of the best feature story of 1984. Along with these duties, Jean continued her acting career as well, appearing on such television shows as "Simon and Simon," "The World of Disney," "Superior Court," "Divorce Court," and in the mini-series "Space." In addition, she played a district attorney on "International Attorney," a Japanese television show, as well as serving as co-host on "Health Care Report" and "Healthy Lifestyles," with Bruce Jenner. On the big screen, Jean's work includes roles in "Payback," "The Janitor," and "A Year to Remember." After a brief appearance on "The Young and the Restless," Jean joined the ranks of daytime television fulltime when she was cast as Nadine Cooper on "Guiding Light" in February of 1989. Divorced, Jean has been involved in a long term relationship with producer, Gary Rand. In her spare time Jean enjoys aerobics, skiing, photography, and writing.

CRYSTAL CARSON

Born: June 24,1967 in Spaulding, Nebraska
Marital Status: married to Peter S. Bradley, II, July 6, 1990
Height: 5'7" **Eyes:** blue **Hair:** blond
Education: University of Nebraska, B.F.A.
Interests: libertarianism, baking, eating, horseback riding, gardening, golf
Awards: Best New Female Character, Soap Opera Digest; Best Couple (with Anthony Geary), Northwest Afternoon

Daytime Dramas: "General Hospital," Julia Barrett, 1991-

Ironically, it was the death of her father that unknowingly lead Crystal Carson towards an acting career. Her father, who was head of circulation for the Omaha World-Herald, died of cancer when Ms. Carson was only seven years old. Crystal's young mother, now faced with the responsibility of raising three children, took on the additional challenge of her husband's former career. Soon the Carson household became the distribution center for the Omaha World-Herald, with each of the children delivering papers and manning the phone lines. It was this latter responsibility which most often fell on Crystal, the oldest of the children, and to make the job a bit more exciting she began to use different voices when answering the phones. Her mother quickly noticed her daughter's creative flair, and convinced her to enroll in an acting program at the Lincoln Community Playhouse. From that moment on Crystal was hooked on acting, and she hasn't looked back since. Born on June 24 in Spaulding, Nebraska, Crystal divided her school years between working, and acting in both high school and community productions. Today, Crystal has three sisters and two brothers. Her mother, who remarried when Crystal was thirteen is now a registered nurse. Crystal's stepfather is retired. Crystal describes her childhood as "Happy   ." After being awarded a scholarship to Long Island University, she moved to New York and enrolled as a drama major. She eventually returned home, graduating with a B.F.A. in acting from the University of Nebraska. During high school and college , Ms. Carson acquired professional stage experience in numerous summer stock and repertory productions, including "Butterflies Are Free," "Two Gentlemen From Verona," "Inherit The Wind," "Alice in Wonderland," and "Spite The Devil For Awhile." It was during one such regional performance that Ms. Carson was discovered by a talent agent and immediately was flown to Los Angeles for screen tests. These screen tests landed her two film roles, first in "The Zero Boys," and then co-starring with Madonna in "Who's That Girl." Her other film work includes "Cartel," "Fade Away," "Pitch," "Eclipse," and the cult hit "Killer Tomatoes III," where she played tomatologist, Kennedy Johnson. On television, Crystal is now receiving a great deal of attention for her work as Julia Barrett on "General Hospital." The actress was named Best New Female Character in 1991 by Soap Opera Digest, as well as being voted best couple, along with Anthony Geary, in Northwest Afternoon. Along with her daytime work, Ms. Carson has also guest starred on numerous prime time series, including "Midnight Caller," "Cheers," "Charles in Charge," "Dallas," "Night Court," "thirtysomething," and "Simon and Simon." While her on-screen relationship with Geary is naturally tempestuous, her real life romance with Peter Bradley II, a senior Systems Analyst, has been going strong since his car broke down in front of the bar where she was waiting tables. The couple married July 6, 1990 and recently purchased a home in the San Fernando Valley of California. Carson is proud to be involved with the National Cancer Society, and recently took on the duty of official spokesperson for the organization's Discovery Shops. She lists among her interests libertarianism and when she has the time, Crystal enjoys horseback riding, gardening, baking, eating and "playing golf badly."

CHRISTOPHER CASS

Born: September 30, 1958 in Glen Cove, New York
Marital Status: married to Winship Cook on November 28, 1987
Height: 6'   **Eyes:** blue   **Hair:** brown
Education: University of Georgia, B.A. in theater
Interests: baseball, old movies

Daytime Dramas: "Loving," Jack Forbes, 1991-1992

Coming straight from a starring role on Broadway, Christopher Cass joined the cast of "Loving" in 1991, taking over the role of Jack Forbes. A New York native, Cass was raised in Cold Spring Harbor, Long Island, with his brother and twin sister. Cass is the only member on his family bent on acting, his brother is a police detective and his sister works on Wall Street. While Christopher was still in high school, the Cass family moved to Atlanta, Georgia, where he went on to attend Georgia Southern College. Bitten by the acting bug, Cass then transferred to the University of Georgia, from which he received his B.A. in theater. After graduating in 1982, he followed the lead of countless others and moved to New York City to practice his craft. The young actor spent the next several years dividing his time between searching for acting jobs and doing office temp work to pay the rent. Cass eventually began to find stage work in off-Broadway and regional productions. His theater credits include the South African play "Born in the R.S.A.," "Big Time," "Dark Encounter," "Summer and Smoke," "The Good Doctor," and "Much Ado About Nothing." Just prior to his work on "Loving," Cass made his Broadway debut, starring in the play "Stand-up Tragedy." In 1986, Cass moved to Los Angeles, where he began working in television and film. He made guest appearances on ""Capitol" and "Night Court," as well as co-starring in the t.v. film "83 Hours 'til Dawn," and in the feature film "Someone to Watch Over Me," with Tom Berenger. While out west, Cass met his future wife, Winship Cook, an actress, when ironically the two portrayed husband and wife in a stage production. Today, Winship lives in L.A. with their two cats, Buster and Dusty, while Christopher's role on "Loving" required him to be in New York City. The couple, however, spoke to each other several times each day, and along with skyrocketing phone bills, have also amassed impressive frequent flyer mileage. Cass plans to relocated to the west coast now that his "Loving" days are over. A die hard Yankee fan, Cass, who was a serious athlete in school, enjoys working out with weights and playing baseball and croquet. He holds an annual croquet party on July 4th. Also fascinated by Native American culture, Cass spent three summers playing lead in a Texas Indian reservation pageant.

TRICIA CAST

Born: November 16 in Long Island, New York
Marital Status: married to composer Jack Allocco in June of
1989
Height: 5'1" **Eyes:** hazel **Hair:** brown
Education: Saddleback Community College
Interests: tennis, travel, movies
Awards:1992 Annual Soap Opera Award, Outstanding
Younger Lead Actress; 1992 Daytime Emmy nomination,
Outstanding Younger Actress

Daytime Dramas: "Santa Barbara," Kristy Duvall; **"The
Young and The Restless,"** Nina Webster Chancellor Kimble

Confused troubled, and misunderstood are just a few words which could be used to describe Tricia Cast's portrayal of Nina on "The Young and The Restless." Tricia's portrayal, which began as a bit part, has, due to her acting abilities, grown to a major character. She has also garnered two award nominations, bringing home the Soap Opera Award for 1992's Outstanding Younger Actress. Born on Long Island in New York, Tricia always had a yen to be an actress and loved acting in high school plays before attending Saddleback Community College. Pursuing her dream, Tricia moved to Los Angeles, and began her acting career with a featured role in the television series, "The Bad News Bears." She also co-starred with Jason Bateman in the NBC series "It's Your Move" and was on the daytime drama, "Santa Barbara" for nine months, in the recurring role of Kristy Duvall. In real life, Tricia is married to composer Jack Allocco, whose music can be heard on "The Young and The Restless" as well as "The Bold and The Beautiful." Tricia is very concerned about the environment, and gives many hours of her spare time to recycling programs. During her free time, you might find Tricia and Jack either at the beach, on the tennis courts or at the movies.

JOHN CASTELLANOS

Born: April 11 in San Diego, California
Marital Status: engaged to Rhonda Friedman
Height: 6'0" **Eyes:** brown **Hair:** black
Education: San Diego State University
Interests: guitar, piano, tennis, travel

Daytime Dramas: "The Bold and the Beautiful,"
Caroline's lawyer, 1987; **"The Young and the Restless,"**
John Silva

Presently seen as attorney John Silva on "The Young and the Restless," John Castellanos was born on April 11, in San Diego, California. Raised in Spring Valley, where he attended Catholic schools, John excelled in football and baseball, while also developing a strong interest in theater. After studying drama at Grossmont College and San Diego State University, he was invited by Broadway producer Paul Gregory to take part in an exchange program, which enabled John to study at the National Theatre of England. Returning to the U.S., Castellanos quickly found work on stage, appearing in such productions as "Poor Murderer," "Love's Labor's Lost," "Les Liaisons Dangereuses,"

"Tamara," and "The Day You'll Love Me," as well as performing at such events as The Oregon Shakespeare Festival and The Berkeley Shakespeare Festival, and with the American Conservatory Theater. On television, in addition to "The Young and the Restless," Castellanos has guest starred on "Hard Copy," and "Miami Vice," and was also seen in the PBS special, "Prelude to the Fall." On the big screen, John co-starred with James Belushi in "K-9." Away from the set, Castellanos, who speaks Spanish fluently, enjoys playing tennis, and frequently displays his skills in charity tennis events. Castellanos is engaged to "The Bold and the Beautiful" producer, Rhonda Friedman whom he met while on the show. He also donates a great deal of time to the Make-A-Wish-Foundation. Among his other interests: travelling, working around the house, and playing piano and guitar.

BETH CHAMBERLIN

Born: October 1 in Danville, Vermont
Marital Status: single
Height: 5'6" **Eyes:** green   **Hair:** blond
Education: New York University
Interests: skiing, swimming, sports

Daytime Dramas: "Guiding Light," Beth Raines, 1989-1991

An actress and a dancer, Beth Chamberlin portrayed Beth Raines on "The Guiding Light" from 1989 to 1991. Born on October 1 in Danville, Vermont, Beth's family includes her parents, Stanley and Sally who still reside in their home state, and three older brothers. Beth spent much of her childhood working on dairy and horse farms, yet she was also a serious dancer, and would make frequent excursions to New York City to study ballet with the American Ballet Theatre. After graduating high school, she enrolled as a dance/theater major at New York University, and in addition, studied jazz dance with Charles Kelly and is also a student of the Martha Graham technique. Along with dancing, Ms. Chamberlin began to hone her acting skills as well, training at both HB Studios and the William Esper Studios. She got her first acting experience in national commercials, and has since gone on to work on such shows as "All My Children," "One Life to Live," "Divorce Court," and the syndicated pilot, "Personal & Confidential Guest." On the stage, she has appeared in "Flowers for Algernon," "The Effect of Gamma Rays," "Godspell," and "You Can't Take it With You," while she was also seen on the big screen in the film, "The Big Picture." Now living in New York City, Beth, who is single, lists amongst her hobbies: swimming, skiing, and most sports.

CRYSTAL CHAPPELL

Born: August 4 in Silver Spring, Maryland
Marital Status: single
Height: 5'6" **Eyes:** brown **Hair:** brown
Education: University of Maryland, B.F.A.
Interests: running, skiing, tennis, music,
hiking, scuba diving

Daytime Dramas: "Days of Our Lives,"
Dr. Carly Manning, 1990-

A few years back, Crystal Chappell believed that "acting was not a practical way to support yourself." Fortunately, for millions of "Days of Our Lives" fans, Crystal Chappell did not heed her own advice, and since 1990 she is played the beautiful and brilliant, Dr. Carly Manning. Born on August 4 in Silver Springs, Maryland, Chappell, along with the rest of her family, which includes father, Don, a Washington D.C. fireman, mother, Priscilla, and brothers, Don and John, moved around frequently throughout the Southeast. Her parents would purchase shells of houses, and then the entire family would work to rebuild it. Once the house was complete they would move on to a new town, and as a result, Crystal attended a total of seven different schools in Maryland and South Carolina. An artistic girl who read a lot and wrote poetry, Ms. Chappell first began acting in a high school production of "Dark of the Moon." After graduating with honors from Arundel High School in Gambrills, Maryland, she decided to use her drama scholarship to Coast Carolina College to study computer science instead, figuring that this was infinitely more practical. She then opted to study journalism at the University of South Carolina, earning her tuition money by working as an aerobics instructor. However, Chappell soon found the right school when she enrolled in the drama department at the University of Maryland in Baltimore, where she performed in such shows as "Beauty and the Beast" and "Spring's Awakening." This later production reached the finals of the National College Theater Festival, and afforded Chappell the opportunity to perform on stage at the Kennedy Center. Putting practicality aside at this point, Chappell was now entirely committed to acting, spending her summers with the school's "Shakespeare on Wheels" touring company. After graduating in 1988, she moved to New York City, where she continued her acting training, as well as spending a period studying acting, along with a select group of students, at the West Indies home of famed acting coach, Sanford Meisner. Returning to New York, Chappell landed a day role on "All My Children." She then relocated to Los Angeles, landing another temporary daytime role, this time as a doomed drug dealer on "Santa Barbara." After her character was killed off in a week, Chappell vowed never to do another soap, but when the producers of "Days of Our Lives" offered her the role of Carly, and the opportunity to be paired with daytime hero, Peter Reckell, she could not refuse. Now enjoying unqualified success on the show, Chappell is branching out into other acting areas, including a recent performance on stage in Los Angeles in "Love Letters." In her spare time, the actress enjoys running, scuba diving, tennis, skiing, hiking, collecting compact discs, (her current favorite is fiddle music) playing with her cats, Bo and Jesse, and decorating her home with her own arrangements of dried flowers. Chappell, who recently separated from her husband of four years, has been linked romantically with her "Days of Our Lives" co-star, Michael Sabatino.

LESLIE CHARLESON

Born: February 22 in Kansas City, Missouri
Marital Status: separated
Height: 5'6"   **Eyes:** hazel   **Hair:** blond
Education: Bennett College, B.A.
Interests: horseback riding
Awards: voted outstanding theater arts student in her graduating class at Bennett College, nominated three times for Best Actress Emmys

Daytime Dramas: "A Flame in the Wind," Pam; **"As the World Turns,"** Alice Whipple,1966; **"Love is a Many Splendored Thing,"** Iris Garrison, 1967-1970; **"General Hospital,"** Monica Quartermaine, 1977-

Over the past twenty five years Leslie Charleson has established herself as one of the most enduring actresses in daytime drama. She first appeared on the short lived show "A Flame in the Wind," and has since enjoyed an illustrious career on daytime television; receiving no less than three Emmy nominations. Leslie was born in Kansas City, Missouri, from there her family moved to Connecticut, and then to Illinois. As a child Leslie's first love was horses. She was able to develop her interest when her family moved to Rowayton, Connecticut and enrolled her in Margaret Cable Self's New Canaan Mounted Troop. Leslie lived and breathed horses until her family moved again, this time to Lake Forrest, Illinois. She soon discovered her other great passion when she performed the story of "Eloise" for her school. Hearing the audience laugh and applaud, Leslie knew she was onto something. She continued her pursuit of acting at Bennett College in Millbrook, New York, where she was voted Outstanding Theatre Arts student for her graduating class. Leslie moved to New York City and continued her acting training with Uta Hagen at the Herbert Berghot Studio. She landed her first professional role playing Pam on "A Flame in the Wind," a daytime drama whose name was later changed to "A Time for Us." When this show had run its course Leslie continued to work in this medium, first appearing as Alice Whipple on "As the World Turns," and then for three years as Iris Garrison on "Love is a Many Splendored Thing," for which she received her first Emmy nomination. In 1970 Leslie decided to pursue areas outside of daytime drama, and after moving to California she appeared in a number of popular prime time shows. Among these are "Adam 12," "Barnaby Jones," "The Streets of San Francisco," "Medical Center," "Marcus Welby M.D.," "Ironside," and "Happy Days." She also starred in several television motion pictures including, "The Black Box Murders" and "The Norming of Jack 2-3-4." On the big screen Leslie co-starred in the Mike Nichols' film "Day of the Dolphin," with George C. Scott. She also appeared on stage with Tony Curtis in "One Night Stand." In 1977 she returned to daytime drama as Monica Quartermaine on "General Hospital," a role she continues to enjoy today. It was through General Hospital's Anna Lee (Lila Quartermaine) that once again, Leslie rediscovered horses. In the mid 1980's Miss Lee asked Leslie to participate in a charity benefit that helps "special children" through horseback riding. Her first love rekindled, Leslie began riding again, soon owning her own Andalusian horse named Andarra, which she rides leisurely as well as in competition. She has also participated with other Andalusian owners, in the Rose Bowl Parade and the Hollywood Christmas Parade. Away from her television work and horses, Leslie devotes much of her time to fund raising for the Cystic Fibrosis Foundation.

MAREE CHEATHAM

Born: June 2 in Oklahoma City, Oklahoma
Marital Status: single
Height: 5'5" **Eyes:** green **Hair:** blond
Education: Baylor University, Bachelor's Degree
Interests: music, collecting aprons, quilts, Native American
jewelry and folk art, Mexican folk art, gardening,piano, harmon
ica, guitar, pottery, horseback riding and raising birds in an
aviary
Awards: nominated for three Emmy Awards for "Search for
Tomorrow;" 1978 Drama Desk nomination for "Clash by Nights"

Daytime Dramas: "**Days of Our Lives,**" Marie Horton,
1965-1973; "**Search for Tomorrow,**" Stephanie Wyatt,
1974-1984; "**General Hospital,**" Aunt Charlene, 1987

Maree Cheatham is in the true sense of the word , an "artist." Not only an actress, Maree is a potter. Her work has been recognized and shown at the Cambridge Gallery in Beverly Hills. For over twenty five years Marie Cheatham has been one of daytime dramas most beloved actresses and now can be seen as Mary Robeson on primetime in "Knots Landing." Born in Oklahoma City of English/Native American descent (Cherokee, Choctaw and Creek), Maree's family moved around quite a bit, but one thing that remained constant was her love for acting. By the time Maree was in high school she was not only active in the school drama club, but also worked at the Alley Theater in Houston. She then went on to attend Baylor University, and following graduation she worked at the Dallas Theater Center. With this strong theater foundation, Maree moved to Los Angeles, where she appeared on her first daytime drama, playing Marie Horton on "Days of Our Lives," a role she continued to play for the next eight years. She also found time to perform in productions at the Oxford Theater in Los Angeles. Her next prominent role, which began in 1974 and continued for ten years was that of Stephanie Wyatt on "Search for Tomorrow." Again finding time for the theater, this time in New York, Maree understudied for Estelle Parsons and Eileen Heckert in the 1977 Broadway production of "Ladies of the Alamo." In 1978 she received a Drama Desk nomination for her performance in the off-Broadway revival of Clifford Odets' "Clash by Night." Also in 1978, she starred in a revival of the musical "Ok, Kay!" She was also in the off-Broadway musical, "Suds" and in 1980 a play entitled "Six Women on a Stage." Recently she appeared on daytime as Aunt Charlene on "General Hospital." In between her work on daytime television, Maree has also guest starred on a number of prime time series, among them "Hawaii Five-O," "Ben Casey," "Gunsmoke," "Hunter," "and "Cagney and Lacey." Her film work includes roles in "Beetlejuice," "Soul Man," and "Dangerous Curves." Today Maree lives in the San Fernando Valley area in California, where her hobbies are as diversified as her career. She enjoys music, collecting aprons, quilts, native American jewelry and folk art Mexican folk art, gardening, piano, harmonica, guitar, pottery, horseback riding and raising birds in an aviary.

MARILYN CHRIS

Born: May 19 in Brooklyn, New York
Marital Status: married to actor Lee Wallace, December 14, 1975, one son, Paul
Height: 5'4 1/2" **Eyes:** hazel **Hair:** blond
Education: High School of Performing Arts; City College of New York
Interests: reading, gardening, cooking & crocheting
Awards: Variety Critics Poll, Obie Award, Drama Desk Award, Outer Critics Circle Award all for her performance in Kaddish

Daytime Dramas: "One Life to Live," Wanda Wolek, 1972-1976, 1980-

A Brooklyn native, Marilyn Chris is unquestionably one of the most respected actresses working in daytime drama. Marilyn attended the High School of Performing Arts in New York, following which she attended City College. After leaving college, Marilyn began her stage career as a charter member of the Living Theatre. Since then Marilyn has enjoyed many triumphs on stage, among these "Brighton Beach Memoirs," "Lenny," "The Seven Descents of Myrtle," and countless others. For her portrayal of Allen Ginsberg's mother in the off-Broadway drama "Kaddish," Marilyn won four of the theatre's most distinguished awards, an Obie, a Drama Desk Award, a Variety Critics Poll, and the Outer Critics Circle Award. Marilyn appeared in the Long Island Stage production of "Aftershocks," for which she yet again received unanimous critical accolades and in 1992 Marilyn could be seen, along with other daytime stars in Valley Forge and Westbury Music Fair production of "Barefoot in the Park." Marilyn's work in motion pictures includes "Looking Up," with Dick Shawn, "Rhinoceros," "Honeymoon Killers," "Rocky II," and "Love with the Proper Stranger." She is best known to daytime audiences as Wanda Wolek on "One Life to Live," owner of "Heavenly Hash," the most popular hamburger joint in all of Llanview. It is a role Marilyn plays with a great deal of... relish. Her other television work includes roles in the award winning docudrama "Kent State," "Blessings," and "Backstairs at the White House," as well as appearing on such series as "Strike Force," and "Family." Marilyn is married to actor Lee Wallace, whom she has previously directed in "I'm Not Rappaport" and "The Sunshine Boys." When Marilyn is not acting or directing, she relaxes through reading, gardening, cooking and crocheting. She also in involved with the not for profit organization, Equity Fights Aids. Marilyn lives in New York, although she frequently visits her son, Paul Christopoulos in California.

WILLIAM CHRISTIAN

Born: September 30 in Washington, D.C.
Marital Status: single
Height: 5'11" **Eyes:** brown **Hair:** dark brown
Education: Catholic University B.A., American University, M.F.A.
Interests: all sports (mostly softball and rollerblading), writing
Awards: nominated for two local (DC) Emmys for "It's Elementary;" nominated for 1991 Daytime Emmy, Best Supporting Actor

Daytime Dramas: "Another World," Dr. Marshall Reed;
"All My Children," Derek Frye, 1990-

William Christian tells us he wants to write fiction when he grows up and that he loves to write but hasn't had much time lately. That is understandable since he is rapidly becoming one of daytime's most respected actors, earning a daytime Emmy nomination for his first season as Derek Frye on "All My Children." Born on September 30 and raised with his sister, in Washington D.C., Bill describes his youth as a "normal childhood with great memories at my grandparents home in Clifford, Virginia." Education was very important in the Christian household (his mother is a retired elementary school teacher) and after high school Christian studied theater at Catholic University. After receiving his B.A. he decided to postpone his entry into the world of professional actors and enrolled in American University, from which he was awarded a Masters degree. Thus with an extremely sound theatrical base, Christian took the big step and moved to New York City, where he has found work on stage as well as television. Among his theater credits are roles in "Black Eagles" and the off-Broadway production of "The Member of the Wedding," with Esther Rolle at the Roundabout Theater. Along with his work on daytime, which included the role of Dr. Marshall Reed on "Another World," Christian has also guest starred on "The Cosby Show," "Matlock," and "Tattinger's." During his years in Washington, he served as host of a local program called "It's Elementary," for which he was nominated for two local Emmys. Before landing the role of Derek on "All My Children," Christian would occasionally pop up on the show in bit parts. Eagle eyed viewers might remember him as one of the wrestlers who was invited by Bob Georgia to dine at the Chateau. Away from the set of "All My Children," the talented actor enjoys all sports and writing fiction.

THOM CHRISTOPHER

Born: October 5 in Jackson Heights, New York
Marital Status: married to to Judith Leverone, December 1971
Height: 6' **Eyes:** hazel **Hair:** black
Education: Ithaca College, B.A.
Interests: environmental causes, volunteer for Fortune Society
Awards: Theater World Award, Clarence Derwent Award (Noel Coward in Two Keys), 1992 Soap Opera Award nomination, Outstanding Villain; 1992 Daytime Emmy, Outstanding Supporting Actor

Daytime Dramas: "Edge of Night," 1974; **"Love of Life,"** 1977; **"One Life to Live,"** Carlo Hesser, 1990-1992

Thom Christopher is perhaps best known to television audiences as Hawk, on the long running television series "Buck Rogers." Born in Jackson Heights, New York, Thom attended the High School of the Performing Arts, as well as Ithaca College. After receiving his B.A., he embarked on a career that has covered television, movies, and theater. On the small screen Christopher has been seen on, "Murder, She Wrote," "Simon and Simon," "Hunter," and "T.J. Hooker," as well as in the television movies "Betrayed by Innocence" and "Hellinger's Law." His theater work includes the Broadway production of "Noel Coward in Two Keys," with Hume Cronyn and Jessica Tandy. For his performance, Christopher received the Theater World Award and the Clarence Derwent Award. Among his other theater work were roles in "Caesar and Cleopatra," "Emperor Henry IV," "Tamara," and "The Merchant of Venice." Christopher has also starred in the feature films "S.H.E.," "Space Raiders," "Voices," and "Street Hunter." Along with his most recent daytime role on "One Life to Live," Christopher has also had featured roles on the "Edge of Night" and "Love of Life." Off screen, Christopher is married to Judith Leverone, a playwright and personal manager whom he met when she became his agent. The couple lives in New York City, where Christopher is an active volunteer at the Fortune Society, a non-profit organization dedicated to educating ex-offenders. Since his character on "One Life to Live" was killed, Christopher (who is a talented singer) has been auditioning for musical roles at New York's Lincoln Center. He also won the 1992 Daytime Emmy for Outstanding Supporting Actor.

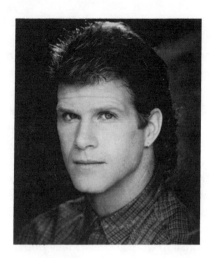

BRIAN PATRICK CLARKE

Marital Status: single, one son, Cary Ryan
Hair: brown
Education: Yale University
Interests: drums, running, jump roping
Awards: Has won Celebrity Division of Los Angeles Marathon since the race was established

Daytime Dramas: "General Hospital," Grant Putnam and Grant Andrews; **"The Bold and the Beautiful,"** StormLogan

Brian Patrick Clarke has enjoyed great success in many branches of the entertainment world. Before becoming an actor he attended Yale University on an academic scholarship, majoring in psychology. Aside from his scholarly pursuits, Clarke also played on the varsity football team as a halfback, linebacker, and place kicker, for which he still holds the record for most field goals in a game, season, and career. Clarke is best known to prime time television audiences for his role on "Eight is Enough" where he portrayed the former baseball player Merle "The Pearle" Stockwell. The NBC movie of the week "Eight is Enough Reunion" afforded Clarke the opportunity to reprise his role. His other television movies included "The Grace Kelly Story," where he co-starred as Jack Kelly opposite Cheryl Ladd. He also appeared as a young John Roosevelt in the television movie "Eleanor and Franklin: The White House Years." On stage Clarke has starred off-Broadway in "A Place Called Heartbreak," portraying Lt. Col. Cord Blass, as well as touring in the Kenley Players Summer Stock production of "Shenandoah." Clarke is known to daytime audiences for his three years on "General Hospital" where he starred in dual roles portraying Grant Andrews and Grant Putnam. After his work on "General Hospital," he starred in such feature films as "Private Road" with George Kennedy," "Sleepaway Camp II," and "Singapore Harbor" with Frank Gorshin. More recently Clarke has been seen on daytime's "The Bold and the Beautiful" where he portrayed Storm Logan. When not in front of the camera, Clarke is a serious athlete who enjoys constant physical challenge. In order to stay in top shape, Clarke likes jumping rope, which for years he did 4,500 times each night. His personal record is 15,000 uninterrupted jump ropes. Today he concentrates more on running and has won the celebrity division of the Los Angeles Marathon every year since the competition began. His best time was in 1988 when he finished the race at just under three hours. Aside from athletics, Clarke also plays the drums and has been known to participated in impromptu jam sessions in many Los Angeles clubs. Clarke resides in southern California and has a son, Cary Ryan Clarke.

JORDAN CLARKE

Born: July 21 in Rochester, New York
Marital Status: married with one daughter, Chelsea
Height: 6'
Education: Cornell University, B.A. in Philosophy, and
M.F.A., Acting
Interests: music, writing
Awards: Best Supporting Actor, 1991 Soap Opera Award;
1992 Soap Opera Award nomination, Outstanding Lead Actor

Daytime Dramas: "Guiding Light," Dr. Tim Ryan, 1975-76;
"Guiding Light," Billy Lewis, 1983-1987, 1989-

Born in Rochester, New York, Jordan Clarke has been intermittently involved with daytime drama since 1975. Clarke was educated at Cornell University, where he received first his B.A. in philosophy, followed by his M.F.A. in acting. Upon graduation he continued his studies at New York University, working with such acting coaches as John Heffernan and Peter Kaas. During these years, Clarke was extremely active in regional theater, among these, the Ithaca Repertory Theater, The Olney Theater, the Long Wharf Theater, and the off-Broadway Shaliko Public Theater, which he co-founded. At the Shaliko, Clarke appeared in such productions as "Shadow of a Gunman" and "Children of the Gods." From 1975 to 1976 Clarke had his first role on daytime television, playing Dr. Tim Ryan on "Guiding Light." He then left New York for California, making guest appearances on "Three's Company," "Knightrider," "The Tony Randall Show," "Fantasy Island," and "M*A*S*H." He also appeared in the television miniseries "The Executioner's Song" and "The Testimony of Two Men." Clarke's television film credits include "Forever," and "Charleston." In 1983, Clarke returned to both New York and "Guiding Light" this time portraying Billy Lewis. He remained with this role for four years, and returned once again in June of 1989. For his work there he was named Outstanding Supporting Actor by Soap Opera Digest Magazine. In his spare time, Clarke, who is married and has a daughter (Chelsea b. 1983), enjoys playing the guitar and trumpet. He also writes poetry, fiction, as well as film scripts. Before his acting career took off, Clarke made his living through an array of jobs, among them running a construction company and raising pure-bred quarterhorses.

ROBERT CLARY

Born: March 1, 1926 in Paris, France
Marital Status: married to the former Natalie Cantor, one
stepson, Michael
Height: 5'2" **Eyes**: hazel **Hair**: brown
Education: Junior High and Art School
Interests: walking, painting

Daytime Dramas: "Days of Our Lives," Robaire LeClair,
1972-1973, 1975-1980, 1981-1983, 1986-1987;
"The Young and the Restless," Pierre Roland, 1973-1974;
"The Bold and the Beautiful," Pierre Jourdan; 1989-

Born Robert Widerman, March 1, 1926, in Paris France, Robert Clary is the youngest of fourteen children. His father was a tailor, his mother a very busy homemaker. He began his career at the age of twelve performing in Paris night clubs, where he was discovered in 1947. This resulted in the recording of a song which went on to become a hit single in America, paving the way for Mr. Clary who has since enjoyed a career both as a singer and an actor of stage and screen. Clary's career has encompassed all facets of the entertainment industry. Television audiences know him best as Louis LeBeau on "Hogan's Heroes" which ran for six seasons and continues to play in syndication around the world. His film credits include "A New Kind of Love" with Paul Newman and Joanne Woodward, "The Hindenburg" with George C. Scott, "Ten Tall Men," "New Faces," and "Thief of Damascus." Clary has appeared on stage since 1952 when he became known as one of the stars of "New Faces of 1952." He has also appeared with Tony Randall in "Around the World in Eighty Days" and on Broadway in "Seventh Heaven," with Bea Arthur, "La Plume de la Tante" and "Sugar." Daytime audiences know Clary for his roles on "The Young and the Restless," "Days of Our Lives" portraying Robaire LeClair, and most recently on "The Bold and the Beautiful" portraying Pierre Jourdan. Clary, a survivor of the Jewish holocaust, lectures throughout the United States and Canada about the holocaust. His talks are in conjunction with the Simon Wiesenthal Center, where he is a volunteer in their outreach program. Since 1989, he has hosted, "A Conversation with Robert Clary," on The Jewish Television Network. Some of his guests include; Carl Reiner, Mel Brooks, Joel Grey, Dick Van Dyke, Ed Asner, Dom De Luise, Steve Allen, Martin Landau, Judith Krantz and Red Buttons. Clary currently lives in Beverly Hills, California with his wife of many years, the former Natalie Cantor, daughter of Eddie Cantor. He has one stepson, Michael and three granddaughters, Kimberly, Stephanie and Jesse.

JESSICA COLLINS

Born: April 1, 1971 in Amsterdam, New York
Marital Status: single
Height: 5'5"   **Eyes:** green   **Hair:** blond
Education: high school
Interests: cooking, fishing
Awards: 1988 Miss Teen New York, First runner up, Miss Teen USA

Daytime Dramas: "Loving," Dinah Lee Mayberry, 1991-

An up and coming actress, Jessica Collins made her daytime debut as Dinah Lee Mayberry, a nanny with a hidden agenda, on "Loving." Born on April 1 Jessica's mother raised her and her twin brothers (two years younger) in Amsterdam, New York. Jessica's parents divorced when she was quite young and her father moved to Oregon. Although she did not see him for many years, today they are quite close. Jessica's first foray into the spotlight was in 1988, when she was named Miss Teen New York, following which she placed first runner up in the Miss Teen U.S.A. pageant. Away from the beauty pageant circuit, Jessica earned extra money working as one of Santa's elves at the local mall. Immediately after graduating high school, Jessica moved to New York City, where she embarked on her acting training, which soon paid off with numerous commercial parts, including a National Dairy Association advertisement for milk. Three years later she was awarded the role of Dinah Lee - a part slated to last less than a month. Before the end of the first week, "Loving" offered Jessica a three year contract. Now living in New York City, Ms. Collins visits her family upstate as much as possible. In her spare time the actress enjoys fishing and cooking, and is particularly partial to Italian food and desserts.

KATE COLLINS

Born: May 6 in Boston, Massachusetts
Marital Status: engaged to Charlie Newell
Height: 5' 5"   **Eyes:** blue/green   **Hair:** blond
Education: Northwestern University, B.A. in theater
Interests: theater

Daytime Dramas: "One Life to Live;" "Guiding Light;" "Search for Tomorrow;" "Another World;" "All My Children," Natalie Hunter,1985-1992

Although she's been a mainstay on "All My Children" since 1985, as well as recently tackling the challenge of a dual role, it is unlikely that Kate Collins will ever equal the same heights (literally) reached by her father. A true hero of the twentieth century, Michael Collins piloted the spacecraft, Columbia, on the Apollo II mission for the historic first lunar landing in July of 1969. Mr. Collins, who is presently a retired Major General from the Air Force, also oversaw the construction of the Smithsonian's Air and Space Museum, as well as serving as it's Director. Today he serves as a consultant, and divides his time between writing and lecturing. Back on the ground, Kate was born in Boston, Massachusetts, the oldest of three children, and raised in Houston and Washington, D.C. It was during her senior year in high school, due largely to the inspiration of Ted Walch, a drama teacher, that Collins decided to dedicate herself to acting. She went on study drama at Northwestern University, and upon graduation moved to New York in search of stage work. Kate made her Broadway debut in "Doubles," playing the only female character, Heather, in an otherwise all male cast. Her other stage credits include "Quiet on the Set," "The Danube," "Blood Moon," and "Clarissa." She has also done a great deal of regional theater, performing with such companies as The Actor's Theater of Louisville, the Woodstock Playhouse, and Drew University's New Jersey Shakespeare Festival. On television, Ms. Collins has made guest appearances on several daytime dramas, including "One Life to Live," "Guiding Light," "Search for Tomorrow," and "Another World," as well as serving as substitute co-host on "Good Morning America." Recently the actress has begun to share her expertise, teaching a course on "Advanced Acting" at Video Associates in New York City. Married once before, Ms. Collins is now romantically linked with theater director Charlie Newell.

DARLENE CONLEY

Born: July 18 in Chicago Heights, Illinois
Marital Status: divorced, three sons, Raymond, Theodore and William
Height: 5' 7"   **Eyes:** green   **Hair:** red
Education: DePaul and Loyola University, two years
Interests: theater, reading, travel, piano, dance
Awards: 1991 Emmy nomination for Best Supporting Actress; 1992 Italia "Umbria Fiction Award"

Daytime Dramas: "The Young and The Restless," Rose DeVille; **"Days of Our Lives,"** Edith Baker; **"Capitol,"** Louie; **"General Hospital,"** Trixie; **"The Bold and the Beautiful,"** Sally Spectra

According to Darlene Conley she had a "short childhood" because at the age of 15 she was discovered by the legendary Broadway impresario Jed Harris. Since then, Darlene has enjoyed a long, illustrious career. Born of Irish-German descent, Conley and her two sisters, Carol and Sharon, were raised on the south side of Chicago. Her father was an accountant, her mother a housewife. After graduating from high school and some college, she began touring with a classical theater company, and went on to great success both in the theater and in the movies. Conley's first role came at the age of fifteen when Jed Harris cast her as the Irish maid in the touring production of "The Heiress" with Basil Rathbone. Following this she toured the country with a classical theatre company as well as performing Shakespeare with the Helen Hayes Repertory Theatre on Broadway. Her other stage credits include the Broadway revival of "The Night of Iguana" with Richard Chamberlain and the David Merrick musical "The Baker's Wife." In Los Angeles she appeared in "Cyrano de Bergerac," "The Time of the Cuckoo," with Jean Stapleton and "Ring Round the Moon" with Michael York. Conley's first film role came when Alfred Hitchcock cast her in "The Birds." She has also worked with John Cassavetes in "Faces" and "Minnie and Moscowitz." Her other film credits include "The Valley of the Dolls," "Play It As It Lays" and "Lady Sings the Blues." Most recently she appeared in "Tough Guys" with Burt Lancaster and Kirk Douglas. No stranger to daytime television, Darlene's credits include "The Young and the Restless," portraying Rose DeVille, "Days of Our Lives," portraying Edith Baker, "Capitol," portraying Louie, "General Hospital," where she played Trixie Monahan and most recently "The Bold and the Beautiful" portraying Sally Spectra. Aside from her work in daytime drama, Conley has also appeared in numerous other television productions, including the mini-series "Robert Kennedy and His Times," and such television movies as "The Fighter," "The Choice," "Return Engagement," and "The President's Plane is Missing." She has also guest starred on dozens of episodic shows, including "Gunsmoke," "Name of the Game," "The Cosby Show," "Murder, She Wrote," "Cagney and Lacey," "Little House on the Prairie," "The Mary Tyler Moore Show," and "Highway to Heaven." Currently single and residing in Los Angeles, Darlene has raised three sons, Raymond, Theodore and William and spends much of her spare time working for an AIDS hospice, AFTRA workshops, PBS, PBS radio and the Museum of Art.

NORMA CONNOLLY

Born: August 20, 1930 in Boston, Massachusetts
Marital Status: single
Height: 5' 5"   **Eyes:** green   **Hair:** blond
Education: Cushing Academy
Interests: reading, travel, swimming
Awards: 1986 Daytime Emmy Nomination for Outstanding Supporting Actress

Daytime Dramas: "The Young Married," Lena Gilroy, 1964-1965; **"General Hospital,"** Ruby Anderson, 1979-

Since 1979, Norma Connolly has portrayed Aunt Ruby Anderson, the voice of reason and comfort on "General Hospital." Whether she's the madam with the heart of gold or the restaurant owner in which everyone confides, viewers can always count on Ruby to wisely guide the troubled residents of Port Charles. For her efforts, the actress was awarded a 1986 Daytime Emmy nomination for Outstanding Supporting Actress. Born on August 20, 1930 in Boston, Massachusetts, Connolly attended the Cushing Academy, as well as studying acting with Leland Powers. Along with "General Hospital," Ms. Connolly was featured on the daytime drama, "The Young Married," and has been seen on the big screen in "The Wrong Man" and "The Other." Her stage credits include "A Streetcar Named Desire," "The Crucible," and "Night of the Iguana." Active behind the scenes as well, she serves on the Board of Directors of the Screen Actor's Guild, is involved with AFTRA , and, additionally donates much of her time to the organization, Hollywood Help. A resident of Los Angeles, Connolly, who is widowed, is the mother of three children, Adam, Philip and Lihana. In her spare time, Norma enjoys swimming, reading and traveling.

JOHN CONSIDINE

Born: January 2 in Los Angeles, California
Marital Status: married to Astrid Considine, two sons,
Kevin and David
Height: 6'3"   **Eyes:** hazel   **Hair:** salt/pepper
Education: UCLA, Phi Beta Kappa
Interests: piano, writing, cooking, gardening

Daytime Dramas: "Bright Promise," Dr. Brian Walsh,
1971-1972; **"The Young and the Restless,"** Philip Chancellor,
1973-1974; **"Another World,"** Vic Hastings, 1974-1976 and
Reginald Love, 1986-1988

A successful actor and writer, John Considine has been intermittently involved with daytime drama for over twenty years. A show business legacy, Considine was born on January 2, in Los Angeles, where his father worked as a film producer for MGM for over twenty years. John's family also included a sister, Erin and a brother, Tim, an actor as well. (he was one of the original brothers in "My Three Sons" and in the "Spin and Marty" and "The Hardy Boys" sereis on the original "Mickey Mouse Club" t.v. show.) After graduating Phi Beta Kappa from UCLA, John began his acting career, which has included film, television, and theater. Among the many feature films in which Considine has appeared: "Fat Man and Little Boy," Made in Heaven," "Trouble in Mind," "Choose Me," "Circle of Power," "When Time Ran Out," "A Wedding," "The Late Show," and "The Greatest Story Ever Told." On the small screen, John has been seen on "Murder, She Wrote," "Hotel," "Taxi," "McGyver," "Simon & Simon," "Eight is Enough," "Lou Grant," "Hart to Hart," and "Highway to Heaven," and in such made for t.v. movies as "Tanner '88," "Rita Hayworth: Love Goddess," "Forbidden Love," "The Waltons: Mother's Day," "The Shadow Box," "Dixie: Changing Habits," and "Marion Rose White." On daytime t.v. Considine has played two roles on "Another World," Vic Hastings and Reginald Love, as well as appearing on "The Young and the Restless" and "Bright Promise." Although he has concentrated chiefly on film and television, this actor also found time to work in several stage productions, including "C.C. Pyle and The Bunion Company," directed by Paul Newman, "Roshomon," and "Bullfight." Along with guest starring on "McGyver," Considine has also flexed his writing talents for that series, scripting four episodes. In addition, this talented writer/actor wrote the Robert Altman film, "A Wedding," as well as episodes of "My Three Sons," "Marcus Welby, MD," "Combat," and the made for t.v. film, "Dixie: Changing Habits," in which he also appeared. The father of two boys, Kevin, 29, and David, 27, Considine and his wife of eight years, Astrid, live in Pacific Palisades, California. John's hobbies include writing, gardening, cooking, and playing the piano.

LINDA COOK

Born: June 8 in Lubbock, Texas
Marital Status: married
Height: 5'5" **Eyes:** hazel **Hair:** blond
Education: 1 year of college
Interests: politics

Daytime Dramas: "Edge of Night," Laurie Ann Karr,
1975-1978, 1984; **"All My Children,"** Lucy Voight;
"Loving," Egypt Masters, 1989-1991

A native of Lubbock, Texas, Linda Cook has portrayed three prominent daytime characters over the past fifteen years, the most recent was Egypt Masters on "Loving." Prior to that role she was seen as Laurie Ann Karr on "Edge of Night" and Lucy Voight on "All My Children." Due to the requirements of her father's career, Linda moved frequently as a child, living in Omaha, Dallas, and Atlanta, where she got her first professional stage experience with the Atlanta Civic Ballet. While still only in high school, Linda toured with the company throughout the Southeast, and after completing a year of college, she decided to pursue her dancing career full time. Joining Atlanta's Alliance Theater Company, Ms. Cook appeared in a variety of musical productions. She made her Broadway debut in "Home Front," with Carroll O'Connor, and later went on to co-star in the Broadway production of "The Wager." Her additional stage credits include "The Marriage of Bette and Boo," "Tartuffe," "As You Like It," "Talley's Fox," "Saigon Rose," and "Crimes of the Heart." She most recently joined fellow daytime performers, Jill Larson and Sloane Shelton, on the New York stage in "Dearly Departed." In addition to daytime, Linda has also guest starred on such shows as "Nurse" and "Newhart." A New York City resident, Cook shares her home with her husband, a scenic designer, and three cats, Spenser, Baxter, and Emily. She devotes much of her spare time to the Starlight Foundation, and lists politics as one of her main interests.

JEANNE COOPER

Born: October 25 in Taft, California
Marital Status: divorced, three children, Corbin, Colin and Caren
Height: 5'6" **Eyes:** blue **Hair:** blond
Education: College of the Pacific/Pasadena Playhouse School
Interests: environmental concerns, human rights
Awards: three Daytime Emmy nominations for Outstanding Lead Actress; Soap Opera Digest Editor's Award for Lifetime Contributions to Daytime Television; 1989 Soap Opera Digest Award for Outstanding Lead Actress, 1989 Woman of the Year, Pasadena Playhouse Alumni and Associates

Daytime Dramas: "The Young and the Restless,"
Catherine Chancellor Sterling, 1973-

Since 1973, Jeanne Cooper has come to define class and talent on daytime television. For her work as Catherine Chancellor Sterling (and occasionally Catherine's lookalike, Marge) on "The Young and the Restless," Cooper has earned three daytime Emmy nominations for Outstanding Lead Actress, a Soap Opera Digest Award for Best Lead

Actress, and a Lifetime Achievement Award from the editor's of Soap Opera Digest. Proving that she is popular with fans and critics alike, Cooper was also voted favorite daytime actress by the magazine's readers. Jeanne was born in Taft, California, the youngest of three children. Her parents, who previously had lived on an Oklahoma Indian reservation, had relocated to California to work in the oil business. After attending the College of the Pacific and the Pasadena Playhouse School, Jeanne got her professional start working with the Civic Light Opera Company and the Revue Theater in Stockton, California. Quickly capturing the attention of film producers, she was hired as a contract player for Universal Pictures, making her motion debut shortly thereafter in "Redhead from Wyoming," with Maureen O'Hara. Cooper's first starring role was opposite Glenn Ford in "The Man from the Alamo," and her additional film credits include "The Boston Strangler," "Tony Rome," "All American Boy," "The Glory Guys," "Kansas City Bomber," and "Let No Man Write My Epitaph." On television, Ms. Cooper was a regular on two series, "Maverick" and "Bracken's Law," while she has appeared as a guest on over 400 prime time shows, among them: "Twilight Zone," "Perry Mason," "The Untouchables," "Four Star Theatre," "Playhouse 90," and "L.A. Law." She received additional Emmy nominations for her work on "Bracken's Law" and "L.A. Law," in which she was cast as the mother of her real life son, Corbin Bernsen. The two are presently teaming up again, this time in the film, "Frozen Assets." Equally at home on the stage, Jeanne has performed in such productions as "The Miracle Worker," "On the Town," "Plain and Fancy," and in a national tour of "Plaza Suite," which starred several daytime favorites. For her achievements, Ms. Cooper was named "Woman of the Year" in 1989 by the Pasadena Playhouse Alumni and Associates. Presently living in Beverly Hills, California, Jeanne, who is divorced, has three children and five grandchildren. Making the most of her recognizability, the actress works with several charities, including D.A.R.E., The Humane Society, The Children's Hospital of Toronto, and as a substance abuse rehabilitation counsellor. She also works as a human rights activist with the Pro-Choice Organization, and supports environmental concerns though such organizations as Greenpeace and the National Wildlife Association.

MICHAEL CORBETT

Born: June 20, in Philadelphia, Pennsylvania
Marital Status: single
Height: 6'1" **Eyes:** blue **Hair:** brown
Education: Boston Conservatory of Music and Drama, B.F.A.
Interests: tennis, real estate, scuba diving
Awards: "Daytime's Favorite Cads," People Magazine

Daytime Dramas: "Ryan's Hope," Michael Pavel, 1980-1981;
"Search for Tomorrow," Warren Carter, 1982-1985;
"The Young and the Restless," David Kimble, 1986-1992

It is no coincidence that every daytime character Michael Corbett has played over the past decade has been shot. First on "Ryan's Hope," then "Search for Tomorrow," and most recently "The Young and the Restless." Corbett has proven himself to be one of daytime's premiere villains, charming yet lethal, and never what he appears. Corbett's ability to play the bad guy even landed him on the cover of People Magazine, who proclaimed him one of "Daytime's Favorite Cads." A native of Philadelphia, Corbett was interested in acting from an early age, however he did not pursue it seriously until many years later. Coming from a conservative family, Corbett's father is an I.R.S. executive and political manager, his mother an artist, and his two brothers a doctor and hospital administrator respectively, Michael decided to study international diplomacy at the University of Pennsylvania. However, during a school production of "Kiss Me Kate," Corbett was discovered by none other than legendary producer/director Harold Prince, who convinced him to devote himself fully to acting. With this ringing endorsement, Corbett transferred to the prestigious Boston Conservatory of Music and Drama, from which he graduated with a B.F.A. in theater. Not one to waste time trudging from audition to audition, the young actor decided to take matters into his own hands. Upon arriving in New York Corbett rented a rehearsal hall and showcased his talents for agents and casting directors, who in turn offered him parts in two Broadway musicals. His first role was in "Nefertiti," a musical extravaganza which did not fare well with neither critics or audiences. Corbett recovered from this initial set back, appearing on Broadway and off-Broadway in such productions as "Grease" and the revival of "Come Back, Little Sheba." On the big screen, Michael appeared in "Heartburn," and on television he has guest starred on "MacGyver," "Today's F.B.I.," "The New Love American Style," and "Women in Prison." In addition Corbett starred in the CBS pilot, "Coed Fever" and in the made for television motion picture "Fire at the Coconut Grove." It is however his villainous roles on daytime drama which have earned him the most recognition. His latest, David Kimble on "The Young and the Restless," was initially slated to be only a temporary assignment, but Corbett's blend of sly charisma and underhandedness quickly caught on with the producers and the fans, and he was soon signed on for a long term contract. Completely removed from acting, Corbett has a second, equally successful career in real estate. At just nine years old he started his own business producing photographs of people's homes, and this interest never faded. Years later, during his stint on "Ryan's Hope," Corbett took his first tax refund check and purchased a small California home, which he renovated and sold at a profit. Since then, the business, known as Highland Properties, has grown tremendously, and currently has holdings on both coasts. When he is not acting, rebuilding, or making personal appearances, Corbett, who is single, lives in Los Angeles, and enjoys tennis and scuba diving.

Melinda Cordell

MELINDA CORDELL

Interests: dance
Awards: theater award for producing "The Country Girl;" Best Actress Award for "Elizabeth Rex"

Daytime Dramas: "The Young and the Restless," Dorothy Stevens, 1980-1982; **"General Hospital,"** Natalie/Natasha, 1983; **"The Young and the Restless,"** Madame Chauvin, 1984-1990

Over the past decade, Melinda Cordell has portrayed two separate characters on "The Young and the Restless." First she was seen as Dorothy Stevens from 1980 to 1982, and then after a few years absence, she returned to the program as Madame Chauvin. In between, Melinda spent a brief but memorable year on "General Hospital," where she took on the double role of Natalie/Natasha. A dancer and an actress, Ms. Cordell's first professional assignment was in a production of "The Gift of the Magi," presented in Monte Carlo by the London Festival Ballet. Over the course of her career, she has danced throughout the world with several prestigious companies, among them the Solov Ballet, The American Ballet Theater, and the American Festival Ballet. Today, Melinda continues to teach dance at the Madilyn Clark Studios, Paradise, and The Dance Center, as well as working as a choreographer and dance consultant in film, television, and music video. On the stage, the actress/dancer made her Broadway debut in "The Star Spangled Girl," and her additional theater work has earned Melinda several prizes, including a Best Actress Award for her performance in "Elizabeth Rex," and a theater award for producing "The Country Girl," at the Callboard Theater. Along with a brief stint on "Search for Tomorrow," Melinda's television work has also included guest roles on several primetime programs, including "Cheers," Lou Grant," "Family," "The Tortelli's," "Little House on the Prairie," and "The Next Step Beyond." She has been seen in the t.v. films: "Fifteen and Getting Straight," "A Brand New Life," "The Secret Life of Miss Leona," "If Birds Could Fly," and "Transplant." Melinda spends much of her spare time continuing her dancing training, as well as passing on her expertise to aspiring performers.

MARGARITA CORDOVA

Born: February 26 in Guadalajara, Mexico
Marital Status: single, two children, David and Angela
Height: 5'5" **Eyes:** brown **Hair:** brown
Education: Los Angles City College
Interests: reading
Awards: Cesar Award for Best Supporting Actress

**Daytime Dramas: "Days of Our Lives;" "General Hospital;"
"Santa Barbara,"** Rosa Andrade, 1984-1987, 1991-

Margarita Cordova is a woman of many talents. Born February 26 in Mexico, Ms. Cordova attended Los Angeles City College, where she graduated as a registered nurse. She also studied acting in her native Mexico, and with famed acting coach, Sandford Meisner. Luckily for her fans, she chose a career in acting and has been busy ever since. Currently seen by daytime audiences as Rosa Andrade on "Santa Barbara," her career has additionally included film, theater, and scores of primetime appearances. On stage, Cordova's credits include, "House of Alba," "Yerma," "Blood Wedding," "Saint Joan," and frequent roles on the Los Angeles stage, working at such theaters as the Old Globe, the Los Angeles Theater Center and as a member of Theatre West. She is also active with the Bilingual Foundation for the Arts, an organization which produces plays in Spanish. For her work, the actress has received the Cesar Award for Best Supporting Actress in a Spanish speaking play. On the big screen, Cordova co-starred in "Pay or Die," "One Eyed Jacks," "Four Horsemen of the Apocalypse," and "Cold Heaven," while she has guest starred on such television programs as "Twilight Zone," "Six Million Dollar Man," "Chico and The Man," "Mission Impossible," "Big Valley," "Wonderful World of Disney," "Divorce Court," "Brave New World," "Police Story," "T.J. Hooker," "Lou Grant," "Flying Nun," "Brady Bunch," "Family Affair," "Night Gallery," "Adam 12," "Dallas," "People's Court," "Archie Bunker," "Mod Squad," "Marcus Welby M.D.," "Room 222," "Virginian," "Gunsmoke," and "Wagon Train," among others. A professional flamenco dancer, Ms. Cordova got to display her talent in a dream sequence on "Santa Barbara." Presently single, Ms. Cordova has two grown children, Angela and David. Margarita believes strongly in giving back to her community and does so by using her areas of expertise. She utilizes her nursing degree by volunteering at local hospitals. She actively seeks roles in Spanish speaking plays, realizing the importance for all communities to appreciate the arts. And, still others know her as their flamenco dance teacher. In what spare time she has, Ms. Cordova loves to read. Prior to joining the cast of "Santa Barbara," Ms. Cordova, who has appeared in several commercials, appeared in "Days of Our Lives," and played a recurring role on "General Hospital."

NICOLAS COSTER

Born: December 3 in London, England
Marital Status: married to Beth Coster in 1982, one son, two daughters form a previous marriage
Education: Royal Academy of Dramatic Arts; New York University
Interests: sailing, theater, scuba diving
Awards: nominated for four Best Actor Daytime Emmys, 1988 Soap Opera Award for Outstanding Supporting Actor

Daytime Dramas: "Young Dr. Malone," Matt Steele, 1962-1963; **"Secret Storm,"** Paul Britton, 1964, 1968-1969; **"Our Private World,"** John Eldridge, 1965; **"As the World Turns,"** John Eldridge, 1966; **"Somerset,"** Robert Delaney, 1970-1972; **"Another World,"** Robert Delaney, 1972-1976, 1980; **"One Life to Live,"** Anthony Makana, 1983-1984; **"All My Children,"** Steve Andrews; **"Santa Barbara,"** Lionel Lockridge, 1984-

Over the past three decades, Nicolas Coster has proven himself one of daytime's most prolific actors, starring in no less than nine daytime dramas. Currently seen as Lionel Lockridge on "Santa Barbara," Coster has been on the show since 1984, earning four daytime Emmy nominations for Best Actor along the way. Since making his daytime debut in 1962, he has starred on "Young Dr. Malone," "Secret Storm," "As the World Turns," it's spin-off "Our Private World," "Another World," it's spin-off "Somerset," "One Life to Live," and "All My Children." Born in London where his father, a New Zealand native, was a Royal Marine Commando Officer during World War II, Nicolas attended the Royal Academy of Dramatic Arts, following which he relocated to the U.S. where he enrolled in the film school at New York University. Although his career has been centered around daytime television, Nicolas has also co-starred in the feature films "Reds," "The Electric Horseman," "All the President's Men," and "Betsy's Wedding," as well as appearing on such prime time shows as "Lobo," "Ryan's Four," "Police Squad," "Dallas," "McGyver," "Matlock," and "Beverly Hills 90210." In addition, the actor's voice has been used in commercials for Toyota, First Union Bank, AT & T (he was their spokesperson before Cliff Robertson), and in various cartoons. Equally at home on stage, Coster is a veteran of twelve Broadway shows, including his most recent role in "Getting Married," with veteran daytimers Linda Thorson and Walter Bobbie. A serious nautical buff, Coster, who is married with three children, two daughters and one son, enjoys relaxing on his boat "Encore," where he puts to use his skills as a licensed skipper with the U.S. Coast Guard. Should, however, he fall overboard, there is no call for concern as Nicolas is also a certified scuba instructor and a founding member of the Cousteau Society.

SUZY COTE

Born: September 17, 1968 in Santa Barbara, California
Marital Status: single
Height: 5'4" **Eyes:** brown **Hair:** brown
Education: UCLA
Interests: swimming, softball, roller skating, bicycling

Daytime Dramas: "Guiding Light," Samantha Marler, 1989-1992

For three years Suzy Cote portrayed teenager Samantha Marler on "Guiding Light." She landed the role during her sophomore year at UCLA, beating more than two hundred other prospective actresses in a nationwide talent search. Born on September 17, 1968 in Santa Barbara, California, Cote and her family, which includes her two sisters, moved to San Luis Obispo, California, when Suzy was in the fifth grade. Having studied dance since the age of six, it is not surprising that by the time she was in sixth grade, Ms. Cote was already performing in numerous community theater productions. Since then she has amassed an impressive list of theater credits, among them "The Great American," "The 49ers," "A Little Night Music," "Gypsy," "Fiddler on the Roof," "The Mikado," "A Christmas Carol," "Wait Until Dark," "The Sound of Music," and "Much Ado About Nothing." Along the way she has been involved with such companies as The Great American Melodrama Company, the Pismo Beach Light Opera, and the Pacific Conservatory of Performing Arts. Since beginning her run on "Guiding Light," Ms. Cote has additionally appeared on "Superior Court," and in two music videos, "Back and Daddy's" and "Night Trap." On the big screen, she has been seen in "The Big Picture," "Back to the Beach," and "Daddy's Little Girl." Suzy has called New York City home for the past three years, and in her spare time enjoys softball, swimming, roller skating, volleyball, and bicycling.

JACQUELINE COURTNEY

Born: September 24, 1946 in East Orange, New Jersey
Marital Status: divorced, one daughter, Jennifer Desiderio
Height: 5'5" **Eyes:** green **Hair:** blond
Education: The Professional Children's School; one year of college
Interests: reading, theater
Awards: Daytime T.V. Best Actress, 1971, 1974; AfterNoon T.V. Best Supporting Actress, 1973 (All Awards for "Another World")

Daytime Dramas: "Edge of Night," Viola Smith, 1961; **"Our Five Daughters,"** Ann Lee, 1962; **"Another World,"** Alice Matthews Frame, 1964-1975; **"One Life to Live,"** Pat Ashley, 1975-1983; **"Loving,"** Diane Winston, 1987

Although not presently on any daytime dramas, Jacqueline Courtney remains a popular television presence. If you haven't seen her recently, you most likely have heard her, as she is now one of the most sought after commercial voice over talents, lending her skills to such products as Weight Watchers and HBO. Born in East Orange, New Jersey, Jacqueline's career began at the age of seven, under the guidance of her mother/manager, Florence. Of these early years, Jacqueline states: "I spent most of my childhood travelling to the city for lessons in singing, dancing, speech etc, and for auditions and work." For the young performer work was readily available, and Jacqueline appeared on such t.v. shows as "The Horn and Hardart Children's Hour," "Route 66," "U.S. Steel Hour," and "The Jackie Gleason Show." She also appeared in commercials and by the age of fourteen, Ms. Courtney landed her first soap opera role, Viola Smith on "Edge of Night." For the next several years she appeared on a number of different daytime programs while attending The Professional Children's School in Manhattan, which Jacqueline found enjoyable. After working on "Edge of Night" and "Our Five Daughters," Jacqueline landed her first long running daytime role in 1964, when she debuted as Alice Matthews Frame on "Another World." She remained with the show until 1975, and her Alice became one of television's most enduring characters. Jacqueline's Pat Ashley on "One Life to Live", which she joined in 1975, was also a very popular character. After years of playing sweet angelic characters, Courtney got to display her versatility on "Loving" in 1987, when she portrayed Diana Winston, a less then virtuous madam of a popular bordello. For her work, she has received numerous awards, including recognition as Daytime TV's best actress of 1971 and 1974, AfterNoon TV's 1973 Best Supporting Actress, and special recognition for being voted number one in one hundred consecutive Daytime TV Reader's Polls. In addition the actress has also worked in documentary films and in various summer stock productions. Ms. Courtney, who presently lives in New York City, is divorced and has one child, Jennifer. An animal lover, Jacqueline is a member of the humane society, and also shares her good fortune by sponsoring a child through the Christian's Children's Fund. She includes among her interests: "audio and speech pathology, reading, walking, going out to dinner and to the theater, going to the movies, and looking for my next job."

CHRISTOPHER COUSINS

Born: September 27 in New York, New York
Marital Status: single
Height: 5'11"   **Eyes:** brown   **Hair:** brown
Education: Boston University
Interests: painting, wood carvings

Daytime Dramas: "Another World," Greg Houston, 1986-1987; **"As the World Turns,"** Colin Crawley, 1990; **"One Life to Live,"** Cain Rogan, 1991-

As con man Cain Rogan on "One Life to Live," Christopher Cousins has had the opportunity to display his wide acting range. Putting to use his mastery of dialects, Cousins has re-appeared in Llanview under several different guises. First he was Hudson King, a British tabloid journalist, then German film director, Heinrich Kaiser, followed by professional gambler, Humberto Calderon, and most recently as Cain Rogan. The talented actor behind all these faces was born in New York City, but raised in Norman Oklahoma, where both his parents worked as college professors. A rebellious child, Cousins originally considered a career as a painter, but after performing in high school productions, decided that acting was his true calling. Moving back east, he attended Boston University, first as a philosophy major and then transferring to the theater department. Cousins spent his summers on a Colorado ranch, training horses, and after graduating from B.U. decided to give painting another try, moving to Mexico to hone his skills. He soon realized, however, that acting was his true ambition, and eight months later moved to New York to pursue this dream. Cousins then began working in regional theater and in independent films, including "Hell High," and most recently, "The Whale Story." He first came to the attention of daytime fans as Greg Houston on "Another World," which he followed up with the role of Colin Crawley on "As the World Turns." Now enjoying the challenge of "One Life to Live," Cousins continues to paint and do wood carvings in his spare time. You may also recognize him as the hairdresser in black, touting Vidal Sasson hair products. The actor lives in Brooklyn, New York, with his girlfriend, Mimi, a photographer and film student.

BARBARA CRAMPTON

Born: December 27, in Levittown, New York
Marital Status: single
Height: 5'4" **Eyes:** blue **Hair:** blond
Education: Castleton State College, B.A.
Interests: horseback riding, skiing, bowling

Daytime Dramas: "Days of Our Lives," Tricia Evans,
"The Young and the Restless," Leanna Love

Leana Randolph, aka the loveable and little bit looney, Leanna Love is convincingly played by Barbara Crampton on "The Young and the Restless." A native New Yorker raised in Rutland, Vermont the trip from Long Island to Vermont was just the start of traveling for Barbara, the daughter of a carnival concessionaire. A serious student, Barbara studied acting in high school and earned a B.A. degree in Theater Arts from Castleton State College in Vermont. While earning her degree, Barbara proved her acting ability by landing the starring roles in "Cabaret," "The Crucible," and "The Importance of Being Ernest," among other dramas. Barbara spent her summers traveling with the carnival throughout the country. After commencement, she went to New York where she was picked for the role of Cordelia in the American Theater of Actors production of "King Lear." Barbara then moved on to Los Angeles to star in the suspense films "From Beyond" and "Reanimator" as well as being seen in "Fraternity Vacation" and "Puppet Master." Barbara made her television debut on the daytime drama, "Days of Our Lives," portraying Tricia Evans, staying with the show for one year. After leaving the show she guested starred on such television series as "Hotel," "The Insiders," "O'Hara," and "Rituals." Barbara has also made a few television movies, among them "Eye to Eye," "Hollywood Wives," "and "Love Thy Neighbor." Currently on recurring status with the show, Barbara is auditioning for primetime roles. When not working Barbara enjoys the outdoors and working out with her stairmaster. She also enjoys horseback riding, skiing and bowling. Most of all she likes to give her free time to the " Make a Wish Foundation" for the terminally ill children.

Dagne Crane

DAGNE CRANE

Born: March 8,1934 in Cleveland, Ohio
Marital Status: married for 31 years, one son
Height: 5'7"   **Eyes:** blue   **Hair:** blond
Education: University of Colorado, B.A.; New York University
Graduate Studies
Interests: animals, aerobics
Awards: Most Popular Actress in Daytime T.V. (AfterNoon T.V.
Magazine)

**Daytime Dramas: "Guiding Light;" "One Life to Live;"
"As the World Turns,"** Sandy Hughes, 1966-1971

A daytime favorite for her portrayal of Sandy Hughes on "As the World Turns," Dagne Crane can now be seen sporadically on "Guiding Light" and "One Life to Live." A native of Cleveland, Ohio, Ms. Crane was born on March 8 and was raised in a convent, where she initially intended to be a nun. However, her ambitions changed, and after receiving her B.A. from the University of Colorado, and continuing with graduate studies at New York University, Ms. Crane embarked on her acting career. Along with daytime, this has included over 350 commercials, a role in such films as Woody Allen's "Bananas," and appearances on the "Today Show" and the "Tonight Show." Voted "Most Popular Actress in Daytime T.V." by   Afternoon T.V. Magazine, Ms. Crane now divides her time between work and home life. She and her husband of thirty one years, live in Ossining, New York, where Dagne is an active Hospice Volunteer, as well as an Emergency Medical Technician and a member of the local ambulance corp. The couple have one son, and in the words of Ms. Crane, "one glorious granddaughter." A local celebrity, Dagne regularly performs her one woman show at the town's library. In addition, the actress keeps busy with aerobic dance classes and on behalf of the Animal Welfare League, often speaks to grade school children on pet responsibility.

MATT CRANE

Born: May 4, 1967 in Kimberton, Pennsylvania
Marriage: single
Eyes: blue   **Hair:** blond
Education: University of Honolulu/American
Academy of Dramatic Arts
Interests: water skiing, surfing, scuba diving

Daytime Dramas: "Another World," Matthew Cory, 1988-

A native of Kimberton, Pennsylvania, Matt Crane joined the cast of "Another World" as Matthew Cory in 1988. Crane was born on May 4, 1967, and attended both the University of Honolulu and the American Academy of Dramatic Arts. After working as a model throughout the world, including stints in Europe, Asia, and Africa, Matt returned to the U.S. and began to flex his dramatic skills on television. In addition to "Another World," which is his first daytime role, the actor has been seen on "Gidget," "Tour of Duty," and in the mini-series, "War and Remembrance." Presently living in New York City, Crane's hobbies include water skiing, swimming, scuba diving, and surfing.

AUGUSTA DABNEY

Born: October 23 in Berkeley, California
Marital Status: married to William Prince
Height: 5'5" **Eyes:** blue **Hair:** blond
Education: University of California at Berkeley
Interests: theater

Daytime Dramas: "Young Dr. Malone," Tracey Malone, 1959-1963; **"Another World,"** Laura Baxter, 1964-1965; **"As the World Turns,"** Ann Holmes, 1966-1967; **"A World Apart,"** Betty Kahlman Barry,1970; **"Guiding Light,"** Barbara Norris, 1970-1971; **"General Hospital,"** Carolyn Chandler, 1975-1976; **"The Doctors,"** Theodora Van Alen, 1980-1981; **"Loving,"** Isabelle Alden, 1983-1987

With featured roles in ten daytime dramas, Augusta Dabney has fortified her position as one of the most prolific television actresses. A California native, Augusta attended the University of California in her home town of Berkeley, following which she moved East to work in the theater. She enrolled at the prestigious American Academy of Dramatic Arts, landing her first Broadway role before completing her studies. This proved to be the start of an illustrious list of stage roles in such productions as "Children of a Lesser God," "Seascape," "Everything in the Garden," and "Who's Afraid of Virginia Woolf." Ms. Dabney's film credits include "Plaza Suite," "Heartbreak Kid," "Violets are Blue," with Sissy Spacek and Kevin Kline, and "Running on Empty." On television, the actress has concentrated chiefly on daytime, beginning with her first role as the wife of "Young Dr. Malone." This part soon spilled over into real life when Augusta married William Prince, the actor in the title role. This husband/wife pairing has since become one of daytime's great couples, and have appeared as husband and wife on "Another World," "As the World Turns," and "A World Apart." In addition, Augusta has been seen on her own in "General Hospital," "Love is a Many Splendored Thing," "One Life to Live," "The Doctors," "Guiding Light," and most recently as Isabelle Alden on "Loving." She has also appeared on episodes of "Nurse," "Lou Grant," "Quincy," "Police Woman," and in the made for television films "F.D.R.-The Last Year," with Jason Robards, and "The Best of Families." Ms. Dabney and Mr. Prince now live in Westchester County, a suburb of New York City. Ms. Dabney has three children by her first husband, actor Kevin McCarthy, James, a writer, Mary, a flower designer, and Lillah, who works in film production.

IRENE DAILEY

Born: September 12, 1920 in New York, New York
Marital Status: single
Height: 5'8"   **Eyes:** blue/green
Education: Cabrini High School, Lee Strasberg Theatre Institute
Interests: theater
Awards: 1960 London Magazine Critics Award, Best Actress, "Tomorrow With Pictures;" 1962 Theater World nomination, "Andorra;" 1964 Drama Critics Circle Award, Best Actress, "The Subject Was Roses;" 1966 Drama Desk Award for Outstanding Contribution to Off-Broadway Theatre, "Rooms;" 1971 Sarah Siddons Award, Best Actress, "The Effect of Gamma Rays on Man-in-the-Moon Marigolds;" 1972 (three) Joseph Jefferson nominations for Best Actress, "The Effect of Gamma Rays on Man-in-the-Moon Marigolds," "The House of Blue Leaves," and "Look Homeward Angel;" 1979 Daytime Emmy, Best Actress, "Another World"

Daytime Dramas: "Edge of Night," Pamela Stewart, 1969-1970; **"Another World,"** Liz Matthews, 1974-

During the course of a career that spans over half a century, Irene Dailey has proven herself a gifted actress of stage and screen, a writer, a recording artist, and a teacher. She is best known to daytime fans as Liz Matthews on "Another World," a role she has played since 1974. Born on September 12, 1920, in New York City, where her father managed the Roosevelt Hotel, Irene was a theater lover from an early age. She shared this passion with her brother, Dan, who went on to become a professional actor as well. Beginning her acting training, which she has continued throughout her career, Irene studied with such renowned acting coaches as Lee Strasberg and Uta Hagen. Taking her expertise, Irene then became a teacher in her own right, and over the years has taught acting, movement, and voice, at many prestigious institutions, including Princeton, Purdue, Northwestern, North Carolina School of the Arts, H.B. Studios, and The School of the Actors Company, an experimental theater school co-founded by Ms. Dailey herself. Since making her stage debut in 1941 in "In Out of the Frying Pan," Ms. Dailey has appeared in scores of theatrical productions, among them: "Tomorrow with Pictures," "Desire Under the Elms," "Night of the Iguana," "Goodwoman of Setzuan," "Andorra," "The Subject Was Roses," "Rooms," "The Cavern," "Threepenny Opera," "Mother Courage," "The Effect of Gamma Rays of Man-in-the-Moon Marigolds," "The House of Blue Leaves," "Look Homeward Angel," "Company," "Long Day's Journey into Night," "Rio Grande," "The Loves of Cass McGuire," and "Lost in Yonkers." For her stage performances Irene has been the recipient of many prestigious awards. Although she has concentrated chiefly on theater, she has appeared in several films, including "Daring Game," "No Way to Treat a Lady," "Five Easy Pieces," "The Grissom Gang," "The Amityville Horror," and "Stacking." On television, in addition to "Another World," Ms. Dailey has co-starred on "Edge of Night," as well as making guest appearances on "Ben Casey," "The Defenders," "Naked City," "Twilight Zone," "Dr. Kildare," and "Perry Mason." For her work on "Another World," she was awarded the 1979 Daytime Emmy for Best Actress. Clearly not one to limit herself, the talented actress has expanded her abilities to other areas, recording three albums, "The Subject Was Roses," "The Wick and the Tallow," and "Of Poetry and Power," a recording suggested by the assassination of President Kennedy. Ms. Dailey has also flexed her writing skills, penning an original play, "Waiting for Mickey and Ava," which was produced at the Ensemble Studio Theatre in 1982, as well as writing "Never Welcomed Never Warmed," a work suggested by Ann Cornelson's "Women of the Shadows." Irene, who is single, now makes her home in Sheffield, Massachusetts. She continues to work in the theater, as well as passing on her knowledge of performing to a new generation of aspiring actors.

MICHAEL DAMIAN

Born: April 26 in San Diego, California
Marital Status: single
Height: 5'10" **Eyes:** blue **Hair:** brown
Interests: music, golf, movies
Awards: Two Youth in Film Awards for "The Young and the Restless;" 1990 BMI Award for "Was It Nothing At All," one of the most recorded songs of that year

Daytime Dramas: "The Young and the Restless,"
Danny Romalotti, 1981-

A phenomenal success as both an actor and singer, Michael Damian has played Danny Romalotti on "The Young and the Restless" since 1981. Born Michael Damian Weir, the youngest of nine children, Michael was raised in San Diego in an extremely musical family. He began his classical piano training at an early age with his mother, a concert pianist, and shortly thereafter began to play the vibes, due largely to the fact that his older siblings were already playing the more traditional instruments. The range of musical talent in the family did not go to waste, as Michael soon formed a band with his brothers and sisters known as The Weirz. After several years of touring around California, as well as releasing two independent albums, Michael decided to leave the band to record his own music. His first single, a cover version of Eric Carmen's "She Did It," soon found its way onto Billboard's Top 100. Along with his musical work, Damian had additionally been studying acting since the age of nine, and this soon paid off when the producers of "The Young and the Restless" discovered the young singer performing his hit song on "American Bandstand." They created the role of Danny specifically for him, and since 1981 Damian has become a daytime favorite, garnering two Youth in Film Awards along the way. His additional t.v. credits include the role of Fly Man on "The Facts of Life." He has also been seen on "Dance Fever" and as the host of "Friday Night Videos." During his decade on "The Young and the Restless," Michael, who has a twenty four track recording studio in his house, has continued to be a vital force in pop music, recording several albums, including "Michael Damian," in 1984, it's follow up, "Love is a Mystery," the popular holiday single, "Christmas Time Without You," and the immensely successful, "Where Do We Go From Here." This last album yielded three top thirty singles, including "Rock On," originally released as part of the soundtrack for the film, "Dream a Little Dream," it went on to sell over a half a million copies. For his efforts, Damian won a Broadcast Music Industry Award for "Was It Nothing At All," as one of the most performed songs of 1990. The actor/singer is presently touring the country in support of his latest album, "Dreams of Summer," which includes the single, "What a Price to Pay." Many of the songs were debuted as Danny Romalotti tunes on "The Young and the Restless." Although no longer performing with his siblings, the majority of Damian's recording are co-produced by two of his brothers, Larry and Tom. Away from his hectic lifestyle, Michael is an avid anti-drug activist, and likes to relax by going to the movies and playing golf.

STUART DAMON

Born: February 5 in Brooklyn, New York
Marital Status: married to Deirdre Ottewill, three children,
Jennifer, Christopher, and Christina
Height: 6'2" **Eyes:** brown **Hair:** brown
Education: Brandeis University, B.A.
Interests: golf, sports
Awards: Theater World, Most Promising Performer of the Year;
Daytime Emmy nominee, Best Actor, 1981, 1982, 1983; 1992
Soap Opera Award nomination for Outstanding Supporting Actor

Daytime Dramas: "General Hospital," Dr. Alan
Quartermaine, 1977-

A three time Emmy nominee, Stuart Damon has played Dr. Alan Quartermaine on "General Hospital" since 1977. One of daytime's most multi-dimensional characters, Damon has invested in his alter ego much of his own intelligence, humor, and worldliness. Born in Brooklyn, New York, Damon's parents were Russian immigrants who had fled their homeland during the Bolshevik Revolution. From an early age Stuart enjoyed performing and making people laugh. At eleven years old he got his first taste of the stage when he portrayed the cowardly lion in a production of "The Wizard of Oz," and followed this up with numerous roles in summer camp productions. Although acting was close to his heart, Damon did not consider this a career option until after he had received his B.A. in psychology from Brandeis University. He had, in fact, chosen to go to law school when he landed a role in a summer stock production, which convinced Damon to put aside the law and pursue his acting ambitions. Stuart spent the next several years working in summer stock and other regional productions, performing in over fifty musical comedies with such co-stars as George Gobel and Jane Powell. His first Broadway role came as a member of the chorus line (which included Damon's dance partner, Elliot Gould) in a production of "Irma La Douce." Also an understudy, Damon eventually took over one of the leads, which lead to a number of other Broadway roles. One of these was in the 1964 production of "The Boys from Syracuse," for which Damon was named the "Most Promising Performer of the Year" by Theater World. Rapidly gaining attention for his Broadway work, Damon was brought to Hollywood in 1965 to star in the t.v. production of Rodgers and Hammerstein's "Cinderella," with Lesley Ann Warren. His performance in this classic gave him world wide exposure, and Stuart was soon offered a starring role in the British television series, "The Champion." Too good to pass up, Stuart, his wife, British actress Deirdre Ottewill-Damon, and their daughter, Jennifer, relocated to England where they lived for the next twelve years. Along with television work, Damon also appeared on stage in several West End productions. In 1977, with his career in a lull, the Damon family returned to the United States, and just two months later Stuart landed the role of Alan Quartermaine on "General Hospital." Since then Damon has appeared in the t.v. Movie of the Week, "Fantasies," and in the feature films "Young Doctors in Love" and "Star 80," as well as a gripping guest turn on Arthur Hailey's "Hotel." In 1982, Damon returned to the stage in a San Diego production of "Camelot," in which he played the King while his wife took on the role of the Queen. Another recent stage accomplishment was the actor's directing debut of the 1988 production of "What's Wrong With This Picture?," at the Back Alley Theater in Los Angeles." When he's not working, Damon and Dierdre (the couple has been married for over thirty years) enjoys relaxing in their Los Angeles home, which they renovated themselves. Along with daughter Jennifer, the Damon family now includes son, Christopher, legal ward, Christina, poodles, Othello and Odette, and cat, Roland. Stuart is a sports fan, particularly golf which he plays regularly. He is also an active fund raiser for the Juvenile Diabetes Foundation; a disease that has afflicted his son, Christopher.

SHELL DANIELSON

Born: in Upland, California
Marital Status: single
Interests: writing, painting, reading

Daytime Dramas: "Santa Barbara," Laken Lockridge,
1990-1991; **"General Hospital,"** Dominique, 1991-

After making her daytime debut as Laken Lockridge on "Santa Barbara" in 1990, Shell Danielson returned to the medium in December of 1991, portraying Dominique on "General Hospital." Born in Upland, California, Danielson hails from a creative family which includes her father, an artist, her mother, a singer/songwriter, and her stepmother, also an artist. Prior to landing her "Santa Barbara" role, Shell spent eight years living in New York City, where she was a model for the prestigious Wilhelmina Modelling Agency. Since moving to Los Angeles, the actress has appeared in numerous commercials. In addition to her daytime roles, she is also an avid writer and hopes to one day have her works published. In her spare time, Danielson, who is single, enjoys drawing, painting, reading, and spending time with her golden retriever, Hailey.

LINDA DANO

Born: May 12 in Long Beach, California
Marital Status: married to Frank Attardi
Height: 5' 7" **Eyes:** hazel **Hair:** brown
Education: University of California at Long Beach, B.F.A.
Interests: fashion, writing, antiques
Awards: 1988 Soap Opera Digest nomination, Outstanding
Comedic Actress; 1988-89 MVP Award, Soap Opera Update;
1989 Ace Award nomination; 1989 Emmy nomination,
Outstanding Talk Show Host; 1992 Soap Opera Digest
nomination, Outstanding Supporting Actress; 1992 Emmy
nomination, Outstanding Supporting Actress; 1992 Dr. Catherine
White Achievement Award from the Catholic Guardian Society

Daytime Dramas: "One Life to Live," Gretel Cummings,
1978-1980; **"As the World Turns,"** Cynthia Haines, 1981-1982;
"Another World," Felicia Gallant, 1983-

An actress, talk show host, and business woman, Linda Dano is approaching her ten year anniversary as Felicia Gallant on "Another World." Born on May 12, in Long Beach, California, Ms. Dano studied art at her hometown's University of California campus. After graduating she quickly found work as a model, which lead to a three year contract with 20th Century Fox Studios. Moving to Hollywood, Linda began working in television, landing a co-starring role on "The Montefuscos," as well as making guest appearances on "Peyton Place," "The Rockford Files," "Emergency,"

"Chips," "Harry O," "Charlie's Angeles," "Barney Miller," "The Hardy Boys," "The Fess Parker Show," and "Braken's World," on which she had a recurring role. She has also been seen in several television films, including "The Nurse Killers," "The Last Survivors," "The War of the Worlds," and "Rage of Angels: The Story Continues." In addition to "Another World," the actress co-starred on two other daytime dramas, "As the World Turns" and "One Life to Live." For several years Ms. Dano stepped out of character and served as co-host of the popular talk show "Attitudes." Disturbed by the shows increasing reliance on tabloid journalism, she decided not to continue as host, and is now planning another talk show more congruent to her own tastes. Equally successful away from television, Linda operates her own fashion consulting firm, Strictly Personal, Ltd., and has even co-authored a romance novel, "Dreamweaver," under the pen name Felicia Gallant. Not one to take her success for granted, Ms. Dano donates much of her time to the Catholic Guardian Society of New York, an organization which provides support for troubled families. For her efforts she was awarded the Dr. Catherine White Achievement Award at a recent charity event. Linda and her husband, advertising executive Frank Attardi, have been married since 1981, and divide their time between their New York and 18th century Connecticut home.

HENRY DARROW

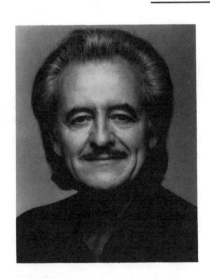

Born: September 13 in New York, New York
Marital Status: married to Lauren Levian, two children, Debe and Tom
Height: 6' **Eyes:** brown **Hair:** brown
Education: University of Puerto Rico
Interests: chess, cooking
Awards: 1990 Daytime Emmy for Best Supporting Actor ("Santa Barbara"); 1985 Golden Eagle Award; 1970 Bambi Award for "High Chaparral"

Daytime Dramas: "Santa Barbara," Rafael Castillo, 1989-1992

At home on both stage and screen, Henry Darrow received a 1990 Daytime Emmy for his work as Rafael Castillo on "Santa Barbara." Born Enrique Tomas Delgado, Darrow lived in New York City with his brother Dennis until the age of thirteen, when his family relocated to Puerto Rico. Convinced her son would be a movie star, Darrow's mother continually enrolled her young son in dance classes, and it was there that Henry first discovered performing. While attending the University of Puerto Rico, where Darrow studied political science and psychology, he was offered a dramatic scholarship, which eventually brought him to the Pasadena Playhouse in California. With his acting career beginning, Darrow, understanding the stereotypes enforced by Hollywood, made the difficult decision of changing his name from Delgado to Darrow. For the next several years the young actor appeared in numerous stage productions and television shows. However, Darrow's big break came in 1965 when he starred in the L.A. stage production of Ray Bradbury's "The Wonderful Ice Cream Suit." The show was seen by a television producer, who then offered Henry the role of Manolito Mantoyo in "High Chaparral." The show became a great success and made Darrow an extremely popular and sought after actor. He divided the next several years between film, television, and theater, even taking time to go to Sweden where he sang Mexican songs in Swedish. Among Darrow's theater credits include roles in "The Rainmaker," "The Fantastiks," "Corridos," "Richard III," and "The Devil Disciple," while he has been seen on the big screen in "Badge 373," "Walk Proud," "Cancel My Reservations," "Losin' It," "The Hitcher," and "Last of the Finest." After "High Chaparral," Darrow starred on other t.v. series, including "Harry O," with David Jansen, "The New Dick Van Dyke Show," "General Hospital," and "Zorro and Son." In addition, Darrow has made quest appearances on over seventy five television shows, including "Dallas," "Dynasty," "Golden Girls," "T.J. Hooker," "Star Trek: The Next Generation," "Quincy," "Kojak," and the mini series "The Centennial." Along with "Santa Barbara," Darrow can also be seen on television as Zorro's father in the Family Channel series "Zorro." Interestingly, the actor has not only guest starred on the earlier series "Zorro and Son," but also provided the voice for the part in an animated cartoon. Thus Darrow is perhaps the only actor involved with three separate Zorro productions. For his work over the years he has won several awards, including the daytime Emmy, Germany's 1970 Bambi Award, and the 1985 Golden Eagle Award. Darrow is married to actress Lauren Levian, with whom he has two children. The family lives in San Fernando Valley, California, where Henry relaxes by cooking (a talent he picked up from his parents who were restaurant owners) and competing in celebrity chess tournaments. Darrow chose to leave "Santa Barbara" in 1992 to work on the feature film, "Time Trax."

DOUG DAVIDSON

Born: October 24 in Glendale, California
Marital Status: married to actress Cindy Fisher, one daughter, Calyssa Rae, son, Caden Douglas
Height: 6' **Eyes:** blue **Hair:** blond
Education: Occidental College, California State University, Northridge
Interests: travel, karate, running, camping, music
Awards: 1990 Soap Opera Award, Outstanding Hero; 1991 Soap Opera Award, Outstanding Hero; 1992 Soap Opera Award, Outstanding Supporting Actor

Daytime Dramas: "The Young and the Restless,"
Paul Williams, 1979-

One of daytime's leading stars, Doug Davidson created dashing detective Paul Williams on "The Young and the Restless" and has played him since 1979. Over the past thirteen years he has helped the show rise to the top of the ratings, as well as being named Outstanding Hero by Soap Opera Digest in 1990 and 1991, and best supporting actor in 1992. Born on October 24 in Glendale, California, Davidson was raised in La Canada-Flintridge, where he discovered acting during his freshman year of high school. The rest of the Davidson family includes two sisters, Donna and Diana, and parents, Donald and Corinne, a chemical engineer and interior designer, respectively. During high school and as a student at Occidental College, where he majored in theater and marine biology, Doug worked as a magazine and catalog model. In addition, he also held a variety of part time employment, including stints as a bartender, cab driver, and waiter. Although he had appeared in several national t.v. commercials, Davidson was discovered by the producers of "The Young and the Restless" when he went to visit a friend on the set. The actor was soon signed on to play Paul Williams, a role that has since earned him legions of fans and a TVQ rating of #1. Along with daytime, Doug has appeared on the big screen in "Fraternity Row," and in the made for television films "I'll Take Manhattan" and "The Initiation of Sarah." He is currently working on his second feature film, currently titled "Ain't Love Grand." There is no release date yet. In 1990, Davidson served as Master of Ceremonies at the Miss California Pageant, as well as serving as co-host of the Kenny Roger's Cerebral Palsy Telethon. Away from the set, Doug works as the co-chairman of "We Tip," an organization which educates people on the reality of urban crime. In addition the actor can also be found donating his time as a YMCA camp director. A world traveller and avid outdoorsman, Doug has camped throughout Europe, and also enjoys waterskiing and scuba diving. Davidson is married to Cindy Fisher, an actress, with whom he has two children, daughter, Calyssa Rae, born on December 27, 1989 one son, Caden Douglas born on May 21, 1992. In his spare time Doug enjoys music (he has played the bagpipes since he was a child), songwriting, running, karate, and playing with his two English sheep dogs, Lucille and Gertrude.

EILEEN DAVIDSON

Born: June 15 in Artesia, California
Marital Status: single
Height: 5'7"   **Eyes:** blue   **Hair:** blond
Education: Orange Coast College
Interests: music, dancing, painting

Daytime Dramas: "The Young and the Restless," Ashley Abbott,1982-1988; **"Santa Barbara,"** Kelly Capwell, 1991-

After six years as Ashley Abbott on "The Young and the Restless," Eileen Davidson has reinvented her daytime persona, and is now seen as Kelly Capwell on "Santa Barbara." The youngest of seven children, Eileen was born in Artesia, California, and raised in nearby La Mirada, where she spent much of her time on the beach. While out dancing one night, Eileen was discovered by a photographer, and this paved the way to a successful modelling career. At nineteen, she moved to Los Angeles, where she decided to enroll in an acting class. From the moment she stepped on stage, Eileen was hooked, and spent the next few years honing her performing skills, continuing her modelling work only to pay for classes. Getting her feet wet, she starred in American Film Institute films and a score of student works as well, and at the age of 22 landed the much sought after role of Ashley Abbott on "The Young and the Restless." After six years on the show, Ms. Davidson, not wanting to restrict herself, felt it was time to seek out new acting challenges. Leaving daytime television, she starred in the feature film "Eternity," with Jon Voight and Armand Assante, as well as in the short lived prime time series, "Broken Badges." Discouraged with the direction her career had taken, Eileen sought some new purpose, which she found in Para Los Ninos, an organization devoted to helping troubled, inner-city youths. She soon found herself immersed in the cause, and although she no longer is able to work there full time, due to her "Santa Barbara" role, she remains a dedicated activist. She is presently learning Spanish to help her communicate better with some of the children. Finding new meaning in charitable work, Ms. Davidson also helped organize the "Housing Now" march on Washington D.C.. Eileen, who was previously married to daytime actor Christopher Mayer, as well as being romantically linked with Nicholas Walker, is now happily involved with Don Diamont, a former castmate on "The Young and the Restless." In her spare time, Ms. Davidson enjoys painting, songwriting, dancing, and playing with her four dogs and two cats. The actress has also recently been influenced by the teachings of the Dali Llama.

TERRY DAVIS

Born: July 23, 1951 in New York, New York
Marital Status: married to TV director, Andrew Weyman, two daughters, Sarah and Karen
Height: 5'4 1/2"   **Eyes:** blue   **Hair:** blond
Education: College of New Rochelle, B.A. in Psychology
Interests: coaching her children, biking, skating, hiking in the canyons

Daytime Dramas: "The Edge of Night," April Cavanaugh Scott,1977-1981; **"Another World,"** Stacey Winthrope, 1982-1984; **"Santa Barbara,"** Madeline Capwell Laurent, 1986-1987

One of daytime's most familiar faces, Terry Davis has had featured roles on "Edge of Night," "Another World," and "Santa Barbara." Terry was born on July 23 in New York City, where she, along with her four siblings, were raised by her father, a self employed laborer, and her mother, a homemaker. After receiving her B.A. in psychology from the College of New Rochelle, Terry embarked on her acting career, which has included television, film, and theater. On stage, Terry appeared off-Broadway in "Toys in the Attic," as well as in such regional productions as "Cabaret," "Bus Stop," "Fiddler on the Roof," and "King Lear." On the big screen, Davis co-starred in "Till There Was You," "Stakeout," and "Romancing the Stone," and has guest starred on several television series, including: "Carol and Co.," "The New Mike Hammer," "Throb," and "Adam 12." Davis resides in Los Angeles with her husband, Andrew Weyman, a television director whom she met on the set of "Edge of Night." The couple have been married since December 1, 1970 and have two daughters, Sarah and Karen. Not presently occupied with the day to day work of a serial, Terry is devoting herself to her children and to various charitable causes. She is on the board of directors at Westland School, and chairs other committees, among them, Community Service, which "adopted" a Head Start Center and they run programs that involve children from both Westland and Head Start. Davis is also a sports enthusiast, and particularly enjoys biking, skating, and hiking in the California canyons. The actress is also active with her children's sporting endeavors. According to Terry: "My kids are playing sports I never had an opportunity to play! So, I coach! This is my third year coaching soccer... & I'm good! Living in L.A. brings us outdoors a lot."

SCOTT DeFREITAS

Born: September 9, 1969 in Newton, Massachusetts
Marital Status: single
Hair: blond
Education: The King School
Interests: hockey, baseball, golf, rollerblading
Awards: nominated for 1988 and 1992 Daytime Emmys, Outstanding Younger Actor; nominated for 1992 Soap Opera Award, Outstanding Younger Leading Actor

Daytime Dramas: "As the World Turns," Andy Dixon, 1984-

Nominated for a 1988 Outstanding Younger Actor Daytime Emmy, Scott DeFreitas has spent the past eight years as Andy Dixon on "As the World Turns." Born on September 9 in Newton, Massachusetts, Defreitas spent his early years in nearby Hudson, before his family, which includes three younger brothers, relocated to Connecticut. Scott began his professional acting career working in commercials, after his neighbor, a casting director, suggested he audition for acting roles. Scott joined the cast of "As the World Turns" at fifteen and upon graduation from high School (The King School) he was offered a full contract. DeFreitas has worked on stage as well, making his New York theater debut in, "Coming of Age in Soho," a production first seen at the New York Shakespeare Festival's Public Theater. In the future, the actor hopes to try his hand at directing. Presently living in New York City, DeFreitas, who is single but involved in a long term relationship, lists amongst his interests, hockey, baseball, golf, and rollerblading.

WANDA DE JESUS

Born: August 26 in New York, New York
Marital Status: single
Eyes: brown   **Hair:** brown
Education: City University of New York, B.F.A.
Interests: meditation, bicycling, dancing

Daytime Dramas: "Another World," Gomez;
"Santa Barbara," Santana Andrade

After several screen and stage successes, Wanda De Jesus is now wowing daytime audiences with her portrayal of Santana Andrade on "Santa Barbara." Born of Puerto Rican heritage, Wanda, along with her two brothers, was the first American generation of the De Jesus family. She was raised on the Upper East Side of New York where her parents ran a restaurant. Mr. and Mrs. De Jesus, firm believers in hard work and discipline, insisted that their young daughter attend parochial school. However, at the age of twelve Wanda discovered acting, when she worked with "The Teenage Performing Arts Workshop," as well as with the "East Harlem Production Troupe." They presented such full fledged musicals as "Pippin" and "The Me Nobody Knows." Hooked on this new passion, Wanda convinced her parents to let her attend the High School of Performing Arts, following which she received her B.F.A. degree from the Leonard Davis Center of the City University of New York. During her schooling years Wanda got her start professionally, appearing in numerous commercials and in stage productions, as well as taking a year off to sing lead with a local punk band, Coney Island White Fish. After graduation, Ms. De Jesus joined the Circle Repertory Theater, where she not only performed on stage, but helped to develop the "Young Playwrights Festival." It was, however, her work with The Public Theater which proved to be her big break, when she helped bring the Ray Ravad play, "Cuba and His Teddybear" to the stage. The production, which starred Robert De Niro, ran for six months at the Public Theater and another year on Broadway. A personal as well as professional triumph, De Jesus also met her longtime beau, actor Jimmy Smits, during the shows run. Wanda's other theater credits include "Dead Man Out," "The Day You'll Love Me," "Miriam's Flowers," and "Summer & Smoke." Moving to California, along with Smits, Wanda began working in television, and along with popular roles on "Santa Barbara" and "Another World," she has also been seen on "L.A. Law," "Matlock," "Civil Wars," "Equal Justice," and in starring roles in "Mariah" and "50 Minute Man." Ms. De Jesus has also begun working on the big screen, co-starring in two recent releases, "Robo Cop 2" and "Downtown." Now a full time Los Angeles resident, Ms. De Jesus spends as much time as possible with her family, and also enjoys bicycling, weight training, dancing, aerobics, and meditation.

JAMES DePAIVA

Born: October 6 in Hayward, California
Marital Status: married to actress Misty Rowe on
June 4, 1986, one daughter, Dreama Marie
Height: 6' **Eyes:** blue-green **Hair:** brown
Education: Stella Adler Training
Interests: spending time with his wife, fixing musical
instruments, his dogs

Daytime Dramas: "General Hospital," 1986
"One Life to Live," Max Holden, 1987-1990, 1991-

After a brief leave of absence from daytime drama, James DePaiva recently resumed the role of Max Holden on "One Life to Live." A native of Hayward, California, and a distant relative of President Andrew Jackson, DePaiva was raised in Livermore, where he initially set out to be a musician. By the age of fifteen, he was playing the electric bass professionally, but soon after, DePaiva decided that his future lay in acting rather than music. He studied drama at a nearby community college, as well as working in community theater and with a repertory company in Solvang, California. With this strong theater base, James moved to Los Angeles to study with famed acting coach Stella Adler. His first big break came on the daytime drama, "General Hospital," where he played a waiter in hot pursuit of Holly Scorpio (Emma Samms). Although he never successfully wooed Holly, he did make an impact on the producers of "One Life to Live," who, in 1987, brought him to New York for the role of Max Holden. Along with his work on "One Life to Live," DePaiva has also appeared on episodes of "Simon and Simon," and "Days of Our Lives." In addition, the actor had a role in the made for television movie, "Commitment to Excellence." On the stage, DePaiva's credits include "The Fifth of July," "The Hasty Heart," "The Desk Set," "The Sound of Music," and "Company." During his twenty month hiatus, DePaiva appeared on PBS's "Mathnet" as well as the Fruit of the Loom commercial with Ed Marinaro and Patrick Duffy. (he kept his clothes on) He was also in the Stella Adler Theatre production of the play, "Permissions." DePaiva and his wife, actress Misty Rowe of "Hee Haw," currently divide their time between the east and west coasts, although both consider California to be their home. They were married June 4, 1986 and became first time parents on July 2, 1992 to daughter, Dreama DePaiva. This is DePaiva's second marriage. The couple recently renovated a cabin in the mountains of California, (coincidentally near the home of Nicholas Walker, who replaced him as Max) where they enjoy spending time with their four dogs, Shiloh, Max, Munchkin, and Daisy May, and pet cockatoo, Cosmo.

MARK DERWIN

Born: October 28, 1960 in Park Forest, Illinois
Marital Status: single
Height: 6'1" **Eyes:** brown **Hair:** brown
Interests: golf, softball, watching sports, movies
Education: Cobleskill College
Daytime Dramas: "The Young and the Restless,"
Adrian Hunter; **"Guiding Light,"** A.C.Mallet, 1990-

Through his roles as a mysterious private investigator and a lethal hit man, Mark Derwin has established himself as a definite presence on the daytime television scene. The youngest of three children, his sister Ann is both mother and secretary, his brother Kevin works for IBM. Born in Park Forest, Illinois, Derwin and his family moved first to Yorktown Heights, New York, and then to North Salem, New York, where Derwin graduated from high school. He then attended Cobleskill College, finding work as a carpenter in his spare time. It was during this time, that he met Michael LaGuardia, an actor and teacher who inspired him to move to Los Angeles and pursue an acting career. Derwin took his advice and moved out west, appearing in "Apres Opera" at the Court Theatre, as well as appearing in a number of student and independent films. Along with a brief part on "Days of Our Lives," Derwin has been featured on two daytime shows, first as hitman Adrian Hunter on "The Young and the Restless," and most recently as A.C. Mallet on "Guiding Light." In addition, Derwin also has a small role in the now defunct prime time series, "Hardball." Mark, who is the proud uncle of Michael, Heather, Stephanie, Alexa, and Jill, presently lives in Manhattan where he enjoys golf and softball, as well as watching sports and going to the movies.

DON DIAMONT

Born: December 31 in New York, New York
Marital Status: single
Height: 6'1" **Eyes:** hazel **Hair:** black
Education: Nina Foch training
Interests: sports, travelling, working with stained glass
Awards: voted Favorite Newcomer-Daytime TV Magazine
(Days of Our Lives)

Daytime Dramas: "Days of Our Lives," Carlo Forenza,
1984; **"The Young and the Restless,"** Brad Carlton, 1985-

Much like his daytime alter-ego, Brad Carlton on "The Young and the Restless," Don Diamont has managed to achieve great success in a short amount of time. Since joining the cast of "The Young and the Restless," Diamont has earned himself a place among daytime's top actors, while the character of Brad has gone from groundskeeper to key player in the Abbott Cosmetic Empire. Born on December 31 in New York, Diamont was raised in Los Angeles, the youngest of four children. After graduating from high school, where he excelled academically and athletically, Don was discovered by a Los Angeles modelling agency, who sent him to Europe to work as a model. Returning to the United States, he continued to pursue this line of work, while at the same time studying acting with Nina Foch. This paid off quickly with the role of Carlo Forenza on "Days of Our Lives," and although Diamont was not on the show for long, he did make enough of an impression to be voted "Best Newcomer" by the readers of Daytime T.V. Magazine. Since joining the cast of "The Young and the Restless" in 1985, the actor has additionally been seen on "The Fall Guy" and "Night of 100 Stars III," as well as in Fruit of the Loom commercials. Presently single, Diamont, who was previously involved with Gloria Loring, is now romantically linked with Eileen Davidson, of "Santa Barbara." He donates much of his spare time to such charitable organizations as the American Cancer Society, Juvenile Diabetes Foundation, and Rancho Los Amigos Hospital. To relax, Diamont, a resident of Sherman Oaks, California, enjoys travelling, football, tennis, basketball, baseball, boxing, swimming, karate, skiing, and working with stained glass. Don, who comes from a Jewish background, recently became interested in his heritage, and is presently preparing for his Bar Mitzvah.

FRANK DICOPOULOS

Born: January 3, 1957 in Akron, Ohio
Marital Status: married to actress Teja Anderson on October 20, 1990
Height: 6'1" **Eyes:** green **Hair:** light brown
Education: Kenyon College, Bachelor's Degree
Interests: art, music, weight training, basketball, tennis, theatre, movies, playing with Sammy
Awards: National Honor Society, National Optimist Award, NCAA Division 3 track record for high hurdles

Daytime Dramas: "Guiding Light," Frank Cooper, 1987-

A native of Akron, Ohio, Frank Dicopoulos came upon his love of acting unexpectedly, while he was a student at Kenyon College. Up to the point that he made this unwitting discovery, Dicopoulos was a star college athlete who aspired to a career as an orthopedic surgeon, and in an effort to maintain his high grade point average he enrolled in a few drama courses. These proved to be much more challenging, and considerably more enjoyable, than Dicopoulos ever imagined, and because of this there is one less orthopedic surgeon in the world today. The oldest of three children, he was born to Catherine and Harry on January 3rd. His father is an attorney who works at the Firestone Tire and Rubber Company, while his mother works in the retail industry. Today, Frank's brother, Alex is a banker, his sister, Penny is an accountant. Dicopoulos continued his collegiate sports career as well, playing football, basketball, and lacrosse, as well as setting an NCAA Division 3 track record for the high hurdles. Upon graduation, Dicopoulos moved to Texas, where, among other things, he managed a tire store and worked as a mechanic. Soon after he was able to devote himself fulltime to his acting career, finding work in commercials and posing for print ads. While still in Texas, Dicopoulos participated in a nationwide talent search to find a replacement for Larry Wilcox on "Chips," although he did not get the role he was one of the four finalists out of the 770 original candidates. Dicopoulos did land another lead television role soon after, albeit without Eric Estrada, in the MTV documentary "Wild Rides," narrated by Matt Dillon. He then hosted ESPN's show, "On The Move," as well as the "Miss Teenage America Pageant." In 1984, Dicopoulos left Texas for Los Angeles where he found steady work on a myriad of television series, among them "The Tracey Ullman Show," "Silver Spoons," "Hotel," "Dynasty," "Falcon Crest," and "O'Hara." Before landing the role of Frank Cooper on "Guiding Light," Dicopoulos also had small parts on three other daytime dramas, "The Young and the Restless," "Capitol," and "General Hospital." In his spare time Dicopoulos enjoys sports, music, theatre, movies, playing with their golden retriever, Sammy, and art, which he both draws and collects. He is also involved with helping to save our earth by volunteering and supporting Greenpeace and Rainforest Alliance. He is also involved in the Actors Fund, American Cancer Society, American Heart Association and Children with Aids. On October 20, 1990 at the Greek Orthodox Holy Trinity Church in New York City, Frank married actress/writer Teja Anderson, who has also appeared on "Guiding Light." The couple resides in New York City.

COLLEEN DION

Born: December 26, 1964 in Newburgh, New York
Marital Status: separated
Height: 5'6" **Eyes:** brown   **Hair:** brown
Interests: ice and roller skating, horseback riding, cooking, baking, making crafts, collecting anything with cows on them

Daytime Dramas: "Search for Tomorrow," Evie Stone, 1985-1986; **"Loving,"** Cecelia Sowolsky, 1986-1987; **"The Bold and the Beautiful,"** Felicia Forrestor

The Forrestor family and the Dion family share one common link, their beautiful, youngest daughter, Felicia Forrestor played by Colleen Dion. Born the youngest of four (3 girls, 1 boy), in upstate New York, Colleen was raised in Crystal Lake, Illinois a suburb of Chicago, where her father works for Kemper Insurance. At the age of fifteen, Colleen decided to enter a Loves Baby Soft modeling contest. She became a finalist which brought her to New York, and she although she didn't win the contest, her modeling career took off. She became a popular teen model, appearing on teen fashion and beauty publication covers. While modelling, Colleen studied acting and landed her first professional job as Evie Stone on daytime's now defunct "Search for Tomorrow." After one year with the show, she moved to "Loving" where she portrayed Cecelia Sowolsky for the next eighteen months. After her stint on "Loving," Colleen relocated to Los Angeles and prior to landing the role of Felicia Forrestor on "The Bold and the Beautiful" she appeared on "Santa Barbara," "Divorce Court" and in the primetime series "Equal Justice." She also showered for a national Coast Soap commercial. On the big screen, Colleen has been seen in "Fatal Charm," and "Lucas." Colleen was married in 1988 to publicist Steve Jensen, just five weeks after they met, in a Las Vegas 24 hour chapel. They separated in 1992. When not working, Colleen enjoys both roller and ice skating as well as horseback riding. She also enjoys the unusual craft of making gifts out of tuna fish cans and cat food cans. She also likes cooking,baking and collecting anything with cows on them - shirts, sheets, mugs and more.

ELLEN DOLAN

Born: October 16, 1955 in Monticello, Iowa
Marital Status: single
Height: 5'5" **Eyes:** brown   **Hair:** brown
Education: University of Iowa, M.A. and M.F.A. in theatre
Interests: music, horseback riding

Daytime Dramas: "Guiding Light," Maureen Bauer, 1982-1986; **"As the World Turns,"** Margo Hughes,1990-

Born in Monticello, Iowa, and raised in nearby Decorah, Ellen Dolan discovered her love of acting in junior high school. She maintained this passion through her college years, receiving her M.A. and M.F.A. in theater from the University of Iowa, as well as spending a summer studying at the Webber Douglass Academy in London. It was at the Milwaukee

Repertory Theater that Ellen made her professional stage debut, and since then has starred in a number of productions, among them, "Mother Courage," "Cat on a Hot Tin Roof," "My Fair Lady," and "Anything Goes." Ellen made her daytime television debut in 1982 as Maureen Bauer on "Guiding Light," a role she created and stayed with for the next four years before moving west to Los Angeles. After being in Los Angeles only a short time, during which she starred in the television movie, "Mother's Day," Doug Marland, the headwriter for "As the World Turns," asked her to return to New York to play the part of policewoman Margo Hughes. Ellen agreed and once again took up residence in New York City, joining the "As the World Turns" cast in January of 1990. In her spare time, Dolan enjoys singing, playing the flute, skiing, and swimming.

AMI DOLENZ

Born: January 8 in Los Angeles, California
Marital Status: single
Height: 5'3" **Eyes:** blue **Hair:** blond
Education: Newbridge High School
Interests: horseback riding
Awards: Star Search Overall Competition

Daytime Dramas: "General Hospital," Melissa

Proving that the apple doesn't fall far from the tree, Ami Dolenz is now embarking on an acting career, just as her father, ex-Monkee Mickey Dolenz, did some twenty five years ago. Her grandfather was the character actor, George Dolenz. Born in Los Angeles, Ami's parents divorced when she was five, and she spent most of her time in Acapulco and Mexico City with her mother, former model Samantha Just Slater. Ami returned to Los Angeles when she was twelve, where she attended Newbridge High School, before getting her big break by winning the overall competition on the show, "Star Search." After winning the competition, Ami appeared in a number of television shows, among them "Silver Spoons," "The Judge," "Star Man," and a recurring role on "Growing Pains," with Kirk Cameron. Aside from her work on "General Hospital," she has appeared in the feature films "Can't Buy Me Love" and as Tony Danza's daughter in "She's Out of Control." Today Ami lives in North Hollywood with her dog, Blondie, where she continues to study voice and acting.

NORMA DONALDSON

Born: in New York, New York
Marital Status: single
Height: 5' **Eyes:** brown **Hair:** black
Education: Saint Alysiusin
Interests: writing, travel, theater, movies

Daytime Dramas: "General Hospital," Dr. Pauline Revelle;
"The Young and the Restless," Lillie Bell

Currently seen as Lillie Bell on "The Young and the Restless," Norma Donaldson was born and raised in New York City. After attending Saint Alysiusin, Ms. Donaldson embarked on her professional acting career, which has included television, film, and theater. In addition to "The Young and the Restless," she appeared briefly on "General Hospital" as Dr. Pauline Revelle, and has also made guest appearances on such shows as "Babes," "Lifestories," "Farewell for the People," "Willow B Woman in Prison," "The Jeffersons," and "Good Times." The actress also played the recurring role of Ms. Watson on "All in the Family" and "Archie Bunker's Place." On the big screen, Donaldson has co-starred in several films, among them "The Five Heartbeats," "House Party," "The Unholy," "Nine to Five," and "Staying Alive," while her theater credits include the Broadway production of "Guys and Dolls," (she played Adelaide) "Purlie," "No Place to be Somebody," "Great White Hope," with James Earl Jones, "Sweet Charity," and "Kiss Me Kate." An accomplished singer as well, she has showcased her vocal skills in concerts with Harry Belafonte, John Davidson, and Lionel Hampton. Away from the set, Donaldson, who lives in Los Angeles, enjoys movies, theater, writing, and travelling, and is also in the process of learning to speak Spanish.

JERRY DOUGLAS

Born: November 12 in Chelsea, Massachusetts
Marital Status: married to Kymberly Douglas on April 6, 1985, two children from a previous marriage
Height: 6'1"   **Eyes:** one blue\one brown   **Hair:** light brown
Education: Brandeis University, Bachelor's Degree in Economics
Interests: golf, going to the movies, reading, watching sports

Daytime Dramas: "The Young and the Restless," John Abbott

Success is something that both John Abbott, the character and Jerry Douglas the actor have in common. John Abbott, businessman, devoted family man and the very epitome of integrity is made real by the fine acting of Jerry Douglas who has portrayed John Abbott on "The Young and the Restless," for the past decade. Born in Chelsea Massachusetts, Douglas grew up in Boston. An athlete at Chelsea High School, Douglas received a football scholarship to Brandeis University. Following commencement, he began to pursue an acting career, studying in New York with Uta Hagen and in California with Jeff Cory. Through the years Douglas has guest starred on more than fifty television shows, among them: "The Greatest American Hero," "Harry O," "The F.B.I.," "Police Story," "The Rockford Files," "House Calls," and "The Streets of San Francisco." His television film credits include "Crash," "Walton's Mountain," and "Night Watch." On the big screen, Douglas' movie credits include, "Looker," "Mommie Dearest," and "Avalanche." His most recent film role, Arthur Kensington in Oliver Stone's controversial film, "JFK" ended up being edited from the film. It had nothing to do with Douglas' acting, it was a matter of a film too long that needed to be shortened. Douglas' talents are also behind the camera; he is a screenwriter, and develops projects through his production company, Jovra Films. Douglas has also worked on "The Other Side of Daytime," a musical variety show he put together that featured other daytime performers. He has also taught "soap seminars" at colleges and universities throughout the country. Douglas, who met his wife Kymberly at a Muscular Dystrophy seminar, when he was hosting the Los Angeles portion of the telethon and she covering the event for a Michigan television station, have been married since 1985. Kymberly has since left her news anchor position and begun acting. She was briefly seen as Michael Crawford's secretary on "The Young and the Restless." He has two children from a previous marriage; Avra (an assistant to actor Marlon Brando) and Jodaman. When not working, Douglas lends his efforts to "Variety Clubs" an organization that gives immediate help to the homeless. In his leisure time he enjoys golf, books, and going to sports events as well as plays.

ROBERT DUBAC

Born: December 15 in Ohio
Marital Status: single
Height: 5'9"   **Eyes:** blue   **Hair:** brown
Education: University of Georgia, B.A.
Interests: yoga, skiing

Daytime Dramas: "Loving," Alex Masters

Having achieved great success in the world of stand up comedy, Robert Dubac has only recently begun to show off his acting ability as well. Born in Ohio, Dubac received his B.A. from the University of Georgia, where he had a triple major of journalism, psychology, and theater. Directly after college he hit the road with his stand up act, first living in Aspen, Colorado, and then moving to Los Angeles. Along the way he opened for various rock and roll bands, and has since graduated to tour with such performers as Linda Ronstadt, Kenny Loggins, The Beach Boys, and The Pointer Sisters. Dubac has also performed his stand up act on "An Evening at the Improv," "Showtime Comedy Club Network," and Joan River's former show, "The Late Show," on which he served as guest host for a week. Along with his role as Alex Masters on "Loving," Dubac has also been seen on television in "Life Goes On," "Hunter," and "Growing Pains." Dubac has had recurring roles on two network series, "Diff'rent Strokes" and "Jack & Mike." He continues to study acting, performing at the Playhouse West in Los Angeles, where he has acted in productions such as "Strange Snow" and "Another Language." In his spare time, Dubac skis and does yoga workouts each day.

CARMEN DUNCAN

Born: July 7 in Lismore, New South Wales, Australia
Marital Status: single, two children, Duncan and Amelia
Height: 5' 4 1/2"   **Eyes:** green   **Hair:** blond
Education: National Institute of Dramatic Arts in Sydney, B.A.
Interests: theater, arts, spending time with friends
Awards: Sammy Award nomination for Best Actress in "Touch and Go;" Australian Film Institute nomination for Best Actress in "Harlequin;" 1992 Soap Opera Award nomination for Outstanding Villainess

Daytime Dramas: "Another World," Iris Carrington Wheeler, 1988-

Hailing from the land down under, Carmen Joan Duncan took over one of daytime's most notorious roles, "Another World's" Iris Carrington Wheeler, in October of 1988. Born to Bob and Rita Duncan on July 7, in Lismore, New South Wales, Australia, Ms. Duncan was educated at the National Institute of Dramatic Arts in Sydney, Australia. Completing her training, she embarked on a successful career, which has included film, television, and theater. Her stage credits include "Cat on a Hot Tin Roof," "Blythe Spirit," "Cactus Flower," "Hamlet," "Romeo and Juliet," "A Man for All Seasons," and "Playboy of the Western World." She has been seen in such feature films as "Harlequin," "Touch and Go," "Now and Forever," "Turkey Shoot," "Dark Forces," and the childrens film, "Platapus Cove." For her work in "Harlequin," the actress received a Best Actress nomination from the Australian Film Institute, as well as receiving a prestigious Sammy Award Best Actress nomination for "Touch and Go." With a string of achievements in her homeland, Carmen decided to head for Hollywood, where she quickly landed guest starring roles on "Matlock," "Riptide," and "Hunter," and a starring role in the made for television film, "Intimate Strangers." Ms. Duncan has lived in New York since she began working on "Another World," and has at the same time continued to work on the stage, receiving great adulation for her performances. Away from the set the busy actress, who has two children, Duncan and Amelia, enjoys visiting art galleries, spending time with friends, and going to the theater. Carmen also donates a great deal of time to Burmese refugee work, Covenant House, Greenpeace, National Epileptic Society, and AIDS research.

BOBBIE EAKES

Born: July 25 in Warner Robins, Georgia
Marital Status: married to David Steen on July 4, 1992
Height: 5'5" **Eyes:** hazel **Hair:** brown
Education: University of Georgia, two years
Interests: singing, cooking, decorating
Awards: Miss Georgia TEEN, Miss Georgia 1992, Top Ten Finalist in Miss America, 1983

Daytime Dramas: "The Bold and the Beautiful," Macy Alexander Forrester, 1989-

A former Miss Georgia TEEN, Miss Georgia, and top ten finalist in the Miss America Pageant, Bobbie Eakes has been a daytime favorite since her 1983 debut as Macy Alexander on "The Bold and the Beautiful." The youngest of five girls, Bobbie was born on July 25 in Warner Robins, Georgia, where her father was a member of the U.S. Air Force. She first discovered performing when she, along with the rest of her sisters, formed the "Eakes Girls," a singing group who toured their home state. Following in her sister's footsteps, Bobbie first entered the beauty pageant circuit with the Miss TEEN Pageant, winning the Miss Georgia Teen Crown and placing first runner up (but taking first place in the talent category) in the national competition. After enrolling in the University of Georgia, Bobbie set her sights on the Miss America Crown, once again being named Miss Georgia, but losing the national title after being named one of the top ten finalists. Taking advantage of her performing experience, Eakes moved to Los Angeles, with the hopes of establishing a singing career, quickly finding work with studio session groups and locally based bands. Although she was offered the opportunity to sing back up for Bob Seeger, Bobbie opted to join "Big Trouble," an all girl band who's first record was produced by Giorgio Moroder. Although the band never enjoyed breakaway success, they did record a song used in the Sylvester Stallone film "Over the Top." Now concentrating chiefly on acting, Bobbie continues to sing, and recently travelled to Nashville to record an album of country songs. Her acting career has been progressing equally well, and along with her "Bold and the Beautiful" role, Bobbie has made guest appearances on several prime time shows, including "Cheers," "The Wonder Years," "Laverne and Shirley," "Full House," "Jake and the Fatman," "21 Jump Street," "Comedy Break," "Werewolf," and "Falcon Crest." Presently living in the San Fernando Valley, Ms. Eakes recently wed writer/actor David Steen, whom she credits with convincing her to pursue her country music career. In her spare time, Bobbie enjoys cooking and decorating.

CANDICE EARLEY

Born: August 18,1950 in Ft. Hood, Texas
Marital Status: married to Bob Nolan on March 14, 1992
Height: 5' **Eyes:** blue/green **Hair:** blond
Education: Trinity University
Interests: computers, antiques
Awards: 1977 Soap Opera Award, Favorite Female Newcomer;
"Outstanding Young Women of America" for two years; 1988
Official Ambassador of Goodwill for the state of Oklahoma; 1988
Daytime Emmy nomination for Outstanding Supporting Actress

Daytime Dramas: "All My Children," Donna Tyler, 1976-1992

After being a mainstay on "All My Children" for over sixteen years, Candice Earley made 1992 her final year as Donna Beck Tyler. Her departure is not a career decision, but rather, in true soap opera fashion, the culmination of a romance that began with a chance meeting on Christmas day 1982. It seems that Candice, who at the time was involved with "One Life to Live" star Clint Ritchie, was on a plane when a fifteen year old girl asked her for an autograph. The girl turned out to be the daughter of Bob Nolan, a successful Arkansas businessman, and Candice quickly struck up a conversation with the family, recommending various restaurants and shows they might want to attend during their stay in New York. A few weeks later Candice received a thank you note from Bob but dismissed any romantic possibilities. One year later, Candice, whose relationship with Ritchie had ended, was shocked to receive a letter from Bob. In the letter he informed her that he had been divorced over the past year and would like to see her the next time he was in New York. Since then the two have been completely devoted, shuttling back and forth between New York and Arkansas. However, Candice feels that it is time to devote herself full time to her marriage, and moved to Arkansas permanently once her "All My Children" tenure ended. She was married on March 14, 1992 at the Dallas Mansion on Turtle Creek, the same place that he proposed in August 1990. The daughter of an army colonel, Candice was born in Texas, but spent the majority of her early years living in Germany. Her father served in the artillery in both World War 2 and the Korean War, as well as serving as an advisor to the South Korean Army. He relocated back to the United States, and Candice spent the remainder of her childhood in Lawton, Oklahoma. It was there that she first appeared in school plays and discovered her love of performing, which she carried with her to her years as a drama major at Trinity University in San Antonio, Texas. After college, Candice joined a San Francisco company of "Hair," and eventually performed in the Broadway production. Clearly a young woman of considerable accomplishments, Candice was listed in "Outstanding Young Women of America" for two consecutive years. Along with "Hair," Ms. Earley has also appeared on Broadway as Mary Magdaline in "Jesus Christ, Superstar" and as Sandy Dumbrowski in "Grease." Among her other stage credits: "The Conjurer," "Civilization and its Discontents," "Gigi," and a national tour of "South Pacific," with Robert Goulet. An accomplished singer and dancer, as well as actress, Candice spent fourteen years training as a classical singer and is schooled in various forms of dance, including jazz, tap, and ballet. She can be found displaying these skills in New York City, where she often performs a cabaret act, many times with fellow soap star, John Gabriel. Another arena in which she performs is in a yearly benefit in her hometown of Lawton. The event is in support of a scholarship fund honoring one of her friends, the late Bill Crawford. For her efforts, the actress was named the 1988 "Official Ambassador of Goodwill" for the state of Oklahoma. Candice spends much of her spare time learning how to use her computer which keeps track of her collection of sheet music as well as her fan mail. Candice also enjoys needlepoint, collecting western art and miniature antiques - a hobby begun when she traveled with various shows, so she would be able to bring home (in her suitcase) souvenirs of all the places she had been.

MICHAEL EASTON

Born: February 16, 1966 in Manhattan Beach, California
Marital Status: single
Eyes: blue   **Hair:** brown
Education: UCLA
Interests: motorcycles, poetry, literature
Awards: People Magazine 50 Most Beautiful People, 1992

Daytime Dramas: "Days of Our Lives," Tanner Scofield, 1990-1992

Voted by People Magazine as one of the world's 50 most beautiful people, Michael Easton is an actor whose talents rival his appearance. A rebel in the true sense of the word, this "Days of Our Lives" star spent several years travelling around the United States, living life on the edge. The results of this can be seen in "Drift," a book of poems the actor wrote during his wild travelling days. Born in Manhattan Beach, California, Easton's childhood was divided between the United States and Ireland, where he lived for several years. While still in high school, influenced by the work of Charles Bukowski, Michael began writing poetry of his own. Following graduation, he enrolled in college, but after bounding around from school to school (seven in all), Easton decided that he wasn't ready to be in a classroom, and embarked on several years of travelling and self exploration. He drifted throughout the country, earning money wherever he could, including a stint as an agitator of attack dogs in training, before deciding it was time to go back to school. He enrolled in UCLA where he studied literature and Greek history, following which he began his formal acting training, working with such coaches as Yvgeny Lansky and Margie Haber. Easton's first break came with the lead in the film "Cold Fire," which lead to a subsequent film role in "The Art of Dying." On stage, Michael has been seen in "Moon Children," "Death of a Salesman," "Loose Ends," "Julius Caesar," and "Dark at the Top of the Stairs." Now enjoying skyrocketing success on "Days of Our Lives," he recently completed a t.v. film, "Night Tide," slated for a fall airing. In his spare time, Easton likes to relax by shooting pool or riding one of his two motorcycles.

LOUIS EDMONDS

Born: September 24, 1923 in Baton Rouge, Louisiana
Marital Status: single
Height: 6' **Eyes:** blue   **Hair:** white
Education: Carnegie Mellon University, Bachelor's Degree
Interests: theater, cajun cooking
Awards: nominated for Daytime Emmy, Best Supporting Actor, 1984, 1985, and 1986

Daytime Dramas: "Young Dr. Malone," Rick Hampton, 1962; **"Dark Shadows,"** Roger Collins/Joshua Collins/Edward Collins, 1966-1971; **"All My Children,"** Langley Wallingford, 1979-

From daytime drama, to the Broadway stage, Louis Edmonds is clearly a man who chooses not to limit himself creatively. Born and raised in Baton Rouge, Louisiana, Edmonds first foray into the spotlight was as a young soprano in the choir. Several years later and several octaves lower, he enrolled in Carnegie Mellon University where he majored in drama and voice. After college, Edmonds spent three years in the navy, following which he moved to New York City where he officially began his extensive theater career. His Broadway credits include roles in "Otherwise Engaged," "Candide," "Passage to India," "Fire," and "Maybe Tuesday." He has been seen off-Broadway in "The Importance of Being Earnest," "Ernest in Love," "Under Milkwood," "The Interview," and regionally in "Billy Budd," "Dearest Enemy," "The Three Sisters," "Anthony and Cleopatra," and countless others. Since joining the cast of "All My Children" in 1979, Edmonds has been nominated for three Best Supporting Actor Daytime Emmys, and has still managed to maintain his thriving stage career. Particularly partial to musicals, the actor has used his time away from daytime to appear as Don Quixote in a Bridgeport production of "Man of La Mancha," as well as in a concert featuring the best of Kurt Weill and Bertolt Brecht at the Library of Congress in Washington D.C.. In addition he has performed in "Leave It to Jane" at Manhattan's Town Hall and as Fagin in "Oliver." His most recent return to the stage was the Los Angeles debut of his cabaret act. Along with "All My Children," Edmonds co-starred in the daytime dramas "Young Dr. Malone," and "Dark Shadows" and in such television programs as "Armstrong Circle Theater," "Hallmark Hall of Fame," and "Studio One." His feature films include "The Exterminator," "The House of Dark Shadows," "The Fifth Arm," and "Come Spy With Me." Still true to his Louisiana roots, Edmonds is a fan of cajun cooking and enjoys making his own gumbo.

BETH EHLERS

Born: July 23 in Queens, New York
Marital Status: married to Dr. William Parsons, June 1991
Height: 5'4" **Eyes:** blue **Hair:** blond
Education: Syracuse University, one year
Interests: travel, reading
Awards: nominated for 1991 Daytime Emmy, Outstanding Younger Actress; nominated for 1992 Soap Opera Award, Outstanding Younger Actress

Daytime Dramas: "Guiding Light," Harley Davidson Cooper Spaulding, 1987-

Since joining the cast of "Guiding Light" as the outspoken Harley Davidson Cooper Spaulding in 1987, Beth Ehlers has been nominated for both a Soap Opera Award and a Daytime Emmy as Outstanding Younger Actress. Born on July 23 in Queens, New York, Ehlers lived on Long Island until moving into New York City at the age of nine. After relocating to Manhattan, she began her acting training, attending school at the Satelite Academy, and appearing in radio and television commercials. Beth attended Syracuse University for one year, but then decided to return to New York City to pursue acting work full time. She continued to do commercials, as well as numerous voice overs, and eventually began landing dramatic roles in both feature films and television. On the big screen, Ms. Ehlers co-starred in "Hiding Out," with Jon Cryer and with David Bowie in "The Hunger," while her t.v. movie credits include "Family Reunion," with Bette Davis, "In Defense of the Kids," with Blythe Danner and Sam Waterston, "Mystery on Fire Island," and the PBS production, "Mother May I." In addition to "Guiding Light," she was also a regular on the series, "Best Times." Beth, who's hobbies include travelling and reading, now shares her New York City home with her husband, Dr. William Parsons, whom she married in June of 1991.

MARIA ELLINGSEN

Born: January 22, 1964 in Reykjvik, Iceland
Marital Status: single
Height: 5' 7"   **Eyes:** blue   **Hair:** blond
Education: New York University, B.A. from experimental Theatre Wing
Interests: mountain climbing, horseback riding, languages, traveling

Daytime Dramas: "Santa Barbara," Katrina Braun, 1991-

A worthy ancestor of the adventurous Vikings, Maria Ellingsen is clearly a woman who believes in challenge and achievement. Born to Haraldur and Asbjoga, and raised with her four siblings (sisters, Elin and Erla; brothers, Orn and Erling) in Reykjvik, Iceland, Maria never seriously considered acting as a career choice. Despite the fact that she was involved in numerous school plays, as well as writing a few scripts of her own, Maria decided to work towards a career in medicine. She soon, however, became disheartened with this choice, and decided that her future lay as a journalist. After graduating from a junior college, Maria found a position on an Iceland newspaper, but the desire to act remained with her, and she soon found herself heading towards America to study theater at New York University. Maria then spent a year in the states working at NYU's Experimental Theater before returning to Iceland, where she enjoyed a string of successful acting assignments. Along with starring roles in four consecutive National Theater of Iceland productions, Maria also found work in film, television, and commercials. The busy actress then parlayed her success into the creation of the Second Stage Theatre Group, whose first production was Sam Shephard's, "Fool for Love." Not only did Maria star in the play, but she also served as the producer as well. Once this was completed Maria decided it was time to return to the United States, moving to New York towards the end of 1990. A few months later Maria auditioned for a role on "Santa Barbara," and in March of 1991, she was chosen to play Katrina Braun. Currently living in Los Angeles, Maria, who is an avid outdoorswoman, spends much of her free time working with children.

JANE ELLIOT

Born: January 17 in New York, New York
Marital Status: divorced, two children, Adrian and Annie Rose
Height: 5'5"   **Eyes:** hazel   **Hair:** auburn
Education: Dalton School
Interests: horseback riding, swimming, bicycling
Awards: 1980 Emmy for Best Supporting Actress; 1980 Soap Opera Award for Favorite Villainess; 1989 Emmy nomination for Outstanding Supporting Actress ("Days of Our Lives"); 1992 Soap Opera Award for Outstanding Supporting Actress

Daytime Dramas: "A Flame in the Wind," Madge Sinclair; **"General Hospital,"** Tracy Quartermaine, 1978-1980; 1989- **"Guiding Light,"** Carrie Todd, 1981-1982; **"All My Children,"** Cynthia Prest,1984-1986; **"Days of Our Lives,"** Angelica Deveraux, 1987-1989

Born and raised in New York City, Jane Elliot went directly from the Dalton school to a profes⟨⟩ Always certain that she wanted to pursue acting, she bypassed college, opting rather to go to Londo⟨⟩ her first role on a British television production of "Come Back, Little Sheba." Returning to the Unite⟨⟩ her first big American break, playing Alan King's daughter in the Broadway production of "The Imposs⟨⟩ was only 18 years old. Following Broadway she returned to television in the daytime drama, "Flame in t⟨⟩ then she has gone on to appear in a number of prime time series, among them, "Knots Landing," "B⟨⟩ Jones," "Police Woman," "The Interns," and "Once an Eagle," as well as in the mini-series "Captain and the Kings " and the television movie, "In the Matter of Karen Ann Quinlan." On the big screen she has been featured in such films as "Baby Boom," "A Change of Habit," and "One is a Lonely Number." It is, however, her work on daytime drama which has brought her the most success. Jane has starred in no less than five series, each time bringing her unique qualities to the role she plays. It is this distinctiveness which earned her an Emmy in 1980 and a nomination in 1989. Jane originated the role of Tracy on "General Hospital" in 1978. Exiting in 1980, Jane gained additional experience on daytime television, appearing in "All My Children," "Days of Our Lives," (where she garnished her second Emmy nomination) "Guiding Light," and in 1989 returned to "General Hospital " as Tracy Quartermaine. An intensely private person, Jane recently spoke publicly about her mothers death in 1991; wanting people to know her mothers death was directly linked to the effects of cigarette smoking. Away from work, Jane enjoys horseback riding, bicycling and swimming. She currently lives outside Los Angeles with her two young children, Adrian and Annie Rose.

PATRICIA ELLIOTT

Born: July 21 in Gunnison, Colorado
Marital Status: single
Height: 5'5" **Eyes:** blue **Hair:** reddish brown
Education: London Academy of Music and Dramatic Art
Interests: yoga, charity work
Awards: Tony Award, Theater World Award, Drama Desk Award for "A Little Night Music;" nominated for Tony for "The Shadow Box;" nominated for Drama Desk Award for "Tartuffe;" 1992 Soap Opera Award nomination for Outstanding Supporting Actress

Daytime Dramas: "One Life to Live," Renee Divine Buchanan

A Tony Award winning actress who lists swimming with dolphins as one of her favorite hobbies, Patricia Elliott is clearly a woman who marches to her own drum. Born in Gunnison, Colorado, Patricia was from an early age a natural ham, and consistently found herself drawn to the stage. An avid reader as well, it was during her youth that she was first introduced to many classic works, in who's stage productions Patricia would later perform. She began her formal training when she left her public relations job at Harvard University to attend the London Academy of Music and Dramatic Arts. Returning to the United States in 1974, Patricia landed her first Broadway role, Countess Charlotte, in the Stephen Sondheim musical, "A Little Night Music." For her debut she earned the triple crown of New York theater: a Tony Award, A Drama Desk Award, and a Theater World Award. Patricia has since added an impressive array of stage credits, including roles on Broadway in "The Shadow Box," "The Elephant Man," with David Bowie, and "A Month of Sundays," opposite Jason Robards. For her work in "The Shadow Box," Patricia earned her second Tony nomination. Off-Broadway and regionally she has appeared in countless productions ranging from tragedy to farce, including "Bunker Reveries," "Misalliance," "Much Ado About Nothing," and "Tartuffe," for which Ms. Elliott achieved her second Drama Desk nomination. Along with roles in the feature films, "Somebody Killed Her Husband," "Natural Enemies," and "Morning, Winter and Night," Patricia has made guest appearances on such television series as "St. Elsewhere," "Spencer: For Hire," and "Hill Street Blues." She has also had featured roles in "Sometimes I Don't Like My Mother," "The Ladies," "The Cartier Heist," "The Adams Chronicles," and the short lived situation comedy, "Empire." Much of Patricia's spare time is devoted to her duties as a board member, along with Tony Randall and Frances Sternhagen, for the "Plays for Living." The goal of this organization, which stages productions at schools, shelters, prisons, and churches, is to educate the audience about many pressing contemporary issues, including AIDS, drug abuse, and racial prejudice. Patricia has thus far been thrilled with the audience response, and is presently planning a benefit which she will direct. Along with swimming with dolphins, Patricia, who lives in Manhattan, spends her free time meditating, bicycling, and spending time with her friends.

MORGAN ENGLUND

Born: August 25, 1965 in Los Angeles, California
Marital Status: married to Pam Ralston, June 1990, one daughter, born in 1992
Height: 6' **Eyes:** blue **Hair:** blond
Education: Monterey Peninsula College; University of Colorado, B.F.A.
Interests: skiing, basketball, guitar, singing, surfing

Daytime Dramas: "Guiding Light," Dylan Shayne Lewis, 1989-

An up and coming actor, Morgan Englund, who has portrayed Dylan Shayne Lewis on "Guiding Light" since 1989, is the son of writer/producer George Englund and popular actress, Cloris Leachman. Born on August 25, 1965 in Los Angles, Morgan was a football star at Palisades High School, continuing with the sport at Monterey Peninsula College. However, after an injury ended his playing days, Morgan decided to take an acting class, and from his first stage performance, in the chorus of "Pippin," he knew that his future was as an actor. For the next few years, Englund devoted himself to theatrical training, studying in the B.F.A. drama program at the University of Colorado, as well as working with the prestigious Circle in the Square Theater in New York City. One of his early stage roles was in a Los Angeles production of "Picnic," which was recorded and later presented on Showtime. On the big screen, Morgan has co-starred in "Phoenix Fire Mystery," with Martin Sheen and James Coburn, and "Beach Balls," while he has appeared in the television film, "The Las Vegas Strip Wars." Along with his role on "Guiding Light," the actor has also been seen on the series "Throb." In 1992 he appeared in an off-Broadway production of Shakespeare's "Twelfth Night." His next stage venture (bringing him full circle) is in an off-Broadway production of "Pippin." In 1990, Morgan married Pam Ralston, a kindergarten teacher, and the couple presently resides in New York City where they had their first child in the summer of 1992. In his spare time, Englund enjoys singing, playing the guitar, biking, basketball, skiing, and surfing. He is also a gourmet cook, and recently displayed his expertise on the "The Image Workshop." He is also a spokesmen for ALS (Lou Gerighs Disease); his brother Max is afflicted with a form of the disease.

TOM EPLIN

Born: October 25, 1960 in Hayward, California
Marital Status: married to Courtney Gibbs, December 31, 1991
Eyes: blue **Hair:** brown
Education: American Conservatory Theater
Interests: race car driving, skydiving, scuba diving, writing
Awards: nominated for 1992 Soap Opera Award for Outstanding Villain

Daytime Dramas: "Another World," Jake McKinnon, 1985-1986, 1988-

An actor and a producer, Tom Eplin is best known to daytime fans as Jake McKinnon on "Another World." Eplin took on the role in 1985, leaving the show the following year and returning in 1988. Born on October 25, 1960 in Hayward, California, Eplin studied acting for three years with the American Conservatory Theater in San Francisco, where he performed in such productions as "Bent"and "Bus Stop." Since then, the actor has continued to study with such coaches as Joan Darling and Alan Rich, and has even conducted his own acting seminars. In addition to daytime, Eplin has made guest appearances on "The Facts of Life," "240 Robert," and "Private Practice," while his feature film credits include, "Discovery Bay," "Sunset Strip," and "Enchanted Evening." Taking time out from acting, Eplin produced the film, "Delta Fever," as well as the television pilot, "Odd Jobs." Eplin now makes his home in Long Beach, New York, and lists amongst his hobbies, writing, race car driving, skydiving, scuba diving, and flying his airplane. Previously married to Ellen Wheeler of "Another World," Eplin recently wed former Miss USA, Courtney Gibbs who originated the role of Galen Henderson on "All My Children." The couple met for the second time at a health and fitness expo and married ten weeks later on New Years Eve.

BRENDA EPPERSON

Born: September 9 in North Hollywood, California
Marital Status: single
Height: 5'9" **Eyes:** blue\green **Hair:** blond
Education: Southern California College
Interests: volleyball, swimming, tennis, running, weight training

**Daytime Dramas: "The Bold and the Beautiful",
"The Young and the Restless,"** Ashley Abbbott, 1988-

Brenda Epperson's story reads like one of the long ago soap operas on radio. Can a little girl from a logging town in Oregon make good in the big city? The answer is yes. Brenda was born in North Hollywood, California but she and her sister were raised in the logging town of Dallas, Oregon. While in high school Epperson often thought of returning to California. These thoughts turned to determination and Epperson left her hometown to pursue an acting career in

Los Angeles. Enrolling in various workshops, Epperson was soon working in commercials as well as modelling. She also appeared on many television shows including, "Saturday Night Live" and "Stop the Music." Although she did appear on "The Bold and the Beautiful," daytime audiences know Epperson from her wonderful portrayal of Ashley Abbott on "The Young and the Restless." She has been working on the show since the fall of 1988 and bears a striking resemblance to her predecessor, Eileen Davidson. Lending her support to "The Missing Children's Foundation," in Oregon, she also acts as their spokesperson. During her leisure time, Epperson, a sports enthusiast, enjoys volleyball, running, swimming, softball, tennis, as well as weight training.

JUDI EVANS

Born: July 12 in Montebello, California
Marital Status: married to Robert Eth
Height: 5'4"   **Eyes:** blue   **Hair:** blond
Education: Pasadena City College
Interests: trapeze, horseback riding
Awards: 1984 Daytime Emmy, Best Supporting Actress
("Guiding Light")

Daytime Dramas: "Guiding Light," Beth Raines,1983-1986;
"Days of Our Lives," Adrienne Kiriakis,1986-1990;
"Another World," Paulina Cory, 1991-

While many actors may describe themselves as former class clowns, few of them have the credentials of Judi Evans. Your average child will earn clown points by putting whoopee cushions on the teacher's desk and calling up the supermarket to see if they have Prince Albert in a can, but Judi opted to wear a wig, a big nose, and floppy shoes and travel with her family's circus between the ages of two and eight. As a baby circus clown, Judi spent these six years performing throughout the western United States, along with her father, a trapeze artist and occasional ringmaster, her mother, and three older, juggling brothers. A native of Montebello, California, Judi enjoyed life on the road until she was eight years old, at which point her family settled down in Monterey Park, California. She initially considered a career in medicine, however after studying drama at Pasadena City College, Judi decided to give acting a whirl. After graduation, and a brief modelling career, she enrolled in acting classes at HB Studios, and nine months later landed her first role, Beth Raines on "Guiding Light." Her sensitive portrayal earned her the 1984 Daytime Emmy for Best Supporting Actress, and Judi remained on "Guiding Light" for the next three years. She followed this with another virtuous daytime heroine, Adrienne Kiriakis on "Days of Our Lives," and is now enjoying her third soap incarnation on "Another World." This latest role is a welcomed departure for Evans, who after years of playing the saintly, weeping type, is finally getting a chance to display her own humor and vibrancy. Judi has also been seen on prime time television, in the movie of the week, "Dreams of Gold." One of the reasons that Judi decided to go to "Another World" was the show's New York base, which allows her to be with her husband, Robert Eth, an importer and designer of men's footwear. The couple resides in New Jersey, where Judi enjoys such pastimes as horseback riding, scuba diving, skiing, and, following in her family's footsteps, (or handprints) the trapeze. Judi also is no stranger to the world of gambling, particularly to shooting craps, which once earned her $3,000 in a mere six hours. She is currently trying to revive her all female poker nights, which she established while living on the west coast.

MICHAEL EVANS

Born: July 27 in England
Marital Status: married
Height: 6'1" **Eyes:** gray **Hair:** gray
Education: Old Vic School of Drama
Interests: gardening, travels to Paris

Daytime Dramas: "The Young and the Restless," Douglas Austin, 1979-1985, 1987-; **"Capitol,"** Jeffrey Martin Sahim, 1986-1987

Since 1979, Michael Evans has come to be known to millions as Douglas Austin, close friend and confidant to Victor Newman on "The Young and the Restless." Born on July 27, Evans was raised and educated in England, receiving his theatrical training at The Old Vic School of Drama in London. Upon graduation, he spent several seasons as a member of The Worthing Repertory Stock Company, appearing in numerous London productions, before moving to New York City in 1950. Evans made his American stage debut in "Ring Around the Moon," which he followed with a starring role on Broadway in "Gigi," opposite Audrey Hepburn. The actor went on to star in the show's national tour. Some of his additional stage credits include "The Sleeping Prince," (on Broadway) and the role of Henry Higgins in the national touring company of "My Fair Lady." Before moving to Los Angeles in 1964, Mr. Evans appeared on several live television programs, among them "Robert Montgomery Presents," "Kraft Theatre," and "Studio One." Once in Hollywood, Michael became a much sought after performer, making guest appearances on such programs as "Hart to Hart," "Charlie's Angles," "The Bob Newhart Show," "The Tony Randall Show," and "Family Ties," while he was also seen in the t.v. movie, "The Hasty Heart." Among his feature film credits are roles in "Bye Bye Birdie," "The Sword and the Sorcerer," and "Time after Time." In 1986, Michael took a brief hiatus from "The Young and the Restless," during which time he appeared as Jeffrey Martin Sahim on "Capitol." In his spare time, Evans enjoys gardening, taking fast walks, and vacationing in Paris with his wife.

SHARON FARRELL

Born: December 24 in Sioux City, Iowa
Marital Status: married to screenwriter, Dale Trevillion
Eyes: blue **Hair:** blond
Interests: painting, horseback riding
Awards: "Newcomer of the Year" in 30th Annual Poll of Motion Picture Exhibitors (for performance in The Reivers); Grand Prix Award for Best Actress for "The Premonition" at the 7th Festival Internationale De Paris Du Film Fantastique Et De Science Fiction; The Pryor Award at the Black Rain Arts and Sciences Institute for "It's Alive;" Miss Brooklyn; Miss Manhattan

Daytime Dramas: "The Young and the Restless," Flo Webster, 1991-

An award winning actress, Sharon Farrell has triumphed over personal tragedy and is now back on top with her portrayal of Flo Webster on "The Young and the Restless." Originally slated to appear in only a handful of episodes, Ms. Farrell so impressed executive producer Bill Bell, that he offered the actress a three year contract. Born in Sioux City, Iowa, Sharon began studying classical ballet at the age of seven. Her combination of talent and diligence quickly earned her much attention, and seven years later she travelled to Denver where she performed with The American Ballet Theater Company. After appearing there for three consecutive summers, Sharon landed a role in the Denver Civic Theater's production of "Oklahoma." Once again her talent garnered a great deal of praise, most notably by The Poet Laureate of Colorado, who cast her as a dancer in "And Perhaps Happiness." During the course of the play, however, her dancing abilities took a backseat to her dramatic abilities, and Ms. Farrell soon became a sought after stage actress. Riding this wave of success, she moved to New York City to work at a children's theater. Unfortunately this proved to be short lived, as the theater went bankrupt soon after, leaving Sharon unemployed in New York City. However, just as her prospects seemed dismal, her life took an unexpected turn when a modelling agent discovered her, and this lead to a string of jobs which included modelling flannel nightgowns in the Montgomery Ward catalog, and a Cosmopolitan cover in September, 1971. Farrell also tried her hand in the beauty pageant circuit, earning the title of Miss Brooklyn and Miss Manhattan. This was intended to be the first victories in a series leading up to Miss Universe, but after landing a role in a summer stock production, Sharon decided to concentrate on her acting. She worked in various regional productions, as well as understudying on Broadway, before landing a featured role in "A Lovely Way To Die," with Kirk Douglas. Quickly establishing herself in the entertainment community, Sharon moved to Los Angeles after catching the eye of Bob Hope, who recruited her to star in the t.v. pilot, "Amy." Once out west, she began working in feature films, earning critical raves for her work in "Marlowe," with James Garner, and "The Reivers," opposite the legendary Steve McQueen. For her work in the latter, she was named "Newcomer of the Year," in The Motion Picture Herald's 30th Annual Poll of Motion Picture Exhibitors. It was at this time, when she was on the brink of major stardom, that Sharon faced the ordeal of a nearly fatal childbirth, during which her lung collapsed and her heart stopped beating for over four minutes. Miraculously, both mother and son survived, yet for the next several years Sharon could not completely recover from the trauma. Unable to perform such basic skills as reading and writing, she spent a great deal of time re-learning all that she had forgotten, but returned to form triumphantly with an Emmy nominated performance on the t.v. series "The Name of the Game," in a segment called "A Hard Case of the Blues." Sharon has since continued to work in television, as a series regular on "Rituals" and "Hawaii Five-O," and making guest appearances on such shows as "Ben Casey," "Dr. Kildare," "My Three Sons," "Wagon Train," "Gunsmoke," "The Fugitive," "I Dream of Jeannie," "Police Story," "McCloud," "T.J. Hooker," "Enos," "The Dukes of Hazzard," "Matlock," and many others. In addition her television film credits include "Rage," "The Baby Brokers," "The Last Ride of the Dalton Gang," and "The Eyes of Charles Sands." On the big screen she has been seen in "Can't Buy Me Love," "The Stunt Man," with Peter O'Toole, "Lone Wolf McQuade," "Night of the Comet," "Sweet Sixteen," "The Fifth Floor," "Separate Ways," "The Premonition," and "It's Alive." Ms. Farrell is also slated to star in two upcoming releases, "Arcade," and "Lonely Hearts," with Eric Roberts. It was while filming "The Premonition" that Sharon met Dale Trevillion, the film's screenwriter. The two fell in love and have now been married for seventeen years. "The Premonition" also garnered Ms. Farrell another prize, the Grand Prix award for Best Actress, presented at the 7th Festival Internationale De Paris Du Film Fantastique Et De Science Fiction. The actress also earned the Pryor Award from the Black Rain Arts and Sciences Institute for her performance in "It's Alive." Sharon's son, Chance Boyer, now in his early twenties, is forging an acting career as well. He was featured on "General Hospital," as well as co-starring with his mother in the film, "One Man Force," which was a true family affair as it was written, produced, and directed by Mr. Trevillion. With her career gaining momentum each day, Sharon likes to relax by riding Brazilia, her Arabian filly, on the seventeen acre ranch she shares with her husband. She also enjoys painting, and has her work displayed at the Parkhurst Gallery in San Pedro, California.

ALAN FEINSTEIN

Born: September 8 in New York, New York
Marital Status: divorced
Height: 6'2" **Eyes:** blue **Hair:** brown
Education: Bronx Community College
Interest: art, theater, weight lifting
Awards: New York Drama Desk Award for "A View From the Bridge"

Daytime Dramas: "Love of Life," Mickey Krakauer, 1965-1968; **"Edge of Night,"** Dr. Jim Fields, 1969-1974; **"General Hospital,"** Gregory, 1988-1990; **"Santa Barbara,"** Jim Sanford, 1991-

An accomplished actor of both stage and screen, as well as a soap opera veteran, Alan Feinstein returned to daytime in 1988 as the mysterious Gregory on "General Hospital." Born in New York City, Feinstein attended Forest Hills High School before enrolling in Bronx Community College as a liberal arts major. A stand out high jumper on the track team, Feinstein never kept the acting profession far from his mind, and upon leaving school he landed his first role in a touring production of "Mister Roberts." His television debut came with a televised Armstrong Circle Theater production, and was quickly followed by Feinstein's first daytime drama, "Love of Life." The actor stayed with the show for three years before transferring to "Edge of Night," where he played Dr. Jim Fields for the next six years. Feinstein went to "Edge of Night" for a day role in a party scene and while there somebody told him about psychiatrist, Jim Fields - a new character slated for a one month run. It turned into a six year month. Not one to limit himself to just one medium, Feinstein has achieved great success both in the theater and feature films. Among his numerous theater credits are roles in "Iphigenia in Aulis," with Irene Papas, "Ghetto," "As is," and "Equus." In addition he appeared with the National Theater of Japan in the 1985 production of "Who's Afraid of Virginia Woolf?." On Broadway, Feinstein performed in "A View From the Bridge," receiving a New York Drama Desk Award for his work, and was cast by Tennessee William's himself to play the role of Stanley in the 1973 Broadway production of "A Streetcar Names Desire." In 1986, the actor tried his hand at directing with a production of "Fat Chance" at the Beverly Hills Playhouse. The experience proved rewarding and in 1992, Feinstein directed a production of "It Had to be You" by Renee Taylor & Joseph Bologna at The Attic Theater in Hollywood. On the big screen he has appeared as Professor Engel in "Looking for Mr. Goodbar," with Diane Keaton and on television he has co-starred in such series as "Jigsaw John" and "The Runaways," as well as in the television movies, "Second Serve," "Alexander, the Other Side of Dawn," and the acclaimed ABC miniseries, "Masada." He also starred in the PBS production of "Fans of the Kosco Show" on the series, "Visions." Currently a resident of Los Angeles, Feinstein, who is divorced, enjoys lifting weights and painting. In the summer of 1988 his art work was exhibited in Beverly Hills.

SUSAN FLANNERY

Born: July 31 in New York City, New York
Marital Status: single
Eyes: blue **Hair:** blond
Education: Stevens College, B.F.A.; Arizona State University, graduate studies
Interests: tennis, swimming, cooking
Awards: Golden Globe Award for "Towering Inferno;" Outstanding Acting Debut in a Motion Picture; 1975 Daytime Emmy-Best Actress (Days of Our Lives); Emmy nomination for NBC miniseries "The Moneychangers"

Daytime Dramas: "Days of Our Lives," Dr. Laura Horton, 1966-1975; **"The Bold and the Beautiful,"** Stephanie Forrester 1987-

An Emmy and Golden Globe winning actress, Susan Flannery was one of the first daytime performers to successfully make the transition from soap operas to feature films. Since 1987, Ms. Flannery has been on familiar ground, portraying Stephanie Forrester on "The Bold and the Beautiful." Prior to that, the actress was known as Dr. Laura Horton on "Days of Our Lives," a role she played from 1966 to 1975, earning a Best Actress daytime Emmy for her work. Born and raised in New York City, Susan received her B.F.A. degree in theater from Stevens College, following which she attended graduate school at Arizona State. After being discovered by legendary producer Irwin Allen, Flannery made her television debut in "Voyage to the Bottom of the Sea." Other television roles have included the t.v. movies, "Women in White" and "Anatomy of Seduction," as well as an Emmy nominated performance in the miniseries, "The Moneychangers." Ms. Flannery also made a memorable impression as Leslie Stewart on "Dallas," a character who went head to head with J.R. Ewing. She made her feature film debut in the adventure epic, "The Towering Inferno," for which she earned a Golden Globe Award for Outstanding Acting Debut in a Motion Picture. Active behind the scenes as well, Flannery co-produced the cable soap opera, "New Day in Eden," and now is one of the directors of "The Bold and the Beautiful." A resident of Los Angeles, Susan, who is a licensed pilot and a gourmet cook, enjoys tennis, swimming, and rooting for her two favorite local teams, the Dodgers and the Rams.

ROBERT FONTAINE

Born: July 11 in Brooklyn, New York
Marital Status: single
Height: 6' **Eyes:** brown **Hair:** brown
Education: Five Towns Junior College
Interests: soccer, music, poetry, painting

Daytime Dramas: "General Hospital," Frankie Greco, 1990-1991, **"Santa Barbara,"** Rafe Castillo, 1992-

Brooklyn born Robert Fontaine made his television debut on "General Hospital," in the role of Frankie Greco. Since 1992 he has been seen as Rafe Castillo on "Santa Barbara." Raised in the Bay Ridge area of Brooklyn, Fontaine attended Bishop Ford Catholic Central High, and later graduated from Five Towns Junior College on Long Island. While at college he appeared in several school productions, and he continued to study acting after college with Gene Frankel, a renowned New York acting teacher. While looking for professional acting work, Fontaine supported himself by teaching private classes, not only in acting technique, but basic and classical guitar as well. As a guitar player he has played in rock bands throughout the tri-state area. Other jobs weren't quite as safe; he worked in New York City as a cab driver and security guard. Aside from his work on daytime drama, Fontaine has appeared in several New York based independent films, including a role as a drug dealer in "China Girl." When he is not working Fontaine enjoys soccer, (a sport he's been playing since he was five and he is also a member of the Danish-American Club) music, poetry, and painting. He keeps in shape by running, weightlifting, and bicycling.

STEVEN MEIGS FORD

Born: May 19, 1956 in Washington, D.C.
Marital Status: single
Height: 6'1"   **Eyes:** blue   **Hair:** blond
Education: California Polytechnic University, two years
Interests: biking, golf, swimming, roping at weekend rodeos

Daytime Dramas: "The Young and the Restless,"
Andy Richards, 1981-1988

A ruggedly handsome man from a powerful political family who has worked as a rodeo roper, a grizzly bear tracker, a film and television actor, a racetrack president, and an owner/breeder of thoroughbreds, Steven Ford's real life surpasses that of any daytime hero. Born on May 19 in Washington, D.C., Ford is the third son of former President and Mrs. Gerald Ford. Choosing not to follow in his father's political footsteps, the younger Ford decided to study animal science at California Polytechnic University in San Luis Obispo. Always interested in animals, as well as in the romantic life of a western cowboy, Ford spent the next several years working in a wide array of jobs. Along with travelling as a roper on the rodeo circuit, Ford spent three months in 1975 tracking grizzly bears in Montana as part of a National Geographic study. In 1979 he decided to try his hand at acting and quickly landed film and television roles. Best known for his nine years as Andy Richards on "The Young and the Restless," Ford also made guest appearances on "Happy Days," "Columbo," "Murder, She Wrote," and "Circus of the Stars," as well as appearing in such films as "Young Doctors in Love," "Cattle Annie and Little Britches," and most recently as Meg Ryan's boyfriend in "When Harry Met Sally." In 1990, Ford decided to leave acting and devote himself fully to his work with thoroughbred horses. He has been involved with racing and breeding for over twelve years, and along with his position as president of Goodwood Thoroughbreds Inc., he was most recently named Associate Vice-President of Turfway Park, a race course in Kentucky. As a representative of this establishment, Fords travels around the country, speaking at symposiums and conventions. In addition, Steven, who is single, owns his own ranch in San Luis Obispo, where he raises thoroughbreds and can often be found sharpening his rodeo roping skills. On his new life, Steven writes: "I might go back to acting one day but right now I am happily developing a new career." Since he wrote that, he began hosting the new t.v. reality series, "Secret Service." Ford presently serves as a member of the Board of Directors for The National Cowboy Hall of Fame, as well as on the board of the President Gerald R. Ford Museum. To relax he enjoys swimming, biking, skiing, and playing golf.

DAVID FORSYTH

Born: September 18 in Long Beach, California
Marital Status: single
Height: 6'2" **Eyes:** blue **Hair:** brown
Interests: sailing, water skiing, running, racquetball

Daytime Dramas: "Texas," T.J. Canfield, 1981-1982;
"As the World Turns," Burke Donovan, 1983;
"Search for Tomorrow," Hogan McCleary, 1983-1986;
"Another World," Dr. John Hudson, 1987-

Only acting professionally since 1979, David Forsyth has managed, during that brief time, to bring four memorable daytime characters to the screen. Currently seen as Dr. John Hudson on "Another World," Forsyth has additionally appeared on "Texas," "Search for Tomorrow," and "As the World Turns." Born on September 18 in Long Beach, California, the son of a Marine Corp colonel, David himself served as a corpsman with the First Marines in Vietnam from 1968 to 1969. Following this, he continued to work with the military in South East Asia and Central America, as well as spending four years as a fire fighter, four years as a paramedic, and three years as a surgical technician, before eventually committing himself to acting. Along the way, Forsyth also became a certified scuba diver and an underwater rescue specialist. Breaking into acting, he began working on stage, appearing in such productions as "The Unsinkable Molly Brown," "A Funny Thing Happened on the Way to the Forum," "The Boyfriend," and "God's Favorite." Away from the "Another World" set, where he has worked since 1987, Forsyth, a New York City resident, enjoys water skiing, racquetball, sailing, and running.

MICHAEL FOX

Born: February 27, 1921 in Yonkers, New York
Marital Status: married to Hannah Fox, two children, David and Jennifer
Height: 5'11" **Eyes:** hazel **Hair:** grey
Education: Indiana University
Interests: sailing, travel, old films, history

Daytime Dramas: "Clear Horizons," Ziggy, 1961-1962;
"The Bold and the Beautiful," Saul

A veteran of stage, film, and television, Michael Fox has, over the course of his illustrious career, worked with some of Hollywood's legendary performers, among them, Paul Muni, Mae West, Joan Crawford, Bette Davis, and Dorothy Gish. He currently is seen as Saul on "The Bold and the Beautiful." Born on February 27, 1921, Fox tells us he has "been in over 100 feature films, 300 t.v. shows and more plays than I can remember." He began his stage career during the late 1940's, appearing on Broadway in "The Story of Mary Suratt," with Dorothy Gish, while some of his additional stage credits include national tours of "Gaslight" and "Sextette," with Mae West. During the '50's, Fox worked under contract to both Columbia Pictures and Warner Brothers, and has since appeared in scores of films, among them, "Young Frankenstein," "The Longest Yard," "Quicksilver," and "Whatever Happened to Baby Jane?" On television, in addition to his role on "The Bold and the Beautiful," the actor co-starred in "Clear Horizons," one of the first daytime dramas, as well as making guest appearances on such shows as "The Hogan Family," "Cagney & Lacey," "MacGyver," "Quincy," "St. Elsewhere," "Simon and Simon," "Knight Rider," "Perry Mason," "Dallas," "Falcon Crest," and "General Hospital." Over thirty years ago Fox founded the Theater East, an elite actor's organization which continues to thrive into the nineties. During the 1970's, Fox took time away from performing to produce a series of topical documentaries for KNBC-TV in Los Angeles. The films dealt with such issues as women's rights, prison overcrowding, and welfare. This is not unusual from a man who includes history as one of his interests. He is also very involved with Actors Equity Association and is the retired West Coast Chair. A Van Nuys resident, Michael has been married to wife, Hannah, for over forty years, and together they have raised two children, David and Jennifer.

DON FRABOTTA

Born: December 23, 1941 in Milford, Massachusetts
Marital Status: single
Height: 5' 6 1/2" **Eyes:** brown **Hair:** brown
Education: LA Valley College; Graduate of Pasadena Playhouse
Interests: people, reading, gardening, walking, raising hybrid roses,bicycling, theater, movies,

Daytime Dramas: "Days of Our Lives," Dave, 1974-

A quiet daytime veteran, Don Frabotta has played Dave on "Days of Our Lives" for close to twenty years. Born on December 23, 1941, Frabotta, along with his two brothers, Frank and Richard, were raised in Milford, Massachusetts, where he has happy memories of a "small town life and good childhood. After honing his skills at the Pasadena Playhouse and LA Valley College, Frabotta began landing roles in television, film, and theater. Along with his long running part on "Days of Our Lives," Frabotta's additional t.v. credits include, "The New Love American Style," "Romance Theatre," "Susan and Sam," "Backlot, USA," "Theatre Beat," and a brief role on "General Hospital." On the big screen, the actor has been seen in "Morax Chant" and "Josie's Castle," while he has performed on stage in such productions as, "One Flew Over The Cuckoo's Nest," "Witness," "Vine Street," "My Sister Eileen," "A Very Sick Man," "Grace, George & God," "Anastasia," and "The Beaux Stratagem." Don, who is fluent in French, German, and Italian, lives in Los Angeles. He is unmarried and lists among his hobbies; people, theater, movies, reading, gardening, bicycling, and raising hybrid roses.

GENIE FRANCIS

Born: May 26, 1962 in Englewood, New Jersey
Marital Status: to actor Jonathan Frakes
Height: 5'5" **Eyes:** blue **Hair:** blond
Interests: theater, pets
Awards: 1981 Soap Opera Award for Favorite Lead Actress

Daytime Dramas: "General Hospital," Laura Baldwin
Spencer, 1976-1981, 1983, 1984; **"Days of Our Lives,"**
Diane Colville, 1987-1989; **"All My Children,"** Ceara Connor,
1990-1992

Few performers have played such an integral part in the history of daytime television as Genie Francis. As one half of the legendary Luke and Laura pairing, Genie reached heights of superstardom rarely achieved by any daytime player. Her onscreen wedding to co-star Tony Geary, in November of 1981, became the single most watched event in the history of daytime television, and even landed the happy couple on the cover of Newsweek. All this occurred, amazingly enough, before Ms. Francis's twentieth birthday. A native of Englewood, New Jersey, Genie was born on May 26, 1962. The daughter of character actor and drama coach Ivor Francis, Genie landed her first role at 13, when she guest starred on the popular series "Family." With this one credit to her name she embarked on her five year "General Hospital" stint, from 1975-1981, after which she moved on to prime time, starring as Tyger Hayes in the popular mini-series, "Bare Essence." The actress proved equally at home as Tyger, and reprised the role when "Bare Essence" became a weekly series. In addition, Genie co-starred in the mini-series "North and South," and has made quest appearances on numerous shows, including "Murder, She Wrote," and "Hotel." Also a stage actress, she has performed in productions ranging from, "Crimes of the Heart" to "See How They Run," and she most recently appeared in "Defying Gravity," which was presented at the Williamstown Theatre Festival. Until recently, a featured player on "All My Children," Ms. Francis has also been seen as Diane Colville on "Days of Our Lives," as well as returning to "General Hospital" in 1983 and 1984. Not on a soap at this time, the rumor mill is working overtime about a Luke and Laura reunion on "General Hospital." Currently maintaining homes in both New York and Los Angeles, Genie shares this busy lifestyle with husband Jonathan Frakes, a co-star on "Star Trek: The Next Generation." Both animal lovers, the couple have three cats, Bix, Chloe, and Alfred, a dog, Gracie, and a goldfish, Thelonius.

ED FRY

Born: May 22 in Chicago, Illinois
Marital Status: single
Hair: brown
Education: Trinity University, B.A.
Interests: bowling, golf, scuba diving
Awards: Muscular Dystrophy Association, "Man of the Year"

Daytime Dramas: "Another World," Adam Cory, 1986-1988;
"As the World Turns," Larry McDermott, 1990-

Best known to daytime audiences as Larry McDermott on "As the World Turns," a role which he began in 1990, Ed Fry donates his time away from the set to his work with two charitable organizations, Earth Action and the Muscular Dystrophy Association. A Chicago native, Fry was raised in Dallas, getting his first performing experience at the age of five, putting on puppet shows for the neighborhood kids. After attending Trinity University, where he majored in history and theater, (minoring in political science and music) Fry tried an assortment of jobs, including banker, butcher, salesman, politician, teacher, and model, before committing himself fully to acting. Since making this decision, Ed has gone on to perform on stage in such productions as "Noyes Fludde," "Death of the Bishop of Brindisi," "Saul," "Indians," "Company," "Miss Julie," "Wooed and Viewed," "The Author's Voice," and "Travelling Squirrel," while he has been seen on the big screen in "Bermuda Triangle," "Night Magic," and "Rude Awakening." Fry made his television debut in 1986 as Adam Cory on "Another World," and has additionally appeared on "Working it Out" and "This Far and No More," a PBS production. An avid environmentalist (and vegetarian), Fry serves on the board of directors of Earth Action, a New York based non-profit organization. The actor is also extremely active with the Muscular Dystrophy Association, co-hosting the New York portion of the Jerry Lewis telethon, and serving as the national chairperson for the organizations Amyotrophic Lateral Sclerosis Division. Sadly, this disease is one which has profoundly affected Fry's life. In 1988, he narrated and starred in a public service film which documented his mother's bout with the illness (also known as Lou Gerigh's disease). The film was honored at the New York Film festival and also earned Ed the "Man of the Year" award from the Muscular Dystrophy Association. Unfortunately he could not share this with his mother, who died just six weeks after the filming. Presently single, Fry lives in Manhattan, and his interests include scuba diving, golf, bowling, and whistling, a pastime he has enjoyed since the age of two.

EILEEN FULTON

Born: September 13, in Asheville, North Carolina
Marital Status: single
Height: 5'2" **Eyes:** hazel **Hair:** blond
Education: Greensboro College
Interests: music, community service
Awards: 1990 Editor's Award from Soap Opera Digest

Daytime Dramas: "As the World Turns," Lisa McColl, 1960-

Since she joined the cast of "As the World Turns" over thirty years ago, Eileen Fulton has proven herself time and time again to be one of the most appealing and exciting actresses to ever grace the screen. As Lisa she set the standard to which all future soap opera villainieses will forever aspire. Born Margaret Elizabeth McLarty in Asheville, North Carolina, Eileen studied dramatics and music at nearby Greensboro College. Her talent was apparent even then as she received Best Actress awards for her performances in "Candide" and "Thirteen Clocks." Upon graduation, Eileen continued to study acting, supporting herself through a wide array of jobs, among them selling hats at Macy's and posing for photographs used on the cover of "True Confessions" magazine. She moved to New York City in 1956, shortly after making her professional debut in Manteo, North Carolina, where she appeared in "The Last Colony." While in New York Eileen studied at the Neighborhood Playhouse, and soon after embarked on an impressive stage career, including roles in "Abe Lincoln in Illinois," "Sabrina Fair," "Any Wednesday," "Cat on a Hot Tin Roof," and "The Owl and the Pussy Cat." Her work in films has included feature roles in "Girl of the Night" and "My Friend Alex." In 1960 Eileen joined the cast of "As the World Turns," in a role that was supposed to be temporary. She was a walk on - a date for Bob Hughes. However, Eileen injected such a perfect mixture of enthusiasm and malicious charm into her character that the producers and the fans alike decided they wanted to see more. The results were phenomenal as Eileen quickly became the undisputed superstar of daytime dramas, inciting in her fans a love and excitement bordering on fanaticism. She was even forced to hire body guards to keep the more overzealous of these groupies at bay. During this period, Eileen continued her stage work as well, and during one particularly tumultuous stretch she would work on "As the World Turns" in the morning, perform in a matinee of "Who's Afraid of Virginia Woolf," followed by an evening performance in "The Fantasticks." In the mid-sixties, Irma Phillips, creator of "As the World Turns," brought Eileen and her character of Lisa into unchartered territory when she headed the cast of the prime time series "Our Private World." This effort proved to be short lived and Lisa returned to daytime, where since 1960 she has probably been through more than any other television character, including 36 romances, six marriages, amnesia, murder trials, and even a Mexican mudslide. Eileen wrote, along with Brett Bolton, of her adventures in the book, "How My World Turns." In addition to her acting career, Eileen has also continued to cultivate her musical talent, touring the country with her own musical variety show, as well as recording four albums. She can also be heard on television, selling everything from Chevrolets, to Kool Aid to J.C. Penney stores. Away from her hectic professional life the actress is active in a number of charities, including UNICEF, the March of Dimes, and Cerebral Palsy. Eileen is also an avid supporter of the Equal Rights Amendment and provides a scholarship for the Neighborhood Playhouse School of the Theatre. She currently divides her time between her homes in New York City and Connecticut. In 1990, Eileen was awarded Soap Opera Digest's Editor's Award.

DON GALLOWAY

Born: July 27 in Brooksville, Kentucky
Marital Status: married to Linda Galloway
Height: 6'2" **Eyes:** brown **Hair:** brown
Education: University of Kentucky

Daytime Dramas: "The Secret Storm," 1962;
"General Hospital," Dr. Buzz Stryker, 1985-1987

Born in Brooksville, Kentucky, Don Galloway is best known to television audiences for his portrayal of Sgt. Brown on the television series "Ironside." Galloway attended Bracken County High School, and upon graduation he entered the U.S. Army. During his years in the service he served as a radar operator, spending most of his time in Kaiserslautern, Germany. After completing his years with the army, Galloway then enrolled in the University of Kentucky, and upon graduation he finally decided to embark on the acting career which had long been his dream. He was placed under contract with Universal Studios for twelve years, eight of which he spent on "Ironside." Galloway's other television roles include a co-starring role in "Arrest and Trail," and quest appearances on "The Fall Guy," "Scarecrow and Mrs. King," "Knight Rider," and "Crazy Like a Fox." Aside from his most recent work on "General Hospital," Galloway also starred in "The Secret Storm," an early work of "GH" producer Gloria Monty. Among his feature films are "The Rare Breed," "Rough Night in Jericho," and "The Big Chill." And for those that don't recognize Don from his many television and movie credits, he may look familiar from his many commercials.Also active behind the camera, Galloway is a partner in BGP Productions Inc. Don is married to Linda Galloway, an actress/writer, and they have two children, Tracey and Jennifer.

TERRI GARBER

Born: Dec. 28 in Miami, Florida
Marital Status: divorced, one child
Eyes: brown   **Hair:** brown
Education: Boston University, Northern University
Interests: travel

Daytime Dramas: "Texas," Allison Linden, 1982;
"Santa Barbara," Suzanne Collier, 1991-

The role of Suzanne Collier on "Santa Barbara" afforded actress Terri Garber a rare opportunity, she actually got to play someone nice. Best known for her wicked roles on "Dynasty" and in parts one and two of the acclaimed mini-series "North and South," Terri was cast against type as Suzanne, an artist childhood friend of Eden Castillo. Hailing from Florida, Terri studied acting at a number of schools, including Northern University, Boston University, and the American Academy of the Dramatic Arts. Her first professional role came when she was sixteen, appearing in a production of "Romeo and Juliet." Daytime audiences first came to know Terri, and her ability to play wicked women, when she starred as Allison Linden on the short lived soap "Texas." Following it's cancelation the actress spent the next several years shuttling between New York and Los Angeles where she worked both on stage and screen. Terri's theater credits include "The Ladies Room," "Cyrano De Bergerac," "The Drunkard," and "Camille." In addition she has performed in the feature films "Beyond My Reach" and "Toy Soldiers." Along with her work on daytime t.v., she has been a regular on "My Two Dads" and "Mr. Smith," as well as quest starring on such shows as "Murder, She Wrote," "Jake and the Fatman," and numerous other series. In addition she appeared in two pilots, "Lone Star" and "Sporting Chance." However of all of Terri's roles, it is her work on "Dynasty," in the role of Leslie Carrington, and in the "North and South" mini-series which has brought her the most acclaim and recognition. However, her years on "Dynasty" ended with her character getting beaten up and left for dead in an isolated cabin. With such a collection of malicious characters, it seems surprising that the producers of "Santa Barbara" would cast Terri as a sweet natured, decidedly bohemian artist. Yet Terri has assumed the role naturally, the only concession being that she must wear a wig to match her character's long flowing hair. One of the perks of returning to daytime television is that it allows Terri, who is now divorced, more time with her daughter, Molly Elizabeth, born in July of 1986. The two often travel, as well as go to the movies and to the zoo.

CARRINGTON GARLAND

Born: in Los Angeles, California
Marital Status: single
Hair: blond
Education: Pepperdine University; Fashion Institute
Interests: gymnastics, swimming, skating, sailing

Daytime Dramas: "Santa Barbara," Kelly Capwell

After an extended search, Carrington Garland was chosen from thousands of hopefuls for the role of Kelly Capwell on "Santa Barbara." A Los Angeles native, Carrington is the daughter of actress, Beverly Garland, best known for her work as Fred McMurray's wife on "My Three Sons." After studying theater and journalism at Pepperdine University, Carrington continued her education at the Fashion Institute, where she earned an honors degree in fashion merchandising. In addition to her work on "Santa Barbara," Garland's t.v. credits include "Divorce Court," "For the Record," and "Scarecrow and Mrs. King." Also active in feature films, she has been seen in such movies as "Stallions," "Darkness in Spring," "Roller Boogie," "L.A. Woman," and "America, Another Way to Go." Away from the set, Garland enjoys gymnastics, ice skating, roller skating, swimming, and sailing.

JOY GARRET

Born: March 2, 1945 in Fort Worth, Texas
Marital Status: single
Height: 5'6"   **Eyes:** blue   **Hair:** blond
Education: Texas Wesleyan University, B.A.; Master's credits at California State; American Academy of Dramatic Arts
Interests: bowling, rollerskating, singing
Awards: 1989 Soap Opera Award, Outstanding Supporting Actress

Daytime Dramas: "The Young and the Restless," Boobsie Caswell Austin, 1984-1985; **"Days of Our Lives,"** Jo Johnson, 1987

An accomplished actress, Joy Garrett was born March 2 in Ft. Worth, Texas where her father was a building contractor, her mother a hairdresser. Blessed with both brains and beauty, Ms. Garrett received her Bachelors Degree from Texas Wesleyan University, worked on her masters at California State and attended the American Academy of Dramatic Arts on a full scholarship. Along the way, she served a year as Miss Ft. Worth. Her list of professional credits ranges from Broadway: "Grease," (as Betty Rizzo) "Inner City," and "The Candy Apple," to off-Broadway, to regional theater. She has co-starred with Joe Namath, as Adelaide in "Guys and Dolls," with Gene Barry in "On a Clear Day," with Van Johnson, as Rosemary in "How to Succeed in Business" and more. On the big screen she has starred with Trevor Howard in "Who." Her t.v. credits include "Magnum P.I.," "Night Court," "Quincy," "Remington Steele," and made for television movies, "Callie and Son," "Having Babies," "Baby Brokers" and "Hotline." When not performing, Joy , a resident of a California enjoys bowling, rollerskating and singing.

MAUREEN GARRETT

Born: August 18 in Rocky Mount, North Carolina
Marital Status: single
Height: 5'7" **Eyes:** brown **Hair:** auburn
Education: Universitat Munchen; Temple University; Villanova
Interests: yoga, swimming
Awards: nominated for Daytime Emmy for Outstanding Supporting Actress, 1991, ("Guiding Light")

Daytime Dramas: "Guiding Light," Holly Thorpe Lindsay, 1976-1981, 1989-; **"Ryan's Hope,"** E.J. Ryan, 1981-1982

Born the daughter of an army officer in Rocky Mount, North Carolina, Maureen Garrett spent much of her childhood shuttling with her family between Europe and The United States. In keeping with this fashion Maureen also divided her studies internationally, first at the Universitat Munchen in Germany, followed by two American universities, Temple and Villanova. Since leaving college she has cultivated several successful careers, both in and out of the acting profession. As an actress she has been involved with daytime drama since 1976 when she first took on the role of Holly of "Guiding Light," a role for which she received a daytime Emmy nomination for Outstanding Supporting Actress in 1991. Maureen also played E.J. Ryan on "Ryan's Hope" from 1981 to 1982, as well as appearing in numerous television commercials. Her stage work includes a wide array of regional theater in such productions as "Les Liasions Dangereuses," "As You Like It," and "Quartermaine's Terms." Not one to limit herself to time established works, Maureen has also toured the country in productions of new American Plays, among them "Beastly Beatitudes of Balthazar B," "Mrs. California," and "Last Looks." While she has accomplished a great deal as an actress, Maureen has done likewise in a myriad of endeavors, both in and away from the entertainment business. During her years in Germany she worked as an editor for an American newspaper, she has also been a freelance photographer, a stage manager, a Head-Start teacher, and served as assistant director of the Philadelphia International Film Festival. During one two year stretch, from 1983-1985, Maureen put her acting career completely on hold to run an art and architectural furniture business in Bridgehampton, N.Y., but eventually she decided to return to the stage where she has since remained. In her spare time the multi-lingual actress (Maureen speaks German and French) enjoys swimming and yoga.

LARRY GATES

Born: September 24, 1915 in St. Paul, Minnesota
Marital Status: married to Judith Seaton
Height: 6' **Eyes:** blue **Hair:** white
Education: University of Minnesota
Interests: tree farming
Awards: nominated for Daytime Emmy for Best Supporting Actor, 1986; Daytime Emmy for Best Supporting Actor, 1985 ("Guiding Light"); 1963 nominated for Tony Award

Daytime Dramas: "Guiding Light," H.B. Lewis, 1983-

A television and theater veteran, Larry Gates has portrayed H.B. Lewis on "Guiding Light" since 1983, a role which earned him a 1985 Daytime Emmy for Best Supporting Actor, and a nomination in that same category the following year. Born on September 24, 1915 in St. Paul, Minnesota, Gates was raised, along with his sister, by his father, an advertising executive, and his mother, a homemaker. After attending the University of Minnesota, Larry began working in the theater, appearing in Broadway and regional productions, as well as regularly participating in the American Shakespeare Festival and the Shaw Festival. A much lauded performer, he received a Tony Award nomination in 1963. On the screen, Gates has been seen in over twenty five feature films, while his television credits include roles on "The F.B.I," "Playhouse 90," "U.S. Steel Hour," and many others. A long time resident of West Cornwall, Connecticut, where he lives with his wife, Judith Seaton, Larry has served as chairman of the town's Park and Recreation Department, and on his own enjoys tree farming.

ANTHONY GEARY

Born: May 29, 1947 in Coalville, Utah
Marital Status: single
Eyes: blue   **Hair:** blond
Education: University of Utah
Interests: writing, travelling
Awards: Daytime Emmy nominations for Outstanding Lead Actor, 1981, 1983; Daytime Emmy for Outstanding Lead Actor, 1982; Soap Opera Award, Favorite Lead Actor for 1980, 1981, 1982

Daytime Dramas: "Bright Promise," David Lockhart, 1971; **"The Young and the Restless,"** George Curtis, 1973; **"General Hospital,"** Luke Spencer, 1978-1984; and as Bill Eckert, 1991-

When Anthony Geary first signed on to join the cast of "General Hospital" in 1978, he was slated to take on the role of Mitch Williams, a powerful Port Charles politician. However, the show's executive producer, Gloria Monty, decided that Geary's talents could be put to better use, and as a result the character of Luke Spencer was created. With his street smart edge, sarcastic demeanor, and decidedly off-beat appearance, Geary's Luke was a far cry from the traditional daytime leading man, but soap fans quickly became fascinated with the character, and Geary's popularity skyrocketed. Over the next several years, the actor became a media superstar, and formed, along with Genie Francis, daytime's greatest couple, Luke and Laura. Their wedding in 1981, remains the single most watched event in daytime history. Equally lauded by his peers for his work, Geary earned three consecutive Daytime Emmy nominations, taking home the prize for Outstanding Lead Actor in 1982, as well as being named Favorite Actor at the Soap Opera Awards in 1980, 1981, 1982. Leaving "General Hospital" in 1984, Geary returned to the show in 1991 as Bill Eckert. A native of Coalville, Utah, Anthony was born on May 29, 1947. After winning a scholarship to study theater at the University of Utah, Geary got his first big break when he was discovered by Jack Albertson, who then cast him as his son in a touring production of "The Subject was Roses." Eventually settling in Hollywood, Geary worked various jobs, from selling toys in a department store to working in the chorus of a Las Vegas production. He soon, however, found work on prime time television, and went on to guest star on dozens of shows, among them "Room 222," "All in the Family," "Starsky and Hutch," "The Mod Squad," "Barnaby Jones," "Marcus Welby," "Six Million Dollar Man," and "The Streets of San Francisco." Also active on the big screen, he appeared in the acclaimed film "Johnny Get Your Gun," as well as in "Educated Heart" and the never released "Blood Sabbath." Among his more recent feature films, "Ammo," with

Annie Potts, "The Whistle Stop Girl," and "Scorchers," with Faye Dunaway and James Earl Jones. In 1971, Geary made his daytime debut as David Lockhart on "Bright Promise," which was followed by another daytime role, George Curtis on "The Young and the Restless." After earning superstar status on "General Hospital," he began working in prime time as well, appearing in such t.v. films as "Intimate Strangers," "Sins of the Past," "The Great Pretender," and "Do You Know the Muffin Man?" He has continued to work on stage as well, and additionally portrayed Julius Caesar in a videotape production of "Anthony and Cleopatra," with Lynn Redgrave and Timothy Dalton. To keep his performing skills sharp, Geary works with the Los Angeles Theatre Center classics lab, and also participates in weekly group readings of classic plays. An aspiring writer as well, Geary has not only penned several screenplays and short stories, but also writes music. He currently lives in the Hollywood Hills with his two cats.

TIMOTHY GIBBS

Born: April 17
Marital Status: single
Interests: sports, travelling, writing

Daytime Dramas: "Santa Barbara," Dashell Nicholls

(ATTENTION: aspiring actors. The following story of Timothy Gibbs might prove too painful to read. Please use caution.) After working successfully as a model and actor since his pre-teens, Timothy Gibbs decided that he should pay his dues. He followed the lead of thousands of other hopefuls and got a job waiting tables. Two months later, Gibbs, who looks like a cross between Mel Gibson and Kevin Costner, was offered a contract by the producers of "Santa Barbara," and has since become one of daytime's most popular stars. Gibbs first came on the scene, after overcoming his parent's objections, as a child actor, appearing in commercials and on television. This eventually lead to a regular role on "Father Murphy," with Merlin Olson. His other television credits include roles in the now defunct series, "The Rousters," and in numerous television movies, among them, "Deliberate Stranger," "Police Story," "Family Honor," and "Contract for Life." On the big screen, Gibbs has appeared in "The Kindred," "Just Between Friends," and "A Letter From Brian." Just like Dashell "Dash" Nicholls, his character on "Santa Barbara," the young actor takes a keen interest in environmental concerns. In his spare time Gibbs, who is unmarried, enjoys sports, travelling, and is working on a feature film screenplay. He is currently working on the soon to be released miniseries, "Secrets."

RICKY PAULL GOLDIN

Born: January 5 in San Francisco, California
Marital Status: single
Height: 5'10" **Eyes:** brown **Hair:** brown
Education: Storm King School
Awards: Daytime Emmy for Outstanding Younger Lead Actor, 1991; 1992 Soap Opera Award nomination for Outstanding Younger Lead Actor

Daytime Dramas: "Another World," Dean Frame, 1990-

Having spent the last several years flirting with television stardom, Ricky Paull Goldin's role on "Another World" has at last pushed the young actor into the spotlight. Born in San Francisco, Goldin's family moved around quite a bit, living in Hawaii, England, Ireland, and New York City. While growing up, Ricky's parents were both in the entertainment industry, giving him an up close insight into the life of an actor. His father Paul Goldin, was a popular performer who today works as a clinical psychologist in Dublin, while Ricky's mother, P.J. Goldin, was an actress. Although he rarely sees his father anymore, Ricky and his mother remain extremely close. As a result of his family's extensive travelling, Goldin attended a grand total of twenty two schools before his 1985 graduation from The Storm King School, located in upstate New York. Prior to that he spent two years on Long Island at Lawrence High School. During his time in school Ricky also began to establish himself as a serious young actor. He made his stage debut as the magicians assistant in the London production of "The Magic Show," and his other stage work includes roles in the McCarter theatre production of "Three Plays by Thornton Wilder," and on Broadway in "On Golden Pond," co-starring Frances Sternhagen and Tom Aldredge. Goldin also played the lead in the off-Broadway hit, "Feathered Serpent," and in the Joseph Papp Public Theatre production of "The Nest of the Wood Grouse." After it's New York run, this work was taken on the road to Washington D.C., where Goldin and cast performed for President and Mrs. Reagan. Best known for his television work, Goldin made his small screen debut on "Romper Room" at the age of four, but did not return to television until 1981, when he co-starred in the television movie "Coach of the Year," with Robert Conrad. In addition Goldin has starred in several ABC Afterschool Specials, including "The Movie Star's Daughter," "Words to Live By," "The Third Dimension," and "Rocking Chair Rebellion," and made quest appearances on "The Hitchhiker," "Bobby and Sarah," "MacGyver," "Baywatch," "21 Jumpstreet," "Kate and Allie," and "Alf." Goldin also performed alongside Sam Waterston, Christine Lahti, and Mary Stuart Masterson in the t.v. movie "Love Lives On." He reunited with former co-star Robert Conrad on the NBC pilot "Hard Knox," and had a featured role on the short lived series "Hail to the Chief," with Patty Duke. Not one to limit himself to the small screen, Ricky made his feature film debut in "Piranha II-The Spawning," and has since gone on to star in "Hyper Sapien," the 1989 remake of "The Blob," "The Insinkable Shecky," with Milton Berle, "Lambada-Set the Night on Fire," "Mirror, Mirror," and "Pastime," with Jeffrey Tambor. After several years in Los Angeles, Goldin returned to New York for the role of Dean Frame, rock 'n roll rebel on "Another World." The actor had previously worked briefly in daytime, originating the role of Rick on "Ryan's Hope." For his first season on "Another World," Goldin was awarded a daytime Emmy for Outstanding Younger Lead Actor. Although he considers himself an actor first and foremost, he does share his characters love of music, and has even written the lyrics for a love song which was used on the show. Away from the set Goldin has several pets, including many dogs, a ferret named Kazoo, and a boa constrictor named Anteus.

NANCY GRAHN

Born: April 28 in Skokie, Illinois
Marital Status: single
Height: 5'6" **Eyes:** brown **Hair:** brown
Education: Neighborhood Playhouse
Interests: community service, charity work, writing
Awards: 1989 Daytime Emmy for Outstanding Supporting
Actress

Daytime Dramas: "One Life to Live," Beverly Wilkes;
"Santa Barbara," Julia Wainwright Capwell, 1985-

One of daytime's most popular and respected actresses, Nancy Grahn has portrayed Julia Wainwright Capwell on "Santa Barbara" since 1985. Along the way, she earned a 1989 Daytime Emmy for Outstanding Supporting Actress. Born on April 28 in Skokie, Illinois, the middle child of three girls, where her parents worked with adults with Down's Syndrome, Nancy was taught from an early age that the most important thing one can do is to help others. Taking this advice to heart, Grahn has used her celebrity status to benefit a number of worthwhile causes. She formed "Daytime For Choice," a powerful pro-choice organization, as well as serving as a spokesperson for the National Victims Center. In addition, the actress also works with AIDS patients and with the environmental protection group, ECO. She also spent three years volunteering with the San Fernando Family Guidance Clinic, working with children who are victims of incest. Encouraging this sort of participation in her fans, Grahn sponsored a contest which awarded a free trip to California, and a tour of the "Santa Barbara" set, to the fan who had logged the most hours of charitable work. As for acting, Nancy's career began at the age of twelve, when she starred in a production of "Guys and Dolls," presented at the Goodman Theater in Chicago. She continued this trend for the next several years, performing in professional productions, while still attending high school full time, where she was an honors student, class president, and homecoming queen. Graduating in 1976, Grahn moved to New York City where she attended the Neighborhood Playhouse. She was able to parlay a two day run as Beverly Wilkes on "One Life to Live" into a one year recurring role. After leaving this show, she moved to Los Angeles, landing guest spots on such programs as "Little House on the Prairie," "Magnum P.I.," "Simon and Simon," "Quincy," "Knight Rider," and "Murder, She Wrote," as well as in the t.v. films, "Kids Don't Tell" and "Obsessed with a Married Man." A California resident, Grahn, who is single, uses her time away from "Santa Barbara" to develop her writing skills, and is presently at work on several plays.

BERNARD GRANT

Born: in New York, New York
Marital Status: married to Joyce Gordon, two children,
Mark and Melissa
Height: 5'11" **Eyes:** brown
Education: College of the City of New York
Interests: writing, music, tennis, travel,

Daytime Dramas: "Guiding Light," Dr. Paul Fletcher,
1956-1970; **"One Life to Live,"** Steve Burke, 1970-1975

A daytime favorite, Bernard Grant has had starring roles on two popular programs, "One Life to Live" and "Guiding Light," as well as making guest appearances on "Somerset," "Search for Tomorrow," "Edge of Night," "Three Steps to Heaven," and "Date With Life." Born in the Bronx and raised in New York City since the age of five, where his father worked as a manufacturer, Grant received his education at George Washington High School and the College of the City of New York. Throughout his extensive career, he has actively pursued stage work, starring in scores of off-Broadway, regional, and summerstock productions. On television, in addition to his daytime work, Grant has guest starred on such shows as "Gimme a Break," "All in the Family," and "Maude," while his voice has been heard in over two thousand radio dramas. The actor has also applied his vocal skills to foreign films dubbed into English, substituting for such renowned actors as Marcello Mostroianni. A lifetime New York City resident, Grant is married to Joyce Gordon, a t.v. spokeswoman, with whom he has two children, Mark and Melissa. In his spare time, Bernard enjoys tennis, travel, sketching, classical music, and writing short stories.

STACI GREASON

Born: May 23, 1964 in Denver, Colorado
Marital Status: single
Height: 5'4 1/2" **Eyes:** hazel **Hair:** brown
Education: Loretto Heights College; University of Colorado
Interests: writing, Buddhism

Daytime Dramas: "Days of Our Lives," Isabella Toscano,
1989-1992

Once responsible for answering the fan mail for such programs as "The Cosby Show," "A Different World," and "Roseanne," Staci Greason, who is known to millions as Isabella Toscano on "Days of Our Lives," is now receiving plenty of fan mail of her own. Born on May 23, 1964 in Denver, Colorado, Staci grew up in the nearby town of Evergreen with her younger sister, Julie. Her father was a salesman, her mother a homemaker. After studying musical theater at Loretto Heights College, as well as attending the University of Colorado, she made the move to Los Angeles and began looking for acting work. She spent several years working an array of odd jobs while getting her feet wet in film and theater. On the big screen, Staci has been brutally murdered in three horror films, "Friday the 13th Part VII," "Final Curtain," and "Terror Night," while she has been seen on stage in "The Session," a production presented by Los Angeles' Gifted Young Artists Company. Originally hired only temporarily for the role of Isabella on "Days of Our Lives," the actress quickly found her niche on the show, and became one of the program's most popular performers. Staci has chosen to leave the show when her contract expires towards the end of 1992, and for the time being, leave show business as well. Her immediate plans are to finish her college education. Presently single, Staci is romantically involved with Tom Kellogg, a playwright, with whom she shares an interest in Buddhist philosophy.

BRIAN GREEN

Born: March 9, 1962 in Columbus, Indiana
Marital Status: single
Height: 5' 11 1/2" **Eyes:** blue **Hair:** brown
Interests: music, the gym
Awards: National Teen Talent Contest, 1st Prize, Vocal Competition; 1989 Tony Award nomination-Best Actor for "Starmites"

Daytime Dramas: "Days of Our Lives," Alan Brand; **"Another World,"** Sam Fowler, 1991-

A Tony nominated performer, Brian Lane Green is now the fourth actor to portray Sam Fowler on "Another World." Initially he had auditioned to be number three, but lost to Danny Markel. A native of Columbus, Indiana, Green is the second of two boys, the older brother Bart, a writer. The family relocated to Cleveland, Tennessee, where Brian's father, Dr. Hollis Green, worked as a minister as well as serving as president of the nearby Oxford Graduate School. A dedicated singer to this day, Brian began this facet of his career at the age of five, and even exercised his talents for the now disgraced PTL ministry. At sixteen, he entered a National Teen Talent Contest, bringing home first prize in the vocal competition. Continuing this winning streak, Green received a high school drama award for his performance as Tevye in a school production of "Fiddler on the Roof." After studying business and psychology in college, Green began his performing career, singing, modelling, and appearing in commercials. Eventually moving to Los Angeles, he landed several guest starring roles on such shows as "Matlock," "Hotel," "Murder, She Wrote," Highway to Heaven," and "The Law and Harry McGraw." Green's daytime debut was as Alan Brand on "Days of Our Lives." After playing this role for a year, the actor relocated to New York City, landing the lead role in the Broadway musical, "Big River," which he followed with another lead role in "Starmites," for which he received a Best Actor Tony nomination, an incredible achievement for such a young performer. Not putting his vocal talent to waste, Green continues to sing with The Tonics, a four person singing group who perform throughout New York City. Away from the set of "Another World," Green, who is unmarried, enjoys playing the piano, going to the movies, and working out.

JAMES MICHAEL GREGARY

Born: in Baltimore, Maryland
Marital Status: single
Eyes: brown   **Hair:** brown
Education: University of Maryland
Interests: swimming, travel, reading, blackjack

Daytime Dramas: "The Young and the Restless," Clint Radison

Although not yet on the Hollywood Walk of Fame, James Michael Gregary did receive a star on Ocean Boulevard in Myrtle Beach, South Carolina, for the Sun Fun Festival and his efforts in promoting the Myrtle Beach area. An actor and director, James' career has already included television, theater, and feature films. He is presently seen as Clint Radison on "The Young and the Restless," and prior to that made appearances on "Ryan's Hope," "As the World Turns," "Another World," and "Search for Tomorrow." Born in Baltimore, Maryland, of Greek descent, Gregary attended the University of Maryland, where he majored in voice and theater. Upon graduating, he went to work as the production coordinator/assistant director of the Susquehanna Theater Festival, displaying both his directing and acting talents in such productions as "Grease," "Godspell," "Bye Bye Birdie," "Mame," "West Side Story," and "Dames at Sea." The actor, who frequently performs in regional theater and on the cabaret circuit, recently made his off-Broadway debut in "Five After Eight." Also establishing himself as a film actor, Gregary co-starred with F. Murray Abraham in "The Favorite," and is slated to star in the t.v. movie "Intimate Power," which will be seen sometime in 1992. He has additionally worked as a guest star on the series, "Leg Work." Now living in Los Angeles, Gregary's hobbies include swimming, reading, travelling, working out, and playing blackjack.

STEPHEN GREGORY

Born: in New York, New York
Marital Status: single
Eyes: blue   **Hair:** blond
Education: New York University; The American Academy
Interests: writing, sports

Daytime Dramas: "As the World Turns," Timothy Hamilton; **"The Young and the Restless,"** Chase Benson

From the time he was in the third grade, when he was awarded the hotly contested role of Inspector Hound in the play, "The Real Inspector Hound," Stephen Gregory knew that performing was his true calling. Born the youngest of seven children, Gregory was raised in New York City, where like many other children, he was an avid t.v. watcher. Gregory's professional career began at the age of fourteen when he joined a New York repertory theater company, and by sixteen he was working steadily in commercials. Gregory's first big break came with the role of Timothy Hamilton on "As the World Turns," which he played for a little less than a year. Despite the fact that this character was somewhat shy and bookish, Gregory was subsequently cast as a sleazy bad guy in the film "The Heavenly Kid." After attending New York University film school for a spell, Gregory officially moved to Los Angeles, where he continued to find steady television work, guest starring on such shows as "St. Elsewhere," "Star Trek: The Next Generation," "Houston Knights," and "21 Jump Street." In between assignments, Gregory also picked up some extra money modelling for the cover of a teen romance novel. In his spare time, Gregory enjoys biking, travelling, sailing, movie going, skiing, and swimming, as well as writing screenplays and short stories. The actor also actively lends his support to the Juvenile Diabetes Foundation. On the weekends, Gregory can often be found visiting his family in Maine.

MICHAEL GUIDO

Born: January 13, 1950 in Queens, New York
Marital Status: married to Arlene Lencioni
Height: 5'10" **Eyes:** brown **Hair:** brown
Education: University of South Florida, B.F.A.;
Brandeis University, M.F.A.
Interests: softball, volleyball, antiques
Awards: 1991 Theatre Artist and Friends, Best Actor Award for "Beau Jest"

Daytime Dramas: "All My Children," Neil Berniker, 1990-

Since joining the cast of "All My Children" over two years ago, Michael Guido has gradually moved from the sidelines to center stage. Initially his character, Lieutenant Neil Berniker, was little more than a face in the crowd, but with the mayhem that has recently swept through Pine Valley, audiences see a lot more of the tough but honest crime fighter. Born on January 13, 1950 in Queens, New York, Guido spent most of his childhood, along with his two siblings, in Atlanta, Georgia. Describing his early years, Guido writes of his "loving parents" and "wonderful childhood." After receiving two theater degrees, a B.F.A. from the University of South Florida and an M.F.A. from Brandeis University, Guido began acting professionally, working in film, television, and theater. Michael has been seen on the big screen in "Snakes" and "Home Alone," as well as in scores of regional theater productions. A highly respected actor, Guido received the Theatre Artists and Friends Best Actor Award in 1991, for his work in the Chicago production of "Beau Jest." Married for more than seven years to Arlene Lencioni, Guido divides his time between his Chicago and New York homes. In his spare time, he enjoys softball, volleyball, and going to antique flea markets.

DEIDRE HALL

Born: October 31, 1947 in Milwaukee, Wisconsin
Marital Status: married to Steve Sohmer, December 31, 1991
Hair: blond
Education: Los Angeles Community College
Awards: nominated for three Best Actress Daytime Emmys;
Soap Opera Award for Outstanding Lead Actress, 1982, 1983,
1984, 1985; 1986 Soap Opera Digest Award for Outstanding
Contribution to Daytime Drama; named Best Actress over 100
times in Daytime T.V. Magazine Reader's Polls; 1992 Peoples
Choice Award nomination for Favorite Daytime Female
Performer

Daytime Dramas: "The Young and the Restless,"
Barbara Anderson, 1973-1975; **"Days of Our Lives,"**
Dr. Marlena Evans Brady, 1976-1987, 1991-

A star of daytime and primetime, Deidre Hall has over the past fifteen years become one of the most popular and well respected television actresses. From 1976 to 1987, she appeared as Dr. Marlena Evans on "Days of Our Lives," a role she returned to triumphantly in 1991. Among the scores of accolades heaped on Ms. Hall for her daytime work are three daytime Emmy nominations, five Soap Opera Awards for Outstanding Lead Actress, a 1986 Soap Opera Digest Award for Outstanding Contribution to the genre, and over one hundred times placing atop the list of favorite soap actresses in Daytime T.V. Magazine's monthly reader's poll. Most recently, she was nominated for a People's Choice Award for Favorite Daytime Performer. Born on October 31, 1947 in Milwaukee, Wisconsin, Hall was raised in Lake Worth, Florida, where she began her show business career at the age of twelve, when she was named Junior Orange Bowl Queen. She went on to study psychology at Palm Beach Junior College and Los Angeles Community College, earning tuition money through modelling and a stint as a disc jockey at an all women's radio station. Moving out to California, Hall quickly began landing television roles, and has since made guest appearances on such shows as "Perry Mason," "Columbo," "Murder, She Wrote," "Wiseguy," "Circus of the Stars," "The Bob Hope Comedy Special," and "NBC 60th Anniversary Celebration." Prior to joining "Days of Our Lives," Ms. Hall portrayed Barbara Anderson on "The Young and the Restless" from 1973 until 1975. The actress has also starred in several television films, among them, "And the Sea Will Tell," "A Reason to Live," "Take My Daughters, Please," "For the Very First Time," and the upcoming, "Woman on a Ledge" which will also star daytime's Leslie Charleson and Colleen Zenk Pinter. In 1987, Hall left "Days of Our Lives" to concentrate on her prime time program, the critically acclaimed, "Our House." Now back as Marlena, plans are in the works for a spin off from "Days of Our Lives," in which Hall will be the lead character. She's been a star on both daytime and primetime, but two roles that she turned down were "Dynasty's" Kyrstle and "Moonlighting's" Maggie. Away from soap operas, she can also be seen in many national commercials, and is a spokesperson for both Dexatrim and Halls, as well as running two video companies, Customs Last Stand and Tinselvania Video. Deidre, who has been married twice before, recently wed novelist/producer Steve Sohmer. They are expecting their first child, by a surrogate mother, during the summer of 1992.

TOM HALLICK

Born: June 13 in Buffalo, New York
Marital Status: divorced, one daughter, Ashley
Height: 6'1" **Eyes:** brown **Hair:** brown
Education: Florida Southern College, B.A.
Interests: politics, travel, golf, tennis
Awards: Best Actor (three years in a row) by "Daytime T.V." and "T.V. By Day"

Daytime Dramas: "The Young and the Restless," Brad Elliot, 1973-1978; **"Days of Our Lives,"** Maxwell Hathaway, 1984

One of the stars of daytime television, Tom Hallick achieved phenomenal success during his years as Brad Elliot on "The Young and the Restless." Aside from winning the hearts of millions, Hallick's efforts also earned him three consecutive Best Actor awards from two popular magazines, "Daytime T.V." and "T.V. By Day." Born on June 13, in Buffalo, New York, where his father worked as a real estate developer, Hallick was interested in theater from an early age, and first performed on stage at Amherst High School. After graduating from Florida Southern College, where he organized the schools first repertory company, Hallick jumped immediately into professional entertaining, first as the host of a radio show, followed then by his own talk show, and eventually hosting a local t.v. variety program. With a strong amount of experience, Hallick moved to New York City, where he embarked on a career which has included television, film, and theater. On stage, Tom has appeared in over 105 productions, including a record breaking two year run in "Plaza Suite," which broke box office records at Pittsburgh's Heinz Hall, the Eastman Theatre, in Rochester, and the Milwaukee Performing Arts Center. One of his most recent stage triumphs was in "Same Time, Next Year." Tom's feature film credits include starring roles in "Dark Eyes," "Hangar 18," "Beyond Death's Door," and with George Kennedy in "The Rare Breed," while he has starred in such television films as, "Fast Friends," "The Time Travellers," "The Return of Captain Nemo," and as the title character in "The Story of Solomon." Although he is best known for his work on "The Young and the Restless," Hallick has additionally been seen as Maxwell Hathaway on "Days of Our Lives," and in the Showtime series, "Loving Friends and Perfect Couples," as well as making guest appearances on "Simon and Simon," "Dynasty," "Matlock," and "Murder, She Wrote." Hallick also holds the honor of being the first host of "Entertainment Tonight." Although it remains to be seen whether he will enter the political ring, Hallick certainly will have the right connections should he choose to do so. He has served as a surrogate speaker for Presidents Reagan and Bush, and has even introduced President Reagan and served as Master of Ceremonies at the National Orange Show Stadium rally, an event attended by thirty thousand people. Additionally, Hallick has performed with the Air Force Band and Choir at Constitution Hall, and hosted a historic reenactment of George Washington's inauguration at Mount Vernon, Virginia. He has also participated in the two most recent presidential inaugurations in Washington, D.C.. Using his influence, Hallick helped in the initiation of the Democracy Corps, an organization devoted to helping newly emerging Eastern Europe democracies. An ardent environmentalist, Tom is active with the Audobon Society, the Defenders of Wildlife, and travels frequently to Yellowstone and Glacier National Parks, where he works to prevent the grizzly bears from slipping into extinction. In his spare time, the actor enjoys tennis and golf, exhibiting these skills in pro tournaments around the world, from the Bob Hope Desert Classic to the Australian Open. He also enjoys travelling, and recently embarked on his second African photographic safari. Presently living in Marina Del Rey, California, Hallick, who is divorced, has one daughter, Ashley, a graduate from the University of South Florida.

BRADLEY HALLOCK

Born: April 8, 1983 in Newport Beach, California
Marital Status: single
Height: 58" **Eyes:** blue   **Hair:** blond
Education: currently in grade school
Interests: sports, Nintendo, gymnastics, baseball cards
Awards: Golden Pencil Award, Honorable mention in the "Invent America" competition

Daytime Dramas: "Days of Our Lives," Eric Brady, 1986-

Born on April 8, 1983, Bradley Matthew Hallock has spent six of his nine years portraying Eric Brady on "Days of Our Lives." Along the way he has had several on-screen parents, including Wayne Northrop, Deidre Hall, and Drake Hogystyn. A native of Newport Beach, California, Brad, who has one sister, Allison, lives in nearby Irvine, where his father, Scott, owns a coin and jewelry manufacturing business. In addition to his daytime work, the young actor has also been seen in television commercials for McDonalds, The Gap, and many more, and also frequently performs in school plays. Presently in the fourth grade, Brad is enrolled in the gifted classes, as well as having held the position of Mayor in his third grade class. An excellent student, he was the recipient of "The Golden Pencil Award," and received honorable mention in the "Invent America" competition. Equally adept on the playing field, the young actor was named an all star in two sports, basketball and baseball (his current team is the Angels), and also has played soccer for the past four years. Away from school and the set, Brad enjoys gymnastics, collecting baseball cards, playing Nintendo, and is a die hard L.A. Lakers/Magic Johnson fan.

CHARLES JAY HAMMER

Born: November 16 in San Francisco, California
Marital Status: married to Dene Nardi, four children
Education: University of the Pacific; Neighborhood Playhouse School of the Theatre
Interests: reading, baseball, movies
Awards: nominated for Writer's Guild Award for work on "Guiding Light"

Daytime Dramas: "Texas," Max Dekker, 1981;
"Guiding Light," Fletcher Reade, 1984-

Born and raised in San Francisco, California, Charles Jay Hammer has achieved great success on daytime drama, not only as an actor, but as a writer as well. A fourth generation Californian, Hammer attended college, appropriately enough, at the University of the Pacific, following which he moved to New York where he began his formal acting training. During this period he worked at the Neighborhood Playhouse School of the Theatre, and studied with such coaches as Sanford Meisner, Bobby Lewis, and William Espes. Hammer devoted much of his early career to the stage, appearing off-Broadway in "Passing Through From Exotic Places," with Vincent Gardenia and Robert Loggia, and in a plethora of summer stock productions. He most recently appeared on the London stage in "Serenading Love," an American version of "Phantom of the Opera." Hammer then returned to California where he embarked on a successful string of television appearances, including a one season stint as Aran Willis on "The Jeffersons," and a recurring role on "The Blue Knight," which also starred George Kennedy and Gerald McRaney. Among the other shows in which he has appeared: "Kojak," "Mannix," "Emergency," "Adam-12," and in such television movies as "F. Scott Fitzgerald in Hollywood," "The Mark of Zorro," and "A World Apart." Hammer then returned to New York where he played Max Dekker in the short lived daytime drama, "Texas." After the demise of this show, he remained with daytime drama as a writer for "Guiding Light," receiving a Writer's Guild nomination for excellence in daytime drama. In 1984 the role of cynical reporter Fletcher Reade was created, and after some persuading Hammer agreed to take the part. While the role was initially supposed to be temporary, it soon became popular with the producers and the fans alike, and a short time later Hammer signed a long term contract. When not on the set, the actor, who lives in New York City, enjoys reading, water polo, and following his favorite team, the Yankees. Hammer is married to actress Dene Nardi, with whom he has three sons and a daughter.

SCHAE HARRISON

Born: April 27 in California
Marital Status: single
Height: 5'6" **Eyes:** blue **Hair:** blond
Interests: tennis, rollerskating, horseback riding
Awards: 1992 Soap Opera Award nomination for Outstanding Comic Performance

**Daytime Dramas: "General Hospital;"
"The Bold and The Beautiful,"** Darla

Blond, blue eyed, and boasting an array of talents, Schae Harrison began dancing at the age of four. Born Schaeffer (a family name) Harrison and raised in Orange County, California, she studied all aspects of the dance medium, from ancient theories through modern movement. Using these very talents, she has worked on the cheerleading-dance squad for the NFL Seattle Seahawks, a position she held for over three years, performing for the more than 60,000 fans at each game. On a smaller scale, Schae was a cheerleader at Canyon High School in Anaheim. Professionally, Schae studied theater in college, as well as with private acting coaches. She has appeared in many primetime shows, including "Throb," "Night Court," and "Freddy's Nightmares." In addition to these credits, Ms Harrison has also hosted her own cable aerobics workout program and appeared on daytime's "General Hospital." Her feature film credits include, "Twice in a Lifetime," with Ann-Margaret and Gene Hackman. To add to her list of talents, Schae has a beautiful singing voice and recently finished working on a demo tape of pop ballads. When the busy actress has spare time, she enjoys tennis, rollerskating at the beach, working out and horseback riding. Schae is also an active supporter of the National Special Olympics Organization.

SUSAN HASKELL

Born: June 10 in Toronto, Canada
Marital Status: single
Height: 5' 8 1/2" **Eyes:** blue **Hair:** brown
Education: Tufts University, Bachelor's Degree in
Biopsychology; American Academy of Dramatic Arts,
Associate's Degree
Interests: snow/water skiing, antiquing, writing poetry, traveling

Daytime Dramas: "One Life to Live," Marty Saybrooke, 1992-

Fortunately for Susan Haskell, whose motto is "A smile is a curve that can set a lot of things straight!" the past year has given the young actress a great deal to smile about. Cast on "One Life to Live" as a lupus patient, Haskell's character, Marty Saybrooke, enjoyed a far better fate than that of her roommate, Megan. (Jessica Tuck) Born on June 10 in Toronto Canada, Haskell hails from what she refers to as the "best loving family in the world." Her family includes her parents, Robert and Marilyn, brother Roger, an attorney and her sister, Carolyn, a part time model and actress. After graduating cum laude with a degree in biopsychology from Tufts University, Ms. Haskell went on to receive another degree from the American Academy of Dramatic Arts. Along with "One Life to Live," she has also been seen on the television show, "My Secret Identity," and in the feature film, "Strictly Business." Now a resident of New York City, Ms. Haskell donates her time to several charitable organizations, including the Make-A-Wish Foundation, Impact (a Christian organization) and the Lupus Foundation. In her spare time, she enjoys skiing (snow/water) running, antiquing, writing poetry and traveling to such locations as Europe, Africa and the Orient.

DON HASTINGS

Born: April 1, 1934 in Brooklyn, New York
Marital Status: married to Leslie Denniston, one daughter,
Katherine Scott; three children from a previous marriage, Julie,
Jennifer and Matthew
Height: 5'11" **Eyes:** blue **Hair:** brown
Interests: music, writing
Awards: 1992 Soap Opera Award nomination for Outstanding
Lead Actor

Daytime Dramas: "Edge of Night," Jack Lane, 1956-1960;
"As the World Turns," Bob Hughes, 1960-

With a career that spans well over a half a century, Don Hastings has proven himself time and time again to be an actor of the highest order. Since his career began at the age of six, the actor has earned such distinctions as being a child star on Broadway, being one of the first television teen idols, and speaking the very first line on a long running daytime drama. Hastings a Brooklyn native, began his career in 1940 when he went to see his brother Bob sing on a radio program. After hearing that Don could sing, he was asked to audition, and soon began performing on the radio show "Coast to Coast on a Bus." His older brother Bob continues to act, recently playing Captain Burt Ramsey on "General Hospital." After making his radio debut the younger Hastings then began his stage work, touring with the national company of "Life With Father" in 1941, which was followed by his Broadway debut three years later in "I Remember Mama." Three successive Broadway roles then followed for Hastings, "On Whitman Avenue," "A Young Man's Fancy," and "Summer and Smoke," continuing his work in television and radio. At the end of the 1940's he began to concentrate on television full time, starring as the ranger on "Captain Video" for six years, and in the process becoming one of the first t.v. teen idols. Among the other radio and television programs in which Hastings was involved: "Studio One," "Crunch and Des," "A Date With Life," and "Modern Romances." In 1956 he joined the world of daytime television on the serial "Edge of Night." As Jack Lane, Hastings has the distinction of speaking the first line in the premiere show of that long running series. He remained in that role for four years, before joining the cast of "As the World Turns" in 1960, where he has remained ever since, not only as an actor but serving as a writer as well. (He wrote under the name of J.J. Matthews - which is in honor of his oldest three children) In addition Hastings has continued his stage work, touring with his co-star Kathryn Hays in a show called "Hastings and Hays on Love," as well as appearing with Ms. Hays in the off-Broadway production of "Algonquin Sampler." Hastings is married to actress Leslie Denniston, whom he met when both were on "As The World Turns. They have one daughter, Katherine Scott, born in September 1982. The actor also has two daughters (Julie and Jennifer) and a son (Matthew) from a previous marriage.

SUSAN SEAFORTH HAYES

Born: July 11, 1943 in San Francisco, California
Marital Status: married to Bill Hayes on October 12, 1974
Height: 5'3 3/4" **Eyes:** blue/grey **Hair:** brown
Education: Los Angeles City College, A.A.
Interests: grand opera
Awards: nominated for Daytime Emmy for Best Actress, 1975, 1976, 1978, 1979; 1983 Emmy for Outstanding Contribution to Daytime Television; 1977 Soap Opera Award for Best Actress; voted favorite performer by 1977 Photoplay; 1976, 1977 Daytime T.V. Magazines

Daytime Dramas: "General Hospital," Dorothy Bradley, 1963; **"The Young Marrieds,"** Carol West, 1964-1966; **"Days of Our Lives,"** Julie Williams, 1968-1984; 1985-; **"The Young and the Restless,"** JoAnna Manning, 1984;

During the 1970's, "Days of Our Lives" found itself at the forefront of daytime drama, not only in the ratings, but as groundbreaking television. At the center of this phenomenon was Susan Seaforth Hayes. During her years on the show, (she was a regular from 1968 to 1984 and returned in 1985) Ms. Hayes garnered four daytime Emmy nominations, a Soap Opera Award for Best Actress, and was named favorite actress by both Photoplay Magazine and Daytime T.V. magazine. In 1983, she received a special Emmy for her contributions to daytime television. Born on July 11, 1943 in San Francisco, Susan was raised by her father, a builder and her mother, Elizabeth Harrower, an actress and soap opera writer. She made her acting debut at the age of four in a production of "Madame Butterfly," and for the next several years found frequent work in the theater and on film and television. At the age of eleven Susan faced the wrath of American children when she guest starred on "Lassie," portraying a mean little girl who feeds poisoned meat to the series star; other programs on which she has guest starred include "My Three Sons," "Kissin' Cousins," "The F.B.I.," "Ironside," "Adam 12," and "Matlock." The actress's feature film credits include "Five Pennies," "Angel in My Pocket," and "Billy." After graduating with a degree in history from Los Angeles City College, Susan continued her acting career, and soon found a name for herself on daytime drama. In addition to "Days of Our Lives," she has appeared on "General Hospital," "The Young and the Restless," and "The Young Marrieds." Her years as Julie Williams on "Days of Our Lives," proved equally successful personally, as Susan met her future husband, actor Bill Hayes, on the set. The two have now been happily married for eighteen years and frequently tour the country in theatrical productions. Now living in North Hollywood, Ms. Hayes continues to be interested in history and politics. An active political force, she has in the past worked for Barry Goldwater's presidential campaign, and has also addressed the platform committee at the Republican National Convention. Susan's other interests include opera, travelling, and gardening, particularly roses, her favorite flower.

KATHRYN HAYS

Born: July 26 in Princeton, Illinois
Marital Status: single, one daughter, Sherri
Eyes: brown   **Hair:** brown
Education: Northwestern University
Interests: theater
Awards: nominated for two Emmy Awards in 1969 for "Star Trek" and "High Chaparral"

Daytime Dramas: "Guiding Light," Leslie Jackson, 1971; **"As the World Turns,"** Kim Hughes, 1972-

A respected stage actress and a long time soap opera favorite, Kathryn Hays was one of the key players in establishing "As the World Turns" as the premiere daytime drama of the 1970's. Born on July 26 in Princeton, Illinois, Hays attended a junior college in Joliet, Illinois before enrolling at Northwestern University. A former model, her career has included tremendous success in television, feature films, and on the stage. In addition to her daytime work, which also included one year as Leslie Jackson on "Guiding Light," Ms. Hays has guest starred on over fifty prime time programs, including a starring role in "The Road West." For the 1969-1970 television season, she received two Emmy nominations for her work on "High Chaparral" and "Star Trek" (a guest role she is still recognized for, more than two decades later). She also demonstrated her vocal talents in a CBS music special, "After Hours: Getting to Know You." Equally at home on stage, Hays has appeared on Broadway in "Mary, Mary," with Barbara Bel Geddes, and "The Irregular Verb to Love," with Claudette Colbert. She has also worked with the Los Angeles Civic Light Opera, and appeared in scores of off-Broadway and regional productions, including "Two by Two," "Show Boat," "Dames at Sea," "Can-Can," "Same Time Next Year," "A Little Night Music," and "Follies," a production which was videotaped and is now a permanent part of the collection of American musicals kept at the Lincoln Center Library of the Performing Arts. Fans of "As the World Turns" have also gotten the opportunity to see Kathryn perform with her co-star, Don Hastings, in a musical concert entitled, "Hastings and Hays on Love." The two have also appeared together in the off-Broadway production, "Algonquin Sampler." Ms. Hays has in addition worked extensively in feature films, appearing in "Counterpoint," "The Savage Land," "Yuma," "Ride Beyond Vengeance," and "Lady Bug, Lady Bug," among others. Now a resident of New York City, Kathryn is the mother of one daughter, Sherri.

SHARI HEADLEY

Born: July 15 in Brooklyn, New York
Marital Status: single
Height: 5'8" **Eyes:** brown **Hair:** black
Education: Queens College
Interests: bowling, movies
Awards: Face of the Eighties, Ford Modelling Agency
and The New York Post

Daytime Dramas: "All My Children," Mimi Reed, 1991-

A model and an actress, Shari Headley burst on the scene in 1988, starring with Eddie Murphy in "Coming to America." The youngest of four children, Shari was born and raised in New York City, where she initially planned on a career in medicine. However, while Shari was enrolled in the pre-med program at Queens College, her sister, Sabin, sent in a picture of Shari to the Ford Modelling Agency. The picture made quite an impression and the younger Headley went on to be named the Face of the Eighties, working on many make-up and beauty ads. Commercials came next and then appearances on prime time followed. With such a strong start, Shari decided to put aside medicine and focus on her modelling and acting careers, both of which took off immediately. It went so well in fact, that her very first role was a co-starring part in one of 1988's biggest hits, with one of Hollywood's biggest stars - "Coming to America" with Eddie Murphy. Although she had no formal acting training, Shari proved to be a natural in front of the camera, and has since enjoyed great television success, including roles on two ABC television series, "Gideon Oliver," with Louis Gossett, Jr., and "Kojak," in which she starred as Trish Van Hogan. Among the other prime time shows on which Shari has appeared: "Miami Vice," "The Cosby Show," "Matlock," and a singing/acting role on "Quantum Leap." Presently Shari lives in New York and is engaged to a man named Reggie, who like her character on "All My Children," is also involved in law enforcement.

RICK HEARST

Born: January 4, 1965 in Howard Beach, New York
Marital Status: married to Donna Smoot, one son, Nicholas
Eyes: brown **Hair:** brown
Education: University of Texas (two years); Circle in the Square
Professional Workshop
Interests: karate, cooking, shooting pool
Awards: 1991 Daytime Emmy, Outstanding Young Actor;
1992 Soap Opera Award nomination for Outstanding Younger
Leading Actor, ("Guiding Light"), 1992 Daytime Emmy
nomination for Outstanding Younger Actor

Daytime Dramas: "Days of Our Lives," Scott Banning
1989-1990; **"Guiding Light,"** Alan-Michael Spaulding,1990-

Actor, family man, martial artist, cat owner, these are just a few of the descriptions that fit Rick Hearst, one of the hottest young actors in daytime drama. Born Rick Herbst on January 4, 1965 in Howard Beach, New York, the actor first came upon his love of performing in first grade. It seems that the boy who was supposed to be the ringmaster in the school play was too frightened to remember his lines, so young Rick took over the role and instantly felt right at home in the spotlight. Growing up, his family moved around quite a bit, living in New York, New Jersey, and Texas, where Hearst attended Plano Senior High School. Although initially rejected by the University of Texas, he auditioned and won a Morton Brown Acting Scholarship which enabled him to attend the University. It was there that he met Donna Smoot, a fellow actor and theater lover. Although they met when he was a freshman and she a senior, the two quickly overcame the age difference and began living together only six months after their first date. At the University of Texas theater Hearst starred in such productions as, "Joseph and the Amazing Technicolor Dreamcoat," "West Side Story," and "Born Again." After two years in Texas, Hearst decided that he needed more rigorous acting training, and so he and Donna moved to New York City where Rick spent two years at the Circle in the Square Professional Workshop. During this time he was featured in the company's production of "Spring Awakening." Hearst's film work includes, "Crossing the Line" and "Brain Damage," a low budget horror film which answered the burning question: what would Rick Hearst look like if the top of his head exploded and emitted electrical sparks. Suffice it to say that this experience is not a personal favorite for Hearst, but he quickly bounced back, landing the role of Scott Banning on "Days of Our Lives." He stayed with the show for one year, but was released from his contract one month shy of his wedding day. (he and the producers disagreed on the direction his character should take) Hearst began to audition for other roles, and his tenacity was rewarded with the role of Alan-Michael Spaulding on "Guiding Light." The couple married on June 9, 1990, in Plano, Texas and honeymooned in France, a trip they won at a celebrity road rally. Since then the actor has been on a definite winning streak, winning a 1991 Daytime Emmy for Outstanding Young Actor and becoming a proud father of Nicholas, born on June 26, 1991. In 1992, Rick and fellow daytimer, Morgan Englund formed a rock band called 2C. They can be seen playing various New York clubs, including the very popular, China Club. The Hearst family currently lives outside New York City, where Rick is pursuing his black belt in karate.

DAVID HEDISON

Born: May 20 in Providence, Rhode Island
Marital Status: married to Bridget Hedison, two daughters, Alexandra and Serena
Eyes: brown   **Hair:** salt and pepper
Education: Brown University, B.A.
Interests: photography, theater, tennis, skiing
Awards: Theater World Award ("A Month in the Country")

Daytime Dramas: "Another World," Spencer Harrison, 1991-

While he has played a great many roles since, David Hedison is perhaps best known as the title character in the 1958 cult classic, "The Fly." After years of working in film, television, and on stage, Hedison recently made his daytime debut as Spencer Harrison on "Another World." Born Albert David Hedison, Jr. on May 20 in Providence, Rhode Island, where his father was a jewelry manufacturer, David's first acting experience was in a high school production of "The Youngest." Dividing most of his childhood between Providence and Boston, he eventually enrolled as an English major at Brown University, where he also continued to star in school productions. Upon graduation, Hedison moved to New York City, working as an apprentice at the Neighborhood Playhouse, while earning money through a wide range of part time jobs, from Fuller Brush salesman to silver polisher at the Waldorf/Astoria Hotel. His first professional acting experience was on live television programs, but his big break came when he earned a Theater World Award for his performance opposite Uta Hagen in the Broadway production of "A Month in the Country," directed by Sir Michael Redgrave. This performance also caught the attention of a talent scout for 20th Century Fox, who recruited Hedison to Hollywood, where he was cast as The Fly. Following this work, he went on to star in such films as, "The Enemy Below," with Robert Mitchum, "The Greatest Story Ever Told," "The Naked Face," "Ffolkes," "The Undeclared War," and two James Bond films, "Live and Let Die" and "License to Kill." Hedison's first major television character was Captain Crane on the popular series, "Voyage to the Bottom of the Sea," and he has additionally been seen in "Five Fingers," "Hotel," "Murder, She Wrote," "Dynasty," "Newhart," "Family," and as Roger Langdon on "The Colbys," as well as appearing in the mini-series, "A.D.," and in the BBC production of "Summer & Smoke," with Lee Remick. He has continued to work on stage as well, starring on Broadway in "Clash by Night," in the national tour of Neil Simon's, "Chapter Two," and in the California premieres of "Forty Deuce," "Come Into My Parlor," and "Return Engagements." Most recently, Hedison starred in the London production of "Catch Me If You Can." David and his wife of more than twenty years, Bridget, are the proud parents of two daughters, Alexandra and Serena, both of whom are now UCLA students. Although the couple is now dealing with a bi-coastal marriage, ("Another World" is produced in New York) they see each other frequently and talk on the phone several times each day. To relax, Hedison enjoys tennis, skiing, swimming, and photography.

WAYNE HEFFLEY

Born: July 15, 1927
Marital Status: divorced, four daughters, Devon, Patricia, Kendis, and Dominique, one son, Michael
Height: 5'10 1/2" **Eyes:** blue
Education: high school
Interests: theater, chess, reading, writing, walking

Daytime Dramas: "Days of Our Lives," Vern Scofield, 1988-

An acting veteran, Wayne Heffley's career has spanned theater, television, and over six hundred feature films. Best known to daytime fans as Vern Scofield on "Days of Our Lives," Heffley, who has one brother, Carl, was born on July 15, 1927. He describes his childhood as "hectic." After graduating from high school he immediately embarked on his professional career, working in the theater with the Stage Society Repertory Group, and appearing in hundreds of feature films, among them "Tora!Tora! Tora!," "King Kong," "Orca," and "The Towering Inferno." On the small screen, in addition to his five years on "Days of Our Lives," Heffley has guest starred on such shows as "Playhouse '90," "Hallmark Hall of Fame," "Little House on the Prairie," "Highway Patrol," "White Shadow," "Evening Shade," "Murder, She Wrote," and "Hill Street Blues." Currently a resident of Glendale, California, Wayne, who is divorced, has one son, Michael, and four daughters, Devon, Patricia, Kendis, and Dominique. In his spare time, the actor enjoys chess, reading, writing, walking, and going to the theater.

JON HENSLEY

Born: August 26 in Browns Mills, New Jersey
Marital Status: single
Eyes: blue   **Hair:** brown
Education: New York University, one year; London Academy of Music and Dramatic Arts
Interest: sports, music
Awards: Nominated for Daytime Emmy as Outstanding Younger Leading Actor, 1985 ("As the World Turns")

Daytime Dramas: "One Life to Live," Brody Price; **"As the World Turns,"** Holden Snyder, 1985-1988, 1990-

One of the rising young stars of daytime drama, Jon Hensley was born in Browns Mills, New Jersey and raised in Bucks County, Pennsylvania. Opting against going into his family's restaurant business, Hensley enrolled in New York University as a journalism major. After his first year Hensley decided that his future was as an actor. Much of his early work was on stage, both in school and in the Bucks County Playhouse, where he was seen in a production of "As You Like It." Along with this he appeared in numerous commercials and print ads before making his daytime debut as Brody Price on "One Life to Live." Joining the cast of "As the World Turns" in October of 1985, Hensley made an immediate impression, receiving an Emmy nomination for Outstanding Younger Leading Man. He remained with the show for three years before taking time off to travel to California and London, where he studied Shakespeare at the London Academy of Music and Dramatic Arts. In the spring of 1990, Hensely returned to the show. Away from the set the young actor is a sports enthusiast as well as an aspiring song writer.

ANTHONY HERRERA

Born: January 19 in Wiggins, Mississippi
Marital Status: single, one daughter
Height: 6'2" **Eyes:** brown **Hair:** black
Education: University of Mississippi, Bachelor's Degree; Stella Adler training
Interests: squash, ballroom dancing
Awards: CINE Golden Eagle Award for the film "Mississippi Delta Blues"

Daytime Dramas: "The Young and the Restless," Jack Curtis, 1975-1977; **"As the World Turns,"** James Steinbeck, 1980-1983; 1986-1987; **"Loving,"** Dane Hammond, 1983-1986; 1988-1991

Born and raised in Mississippi, Anthony Herrera has been a strong presence on daytime drama since 1975 when he first starred in "The Young and the Restless." Since then he has also starred in "As the World Turns" and "Loving," portraying Dane Hammond, a role he created. Herrera attended the University of Mississippi where he had a double major of zoology and English literature. Upon graduation he decided against attending medical school, and instead moved to New York City to study acting with Stella Adler. Along with his extensive work on soap operas, Herrera also made guest appearances on "The Rockford Files," "The Incredible Hulk," and "Emergency," as well as appearing in the feature film "Helter Skelter." Herrera has also enjoyed great success as a writer/director/producer of short films. One such work, entitled "Mississippi Delta Blues," won the CINE Golden Eagle Award, and his adaption of Eudora Welty's "The Wide Net," which aired on the PBS series "American Playhouse," was received with unanimous critical praise. When not working, Herrera tries to spend as much time as possible with his daughter. He also enjoys playing squash, ballroom dancing, and visiting his home in Mississippi.

LAURA HERRING

Born: March 3 in Los Mochis, Mexico
Marital Status: single
Height: 5'7" **Eyes:** brown **Hair:** dark brown
Education: Aiglon College
Awards: Miss El Paso; Miss Texas; Miss USA, 1985;
International Star Search Champion

Daytime Dramas: "General Hospital," Carla Greco, 1990-1991

Born in Los Mochis, Mexico, Laura Herring is a beautiful new edition to daytime drama. Laura first came to the United States at the age of eleven with her mother and two sisters, first living in San Antonio, Texas, and later El Paso. For her senior year of high school, Laura studied at Aiglon College in Switzerland, and from there was chosen to spend a summer doing social work in India. Laura then returned to El Paso where she enjoyed a phenomenal string of success in beauty pageants. First she was named Miss El Paso, which was followed by the title of Miss Texas, and in 1985 she became the first Hispanic to be crowned Miss USA. This exposure lead to Laura's first acting assignment in the television film, "The Alamo: Thirteen Days of Glory," in which she starred opposite Raul Julia. The experience proved to be so rewarding that Laura, who had never planned on a career as an actress, decided to pursue this profession full time. She spent the next four years studying with Stella Adler, Alan Rich, and Morgan Shepard, and has since made a number of television appearances. She was featured in the telefilm "Desperado II," as well as on such prime time series as "Alien Nation" and "Beauty and the Beast." Along with these acting assignments, Laura has also been seen as a co-emcee for such events as the 1990 tournament of Roses Parade, and the 1989 and 1990 Miss USA Pageants, as well as participating in "The People's Choice Awards" and "The Golden Eagle Awards." In 1989, Laura, representing Mexico on the popular talent show, "Star Search," hosted by Ed McMahon, became the International "Star Search: Champion." She has also been featured on information shows such as "Good Morning America," "20/20," "Entertainment Tonight" and others. Recently Laura also made her motion picture debut in "The Forbidden Dance," and has since appeared in the film "Better Watch Out" and "Dead Women in Lingerie."

LYNN HERRING

Born: September 22 in Enid, Oklahoma
Marital Status: married to Wayne Northrop on May 9, 1981, one son, Hank
Height: 5'7" **Eyes:** hazel **Hair:** brown
Education: Louisiana State University, Bachelor's Degree in Psychology
Interests: animals, skiing, tennis, crossword puzzles,gardening
Awards: 1977 Miss Virginia; 1978 runner up in Miss USA pageant; nominated for 1988, 1991 Daytime Emmy for Outstanding Supporting Actress; Soap Opera Award for Outstanding Villainess, 1989, 1991

Daytime Dramas: "General Hospital," Lucy Coe, 1986-1992; **"Days of Our Lives,"** Lisanne Gardener, 1992-

With the character of Lucy Coe on "General Hospital," Lynn Herring created the only daytime vixen of the past decade who could give Erica Kane a run for her money. Originally cast for only a thirteen week storyline in 1986, Herring made such an immediate impression that she stayed on the show for the next six years, during which time she became the unrivalled bad girl of Port Charles. Along the way, the actress behind the vamp was nominated for a Daytime Emmy as Outstanding Actress, as well as twice being named Outstanding Villainess at the Soap Opera Awards. In 1992, Herring left behind Lucy and took on the role of Lisanne Gardener on "Days of Our Lives." Born in Enid, Oklahoma, the daughter of an Air Force officer, Lynn, along with the rest of her family, relocated constantly, and by the time she graduated from Woodson High School in Fairfax Virginia, she had attended a total of fifteen different schools, spread out among ten states and Puerto Rico. Although she grew up all over, Lynn considers the town of Jennings, Louisiana, where many of her relatives still live, as her hometown. She moved on to Louisiana State University, where during her sophomore year she won the 1977 title of Miss Virginia, and was named a runner up in the Miss USA Pageant the following year. After receiving her degree in psychology, Ms. Herring waived several graduate school scholarship offers from USC, UCLA, and Loyola-Marymount, and opted to move to New York to work as a model. She spent the next year modelling, and acting in off Broadway productions, honing her skills with the Actors Company. In 1980, Lynn headed cross country, where her time was divided between acting assignments and her pursuit of a Masters degree from Loyola-Marymount. Her first big break was a part in the feature film "Roller Boogie," and this was quickly followed by a great deal of television work, from commercials to guest starring roles on "Riptide," Arthur Hailey's "Hotel," "T.J. Hooker," and "The Colbys," as Ricardo Montalban's secretary, Lena. In 1981, Lynn married actor Wayne Northrop, whom she now co-stars with on "Days of Our Lives." The couple live in the Topanga Canyon area of Los Angeles with their son, Hank born January 9, 1991. In her spare time, Lynn enjoys skiing, tennis, gardening, horseback riding, crossword puzzles, and tending to the family's three cats, two dogs, two horses, and five chickens.

BRIGHTON HERTFORD

Born: June 11, 1986 in Tarzana, California
Marital Status: single
Height: 43" **Eyes:** blue   **Hair:** light brown
Education: entering first grade
Interests: movies, bowling, dancing, swimming
Awards: nominated for a Youth in Film Award

Daytime Dramas: "General Hospital," Barbara Jean Jones, 1986-

While most actors can recall with vivid detail their first acting experience on a daytime drama, Brighton Quinn Hertford remembers nothing of her first day on the job as Barbara Jean Jones on "General Hospital." This is understandable considering the young actress was just four months old when she debuted in 1986. Since then fans have been able to watch Brighton grow up in front of the camera, and along the way she has received a nomination for Youth in Film Award. Amazingly enough, she had already amassed another soap opera credit before joining "General Hospital," a brief (naturally, non-speaking) appearance on "The Young and the Restless." A native of Tarzana California, Brighton was born on June 11, 1986. Not the only performer in the family, her brother, Whit, has been seen on "Full House" and in the feature film, "Nightmare on Elm Street Part V," while her sister, Chelsea, co-stars as Casey MacGillis on "Major Dad." In addition to her work on "General Hospital," Brighton has also guest starred on "The Royal Family" and "Drexell's Class." Still a resident of California, Brighton is enjoying a fun-filled childhood with many friends and a large family. She is slated to start the first grade in the fall of 1992, and in her spare time enjoys dancing, swimming, going to the movies, bowling, and visiting the batting cages. Also a well-travelled young girl, Brighton has visited London, New York, Seattle, Utah and Hawaii.

DRAKE HOGESTYN

Born: September 29 in Fort Wayne, Indiana
Marital Status: married to Victoria Hogestyn, four children
Hair: brown
Education: University of South Florida
Interests: baseball
Awards: Daytime T.V. Magazine, Best Kisser

Daytime Dramas: "Days of Our Lives," Roman Brady/ John Black, 1986-

A native of Fort Wayne, Indiana, Drake Hogestyn took over the role of Roman Brady on "Days of Our Lives" in 1986, and has since proven himself one of daytime's top leading men. As of now, he is the only male soap opera star to be a guest on "The Tonight Show," starring Johnny Carson. And recently he was voted "Best Kisser" in Daytime T.V. Magazine reader's poll. In 1991, Wayne Northrop returned to the role of Roman, and Hogestyn's identity on the show was changed to John Black. Growing up, Hogestyn originally intended on becoming a dentist, pursuing this as an undergraduate at the University of South Florida. Also a talented baseball player, (he was at the University on a baseball scholarship) Hogestyn put aside his dentist dreams to play minor league ball for the New York Yankees. Through 1978 he played third base for the Yankee farm team, but decided on pursuing an acting career when an injury ended his playing days. Today however, Hogestyn keeps his baseball skills in tact as a member of the Hollywood All Stars' Baseball Team. As an actor, his first big break came when he entered a national talent search conducted by Columbia Pictures, becoming one of only thirty chosen winners out of a field of 75,000 aspirants. Hogestyn went on to work on numerous television productions, including a starring role in the series, "Seven Brides for Seven Brothers." Today the actor lives in Malibu, California, along with his wife, Victoria, and four children.

Anna Holbrook

ANNA HOLBROOK

Born: April 18 in Fairbanks, Alaska
Marital Status: married to Bruce Holbrook, daughter, Johanna, born October 1990
Hair: blond
Interests: horseback riding, photography, singing, tennis, skiing

Daytime Dramas: "Another World," Sharlene Hudson, 1988-1991

A former "Another World" star, Anna Holbrook left the role of Sharlene Hudson (and her troubled twin, Sharly) in 1991 to take care of her new baby, Johanna Catherine. Anna was born on April 18 in Fairbanks, Alaska, and over the course of her career has worked consistently in regional theater, appearing in such productions as "Crimes of the Heart," "Pal Joey," and "The Children's Hour." Along with "Another World," she has additionally been seen on television in "Benji," "Dallas," and "Johnny Blue." Anna is married to Bruce Holbrook, an airline pilot. Former childhood sweethearts, the couple have been married for over twelve years, and are now enjoying family life with daughter, Johanna. In her spare time, Anna, who is an accomplished horseback rider, enjoys photography, singing, skiing, and tennis. Although she left "Another World" in 1991, she recently reunited with many of her former castmates when she arranged a charity basketball game to benefit Covenant House, an organization dedicated to helping homeless and runaway children.

SCOTT HOLMES

Born: May 30 in West Grove, Pennsylvania
Marital Status: married to Pamela Holmes, one son, Taylor
Height: 5'9" **Eyes:** hazel **Hair:** black
Education: Catawaba College, B.A.
Interests: sports, cooking

Daytime Dramas: Ryan's Hope," David Greenberg, 1984-1985; **"As the World Turns,"** Tom Hughes, 1987-

Like many accomplished actors, Scott Holmes proclaims music to be his first love. He recently played with fellow co-stars, Rex Smith and Mary Ellen Stuart in New York's famed Russian Tea Room. Born on May 30 in West Grove, Pennsylvania, Holmes first came across this passion at the age of five when his father bought him a piano, and over the years he has continued to cultivate this talent along with his acting. Growing up in Oxford, Pennsylvania, Holmes was a member of the state choir, as well as playing trumpet in the state band. In addition, he was an active member of the drama club and during his senior year served as a student council president. Holmes continued his education at Catawaba College in Salisbury, North Carolina, receiving his B.A. in music and drama and appearing in such productions as "Hello Dolly," "Luv," and "A Funny Thing Happened on the Way to the Forum." While at Catawaba, Holmes met his future wife, Pamela, who after graduation choreographed a touring production of "Godspell," in which her future husband starred. Following this Holmes spent a season with the Pittsburgh Civic Light Opera Company, as well as appearing in "Shenandoah" with Howard Keel. Among Holmes' other stage credits are roles on Broadway in "Grease," the original cast production of "Evita," "The Rink," and "Jerome Kern Goes to Hollywood." The actor also appeared in the original Los Angeles cast of "Evita," as well as touring with "Nightclub Confidential." Holmes first venture into daytime television was as David Greenberg on "Ryan's Hope," a role he played from 1984 to 1985. In the summer of 1987 Holmes returned to daytime as Tom Hughes on "As the World Turns." Away from the set Holmes remains a sport enthusiast, playing many of the same sports he did in high school, among them baseball, basketball, volleyball and swimming. He also enjoys cooking for his wife and son Taylor, who was born in August of 1987.

BABS HOOYMAN

Born: May 6 in Glen Ellyn, Illinois
Marital Status: married to Jeff Baker
Height: 5'5"   **Eyes:** blue   **Hair:** brown
Education: St. Norbert College, B.A.; Southern Methodist University, B.F.A.
Interests: writing, comedy, music, reading, interior design

Daytime Dramas: "All My Children," Ethel Gadinsky, 1983-

An actress/writer/director, Babs Hooyman has portrayed Ethel Gadinsky (the faithful Glamorama employee) on "All My Children" since 1983. Born on May 6 in Glen Ellyn, Illinois, the youngest of four children, Hooyman was raised in Appleton, Wisconsin, where her father worked as an interior designer and furniture salesman, while her mother owned an antique shop. She enjoyed what she describes as "a happy, imaginative, and spirited childhood." After earning her B.A. from St. Norbert College and her M.F.A. in acting from Southern Methodist University, Hooyman began working extensively in off-Broadway and regional theater. Along the way she has received numerous acting awards for her work in college and community theater. Not only an actress, she has directed several regional productions, as well as writing and starring in her own one woman show, "A Tale of One City." On the big screen, she appeared with George C. Scott in "Exorcist III," and guest starred on the television program, "Big Brother Jake." In addition, Hooyman has been seen in dozens of commercials. Away from the set of "All My Children," Babs frequently appears at AIDS benefits, and is also a member of The 200 Club in her hometown of Upper Montclair, New Jersey. The actress is married to Jeff Baker, and the couple are currently expecting their first child in July 1992. In her spare time, Babs lists amongst her hobbies, reading, music, stand up comedy, race walking, interior design, refinishing furniture, antiques, and writing.

KAITLIN HOPKINS

Born: February 1, 1964 in New York, New York
Marital Status: single
Height: 5'6" **Eyes:** blue **Hair:** auburn
Education: Carnegie-Mellon University; Royal Academy of Dramatic Arts
Interests: reading, theater, singing, travelling, skiing, museums
Awards: 1991 Miss Golden Globe

Daytime Dramas: "One Life to Live," Paula Simms;
"Another World," Kelsey Harrison, 1992-

Considering her familial ties, it is no surprise that Kaitlin Hopkins has established herself as a talented actress and singer. Included in Kaitlin's family is her mother, the Tony Award winning actress Shirley Knight, her father, Gene Persson, a successful producer, and her stepfather, playwright John Hopkins. Born in New York City on February 11, 1964, Kaitlin first began singing in church, alongside her mother, at the age of three. Two years later, the family moved to London, returning to the U.S. when Kaitlin was twelve years old, at which point she entered the Williston Academy in Northhampton, Massachusetts. It was there that she got her first stage experience, and continued to study theater at Carnegie-Mellon University. Kaitlin also trained in London, receiving a degree in classical theater at the Royal Academy of Dramatic Arts. As a stage actress, Ms. Hopkins has appeared in "Come Back, Little Sheba," an off-Broadway production which also starred her mother, "Bill of Divorcement," with Christopher Walken, "A Victorian Scandal," "The Children's Hour," with Joanne Woodward, "All Summer Long," "The Seagull," "The Master and Margarita," and Kaitlin's favorite musical theater role, Velma in "My Favorite Year." On the big screen, the actress has appeared in "Turk 182," "Spirits," "Runaway Dreams," and "Prisoners," while her television credits include "Gabriel's Fire," "Veronica Claire," the television films "Trial of a Terrorist," "Police Story," and "My Life and Times." On daytime television, Ms. Hopkins briefly portrayed Paula Simms on "One Life to Live," and is presently seen as Kelsey Harrison on "Another World." In 1991, she followed in the distinguished footsteps of Angelica Houston and Melanie Griffith when she held the title of Miss Golden Globe, an honor bestowed by the Foreign Press Association. Not letting her vocal abilities go to waste, Kaitlin stars in her own cabaret act, "Kaitlin Hopkins...In a Heartbeat," as well as singing a mixture of country/rock/blues with the "Kaitlin Hopkins and the Buckskin Bullet Band." Now living in her hometown of New York City, Kaitlin, who is single, is linked romantically with actor Judge Rheinhold. In her spare time, she enjoys travelling, reading, and many outdoor activities, among them skiing and whitewater rafting.

JAMES HORAN

Born: December 14 in Louisville, Kentucky
Marital Status: single
Height: 6'2" **Eyes:** blue **Hair:** light brown
Education: Centre College, B.A.; University of Iowa, Master's Degree
Interests: singing, martial arts

Daytime Dramas: "Another World," Denny Hobson, 1981-1982; **"Edge of Night,"** Sky Witney; **"General Hospital,"** Brett Madison, 1985-1987; **"All My Children,"** Creed Kelley; **"Loving,"** Clay Alden

One of the key ingredients to any good soap, is the character audiences "love to hate," and few actors in daytime drama have fit into that niche more comfortably than James Horan. Born and raised in Louisville, Kentucky, Horan was a star athlete in high school, and continued his success at nearby Centre College, where he lettered in football and track. While at college, Horan's focus shifted from athletics to acting, and he began to appear in school productions. His first stage appearances was as the Marquis de Sade in the school production of "Marat/Sade," and from that moment on Horan knew that his future was as an actor. Driven by this new found passion, Horan enrolled in the masters program at the University of Iowa, where he continued to hone his performing skills. With this solid training, Horan then moved to Hollywood, spending two years as a member of the Colony at the Studio Theater Playhouse theater company. From there he travelled to New York where he began his work on daytime television, appearing on "The Guiding Light," "The Edge of Night," "Another World," "Romance Theater," "All My Children," and ""General Hospital." His other television work includes guest roles on "Dynasty," "Remington Steele," "The Dukes of Hazzard," and "Hunter." Horan made his motion picture debut in "Chattanooga Choo-Choo," which co-starred Barbara Eden and George Kennedy, and has appeared on stage in the Vietnam drama "Strange Snow," for which he received unanimous critical praise. Other stage credits include the New York production of "Duse, Duncan, and Craig." He has also appeared in "The Dream," at Manhattan's U-BU Repertory Theatre. An accomplished singer, as well as actor, Horan performs in nightclubs and fundraising events, and recently toured England in the title role of an original American production of "Phantom of the Opera." Taking a break from daytime, Horan is considering becoming bi-coastal, and pursuing acting jobs on the west coast as well as New York. In his spare time Horan, who reads and speaks German, enjoys running and martial arts.

ALLISON HOSSACK

Born: January 26 in Steinbach, Manitoba, Canada
Marital Status: single
Height: 5'8" **Eyes:** blue-green **Hair:** blond
Education: Brandon University
Interests: dance, singing, water skiing, diving, cycling
Awards: numerous piano competitions

Daytime Dramas: "Another World," Olivia Matthews, 1989-1992

A respected stage actress, Allison Hossack made her television debut in 1989 with the role of ballet dancer, Olivia Matthews on "Another World." Hailing from Canada, Hossack was born on January 26 in Steinbach, Manitoba, and raised in the town of Killarney. She has two older brothers and one younger sister. At the age of six, she began her classical piano training, a skill which earned her top prizes in numerous musical competitions and eventually a scholarship to Brandon University. It was at college that she first began working in theater, changing her major from piano to voice and drama. Allison honed these skills over the summer, spending three seasons working on The Rainbow Stage in Winipeg, where she appeared in such productions as "The Pirates of Penzance," "The Sound of Music," and "Mame." She also studied classical theater at the Banff School in Alberta, showcasing these skills as Titania and Puck in "A Midsummer Night's Dream." Returning to school, Ms. Hossack was performing in a production of "Paper Wheat," when she was discovered by a talent scout, who encouraged her to star in the Muskoka Festival presentation of "They're Playing Our Song." Since then, the actress has gone on to appear in such plays as "Eight to the Bar," "Bedfull of Foreigners," and "Paper, Planets...and other things." A talented singer as well, Ms. Hossack displayed her soprano voice in the opera, "The Medium." Since making her t.v. debut on "Another World," she has gone on to make her movie debut in the Canadian film, "White Light." Allison, who is single, lives in New York City, and lists amongst her hobbies, jazz singing, water skiing, diving, and cycling. She is also a trained ballerina and gymnast, two attributes which suited her perfectly to the role of Olivia Matthews.

DEE HOTY

Born: on August 16
Marital Status: single
Height: 5'9" **Eyes:** blue **Hair:** brown
Education: Otterbein College
Interests: reading, working out, swimming, cooking
Awards: nominated for Outer Critics Circle Award for "City of Angels;" nominated for Tony Award for "The Will Rogers Follies;" 1992 Distinguished Alumnus Award, Otterbein College

Daytime Dramas: "Guiding Light," Mrs. Crown; **"Capitol,"** Andrea; **"As the World Turns,"** Karen Martell, 1992-

With her much lauded performances in "City of Angels" and "The Will Rogers Follies," Dee Hoty has over the past few years established herself as one Broadway's premiere actress. Her performance in the former earned her an Outer Critics Circle Award nomination, while she received a Tony nomination for the latter. On daytime, the talented actress has been seen in recurring roles on "As the World Turns," "Capitol," "Guiding Light," "Ryan's Hope," and "Loving." Born on August 16, Hoty, along with her three siblings, were raised in Lakewood, Ohio, where their parent's were in the restaurant business. She began her career at the Cleveland Playhouse, after studying drama at Otterbein College. Since then, Hoty has built up an impressive list of stage credits, including roles on Broadway in "The Will Rogers Follies," "City of Angels," "Me and My Girl," "Big River," "The Five O'Clock Girl," and "Shakespeare Cabaret." Additionally she has been seen in such off-Broadway and regional productions as "Barnum," with Stacey Keach, "Personals," "Maybe I'm Doing It Wrong," "Forbidden Broadway," "Vanities," "The Golden Apple," "Quilters," "Is There Life After High School," "First Monday in October," "The Club," "Richard III," and "Pal Joey," among others. On the big screen, Hoty has co©starred in "Harry and Walter Go to New York," while her many television credits include "Spenser:

For Hire," "Hi Honey, I'm Home," "Ron Reagan is the President's Son," "The Equalizer," "St. Elsewhere," "It's Your Move," and "An Uncommon Love." Since graduating from college, Ms. Hoty has continued to work with the Otterbein Theatre Development Fund, and out of recognition for her efforts, she received a 1992 Distinguished Alumnus Award. She is also an active member of Broadway Cares and Equity Fights AIDS. Presently living in New York City, Hoty, who is single, enjoys reading, working out, swimming, and cooking. She can soon be seen along with Keith Carradine in the national tour of "The Will Rogers Follies," opening August 1992 in San Francisco.

ELIZABETH HUBBARD

Born: November 22 in New York, New York
Marital Status: divorced, one son, Jeremy
Hair: blond
Education: Radcliffe College; Royal Academy of Dramatic Arts
Interests: theater, writing, travelling
Awards: 1974 Daytime Emmy, Best Actress ("The Doctors"); seven Daytime Emmy nominations for Outstanding Lead Actress ("As the World Turns"); nominated for Soap Opera Award, Outstanding Lead Actress (ATWT); Emmy Award for "First Ladies' Diaries;" Clarance Derwent Award for "The Physicists"

Daytime Dramas: "Guiding Light," Anne Benedict Fletcher, 1962; **"Edge of Night,"** Carol Kramer, 1963; **"The Doctors,"** Dr. Althea Davis, 1964-1982; **"As the World Turns,"** Lucinda Walsh Dixon, 1984-

A longtime soap opera favorite, Elizabeth Hubbard has portrayed Lucinda Walsh Dixon on "As the World Turns" since 1984, and over the past eight years has received a Soap Opera Award nomination and a total of seven Daytime Emmy nominations for Outstanding Lead Actress. Prior to that, Ms. Hubbard spent seventeen years as Dr. Althea Davis on "The Doctors," receiving a 1974 Best Actress Daytime Emmy for her work. In addition, Ms. Hubbard has also appeared on "Edge of Night" and "Guiding Light." Born in New York City, where her mother was a highly respected doctor, Elizabeth attended Radcliffe College, as well as the Royal Academy of Dramatic Arts in London, where she was awarded the prestigious silver medal. She continues to study acting to this day, and along the way has worked with such coaches as the famed Lee Strasberg and Harold Cluman. An accomplished stage actress, her Broadway credits include "Joe Egg," "Children! Children!," "John Gabriel Borkman," "Present Laughter," "Dance a Little Closer," "I Remember Mama," with Liv Ullman, "A Time for Singing," "Look Back in Anger," and "The Physicist," a performance which earned her the Clarance Derwent Award. Off-Broadway and regionally, she has been seen in such productions as "War and Peace," "Uncle Vanya," "The Boys from Syracuse," "The Threepenny Opera," "Blithe Spirit," and "Macbeth." Hubbard has also worked in feature films, co-starring in such popular movies as "Ordinary People," "The Bell Jar," and "I Never Sang for My Father." She has proven herself an Emmy caliber performer on prime television as well, taking home the prize for her portrayal of Edith Wilson in the NBC special, "First Ladies' Diaries," while she was additionally seen in the PBS special, "Ceremony of Innocence." Elizabeth, who is single, currently resides in New York City with her son Jeremy born September 1971, and lists amongst her hobbies writing and travelling.

FIONA HUTCHISON

Born: May 17 in Miami, Florida
Marital Status: single
Height: 5'4"   **Eyes:** blue-gray   **Hair:** honey blond
Education: Royal Ballet School/School of American Ballet
Interests: horseback riding, scuba diving, ballet, driving fast cars

Daytime Dramas: "As the World Turns," Sheila, 1985; **"Guiding Light,"** Molly Patterson, 1986; **"One Life to Live,"** Gabrielle Medina, 1987-1991; **"Guiding Light,"** Jenna Bradshaw, 1992-

A rare individual of talent, poise, and perseverance, Fiona Antionette Hutchison is a woman who refuses to let adversity stand in her way. Born on May 17, in Miami, Florida, where her parents were en route from England to Jamaica, Fiona began life as a dual citizen of the United States and Great Britain. She spent her first ten years living in Jamaica, beginning her classical ballet training at the age of four. An artistic upbringing, Fiona was encouraged to express herself creatively from an early age, this attitude was emphasized most significantly by two prominent artists, her mother, June, and Barrington Watson, a popular Jamaican painter. At the age of ten, Fiona and her family relocated to South Carolina, where once again dancing became an integral part of her life, this time as a member of the Columbia City Ballet. A year later, Ms. Hutchison received a scholarship to London's Royal Ballet School, and after studying in Europe, a second scholarship, this one to the School of American Ballet in New York City, brought Fiona back to the United States. The talented dancer made her professional debut with the American Ballet Theatre, where she worked with the likes of Natalia Makarova and Mikhail Baryshnikov. Following the death of her father, Fiona moved to Florida at the age of eighteen to be with her mother. There she danced with the Miami Conservatory, but her life changed drastically when she suffered a lower spine injury during a rehearsal of "Giselle," an injury that threatened her ability to ever walk again, let alone dance. The next several years were devoted to gruelling rehabilitative therapy, and as a testimony to Fiona's determination and strength of character, she not only regained her ambulatory skills, but has even managed to dance again. While this recovery is truly miraculous, the injury could not be ignored, and Fiona had no other choice but to explore alternate career avenues, the first being a series of modelling assignments for such companies as Maybelline and Loreal. This was soon followed by Hutchison's acting debut, in the television movie, "Mirrors," which lead to small roles on two daytime dramas, "Guiding Light" and "As the World Turns." In 1987, the actress landed her first starring daytime role as Gabrielle Medina on "One Life to Live." She remained on this show for four years, and recently returned to soaps as the sophisticated, eccentric jewel thief, Jenna Bradshaw on "Guiding Light." Along with her television work, Ms. Hutchison has also been seen on the big screen in "Biggles, Adventures in Time," and in the 1987 cult film, "American Gothic," which also starred Rod Steiger and Yvonne DeCarlo. Clearly a person who seeks out a challenge, Fiona has worked extensively on stage as well, portraying Ophelia in a workshop production of "Hamlet," working with the New England Stage Company, and appearing off-Broadway in "Private Lives," and most recently with Tatum O'Neal in "A Terrible Beauty," at the Provincetown Playhouse in New York City. Although her professional dancing career is a thing of the past, Fiona regularly teaches dance classes, and has displayed her skills on television, in a "One Life to Live" fantasy sequence which she also choreographed, and on stage with the Columbia City Ballet, where she danced the role of the Black Queen in a production of "Swan Lake." Taking control of her own career, Fiona recently started her own production company, Hutchison Enterprises, with offices in New York and London. Among the projects in the works for the new company: a situation comedy and a BBC series of documentaries focusing on Jamaican artists, including Barrington Watson, Fiona's early influence. Another potential undertaking for Hutchison Enterprises is "We Can Be" a documentary on one of Fiona's favorite organizations, the

Foundation for Exceptional Children, which encourages the artistic endeavors of exceptional children. The busy actress also sponsors acting seminars, the first one, held in Montclair, New Jersey, proved very successful. Away from her hectic professional life, Fiona, who is single, enjoys such leisure activities as swimming, cooking, horseback riding, scuba diving, and driving fast cars. She presently lives in New York City.

VINCENT IRIZARRY

Born: November 12 in Queens, New York
Marital Status: separated, one daughter, Siena Sophia
Eyes: brown **Hair:** brown
Education: Berklee College of Music, Lee Strasberg Theatre Institute
Interests: music, photography, writing
Awards: nominated for 1986 Daytime Emmy, Outstanding Younger Leading Man ("Guiding Light")

Daytime Dramas: **"Guiding Light,"** Lujack, 1982-1985; **"Santa Barbara,"** Scott Clark, 1988-1990; **"Guiding Light,"** Nick McHenry, 1991-

Few daytime actors are so readily identified with a role as Vincent Irizarry is with the character Lujack, on "Guiding Light." From 1982 to 1985, Irizarry won the hearts of millions for his portrayal of the tough but tender Brandon Lujack, a role which earned him a daytime Emmy nomination in 1986. After leaving the show, the actor worked on several other projects, but in 1991 returned to "Guiding Light," this time as Nick McHenry. A New York City native, Irizarry was born on November 12, and was interested in music from the age of ten. A classically trained pianist, he studied music in high school and then at the Berklee College of Music in Boston. While still in school, a teacher suggested that Vincent try his hand at acting in a school play, an experience that proved so positive that he decided to put aside his music and pursue acting. Remaining in Boston, Irizarry appeared in many local stage productions, before moving to New York in 1979 where he was offered a scholarship to study at the famed Lee Strasberg Theatre Institute. Over the next few years, Vincent landed several off-Broadway roles, while continuing his acting training, as well as studying jazz dance with the Morelli Ballet. His theater credits include roles in "The Death of Von Richthoven," presented at the New York Shakespeare Festival, and as Paul McCartney in "Lennon." At the audition for this role, Irizarry lied about his ability to play the bass, and then spent the next several weeks practicing for fifteen hours every day. Fortunately his music skills had not abandoned him, and come the first day of rehearsal he was able to play all the songs. After only three days as Lujack on "Guiding Light," Irizarry was offered a long term contract, which kept him on the show for the next four years. Following this run, he moved to Los Angeles, where he starred in the television movie "Firefighters," and two popular mini-series, "Echoes in the Darkness" and "Lucky/Chances." In addition he landed guest starring roles on "L.A. Law" and "Mancuso," and co-starred in the feature films, "Heartbreak Ridge," with Clint Eastwood, and "Marie - A True Story." It was however, his work in the television film "Circus," which prompted the producers of "Santa Barbara" to create the role of Scott Clark specifically for Irizarry, who remained with the character for the next two years. Now back in New York, and back on "Guiding Light," he is hoping to create the same excitement around Nick that surrounded Lujack. Vincent recently separated from his wife, actress Signy Coleman (ex Celeste, Santa Barbara), with whom he has one daughter, Siena Sophia, born in 1990. He currently resides in New York City, where he enjoys opera, photography, writing poetry, and honing his classical piano skills.

PAULA IRVINE

Born: June 22, 1968 in Hollywood, California
Marital Status: single
Height: 5'2" **Eyes:** blue **Hair:** blond
Interests: theater

Daytime Dramas: "Santa Barbara," Lillie Blake, 1991-

Born on June 22, 1968, in Hollywood, California, Paula Irvine came upon her love of acting from her grandmother, Kate Doreen Irvine, who herself had been a stage actress in Scotland. Thrilled by her grandmother's stories, Paula, who grew up in Agoura, California with her two sisters, talked about acting so much that her parents enrolled her in drama classes when she was only five years old. She continued to train throughout her childhood, and in addition also developed her dance skills, working for a time with the Los Angeles Ballet Company. Irvine's first professional acting work was providing voice overs for Disney, Superscope, and Hanna-Barbera, and she made her television debut, (body and voice) at the age of seventeen in the t.v. movie, "My Dissident Mom," with Annie Potts. Since then she has guest starred on such shows as "Beverly Hills 90210," "Growing Pains," "Super Mario Brothers," and "A Year in the Life." On the big screen, Ms. Irvine has appeared in "Phantasm II," "Doing Time on Planet Earth," and "Party Camp." Since 1991, the actress has portrayed the energetic Lillie Blake on "Santa Barbara." In between acting assignments, Paula has taken on a number of jobs, the most recent of which was as a Jeep salesman, an occupation which proved profitable both financially and as an acting exercise. Paula, who is single, still lives in Agoura, and remains close with her family and childhood friends.

ANDREW JACKSON

Born: September 11, 1962 in Ontario, Canada
Marital Status: single
Height: 6'3" **Eyes:** blue **Hair:** blond
Education: McMaster University, B.A. in English
Interests: scuba diving, music, sketching, hockey
Awards: Tyrone Guthrie Award for Most Promising Young Actor at Stratford Theater Festival, 1987

Daytime Dramas: "All My Children," Dr. Stephen Hamill, 1991-

As a Canadian citizen, Andrew Jackson, the actor, will never be allowed to hold the same office as his famous ancestor, Andrew Jackson, the United States President. On the other hand it is equally unlikely that Andrew Jackson, the president, will ever enjoy the popularity with daytime fans enjoyed by Andrew Jackson, the actor. Born on September 11, 1962 in Ontario, Canada, Jackson grew up amidst a highly artistic family, which includes his father, a retired armed forces minister and an accomplished trumpet and cornet player, his mother, a high school music teacher, and sister

Deborah, an actress/composer. Andrew's first stage triumph was as Fagin in a high school production of "Oliver," following which he went on to study English at McMaster University. After attending the National Theater School, he landed his first professional role in a futuristic Toronto production of "Macbeth," and continued with the classical motif over the next four years at the famed Stratford Theater. Among the plays in which he performed: "Julius Caesar," "The Merry Wives of Windsor," "Love for Love," "Titus Andronicus," "Comedy of Errors," "The Merchant of Venice," "The Two Gentlemen of Verona," "Trolius and Cressida," "Pride and Prejudice," and "As Is." In 1987, Jackson was awarded the Tyrone Guthrie Award (Jean A. Chalmers Award), a prize given to the most promising young actor at the Stratford Theater Festival. Jackson's big screen credits include "Heavy Metal Summer" and "Red Blooded American Girl," while he has been seen on the small screen in episodes of "Top Cops," "Friday the 13-The Series," "Alfred Hitchcock Presents," and since 1991 as Dr. Stephen Hamill on "All My Children." Now living in New York City, (in the same building as Madonna) the single actor enjoys ice skating, skiing, and scuba diving, an activity he has even attempted in the shark infested waters of the Bahamas. Jackson, following in his father's musical footsteps, also plays both trumpet and synthesizer.

JOANNA JOHNSON

Born: December 31, 1961 in Phoenix, Arizona
Marital Status: single
Height: 5'7" **Eyes:** blue **Hair:** blond
Education: University of Southern California, B.A.
Interests: directing, writing, travelling, sports

Daytime Dramas: "The Bold and the Beautiful,"
Caroline Spencer, 1987-1990; Faith Roberts, 1991-

An actress and director, Joanna Johnson recently returned to "The Bold and the Beautiful" after a one year absence. From 1987 to 1990 she portrayed Caroline Spencer, and now has reappeared as Caroline's brunette cousin, Faith Roberts. Joanna was born on December 31, 1961 in Phoenix, Arizona, where her father is a produce broker. Her mother died, unexpectedly , of a heart attack several years ago. The third of four children, (three girls, one boy) Joanna's initial show business ambition was to become a director, a skill she pursued at USC film school, where she produced and directed several student projects. After receiving her degree she put her skills to work, writing and producing medical training films for the Hospital Satellite Network. Deciding that a good director must understand actors, Ms. Johnson began acting training with Darryl Hickman and at Peggy Feury's Shakespeare Workshop, where her talent soon caught the attention of producers. Her first role was as a guest star on "The New Mike Hammer," which was followed by a part in the feature film, "Killer Party." Joanna's additional t.v. credits include "Twilight Zone" and "Riptide." In between acting assignments, she held a number of odd jobs, among them a stint as an assistant manager of a West Hollywood art gallery. Although back in front of the screen, Joanna still pursues work behind the screen, writing, and hopefully, soon again as a director. Away from "The Bold and the Beautiful," the actress donates her time to Project Angel Food and the Family Assistance Program. A serious athlete, Joanna lists amongst her hobbies, jogging, horseback riding, tennis, boxing, and weightlifting.

MELINA KANAKAREDES

Born: April 23 in Akron, Ohio
Marital Status: engaged to Peter Constantinides
Height: 5'7" **Eyes:** green **Hair:** brown
Education: Point Park College, Bachelor's Degree
Interests: swimming
Awards: 1977 first runner-up, Miss Ohio Pageant; Miss Columbus 1986; 1992 Soap Opera Award nomination for Outstanding Female Newcomer

Daytime Dramas: "Guiding Light," Eleni, 1991-

A woman of talent, beauty, and a really long name, Melina Kanakaredes was born on April 23 in Akron, Ohio. Her father owns an insurance agency, her mother a candy store, yet from an early age Melina knew that she wanted to be an actress. The youngest of three girls, she began singing and dancing professionally at the age of eight, when she portrayed Becky Thatcher in a local musical production of "Tom Sawyer." Melina continued her regional theater work while attending Litchfield Junior High and Firestone Senior High School, moving on to Ohio State upon graduation. She remained at this school for only a year before transferring to Point Park College in Pittsburgh. However, during that one year she met Peter Constantinides, to whom she is now engaged. While at Point Park College, Melina embarked on a successful modelling career, as well as working in commercials and industrial films. She continues to appear in numerous commercials; watch for her in Sony, Diet Rite Cola, Hyundia, K-Mart, Rave and Semicid contraceptives. In addition she was also named Miss Columbus in 1986, and was the first runner up in the Miss Ohio Pageant of the following year. After graduating cum laud with a degree in musical theater, Melina moved to New York City where she found work in such stage productions as the off-Broadway musical "State of the Art," at Steve McGraw's cabaret. Her other theater credits include "Evita," "42nd Street," "Romeo and Juliet," "Candide" and most recently as Mary Magdalene in "Jesus Christ Superstar" at the Fulton Theatre in Pittsburgh. On television Melina has appeared in the made for cable film "Cartes," as well as on "One Life to Live" and "Comedy Shorts" which aired on HA Cable Network, now known as Comedy Central. In April of 1991 she debuted as Eleni on "Guiding Light," and from the moment she auditioned, it was clear that no other actress could play the part. Her accent, which Melina borrowed from her grandmother, added a perfect touch of authenticity; not to mention the fact that Frank Dicopoulus, who plays Frank Cooper, happened to be an old friend of the Kanakaredes family. (Frank was unaware that she was auditioning) Off screen she is involved with the Starlight Foundation. For Melina, family remains the most important influence in her life, and she makes regular trips back to Ohio to visit her parents and sisters.

LENORE KASDORF

Born: July 27 in Fort Totten, New York
Marital Status: divorced, one daughter, Vanessa
Height: 5'5" **Eyes:** hazel **Hair:** brown
Education: Butler University
Interests: camping, animals, horseback riding, gardening, reading

Daytime Dramas: "Guiding Light," Rita Stapleton Bauer, 1975-1981; **"Days of Our Lives,"** Dr. Stephanie Kimball, 1983; **"Santa Barbara,"** Caroline Wilson, 1986-1987

A popular actress, Lenore Kasdorf's career has included television, feature films, and theater. On daytime, she has portrayed prominent roles on "Days of Our Lives," "Santa Barbara," and "Guiding Light." Born on July 27, in Fort Totten, New York, an army post where her father was an officer, Lenore's family also includes her mother, a homemaker, and one older sister. After attending Butler University, where she majored in English and minored in psychology, Lenore relocated to Los Angeles to pursue a professional acting career. Since then she has co-starred in such feature films as "L.A. Bounty,""Nervous Ticks," "The Kid," "Missing in Action," and "Where Does it Hurt?," while she has had appeared on dozens of television shows among them, a recurring role on "Coach," "Pros and Cons," "Beverly Hills 90210," "In the Heat of the Night," "21 Jump Street," "Jake and the Fatman," "Murder, She Wrote," "Houston Knights," "Airwolf," "Riptide," "Moonlighting," "Highway to Heaven," "Matlock," "Simon and Simon," "The A Team," and "Magnum P.I.." Ms. Kasdorf has additionally been seen in several television movies and pilots, including "The Woman who Sinned," with Susan Lucci, "Dinner at Eight," "A Different Affair," "Covenant," and "Two and a Half Dads." A theater actresses as well, she has performed on stage in "Everything in the Garden," "The Balcony," "The Death of Bessie Smith," "Period of Adjustment," "Natural Affection," and "Star Spangled." For many years, Ms. Kasdorf served on S.A.G. committees, but now devotes much of her spare time to animal shelters and helping relocate lost pets, as well as serving on the P.T.A. at her daughter, Vanessa's school. Although she realizes the importance of committee work, Kasdorf prefers the hands on involvement of the work she is doing now. A Los Angeles resident, Lenore, who is divorced, lists amongst her interests camping, biking, horseback riding, water skiing (which she use to do competitively), gardening, reading, cooking, making wreaths and baskets, and according to Ms. Kasdorf, "when I'm being good, working out."

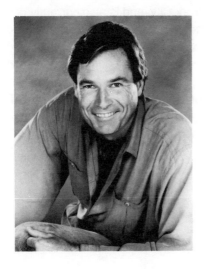

BEAU KAYZER

Born: May 27 in suburban Toronto, Canada
Marital Status: single
Height: 6'3" **Eyes:** hazel **Hair:** brown
Education: The Stella Adler Acting School
Interests: tennis, guitar, traveling

Daytime Dramas: "The Young and the Restless," Brock Reynolds, 1974-1980, 1984-

Knowing that he wanted to pursue a career in acting and music, Beau Kazer left high school at sixteen. Born May 27 outside of Toronto, Canada, Beau spent three years honing his skills at the Stella Adler Acting School. After graduation Beau quickly secured guest starring roles on television shows such as "Love Boat," "Harry O," "Hart to Hart," and "Barnaby Jones." He was also featured in the NBC mini-series "Glitter Dome," and starred in the NBC pilot "Hardcase," a police drama. Beau originated the role of Brock Reynolds in 1974 and enjoys playing the compassionate son of Kay Chancellor. His feature film debut was in the critically acclaimed/box office hit, "Taxi Driver" starring Robert DeNiro and Jodie Foster. When not working Beau enjoys traveling, playing tennis and playing his guitar. He has composed several albums of his music.

SUSAN KEITH

Born: September 30 in Milwaukee, Wisconsin
Marital Status: married to actor James Kiberd on May 17, 1986
Height: 5'3" **Eyes:** blue **Hair:** strawberry blond
Education: Goodman School of Drama
Interests: cooking, sports

Daytime Dramas: "One Life to Live," Samantha Vernon, 1979; **"Another World,"** Cecile de Poulignac, 1979-1981; **"Loving,"** Shana Vochek, 1983-1989, 1991-

An actress and a writer, Susan Keith's portrayal of Shana Vochek on "Loving" has been one of daytime television's highlights for almost ten years. Originally set on another vocation, Susan, who hails from Crystal Lake, Illinois, studied speech therapy at Illinois' Barat College, before deciding on pursuing her acting dream. She transferred to The Goodman School of Drama in Chicago, landing her first role, Samantha Vernon on "One Life to Live," just prior to her graduation. Relocating to New York City, Susan made her daytime debut in 1979. However, after a short time she moved onto her next soap opera role, Cecile de Poulignac on "Another World," whom she portrayed for the next two years. In 1983, the producers of "Loving" offered her the part of Shana, the beautiful and strong willed lawyer, a role for which Susan is ideally suited. For the next six years the actress won the hearts of daytime fans, who protested greatly when she left the show. Not one to disappoint the public, Susan returned to "Loving" in 1991. An aspiring writer, Susan spends much of her time working at The Writers Theater in New York City, and is also currently developing a television project for a major production company. Susan's most recent theatrical work was the production of "A Doll's House," presented at The Actors Outlet. Regarding her personal life, Susan makes up one half of what could be called todays first couple of daytime drama. She and her husband, James Kiberd of "All My Children," live in a 120 year old Victorian home in the suburbs of New York City, with their dog, Omen, and cat, Caliban. The couple met when Susan auditioned, with James, for the role of Shana - he advised the producers not to pick her; she appeared cold. The mutual dislike obviously dissipated and even though they no longer work together, they work in the same building, and the now happy couple get to commute to work together. A gourmet cook and sports lover, Susan spends much of her free time hiking, ice skating, bowling, and developing her Tai Chi skills.

PETER KELEGHAN

Born: September 16, 1959
Marital Status: married for ten years, one daughter, Shauna
Height: 6'1" **Eyes:** blue **Hair:** brown
Education: York University, B.A.; London Academy of
Music and Dramatic Arts
Interests: airplanes, movies, animals

Daytime Dramas: "General Hospital," Barry Durbin, 1992-

A new face on the daytime scene, Peter Keleghan made his soap opera debut as Barry Durbin on "General Hospital." Born on September 16, 1959, Keleghan was raised, along with his sister Teresa, in Montreal, Canada. According to Keleghan the atmosphere at home was "very loving." After receiving his B.A. from York University, Peter attended the London Academy of Music and Dramatic Arts, following which he began his professional career, working in both London and the United States. On stage, Keleghan has performed with the Second City organization, appearing in such productions as, "Waiter, Waiter, There's Soup On My Fly," "The Duck Stops Here," and "Reach Out And Punch Someone," while his additional theater credits include "Cyrano De Bergerac," "Caesar And Cleopatra," "Twelfth Night Blues," "Suits," "Tartuffe," "Uncle Vanya," and "Richard III." Along with "General Hospital," Peter has guest starred on such shows as "This Just In," "Cheers," "Davis Rules," "Baby Talk," "Top Cops," "Street Legal," "Sunday Funnies," "Super Dave Osborne," and as a writer/co-star on "The Comedy Mill." In addition, the actor has worked in commercials and provided voices for cartoon characters. Now living in Los Angeles, Keleghan and his wife of ten years recently became the proud parents of their first child, Shauna Taylor. An active supporter of Greenpeace, Peter, who is a licensed private pilot, enjoys going to the movies and playing with Jackson, his seven year old Sheltie.

JAMES KIBERD

Born: July 6 in Providence, Rhode Island
Marital Status: married to actress Susan Keith on May 17, 1986
Height: 6' **Eyes:** brown **Hair:** light brown
Education: University of Pennsylvania
Interests: art, theater
Awards: Best Actor from Soap Opera Digest, 1983 ("Loving"); Best Single Scene, Soap Opera Digest, 1985; 1992 Soap Opera Award nomination for Outstanding Comic Performance

Daytime Dramas: "Loving," Mike Donovan, 1983-1985;
"All My Children," Trevor Dillion, 1989-

One of daytime's finest actors, James Kiberd manages to translate his own eccentricities and passions onto the screen, in the process creating some of television's most vivid characterizations. Kiberd is a man who requests no novocaine from the dentist, frequently rewrites his own scenes, and upon joining the cast of "All My Children," presented the writers with a fifteen page exegesis of what he believed to be his character's life story. Yet despite the waves he certainly must create, the results of his efforts are obvious to anyone who has seen him on either "Loving" or "All My Children." Known for years as an artist, Kiberd, a native of Providence, Rhode Island, began painting portraits as a child. His teenage years found the young artist developing an abstract style, which eventually evolved into a more traditional figurative approach during his stint at the University of Pennsylvania's Graduate School of Fine Arts. Not a great student, Kiberd often found himself at odds with the system, and after jumping from undergraduate sophomore to graduate student, he decided to leave school entirely and go to Europe. Returning to the United States, James settled in an artist's colony, located in New York's Rockland County. For the next few years he concentrated on his art work, and continues to paint prolifically. His talents have been recognized by such organizations as the New York State Council on the Arts, the National Endowment for the Arts, and the America the Beautiful Fund. Among his most recent works are oil paintings which depict a widely divergent range of subjects, from an Indian summer, to the Berlin Wall, to the injustices of South Africa. Towards the end of the seventies, Kiberd served as executive director of a local cultural institution, assisting the bi-lingual community in developing it's own cultural and artistic identity. For his efforts the community opened an art gallery in Kiberd's honor. In 1980, Kiberd finally branched out into acting when he joined Rockland County's Penguin Repertory Company. A fan of both the classics and experimental theater, Kiberd's stage credits include "Death of a Salesman," "The Seagull," "Who's Afraid of Virginia Woolf," "Recent Developments in Southern Connecticut," and "Veteran's Day." Never one to settle, Kiberd continues to study his craft with Uta Hagen. His first foray into daytime drama was as the emotionally wounded Vietnam veteran, Mike Donovan on "Loving." His raw, passionate performance earned him a 1983 Best Actor Award from Soap Opera Digest, who again singled out Kiberd's work two years later. This 1985 award was in recognition of the emotional scenes surrounding his character's visit to the Vietnam Memorial in Washington D.C. Along with "All My Children," Kiberd has also appeared on "Another World," "As the World Turns," and "Spencer: For Hire." In the past, Kiberd has shared his expertise with aspiring actors at the Warren Robertson Studio, where he co-developed "the core technique," an acting style which relies on, among other things, repetitive sound and movement. The award winning actor married Susan Keith of "Loving" in 1986, and the two presently live in a 120 year old Victorian home in Westchester County, New York. The couple are proud owners of a siamese cat and a rottweiler dog.

Amelia Kinkade

AMELIA KINKADE

Born: December 31 in Denton, Texas
Marital Status: single
Height: 5'5" **Eyes:** brown **Hair:** brown
Education: Interlochen Arts Academy
Interests: writing, cooking, dancing, travelling, singing

Daytime Dramas: "The Young and the Restless," Vivian Peterson

Since her first big break, starring in the Stray Cats video, "Sexy and Seventeen," Amelia Kinkade has landed roles in both film and television, and can now be seen as Vivian Peterson on "The Young and the Restless." Born on December 31 in Denton, Texas, Kinkade was raised in nearby Forth Worth, before relocating to Michigan at the age of ten. A straight A student, she graduated two years early from the renowned Interlochen Arts Academy, following which she moved to Los Angeles in search of acting roles. After appearing in the "Sexy and Seventeen" video, Amelia quickly found work in other music videos, following which she began to become a familiar face in national commercials, most notably as the featured model for Redekin hair products. During this time, she continued to hone her acting skills, studying at the Creative Actor's Workshop and with such coaches as Robert Lewis and Lilyan Chauvin. This soon paid off, and Amelia found herself a much sought after television guest star, appearing on such shows as "Fame," "The Golden Girls," "Misfits of Science," "Mama's Family," "Dirty Dancing," "Knightrider," "Capitol," and "General Hospital." The actress' feature film credits include: "Night of the Demons," "Body Rock," "Breakin' II," "Fast Forward," "Girls Just Want to Have Fun," "Kissing Dangerously," and "Roadhouse." Several of these films displayed Amelia's dancing expertise, while she is additionally a trained choreographer, a task she took on for the television series, "What a Country." Presently living in Los Angeles, Kinkade, who is single, enjoys dancing, singing, playing the piano, traveling, cooking, and renting old movies. She also returned to school recently, studying screenwriting at UCLA. A strong believer in animal rights, Ms. Kinkade donates much of her spare time to the organization, PETA (People for the Ethical Treatment of Animals).

MAEVE KINKEAD

Born: May 31 in New York, New York
Marital Status: married to Harry Streep, December 31, 1980, two children, Abraham and Maude
Height: 5'5" **Eyes:** blue **Hair:** black
Education: Radcliffe, Harvard University, London Academy of Music and Dramatic Arts
Interests: theater, dance
Awards: 1992 Daytime Emmy-Outstanding Supporting Actress; 1985 Daytime Emmy nomination-Outstanding Supporting Actress; 1992 Soap Opera Award nomination-Outstanding Supporting Actress

Daytime Dramas: "Another World," Angie Perrini, 1977-1980; **"Guiding Light,"** Vanessa Lewis, 1980-

A television and theater actress, Maeve Kinkead has portrayed Vanessa Lewis on "Guiding Light" since 1980, along the way earning two Daytime Emmy nominations for Outstanding Supporting Actress, a prize she took home in 1992. She was additionally nominated for a Soap Opera Award in the Supporting Actress category. Prior to joining "Guiding Light," Ms. Kinkead appeared on "Another World" for three years as Angie Perrini. Born on May 31 in New York City, where both her parents worked for the New Yorker magazine, Maeve attended Radcliffe College, with the initial intention of becoming an English teacher. However, after becoming involved with productions at Harvard's Loeb Drama Center, she quickly found her focus shifting to the stage. While in school, Kinkead performed in several productions, including "Coriolanus," "Tis Pity She's a Whore," "The Rivals," "Peer Gynt," and "A View from the Bridge." The actress also worked with The Concord Players in "The Three Sisters," a role she re-created for a Boston Public Television presentation. Moving to London, Ms. Kinkead studied at the London Academy of Music and Dramatic Art, where she took part in such classics as "The Importance of Being Earnest," "Twelfth Night," and "Patience." Since 1980, Maeve who lives in a suburb of New York, has been married to Harry Streep, a dancer/choreographer, with whom she has two children, Abraham (10/81) and Maude (8/84). Show business runs in their family- Maeve's sister in law is award winning actress, Meryl Streep.

MICHAEL E. KNIGHT

Born: May 7 in Princeton, New Jersey
Marital Status: married to actress Catherine Hickland on June 27, 1992
Height: 6'1" **Eyes:** blue **Hair:** light brown
Education: Wesleyan University, Bachelor in Theater Arts
Interests: theater
Awards: Daytime Emmy for Outstanding Younger Leading Man, 1986, 1987; nominated in 1985

Daytime Dramas: "All My Children," Tad Martin, 1982-1986, 1988-1990

Michael Knight established himself as one of daytime's premiere actors with his portrayal of Tad Martin on "All My Children." During his six years as Tad, Knight earned two Daytime Emmys for Outstanding Younger Leading Man, and was nominated a third time. He was also invited, with then co-star Patrick Stuart, to a White House reception given by President and Mrs. Bush. Born on May 7 in Princeton, New Jersey, Knight, along with his two brothers, spent most of his childhood in Ojai, California, where his father was a faculty member at a boys preparatory school, which Michael attended. The family relocated a second time, to San Francisco, where Michael lived until enrolling at Wesleyan University in Middletown, Connecticut. Committed to acting since the age of twelve, he majored in theater arts at Wesleyan, graduating in just three years and immediately moving to New York City, where he continued his training at the Circle in the Square Theater. After graduating from this institution in 1982, he began his professional career, concentrating chiefly on stage work. Since then, Knight has worked in several theatrical productions, among them, "Absurd Person Singular," "Enemies," and "Call Back- A Duel in One Act," an off off-Broadway production that he starred in as well as produced. Recently Michael appeared off-Broadway in "House Games," reprising a role he had originally played in an American Stage Company production at Farleigh Dickinson University. Along with his work on "All My Children," the actor has guest starred on "Matlock," and appeared in the television film, "Charles and Diana," as well as being seen on the big screen in "Date with an Angel" and "Baby It's You." He was most recently seen in the 1992 series, "Grapevine." Married in 1992 to actress Catherine Hickland, who (consider this) was previously married to David Hasselhorf, most famous for playing the role of *Michael Knight* on "Knight Rider."

MIA KORF

Born: November 1 in Ithaca, New York
Marital Status: married to Jeffrey LeBeau, July 7, 1991
Height: 5'6" **Eyes:** brown **Hair:** black
Education: Cornell University, Julliard School of Music
Interests: fresh water fishing, basketball, racquetball, jewelry design, cooking, collector of antique watches and old pez dispensers

Daytime Dramas: "Another World," "Loving," Mei Lin'g; **"One Life to Live,"** Blair, 1991-

While all actors inject some of their own personalities into the parts they play, the character of Blair on "One Life to Live" bore a striking resemblance to Mia Korf long before she was even cast. Both are from upstate New York, both are Scorpios, and both enjoy designing their own jewelry; of course Mia isn't a mystery woman who blew into town for the sole purpose of carrying out an elaborate revenge plot, but the similarities had to end somewhere. Born on November 1 in Ithaca, New York, Mia was a serious musician from an early age, studying classical violin for eighteen years, most recently at the Julliard School of Music. She opted for a college close to home, majoring in drama at Cornell University, where she developed an affinity for stage work. Since leaving school, Mia has been involved with a number of prestigious theatrical productions, including "The Seagull," "Three Sisters," "Godspell," Viola in "Twelfth Night," Maria Shabata in "O' Pioneers!," Perdita in "The Winter's Tale," and "Two Gentlemen of Verona," which was presented by the New York Shakespeare Festival. On television Mia has been seen as Dr. Rosenthal, Blair Brown's OB-GYN in "The Days and Nights of Molly Dodd," "Dream Street," "True Blue," "Another World," "Loving," and numerous commercials. In July of 1991, just one month before joining "One Life to Live," Mia was married to actor Jeffrey LeBeau. Despite the time constraints the couple did manage to visit Paris and Belgium for their honeymoon, a trip no doubt made easier by Mia's fluency in French. When she's not working Mia enjoys fresh water fishing, basketball, collecting antique watches and pez dispensers, and designing her own jewelry. This last hobby, which she shares with her on-screen alter ego, has turned into a possible business venture for Mia, whose jewelry can often be seen on "One Life to Live." The actress hopes to start a possible mail order company with her husband, from which the profits would go to various charities, such as the GMHC (Gay Men's Health Center), The Actor's Fund, and Equity Fights AIDS - three charities Mia actively supports.

ALLA KOROT

Born: November 1, 1970 in Odessa, USSR
Marital Status: single
Eyes: brown   **Hair:** brown
Education: UCLA
Interests: skiing, horseback riding, travelling, opera, bowling
Awards: 1992 Soap Opera Award, Outstanding Newcomer;
1991 Daytime Emmy nomination, Outstanding Younger Actress;
1987 Miss California T.E.E.N.

Daytime Dramas: "Another World," Jenna Norris, 1990-

From Soviet citizen, to American ballerina, to daytime drama star, Alla Korot's life has taken many changes during the course of her twenty one years. Alla was born on November 1, 1970 in what was then Odessa, USSR, where her father, Alex, worked as an engineer/broker/musician, and her mother, Elena, a business entrepreneur and musician. The family immigrated to San Francisco when Alla was six years old. It appears she adjusted well to American life, dividing up her school years between academics and the arts, attending Mercy High School, the Nova Academy (a performing arts school),and UCLA, along the way pursuing numerous performing avenues. She began studying ballet at the age of nine, and later spent six years touring with the Ballet Celeste International. Alla also dabbled in jazz and modern dance, skills she displayed as a featured soloist at Mercy High School. In 1987, she won the title of Miss California T.E.E.N., beating out 110 other contestants in this contest which stressed academics and achievements. Moving to Los Angeles, Ms. Korot enrolled at UCLA, but soon began to pursue acting roles, appearing in such feature films as "Angelique" and "Night of the Cyclone." In 1990, she joined the cast of "Another World" as Jenna Norris, and has since earned a Soap Opera Award for Outstanding Newcomer, as well as a daytime Emmy nomination for Outstanding Younger Actress. In addition, she recently made a guest appearance on "Parker Lewis Can't Lose." Alla, who is single, now lives in New York City, where her hobbies include dancing, skiing, horseback riding, bowling, travelling, and going to the opera.

LAUREN KOSLOW

Born: March 9 in Boston, Massachusetts
Marital Status: married to Nick Schillace, two children,
Zachary and Milli Kate
Hair: brown
Education: Virginia State University, Bachelor's Degree
Interests: drawing, travelling
Awards: award for production design at American College
Theater Festival

Daytime Dramas: "The Young and the Restless,"
Lindsay Wells, 1984-1986; **"The Bold and the Beautiful,"**
Margo Lynley, 1987-1992

Over the past eight years, Lauren Koslow has portrayed two popular daytime characters, Lindsay Wells on "The Young and the Restless," and most recently Margo Lynley on "The Bold and the Beautiful." A Boston native, Lauren, who was raised in Massachusetts and Rhode Island, attended the University of Massachusetts, where she studied sculpture and wildlife management. Moving south, she transferred to Virginia State University, pursuing a degree in the theater arts, specifically costume design. Her work on a production of "Waiting for Godot" earned Lauren an award at the American College Theater Festival, at the Kennedy Center in Washington D.C.. After graduating, she signed on as a costume designer/actress with a summer stock theater company in Virginia. Following a season, during which she worked on such productions as "Idiot's Delight" and "The Good Doctor," Lauren switched over to full time actress, and went on to perform in numerous regional productions, among them "Cat on A Hot Tin Roof," "How the Other Half Lives," "Never Too Late," "Ten Little Indians," "Dial M for Murder," and "The Importance of Being Earnest," as well as in the Atlanta Shakespeare Festival productions of "Two Gentlemen of Verona" and "Tartuffe." Looking to pursue television work, Koslow then moved to Los Angeles, where she landed roles on such programs as "Harper Valley P.T.A.," "The New Mike Hammer," "House Calls," "The A Team," and "Spies." Since 1988 the actress has been married to Nick Schillace, a make up artist for "Knots Landing," and the couple have two children, Zachary and Milli Kate (October 1990). Zachary can be seen as baby Mark on "The Bold and the Beautiful." Away from the set, Lauren enjoys travelling, painting, and taking car of her pets, which include two cats, George and Martha, and a pit bull, Butch.

WORTHAM KRIMMER

Marital Status: married to Mary Wortham-Krimmer, one son,
Max
Eyes: brown **Hair:** brown
Education: University of California at Berkeley
Interests: the environment, sailing

Daytime Dramas: "Days of Our Lives," Cal Winters;
"One Life to Live," Rev. Andrew Carpenter, 1991-

Once set on being an environmental lawyer, Wortham Krimmer was in the midst of law school when he received a scholarship offer from the American Conservatory Theater in San Francisco. Although committed to his legal studies, Krimmer, who had acted in school and community productions, decided to follow his heart and pursue an acting career. Luckily, Krimmer came to this decision *before* taking his mid-term exams. Wortham, who worked for a spell at the Environmental Protection Agency, continues to dedicate himself to environmental causes, most recently producing the educational video, "What You Can Do To Save The Planet," which was shown to grade school children throughout California. Since deciding on acting, he has appeared in several stage productions, including, "Tamara," "The Cherry Orchard," "Richard III," and "A Month in the Country," while his television credits include, "Knots Landing," "Newhart," "Cop Rock," "Hill Street Blues," and recurring roles on "The Paper Chase" and "Max Headroom." Now playing one of daytime's most compassionate characters, the Reverend Andrew Carpenter on "One Life to Live," Krimmer was previously seen on daytime, originating the role of Cal Winters on "Days of Our Lives." In addition, he will soon be making his feature film debut opposite Janet Leigh in "Sensei." The actor's real name is Robert Krimmer, but changed his name to Robert Wortham Krimmer when he married Mary Wortham fifteen years ago. Soon however, he was told that the full three names was too long, and so out of admiration for Mary, and all the support she gave him, he dropped the Robert from his professional name. Since they met at their Colorado college, Mary has been extremely successful as well, starting her own health and fitness company, and now flexing her skills as a photographer. Her work was most recently exhibited in Los Angeles, where she received glowing reviews. The couple, along with their son, Max, now live in suburban New York, and they spend a great deal of time enjoying the outdoors.

ILENE KRISTEN

Born: July 30 in Brooklyn, New York
Marital Status: single
Height: 5'2" **Eyes:** blue **Hair:** blond
Education: Professional Children's School
Interests: running, singing
Awards: Best Supporting Actress by T.V. Guide, 1990

Daytime Dramas: "Ryan's Hope," Deila Reid Ryan Ryan Coleridge Crane III, 1975-1978, 1982-1983, 1986-1989; **"One Life to Live,"** Georgina Whitman; **"Loving,"** Norma Gilpin

She is best known to daytime audiences as the oft married vixen Deila Reid Ryan Ryan Coleridge Crane III, on "Ryan's Hope." More recently she portrayed the antithesis of her old character, the warm hearted Norma Gilpin on "Loving." Born and raised in New York City, Ilene Kristen attended the Professional Children's School. Since then her career has branched off into numerous directions. She has appeared on Broadway in "Henry Sweet Henry" and "Grease," and off-Broadway in "Light Up the Sky," "Strange Behavior," and "Mayor," in which she had the honor of playing Leona Helmsley. Kristen has also appeared on the television series, "Family " and many t.v. specials. Away from her dramatic roles, Kristen is also an accomplished singer, performing in many of New York's top night clubs. Off screen, Ilene spent much of her time volunteering at the now closed Prince George Hotel homeless shelter in New York City, and she still works closely with many of the former residents. To keep in shape she tries to run six miles each day.

JOE LANDO

Born: December 9 in Chicago, Illinois
Marital Status: single
Height: 5'11"   **Eyes:** blue   **Hair:** brown
Education: Prairie View High School; Vincent Chase training
Interests: photography, cooking, camping

Daytime Dramas: "One Life to Live," Jake Harrison

Joe Lando makes his daytime debut with the role of Jake Harrison on "One Life to Live." Born in Chicago and raised in Prairie View, Illinois, Lando was raised on old movies, and always knew that he wanted to be an actor. After graduating high school, Lando chose not to go into the family fishing business, and with $400 in his pocket moved from Prairie View to Los Angeles, where he studied acting with Vincent Chase. Lando supported himself by working with caterers on such movies as "Silkwood," and as a chef in various restaurants, including Santopierto's; a popular restaurant owned by Vanna White's husband. Joe landed t.v. work on the series "Nightingales," as well as in the pilot "Pros and Cons." Aside from catering food to feature films, he taught Kevin Kline and Tracey Ullman how to twirl pizza dough for their roles in "I Love You to Death," a movie he was also featured in. (he was given credit as a technical advisor for his pizza throwing lessons). He also appeared in the film, "Star Trek IV" Away from his work on "One Life to Live," Lando enjoys practicing his culinary skills, as well as being an avid outdoorsman, who lists among his favorite pastimes hiking, camping, and rock climbing. Since leaving "One Life to Live" in 1991 (he did come back briefly in 1992), Joe has signed a contract with CBS to star in a series pilot.

CHARLEY LANG

Born: October 24 in New Jersey
Marital Status: single
Height: 5'11"   **Eyes:** brown   **Hair:** brown
Education: Catholic University, B.F.A. in Drama
Interests: directing, swimming, painting, sign language
Awards: Golden Eagle Award for directing "Once In A Blue Moon;" Helen Hayes Award for directing the play, "The Foreigner;" Walter Kerr Award for Outstanding Artistic Achievement at Catholic University

Daytime Dramas: "Days of Our Lives," Robert Stemkowski, 1991-1992

An up and coming actor and director, Charley Lang recently made his daytime debut on "Days of Our Lives." Born on October 24, Lang and his family travelled between their London and New Jersey homes. Along with Charley, the Lang family consists of three boys and two girls, as well as Charley's father, a biochemical engineer, and his mother, an assistant to Calvin Klein. After graduating from Depaul High School, in Wayne, New Jersey, Lang enrolled as a drama major at Catholic University. Receiving his B.F.A., he quickly found work on the stage and screen. He has appeared on Broadway in "Da," "Strange Interlude," "Mass Appeal," and "Once A Catholic," and on the big screen in "Bird," "Ragtime," and "Danger Sign." In addition to his work in the made for television movies "Kent State," "First Affair," "The Gentlemen Bandit," "The Late Great Me," and "Mister Roberts," Lang has guest starred on numerous prime time series, including "L.A. Law," "Murphy Brown," "Reasonable Doubts," "Matlock," "Tour of Duty," "Alien Nation," and "Star Trek: The Next Generation." Equally passionate about directing, Lang has called the shots on several theatrical productions as well as the film "Once In A Blue Moon." Seen on Showtime in 1991, this work earned Lang the Golden Eagle Award. He has additionally been recognized with the Walter Kerr Award, for Outstanding Artistic Achievement at Catholic University and the Helen Hayes Award for his direction of the play "The Foreigner." Lang recently directed a music video for the Johnny Mathis song, "Misty." The video is released to bars and clubs and audiences are invited to sing along to them, a popular new concept called karaoke. The Japanese have been doing this in the Orient for a few years with great success. Lang, who is unmarried and lives in Los Angeles, is a volunteer with Project Angel Food, as well as being on the board of directors of the Ensemble Studio Theater in L.A.. Charley lists among his interests, directing, swimming, movies, sign language, and painting.

KATHERINE KELLY LANG

Born: July 25 in Los Angeles, California
Marital Status: married to Skott Snider, one son, Jeremy
Eyes: blue   **Hair:** blond
Education: Beverly Hills High School
Interests: horseback riding, surfing, tennis, skiing
Awards: 1990 Soap Opera Award nomination for "Outstanding Heroine;" Two consecutive M.V.P. Awards from Soap Opera Update Magazine

Daytime Dramas: "The Young and the Restless," Gretchen; **"The Bold and the Beautiful,"** Brooke Logan,1987-

One of daytime's most popular actresses, Katherine Kelly Lang has portrayed Brooke Logan on "The Bold and the Beautiful" since the show's premiere in 1987. For her work, she received a 1990 Soap Opera Digest nomination for "Outstanding Heroine," and in addition was twice named Most Valuable Player, an award presented annually by Soap Opera Update Magazine. Born in Los Angeles, Lang hails from a show business family, which includes her father, Keith Wegeman, a former Olympic Long Jump Skier who went on to appear as the Jolly Green Giant on television, her mother, Judith Lang, a film and television actress, and her grandfather, Charles Lang, a renowned cinematographer. Katherine got her professional start shortly after graduating from Beverly Hills High School, when she landed the lead role in "Skate Town U.S.A.," a film which also marked the big screen debut of Patrick Swayze. Following this role, Lang went on to appear in several other feature films, among them "Evilspeak," "The Nightstalker," and "Delta Fever." On television, she has guest starred on such shows as "Happy Days," "Masquerade," "Magnum P.I.," "The Last Precinct," "Crazy Like a Fox," and "First and Ten," while she has additionally starred in the television film, "Mr. Boogedy." Before joining the cast of "The Bold and the Beautiful," Lang had a brief stint at Gretchen on "The Young and the Restless." The quintessential California beauty, she has also been seen in several Beach Boys music videos. When not on the set, Ms. Lang is a much sought after international model, as well as devoting much of her time to voice, jazz dance, and ballet training. A long time sports fan, Katherine enjoys tennis, surfing, skiing, mountain biking, and jogging. In addition, she owns several Arabian horses, and frequently competes in both twenty five and fifty mile cross country endurance races throughout southern California. Lang shares her Malibu home with husband, Skott Snider, a director. The couple have one child, Jeremy (born September 1990), and are expecting their second child in the fall of 1992. Jeremy can be seen reprising his role as the loving son on "The Bold and the Beautiful," where he appears as Eric Junior.

JILL LARSON

Born: October 7, 1947 in Minneapolis, Minnesota
Marital Status: divorced
Height: 5' 8 1/2" **Eyes:** blue **Hair:** strawberry blond
Education: Hunter College, B.F.A.; Circle in the Square Professional Acting Program, two years
Interests: entertaining, hiking, cooking, carpentry, skiing, antiques
Awards: 1991 Daytime Emmy nomination for Best Supporting Actress; Student Academy Award for film, "Gibbs Garden"

Daytime Dramas: "As the World Turns," Judith Clayton; **"One Life to Live,"** Ursula Blackwell, 1988; **"All My Children,"** Opal Cortlandt, 1989-

When Jill Davis Larson joined the cast of "All My Children" in 1989, she faced a considerable challenge. Not only would she have to play the always flamboyant Opal Cortlandt, but she would also be replacing Dorothy Lyman, whose portrayal had earned her two daytime Emmys. Three years and an Emmy nomination later, it is clear that Larson was up to the task. Hailing from Minnesota, where her father was an aerospace engineer and her mother an interior decorator, Jill, the oldest of four girls, says, "I started acting professionally at age 10 and have never stopped!" After receiving a degree in communications from Hunter College, Larson began to devote herself fully to the stage, studying drama with Circle in the Square Professional Theater Program. Primarily a theater actress, Larson's stage credits include "The Glass Menagerie," "Life With Father," "Romantic Comedy," and title roles in "Agnes of God" and "Gypsy." In 1992, Jill, along with veteran daytime performers Linda Cook and Sloane Shelton appeared in "Dearly Departed" at the Second Stage Theater in New York City. On television, along with roles on "One Life to Live" and "As the World Turns," Jill has made guest appearances on "Kate and Allie," "The Equalizer," "Late Night with David Letterman," and in the afterschool special, "Over the Limit." Larson is also a founding member and president of GLM Productions. The company, which concentrates chiefly on theatrical productions, recently presented the off-Broadway revue, "Serious Bizness," and in addition co-produced the film "Gibbs Garden," a documentary on the life of a painter infected with the AIDS virus. Nominated for a student Academy Award, the film brought attention to the artist, whose work was later exhibited in a show co-curated by Ms. Larson. For relaxation, the actress, who is single, is an avid yoga practitioner and also enjoys cooking and embarking on home improvement projects. She divides her time between her New York City apartment, and Pennsylvania weekend home.

CAROL LAWRENCE

Born: September 5, 1934 in Melrose Park, Illinois
Marital Status: divorced, two children, Michael and Chris
Eyes: brown   **Hair:** brown
Interests: singing, mountain climbing, cooking

Daytime Dramas: "General Hospital," Angela Eckert

A legendary performer, Carol Lawrence has been entertaining audiences around the world for over thirty years. She burst onto the scene in 1960, when at the age of twenty, she created the role of Maria in the original Broadway production of "West Side Story." Although landing the role was no picnic; (she had to audition thirteen times) she eventually won the approval of Jerome Robbins, and quickly established herself as one of her generation's premiere theater actresses. Her thirteen auditions helped lead to the ruling known in the industry as the "Carol Lawrence Rule," allowing a performer to audition three times for a role, and being paid for any audition thereafter. Born Carolina Maria Laraia on September 5 in Melrose Park, Illinois, Ms. Lawrence began her career singing in local Chicago clubs. Moving to New York in the mid 1950's, she began searching for Broadway roles, and along with "West Side Story," appeared in "Shangri-La," "Subways are for Sleeping," and "I Do! I Do!." In addition, Lawrence toured the country in productions of "Funny Girl," with James Mitchell of "All My Children," "Sugar Babies," and "The Sound of Music." On television, she was seen for many years as the spokesperson for General Food's International Coffees, as well as appearing on an episode of "Murder, She Wrote," and in scores of variety shows. Ms. Lawrence can currently be seen as Angela Eckert on "General Hospital." For the past two decades, the actress has performed her musical act around the world, appearing on cruise ships, and as a popular act in Las Vegas, Atlantic City, and Tahoe. When not working, Carol spent much of the early 1980's travelling to Somalia as a representative of World Vision, an organization dedicated to alleviating world hunger. Lawrence was married for seventeen years to actor/singer Robert Goulet, with whom she had two children, Michael and Chris. Now living in Los Angeles, the actress/singer enjoys cooking, (her food is often used in dinner scenes on "General Hospital") aerobics, and mountain climbing, and has even scaled the Grand Teton in Jackson Hole, Wyoming. Lawrence displayed her aerobics skill in the best selling video, "Broadway Bodies." She also wrote her autobiography, entitled "Carol Lawrence: The Backstage Story."

ELIZABETH LAWRENCE

Born: September 6, 1922 in West Virginia
Marital Status: single
Height: 5'7" **Eyes:** blue **Hair:** grey
Education: M.S. in Special Education
Interests: chamber music, gardening
Awards: nominated for Best Supporting Actress Daytime Emmy, 1980, 1981, 1984; "Afternoon T.V." Magazine, Editors Award

Daytime Dramas: **"The Road of Life,"** Francie Brent, 1954-1955; **"Edge of Night,"** Constance Johnson, 1962-1963; **"A World Apart,"** Betty Kahlman Barry, 1970; **"The Doctors"** Virginia Dancy, 1976-1978; **"All My Children,"** Myra Murdoch Sloan, 1979-1991

An accomplished actress of television, stage, and screen, Elizabeth Lawrence first became involved with soap operas back in the days of radio. Since then she has starred on several popular daytime television dramas, including, "The Doctors," "Edge of Night," "The Road of Life," "A World Apart," and as Myra Murdoch Sloan on "All My Children," from 1979 to 1991. For her work on this program, Ms. Lawrence was nominated three times for Daytime Emmys, as well as receiving an Editors Award from "Afternoon T.V." Magazine. Born on September 6, 1922, in West Virginia, Elizabeth received her M.S. degree in special education, putting these skills to use as a teacher from 1972 to 1979. She began her performing career on radio, where she could be heard on such shows as "Nora Drake" and "Right to Happiness." On television, in addition to her more prominent daytime roles, Elizabeth has guest starred on "Somerset," "Hidden Faces," "As the World Turns," "Guiding Light," and "Search for Tomorrow," and on a great many prime time shows, most recently the acclaimed series, "Law and Order." An accomplished stage actress, she has amassed an impressive list of credits, among them, Broadway productions of "Look Homeward Angel," "All The Way Home," "Matter of Gravity," with Katherine Hepburn, and "Strange Interlude," with Glenda Jackson, as well as regional and summer stock theater. On the big screen, Lawrence has co-starred in such popular films as "Sleeping with the Enemy," as Julia Robert's blind mother, and "We're No Angels," with Robert DeNiro and Sean Penn. For close to fifty years, Elizabeth has lived in New York City, and has done her share of community service, including an eight year stint as a City Auxiliary Police Officer, and now a NYC Citizen Street Tree Pruner. The actress' interests include chamber music, gardening, and her red setter dog.

LEE LAWSON

Born: October 14 in Queens, New York
Marital Status: divorced, three children, Chris, Leslie and Gabriella
Height: 5'2" **Eyes:** brown **Hair:** red
Education: Boston University, Graduate of the American Theatre Wing
Interests: education, theater, cat fanatic
Awards: Outer Critic's Circle Award for "Suggs;" Clio Award for "Sanforized" commercial

Daytime Dramas: **"Love of Life,"** Barbara Sterling Latimer, 1963-1970; **"One Life to Live,"** Wanda Wolek, 1978-1980; **"Guiding Light,"** Bea Reardon, 1980-1987

Since making her daytime debut in 1963 as Barbara Sterling Latimer on "Love of Life," Lee Lawson has gone on to star on both "One Life to Live" and "Guiding Light." Born on October 14, in Queens, New York, Lee came from a creative family, which also includes her sister, Susan Gray, an artist, and her mother, Lou Lawson, a novelist. After attending Forest Hills High School, Lee went on to study at the American Theatre Wing at Boston University, following which she began her professional stage career. A prolific actress, she has appeared on Broadway in "Teible and Her Demon," "An American Millionaire," "My Daughter Your Son," "Agatha Sue, I Love You," and "Cactus Flower," while her off-Broadway and regional credits include, "The Birthday Party," "Scenes from an American Life," "Suggs," for which she won a New York Outer Critic's Circle Award, "The Plough and the Stars," "The Way of the World," "Jack Be Nimble," "The Unemployed Saint," "Waltz Me Around Again," "The Button," "Firebugs," "Les Liasons Dangereuses," and "The Married Bachelor." On television, in addition to daytime, Ms. Lawson has been a regular on "New York TV Theatre," "The Mason Reese Show," and "NY Ensemble Players," while she has guest starred on such shows as "Maude," "Kojak," and "Equal Justice," among others. Also a familiar face in commercials, the actress received a Clio award for her work in the "Sanforized" advertisement. Devoting much of her spare time to helping people with substance abuse problems, Lee is a certified alcohol and drug counselor, and has applied these skills as an assistant administrator for AFTRA Industry Program for Alcohol and Drug Abuse. She is also a member of the West Side Alcohol Coalition in Los Angeles, and additionally is a member of the Parents for Education organization. A resident of Beverly Hills, California, Lee, who is divorced, is the mother of three children, Chris, a playwright, and Leslie and Gabriella, both whom are college students. A self proclaimed cat fanatic, Lee shares her home with her three cats.

CHRISTIAN LeBLANC

Born: August 25, 1958 in Fort Bragg, North Carolina
Marital Status: single
Height: 5'10" **Eyes:** brown **Hair:** brown
Education: Tulane University, Bachelor's Degree
Interests: painting, gymnastics, skiing, ice skating

Daytime Dramas: "As the World Turns," Kirk McColl, 1983-1985; **"The Young and the Restless,"** Michael Baldwin, 1991-

Last seen by daytime audiences in 1985 as Kirk McColl on "As the World Turns," Christian Le Blanc returned to the soap world in 1991, playing the much older and more mature Michael Baldwin on "The Young and the Restless." Born Christian Jules Le Blanc the second of eight children (six boys two girls), on August 25, 1958, in Fort Bragg, North Carolina, Christian was the son of an oft decorated Green Beret Officer. In accordance with their father's job, the family relocated frequently, living throughout the United States and in Germany before settling down in New Orleans when Christian was eleven years old. Although he had acted in some high school productions, Le Blanc enrolled as a pre-med major at Tulane University. However, after landing a role in a production of "You're a Good Man, Charlie Brown," he shifted his ambitions towards acting. Since then, Le Blanc has consistently worked at honing his craft, studying with several acting coaches, including Pat Muller, Max Gartenberg, Bob McAndrew, Janet Alhanti, and Robert Jones. He has also worked on his dancing and singing skills with David Jones and Carol D'Andrea, displaying his footwork at the New York Conservatory, where he worked with the renowned jazzman, Phil Black. Following "You're a Good Man Charlie Brown," Le Blanc went on to appear in such Louisiana stage productions as "Pippin," "Guys and Dolls," "Grease," "The Fresca Wars," "Arc Light," and "Fairy Tale." His first television part was on the PBS series, "Edit Point," following which he took on the role of the rebel/loner Kirk on "As the World Turns." After two years on the show, Le Blanc decided to explore new acting avenues. He relocated to the west coast, and soon landed guest starring roles on "Monsters," "Superior Court," "Hotel," "Riptide," "Brand New Life," "Cheers," "Gabriel's Fire," and two television films, "Seeds of Tragedy" and "Green Leaves, White Death." The actor also was seen in the role of Junior Abernathy on "In the Heat of the Night" and "Earth Force," a short lived show shot entirely on location in Australia. Before returning to daytime, Le Blanc, who is fluent in French, Spanish, and Russian, took time off to travel throughout the world, including stints in Europe, Israel, and Egypt. Now back in the U.S.A., and relishing his new daytime role, Christian, who is single, lists amongst his hobbies water and snow skiing, ice skating, and gymnastics. He is also an aspiring painter, and is in the process of having his work displayed.

JEAN LeCLERC

Born: July 7 in Montreal, Canada
Marital Status: single
Height: 6' **Eyes:** brown **Hair:** brown
Education: University of Quebec
Interests: restoring antiques and historic homes, cooking, avid collector of wooden duck decoys
Awards: Fleur de lys Awards for Best Actor ("Waiting for Godot") and Best Supporting Actor ("Lion in Winter")

Daytime Dramas: "The Doctors," Jean Marc Gauthier, 1982; **"One Life to Live,"** Peter Russo; **"All My Children,"** Jeremy Hunter, 1985-1992; **"Loving,"** Jeremy Hunter, 1992-

Choosing a career in acting often means sacrificing a more reliable and conservative profession for something far riskier. In the case of Jean LeClerc it meant leaving his medical studies for the stage. Born and raised in Montreal, LeClerc was studying pre-med at the University of Quebec, while simultaneously getting his feet wet in the world of acting. Eventually it came to a point where a commitment had to be made, and after landing a guest appearance on a prime time CBS series, LeClerc decided to give up medicine. Jean quickly found work in the theater, where he has continued to thrive ever since. Among his many stage credits are roles in the Broadway production of "Dracula," "Waiting for Godot," "Tale of the Wolfe," "A Lion in Winter," and "Beckett." For his work in "Waiting For Godot," LeClerc was awarded the Fleur de lys Award (the Canadian equivalent of the Tony Award) for Best Actor, and was awarded the prize again for his supporting performance in "A Lion In Winter." One of his most recent stage ventures is a production of "Love Letters," opening late 1992 at Le Theatre Rideau Vert in Montreal. Not only will LeClerc star in the show's first week, but he will also be translating the play and serving as it's producer. Also a popular guest star on many prime time series, LeClerc has appeared on the final episodes of "The Days and Nights of Molly Dodd," "T.J. Hooker," "The Devlin Connection," "Justice Express," and the miniseries "Misfortunes of the Rich," while he has been seen on the big screen, with Victoria Tennant, in "Whispers." LeClerc, in addition, hosted a six hour gala program, which aired on the A&E Cable Network, commemorating the 200th anniversary of the French Revolution. But it is certainly Jean's daytime work which has brought him the most popular success. Before landing the role of Jeremy on "All My Children," LeClerc appeared on a number of other soap operas, including "The Doctors," "Edge of Night," "As the World Turns," and "One Life to Live." Off camera, LeClerc's voice is often used for commercials, most notably the FTD spots, both French and English versions. Much of LeClerc's free time is devoted to charitable causes. The actor serves as national fund-raising chairman for the Cystic Fibrosis Foundation, and recently was personally responsible for a $13,600 donation; this occurred when a Dallas woman paid the impressive sum for the opportunity to have lunch with LeClerc and receive a personalized tour of the "All My Children" set. Jean also donates his efforts to the Make-A-Wish Foundation, the American Cancer Society, for which he serves as Co-Captain for their Surf All

Stars, and as a key member of the soap opera softball team, which raise money to help children stricken with disease. In his spare time, LeClerc enjoys restoring antiques and historic houses, including his own weekend home, a restored nineteenth century flour mill with a waterfall in the living room. Located outside of Montreal, the house was recently declared a historic landmark by the Canadian Government. Jean also enjoys cooking and collecting wooden duck decoys. In 1991, to help boost the ratings of "Loving," Jean LeClerc took his character, Jeremy and on screen wife, Ceara (Genie Francis) to the mythical town of "Corinth." The month proved to be a success for everyone and in 1992 Jean took his character to Corinth for a more permanent stay.

ANNA LEE

Born: January 2, 1913 in Igtham, Kent, England
Marital Status: widowed, four children, Caroline and Venetia Stevenson, Stephen Stafford, Jeffrey Byron
Height: 5' 5"   **Eyes:** blue   **Hair:** white
Education: Central School of Speech Training Dramatic Arts
Interests: collecting antiques, gardening, embroidery
Awards: awarded by Queen Elizabeth in 1983, the MBE (Member of the Most Excellent Order of the British Empire), she received the award at Buckingham Palace; Soap Opera Award, Favorite Mature Actress, 1982, 1983; Soap Opera Award, Outstanding Supporting Actress, 1988

Daytime Dramas: "General Hospital," Lila Quartermaine, 1978 -

Through her work in film and television, Anna Lee has been entertaining the world for over seven decades. She was born Joan Boniface Winnifrith on January 2, 1913, in the village of Igtham, Kent, England. Her father was the Rector of St. Peter's Church. Anna first began to study acting when, at the age of seventeen, she enrolled at the Central School of Speech and Training and Dramatic Art at the Royal Albert Hall in London. After studying with Elsie Fogary, Anna went on to join the London Repertory Theatre appearing in plays such as "The Constant Nymph," and "Jane Eyre." In 1935, she signed a motion picture deal and through 1939 starred in over a dozen films. Among these were "King Solomon's Mines," with Paul Robeson, "The Camels are Coming," "Passing of the Third Floor Back," "Young Man's Fancy," "Return to Yesterday," and "Non-stop New York." After this string of British films, she left for the United States in 1939 to star opposite Robert Coleman in "My Life with Caroline." In 1940 she began her longtime association with director John Ford when he cast her as Bronwen in the Academy Award winning film "How Green Was My Valley." Anna went on to work with John Ford eight more times over the next twenty-five years. She has made several wartime pictures, among them "Seven Sinners" and "Flying Tigers," both of which starred John Wayne. She also appeared in "Comandos Strike at Dawn," with Paul Muni, "Flesh and Fantasy" with Edward G. Robinson and Charles Boyer, and the Fritz Lang film "Hangmen Also Die." With the outbreak of World War II, Anna took a hiatus from her film career to volunteer with the U.S.O. and performed for Allied troops in North, Central, and East Africa, Iran, and Cicily. On these tours she appeared with Jack Benny and Adolph Menjou. This proved to be such a complete success that at the special orders of General Patton, she spent several months travelling throughout the Mediterranean visiting field hospitals. In gratitude, Patton made Anna an Honorary Private in the Sixth Army. After returning from the war she continued her film career with such films as "Bedlam," "The Ghost and Mrs. Muir," "G.I. War Brides," "High Conquest," and "Fort Apache." Looking for a change in 1950, Anna moved to New York to work in the then brand new medium of television. Her first job was in the live weekly show "A Date With Judy," which she appeared in for the next four years. During this time she also appeared as an "anchor-man" every Thursday evening on the CBS panel show "Its News to Me," along with John Daly and later, Walter Cronkite. Her other television work during this time included many "live" shows, including "Pulitzer Prize Playhouse," "Kraft Theatre," "Studio One," "Robert Montgomery Presents," and "Ford Theatre." In 1957 Anna decided to renew her film career opposite Jack Hawkins in John Ford's "Gideon of Scotland Yard," as well as appearing in "The Last Hurrah," "Horse Soldiers," "This Earth is Mine," "The Prize," "The Crimson Kimono," "Whatever Happened to Baby Jane?" "In Like Flint," "The Sound of Music," (she played Sister Marghereta - the nun who stole the Nazi's car parts, allowing the Von Trapps to escape) and "Seven Women." Along with these films Anna continued her television work on the shows "Eleanor and Franklin," "Scruples," and "The Night Rider." Anna has made special guest appearances on many shows including "Maverick," "Dr. Kildare," "The FBI," "Mr. Novak," "Mission Impossible," "Perry Mason," "Mannix," "Family Affair," and "Glitter." Since 1978 daytime audiences have known her as Lila Quartermaine on "General Hospital," a role she cherishes for the diversity of the character and the closeness of her television "family." In her non-professional life Anna was happily married to the novelist and poet Robert Nathan, until his death in 1985. Nathan is best known for such works as "Portrait of Jennie," "The Bishops Wife," and "One More Spring." The year following her husbands death, Anna also lost her eldest son. Another son is actor Jeffrey Byron who portrayed Dr. Jeff Martin on "All My Children" and Richard Abbott on "One Life to Live." Today Anna resides in California, and keeps busy with her grandchildren and as the chairman of the Royal Oak Foundation of California, an affiliate of the National Trust of Great Britain, which works to preserve places of historical interest and natural beauty throughout the United Kingdom. Along with this, Anna is presently writing her autobiography and also enjoys gardening, embroidery, and collecting antiques.

EDIE LEHMANN

Born: September 25 in Buffalo, New York
Marital Status: single
Height: 5'9"   **Eyes:** brown   **Hair:** blond
Education: University of Southern California
Interests: music, exercise
Awards: 1975 California Junior Miss; Creative and Performing Arts Award,1975 America Junior Miss Pageant

Daytime Dramas: "General Hospital," Katherine Delafield, 1988-1991

An established singer and pianist, Edie Lehmann's delve into the realm of daytime acting came quite by accident. Initially she had hoped that it would be her hands which would be featured on screen, specifically as the hands of Katherine Delafield on "General Hospital." However, after seeing her audition, the producers as well as co-star Tristan Rogers, decided that Edie should play the part herself, hands and all! Born in Buffalo, New York, Edie began her musical training at the age of four, and by the time she was six she had performed in many recital halls throughout New York City. Two years later her family moved to California, where Edie continued her study of music at the University of Southern California (USC) focusing not only on piano, but chamber music and music theory. She continued studying at USC after graduating from Polytechnic High School in Simi Valley, California. During these years she continued to perform in concert halls in the United States and Europe, winning several major awards. In 1975 Edie won the title of California's Junior Miss, and went on to represent her home state in the America Junior Miss Pageant. Although she did not win the title, she did take home the Creative and Performing Arts Award. While working on "General Hospital," Edie continued her music career, singing in commercials, numerous albums as well as television themes and motion picture soundtracks. She chose to leave the show to devote herself fulltime to her first passion - music. She currently lives in Los Angeles where she enjoys exercising and walking on the beach.

ROBERTA LEIGHTON

Born: June 23 in Minneapolis, Minnesota
Marital Status: married to Corey Young on August 20, 1988
Eyes: blue   **Hair:** blond
Education: Stephens College, two B.F.A.'s in writing and acting
Interests: poetry, horseback riding, writing, water/jet skiing

Daytime Dramas: "The Young and the Restless,"
Dr. Casey Reed, 1978-1981, 1984-1991; **"General Hospital,"**
Shirley Pickett, 1983; **"Days of Our Lives,"** Ginger Dawson,
1991-1992

Had it not been for a simple twist of fate, daytime drama fans may never have known the name Roberta Leighton. It seems that some time ago Ms. Leighton came to a point where a decision had to be made - should she go to New York and work on the stage or head to California for film/television work? Her decision making technique was very scientific - she flipped a coin. Heads, Los Angeles; Tails, New York. When the coin said go west, she did. A Minneapolis native, Roberta was born on June 23 to Norma and Gordon Weimar. She has one sister, Judith. In 1975 she moved to Los Angeles to study acting at the prestigious Guthrie Theater. After a brief stint there, Roberta moved to Missouri where she enrolled at Stephens College, from which she received two B.F.A. degrees, one in acting, the other in writing. She spent the next three seasons in summer stock, where she performed in such productions as "The Taming of the Shrew," "Anything Goes," "Sweet Charity," and "Midsummer's Night Dream." After this Roberta tossed the fateful coin and moved back to Los Angeles. She quickly found work on television and in film, appearing in such features as "Stripes" and "One on One," and making guest appearances on numerous prime time series, including "Cheers," "Dukes of Hazzard," "The Blue Knight," "Barnaby Jones," "Baretta," and "Switch." She is best known to daytime fans as Dr. Casey Reed on "The Young and the Restless," a role she played for over ten years. Ms. Leighton is now, however, enjoying the new challenge of playing Ginger Dawson on "Days of Our Lives," a character without Dr. Reed's medical expertise, but a far more adventurous attitude. Initially, Roberta was not looking to start on another soap. She had just reached the end of a difficult few years, fraught with a myriad of health problems, when she decided to take a much needed vacation. While she was travelling through Russia she received word from her husband that "Days of Our Lives" had a part for her to play, and when Roberta saw how different the role was from her previous daytime work, she simply could not turn it down. Although her acting career is going stronger than ever, Roberta continues to cultivate her writing skills, and hopes to see this develop further. She has written several screen plays and television scripts, and has had some of her poetry published in anthologies. She shares this passion with her husband, former "General Hospital" cast member, Corey Young. Ms. Leighton has previously been romantically linked with such daytime luminaries as David Hasselhoff and Anthony Geary. In her spare time Roberta enjoys horseback riding, (western and English) golf, scuba diving, and water/jet skiing. She devotes much of her time to the National Kidney Foundation, and as a fundraiser for St. Judes Hospital.

TERRY LESTER

Born: April 13 in Indianapolis, Indiana
Marital Status: single
Height: 6'2" **Eyes:** blue **Hair:** blond
Education: Depauw University, Bachelor's in Political Science
Interests: music, skiing, biking, tennis, golf, computers, reading, motorcycling, travel, philosophy, mysticism, snorkeling
Awards: nominated for four Daytime Emmys for Best Actor, 1983, 1984, 1985, 1986

Daytime Dramas: "The Young and the Restless," Jack Abbott, 1980-1989; **"Santa Barbara,"** Mason Capwell, 1989-1990

During the 1980's "The Young and the Restless" became the top rated show on daytime television, and a large portion of the credit should go to Terry Lester. Earning four daytime Emmy nominations for his portrayal of playboy Jack Abbott, Lester was the cornerstone of the popular series. Born on April 13, in Indianapolis, Indiana, Lester was clearly not your average child. He began reading the newspaper at the age of three, and a short time after that commenced his classical piano training. Still a music lover to this day, Lester continues to play the piano as well as exercise his vocal talents. Along with music, Lester's childhood interests ranged from sports to politics; he competed on the swim team as well as serving as student body president at the age of fifteen. On a larger political scale, Lester also worked on the successful campaign of Governor Edgar Whitcombe. After receiving his degree in Political Science from Depauw University, he enlisted in the army. While in the army, Terry studied and taught Russian at the Defense Language Institute at Monterey, California. Also during his stint in the service, Lester began his modelling career, which soon lead to acting roles. On prime time television he co-starred on "Dallas," "Hotel," "Eight is Enough," "Flying High," and in several movies of the week, including "In Self Defense," "Blade In Hong Kong," "Once Upon A Spy," and "Kiss Meets The Phantom." On the big screen, Lester has been seen in "Airport '75" and "Racquet," while his stage credits include "Kiss Me Kate," "Drood," "Bus Stop," and "Oklahoma." After leaving "The Young and the Restless," Lester spent a year on "Santa Barbara" before embarking on a self imposed hiatus. After ten years of daytime work, the actor decided to take a break from the gruelling schedule of episodic television. He has spent this time working as an animal shelter volunteer and with the charity organization, Rancho Los Amigos. Terry has also been getting back into peak physical shape, working out, skiing, and bicycling. The actor's other hobbies include writing, tennis, golf, computers, reading, and travelling. Lester's fans will be happy to know that he is certainly not on a permanent vacation, and hopes to return to television in the near future.

DAVID LEWIS

Born: October 19 in Pittsburg, Pennsylvania
Marital Status: single
Height: 6'1" **Eyes:** blue **Hair:** auburn-gray
Interests: theater, directing
Awards: Clarance Derwent Award for "The King of Hearts;
Daytime Emmy for Outstanding Supporting Actor 1981;
nominated in same category 1982, 1983; Soap Opera Award
for Favorite Mature Actor, 1980, 1981, 1982, 1983

Daytime Dramas: "Bright Promise," Henry Pierce, 1969-
1972; **"General Hospital,"** Edward Quartermaine, 1978-

Since he began working in the theatre in 1933, David Lewis has enjoyed a career spanning many facets of the entertainment industry. Working as both an actor and director, Lewis has been involved in some 400 stage productions, as well as a widely divergent range of film and television work. Born in Pittsburg, Pennsylvania, Lewis began his career in 1933 as an apprentice at the Eerie Playhouse. (A.K.A. The Erie Civic Theater Association) He remained there for twelve years, working his way up through juvenile roles to become the leading man of the company, and eventually being appointed assistant to the director and founder, Henry Vincent, and finally, director of the theater. Having reached the top in Eerie, Lewis then headed for New York City, where for the next decade he established a name for himself both in stock productions and on Broadway. On Broadway he performed in works such as "The Wild Duck," and "King of Hearts," winning the Clarance Derwent acting award for the latter. Along with this work he also acted in, as well as directed countless summer stock productions, and spent two years touring Canada and this country as a leading player in the Margaret Webster Shakespeare Company. Clearly a man who loves his craft, Lewis also devoted much of his time to his work as an acting instructor and director at the Abbe Theater School in New York City which was operated by Gloria Monty and Robert O'Bryne. David later moved to Chicago to become the director of The Showcase Theater of Evanston. After completing over twenty productions, it was back to New York to work, once again, on "The King of Hearts." After seeing him in "The King of Hearts, " filmmaker Michael Cutiz convinced Lewis to move to Hollywood to work in movies. Lewis obliged and went on to appear in numerous films including "Generation," "John Goldfarb, Please Come Home," "A Girl Named Tamiko," "The Boston Strangler," "The Apartment," "Kid Galahad," "The Absent-Minded Professor," and "The Spiral Road." He also appeared on the small screen in such shows as "Good Times," "Medical Center," "Barnaby Jones," and "The Streets of San Francisco," as well as the t.v. movies "Rich Man, Poor Man," and "Eleanor and Franklin: The White House Years." Along with his work on "General Hospital," for which he has won a Daytime Emmy as Best Supporting Actor as well as four Soap Opera Awards, Lewis also worked on the daytime drama "Bright Promises" (another Gloria Monty show) from 1969 to 1972 and has appeared on "The Young and the Restless" and "Days of Our Lives."

JENNIFER LIEN

Born: August 24, 1974 in Illinois
Marital Status: single
Height: 5'4"   **Eyes:** blue   **Hair:** blond
Education: Professional Children's School, 1992 Graduate
Interests: singing, writing, painting, football, basketball, track

Daytime Dramas: "Another World," Hannah Moore, 1991-

Born on August 24, 1974 to Tore and Delores, Jennifer Lien was five years old when she told her parents she wanted to be an actress. Her parents responded, as any loving parent would, and told Jennifer she could be anything she wanted to be, as long as she was willing to work at it...and she has. After attending Central Junior High School in Steeger, Illinois, and Bloom Trail High School in Chicago, Ms. Lien enrolled in the Professional Children's School, graduating in 1992. In addition, she also studied at the Illinois Theatre Center Drama School. Among the many stage productions in which the young actress has appeared: "Scapino," "When Are You Coming Back Red Ryder?," "Othello," "The Tempest," "Androcles and the Lion," "Show Boat," "Emergency Room," "Picnic at Hanging Rock," "Our Town," and "Edmond." In 1991, Jennifer made her daytime debut as the orphan, Hannah Moore on "Another World." The producers were so impressed by Ms. Lien, she was quickly offered a three year contract. Other television credits include the prime time series, "Brewster Place." Orphaned only on television, Jennifer comes from a close knit family, which includes her brother Tore Anthony, her sister Theresa, her brother-in-law, Paul Wilson and the youngest members of the family, Jennifer's niece and nephew, Mary and Robert Wilson. Jennifer, who resides in New York City, lists amongst her interests, singing, football, writing, painting, basketball and track.

KATE LINDER

Born: November 2 in Pasadena, California
Marital Status: married to Ronald Linder, February 14, 1976
Height: 5'4"   **Eyes:** brown   **Hair:** brown
Education: San Francisco State College, Bachelor's in Theatre Arts
Interests: tap dancing, charity work, theatre
Awards: L.I.F.E.'s Volunteer Award, 1991; 1985 "Bronze Halo Award" from Southern California Motion Picture Council

Daytime Dramas: "The Young and the Restless," Esther Valentine, 1982-

Probably the only actress on daytime drama to moonlight as a flight attendant, Kate Linder spent several years dividing her time between her role as Esther Valentine on "The Young and the Restless," and working as a stewardess for Transamerica Airlines. Born and raised in Pasadena, California, Kate's life as a performer began at the age of three, when she enrolled in dance classes. It was, however, her seventh grade history teacher who can be credited with pointing Kate towards an acting career, when he decided that history reports should be presented as dramatic skits. From that moment Kate was hooked, and spent the next several years involved with a myriad of school productions, among them "L'il Abner" and "Jesus Christ Superstar." After completing high school, Kate decided to study theater at the American Academy in New York City, however her father, a C.P.A., convinced her to enroll in a liberal arts college for two years. The deal was that if after two years she still wanted to try life in New York, he agreed to help out financially. Honoring this arrangement Kate enrolled at San Francisco State College, and quickly became so involved with school and regional productions that she never did actually make it to New York City. It was during her years at college that the young actress embarked on her second career as a flight attendant for Transamerica Airlines. This small operation flew exclusive champagne flights to Monaco and Tahiti, and gave Kate her first taste of life as a world traveller. Upon graduation she remained in San Francisco, where if she was not working on stage, she could surely be found jet setting off to some exotic destination. In addition, Kate also found time to work in the University's activities office, and it was there that she met her future husband, Ronald Linder, a professor and one of the worlds leading experts on drug abuse. After a Valentine's Day wedding, the couple relocated to Los Angeles, where Ron began teaching at UCLA and Kate found work on television. Among the shows on which she appeared: "Archie Bunker's Place," "Bay City Blues," and "Dream Girl." In 1982, the character of Esther Valentine (in honor of Kate's wedding day) was introduced to "The Young and the Restless" fans with the line "dinner is served." Since that fateful day countless other dinners have been prepared and Esther has become a key member of the Chancellor household. Kate, who still loves to travel, only recently gave up her flight attendant career, and now devotes much of her spare time to the LIFE (Love is Feeding Everyone) organization. LIFE, founded by Valerie Harper and Dennis Weaver, is responsible for feeding 100,000 people in the L.A. area each week. Kate also serves as the spokesperson/fundraising chairperson for Escalon, a school for children with learning disabilities.

TERI ANN LINN

Born: April 7 in Hawaii
Marital Status: married to photographer Richard Hume
Height: 5'9" **Eyes:** green **Hair:** blond
Education: University of San Diego
Interests: sports, singing
Awards: 1982 Mother/Daughter Division of U.S. Open, 1981 Miss Hawaii USA, 4th runner up, Miss USA

Daytime Dramas: "The Bold and the Beautiful," Kristen Forrester, 1987-1991, 1992

If one were to search for the most beautiful woman in daytime drama the process could be endless. However, if one were to search for the most beautiful woman, with the most blistering serve and best cross court backhand, it's a pretty safe bet that Terri Ann Linn would be the clear winner. A native of Hawaii, the actress spent much of her childhood on the tennis court, and as a teenager was the number one ranked junior in her home state. Coming from an extremely athletic and outdoorsy family, this was no surprise. Teri's father is an insurance agent, while her mother has worked as a teacher, model, and currently is a professional tennis player, ranked in the top twenty of her age group. Teri's older brother is a commercial airline pilot. Perhaps the family's proudest moment on the court came in 1982, when Teri and her mother won the mother-daughter division of the U.S. Open. During her years as a tennis sensation, the future "The Bold and the Beautiful" star would go through as many as twelve racquets a year, some of them worn out from use, others became "worn out" after being smashed against the ground in frustration by a highly competitive teenage girl. Away from the pressures of the court, Teri attended Panahou High School, from which she was awarded a tennis scholarship to California's Pepperdine University. At Pepperdine, one of the top ranked tennis schools in the country,

Teri was ranked #5 on the ten person squad. Not use to such tough competition, she trained even more rigorously than before, spending as much as eight hours a day on the court, as well as lifting weights and running six miles each day. Teri left Pepperdine when she received a scholarship offer from the University of San Diego, where she played volleyball as well as tennis. While at San Diego, Linn first began to look towards acting as a possible career choice. Years before she had appeared on an episode of "Hawaii Five-O," along with Tim Matheson and Kurt Russell, and this had left an indelible impression on her. In 1981 Teri returned to Hawaii where she won the title of Miss Hawaii U.S.A., which was followed by a fourth runner up showing in the subsequent Miss U.S.A. pageant. With this exposure, Teri decided to move to Hollywood and officially begin her acting career, which immediately took off with a slew of commercials, as well as guest appearances on such shows as "Hill Street Blues," "Magnum P.I.," "Mike Hammer," "Riptide," and "Dallas." She also co-starred in the motion picture, "Hanauma Bay." Along the way Teri has earned the reputation as an adventurous type, preferring to do her own stunts rather than hand the task over to a double. In 1986, she was the first actress cast in the soon to be premiered daytime drama "The Bold and the Beautiful," and since then Teri has enjoyed tremendous success. While her tennis play is now limited, she still manages to compete in charity events, as well as continue to study drama and dance. Teri is married to fashion photographer Richard Hume and presently serves as the spokesperson for the "Blind" Institution.

BRAD LOCKERMAN

Born: March 9 in Milford, Connecticut
Marital Status: single
Height: 6' 2"   **Eyes:** hazel   **Hair:** dark brown
Education: University of Pittsburgh (three semesters)
Interests: golf, chess, reading

Daytime Dramas: "Capitol," Zed Diamond, 1984-1987;
"General Hospital," Casey Rogers/Shep Casey, 1990-1991

There is perhaps no greater testimony to Brad Lockerman's unique talent than the fact that he has never gotten a role in a soap opera for which he actually auditioned. Two times he tried to get parts on daytime dramas, first on "Capitol," and most recently on "General Hospital." In both instances he failed to get the part, yet each time the producers were so impressed by him that they created a new role tailored specifically to Brad's unique qualities. Lockerman was born in Milford, Connecticut, but his family moved to Pittsburgh a few years later. A serious baseball player, Lockerman was a star pitcher for North Hills High School and had ambitions of a professional baseball career. However, in 1975, the night before he was scheduled to try out for the Pittsburgh Pirates, he broke his shoulder in a motor bike accident. With a sports career no longer a possibility, Lockerman enrolled at the University of Pittsburgh. He spent three semesters studying chemistry and drama before deciding to take some time away from school. During this time he did a number of different jobs: he tended bar, drove a truck, and worked as a greens keeper at a golf course (a game his father taught him to play when he was six years old - he now has a scratch handicap). In 1978 Lockerman decided it was time to pursue an acting career, and spent the next few years studying in New York and Los Angeles, supporting himself by appearing in print ads for Gentleman's Quarterly. His first big break came when the producers of "Capitol" created the role of Zed Diamond for Lockerman. He remained in that role for the next four years, and returned to daytime drama in 1990 when he began his work on "General Hospital." His role on "GH" was truly a unique one, having originally appeared as an alien claiming to be Casey Rogers, and then reappearing as television reporter Shep Casey. Away from the set Lockerman enjoys reading, serving as a referee for children's basketball games, and playing golf. Since leaving the show, Lockerman starred in the Los Angeles production of A.R. Gurney's play, "Love Letters" and also shot a television pilot titled "Divorce Law."

NIA LONG

Born: October 30, 1970 in Brooklyn, New York
Marital Status: single
Height: 5'2" **Eyes:** brown **Hair:** brown
Education: Santa Monica College
Interests: music, writing, dance

Daytime Dramas: "Guiding Light," Kathryn Speakes, 1991-

1991 can certainly be considered a good year for Nia Long. First she joined the cast of "Guiding Light," and in doing so, became only the third African-American performer in the show's thirty year history to become a contract player. Then she exploded onto the big screen as Brandi, in the critical/box office smash, "Boyz N The Hood." Only twenty one years old, Ms. Long was born on October 30, 1970, in Brooklyn, New York, where her father, Doc Long, was a poet and a teacher, and her mother, Talita, an artist and singer. After relocating to Los Angeles with her mother, Nia first became interested in acting in the third grade when her best friend, Regina King (of the sit-com "227") invited her to come to an acting class at Kane/Bridge Academy. Taking an instant liking to the class, Nia continued her acting studies through her years at Westchester High School and Santa Monica College. Putting her skills to the test in several mediums, Ms. Long has appeared on stage in "Self Defense," "Rites of Passage," and "A Girl's Dormitory," while her film credits include "Buried Alive" and "B.R.A.T. Patrol." She recently finished filming a starring role in the feature film, "Made in America" starring Whoopi Goldberg and Ted Danson. The movie's producers are Carol Burnett and Michael Douglas. In addition to her daytime work, she has also guest starred on "227," "Silver Spoons," and "My Two Dads," as well as displaying her dancing skills in two music video, Bell Biv Devoe's, "Do Me" and Special Generation's, "Spark of Love." A singer in her own right, Nia hopes to record her own album in the near future; she is particularly fond of jazz and rhythm and blues. The actress/singer/dancer, who has lived in New York City since 1991, lists amongst her hobbies, writing, shopping, and eating chocolate.

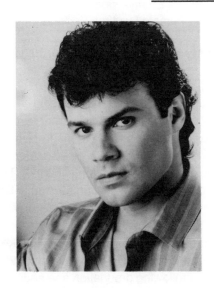

JOHN LOPRIENO

Born: October 7 in Chicago, Illinois
Marital Status: married to Lisa Brien, one daughter Anna, one daughter, Danielle from a previous marriage
Height: 6' **Eyes:** brown **Hair:** brown
Education: Lewis University, B.A.; University of Minnesota, M.F.A.
Interests: baseball, weightifting, jogging, writing

Daytime Dramas: "Search for Tomorrow," Danny Walton, 1985-1986; **"One Life to Live,"** Cord Roberts, 1986-1991

John Loprieno, who most recently portrayed Cord Roberts on "One Life to Live," has become one of the most popular male stars in daytime drama. Loprieno attended high school in Elk Grove Village, Illinois, where along with playing baseball and football, he first became interested in acting. After appearing in numerous high school productions he continued his education at Lewis University in Romeoville, Illinois, where he received his undergraduate degree in theater. From there he received his masters in acting from the University of Minnesota, appearing in many productions, including "The Elephant Man," "Pippin," "West Side Story," "Grease," and "Guys and Dolls." Loprieno then move to Chicago where he divided his time between acting and teaching, before landing his first big role as Danny Walton on "Search for Tomorrow." He remained with the show for a year before beginning his work on "One Life to Live." He continued, however, to work on stage, most recently appearing off-Broadway in the Circle in the Square production of "The Rothchilds." Presently Loprieno lives in Ridgewood, New Jersey with his second wife Lisa, their daughter Anna Elise, born on October 11, 1991, and John's daughter, Danielle (he and his first wife share joint custody). John and Lisa met in 1988, when, as a Florida shopping mall marketing director, Lisa set up a promotional appearance with John. They began a long distance friendship that blossomed into romance. In an effort to share his expertise and foster young talent, Loprieno and Lisa established the Theatrical Education Workshop, a nonprofit theater company which provides classes for potential actors. Here John can pass on his knowledge not only of acting, but of stage combat, fight choreography, and stand up comedy. Since leaving "One Life to Live," John has been very active in raising his children, as well as writing and producing the comedy "Almost Paradise." He plans on playing the lead role. In his spare time John enjoys jogging, weightlifting, racquetball, and baseball, as well as spending time with his family.

SUSAN LUCCI

Born: December 23 in Westchester County, New York
Marital Status: married to Helmut Huber in 1969, two children, Liza and Andreas
Height: 5' 3" **Eyes:** dark brown **Hair:** chestnut
Education: Marymount College
Interests: tennis, skiing, travelling
Awards: 1985 People Magazine Reader's Poll for Best Soap Actress; 1988 Soap Opera Digest Award for Outstanding Contribution to Daytime Television; 1989 Canadian TV Guide People's Choice Award for Best Soap Actress; the Italian-American Welfare League's "Woman of the Year;" nominated for thirteen Best Actress Daytime Emmys since 1978; 1991 People's Choice Award for Favorite Female Daytime Performer

Daytime Dramas: "All My Children," Erica Kane, 1970-

The undisputed queen of daytime drama, Susan Lucci defines the genre...she is the genre. Since 1970, when "All My Children" debuted, millions the world over have come to relish the exploits of Lucci's Erica Kane, seeing her through numerous marriages, countless love affairs, plane crashes, kidnappings, nun impersonations, helicopter rescues, and anything else that one can possibly imagine. Along the way the character has gone from a bratty teenager named Erica Kane, to a decidedly more worldly, corporate executive named Erica Kane Martin Brent Cudahy Chandler Montgomery Montgomery Chandler. In 1991, Lucci received the first People's Choice Award for Favorite Female Daytime Performer, and has additionally received a 1988 Soap Opera Digest Award for "Outstanding Contribution to Daytime Television," the 1989 Canadian TV Guide People's Choice Award for Best Soap Actress, the 1985 People Magazine Reader's Poll Award for Best Soap Actress, and was named "Woman of the Year" by the Italian-American Welfare League. Although Lucci has now been nominated for an amazing thirteen daytime Emmys, she is yet to take home the prize, but the talented actress continues to enjoy a rich, rewarding life nonetheless. Born on December 23, 1948 in Westchester County, New York, Susan attended Marymount College, and following graduation she auditioned for the role of Tara Martin on "All My Children," but fortunately was cast as Erica Kane. She continued to study acting in Harold Clurman's midnight classes, and over the course of her run on "All My Children," has found great success on prime time as well. Among the many t.v. movies in which Lucci has starred: "Lady Mobster," "Mafia Princess," "Invitation to Hell," "Anastasia," "Secret Passions," "The Woman who Sinned," "Double Edge," and "The Bride in Black," as well as on the big screen in "Young Doctors in Love." Additionally, she has appeared on "Dallas," "Fantasy Island," "Love Boat," and in such t.v. specials as "How to Attract the Right Man," parts one and two of "Night of 100 Stars," the A&E program, "The Class of the Twentieth Century," and as the host of "Saturday Night Live." She has also been seen as a spokesperson for Ford, Sweet Ones, Wendys, and on the QVC network, through which her line of hair care products, The Susan Lucci Collection, are sold. All this phenomenal success has established Lucci as a television superstar, and she has been featured on "The Oprah Winphrey Show" and the ABC News program, "20/20." To escape her hectic professional life, Susan enjoys skiing, tennis, and travelling. A far cry from her on-screen alter ego, Ms. Lucci has been happily married to Helmut Huber, a former chef, and now her manager, since 1969, with whom she has two children, Liza Victoria, born in 1975, and Andreas Martin, born in 1980. The family lives in a suburb outside New York City.

ROBERT LuPONE

Born: July 29 in Brooklyn, New York
Marital Status: divorced
Height: 5'9 1/2" **Eyes:** brown **Hair:** brown
Education: Julliard School of Music, B.F.A.
Interests: scuba diving, sailing
Awards: 1985 Daytime Emmy nomination for Outstanding Supporting Actor ("All My Children"); 1976 Tony Award nomination, Outstanding Supporting Actor for "A Chorus Line;" 1973 Joseph Jefferson Award for Best Actor.

Daytime Dramas: "Ryan's Hope," Chester Wallace, 1980; **"Search for Tomorrow,"** Tom Bergman, 1983; **"All My Children,"** Zach Grayson, 1984-1985; **"As the World Turns,"** Neal Cory, 1985-1986; **"Loving;" "Another World;" "Guiding Light,"** Leo Sharpe, 1991-

Of all the characters Robert LuPone has played over the course of his career, the characters named Zach seemed to have brought him the most accolades. His performance on Broadway, as Zach in the original cast production of "A Chorus Line" earned him a Tony award nomination, while his role as the villainess Zach Grayson on "All My Children" earned him an Emmy nomination. Born on July 29, 1946, at the Brooklyn Naval Hospital to Orlando and Louise, Bob grew up on Long Island with his twin brother, William, and sister Patti. Patti, like her brother, has achieved great success on Broadway, and in television as the star of the acclaimed series, "Life Goes On." Today, Bob's father is a retired professor emeritus at San Diego State University, and his mother is an administrative assistant at C.W. Post College. Aside from his role in "A Chorus Line," Bob has also starred on Broadway in "St. Joan," "Late Night Comic," and the Circle in the Square production of "Zoya's Apartment." Equally at home in feature films, he has starred in the Oliver Stone movie, "The Doors," "Jesus Christ Superstar" and "Melaney Rose." On daytime television, LuPone has been seen on and off the soaps since 1980, currently playing on "Guiding Light." Annually, Robert directs an original play at the Newport Festival for the Shake-A-Leg Group, an organization of physically challenged people. He is also founder and president of the Manhattan Class Company, a not-for-profit theatre company that brings original works to the stage. Away from his professional and charitable work, Bob, who lives in New York City, enjoys sailing and scuba diving.

JOHN LUPTON

Born: August 22, 1928 in Highland Park, Illinois
Marital Status: married to Dian Friml, three children, Rollin, Ed and Tony
Height: 5'11" **Eyes:** blue **Hair:** gray
Education: American Academy of Dramatic Arts
Interests: sculpting, sports, theater, tennis, gardening

Daytime Dramas: "Never Too Young," Frank Landis, 1965; **"Days of Our Lives,"** Tommy Horton, 1965-1972, 1975-1979

A popular actor of stage, television, and film, John Lupton is best known to daytime audiences as Tommy Horton, Jr. on "Days of Our Lives." Born on August 22, 1928 in Highland Park, Illinois, John, along with his sister, were raised by his father, a newspaperman with the Milwaukee Journal, and his mother, a homemaker. After graduating from Shorewood High School, where he played football and tennis, John enrolled at the American Academy of Dramatic Arts in New York City. Once completing his course of study there, Lupton embarked on a professional acting career, gaining initial experience with the Port Players and at the Edwin Strawbridge Children's Theatre. Among his numerous stage credits are roles in "Plaza Suite," "Born Yesterday," "The Glass Menagerie," "Calculated Risk," "Arms and the Man," "The Decent Thing," "Period of Adjustment," and with Katherine Hepburn in the national touring company of "As You Like It." In 1950, Lupton was placed under contract by MGM studios, and over the next two years starred in such films as "Story of Three Loves," "Julius Caesar," "Diane," "All The Brothers Were Valiant," "Escape From Fort Bravo," and "Scandal At Scourie." Independent of MGM, the actor's additional film credits include "Midway," "Airport '75," "Day of the Wolves," "Cool Breeze," "Napoleon and Samantha," "The Greatest Story Ever Told," "Great Locomotive Chase," "Man in a Net," with Alan Ladd, "Man with a Gun," with Robert Mitchum, "Glory," "Fun Fever," and "Durango." On the small screen, John was a regular for two seasons on "Broken Arrow," and has guest starred on over 150 prime time shows, among them "Studio One," "Playhouse 90," "G.E. Theatre," "Laramie," "Wagon Train," "Alfred Hitchcock," "Gomer Pyle," "Gunsmoke," "The Virginian," "Marcus Welby," "Mannix," "Ironside," "I Spy," "Cannon," "Rockford Files," "Kung Fu," "Police Story," "Hunter," and "Charlie's Angels," In addition, Lupton co-starred in such t.v. movies as "Miracle on Ice," "Bare Essence," "Red River," and "Sidney Shore." On daytime t.v., along with "Days of Our Lives," he appeared as Frank Landis on "Never Too Young." John, who lives in Los Angeles, is now married to his second wife, Dian Friml, (granddaughter of composer Rudolf Friml) and the couple have three children, daughter Rollin, and stepsons Ed and Tony. Along with donating his time to the Special Olympics and Multiple Sclerosis, Lupton enjoys tennis, gardening, sculpting, and the theater.

PHYLLIS LYONS

Born: August 20 in North Brunswick, New Jersey
Marital Status: single
Height: 5'4" **Eyes:** green **Hair:** blond
Education: Rutgers University, M.F.A.
Interests: fine arts, running, aerobics
Awards: 1991 Soap Opera Award nomination, Outstanding Female Newcomer
Daytime Dramas: "All My Children," Arlene Vaughan, 1990-

When Phyllis Lyons took on the role of recovering alcoholic, Arlene Vaughan on "All My Children," the producers intended the character to be only temporary. However, the talented actress brought such a passion and focused intensity to the role that she was awarded a contract. A native of North Brunswick, New Jersey, Phyllis traces her love of acting back to high school, when she appeared in a school production of "Fiddler on the Roof." The experience proved to be so powerful that she immediately knew that she had found her calling. After receiving her MFA degree in theater from Rutgers University, Phyllis began working onstage at the Williamstown Theater Festival, New York's Public Theater, and The Baltimore Center Stage. Among her stage credits are roles in "As You Like It," "Romeo and Juliet," and "Fool for Love." On television she has appeared on "L.A. Law" and a CBS pilot called "Hot Prospects." Since joining "All My Children," Phyllis has had the considerable challenge of playing an alcoholic, afraid to face a drunk driving conviction that could land her behind bars and putting the blame on her daughter. The fact that daytime audiences have responded sympathetically to such a character is a testimony to the deft sensitivity of Phyllis' performance. In her spare time, Ms. Lyon's keeps in shape through running and aerobics, and also enjoys visiting museums.

ROBERT MAILHOUSE

Born: January 22 in New Haven, Connecticut
Marital Status: single
Height: 6'4" **Eyes:** brown **Hair:** brown
Education: Catholic University, B.A.
Interests: music
Awards: 1992 Soap Opera Award, Outstanding Comic Performance ("Days of Our Lives")

Daytime Dramas: "Days of Our Lives," Brian Scofield, 1990-1992

Although he originally auditioned for the role of Lawrence Alamain on "Days of Our Lives," Robert Mailhouse instead wound up as the decidedly more comic Brian Scofield. (The role of Alamain went to Michael Sabatino) Fortunately for Mailhouse his new role turned out to be a perfect match and since joining the show the actor has earned a Soap Opera Award for Outstanding Comic Performance. Born on January 22 in New Haven, Connecticut, Robert received his B.A. in acting from Catholic University, following which he began working on stage and in commercials. You can catch him in an Oscar Mayer Lunchables. Among his numerous theater credits are roles in "Actor's Nightmare," "The Glass Menagerie," "Equus," "The Homecoming," "Betrayal," "Julius Caesar," and "Sexual Perversity in Chicago." Additionally, Mailhouse performed in a stage reading of "The Dinner Party," opposite the late Geraldine Page. Moving from New York to Los Angeles, the actor began to concentrate on television work, making a guest appearance on "Kay O'Brien," as well as brief stints on two daytime dramas, "One Life to Live" and "Ryan's Hope." Mailhouse almost reached prime time stardom when he was slated to take on the Tom Hanks' role in a television version of the film, "Big," but unfortunately the project never got off the ground. Away from the set, Mailhouse, who lives in Los Angeles with his labrador, Gus, is active with both Amnesty International and Greenpeace. He owns three classic motorcycles, having been, since childhood, a motorcycle enthusiast. Mailhouse also flexes his musical skills as the topless drum player in a punk band called BFS which features actor, Keanu Reeves. The band can be seen playing the L.A. underground clubs. He has also played keyboard in a garage band, which featured Antony Alda and again, Keanu Reeves.

BETH MAITLAND

Born: May 12 in Rapid City, South Dakota
Marital Status: married
Eyes: blue   **Hair:** blond
Education: Arizona State Theatre University; Los Angeles Film Industry Workshop
Interests: horseback riding, dancing, swimming
Awards: 1985 Daytime Emmy for Best Supporting Actress

Daytime Dramas: "The Young and the Restless,"
Traci Abbott, 1982-

Since 1982, Beth Maitland has come to be known by millions as Traci Abbott on "The Young and the Restless." For her work, the popular actress was awarded the 1985 Daytime Emmy for Best Supporting Actress. Born on May 12 in Rapid City, South Dakota, Maitland moved to Scottsdale, Arizona at the age of seven. Always interested in the theater, she attended Arizona State Theatre University in Tempe, after graduating from Coronado High School in Scottsdale. She made her professional stage debut when she was just thirteen years old, and has since gone on to appear in many productions, among them "The Skin of Our Teeth," "Candide," "A Midsummer Night's Dream," and "The Crucible." In 1978, Beth moved to Los Angles, where she worked developing nightclub acts for John Davidson's "Singer Summer Camp," while at the same time continuing her acting training at the Los Angeles Film Industry Workshop. She eventually joined the faculty of the school, teaching classes in acting and daytime drama. In addition to "The Young and the Restless," Ms. Maitland's t.v. credits include "Situation Comedy," "Good Time Harry," "The New Love American Style," and a Carol Burnett special, "California Suite." Away from the set, she devotes much of her time to three charitable organizations; The American Heart Association, The American Cancer Society, and Bill Cosby's Committee for Literacy. She has also recently sued the makers of Static Guard, in the hopes that they will put warning labels on their products, stating that the contents in the can are flammable and should be sprayed prior to putting on your clothes. This came after Ms. Maitland's shirt, that she was wearing, caught fire when sprayed with Static Guard. Any monetary compensation from her suit will be donated to a burn unit. Beth, who is married, recently purchased a ranch in northern California, where she and her husband keep their five horses, five dogs and one cat. A talented equestrian, she trains and raises her own horses, as well as riding in various competitions. In addition, Ms. Maitland's other hobbies include singing, swimming, bicycling, racquetball, and jazz, tap and modern dance.

KRISTINA MALANDRO

Born: October 30 in Indianapolis, Indiana
Marital Status: single, one son, Peter John, born in 1990
Height: 5'6" **Eyes:** blue **Hair:** blond
Education: Indiana Central University; Purdue University at Indianapolis
Interests: wildlife protection, camping, ice skating, swimming
Awards: People Magazine, 50 Most Beautiful People in the World

Daytime Dramas: "General Hospital," Felicia Cummings Jones, 1984-1991, 1992-

Selected by People Magazine as one of the fifty most beautiful people in the world, Kristina Malandro has also proven herself one of daytime's brightest stars since joining the cast of "General Hospital" in 1984. Kristina's love of performing developed at a very early age, and progressed steadily during her childhood in her hometown of Indianapolis. These years were spent studying dance and appearing in both high school and local theatrical productions. Kristina enrolled as a drama major at Indiana Central University, and continued her studies at Indiana University-Purdue University at Indianapolis. Along with her extensive involvement with the University Theater Group, Kristina also got her feet wet professionally, through modelling and commercial work. With graduation looming in the not too distant future, Kristina followed the advice of her brother and sent her pictures and resumes to a modelling consultant, who in turn suggested her for various daytime roles. After auditioning for parts on "All My Children" and "Ryan's Hope," Kristina landed the role of Felicia Cummings on "General Hospital." This part has since proved a resounding success, both professionally and personally. Mirroring Felicia's romance with Frisco Jones, is Kristina's real life pairing with Jack Wagner, with whom she has had a child, Peter John, born September 4, 1990. The happy family resides in Los Angeles. Kristina is extremely active away from the set, and lists among her hobbies camping, river rafting, mountaineering, ice skating, swimming, and gymnastics. In 1989 Kristina took some time to travel to Europe and Africa, and was deeply moved by the experience. Upon returning she became a board member of the Africa Wildlife Foundation, and frequently appears on television and in print to discuss the dangers faced by African wildlife. Kristina left "GH," again in 1991 citing she wanted to spend more time with her family. Fans were happy about her 1992 return.

EDWARD MALLORY

Born: June 14 in Cumberland, Maryland
Marital Status: married to Suzanne Zenor, two sons, John and Shay
Height: 6' **Eyes:** blue
Education: Carnegie Mellon University, B.F.A . in Drama
Interests: remote control airplanes, piano
Awards: 1972 and 1973 Best Actor Award from Daytime T.V. Magazine

Daytime Dramas: "Morning Star," Bill Riley, 1965-1966;
"Days of Our Lives," Dr. William Horton, 1965-1980, 1992

For fourteen years, Edward Mallory portrayed Dr. William Horton on "Days of Our Lives," and since leaving the show has continued to be a powerful daytime force behind the camera, directing episodes of "The Young and the Restless," "General Hospital," "Generations," "Rituals," "All My Children," "Group One Medical," and "Days of Our Lives." Born on June 14, Edward was raised, along with his two siblings Carol Ann and David, in Cumberland, Maryland, where his father owned and operated a cafe. An extremely happy time, Mallory still keeps in touch with many of his childhood friends. After attending a military academy, Mallory studied drama at Carnegie Mellon University, eventually earning his B.F.A. degree before enrolling in the officer's candidate school at Fort Benning. Upon graduation, he was commissioned as a second lieutenant in the infantry. In 1966, after starring on another daytime drama, "Morning Star," Mallory joined the cast of "Days of Our Lives," and over the next fourteen years earned two Best Actor Awards from Daytime T.V. Magazine, in 1972 and 1973. He returned to the role for a brief appearance in July of 1991. In addition to daytime, the talented actor made numerous prime time t.v. appearances and starred in the feature films "Diamond Head" and "Experiment in Terror." Along with his scores of soap opera directing credits, he also called shots on the documentary, "Remembering World War II." Mallory and his wife, former "Days of Our Lives" star Suzanne Zenor, share a home in Topanga, California. The couple have two sons, Shay and John. For over a decade Edward has donated his time as a member of the Board of Directors for the Theatre East Workshop, three years of which he served as president. To relax, the actor/director enjoys playing the piano and flying radio controlled airplanes.

LARKIN MALLOY

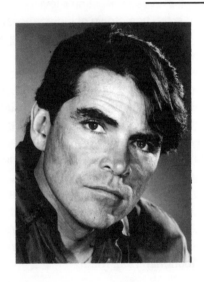

Born: September 24 in New York, New York
Marital Status: single
Height: 6' **Eyes:** brown **Hair:** brown
Education: Iona College
Interests: theater, skiing, travelling, bicycling
Awards: nominated for 1984 Daytime Emmy for Best Actor ("Edge of Night"); two Afternoon T.V. Best Actor Awards ("Edge of Night"); 1973 New York State Theater Festival, Best Actor

Daytime Dramas: "Edge of Night," Schuyler Whitney, 1980-1984; **"Guiding Light,"** Kyle Sampson, 1984-1986; **"All My Children,"** Travis Montgomery, 1986-1991; **"Loving,"** Clay Alden, 1992-

A daytime favorite, Larkin Malloy has starred as a leading man on four daytime dramas since making his soap debut in 1980. His first role, Schuyler Whitney on "Edge of Night," earned him two Afternoon T.V. Best Actor Awards and a 1984 daytime Emmy nomination for Best Actor. Since then, Malloy has resurfaced on "Guiding Light," "All My Children," and most recently replacing James Horan as Clay Alden on "Loving." After many negotiations, the actor committed himself to this last role just twenty four hours before he was to go before the cameras, and thus was forced to wear his own clothes on his "Loving" debut, since there was no time for a wardrobe fitting. Born Thomas Larkin Malloy (Larkin is his mother's maiden name), the youngest of four, on September 24 in New York City, he was the first generation of his family born in America, his parents having come to New York from the County of Sligo in Ireland. After attending Fordham Preparatory School, Malloy went on to Iona College, where he performed in numerous school productions. Beginning his professional career, the young actor concentrated chiefly on stage work, appearing in such productions as "Romeo and Juliet," "A Christmas Carol," "Mr. de Molier," "Cyrano de Bergerac," "Idiot's Delight," "The Three Sisters," and "Taming of the Shrew." In 1973, Larkin was awarded the Best Actor prize at the New York State Theater Festival. To this day he continues to hone his acting skills in workshops and classes, and is also in the process of organizing a Los Angeles based classical theatre company. Along with his work on "Loving," he hopes to continue to explore theatrical roles. In his spare time, Larkin, who is single, enjoys sailing, travelling, skiing, reading, and bicycling.

AMELIA MARSHALL

Born: April 2 in Albany, Georgia
Marital Status: engaged to marry musician Daryl Waters in November 1992
Eyes: brown   **Hair:** brown
Education: University of Texas at Austin, Bachelor's Degree
Interests: reading, knitting, baking

Daytime Dramas: "One Life to Live," Miranda;
"Guiding Light," Gilly Grant, 1990-

With skills ranging from acting/singing/dancing to repairing telephones and climbing telephone poles, it seems pretty clear that Amelia Marshall is adequately prepared for the future. Presently concentrating on acting, she has portrayed television producer Gilly Grant on "Guiding Light" since 1990. Amelia was born on April 2 in Albany, Georgia, where her father, David, worked as an executive for a large insurance company. The rest of the Marshall family includes Amelia's mother, Catherine, a math teacher, older sister, Valerie, a business executive, and younger brother, David Jr., presently an undergraduate at Princeton. The family relocated frequently, living in Amityville, New York, Atlanta, Georgia, and eventually Houston, Texas. Always interested in singing, Amelia got her first opportunity to develop this talent when she was accepted into the vocal music program at the High School for the Performing and Visual Arts. However, after a brief time at the school, she found her interest shifting from singing to dancing, and Amelia began to devote herself to this new found passion. She studied with the Houston Ballet, and eventually became a member of the Houston Jazz Ballet, directed by Patsy Swayze. While continuing her dance training, Ms. Marshall also found the time to attend the University of Texas at Austin, where she earned a degree in Business Administration, and at the same time honed her dance skills as a school cheerleader. After graduating, she went to work as a telephone repair supervisor for Southwestern Bell, and over the subsequent two years learned how to repair telephones and climb telephone poles. Eventually, she returned to entertaining, and has since appeared in numerous theatrical productions, including roles on Broadway in Bob Fosse's "Big Deal," "Harrigan and Hart," and "Porgy and Bess," while she has been seen off-Broadway in "Skyline" and "Applause." Marshall's additional theater credits include "Cats," "West Side Story," "Queenie Pie," "Sweet Charity," and "A...My Name is Alice," and she has also performed in "Treemonisha," with the Houston Grand Opera. Prior to joining the cast of "Guiding Light," she had a brief run as Miranda on "One Life to Live," and was additionally seen in two television specials, "Robert Klein on Broadway" and the PBS program, "The History of Dance." Now a resident of New York City, one of Amelia's favorite hobby is to visit amusement parks. She also enjoys knitting, baking, reading and gardening.

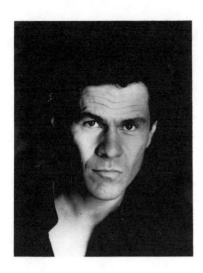

A MARTINEZ

Born: September 27 in California
Marital Status: married to Leslie Bryans, one son, Dakota Lee, and one daughter, Devin Makena
Eyes: brown   **Hair:** brown
Interests: cycling, baseball, music
Education: UCLA
Awards: 1988 Soap Opera Award for Outstanding Hero; 1990 Daytime Emmy Award for Best Actor; 1990 Soap Opera Award for Outstanding Lead Actor; 1990 Soap Opera Award for Outstanding Super Couple (with Marcy Walker); 1987, 1988, 1989, 1992 Daytime Emmy nomination for Outstanding Lead Actor

Daytime Dramas: "Santa Barbara," Cruz Castillo, 1984-1992

Adored by fans across the world, A Martinez is one of daytimes most talented actors. A California native, born Adolf (a family name, but he was always known as A) Martinez grew up with a passion for music. At the age of twelve this accomplished musician made his professional debut at a talent competition held at the Hollywood Bowl. Appearing in front of an audience of over 15,000, he performed his rendition of "Kingston Market." Martinez attended UCLA, where in the Hollywood tradition, he was "discovered" in acting class and made his motion picture debut in "Born Wild," playing opposite Patty McCormick. He has played opposite many of Hollywoods greatests including John Wayne in "The Cowboys," "Once Upon A Scoundrel," with Zero Mostel, "Shoot the Sundown," with Christopher Walken and Margot Kidder, "Beyond the Limit" with Michael Caine and Richard Gere and as Meryl Streep's, butler/lover in "She-Devil." Martinez also starred in George Harrison's Handmade Film "Pow Wow Highway" a film which won critical acclaim at a series of international film festivals. He has also appeared in "La Chiva" and "In Circumstantial Evidence." His numerous television credits including a starring role in the critically acclaimed "Seguin" for American Playhouse, the television movies "The Young Pioneers," "Walk Softly Through the Night," "The Far Turn," "A Matter of Honor," "Manhunt: Search for the Nightstalker," "Not of This World," "Criminal Behavior" with Farrah Fawcett and the NBC Christmas movie, "The Nick of Time." Martinez has held starring roles in the series "Whiz Kids," with Max Gail as well as "Cassie & Company" opposite Angie Dickinson. No stranger to prime time, he has also guest starred on "Quincy," "Police Story," "Baretta," "Kung Fu," "The Streets of San Francisco," "Barney Miller," and "L.A. Law" where he portrayed a convicted killer sentenced to the gas chamber. Daytime audiences know Martinez for his portrayal of Cruz Castillo on "Santa Barbara." His role on the show has garnered him a Daytime Emmy as well as numerous Soap Opera Awards. Martinez is married to Leslie Bryans and together they have a son, Dakota Lee and a daughter, Devin Makena. In his spare time he enjoys baseball and cycling. Pursuing his musical talents, Martinez continues to write music in a unique style which he deems "L.A. Rock." His composition "Last Light of the Moon" was performed on "The Tonight Show." 1992 marked A's last year with "Santa Barbara" and first year as a regular on the hit series, L.A. Law.

MARISOL MASSEY

Born: November 10 in Puerto Rico
Marital Status: single
Height: 5'7" **Eyes:** green **Hair:** brown
Education: Emerson College, Bachelor's Degree
Interests: hiking, horseback riding, dance, music

Daytime Dramas: "Loving," Abril Domecq

Marisol Massey first became known to television audiences as the original hostess of the MTV game show, "Remote Control." Today, however, daytime audiences know her best as the good natured Abril Domecq on "Loving." Born of Puerto Rican/British decent, Marisol was raised in Puerto Rico before relocating to Boston, where she attended Emerson College. After graduating with a degree in business and theater arts, Marisol moved to New York where she was signed by the Elite Modeling Agency. Since then Marisol has divided her time between modelling and her acting career. Aside from her work on "Loving," she appeared in the film "Second Sight," with Bronson Pinchot, as well as on stage in "The Have Little," a play by Migdalia Cruz, which won the prestigious, International Blackburn Award for women writers. In her spare time Marisol enjoys water sports, hiking, horseback riding, and dancing. She also donates much of her time to working with troubled children at the Youth Risk Center.

MARIE MASTERS

Born: February 4 in Cincinnati, Ohio
Marital Status: divorced, two children, twins Jenny and Jesse
Height: 5'4" **Eyes:** green **Hair:** brown
Education: Marion College, Bachelor's Degree
Interests: art

Daytime Dramas: "Love of Life," Hester Ferris, 1966-67;
"As the World Turns," Dr. Susan Stewart,1968-79; **"One Life to Live,"** Helen Murdoch, 1982; **"As the World Turns,"** Dr. Susan Stewart, 1986-

Since her daytime drama debut in 1966, Marie Masters has proven herself to be one of television's most enduring and popular actresses. Born on February 4 in Cincinnati, Ohio, Marie was, from an early age, an extremely artistic and creative child. She came upon her desire to act at the age of ten when she attended her first play, a summer stock production. Marie became determined from that moment to become a professional actress. A sculptor as well as an actress, she received a scholarship to study art, graduating cum laud from Marion College in 1963. During her college years Marie honed her acting skills in summer stock productions, and after graduation moved to New York City, where she studied with acting coaches Wynn Handman and Uta Hagen. While still trying to find work as an actress, Marie supported herself by working at the city desk of "Women's Wear Daily." The world of journalism proved only a temporary stop however, as Marie made her New York stage debut a short time later in the off-Broadway production of "A Sound of Silence." Among her other stage credits are roles on Broadway in "There's a Girl in My Soup," and in regional productions of "Hay Fever," "The Trojan Woman," and "The Country Girl." Marie has also appeared in the feature films "Scream For Help" and "Slayground." On television, the actress has appeared in three daytime dramas, "Love of Life," "One Life to Live," and "As the World Turns." Marie originally joined the cast of "As the World Turns" in 1968, remaining with the show for eleven years before deciding to move to Los Angeles. With her heart in New York, Marie returned to the east and eventually back to the role of Dr. Susan Stewart. Her other television work includes guest appearances on "Kate and Allie," "Here's Boomer," and "King's Crossing," as well as numerous commercials. In 1991, she starred in the off-Broadway play, "Nothing to Dream About." Along with acting, Ms. Masters, who lives in New York City, is busy cultivating her skills as a director and a sculptor. Twice divorced, Marie is the mother of twins, Jenny and Jesse, who recently graduated from college. Jenny made her television debut in 1974 playing Susan Stewart's daughter Emily on "As the World Turns."

ROBIN MATTSON

Born: June 1 in Los Angeles, California
Marital Status: single
Hair: blond
Education: Santa Monica College
Interests: aerobics, cooking, attending classical concerts, most sports
Awards: nominated in 1982, 1983 Daytime Emmy for Outstanding Supporting Actress ("General Hospital"); 1986 nomination for Outstanding Supporting Actress ("Santa Barbara") 1981, 1982, 1983 Soap Opera Award for Favorite Villainess; 1988, 1989, 1990 Soap Opera Award for Outstanding Comic Performance

Daytime Dramas: "Guiding Light," Hope Bauer, 1976-1977; **"General Hospital,"** Heather Weber, 1980-1983; **"Ryan's Hope,"** Delia Ryan, 1984; **"Santa Barbara,"** Gina DeMott Capwell, 1985-

She began her professional career at the tender age of seven and today Robin Mattson is a talented actress who brings a spark to every character she portrays. Born and raised in Los Angeles, Robin's early credits include the television sitcom, "The John Forsythe Show," and "Daniel Boone." She made her feature film debut in Ivan Tors', "Namu, The Killer Whale." The legendary producer was so impressed with her performance that he placed Robin under contract and she went on to appear in "Island of the Lost," "Flipper," and "Gentle Ben." Taking some time to further her education, Robin enrolled in Santa Monica College. After college she starred in the feature films, "Take Two" with Grant Goodeve, "In and Out" with Sam Bottoms, and "Return to Macon County" with Nick Nolte. She recently shot a yet to be released feature film, "Bardo."   Robin's television credits are extensive, appearing in many prime time series including, "Charlie's Angels," "Barnaby Jones," "The Dukes of Hazard," and "Fantasy Island." She has also appeared in many television movies among them, "Fantasies," "Are You in the House Alone?," "Doctor's Private Lives," and "Mirror, Mirror." A veteran of daytime dramas, Robin has portrayed the loyal daughter, Hope Bauer on "Guiding Light," sexy blond, Delia Ryan on "Ryan's Hope," and the ever conniving, Heather Weber on "General Hospital," and her longest running role as Gina DeMott Capwell on "Santa Barbara." Along the way she has been nominated for Emmy Awards for her roles on "General Hospital" and "Santa Barbara." She has also won numerous Soap Opera Awards for both shows in two categories - outstanding villain and comic performance. Robin's versatilities can also be witnessed behind the camera. She produced the NBC Movie of the Week, "False Witness," starring Phylicia Rashad and Philip Michael Thomas. In what spare time she has, Robin loves going to classical concerts and, growing up the daughter of a chef, it is no coincidence that Robin loves to cook. She also enjoys most sports and aerobics workouts. Single, Robin has been involved with actor/writer John Vargas (ex-Rico, "General Hospital") for many years.

BRAD MAULE

Born: October 11 in Rotan, Texas
Marital Status: married to Laverne Bullard on December 12, 1984, three children, Michael, Hunter and Lily
Height: 6" **Eyes:** blue **Hair:** light brown
Education: Stephen F. Austin College, B.F.A.
Interests: guitar, songwriting, painting
Awards: 1984 Dramalouge Award for "Marry Me a Little"

Daytime Dramas: "General Hospital," Dr. Anthony Jones, 1984-

A small town boy decides to leave his family's ranch and go off to Hollywood to pursue fame and fortune as an actor and a singer. While this may sound like a movie of the week, it just so happens to be the story of Brad Maule. Or as Maule describes it, he lived on the "family farm (which was like) "The Last Picture Show" on a good day." Raised in Rotan, Texas and raised on a cattle and cotton ranch, Maule opted not to follow in the ranching footsteps of his parents, George and Josie, but rather try his hand at a career in show business. Maule got his first taste of the spotlight when he appeared in high school productions. A true product of small town life, Maule attended one of America's last country schools, which averaged about 13 students in each grade. After what must have been a quick graduation ceremony, Maule moved on to Stephen F. Austin College, where he continued his theatrical studies. (Years later, after landing his role on "General Hospital," Maule established a scholarship at his alma mater, which would provide financial support to a student who wished to study drama.) After college Maule's next move was to Hollywood where he embarked on a successful string of stage appearances. At the Westwood Playhouse he appeared in Billy Barne's musical revue, "Movie Star," as well as being featured in "Somethin's Rockin' in Denmark" and the Stephen Sondheim musical, "Marry Me a Little." For his performance in "Marry Me a Little," a two character musical, Maule was awarded the Dramalogue Award. On television, along with "General Hospital," he has made guest appearances on "Charlie's Angeles," "Three's Company," The White Shadow," and "Too Close for Comfort." He was also in the t.v. movie, "Malibu." Like his t.v. wife, Jacklyn Zeman, Maule has also served as co-host on "The Home Show." While primarily known for his acting, Brad has also earned a reputation for his musical abilities. A singer and a songwriter, he recently headlined at the famed Palomino Club, and has performed on such shows as "The Mike Douglas Show," "The Merv Griffin Show," "The John Davidson Show," and at the American Music Awards. Musically Maule's taste are a little bit country (he was once a backup singer for Bobbie Gentry of "Ode to Billy Joe" fame), and in 1991 released his first album, "Living it Up," for which he not only wrote and performed all the songs, but designed the album cover as well. Maule and his wife, Laverne, live in Sherman Oaks with their three children, Michael Benjamin, Hunter Nix, and Lily Alexandra Nix. Away from his hectic work life, Maule enjoys playing the guitar, songwriting and painting.

PEGGY McCAY

Born: November 3 in New York, New York
Marital Status: single
Height: 5' 3"   **Eyes:** brown   **Hair:** blond
Education: Barnard College, Columbia University, B.S.
Interests: health, environmental issues, animal protection,
vegetarianism to save the earth
Awards: nominated for Best Actress Daytime Emmys, 1986,
1987 ("Days of Our Lives"); nominated for Best Actress Emmy,
1987 ("Cagney and Lacey"); 1991 Best Actress Emmy ("The
Trials of Rosie O'Neil"); John Henry Foundation Award, 1991

Daytime Dramas: "Love of Life," Vanessa Dale, 1951-1955;
"For Better or Worse," 1959-1960; **"The Young Marrieds,"**
1964-1966; **"General Hospital,"** Iris Fairchild, 1967-1970;
"Days of Our Lives," Caroline Brady, 1985-

An Emmy award winning performer, Peggy McCay has established herself as one of daytime's, and primetime's, best actresses. For the past seven years she has portrayed Caroline Brady on "Days of Our Lives," earning two Daytime Emmy nominations for best actress. In addition, Ms. McCay has been seen on "Love of Life," "For Better or Worse," "The Young Married," and "General Hospital." Born on November 3 in New York City, where her father was a building contractor, her mother an artist, Peggy attended small, private convent schools, following which she enrolled at Barnard College as a writing major. She began her professional career at nineteen when she toured with the Margo Jones Repertory Company in "Summer and Smoke," while she landed her first television role, in a Kraft Theatre production just two weeks after her college graduation. A long time member of the prestigious Actor's Studio, Peggy has been involved with the theater throughout her career, sharing her expertise as an acting teacher at Pasadena's American Academy of Dramatic Arts. On television, in addition to daytime, she appeared for six seasons as Marion Hume on "Lou Grant," as well as making frequent guest appearances on such shows as "Cagney and Lacey" and "The Trials of Rosie O'Neil." In 1987, McCay became the first actress in television history to be nominated for both daytime and primetime Best Actress Emmys, the former for her work on "Days of Our Lives," the latter for a guest role on "Cagney and Lacey." Although she did not take home the prize in 1987, her performance in a 1991 episode of "The Trials of Rosie O'Neil," in which she played a mentally ill homeless woman, earned her the year's Emmy for Best Actress. She was similarly honored by the John Henry Foundation, an organization promoting a positive representation of the mentally ill. In addition to her extensive television work, Ms. McCay appeared in the feature films, "Murphy's Romance" and "Getting Dead," and put her writing skills to work when she scripted and starred in "The Caroline Brady Rap," a 1991 production presented in front of two thousand people at the Greek Theater in Los Angeles. Presently living in L.A., Peggy, who is single, donates her energies to animal protection, the preservation of the wilderness, and promoting vegetarianism as a means to both good health and environmental protection.

CADY McCLAIN

Born: October 13 in Burbank, California
Marital Status: single
Height: 5'3" **Eyes:** blue **Hair:** strawberry blond
Education: high school
Interests: theater, dancing, drawing
Awards: 1991 Daytime Emmy for Outstanding Ingenue;
1992 Soap Opera Award nomination for Outstanding Younger
Leading Actress; 1992 Daytime Emmy nomination for
Outstanding Younger Actress

Daytime Dramas: "All My Children," Dixie Cooney, 1989-

While Cady McClain's performance as Dixie Cooney Chandler Martin Lawson on "All My Children" may have earned her a daytime Emmy, it is her tap dancing abilities which landed her in the Guiness Book of World Records. Dancing from an early age, Cady was just nine years old when she, along with 499 fellow tap dancers, became the largest group to perform the same routine, thus landing themselves in the record books. A California native, the rest of Cady's family includes her father, an attorney, her mother, an artist, and older sister Molly, a Yale graduate. Although she graduated from high school at sixteen, academics never had much appeal for Cady, who was instead devoted to performing from an early age. Cady began appearing in commercials at the age of ten, the first of which (for Band Aids) called on the young actress to wash a horse and sing. Unfortunately the horse stepped on her foot, breaking her toe, but Cady handled it like a pro and went on to do many more commercials, eventually progressing to film and television roles. On television, she portrayed Erin Shienfeld on "St. Elsewhere," as well as guest starring on such shows as "Cheers," "Spencer: For Hire," "Lou Grant," "Just a Regular Kid: An AIDS Story," an ABC afterschool special, and the television film "Who Will Love My Children." On the big screen, Cady appeared in "My Favorite Year," as Peter O'Toole's daughter, Tess, "Simple Justice," and "Pennies for Heaven," in which she put her tap dancing skills to use. Equally at home on stage, Ms. McClain's theater credits include "A Little Night Music," "Happy Birthday and Other Humiliations," "Dames at Sea," "Wait Until Dark," "The Miracle Worker," "Finian's Rainbow," "The Music Man," "Quiet on the Set," and in 1992 alongside fellow soap stars, Walt Willey, Marilyn Chris, and Bernie Barrow, in "Barefoot in the Park," presented at the Music Fairs at Valley Forge and Westbury. Away from the "All My Children" set, Cady continues to hone her tap dancing skills, and likes to relax by drawing fantasy cartoon animals.

JUDITH McCONNELL

Born: September 6 in Pittsburgh, Pennsylvania
Marital Status: single, one daughter, Gwendolyn, born
October 12, 1990
Eyes: blue **Hair:** blond
Education: Carnegie Mellon University
Interests: skiing, swimming, body surfing, scuba diving
Awards: Miss Pennsylvania; Contestant in Miss America
Pageant

Daytime Dramas: "General Hospital," Augusta McCloud,
1973-1975; **"As the World Turns,"** Valerie Conway, 1976-
1979; **"Another World,"** Miranda Bishop, 1980-1981; **"One
Life to Live,"** Eva Vasquez, 1983; **"Santa Barbara,"** Sophia
Capwell, 1984-

A veteran of five daytime dramas, Judith McConnell has been seen as Sophia Capwell on "Santa Barbara" since 1984. Her first foray into daytime was in 1973, when she portrayed Augusta McCloud on "General Hospital," and this was followed by roles on "As the World Turns," "Another World," and "One Life to Live." Born on September 6 in Pittsburgh, Pennsylvania, Ms. McConnell began her theater career while still in high school, as well as additionally taking the time to study ballet and tap dancing. Continuing her training, she enrolled as a drama major at Carnegie Mellon University, during which time she also entered the beauty pageant circuit, taking home the title of Miss Pennsylvania and competing for the Miss America crown. After leaving school, McConnell performed in scores of regional productions, eventually reaching the off-Broadway stage in "Something for the Boys." On television, in addition to her prolific daytime work, the actress was seen in the pilot, "Judd for the Defense," as well as making guest appearances on such shows as "Mannix," "Cannon," "Star Trek," "Wild Wild West," and "Harry O." Ms. McConnell, who is single, presently lives in the Hollywood Hills, sharing her home with Gwendolyn, her recently adopted daughter. In her spare time, Judith enjoys swimming, water skiing, snow skiing, body surfing, and scuba diving.

JOHN McCOOK

Born: June 20 in California
Marital Status: married to actress Laurette Spang on February 16, 1980, three children, Jake, Bucky and Molly; one son, Seth from a previous marriage
Hair: salt/pepper
Education: Long Beach State College
Interests: scuba diving, remodeling his house
Awards: 1977 Soap Opera Award for Favorite Male Newcomer ("The Young and the Restless"); M.V.P. Award from Soap Opera Update Magazine, ("The Bold and the Beautiful")

Daytime Dramas: "The Young and the Restless," Lance Prentiss,1976-1980; **"The Bold and the Beautiful,"** Eric Forrester, 1987-

Talented and successful, traits found in both Eric Forrester and John McCook, the actor who portrays him. A California native, McCook worked at Disneyland while attending Long Beach State College. His professional career began in the chorus at the San Diego Circle Arts Theatre. After this brief stint, he appeared at Melodyland in productions of "Guys and Dolls," with Hugh O'Brian and Betty Grable, "Firefly" with Anne Marie Alberghetti, and "Flower Drum Song," with Pat Suzuki. Moving to New York, McCook appeared in the City Center revival of "West Side Story" where he was discovered by scouts from Warner Brothers, and was one of the last three actors personally signed by Jack Warner himself. McCook later went on to sign with Universal Studios as a contract player before being drafted. He served in the army for two years, playing the piano and conducting the men's chorus. After his release, McCook enjoyed an extensive career in the theater, appearing in "Barefoot in the Park," with Virginia Mayo, "Mame," with Ann Miller, and numerous other shows including "They're Playing Our Song," "Seven Brides for Seven Brothers," "The Pirates of Penzance," "42nd Street," "Man of La Mancha," and "Oklahoma." A veteran television actor, McCook portrayed Lance Prentis, a core character on "The Young and the Restless" and today he portrays another character he originated, the leader of Forrester Creations, Eric Forrester on "The Bold and the Beautiful." His talented portrayals on both shows have earned him awards from Soap Opera Digest and Soap Opera Update Magazine. McCook married Laurette Spang, a former television actress, now a writer on February 16, 1980. Together they have three children, Jake, Bucky, and Molly. McCook also has a son, Seth from a previous marriage. When not at work, he enjoys scuba diving, as well as spending time remodeling their house.

KIMBERLY McCULLOUGH

Born: March 5, 1978 in Bellflower, California
Marital Status: single
Height: 4'10" **Eyes:** brown **Hair:** brown
Education: enrolled in La Mirada High School
Interests: dancing, singing, collecting European dolls
Awards: 1986, 1987 Youth in Film Awards; 1986 Soap Opera Award for Best Juvenile in a Daytime or Primetime Program; 1987 Daytime T.V. Magazines Top Ten Actress on Soap Operas; 1989 Daytime Emmy for Best Juvenile Performer; 1990 Emmy nomination for Best Juvenile in a Drama Series; 1992 Soap Opera Award nomination for Outstanding Younger Actor

Daytime Dramas: "General Hospital," Robin Scorpio, 1985-

Kimberly McCullough is a true rarity in the world of daytime drama, a child actress who has played the same character for over five years. Since August of 1985 Kimberly has played Robin Scorpio, and audiences have been able to watch her grow up on screen. This has propelled the teenaged McCullough to the ranks of daytime dramas top actresses. Kimberly was born in Bellflower, California, from which her family moved first to Huntington Beach, then to Fresno, and eventually to her present home in La Mirada. Kimberly first worked professionally when she was but seven months old, appearing in a diaper commercial with Juliet Mills. By the age of five she was dancing at trade shows in Las Vegas, as well as appearing (and dancing) on television in such shows as "Fame," "Solid Gold," and "The People's Choice Awards." Kimberly also performed in the films "Electric Boogaloo," "Breakin' 2," and "Purple People Eater," as well as on stage in the Los Angeles production of "Les Miserable." Most recently, Kimberly was seen in the 1992 blockbuster, "Bugsy" as Warren Beatty's daughter. It was not until 1985 that Kimberly began to study acting seriously, yet in August of that same year she landed the role of Robin on "General Hospital," a role which has brought her great success. Among the accolades bestowed on this young star have been two Youth in Film Awards for 1986 and 1987, a Soap Opera Award for Best Juvenile in a Daytime or Primetime Drama, amd a Daytime Emmy Award in 1989 for Best Juvenile performer under the age of 21. Kimberly was again nominated for this award the following year, as well as being voted #8 in a Daytime T.V. magazine readers poll on the top ten actresses in soap operas. Despite all these "extracurricular" activities, Kimberly has still managed to maintain a high grade average at her school in La Mirada. Away from school and work Kimberly likes to play video games, collect dolls, and ride her bike.

TODD McKEE

Born: November 7
Marital Status: single
Eyes: brown **Hair:** brown
Education: University of Southern California
Interests: snowboarding, tennis, windsurfing
Awards: 1992 Soap Opera Award nomination for Outstanding Younger Lead Actor

Daytime Dramas: "Santa Barbara," Ted Capwell, 1984-1989; **"The Bold and The Beautiful,"** Jake Maclaine, 1990-1992

Todd McKee made his professional debut as Ted Capwell on daytime's "Santa Barbara" and remained with the show for five years. Todd along with then co-star, Lane Davies took a hiatus from show business and traveled around the world, making stops in Kenya, Greece, Europe, and Thailand. When he returned to the states he auditioned for the role of Jake and joined the cast of "The Bold and the Beautiful" in March of 1990. Todd was educated at the University of Southern California. Always striving to improve, this talented actor frequently attends lectures, workshops, and theater classes. Todd also takes classes in stand up comedy as well as improvisation. On the set you may see him in tennis whites swinging a racquet, off the set it is likely you will see him swinging a sledge hammer wearing a tool belt and painters cap. His main interest off camera is renovating old houses, a hobby he and his brother Jon share. Home #1 was once owned by the late Victor French of "Highway to Heaven," and now, three houses later he is finding this work rewarding both mentally as well as monetarily. In what little spare time he has, he enjoys windsurfing and snowboarding. Like his character, he also enjoys tennis.

CHRISTOPHER McKENNA

Born: October 18 in Queens, New York
Marital Status: single
Height: 5'8"   **Eyes:** brown   **Hair:** light brown
Education: Watertown High School
Interests: writing, computer games, chess, "dungeons and dragons"
Awards: 1990 Best Actor Award from Laurel Cablevision "Our Father"

Daytime Dramas: "One Life to Live," Joey Buchanan, 1991-

By thirteen years of age, Christopher McKenna had already worked in theatre, film, and television. Since 1991, he has portrayed Joey Buchanan on "One Life to Live." Born in Queens, New York on October 18, his first foray onto the stage came at the age of seven when he appeared as Dopey in "Snow White and the Seven Dwarfs," which was presented by the Youth Theatre Ensemble. Enthralled by the experience, Christopher spent the next several years honing his skills, training at The Dance Theatre of the Arts, Georgianna Talent and Modeling School, Post College Summer Workshop, and with voice coach Richard Miratti. Along the way, the young actor has performed in numerous community and regional productions, including "Life with Father," "A Christmas Carol Revisited," "Ah, Wilderness," "Winnie the Pooh," and "Hans Christian Anderson." In addition to his work on "One Life to Live," he has also been seen in the much acclaimed HBO movie, "Gunplay: The Last Day in the Life of Brian Darling," as well as in the Connecticut Public Television productions of "That Time of Year," "Blitz," and "Our Father." For this last presentation, Christopher received the 1990 Best Actor award from Laurel Cablevision. Also landing roles on the big screen, his feature film credits include "Oppositional Conduct," and "The Boy Who Cried Bitch." Although he works in New York City, Christopher, along with his family, which includes younger brother Ryan, reside in Connecticut, where he attends classes at Watertown High School. In his spare time he enjoys playing "Dungeons and Dragons," chess, computer games, basketball, swimming, rollerblading, going to the movies, and writing. Hoping for a long career in front of the camera, Christopher's acting role model is Tim Curry.

KURT ROBIN McKINNEY

Born: February 15 in Louisville, Kentucky
Marital Status: married to Maronda McKinney in April 1986
Height: 5'10" **Eyes:** blue **Hair:** brown
Education: University of Louisville
Interests: swimming, tennis, karate, kickboxing
Awards: 1990 Soap Opera Award, Outstanding Male Newcomer

Daytime Dramas: "Days of Our Lives," "General Hospital,"
Ned Ashton, 1988-1991

His debut as Ned Ashton on "General Hospital" made Kurt Robin McKinney one of daytime dramas premiere leading men. Born and raised in Louisville, Kentucky, McKinney began his career as a model, both in print ads and commercials. He soon, however, decided that he wanted to pursue a career in acting, and in 1984 McKinney left for Los Angeles. After arriving in L.A., Kurt enrolled in acting classes and he soon found work in commercials, various television shows, as well as industrial films. In between stints, Kurt also worked as a car salesman. His t.v. credits include, "Highway to Heaven," "Alf," "Roomies," and "Gimme a Break" as well as the daytime drama, "Days of Our Lives." Before joining "General Hospital" in August of 1988. Kurt had a leading role in the feature film, "No Retreat, No Surrender." McKinney makes his home in the San Fernando Valley area of Los Angeles, where he lives with his wife Maronda. Kurt met his wife while in his late teens back in Louisville. Although they lived less than a mile apart while growing up, they didn't meet each other until in their late teens, when both worked together as lifeguards. Maronda enjoys a successful career as a regional sales director for a travel business. Together they share a Spanish-style home in the San Fernando Valley. The McKinney's share their home with two Chihuahuas, Carla, and her puppy, Candy. In his spare, time McKinney is a sports enthusiast, and enjoys weightlifting, karate, tennis, motorcycling, and kickboxing.

BEVERLEE McKINSEY

Born: August 9, 1940 in McAlester, Oklahoma
Marital Status: widowed, one son, Scott
Height: 5' 5" **Eyes:** green **Hair:** blond
Education: University of Oklahoma, B.F.A.
Interests: theater
Awards: nominated for Best Actress Daytime Emmys, 1977, 78, 79, 80, ("Another World"); 1977, 1978 Soap Opera Award for Outstanding Villainess ("Another World"); 1990 Soap Opera Update, Most Valuable Player Award ("Guiding Light"); 1992 Soap Opera Award nomination for Outstanding Lead Actress

Daytime Dramas: "Love Is a Many Splendored Thing,"
Julie Richards/Martha Donnelly, 1970-1971; **"Another World,"** Emma Frame Ordway, 1972; Iris Cory Carrington, 1972-1980; **"Texas,"** Iris Cory Carrington, 1980-1981; **"Guiding Light,"** Alexandra Spaulding, 1984-1992

One of daytime's legendary performers, Beverlee McKinsey has, over the past twenty years created some of televisions most memorable characters. She is perhaps best known as Iris Cory Carrington on "Another World," a role she played from 1972 to 1981, along the was earning four daytime Emmy nominations and twice voted Best Villainess by Soap Opera Digest. The character was so popular that Ms. McKinsey recreated the role as the star of the short lived program, "Texas." Since 1984, she has starred as Alexandra Spaulding on "Guiding Light." For her work on the show she received a Soap Opera Award nomination for Outstanding Lead Actress, as well as winning the 1990 Most Valuable Player Award from Soap Opera Update. Born on August 9, 1940, in McAlester, Oklahoma Beverlee describes her early years as a "very simple childhood - no theatrics." A natural performer, she received her B.F.A. degree from the University of Oklahoma, following which she got her professional start as the host of "Make Believe Clubhouse," a children's show on Boston's public television. Moving to New York City, McKinsey soon found work on the New York stage, appearing on Broadway in "Barefoot in the Park," and "Who's Afraid of Virginia Woolf," a role she recreated in London. Her off-Broadway and regional credits include "Love Nest," "P.S. 193," "Dutchman," "Valpone," and "Mert and Phil," a Joseph Papp production presented at New York's Lincoln Center. Beverlee made her daytime debut as Julia Richards/Martha Donnelly on "Love is a Many Splendored Thing," before moving onto "Another World," where she was initially cast as Emma Frame Ordway, but soon took on the more suitable role of Iris. A popular guest star on prime time shows, the actress has appeared on "Hawaii Five-O," "Remington Steele," "Mannix," "Cannon," "The Virgianian," "McMillan and Wife," and many others, while she has starred on the big screen opposite Clint Eastwood, in "Bronco Billy." Also a much sought after guest on talk shows and game shows, she has been seen on "Phil Donohue," "Today," "The Hollywood Squares," "The Merv Griffin Show," and "Tomorrow." Now living in New York City, Beverlee is a widow, having lost her husband, (actor Berkeley Harris of "Love is a Many Splendored Thing") a few years back. She has one son, Scott, who formerly worked as a director on "Guiding Light."

DANIEL McVICAR

Born: June 17 in Independence, Missouri
Marital Status: married to Darling McVicar, two children, Thomas Henry and Margaret Lee
Height: 6'4" **Eyes:** brown **Hair:** black
Education: California Institute of Art; Royal Academy of Dramatic Arts
Interests: jazz, golf, music

Daytime Dramas: "The Bold and the Beautiful,"
Clarke Garrison, 1987-1992

Quickly establishing himself as one of daytime's hottest leading men, Daniel McVicar has portrayed fashion designer/playboy Clarke Garrison on "The Bold and the Beautiful" since 1987. Born in Independence, Missouri, one of twelve children, Daniel spent most of his childhood in Colorado. He first became interested in acting while in high school, and at the age of nineteen decided to pursue this option fully, moving to Los Angeles and enrolling at the California Institute of Art. While attending this school, McVicar received additional training with Stella Adler, and as a member of the Comedy Store's Improvisation Troupe. After spending a year at the Royal Academy of Dramatic Arts in London, McVicar returned to the states and began working an array of odd jobs while looking for acting assignments. His television debut came as an extra on "The Young and the Restless," but his audition, during which he read a monologue from a Eugene O'Neil play, made an impression on the producers, who recommended him for the role of Clarke on "The Bold and the Beautiful." Since then, Daniel has also guest starred on "Highway to Heaven," as well as appearing on stage in "Othello" and "Guys and Dolls." The actor is now preparing his feature film debut, opposite Margaux Hemmingway and Appolonia, in "A Woman's Secret." The movie is being produced by Mirage, an Italian production company who sought out McVicar due to the tremendous popularity of "The Bold and the Beautiful" in Italy. Living in Santa Monica, California, Daniel and his wife, Darling, are the proud parents of two children, Thomas Henry (Hank) and Margaret Lee (Maisey). In his spare time, the actor enjoys golf, jazz, and jogging, and recently competed in the Los Angeles Marathon.

KEN MEEKER

Born: March 31 in New York, New York
Marital Status: single
Height: 6'3" **Eyes:** brown **Hair:** brown
Education: SUNY Binghamton, Bachelor's Degree;
Lee Strasberg Theatre Institute
Interests: music, volunteer work

Daytime Dramas: "One Life to Live," Rafe Garretson,
1980-1990

Born and raised in New York City, Ken Meeker first discovered acting while attending the State University of New York at Binghamton. He appeared in more than twenty school productions, and upon graduation he enrolled in the Lee Strasberg Theatre Institute. While still a student at the institute, Meeker received a development contract from ABC, which lead to his role as Rafe Garretson on "One Life to Live." Meeker has also appeared on stage, making his professional stage debut, touring with Lana Turner in the comedy-thriller "Murder Among Friends," as well as appearing as "Captain Camera" on public television in the cult hit "Adventures in Photography." Meeker also is very active in country music, both as a singer and songwriter. He frequents Nashville where he has performed on the cable show "Nashville Now," and has also performed in New York clubs with his band, Ken Meeker and the Metro Mountaineers. When not working, Meeker donates a large portion of his spare time to public service work - something he began in high school when he volunteered to be a big brother. He is involved with a theatrical workshop for psychiatric patients, supportive care for the terminally ill, as well as being a long time volunteer at a homeless shelter at St. Paul's Chapel in lower Manhattan. A member of the organization Partnership for the Homeless, Meeker believes that helping out those less fortunate is an essential facet of a balanced and fulfilling life.

TOMMY J. MICHAELS

Born: February 8, 1981 in Staten Island, New York
Marital Status: single
Height: 4'6" **Eyes:** blue **Hair:** blond
Education: currently in grade school
Interests: soccer, outer space

Daytime Dramas: "As the World Turns," Stephen Barclay;
"All My Children," Timmy Hunter, 1988-

When asked about their future plans, most actors who have enjoyed success on television and the Broadway stage would probably aspire to feature films, more theater, perhaps directing. Pose the same question to Tommy J. Michaels and the response is a tad different: "When I grow up I want to be an astronaut." (He should be able to get a lot of information from his TV mother's real father, astronaut, Michael Collins.) Not your average response, but considering that this particular actor is only eleven years old, it seems to make perfect sense. After three years on "All My Children," roles in two Broadway plays, "Les Miserable" and "The Grapes of Wrath," and a CBS Movie of the Week, "Littlest Victims," Tommy is proving himself to be a young actor with a bright future. The first child for Tom and Diane Michaels, Tommy was born on February 8, 1981, on New York's Staten Island. He first considered acting at the age of four while watching "Sesame Street." Tommy told his mother that he wanted to do what the kids on t.v. were doing, and after two years of modelling work, the six year old actor made his television debut in a commercial for cold medicine. The script called for Tommy to cough, and since he has asthma, he was a natural for the role. Following his lead, Tommy's younger siblings, Brian and Lauren, have both begun working as actors and models. Brian's most recent role was in the acclaimed film "The Fisher King." Although the pace of a three actor family is hectic, the Michaels have strived to give their children a "normal" lifestyle. Tommy attends public school, where he maintains an A average, as well as playing soccer, basketball, and baseball. He also believes in helping those less fortunate, and is honorary chairman for the Make a Wish Foundation - Kids Helping Kids Campaign. In between school and acting assignments, (currently he is working on recording an album for a new Broadway show) Tommy enjoys sports, especially soccer, baseball and swimming. He also enjoys outerspace, playing Nintendo, and other computer games.

TRACEY MIDDENDORF

Born: January 26, 1971 in Miami, Florida
Marital Status: single
Height: 5' 6 1/2"   **Eyes:** brown   **Hair:** brown
Education: State University of New York at Purchase
Interests: theater

Daytime Dramas: "Days of Our Lives," Carrie Brady, 1992-

Tracey Middendorf's professional acting debut, as Carrie Brady on "Days of Our Lives," was made all the more nerve wracking, considering that her performance would come on a special prime time episode of the popular daytime drama. However, the young actress handled the pressure well, and is now completely at home in her new role. Born on January 26, in Miami, Florida, Tracey, who is distantly related to James Dean, spent most of her childhood in Georgia where her parents were in the restaurant business. Moving north, she enrolled as a theater major at the State University of New York at Purchase, where she performed in such plays as "Getting Out," and "Reckless." Leaving college during her junior year, she moved to New York City and waited tables at The Penguin Cafe. At the same time she found an agent and began going on auditions. When she was offered the role of Carrie Brady, she relocated to Los Angeles and lives there with her two cats, Lucy and Calvin.

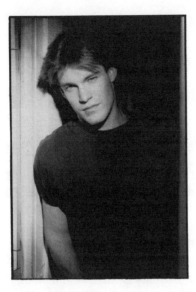

JUDSON MILLS

Born: May 10, 1969 in Washington, D.C.
Marital Status: married to actress Christiaan Torez,
May 10, 1990
Height: 5'11"   **Eyes:** blue   **Hair:** blond
Education: Barry University; American Academy of Dramatic
Arts
Interests: motorcycles, mountain climbing, canoeing, billiards,
skydiving, golf, water sports, skiing, singing, playing music with
his father and brother

Daytime Dramas: "As the World Turns," Hutch Hutchinson,
1991-

May 10th is clearly a big day in the life of Judson Mills. The first big May 10th was in 1969 when he was born; the next big May 10th was in 1990 when Judson got married; and in 1991 he landed the plum role of Hutch Hutchinson on "As the World Turns," on, you guessed it, May 10th. Raised in Virginia, in a stone house built by George Washington, (and now a national landmark) Judson comes from a close knit family. This includes his father, James, an attorney for the Federal Trade Commission, his mother, Patricia, and his younger brother Jason. Judson describes his brother as "a musician and artist; he plays drums & sings. He is now designing ties for Nicole Miller in New York, but still lives in Virginia." His parents, who have been happily married for over twenty years, and very much a product of the sixties, created a communal type of atmosphere for the Mills home. Judson's father would spend his free time playing guitar and drums, while his mother's hobbies include beekeeping, rug making, spinning, weaving, and dying her own wool. Judson describes his family with love and says they are "very, very close." A rebellious type as a child, Judson credits his parents with letting him make his own mistakes, but always being there for him nonetheless. During his school years at High Mowing Prep, Judson considered a career in football, but a performance in a school play convinced him to pursue acting instead. With his goals set he began his study of drama, first at Barry University, and then at the American Academy of Dramatic Arts. It was at the later that he met Christiaan Torez, formerly of "One Life to Live" and daughter of ex-Yankee pitcher, Mike Torez. The two immediately hit it off, and a few months later decided one afternoon to get married. Twenty four hours later, on May 10th, the couple wed in a New York City courthouse. Over the next year Christiaan found work playing Stephanie Hobart on "One Life to Live," while Judson continued his search for the right role. This day came on May 10, 1991 when Judson was informed that he had won the role of Hutch, a joyous moment tempered by the fact that Christiaan lost her "One Life to Live" role on the same day. Since joining the cast of "As the World Turns," Judson has become one of daytime's hottest properties. The actor continues to work on stage as well, appearing in such productions as "Lone Star," "Orpheus Descending," and "Picnic." In his spare time Mills, who considers himself an outdoorsman, enjoys a number of hobbies, among them camping, fishing, hunting, golf, skydiving, skiing, water sports, playing music with his father and brother, (he used to be in a band) and tending to his two boa constrictors, Romeo and Juliet and his python, Cleopatra. He is also an avid motorcyclist, and hopes to one day ride across America with his father.

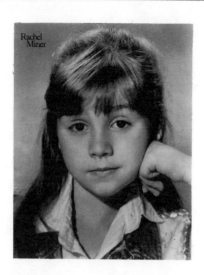

RACHEL MINER

Born: July 29, 1980 in New York, New York
Marital Status: single
Height: 4'6" **Eyes:** hazel **Hair:** blond
Education: currently in junior high
Interests: sports, reading, writing, dance, animals
Awards: 1991 Youth in Film Award, Best Younger Actress in a Daytime Drama

Daytime Dramas: "Guiding Light," Michelle Bauer, 1990-

The winner of the 1991 Youth in Film Award for Best Younger Actress in a Daytime Drama, Rachel Miner has been winning the hearts of millions since joining the cast of "Guiding Light" in 1990. Born on July 29, 1980, in New York City, where her father, Peter Miner, works as a director on "One Life to Live," Rachel has, over the course of her brief career, worked with some of the entertainment industry's biggest names. Her film credits include roles in "Freejack," Woody Allen's "Alice," "Spring Pageant," "Count Cagliostro's Den," "Don't Start," and in a New York University student film, also called "Alice." A stage actress as well, Ms. Miner has been seen in such productions as "A Doll's House" and in a staged reading of "Macbeth." In addition to her work as Michelle Bauer on "Guiding Light," she has appeared on "Shining Time Station," the PBS Holiday Special, "Tis A Gift," "One Life to Live," and numerous t.v. commercials. Currently in junior high school, Rachel frequently attends fundraising events and benefits, as well as working with her school's community service group. Away from school and work, the busy young actress list among her hobbies: horseback riding, figure skating, tennis, soccer, softball, rollerblading, skiing, tap dancing, singing, writing, reading, and taking care of her pets and other animals.

ANN MITCHELL

Born: October 23 in Providence, Rhode Island
Marital Status: divorced
Height: 5'4" **Eyes:** blue **Hair:** black
Education: Norwalk High School
Interests: architecture, art, swimming, documentaries

Daytime Dramas: "As the World Turns," Jane Bingham, 1985-

A singer and an actress, Ann Mitchell has been an entertainer for over half a century. Born on October 23 in Providence, Rhode Island, Ann's introduction to show business came courtesy of her father, who worked as a master of ceremonies and conductor on the vaudeville circuit. Ann, along with her sister Jane, would accompany him on the road, and after Ann graduated from high school in Norwalk, Connecticut, she officially began her career, singing with Paul Whiteman's Band. Following this she spent several years singing with the legendary Stan Kenton, who was recruited to appear on "The Bob Hope Show." It was on this program that Ann got her first taste of acting, a thrill that she thoroughly enjoyed. Over the next several years, Ms. Mitchell sang in nightclubs in New York and Paris, as well as continuing her acting training, which soon paid off with roles on stage in "The Importance of Being Earnest," "She Stoops to Conquer," "The Comedy of Errors," "High Spirits," and "Once Upon a Mattress." In addition to her appearances on "The Bob Hope Show," Mitchell also guest starred on "Perry Mason," "Guiding Light," and scores of commercials. Since 1985 she has been seen as dutiful secretary, Jane Bingham on "As the World Turns." Divorced from her first husband more than three decades ago, Ann has chosen not to remarry. She presently lives in New York City, where she list among her interests, architecture, documentaries, art, and swimming.

JAMES MITCHELL

Born: February 29 in Sacramento, California
Marital Status: single
Height: 5'10" **Eyes:** brown **Hair:** gray
Education: M.F.A.; Honorary Doctorate in Fine Arts from Drake University
Interests: theater, movies, cooking
Awards: 1980 Soap Opera Digest Award, Outstanding Villain; nominated for seven Daytime Emmys for Outstanding Lead Actor

Daytime Dramas: "Edge of Night," Captain Lloyd Griffin, 1964; **"Where the Heart Is,"** Julian Hathaway, 1969-1973; **"All My Children,"** Palmer Cortlandt, 1979-

After many successful years as an actor and a dancer, James Mitchell began the second stage of his career with the role of Palmer Cortlandt on "All My Children." Mitchell spent years performing on Broadway and in films, but like all dancers, his retirement came at an early age. After a four year draught during which job opportunities were few and far between, Mitchell was offered the part of Palmer in 1979, and has since maintained his status as one of daytime's leading villains. Born on February 29, in Sacramento, California, (no dancer/leap year jokes please) James began his career as a dancer on Broadway, playing lead roles in such productions as "Mack and Mable," "Carnival," "Paint Your Wagon," "Brigadoon," and "Bloomer Girl,"(the last three were highly acclaimed Agnes DeMille productions) as well as touring the nation in "Funny Girl," with Carol Lawrence, "The Threepenny Opera," and "The King and I." Also active backstage, Mitchell worked as assistant director on the Los Angeles Civic Light Opera Production of "Annie Get Your Gun," with Debbie Reynolds. Renowned for his dancing prowess, Mitchell has appeared with the Agnes DeMille Dance Theater, and in addition toured the United States, Europe, and South America with the American Ballet Theater. His film work includes "That's Dancing," the artistic director in "The Turning Point," "The Bandwagon," with Fred Astaire, "Oklahoma,"(he played Curly in the dream ballet production) and "Deep in My Heart," with Cyd Charisse. Mitchell reteamed with Charisse in her 1965 television special and the Academy Awards presentation of the following year. As an actor, Mitchell has been featured on several daytime dramas, including "Edge of Night," and a four year stint as Professor Hathaway on "Where the Heart Is." For his work on "All My Children," the actor was named favorite villain of 1980 by Soap Opera Digest. However, in keeping with the pattern set by his co-star Susan Lucci, he has never won a daytime Emmy, despite being nominated seven times for outstanding lead actor. A respected teacher, Mitchell has taught theater at Yale University, the Julliard School, and Drake University in Des Moines, Iowa, from which he received an honorary doctorate in fine arts. Mitchell chooses to concentrate his teachings on movement for actors, which combines his expertise of both dance and drama.

CARRIE MITCHUM

Born: June 15 in Los Angeles, California
Marital Status: single
Eyes: brown **Hair:** brown
Education: Dartmouth College; University of California at Santa Barbara; Neighborhood Playhouse
Interests: swimming, skiing, tennis, horseback riding

Daytime Dramas: "The Bold and the Beautiful," Donna Logan, 1987-1991

Born into a family of successful actors, it is no surprise that Carrie Mitchum is herself a talented actress. Born Caroline Elizabeth Day Mitchum, Carrie is a third generation actress. Her grandfather is the legendary actor Robert Mitchum and her father is the multi-talented Christopher Mitchum. The oldest of four children, she has two brothers, Bentley and Kian and a sister, Jenny. She was born June 15 in Los Angeles, but as a child she often traveled with her family in Europe while her father worked on various films. Educated abroad, she spent one year in England and four years in Spain where she learned to speak fluent French and Spanish. When Carrie moved back to the states, she was enrolled in a New England prep school where she pursued her interest in horses; a love she developed at the age of four when she was given her first horse. Over the years she has won numerous medals and trophies. After prep school, she went on to Dartmouth College in New Hampshire, transferring after one year to the University of California at Santa Barbara. While at UCSB Carrie's interest in acting peaked and she appeared in many student productions. Still not positive she wanted to become an actress, Carrie worked with a brokerage firm on Wall Street in New York. When she finally decided to pursue an acting career, she studied with the respected Sanford Meisner and Ron Stetson at the renowned Neighborhood Playhouse. Her first professional roles were in the stage productions of "Two Gentlemen of Verona" and the "Children's Hour." Relocating to Los Angeles, Carrie originated the role of Donna Logan on "The Bold and the Beautiful" in 1987. When not in front of the camera, Carrie may be found in front of the stove as she loves to cook. A sport enthusiast, she enjoys horseback riding, swimming, snow skiing, and tennis.

KAREN MONCRIEFF

Born: December 20, 1963 in Sacramento, California
Marital Status: married to Michael Price
Eyes: brown **Hair:** brown
Education: Northwestern University, B.S.
Interests: theater, charity work
Awards: Miss Illinois, 1985

Daytime Dramas: "Guiding Light," Patricia Murphy, 1986; **"Days of Our Lives,"** Gabrielle Pascal, 1987-1989; **"The Bold and the Beautiful,"** Michelle Brookner; **"Santa Barbara,"** Cassie Benedict

Since beginning her professional career in 1986, Karen Moncrieff has been seen in three popular daytime roles, Patricia Murphy on "Guiding Light," lawyer/spy Gabrielle Pascal on "Days of Our Lives," and most recently as Cassie Benedict on "Santa Barbara." A native of Sacramento, California, Moncrieff was raised in Rochester, Michigan, and from an early age was interested in the arts. She would frequently go to the theater with her mother, and on her own performed in many junior high and high school productions. A former Miss Illinois, Karen studied drama at Northwestern University, where she performed in such productions as "Learned Ladies," "After the Fall," "Our Town," "The Miser," and "Tis' Pity She's a Whore." After graduating, she moved to New York City and landed her first professional role on "Guiding Light" (she was Ross Marler's legal assistant.) During her time on the show Moncrieff continued her acting training with coaches, William Alderson and Patrick Tucker, and in 1987 she relocated to Los Angeles. Once again she found herself on daytime television, working on "Days of Our Lives" for two years before moving on to "Santa Barbara." In between, she briefly appeared on "The Bold and the Beautiful." Away from the set, Ms. Moncrieff works with several charities, concentrating chiefly on AIDS related causes, as well as other problems which face the young and the elderly. Karen is married to Michael Price, a vice-president of security sales for a premiere investment bank. The two met while both were seniors at Northwestern, and now share their home with cat, J.D.. (stands for James Dean) Now that her stint on "Santa Barbara" is over, Ms. Moncrieff plans to continue auditioning and also pursue her interest in writing.

WILLIAM MOONEY

Marital Status: married to Valorie Goodall, two sons (twins), Sean and Will
Eyes: brown   **Hair:** black
Education: University of Colorado, American Theatre Wing
Interests: theater, writing
Awards: nominated for two Best Actor Daytime Emmys, 1980, 1981 ("All My Children")

Daytime Dramas: "All My Children," Paul Martin, 1972-1982, 1984-1985; **"One Life to Live,"** Paul Martin, 1978-1979, 1982

An actor/writer/director of tremendous accomplishments, William Mooney, who is best known to daytime audiences as Paul Martin on "All My Children," has performed on stage throughout the world. A graduate of the University of Colorado, Mooney's career has covered many areas of the entertainment world. A popular stage actor, he regularly tours the country as author and co-star of the Civil War play "Banjo Reb and the Blue Ghost." He has additionally toured the U.S. and Europe in two critically acclaimed one man shows, "Half Horse, Half Alligator," which was recorded by RCA Victor and filmed for CBS television, and "Damn Everything But the Circus," a show based on the poems of E.E. Cummings. On Broadway, Mr. Mooney has appeared in "Lolita," "A Man for All Seasons," and "A Place for Polly," while his off-Broadway work includes roles in the four play series, "We," and "The Brownsville Raid," both of which were presented by the Negro Ensemble Company. Among his additional theater credits: "The Upper Depths," "The Truth," "Crossing the Bar," "Alone Together," "My Fair Lady," "The Music Man," "The Prime of Miss Jean Brodie," "The Sound of Music," "The Tender Trap," "Period of Adjustment," with William Shatner, "Golden Rainbow," "Ilya Darling," with Cyd Charisse, "The Secretary Bird," three Yukio Mishima Noh plays, and the Manhattan Punch Line One-Act Play Festival. Also active behind the scenes, Mooney has directed such productions as the original musical "Jam" at tNew York's AMAS Repertory COmpany, "The Truth," "The Desert Song," "Amahl and the Night Visitors," "Oklahoma," "Candide," "The Merry Widow," "Damn Yankees," "Threepenny Opera," "Pippin," and "The Robber Bridegroom." For years the actor has taken time away from the theater to co-star in several feature films, including "Second Sight," "Beer," "A Flash of Green," "C.A.T. Squad," "Network," and "The Next Man." On television, in addition to his long running role on "All My Children," for which he received two daytime Emmy nominations for Best Actor, Mooney has appeared on "One Life to Live," "All that Glitters," "Loving," "Ryan's Hope," "Texas," "Guiding Light," "The Today Show," "The Mike Douglas Show," and a PBS Christmas Special. He is also the co-author of "ASAP—The Fastest Way to Create a Memorable Speech," a main selection of the Fortune Division of Book of the Month Club. Now living in East Brunswick, New Jersey, Mooney is married to Valorie Goodall, a professor of music at Rutgers University. The couple have two children, twins, Sean and Will.

ALLAN DEAN MOORE

Born: November 19 in East Palo Alto, California
Marital Status: single
Height: 5'11" **Eyes:** brown   **Hair:** brown
Education: Howard University
Interests: horticulture, golf, cooking, basketball, reading, movies

Daytime Dramas: "One Life to Live," Kerry Nichols

Allan Dean Moore most recently became known to daytime audiences as the aspiring raper Kerry Nichols on "One Life to Live." Moore was born and raised in East Palo Alto, California, one of four boys and one girl. He discovered acting while in high school but after graduation he opted for a more "responsible" route and enrolled at Howard University where he studied electrical engineering. During this time he also did a little modeling, but soon realized acting was what he wanted to pursue full time. With this decision made, Moore moved to Los Angeles where he began to study with several acting coaches, among them Al Mancini and Cal Bartlett. His persistence paid off and he was awarded his first major role on "Hill Street Blues." Following this Moore made several film appearances in such works as, "Lethal Weapon 2," "Colors," and "The Iron Triangle." Moore also worked on the stage as well in regional productions of "Jonin," "Film at Eleven," "Or," "Fernando the Bronx is Burning," and "A Children's Christmas Celebration." In his spare time Moore is an avid horticulturalist, and hopes he can populate his Manhattan apartment with as many plants as he had in his Los Angeles home. Along with this he enjoys most sports, including basketball, cooking, and golf.

SHELLEY TAYLOR MORGAN

Born: September 3 in Charleston, West Virginia
Marital Status: single
Height: 5'5" **Eyes:** grey-green **Hair:** blond
Education: Emerson University High; UCLA
Interests: fashion, interior design

Daytime Dramas: "General Hospital," Lorena Sharpe, 1984-1986; **"Days of Our Lives,"** Anjelica Deveraux

Although primarily known for her acting, Shelley Taylor Morgan has additionally carved out a niche for herself as a popular contributor to "The Home Show." Initially she was asked on as a guest, but her natural effervescence and flair for interior design and fashion quickly caught on with "Home" viewers, and she has since become a vital part of the show. A native of Charleston, West Virginia, Shelley was born on September 5 to Cleonne and Leon Stein. Her parents, both of whom were film buffs, often took their young daughter to the movies, where she quickly came to share in her parent's enthusiasm. Shelley recalls being particularly impressed with the special effects used in "Moby Dick." After the family moved to Los Angeles, Ms. Morgan attended Emerson Junior High and University High, from which she graduated with honors, earning special recognition as the class's outstanding business student. She initially entered the work force as a secretary, putting to use her exemplary typing (100 words per minute) and shorthand (140 words per minute) skills. Shelley found a job at the Medical Genetics division of UCLA, but soon decided that it was time to pursue her acting dream. In 1978 she took a commercial acting class at UCLA, and soon after found work in film, theater, and television. On the big screen, Ms. Morgan has been seen in "Cross My Heart," "Scarface," "My Tutor," "Black Panther," and "The Sword and the Sorcerer," while her stage credits include "Aspirins & Elephants," "Backbone of America," "The Mind With The Dirty Man," with Don Knotts and Rue McClanahan, "Norman, Is That You?," and "Steambath." Along with many commercials, Shelley's t.v. work has been both as an actress and a co-host of such shows as "A.M. Los Angeles," "Celebrity Update," "It's A Great Life," "VTV," and various telethons including the "Children's Miracle Network." Her acting assignments have included two popular daytime roles, Anjelica Deveraux on "Days of Our Lives" and Lorena Sharpe on "General Hospital." Shelley has also made guest appearances on "Tales from the Crypt," "Totally Hidden Video," "Webster," "An Evening at the Improv," "Archie Bunker's Place," and three movies of the week: "Marilyn: The Untold Story," "Intimate Agony," and "Sunset Limousine." Of all the characters Shelley has portrayed, perhaps her most memorable is that of Kitty O'Hearn, a detective on the popular series "Hunter." Presently living in Westwood, California, the 5'5" actress devotes much of her free time to Friends of Animals, a local organization which finds homes for lost pets.

RONN MOSS

Born: March 4, 1952 in Los Angeles, California
Marital Status: married to actress Shari Shattuck
Height: 6' 2"   **Eyes:** brown   **Hair:** brown
Education: studied with acting coach Peggy Feury
Interests: martial arts, photography, painting, cycling, skiing
Awards: Ronn's band, Player, named one of Best New Single
Artists of 1978

Daytime Dramas: "The Bold and the Beautiful,"
Ridge Forrester, 1987-

A film and television actor, as well as a chart topping recording star, Ronn Moss has enjoyed a widely diverse and successful career. As Ridge Forrester on "The Bold and the Beautiful," he has been a key player on the show since it's debut in 1987. Born in Los Angeles, California on March 4, 1952, Moss grew up in a show business environment, his father being a successful record executive. Following in the family tradition, the future actor's first passion was rock and roll. He began playing the drums at the age of eleven, and soon added guitar and electric bass to his repertoire. As a teenager, Moss played in a variety of bands that performed first at weddings and bar mitzvahs, and eventually in Los Angeles nightclubs. His music career took off in 1976 when he formed the group, Player, with three other musicians. Discovered by Robert Stigwood, a famed music impresario, the band was signed to RSO records, and went on to record three albums, "Player," "Danger Zone," and "Room with a View." (The last album was recorded with a different record label) Player quickly became a much sought after group, touring with such acts as Gino Vanelli, Boz Scaggs, Eric Clapton, Heart, and The Little River Band. In 1978, the band enjoyed it's biggest success, when their single, "Baby Come Back," spent three weeks at number one on the singles chart. This earned the band special recognition on Billboard's Honor Roll as one of the years best new single's bands. In 1981, Moss left the group in the hopes of forging an acting career, honing his skills with such coaches as Charles Conrad, Chris O'Brien, Kathleen King, and Peggy Feury. He was eventually discovered by an ABC talent scout, and has since gone on to appear in several feature films, among them, "Hard Ticket to Hawaii," "Hot Child in the City," and "Hearts and Armour," an Italian film in which Moss played the lead role. Although his role in "Hot Child in the City" was brief, he did develop a rapport with the film's star, Shari Shattuck, and the two eventually married in a ceremony during an African safari. Ronn and Shari are slated to co-star again, this time in an Italian mini-series, "The Baron." The couple live in the Hollywood Hills, where Ronn's hobbies include photography, painting, skiing, rollerskating, cycling, and the martial arts.

MICHAEL NADER

Born: February 18 in St. Louis, Missouri
Marital Status: married March 20, 1992 to Beth Windsor, one daughter from a previous marriage
Eyes: brown **Hair:** brown
Education: Santa Monica City College
Interests: environment, philosophy

Daytime Dramas: "As the World Turns," Kevin Thompson, 1976-1978; **"All My Children,"** Dimitri Marick, 1991-

From the beach blanket movies of the sixties, to the prime time world of the Carrington's and the Colby's to the always interesting world of Pine Valley, Michael Nader is an actor who has enjoyed great success and popularity. He began studying acting in high school, and shortly thereafter was discovered surfing by a talent coordinator, who went on to cast him in several of the legendary Annette Funicello/Frankie Avalon beach party movies. Nader followed this with a semi-regular role on the series "Gidget," after which he relocated to New York City. While in New York, Nader studied at The Actor's Studio and the Herbert Berghof Studios, and supported himself by modeling for the Zoli Agency, appearing on many major magazine covers. In Manhattan, he starred off-Broadway in "Are You Now or Have You Ever Been...?," and his other stage work includes the West Coast premiere of Tennessee Williams' "Vieux Carre." Nader has appeared on the big screen in "Final Analysis" with Richard Gere and Kim Bassinger, but he is best known as Dex Dexter on the hit series "Dynasty." He played this role for six years, from 1983 to 1989, earning legions of fans along the way. Other television work includes two years on "As the World Turns," as well as roles in "The Flash," and Alexi Theopolous in the NBC prime time series, "Bare Essence," with Genie Francis. Nader has also starred in the television movie, "Lady Mobster," with Susan Lucci, as well as "Nick Night" with Rick Springfield and the mini-series "The Great Escape." Nader, who has a daughter, Lindsay, from a previous marriage, recently wed actress Beth Windsor (ex-Frankie Bridges, Capitol). A self described loner, the actor likes to donate much of his spare time to working with addicted youths and supporting environmental causes.

CHRISTINE TUDOR NEWMAN

Born: June 22 in Baltimore, Maryland
Marital Status: married to Craig Newman in October, 1987
Height: 5'8" **Eyes:** blue **Hair:** light brown
Education: Peabody Conservatory of Music; University of Florida at Gainesville, B.F.A.
Interests: travel

Daytime Dramas: "Loving," Gwyneth Alden, 1984-1989, 1991-

An actress and activist, Christine Tudor Newman has portrayed the powerful Gwyneth Alden on "Loving" since 1984. Born on June 22 in Baltimore, Maryland, the youngest of five children, Newman began performing while in junior high. Her vocal skills earned her a scholarship to the Peabody Conservatory of Music in Baltimore, following which she received her B.F.A. in theater from the University of Florida at Gainesville. There she not only honed her performing skills, but also studied set building, costume design, and direction. After graduating, Newman began working on stage, and has since appeared in such productions as "Cat on a Hot Tin Roof," "Pajama Tops," and "Plaza Suite," while her feature film credits include "The Final Mission" and "Deadly Games." Along with her role on "Loving," the actress has also co-starred in the television film, "Having Babies, Part II." While in college, Christine began doing volunteer work with developmentally disabled teenagers, and is now a partner in "Youth at Risk," a program dedicated to helping troubled teens, particularly those involved with gangs. In order to increase celebrity involvement with "Youth at Risk," Newman created the Celebrity Development Division of the Breakthrough Foundation. Since 1987, Christine has been married to Craig Newman, a sales executive for a medical supply company. The couple live in New York City, and enjoy travelling to Hawaii and the Caribbean.

DAVID B. NICHOLS

DAVID BRUCE NICHOLS

Born: January 16, 1946 in Sydney, Nova Scotia
Marital Status: married to Lynda Nichols, three children, Andrew, Graham, and Leslie
Height: 6'1" **Eyes:** green **Hair:** sandy
Education: Ryerson Polytech, B..A. in English
Interests: skiing, sailing, reading, tennis, travel
Awards: Head Boy, Senior Year High School

Daytime Dramas: "As the World Turns,"
Benjamin Reynolds,1991-

Previously seen as a dayplayer on "Another World" and "One Life to Live," David Nichols most recent daytime role is that of Benjamin Reynolds on "As the World Turns." Born on January 16, 1946, in Sydney, Nova Scotia, David first stage experience was as a singer in music festival competitions. After graduating from high school, he attended college on a music scholarship, dividing his studies between English and music, following which he continued his vocal training in radio and television at Ryerson Polytech in Toronto. In addition to his daytime work, Nichols has co-starred on dozens of programs, among them "Counterstrike," "Honor Bright," "Sweating Bullets," "Dracula, The Series," "The Judge," "Top Cops," "Personals," "Doghouse," "Street Legal," "My Secret Identity," "Alfred Hitchcock Presents," "Taking Care of Terrific," "Diamonds," "Check it Out," "Street Justice," "Night Heat," "Loving Friends and Perfect Couples," "Cagney and Lacey," "The New Avengers," and "Littlest Hobo," while he has been seen in such feature films as "Amerika," "C.A.T. Squad," "Ruling Passion," and "Deadly Business." A sought after television and radio host as well, the actor has lent his talents to several shows, including, "Your Money Today," as co-host, writer, and researcher, "CBC TV News and Public Affairs," "CBC TV Variety," as well as appearing in numerous commercials. Also a stage actor, David's theater credits include, "Tom Foolery," "Little Pink Lies," "Carousel," and "Brigadoon." Nichols presently lives in New York City, with his wife, Lynda, and children, Andrew, Graham, and Leslie. In his spare time he enjoys reading, tennis, skiing, music, travel, and sailing on his 23 foot sailboat.

JANIS PAIGE

Born: September 16, 1925 in Tacoma, Washington
Marital Status: married three times, widowed in 1976 from composer Ray Gilbert
Height: 5'5 1/2"   **Eyes:** green   **Hair:** blond
Education: Stadium High School
Interests: horseback riding, wine, basketball, gourmet cooking

Daytime Dramas: **"General Hospital,"** Iona Huntington; **"Capitol,"** Laureen Clegg, 1987; **"Santa Barbara,"** Minx Lockridge, 1991-

Currently seen as Minx Lockridge on "Santa Barbara," Janis Paige has enjoyed triumphs on stage, film, and television, since beginning her professional performing career almost fifty years ago. Born on September 16, 1925 in Tacoma, Washington, Paige first began performing on stage at the age of five, competing in amateur contests. After graduating from Stadium High School, her big break came when her vocal skills caught the attention of Louis B. Mayer's assistant, who saw Paige perform at the Hollywood Canteen. She made her film debut shortly thereafter in "Bathing Beauties," following which she became a contract player with Warner Brothers. Over the next several years, Paige appeared in numerous films, among them "Hollywood Canteen," "Of Human Bondage," "Silk Stocking," with Fred Astaire, "Two Guys From Milwaukee," "Her Kind of Man," "Wallflower," "One Sunday Afternoon," "Winter Meeting," "Romance on the High Seas," and "The Caretakers." An equally skilled stage actress, Janis debuted on Broadway in 1952 opposite Jackie Cooper in "Remains to be Seen," and three years later co-starred with John Raitt in the premiere Tony Award winning production of "Pajama Game." Additional stage credits include "Applause," "Sweet Charity," "Hello, Dolly," "South Pacific," "Lovers and Other Strangers," "Mame," "Here's Love," "Alone Together," and "Gingerbread Lady." A tireless performer, Paige has also appeared in nightclubs across the country, as well as taking part in Bob Hope's USO shows, including his first tour of Viet Nam. On television, the actress starred in her own series, "It's Always Jan," and played recurring roles on "Eight is Enough," "Trapper John M.D." "Lanigan's Rabbi," with Art Carney, and "All in the Family." Ms. Paige has also guest starred on dozens of programs, including "Charlie's Angels," "Fantasy Island," "All's Fair," "Columbo," "Police Story," "Mission Impossible," and "Shade of L.A." Prior to taking on the role of Minx Lockridge on "Santa Barbara," Paige appeared on two other daytime dramas, "Capitol" and "General Hospital." In 1976, Janis' husband of twenty four years, Oscar winning songwriter Ray Gilbert, passed away, and since then, Janis has taken control of her husband's music publishing company, Ipanema Music Corporation. Along with owning the rights to her late husband's musical catalogue, which includes such songs as "Zip-A-Dee Doo Dah," (which her husband wrote) Janis is presently overseeing the release of a video, "We think the World is Round," an animated musical written by Mr. Gilbert depicting Christopher Columbus' arrival in America. In the video, Janis provides the voice of Columbus' ship, the Nina. Away from show business, Paige is the founder (and former president) of the Sunset Plaza Civic Association, and is presently the vice president of the Beverly Highlands Home's Association. As a result, she frequently can be found in City Hall, where she serves as a lobbyist on behalf of homeowners. To relax, Janis, who lives in Los Angeles, enjoys horseback riding and working out daily, and lists amongst her other interests, baseball, basketball, gourmet cooking, fine wines, and collecting art.

MICHAEL PALANCE

Born: March 27 on Long Island, New York
Marital Status: single
Height: 6' **Eyes:** blue **Hair:** brown
Interests: music, softball

Daytime Dramas: "Guiding Light," Kevin Stanton, 1987-1988; **"Ryan's Hope,"** Robert Rowan,1988-1989; **"One Life to Live,"** Dr. Dan Wolek, 1989-1991

While he may be one of the younger stars of daytime drama, Michael Palance has nonetheless appeared in three popular soap operas, "Guiding Light," "Ryan's Hope," and most recently, "One Life to Live." Born on Long Island, New York, Palance spent his free time studying acting, while maintaining a full high school course load. He was planning to begin New York University, when he was offered the role on "Ryan's Hope." Unable to turn down the opportunity, Palance put his college plans temporarily on hold. Along with his work on daytime television, he has also appeared in the NBC pilot "Down Delaware Road," and has performed with the Ensemble Studio Theater in New York, participating in their 1988 Octoberfest reading of "Princess Grace and the Fazzaris." In his spare time, Palance enjoys listening to music, everything from hard rock to classical.

ELLEN PARKER

Born: September 30 in Paris, France
Marital Status: married to Dr. Mack Lipkin since 1987
Height: 5' 6" **Eyes:** blue **Hair:** brown
Education: Bard College, Bachelor's Degree
Interests: painting, gardening, cooking, reading

Daytime Dramas: "Guiding Light," Maureen Reardon Bauer, 1986-

A Broadway actress, Ellen Parker has portrayed Maureen Bauer on "Guiding Light," since 1986. Born on September 30, in Paris France, where her father worked as a sculptor, her mother a chef, Ellen and her brother, Paul spent most of their childhood in New York City. After studying theater at Bard College, she continued her acting training with Warren Robertson, and over the course of her career has achieved success in films and theater. On Broadway, Ms. Parker has appeared in "The Heidi Chronicles," "Equus," "Plenty," and "Strangers," while her additional stage credits include "Translations," "Dusa, Fish, Stas, and Vi," "Absent Friends," "Uncommon Women and Others," (a role she re-created for a PBS special presentation) "Isn't It Romantic," "Fen," "Sweet Talk," "Aunt Dan and Lemon," and "The Scare." The actress is also a frequent performer at several regional theaters, among them the Yale Repertory Theatre,

The Long Wharf Theatre, and Baltimore's Center Stage. On the big screen, Ellen has co-starred in "Kramer vs. Kramer," "Night of the Juggler," "Dreamlover," "Zits," and "Desperate Hours." Along with her work on daytime, her prime time credits include guest appearances on "Bay City Blues" and "Love Sydney," and the mini-series "Kennedy," in which she played the part of Ethel Kennedy. Ellen, who has been married to Dr. Mack Lipkin since 1987, lists amongst her hobbies painting, cooking, reading, gardening, and "long walks everywhere."

RIA PAVIA

Born: October 8, 1967 in Cleveland, Ohio
Marital Status: engaged to actor, Matt Adler
Height: 5'0" **Eyes:** hazel
Education: UCLA
Interests: dancing, biking, reading

Daytime Dramas: "Santa Barbara," Elaine Bernowski, 1992-

A new face to daytime drama, Ria Pavia joined the cast of Santa Barbara as Elaine Bernowski in 1992. The actress was born on October 8, 1967 in Cleveland, Ohio, and grew up in Rochester, New York, Michigan, and South Carolina. Ria's family also includes two brothers, her father, an investment banker, and her mother, whom she describes as a "jack of all-trades." Since 1985, the entire Pavia family has been settled in Los Angeles. Always interested in performing, Ria attended the Interlocken Arts Academy, following which she studied drama at UCLA. In addition to her work on "Santa Barbara," Ms. Pavia has also been seen on "The Young and the Restless," "Who's the Boss?," "The Tracey Ullman Show," "Married with Children," "Doctor, Doctor," "Growing Pains," "Hogan Family," and numerous national commercials. Her feature film credits include "She's Out of Control," "Dream a Little Dream," and the upcoming Clive Barker film, "Candyman." It was on the set of "Dream a Little Dream" that she met co-star Matt Adler, and the two are now engaged to be married on March 20, 1983. Presently a resident of Santa Monica, California, Ria is involved with the "meals on wheels" program. In her spare time she enjoys dancing, biking on the beach, improvisation, reading Stephen King and Michael Crichton, and "hanging out" at her parents house with her family.

PATSY PEASE

Born: July 5 in North Carolina
Marital Status: married to Robert Martin, two sons, Russell and Joshua
Eyes: green **Hair:** blond
Interests: martial arts, dancing, singing
Awards: 1986 Soap Opera Award, Outstanding Lead Actress; 1988 "Super Couple" Soap Opera Award (with Charles Shaughnessy)

Daytime Dramas: "Search for Tomorrow," Cissie Mitchell, 1979-1982; **"Days of Our Lives,"** Kimberly Brady, 1984-1990, 1992-

One of the leading daytime heroines of recent years, Patsy Pease is best known to soap fans as Kimberly Brady on "Days of Our Lives," a role she played from 1984 to 1990. Along the way, she and co-star Charles Shaughnessy, received a Soap Opera Award for Super Couple of 1988. Born in North Carolina, Pease eventually moved to New York, where she landed her first daytime role as Cissy Mitchell on "Search for Tomorrow." In addition, the actress has guest starred on such shows as "Remington Steele" and "Trapper John M.D.." Patsy is also a talented singer and dancer, as well as being an accomplished martial artist, specializing in Tai Kwon Do. In 1990, Ms. Pease courageously shared her story in Soap Opera Digest (1/21/92) of the horrors of being raised by a physically, sexually, and emotionally abusive, mentally ill mother, hoping her honesty would encourage others in a similar situation to confront their pain as well. An NBC television movie about her life is currently in the works and Patsy will portray herself in the story. Now living in Los Angeles, Pease is married to musician Robert Martin, with whom she has one child, Russell born August 1990. She has a son, Joshua from a previous marriage. In 1990, when she became pregnant with Russell, Pease opted to leave "Days of Our Lives," on which her character, Kimberly, was to undergo a traumatic pregnancy which would ultimately result in the death of her newborn child. Deciding that this would be too stressful a role to play, and following the advice of several doctors, Ms. Pease left the show. Ironically, when Russell was born, his initial chances of survival were slim, but happily he pulled through. Now two years later, he is a healthy child and his mother has returned to "Days of Our Lives."

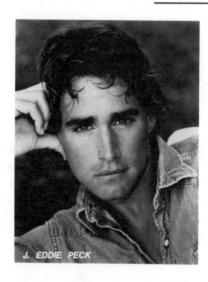

J. EDDIE PECK

J. EDDIE PECK

Born: October 10, 1958 in Lynchburg, Virginia
Marital Status: married to Sonya Peck, one son Austin Colt
Height: 6'2" **Eyes:** blue **Hair:** brown
Education: Missouri Southern State College, Bachelor's Degree
Interests: music, sports

Daytime Dramas: "Days of Our Lives," Hawk Hawkins

Coming from a small town in Missouri, J. Eddie Peck had a difficult time choosing an acting career over a more conservative nine to five job. However, after landing two national commercials during his first week in Los Angeles, it became pretty clear that he had made the right choice. Born on October 10 in Lynchburg, Virginia, John Eddie, and the rest of the Peck family, relocated first to Kansas City, before settling down in Joplin, Missouri, a town which he still considers his home. An extremely orderly and ambitious child, Peck was not the type to waste time, but rather was constantly setting and accomplishing goals. Along with being an A student and a talented athlete, Peck also had the city's third largest paper route by the time he was nine years old. He was selling products door to door at eleven, and purchased his first home when he was just nineteen. Peck originally entered Missouri Southern State College with the idea of a career in medicine, but soon decided that he should pursue his dream and brave the waters of the entertainment business. His first such job was as a d.j., which afforded Peck the opportunity to host his own country western radio show. Not only did this introduce the young student to a whole new way of life, but also helped to pay his school tuition. After receiving his degree in marketing, Peck moved to California, where he quickly found work in television and film. Along with starring roles in the feature films "Dangerously Close," "Lambada, Set The Night On Fire" and "Curse II, The Bite," J. Eddie appeared on such television shows as "Knightrider," "Highway to Heaven," "Murder, She Wrote," "Cheers," "Dark Justice," and a recurring role on "Double Trouble." Peck also was featured in the movie of the week "Breaking Home Ties," with Jason Robards, and as a series regular on "Wildside." Before making his daytime debut on "Days of Our Lives," Peck made a splash on prime time soaps with key roles on "Dallas" and "Dynasty." On the latter he portrayed both the fantasy lover of Emma Samms and the nightmare vision of Joan Collins; on Dallas, he was Tommy McCay, the drug addict son of George Kennedy. Now living in Los Angeles with his wife, Sonya and son, Austin Colt, Peck recently moved his mother, father, and three siblings out west as well. The actor is a passionate family man and spends as much time as possible with his young son. Peck lists basketball, horseback riding, and water sports as his favorite hobbies and his #1 interest is "playing an active role in my son's life."

ASHLEY PELDON

Born: April 2, 1984 in New York
Marital Status: single
Height: 3' 9" **Eyes:** blue **Hair:** brown
Education: presently in grade school
Interests: barbie dolls, ice skating, swimming, reading, Madonna tapes

Daytime Dramas: "Guiding Light," Marah Lewis, 1988-1991

It's not your average seven year old who leads a bi-coastal life, but then again most seven year olds don't have a three film deal with Disney Studios and a major network creating a series for you. Beginning her career at the age of three, Ashley Peldon won the hearts of daytime fans as Marah Lewis on "Guiding Light." The forty three inch actress has since gone on to tremendous success on the big screen. Born on April 2, 1984, Ashley comes from a tight knit family which includes father, Jeffrey, an attorney, mother, Wendy, a college professor, and sister Courtney, a fellow actress who recently starred on Broadway in "Meet Me in St. Louis." During her short career, Ashley has co-starred with such premiere actresses as Bette Midler, Goldie Hawn, and Diane Keaton, in such films as "Stella," "Deceived," "The Lemon Sisters," and "Drop Dead Fred." Ashley also made a guest appearance on "The Torkelsons" guest starring as Patty Duke's daughter and most recently was seen with Delta Burke and Charles Shaughnessy in the t.v. movie "Dayo." An excellent student, Ashley spends her free time playing with Barbie dolls, swimming, ice skating, reading, and listening to Madonna.

LISA PELUSO

Born: July 29, 1964 in Philadelphia, Pennsylvania
Marital Status: single
Height: 5'4" **Eyes:** green **Hair:** brown
Education: high school
Interests: horseback riding, exercise, skiing, ice skating, biking, gardening, Nintendo, arts & crafts, movies, theater, health foods, singing, walks on the beach & in the park

Daytime Dramas: "Search for Tomorrow," Wendy Wilkins, 1976-1986; **"One Life to Live,"** Billie Giordano; **"Loving,"** Ava Rescott Alden Masters, 1988-

Over the past decade, Lisa Peluso has made an indelible impression on the world of daytime drama. Before starring on "Loving," Lisa appeared on "One Life to Live," "As the World Turns," and "Search for Tomorrow," as well as roles in "Love of Life" and "Somorset." Born in July of 1964, Lisa began her career only four months later, when she was chosen as the Philadelphia Phillies "caption baby," appearing in print ads with cute sayings in the captions. By the age of five, Lisa was working in commercials, (to date she has over 100 commercial credits) and at nine she starred on Broadway with Angela Lansbury in "Gypsy." She has also appeared in many regional theater productions, among them, "The King & I." Her feature film work includes the role of John Travolta's little sister in the hit movie, "Saturday Night Fever." Lisa has also had guest starring roles in the primetime series, "Hunter," and "Designing Women." On the personal side, Lisa grew up in Philadelphia with her two sisters and one brother. Her mother is a homemaker and her father a postal worker. Lisa says about her childhood, "My childhood was interesting. I've been an actress and performer since age 5. I began modeling at 4 months old. My childhood was spent working - I went to professional childrens school, studied voice and dance and worked in the theater as a kid... I had many friends from all walks of life & gained immeasurable experience." Aside from working, Lisa donates her time and efforts to various charities; she is the Honorary Chairperson for the ARC (Association for Retarded Citizens), a fundraiser for Juvenile Diabetes, volunteer staff for Hospice, Special Olympics and the Lifeway Program. In her spare time Lisa, who is single and lives in Manhattan, enjoys everything from bowling to antique shopping to amusement parks & arcades to dinner parties.

ANTHONY PENA

ANTHONY PENA

Born: February 18 in San Antonio, Texas
Marital Status: married to Raylene Pena, one daughter, Denisha Michelle, one son, Tony, III
Height: 6' **Eyes:** brown **Hair:** brown
Education: California State University at Fullerton, B.A.
Interests: baseball, travelling, reading, skiing, basketball, University of Oklahoma football and baseball

Daytime Dramas: "The Young and the Restless," Felix, 1980; **"General Hospital,"** Harry Greg, 1981; **"The Young and the Restless,"** Miguel Rodriguez, 1985-

A mainstay on "The Young and the Restless" for over seven years, Anthony Pena has achieved similar success in both theater and feature films. Born on February 18 in San Antonio, Texas to Antonio Sr. and Janie Garza, Pena attended Servite High School, where he excelled in football, baseball, basketball, and track. His family moved to Los Angeles while Anthony was still in high school, and upon graduating he enrolled at California State University at Fullerton, earning his B.A. degree in comparative literature and Native American history. (Pena is one half Native American) While at college, he also earned his credentials to teach troubled children, a skill he put to use as a Juvenile Probation Counselor. After almost being drafted to play baseball for the Cincinnati Reds, Pena decided to give acting a shot, enrolling in classes with acting coaches Bruce Glover and Margo Albert. His first role was on stage in "Zoot Suit," at the Aquarius Theatre, which was followed by another stage role in "Bronze Images." This production, which was presented at the Actor's Studio West, posed particular challenge to Pena, who was called on to play a total of fourteen different characters. Eventually, the production was developed into a two part television special. The actor's next t.v. appearance was on an episode of "Kojak," and encouraged by the positive response, Pena went on to guest star on several more shows, among them "The Master Gunfighter," "Grand Slam," "Hill St. Blues," "Simon and Simon," "Highway to Heaven," "L.A. Law," "Hunter," "Knots Landing," "Quantum Leap," and "MacGyver," while his t.v. film credits include a starring role in "Code Red." On the big screen, Pena has been featured in some of the biggest films of the past several years, including "Born on the 4th Of July," "Colors," "The Running Man," "Marathon Man," "Let's

Get Harry," "Backtrack," with Dennis Hopper and Jodie Foster, "Porky's II," "Megaforce," "Altered States," "Beneath the Darkness," and "River of Gold." Daytime fans know Pena as Miguel Rodriguez on "The Young and the Restless," and he has additionally been seen on "General Hospital," as Harry Greg. Anthony now lives in Santa Ana, California, with his wife of more than twenty years, Raylene, with whom he has two children, Tony and Denisha, both of whom are now in college. The actor is a strong believer in charity, donating his time to the Muscular Dystrophy Telethons, the Cystic Fibrosis Foundation, and the Heart Foundation. In his spare time Anthony enjoys skiing, jetskiing, reading, travelling, and rooting for the baseball and football teams of the University of Oklahoma. Closer to home, he coaches little league baseball and grade school football.

VALARIE PETTIFORD

Born: July 8, 1960 in Queens, New York
Marital Status: engaged to actor and former Philadelphia Phillies pitcher, Tony Rader
Height: 5'8" **Eyes:** brown **Hair:** brown
Education: High School of Performing Arts
Interests: dancing, cooking, crocheting, her pets

Daytime Dramas: "Another World," Courtney Walker;
"One Life to Live," Sheila Price

Valarie Pettiford, best known as Sheila Price on "One Life to Live," is a woman who has enjoyed triumphant success in several areas of the performing arts. She is known not only for her acting skills, but for her extraordinary talents as a singer and dancer. Valarie was born and raised in Queens, where she began studying dance at the age of eight. She continued this at the High School of Performing Arts in New York City, where she changed her focus from ballet to modern dance. Valarie's first big role came when, much to her parents chagrin, she cut school to attend an audition for the film version of "The Wiz." She missed a day of classes but she ended up getting the part, a sacrifice Valarie was more than willing to make. After completing school she continued her dance training, and went on to perform in such stage productions as "West Side Story," "Big Deal," "The Balcony," Sophisticated Ladies," "Grind," " and "Dancing." (The latter three were Broadway productions) Aside from her work in "The Wiz," Valarie has also appeared on screen in "Street Hunter," "The Last Dragon," and "The Cotton Club." Despite the success she was enjoying, Valarie, who is not one to rest on her laurels, decided that she wanted to pursue a career as a dramatic actress. This lead to her work on daytime drama, first as detective Courtney Walker on "Another World," and then as physical therapist Sheila Price on "One Life to Live." Valarie still finds time for her singing career, singing background vocals for Phyliss Hyman, touring with the group, Raw Silk as well as performing as part of the rock group "The Stingers," some of whose members have sung on "One Life to Live." The group recently signed a record deal and will soon be recording their first album. To relax Valarie enjoys her dogs and cats, cooking, crocheting, and spending time with her fiance, Tony Rader, an actor and former pitcher for the Philadelphia Phillies.

GRACE PHILLIPS

Born: May 3, 1964 in Los Angeles, California
Marital Status: single
Height: 5'5" **Eyes:** blue **Hair:** blond
Education: Columbia University, B.A. in East Asian Studies
Interests: rock climbing, opera, knitting, hiking, long distance biking, writing

Daytime Dramas: "One Life to Live," Sara Buchanan, 1991-1992

A rising star, Grace Phillips joined the cast of "One Life to Live" as Sara Buchanan in 1991. Born on May 3, 1964 in Los Angeles, Grace, along with the rest of her family, which includes two sisters and one brother, moved quite frequently, setting up house in Arizona, New Hampshire, Boston, and New York. Her father is a music conductor, her mother a teacher After receiving her B.A. in East Asian Studies from Columbia University (she started out at Princeton), Ms. Phillips soon found work on stage, and in film and television. She appeared in the American Playhouse production of "All the Vermeers in New York," and also won the role of Sam Waterston's daughter in Woody Allen's "Crimes and Misdemeanors." On television, in addition to her daytime work the actress has guest starred on "Herman's Head." Although she had lived in New York City for several years, Phillips relocated to Los Angeles in 1991, only to return to Manhattan a short time later when she won the role of Sara Buchanan. In her spare time, Grace, who is single, enjoys rock climbing, hiking, long distance biking, writing, knitting, and going to the opera.

JEFF PHILLIPS

Born: July 3, 1968 in Westwood, New Jersey
Marital Status: single
Height: 5'10" **Eyes:** hazel **Hair:** blond
Education: Ramapo College, one year, H.B. Studio
Interests: skiing (snow/water), mountain biking, horseback riding
Awards: 1992 Soap Opera Awards nomination, Outstanding Male Newcomer; 1992 Daytime Emmy nomination for Outstanding Younger Actor

Daytime Dramas: "As the World Turns," Kevin Marshall; **"Guiding Light,"** Hart Jessup 1991-1992

Born on the third of July in Westwood, New Jersey, Jeff Phillips has quickly established himself as a favorite among daytime fans. The second of three children, he was raised in Hillsdale, New Jersey and attended Pascack Valley High School, following which he enrolled at Ramapo College as a criminal justice major. After a year the future law enforcement officer decided to change his status to future actor, moved to California and then back to New York City where he believed you had to be if you wanted to learn to be an actor. To support himself, Phillips worked as a busboy at the Hard Rock Cafe, and attended acting classes at the Herbert Berghof Studio. It was there that he was discovered by a casting director for "One Life to Live," on which Phillips made his professional debut. He worked one day on the show and not again for six months. Along with the role of Hart Jessup on "Guiding Light," Phillips has appeared as Kevin on "As the World Turns," as well as making guest appearances on "Another World," and the prime time series "Superforce." He has tested for several other soap parts - among them are: Joey Moscini on "General Hospital," Will Cortlandt and Charlie Brent on "All My Children", and, in the same week, he tested for "All My Children's" Brian Bodine and "Guiding Light's" Hart Jessup. He won the part he wanted. His stage credits include "The Aching Heart of Samuel Kleinerman," "Midnight Cowboy," "Bury the Dead," and "Teach Me How to Cry." An expert skier, Phillips was in the film, "The Art of Skiing." To unwind, the actor is a definite thrill seeker, participating in such activities as bungee jumping, mountain biking, skiing, and sky diving.

DEVON PIERCE

Born: February 6 in Amsterdam, New York
Marital Status: single
Height: 5'3"   **Eyes:** brown   **Hair:** black
Education: Fulton-Montgomery College
Interests: music, golf, biking, travelling
Awards: 1983 Miss Teen USA

Daytime Dramas: "Santa Barbara," Marie;
"The Young and the Restless," Diane Westin

From the time she appeared in her first school play, at the age of three, Devon Pierce knew that she wanted to be an actress. Today, she can be seen fulfilling this dream as Diane Westin on "The Young and the Restless." Born on February 6 in Amsterdam, New York, Pierce was a Navy brat, and as a result, she and her brother, Albert relocated frequently. In 1983, Ms. Pierce earned the Miss Teen USA crown, following which she began to concentrate on acting. After studying literature and language at Fulton-Montgomery College, she moved to New York City in search of theater work, continuing her acting training with such coaches as Stella Adler, Zina Provrndie, and Tracy Roberts. Among the productions in which Pierce has appeared: "The Fantasticks," "All My Sons," "Babes in Toyland," "Fool for Love," and "The Miracle Worker." On television, along with "The Young and the Restless," she spent four months on "Santa Barbara," as Marie, and has additionally appeared in the pilot "Sisters," as well as "The Twilight Zone," "Hunter," "What a Country," "The Tortelli's," "The Wonder Years," and "Freddie's Nightmares." Devon's feature film credits include "Corporate Affairs," "Private Affairs," "Dead Giveaway," "Double Switch," "Cutting Loose," and "The Lords of Magik." Aside from acting, she co-owns a recording studio, "Out of the Closet," where she records her own music, as well as the work of fellow musicians. Ms. Pierce donates much of her spare time to helping children with drug problems. To relax, she enjoys taking long walks, biking, golf, hiking, and travelling.

DANIEL PILON

Born: November 13 in Montreal, Canada
Marital Status: married to Susana Pilon, two children, Alexandra and Max
Height: 6'3"   **Eyes:** hazel-green   **Hair:** brown
Education: University of Montreal, B.A. in Philosophy; Master's credits at McGill
Interests: his children, writing, music, carpentry
Awards: Box Office Champ, Theater Owner's Association of Quebec

Daytime Dramas: "Ryan's Hope," Max Dubujak, 1983-1988; **"Guiding Light,"** Alan Spaulding, 1988-1990; **"Days of Our Lives,"** Gavin, 1992-

A tremendously popular Canadian actor, Daniel Pilon was recognized for his public appeal when he was named Box Office Champ by the Theater Owner's Association of Quebec. Best known to American audiences for his daytime work, Pilon has created three popular characters on "Ryan's Hope," "Guiding Light," and most recently "Days of Our Lives." Born on November 13 in Montreal, Canada, Pilon describes his early days as a "happy childhood in the Northern Climes." After receiving his B.A. in philosophy, and working towards a Masters in history, Pilon embarked on his successful acting career. Now living in Los Angeles, Pilon has been seen in such feature films as "Scanners III," "North of Chiang-Mai," "Malarek," "Obsessed," "Mutations," "The Blood of Others," "The Rebels," "Play Dirty," "Red," and "The Devil Is Amongst Us," and on the small screen in "Sweating Bullets," "Urban Angel," "La Maison Deschesne," "Casablanca," "The Hamptons," the role of Naldo Marchetta on "Dallas," "Hart to Hart," and "The Devlin Connection." The actor and his wife, Susana, recently moved officially from Canada to Los Angeles with their son and daughter, Max (11/14/89) and Alexandra (8/14/88). Daniel lists among his interests music, writing, skiing, judo, cabinet making, carpentry, and most significantly, he says, "My kids."

TONYA PINKINS

Born: May 30, 1962 in Chicago, Illinois
Marital Status: married to Ron Brawer, February 12, 1987, two children, Maxx and Myles
Height: 5' 7"   **Eyes:** brown   **Hair:** brown
Education: Carnegie Mellon University
Interests: reading, writing, scuba diving
Awards: 1992 Tony Award, Drama Desk Award, and Clarance Derwent Award, all for Best Featured Actress in a Musical ("Jelly's Last Jam"); Monarch Award

Daytime Dramas: "As the World Turns," Heather Dalton, 1984-1986; **"All My Children,"** Livia Frye, 1991-

A daytime favorite, equally at home on the stage, Tonya Pinkins' most recent theater role, as Sweet Anita, in the Broadway production of "Jelly's Last Jam," has earned the actress a Tony, Drama Desk and Clarance Derwent Awards for Outstanding Featured Actress in a musical. A Chicago native, Tonya began acting in school productions, and by the time she graduated high school her professional resume already included commercials, regional theater, and a television pilot. Offered admission into several schools, including Yale, Harvard, and Julliard, Tonya opted to enroll at Carnegie Mellon University, following which she began working extensively in the theater. She made her Broadway debut at the age of nineteen in "Merrily We Roll Along," and has additionally been seen in "Joe Turner's Come and Gone," "The Piano Lesson," "A...My Name is Alice," "Ain't Misbehavin'," "An Ounce of Prevention," "Just Say No," "Caucasian Chalk Dance," "Little Shop of Horrors," and "Approximating Mother." She debuted her award winning performance in "Jelly's Last Jam" in the original Los Angeles production, and since the show came to New York, Tonya has established herself as one of the premiere theater performers. Along with the stage, she has also kept busy on television, guest starring on such shows as "Law and Order," "The Cosby Show," "Crime Story," "Miami Vice," and "Spencer, For Hire," while her feature film credits include "Hot Shots," "Beat Street," and "See No Evil, Hear No Evil." In 1992, she completed work on the HBO film, "Strapped." A long time "All My Children" fan, Ms. Pinkins' originally tried to land the role of Angie Baxter in 1981, but was beat out by Debbi Morgan. However ten years later she got another shot, and can now be seen on the show as Livia Frye. Since 1987, Tonya has been married to Ron Brawer, who works as the musical director on "Another World." The couple first met when Tonya was investigating a possible role on "Another World," and they ended up getting married in a Las Vegas Chapel. Returning home, Tonya and Ron did have a somewhat traditional wedding, with family and friends in attendance, by a lake in upstate New York. However, the ceremony, which called for the newlyweds to row across the lake while the deejay played Wagner's "Flight of the Valkyries" and Billy Idol's "White Wedding," was anything but conventional. The two moved from New York City, with their two sons, Maxx and Myles, to Essex County, New Jersey. The couple recently had the opportunity to work together, when Tonya sang "Give Me All Your Love," a song written by her husband, and recorded for the "Another World" primetime special, "Summer Desire." They are also collaborating on an album to be released in 1993, which will also be when Tonya can be heard singing in New York's famed Rainbow Room.

COLLEEN ZENK PINTER

Born: January 20 in Barrington, Illinois
Marital Status: married to actor Mark Pinter
Education: Catholic University of America
Interests: antiques, gardening

Daytime Dramas: "As the World Turns,"
Barbara Ryan Munson, 1978-

A native of Barrington, Illinois, Colleen Zenk joined the cast of "As the World Turns" in 1978. While growing up, Colleen initially set out to be a dancer, devoting much of her time to studying both ballet and jazz. However, a knee injury in her late teens forced her to refocus her aspirations, and so Colleen decided that acting would be a suitable replacement. She studies theater at Catholic University of America, and following graduation began working on the stage in the United States and Europe, where she worked for the Army Special Services. Among her stage credits are roles in "They're Playing Our Song," "Can Can," "Barefoot in the Park" and "Where's Charley?" Colleen first appeared on Broadway in 1981 in "Bring Back Birdie," which starred Chita Rivera and Donald O'Connor. Continuing with a musical theme, Colleen made her film debut in John Huston's "Annie." When not working on "As the World Turns," Colleen devotes much of her time to the March of Dimes and Cystic Fibrosis charities, In addition she enjoys gardening, collecting American antiques from the past two centuries, skiing and golfing. Previously divorced, Colleen and her second husband, actor Mark Pinter, have combined their families and are the parents of five children, three girls and two boys.

Mark Pinter

MARK PINTER

Born: March 7 in Decorah, Iowa
Marital Status: married to actress, Colleen Zenk
Height: 6'1" **Eyes**: hazel **Hair:** brown
Education: Iowa State University, B.A.; Wayne State University, M.F.A.
Interests: golf, theater, gardening, skiing

Daytime Dramas: "Love of Life," Dr. Tom Crawford, 1979-1980; **"Guiding Light,"** Mark Evans, 1981-1983; **"As the World Turns,"** Brian McColl, 1984-1987; **"Loving,"** Dan Hollister,1988-1989; **"Another World,"** Grant Harrison, 1991-

Since 1979, when he made his daytime debut, Mark Pinter has starred on five popular daytime dramas, "Love of Life," "Guiding Light," "As the World Turns," "Loving," and since 1991, "Another World." With each of these shows, Pinter has displayed his acting versatility, equally adept at playing a villain or a hero. Born in Decorah, Iowa, of Norwegian/German descent, Pinter is the youngest of five children. While his older siblings all planned on careers in the business or financial world, young Mark always intended to be an actor, beginning his training with high school productions and then as a theatre arts major at Iowa State University. Following graduation, Mark co-founded The Old Creamery Theater Company in Garrison, Iowa, where he performed in such productions as "The Glass Menagerie." With this key experience under his belt, Pinter was soon accepted into Wayne State University's Hilberry Graduate Repertory Program, eventually earning his Masters degree after completing the challenging course of study. For the next several years, Mark concentrated chiefly on stage work, performing in "The Show Off," "What the Butler Saw," "Equus," "The Shadow Box," and "Who's Afraid of Virginia Woolf," at the Zephyr Theater in Los Angeles. In addition to his plethora of daytime roles, Pinter has been a regular on several nighttime series, including "Secrets of Midland Heights" and "Behind the Screen," as well as making guest appearances on "Charlie's Angels," "Hart to Hart," "The Love Boat," "Hunter," and in the television films "Crash" and "Go West, Young Girl." In 1991, Mark was seen opposite Danny DiVito in the feature film "Other People's Money." The actor has been married for five years to actress Colleen Zenk of "As the World Turns," with whom he is raising five children. (his, hers and theirs) Between 1989 and 1991, a stretch where Pinter was not seen on a daytime drama, he devoted himself fully to raising their newborn son, Morgan. The family lives in Connecticut, where Mark enjoys gardening, skiing, and tending to their two cats, including a prize winning Somali cat, one dog, and couple of raccoons. Pinter is also an avid golfer, and frequently plays in invitational tournaments throughout the country.

PARKER POSEY

Born: November 8, 1968 in Baltimore, Maryland
Marital Status: single
Hair: brown
Education: State University of New York at Purchase

Daytime Dramas: "As the World Turns," Tess Shelby,
1991-1992

Finishing up her senior year at the State University of New York at Purchase, Parker Posey was all set to embark on the poverty and degradation that go along with being a struggling actress, but instead she landed the role of Tess Shelby on "As the World Turns," and quickly found her career in high gear. Born on November 8, 1968 in Baltimore, Maryland, Parker and her twin brother, Chris (who is studying law), were raised in two small Mississippi towns, Monroe and Laurel. Parker began taking ballet lessons at the age of nine, and was committed to this until she was rejected from the ballet program at North Carolina School of the Arts. Following the suggestion of the school's dean, Ms. Posey began to concentrate on acting, eventually earning admission into the prestigious conservatory program at the State University of New York at Purchase. Her audition for the school almost turned disastrous when Parker failed to remember the Tennessee Williams' monologue she had prepared, but fortunately she was saved by her natural charm and improvisational skills, and eventually was one of thirty prospective students (out of 500 applicants) to be accepted into the program. While at the school, she shared an apartment with another future daytime star, Sherry Stringfield of "Guiding Light." Prior to joining the cast of "As the World Turns," Posey, who now lives in New York City, made her television debut in the HBO film, "First Love, Fatal Love," a docudrama dealing with AIDS.

SUSAN PRATT

Born: April 29 in Gainesville, Florida
Marital Status: married to Alfredo Pecora, two daughters,
Sophia and Lorena
Height: 5'6" **Eyes:** blue **Hair:** brown
Education: American Academy of Dramatic Arts
Interests: horseback riding

Daytime Dramas: "General Hospital," Annie Logan,
1978-1982; **"Guiding Light,"** Dr. Claire Ramsey, 1983-1986;
"All My Children," Barbara Montgomery, 1987-1991

After years as a successful model, Susan Pratt made her daytime debut in 1978 as Nurse Annie Logan on "General Hospital." The next four years, spent basking in the glow of such world renowned physicians as Dr. Steve Hardy, Dr.

Noah Drake, and the legendary Quartermaine couple, were certainly not lost on Susan, who soon became Dr. Claire Ramsey on "Guiding Light." During her years in Five Points she must have gone to night school, and in 1987 Susan resurfaced yet again, as magazine editor, Barbara Montgomery on "All My Children." Born in Westchester County, New York, Susan's parents ran a 200 year old inn/restaurant, specializing in French cuisine. Much of her youth was devoted to horseback riding, and Susan regularly showed her horse competitively. Still one of her favorite pastimes, she particularly enjoys dressage. (training a horse in obedience and movement) During her teens, Susan began modelling and appearing in commercials. After completing high school she moved to Europe to model full time. She spent several years working in Paris and Munich before returning to the United States, where she enrolled in the American Academy of Dramatic Arts. Upon graduation Susan relocated to California, and began her television career. Along with her soap opera roles, she has guest starred on "Welcome Back Kotter," "Baretta," "Nancy Drew Mysteries," "Carter Country," and "The Streets of San Francisco." Susan has also appeared in the television films, "A Circle of Children" and "The Death of Ritchie," and in the feature films, "Survival Run" and "Her Alibi," with Tom Selleck. Pratt is married to Alfredo Pecora, a fashion designer, with whom she has two young daughters, Sophia and Lorena. The couple met in Los Angeles, when Susan decided to remodel her bathroom. Pecora, who at the time worked in this field, was selected for the job, and the two have been together ever since. Currently living in New York, the family spends weekdays in their New York City apartment, and weekends at Susan's mother's Westchester home. Following in her mother's footsteps, Sophia has already begun to ride horses competitively.

JOHN PRESTON

Born: September 4 in Cedar City, Utah
Marital Status: single
Height: 6' **Eyes:** hazel **Hair:** dark brown
Education: Southern Utah State College
Interests: music, skiing, horseback riding

Daytime Dramas: "General Hospital," Greg

A native of Cedar City, Utah, John Preston moved to California at an early age, and has been active in the world of show business ever since. He appeared in his first commercial at the age of ten, and a year later performed on stage in "The Music Man." Preston was also involved in the arts while in school, singing in the chorus in junior high, and forming his own band, "Mirage," while in high school. By the time he was sixteen, Preston was supporting himself as a sound mixer for professional music recordings, as well as studying Shakespeare at Southern Utah State College. Returning to Los Angeles, Preston found steady work in commercials and print ads, and appearing on the big screen in the hit film, "The Karate Kid." He also worked on television in such shows as "The Judge" and "The Insiders," on which he had a four episode recurring role. In August of 1987 Preston was hired to appear sporadically as Greg on "General Hospital," however there was such a tremendous audience response that he was hired for full time work in May of the following year. In his spare time Preston enjoys writing music, as well as skiing, skeet shooting, and horseback riding.

LINDSAY PRICE

Born: December 6, 1976 in Arcadia, California
Marital Status: single
Height: 5'6" **Eyes:** dark brown **Hair:** black
Education: currently enrolled at Professional Children's School
Interests: dancing, skiing, horseback riding, volleyball

Daytime Dramas: "All My Children," An Li Chen, 1991-

Only the most imaginative of soap opera writers could concoct the real life family history of Lindsay Price. It seems that Lindsay's mother, Diane, was an eleven year old orphan from Korea, when she was selected to come to the United States to perform with a worldwide choir. The couple who selected the young girl were so impressed that they decided to adopt her officially, bringing her into the family which also included their son Bill. A few years later Bill went off to fight in Vietnam, and when he returned he discovered that his adopted sister, six years his junior, had become a beautiful young woman. The two became very close, and eventually decided it would be o.k. to marry. The couple are now the proud parents of Lindsay Price, presently starring as An Li Chen Bodine on "All My Children." Lindsay was born on December 6, 1976 in Arcadia, California, and has over her fifteen years guest starred on numerous t.v. shows, among them "Parker Lewis Can't Lose," "Life Goes On," "Stories for Growing Up," "The Wonder Years," "Family Medical Center," "My Two Dads," "Newhart," "Joe Piscopo HBO Comedy Special," "Hotel," "Finders of Lost Loves," "Airwolf," "General Hospital," "Junior Star Search," and "I'm Telling," while she has been seen in such t.v. movies as "Suspicions" and "Plymouth." Ms. Price's big screen credits include "Hypersapiens" and "The Purple People Eater," with Neil Patrick Harris. Also a talented singer and vocalist, the young actress has displayed these skills on several recordings, including "Aesop's Fables As Told By Michael Mish," "A Kid's View Of The Environment," "Sleepy Train," and "I'm Blue." In addition, Lindsay is also a trained dancer, adept at jazz, tap, and ballet. Since joining the cast of "All My Children" in 1991, Lindsay has lived in New York City, where she attends high school at the Professional Children's School. Although her career is going well, Lindsay says she is "planning on definitely going to college." In her spare time, Lindsay enjoys snow and water skiing, horseback riding, ice skating, dancing, and volleyball.

CLAYTON PRINCE

Born: February 17, 1965 in Philadelphia, Pennsylvania
Marital Status: single
Height: 6' **Eyes:** brown **Hair:** brown
Education: Temple University, one year
Interests: martial arts

Daytime Dramas: Ryan's Hope," Lyndon;
"Another World," Reuben Lawrence, 1988-1990

Currently seen as Jericho "Gibs" Gibson on the popular late night series "Dark Justice," Clayton Prince is best known to daytime audiences as Reuben Lawrence on "Another World." Born on February 17, 1965, Clayton was raised, along with his two older siblings, Joyce and Darnel, in Philadelphia, Pennsylvania. After a stint as a math major at Temple University, Clayton, who had attended the High School of the Creative and Performing Arts, decided to devote himself full time to acting. He studied and performed with the Children's Repertory Theatre, appearing in such productions as "Peter Pan" and "The Grasshopper and the Ant," and has additionally been seen on stage in the Boston production of "American Passion," with Robert Downey Jr. and Laura Dern. On the big screen, the young actor starred in two popular films, Berry Gordy's "The Last Dragon," and as Seaweed in "Hairspray," directed by John Waters. Along with "Another World," Prince's television credits include "Ryan's Hope," "Saturday Night Live," and "The Cosby Show," on which he made an indelible impression as Lisa Bonet's reggae singing boyfriend. According to Prince, at the time he landed his role on "Cosby," he was, as many stuggling actors, living on $7 a day in New York. Presently bi-coastal, living in Bergen County, New Jersey, and California, Clayton, who is single, is an active supporter of The Guardian Angels, an organization of unarmed volunteers who help prevent crime throughout the country. In addition, he also donates his time to the Make A Wish Foundation. Away from the set, Clayton can often be found practicing the martial arts, with particular concentration on karate and aikido.

ELAINE PRINCI

Born: December 14 in Chambersburg, Pennsylvania
Marital Status: single
Height: 5'4" **Eyes:** brown **Hair:** brown
Education: California State University at Northbridge, B.A. in theatre arts
Interests: horseback riding, oil painting, cooking, fencing
Awards: 1992 Soap Opera Award nomination for Outstanding Villainess

Daytime Dramas: "As the World Turns," Miranda Marlowe, 1981-1982; **"Days of Our Lives,"** Linda Anderson/Madame X, 1984-1986; Dr. Kate Winograd; **"One Life to Live,"** Dorian Lord Callison 1990-

Elaine Princi has shown a penchant for playing "the woman you love to hate." From her role in "As the World Turns," to her most recent work on "One Life to Live," few actresses in daytime have portrayed such a wide range of wickedness. Elaine was born in Chambersburg, Pennsylvania where she grew up in a very close knit family with her two sisters Valerie and Carla. She first discovered her love of acting from her father, actor Carl Princi, who starred in such films as "Tender is the Night," and "How to Succeed in Business Without Really Trying." Elaine graduated from California State University at Northbridge with a B.A. in drama. From there she went on to a string of guest appearances on series such as "All in the Family," "Rockford Files'" "Cannon," "That Girl," "Lou Grant," and "Barnaby Jones," as well as a public television production of "A Doll's House." Her t.v. movies include "Helter Skelter," "A Sensitive Passionate Man," "A Suicide's Wife" and "Stroke-Counter-Stroke." Most recently fans can see Elaine on t.v. as a guest on the infomercial for a 900 psychic line. At home on the stage, Elaine has played the lead roles in off-Broadway and regional productions, among them, "Malice Afterthought," "Beehive," "Thirteen," "No Sex Please, We're British," and "Othello." For the past decade Elaine has concentrated mainly on daytime dramas, creating some of the mediums most memorable villains. Among them: Miranda Marlowe on "As the World Turns," and the wicked Linda Anderson/ Madame X on "Days of Our Lives," and her most recent creation Dorian Lord Callison on "One Life to Live." Away from the world of daytime drama Elaine has numerous other pursuits. She has co-authored "The Ancient Rarebit Fantasy," a book for children; she also is in the process of producing a PBS documentary about a lost Inca treasure, (she has traveled through the mountains of Equador searching for Incan treasures missing for over 400 years) as well as being part of a real estate partnership in New York City. When she is not working, Elaine enjoys oil painting as well as sports, particularly fencing and horseback riding. She also loves to cook as well as entertain. She attributes this to her parents who were always entertaining. Elaine also volunteers her time to various organizations and charitable causes, involving herself with Bide-a-Wee, PITA, and homeless shelters.

ROSEMARY PRINZ

Marital Status: married to Joe Patti
Eyes: brown   **Hair:** blond
Interests: theater, music, the beach

Daytime Dramas: "First Love," Amy, 1954-1955; **"As the World Turns,"** Penny Hughes, 1956-1968, 1985-1987; **"All My Children,"** Amy Tyler, 1970; **"How to Survive a Marriage,"** Dr. Julie Franklin, 1974-1975

The star of over two hundred theatrical productions, Rosemary Prinz is also one of the great daytime actresses, best known for her twelve year run as Penny Hughes on "As the World Turns." Throughout her years on the show, Ms. Prinz always made certain that she was given suitable time to pursue stage roles, and thus was able to cultivate two distinct, but thriving careers. Born into an artistic family, Rosemary's father was the renowned cellist, Milton Prinz, who performed with the NBC Symphony Orchestra and was the founder of the New York String Quartet. Rosemary made her professional debut at the age of sixteen at the Craigsmoor Summer Theatre, following which she joined bus and truck tours of such shows as "Joan of Lorrainne," "Kiss and Tell," "Glad Tidings," and "The Second Man." Since then she has steadily worked in the theater, appearing on Broadway in "Tribute" with Jack Lemmon, "Prisoner of Second Avenue," "Three Men on a Horse," "Tonight in Samarkand," with Louis Jordan, "Late Love," and with Walter Mathau in "The Grey-Eyed People." Among the hundreds of off-Broadway and regional productions in which Ms. Prinz has starred: "Steel Magnolias," "Driving Ms. Daisy," "California Suite," "Last of the Red Hot Lovers," "The Apple Tree," "Same Time, Next Year," "Absurd Person Singular," "The Odd Couple," "Cat on a Hot Tin Roof," "Twigs," "Two for the Seesaw," "Lovers and Other Strangers," "Gypsy," "Irma La Douce," "The Owl and the Pussycat," "A Girl Could Get Lucky," "Death of a Salesman," "Long Day's Journey Into Night," "Important of Being Earnest," "A Delicate Balance," "A Little Night Music," and "Another Part of the Forest." The actress's most familiar role is Amanda in "The Glass Menagerie," which she has played in five separate productions, including one presentation in Japan. Along the way, Rosemary has been in scores of national tours, as well as performing in such prestigious regional venues as the Alabama Shakespeare Festival, The American Shaw Festival, the Milwaukee Repertory Company, and the Alley Theater in Houston, to name but a few. Along with "As th World Turns," daytime viewers also came to know Rosemary from her work on "First Love," "How to Survive a Marriage," and originating the role of Amy Tyler on "All My Children." The actress returned to the role of Penny Hughes from 1985 to 1987, and has made prime time guest appearances on "Archie Bunker's Place," "The Mickey Rooney Show," "Hart to Hart," "Knots Landing," and "Laverne and Shirley." In her personal life, Rosemary is married to musician, Joe Patti.

RENEE PROPS

Born: February 15 in Oklahoma
Marital Status: single, one daughter
Eyes: brown   **Hair:** brown
Interests: singing, writing

Daytime Dramas: "As the World Turns," Ellie Snyder, 1988-

Born on February 15 in Oklahoma, Renee Props was raised on a family farm in Litchfield, Arkansas. From an early age she wanted to be an actress, and as a child she pursued this dream appearing in community theater and local commercials. At the age of nine, Props joined the Phoenix Center Stage company, with whom she made her professional debut in "The Sound of Music," following which she remained with the organization, touring the United States and Canada. Her career progressed rapidly, and by the time she was fifteen, she has starred in a European television movie, appeared in several national commercials, and even taken the top prize in a modelling contest. Renee eventually moved to Los Angeles, where she landed roles in such films as "Weird Science," "Forbidden Sun," and "When You're Young." On television, she can currently be seen as Ellie Snyder on "As the World Turns," a role she has played since 1988. Additionally, Ms. Props was a regular on "Hard Knocks," and has made guest appearances on numerous shows, including "Hill Street Blues," and "Murphy's Law." She is also in the process of forging a singing career, and in her spare time has written several plays and short stories. Props now makes her home in New York City, where she enjoys spending time with her daughter, Audra Megyne Charlee Ziegler.

KEITH DOUGLAS PRUITT

Born: October 12 in Wichita, Kansas
Marital Status: single
Height: 6' **Eyes:** brown   **Hair:** brown
Education: Duke University, Bachelor's Degree; City College of New York, Master's Degree
Interests: music, motorcycles, sports

Daytime Dramas: "As the World Turns," Frank Wendell; **"Loving,"** Flynn Riley, 1990-1992

Already a renowned force in the world of modern classical music, Keith Douglas Pruitt is proving himself to be equally adept in the world of professional acting. Born in Wichita, Kansas, Pruitt's family relocated to Fairfax, Virginia when Keith was eight years old. That same year saw the inception of his extraordinary musical abilities, after Keith convinced his parents to let him have a go at the piano lessons which were already causing his older siblings untold misery. For the younger Pruitt the piano proved to be anything but misery, and he has not stopped playing since. At the age of seventeen Keith was awarded a piano scholarship to Duke University, from which he graduated Phi Beta Kappa/ summa cum laude with a degree in political science. Following college, he moved back home for a while, concentrating on his music, and the possibility of an acting career. His first foray into the latter was a series of Army training films, which proved to be excellent experience and further piqued his interest in acting. After saving up enough money, Keith moved to New York City, enrolling in the graduate program at the City University of New York. It was there that he met Daniel Del Tredici, composer-in-residence for the New York Philharmonic, a man who has since proved to be his musical mentor. After receiving his master's degree, Pruitt's first work, "Sonata for Piano," was performed at Merkin Hall in New York City, and received such a positive response that it was subsequently performed in Ireland, Wales, and throughout the United States. His other musical works include "Innocence," which was commissioned by the Regina Symphony Orchestra, and "Dominance and the Seduction," commissioned by the New York Chamber Ensemble. Since then, he has been selected by Robert La Fosse, principal dancer and choreographer of the New York City Ballet, to write a suite of Piano pieces. On the acting front, Pruitt starred as Nick, in the film "Hairspray," as well as playing the role of Frank Wendell on "As the World Turns." He has also appeared on "Ryan's Hope" and "Another World." The role of Flynn Riley on "Loving" was created around the actor's own talents, which has afforded daytime fans the opportunity to see Pruitt act as well as perform some of his musical competitions. Another similarity to his daytime character is his love of motorcycle riding. A serious athlete since high school, the actor/musician/ composer stays in shape by running and weightlifting.

NATHAN PURDEE

Born: August 6 in Tampa, Florida
Marital Status: married to Roberta Morris, November 9, 1991, one son, Taylor Armstrong, born January 14, 1992
Height: 6'2" **Eyes:** brown **Hair:** black
Education: Metropolitan State College
Interests: painting

Daytime Dramas: "General Hospital," Dr. Karlan;
"The Young and the Restless," Nathan Hastings, 1984-1991;
"Santa Barbara;" "One Life to Live," Rocket Gannon, 1992-

In January of 1992, Nathan Purdee joined the cast of "One Life to Live" as Rocket Gannon, ending a six year run as Nathan Hastings on "The Young and the Restless." Born on August 6 in Tampa, Flordia, Purdee, along with his family, relocated frequently, and before he graduated from high school, Nathan had resided in Washington D.C., California, Denver, and Kaiserlautern, Germany. (Nathan is fluent in German) Moving to McMinvelle, Oregon, he enrolled as a criminology major at Lindfield College, with a minor in theater, and soon began appearing in school plays and community theater. After earning his degree in mental health from Metropolitan State College in Denver, Purdee put these skills to work at the Fort Logan Mental Institution. He eventually, however, began working in show business, serving as house manager with Eaton House Broadcasting, a production company. In addition, Purdee was the executive producer of the play, "The Soul of Nat Turner." Encouraged by daytime star Anthony Geary, Nathan continued to study acting as well, and soon made his daytime debut as Dr. Karlan on "General Hospital." In September of 1984, the actor landed the two day role of mob enforcer, Kong, on "The Young and the Restless." But as it happens, two days turned into seven years, and fans of the show got to see Purdee take the character of Kong from street smart con man to the decidedly more upwardly mobile detective, Nathan Hastings. In 1989, Purdee took ten weeks away from the show to appear on "Santa Barbara," where he was a featured player in a storyline depicting an interracial relationship. Away from daytime, the actor recently made his feature film debut in "Dark Streets: The Return of Superfly." Since joining the cast of "One Life to Live," Nathan, who was previously married to actress, Mary Jacobsen, now shares his New York home with his wife, Roberta, and son, Taylor. The family relocated from Los Angeles when Nathan joined the cast of "One Life to Live." A firm believer in supporting local charities, Purdee donates his time as a hospital emergency room volunteer. Along with acting, Purdee is an accomplished artist, and recently sold his first painting to a Parisian Art collector. Prior to that, his work was displayed at Installations I, a popular Encino art gallery.

COLLEEN QUINN

Born: April 24 on Long Island, New York
Marital Status: single
Height: 5' 7" **Eyes:** brown **Hair:** brown
Education: University of North Carolina at Greensboro, B.F.A. in acting
Interests: skating, football, baseball

Daytime Dramas: "Loving," Carly Rescott

Through her role as the manipulative Carly Rescott on "Loving," Colleen Quinn has become one of the most exciting actresses in daytime drama. Raised on Long Island, Colleen attended St. John the Baptist High School in West Islip, where she aspired to become a professional figure skater. Although she sang in the school chorus, it was not until her senior year that Colleen first became interested in acting. She carried this interest over to college, receiving her B.F.A. in acting from the University of North Carolina at Greensboro. After graduating Colleen decided to see some of the world before settling into the life of a struggling actress. Her first stop was Ireland, following which she returned to the states and moved to Nebraska. For Colleen, each of these diverse experiences proved to be a refreshing change of pace, but she eventually returned to New York to pursue her acting career full time. She began studying at the Michael Howard Studio, and later with acting coach Uta Hagen. Among her early roles were small parts on such daytime dramas as "The Guiding Light," and "Ryan's Hope." She also performed off-Broadway and in regional theater in such productions as "Dutchman," "Wild Horse Road," "Grease," and "Beauty Marks," where she first came to the attention of "Loving's" casting director. Recently Colleen performed in the New York production of "Midsummer" and "Ascention Day." Away from her professional life Colleen is an avid sports fan, and is a die hard fan of both the Mets and Notre Dame. She continues skating, as well as watching and playing baseball, softball, and football.

DACK RAMBO

Born: November 13 in Delano, California
Marital Status: single
Height: 6' **Eyes:** blue **Hair:** white
Education: studied with Lee Strasberg and Vincent Chase
Interests: horseback riding, jogging, racquetball
Awards: 1989 "One of Television's Top Ten Hunks"

Daytime Dramas: "Never Too Young," Tim, 1965-1966; **"All My Children,"** Steve Jacobi, 1982-1983; **"Another World,"** Grant Harrison

A long time soap opera favorite, Dack Rambo has appeared on "All My Children," "Another World," and as Jack Ewing on "Dallas." Born on November 13 in Delano, California, Rambo decided at an early age that acting would be a lot easier than life on the family cotton farm. He left home after high school to find that better life as a "star." His career began when he and his twin brother, Dirk, (who died in a car accident at the age of 25) were discovered in church by Loretta Young, who subsequently asked the boys to appear on her t.v. program, "The New Loretta Young Show." Although Dack had always wanted to be an actor, he had never studied the craft. After his successful t.v. debut, he began his training with legendary acting coaches, Lee Strasberg and Vincent Chase. Following this, Rambo made his first venture into daytime television in 1965, co-starring as Tim on "Never Too Young." Since then, the actor has proven himself a prime time favorite as well, starring with Walter Brennan in the series, "The Guns of Will Sonnett, the CBS series "Sword of Justice" and his three year stint on Dallas. He has also been seen in "Paper Dolls," as well as guest starring on "The Love Boat," "Fantasy Island," and "Hotel." Rambo has co-starred in such t.v. films as "Deadly Honeymoon," "Hit Ladies," "Wild Flower," and "Waikiki." On the big screen he has been seen in "The Spring," and Roger Coman's "Welcome to Oblivion." He is also at the helm of his own production company, Dack Rambo productions, and additionally has been successful in the fashion world, serving as the exclusive men's loungewear supplier for Saks Fifth Avenue, Bullocks, Wilshire, and Neiman-Marcus. On the personal side, Dack who is of Italian, French and Native American descent (his family migrated west in a covered wagon) spends much of his free time on his ranch in Earlimart, California. To relax he enjoys horseback riding, racquetball, jogging and tennis. As successful and exciting as Dack's life has been, he has also suffered more than his share of tragedies. Dack, who has a surviving sister and brother, is an avid supporter of Mothers Against Drunk Drivers (MADD). The cause is an emotional one for him - his twin brother was tragically killed by a drunk driver. In 1992, Dack chose to leave his role on "Another World" after learning that he had contracted the HIV virus. Although not leaving the acting profession officially, he has chosen to donate his time to further the education and research of this disease. He has been involved with the originations Search Alliance and the Aids Project, Los Angeles. (213) 962-1600. With these organizations he hopes to help others with the disease as well as educating the public on the reality of AIDS. The address for Search Alliance is 7461 Beverly Boulevard, Suite 304, Los Angeles, CA 90036, phone (213) 930-8820.

GAIL RAMSEY

Born: June 29
Marital Status: single, one son, Quinn
Height: 5'4"   **Eyes:** brown   **Hair:** brown
Education: University of Wisconsin
Interests: golf, tennis, music
Awards: numerous sports awards

Daytime Dramas: "General Hospital," Susan Moore, 1978-1983; **"Generations,"** Laura McCallum

An accomplished actress and golfer, Gail Ramsey has starred on two popular daytime dramas, "Generations" and "General Hospital." Her "GH" stint was under the name of Gail Rae Carlson. Born on June 29, Gail no doubt acquired many of her talents from her parents, Gordon, a golf pro, and Dorothy Hartz, a singer. After attending the University of Wisconsin, where she majored in Public Address as well as Physical Education, (picking up numerous golf and tennis awards along the way) Ramsey moved to Los Angeles where she began her acting training with Darryl Hickman. Since then she has appeared in such motion pictures as "He Loves Me...He Loves Me Not," "Spoiled Rotten," and "Portrait of a Mistress," while her theater credits include roles in "Streetcar Named Desire," "Gentlemen Prefer Blondes," "Bye Bye Birdie," and "The Rainmaker." Along with her work on daytime, Ms. Ramsey has made guest appearances on several prime time programs, including "Matlock," "Mike Hammer," "Adam 12," "O'Hara," "Scarecrow and Mrs. King," and "Hardcastle and McCormick." Now living in North Hollywood with her son, Quinn, Gail, who is single, enjoys golf, tennis, music, skydiving, and mountain climbing. She also donates much of her time to church related charities.

HEATHER RATTRAY

Born: April 26 in Moline, Illinois
Marital Status: single
Height: 5' 7"   **Eyes:** blue-green   **Hair:** honey brown
Education: Skidmore College, B.S.; graduate work at the State University of New York, Albany
Interests: hockey, scuba diving, travel, horseback riding, softball

Daytime Dramas: "The Guiding Light," Wendy; **"As the World Turns,"** Lily Walsh, 1989-

It was during a children's theater group production of "Peter Pan," that five year old Heather Rattray, sitting in the audience, first felt the magic of the stage. Born in Moline, Illinois, Heather grew up on a farm in Cambridge Minnesota as well as in Los Angeles, California. While living on the farm, Heather learned how to ride and handle a gun, skills she was able to use in the films "Across the Great Divide," and "Wilderness Family II," films she began making when she was only eleven years old. Before going to college, she made two more family films, "Shipwrecked" and "Mountain Family Robinson." After attending Oakwood High School in North Hollywood, Heather moved east to attend Skidmore College, graduating with honors and a B.S. in theatre. She also did graduate work at the University of Albany. No stranger to daytime television, Heather portrayed Wendy on "The Guiding Light" prior to taking over the role of Lily. Her stage credits include regional performances in the Empire State Institute for the Performing Arts productions of "Lyle," "Carnival," and a "Christmas Carol." Other regional theater credits include "Under Milkwood," "Fool for Love," "The Big Knife," and "Spoon River." She has also starred in the horror film "Basket Case 2." Heather, who is single, currently lives in New York City. She has an older brother, actor Laird McIntosh, as well as three half brothers. Her cousin Peter Rattray, also an actor, portrayed Scott Phillips on the now defunct, "Search for Tomorrow." Away from the set, Heather enjoys horseback riding, scuba diving, traveling and softball. She is a self proclaimed, die hard hockey fan and absolutely loves the New York Rangers.

PETER RECKELL

Born: in Michigan
Marital Status: separated
Height: 5'11" **Eyes:** brown **Hair:** brown
Education: Boston Conservatory of Music
Interests: theater, bicycling, softball
Awards: nominated for 1992 People's Choice Award, Favorite Daytime Performer; 1985, 1987 Soap Opera Awards for Outstanding Lead Actor; 1986 Soap Opera Award for Outstanding Younger Lead Actor ("Days of Our Lives")

Daytime Dramas: "As the World Turns," Eric Hollister, 1979-1982; **"Days of Our Lives,"** Bo Brady, 1982-1987, 1990-1991

During the 1980's, Peter Reckell became one of daytime's greatest stars, earning millions of devoted fans for his portrayal of the heroic Bo Brady on "Days of Our Lives." Reckell played the part for five years, from 1982 to 1987, returning briefly from 1990 to 1991. Along the way he was nominated for a 1992 People's Choice Award for Favorite Soap Opera Performer, as well as winning three consecutive Soap Opera Awards for Outstanding Lead Actor. Raised in Michigan, Reckell studied theater at the Boston Conservatory of Music, and following graduation put his skills to work in several Broadway productions, including "West Side Story," "Camelot," and "Pippin," as well as in such off-Broadway and regional shows as "The Fantasticks," "Moon Children," and most recently, "Brilliant Traces." He made his daytime debut in 1979 as Eric Hollister on "As the World Turns." After staying with the show for three years, Peter switched over to "Days of Our Lives," where his pairing with Kristina Alfonso resulted in one of soap's great couples, Bo and Hope. After leaving the show in 1987, he made the move to prime time, appearing as Johnny Rourke on "Knots Landing." He returned to "Days of Our Lives" in 1990, but decided to leave the show shortly thereafter in search of new acting challenges, which thus far has included a television movie, "They're Doing My Time," with Cheryl Ladd. A strong believer in education, Reckell donated his time to a fund raising effort to save the journalism program at Lugo-Elgin High School; his appearance on the football field turned stage prompted incredible reaction, and the actor was able to help raise thirty thousand dollars in just three hours. Now living in Los Angeles, Reckell, who enjoys bicycling and softball, recently separated from Dale Kristien, his former "Days of Our Lives" co-star.

QUINN REDEKER

Born: May 12 in Woodstock, Illinois
Marital Status: single, four children
Education: University of Washington; Santa Monica City College
Interests: writing
Awards: nominated for 1989 Daytime Emmy, Outstanding Lead Actor; nominated for 1990 Daytime Emmy, Outstanding Supporting Actor; 1983 Soap Opera Award for Outstanding Villain; 1989 Soap Opera Award for Outstanding Supporting Actor; nominated for two additional Soap Opera Awards; (all for "The Young and the Restless"); 1978 Academy Award nomination, Best Screenplay ("The Deer Hunter")

Daytime Dramas: "The Young and the Restless," Nick Reed,1979; **"Days of Our Lives,"** Alex Marshall, 1979-1987; **"The Young and the Restless,"** Rex Sterling, 1987-

An Emmy nominated actor and an Academy Award nominated writer, Quinn Redeker has enjoyed an illustrious and diverse career spanning over forty years. He is presently seen as Rex Sterling on "The Young and the Restless," a role he has played since 1987, along the way receiving two Daytime Emmy nominations. In addition he has won two Soap Opera Digest Awards, as well as being nominated two other times. Longtime fans of "The Young and the Restless" may recall that Redeker appeared on the show briefly in 1979 as Nick Reed, but left the show to begin an eight year run as Alex Marshall on another popular daytime drama, "Days of Our Lives." Born on May 12 in Woodstock, Illinois, Redeker was raised in Seattle, where he attended Queen Ann High School. A star football player, he was a three year letterman, named all city two years, and earned All American mention for his senior year. After a period at the University of Washington, where he was awarded a football scholarship, Quinn enlisted in the Marine Corps Reserve, for which he relocated, first to Sands Point, Washington, and then to Cherry Point, North Carolina. Continuing in the service, he joined the Air Force Cadets, and subsequentially worked with the outfit in San Francisco, Miami, and Montgomery, Alabama. It was during his time in Miami that Redeker began his show business career, writing, producing, and directing a situation comedy for WTHS-TV. He found the experience rewarding, and decided to move to Los Angeles to pursue a career in comedy. Initially he was forced to work a wide array of jobs to support himself, among them, dance instructor, commercial fisherman, car attendant, carhop, paint mixer, interior decorator, truck driver, washing machine repairman, and auxiliary Santa Monica Police officer. Eventually he decided to return to school, enrolling at Santa Monica City College on a football scholarship. Redeker had hoped to start a business as a painting contractor, but his performing career soon began to take off when a talent scout discovered Quinn performing comedy in a Hollywood night club. Honing his acting skills, he began working with coach Sandy Meisner at 20th Century Fox, and soon landed his first television role, opposite MacDonald Carey, in the series, "Lock Up." Following this, he became a regular on "Dan Raven," and additionally had a recurring role on "Bonanza." Over the course of his career, Redeker has guest starred on over 125 programs, including "Kojak," "Cannon," "The Rockford Files," "Starsky and Hutch," "Barnaby Jones," and "The Love Boat," on which he was cast as the original Captain. Equally at home on the big screen, the actor made his film debut opposite John Wayne in "North of Alaska," after which he displayed his comedic skills in "The Three Stooges Meet Hercules." Among the other films in which Redeker has appeared: "The Christine Jorgensen Story," "Cannibal Orgy," with Lon Chaney Jr., "Airport," "Marriage Go Around," "Where Buffalo Roam," "Coast to Coast," "The Electric Horseman," "The Andromeda Strain," "Ordinary People," and "The Candidate." On stage, he co-starred with Marlo Thomas in "Sunday in New York." In 1976, Quinn sold his first screenplay to Universal Pictures, and has since sold seven more, one of which, "The Deer Hunter," which he co-wrote, received a 1978 Academy Award nomination. Sharing his expertise, he takes time to teach a screen writing class at USC. Now a resident of the San Fernando Valley, Redeker is the father of four college age children.

MELISSA BRENNAN REEVES

Born: March 14 in Eatontown, New Jersey
Marital Status: married to Scott Reeves, one daughter, Emily, born June 1992
Eyes: blue   **Hair:** blond
Education: Lee Strasberg Studios
Interests: skiing, water sports
Awards: nominated for 1991 Daytime Emmy for Outstanding Younger Actress

Daytime Dramas: "Santa Barbara," Jade Perkins, 1984;
"Days of Our Lives," Jennifer Rose Horton, 1985-

Since 1985, Melissa Brennan Reeves has portrayed Jennifer Rose Horton on "Days of Our Lives," a role which earned her a 1992 Emmy nomination for Outstanding Younger Actress. Born and raised in Eatontown, New Jersey, Melissa studied acting at the Lee Strasberg Studios, while she additionally trained as a dancer. Along with "Days of Our Lives," Reeves has also co-starred on "Another World," and as Jade Perkins on "Santa Barbara," as well as appearing in numerous t.v. commercials, all since the age of fifteen. Her movie credits include the HBO Film, "Somewhere Tomorrow." In 1991, Melissa married actor, Scott Reeves (currently on "The Young and the Restless") the two met on the set of "Days of Our Lives" and on June 23, 1992 (the day of the Daytime Emmys), Melissa gave birth to their first child, Emily Taylor Reeves. Nominated for the Emmy, she obviously was unable to attend the ceremonies. The couple lives in Los Angeles, where they keep a plethora of pets. In her spare time, Melissa enjoys skiing and water sports.

SCOTT REEVES

Born: May 16 in Santa Monica, California
Marital Status: married to actress Melissa Brennan Reeves, one daughter, Emily, born June 1992
Eyes: brown **Hair:** brown
Education: Renee Harmon Commercial Workshop; Milton Katselas Acting School
Interests: skiing, travelling, golf, backpacking
Awards: 1991 Emmy nomination for Outstanding Younger Actor

Daytime Dramas: "Days of Our Lives," Jake Hogansen;
"The Young and the Restless," Ryan McNeil, 1991-

When Scott Reeves first joined the cast of "The Young and the Restless," his character, Ryan McNeil, was intended to be only a recurring role, but the actor made an immediate impression, and a short time later he found himself signing a three year contract. The show's producers clearly made the right choice, as Reeves is quickly becoming a daytime favorite, pulling in a 1991 Daytime Emmy nomination for Outstanding Younger Actor. Born on May 16 in Santa Monica, California, Reeves was raised in the San Fernando Valley; his father worked as a Beverly Hills police officer, and his mother owned a publishing company. After graduating from West Valley Christian High School, where he excelled in baseball and football, Scott began his acting training at the Renee Harmon Commercial Workshop and the Milton

Katselas Acting School. Although his career is going well now, he continues to hone his skills with acting coach Carole D'Andrea. Along with numerous national commercials for McDonalds and Diet Coke, among others, Reeves has landed roles on both television and in feature films. On the big screen, the actor had the honor of killing Jason in "Friday the 13th Part VIII: Jason Takes Manhattan," and also appeared in "Edge of Honor" and "Big Man on Campus." His t.v. credits include a guest stint on "The Munsters Today," and co-starring roles in two television movies, "Teen Angel II" and "I Know My First Name is Steven." Daytime fans first came to know Scott when he portrayed Jake Hogansen on "Days of Our Lives." While the role may not have lasted a substantial amount of time, it did introduce Reeves to co-star Melissa Brennan, and the two are now happily married and the proud parents of their first child, Emily Taylor, born on June 23, 1992. The couple live in California with their four dogs, three cats, one bird, and one wild mustang. Away from the joys of parenthood and pet ownership, Reeves' hobbies include water skiing, snow skiing, golf, bicycling, going to movies, backpacking, and taking weekend trips with Melissa along the Northern California Coastline (which will now include their daughter).

JOHN REILLY

Born: November 11 in Chicago, Illinois
Marital Status: married with three daughters and two stepdaughters
Height: 6'1" **Eyes:** brown **Hair:** brown
Interests: writing, tennis, reading spy novels
Awards: Soap Opera Digest "Daytimes Ten Sexiest Men"

Daytime Dramas: "**As the World Turns,**" Dan Stewart, 1974-1976; "**General Hospital,**" Sean Donely, 1984-

Although he was always interested in acting, it was by chance that this talented actor actually entered the entertainment industry. Born on November 11, in Chicago, Illinois, John was a successful businessman, working for ten years as an account executive for a packaging firm. Through his work John met a theatrical producer who, knowing John's interest in acting, asked John to take over a role from an actor he had fired. Although John had never acted before, he received great reviews. The experience proved to be such a success that he continued working as an actor in Chicago, while still holding his executive position. Eventually he was convinced that he should devote himself fulltime to his acting career, which took him out of Chicago and into film, theater, and television. Reilly first appeared on Broadway in Donald Driver's comedy "Status Quo Vadis," in which he co-starred with Ted Danson and Bruce Boxleitner. After leaving New York for Hollywood he enjoyed a string of appearances on popular prime time shows including the recurring role of Roy Ralston on "Dallas," along with recurring roles on "How the West Was Won," and "Hart to Hart." He has also guest starred on "Simon and Simon," Three's Company," "Benson," "The Love Boat," "Lou Grant," "Remington Steele," and "Who's the Boss?" Reilly also starred in the short lived series "Paper Dolls" as well as "The Hamptons," a prime time series where he worked with "General Hospital," producer Gloria Monty. Reilly's feature films include "Deal of the Century," "The Great Waldo Pepper," and "The Main Event." He also starred in such television movies as "Missing Pieces" and "The Patricia Neal Story." In 1974 John made his soap opera debut as Dr. Dan Stewart on "As the World Turns". Currently he can be seen on daytime's "General Hospital" where he portrays Sean Donely, a role that has earned him the honor of "One of Daytime's Ten Sexiest Men" by Soap Opera Digest. Off camera, John's voice can be heard across the country selling Pactel Cellular Phones. In his early career days in Chicago, John did a lot of voice overs, and now, aside from Pactel, he is the voice behind Hallmark cards, a few banks, and even a potato chip ad. In his spare time he enjoys tennis, reading spy novels and writing. (he has completed a screenplay) John is married and has three daughters and two stepdaughters.

SANDRA REINHARDT

Born: March 23, 1967
Marital Status: married to John Reinhardt on December 17, 1989
Height: 5' 7" **Eyes:** hazel **Hair:** blond
Education: two years of college
Interests: sports, sketching, painting, spending time with her animals
Awards: Miss Western Pennsylvania; second runner up, Miss Teen All American Pageant; Miss Pennsylvania; contestant in 1985 Miss USA Pageant

Daytime Dramas: "Another World," Amanda Cory Fowler, 1987-

A former Miss Pennsylvania, Sandra Reinhardt made her daytime debut in 1987 as Amanda Cory on "Another World." Born on March 23, 1967, Sandra was raised in Pittsburgh, Pennsylvania, the youngest of three children. She grew up "in a small middle class neighborhood outside of Pittsburg and loved it." Her professional career began as a model at thirteen, appearing in print ads, commercials, industrial films, as well as on the runway. At the age of sixteen she won the title of Miss Western Pennsylvania, following which she earned the second runner up position in the Miss Teen All-American Pageant. Continuing with the beauty pageant circuit, Reinhardt then won the Miss Pennsylvania crown, and went on to represent her home state in the 1985 Miss USA Pageant. During this time, she additionally honed her acting skills, appearing in such local productions as "The Barber of Seville," "Miss Daisy Drinks a Little," "Bus Stop," and "Crimes of the Heart." Presently living in Brooklyn, New York, Sandra (or as she is known, Sandi) has been married for three years to John Reinhardt. An animal lover, she donates much of her time to the Humane Society, as well as working to promote AIDS awareness. In her spare time, she enjoys horseback riding, running, rollerskating, and bicycling, as well as sketching, painting abstracts, and using acrylics.

JAMES REYNOLDS

Born: August 10, 1950 in Oskaloosa, Kansas
Marital Status: married to Lissa Reynolds, one son, Jed
Height: 6' **Eyes:** brown **Hair:** brown
Education: Washburn University, B.F.A.
Interests: racquetball, reading, basketball, backpacking, coaching
Awards: 1991 Daytime Emmy nomination-Outstanding Lead Actor for "Generations;" National Jewish Hospital, "Man of the Year," 1984, 1985, 1986, 1989, 1990

Daytime Dramas: "Days of Our Lives," Abe Carver, 1981-1990; **"Generations,"** Henry Marshall, 1990-1991; **"Days of Our Lives,"** Abe Carver, 1991-

A popular television and stage actor, James Reynolds has appeared as Abe Carver on "Days of Our Lives" since 1981. He took a hiatus from the show in 1990 to portray Henry Marshall on the now defunct "Generations." For his work on this show, Reynolds received a 1991 Daytime Emmy nomination for Outstanding Lead Actor. Born on August 10, 1950 in Oskaloosa, Kansas, Reynolds, along with his brother Warren, were raised in Kansas City, Missouri. He was an All State high school football star, following which he went on to receive his B.F.A. from Washburn University. A former

Marine and Vietnam veteran, Reynolds' acting career has included over fifty plays, fifty t.v. shows, and ten feature films, while he has additionally worked as a newspaper art critic and magazine editor. Among his many stage roles, he is perhaps best known for his work in two one man shows, "I, Too, Am America," and "Great Art, Great Work," both of which he has performed across the country. Today, the actor also serves as the managing artistic director of the DeLacey Street Theater in Pasadena. On television, Reynolds was a series regular on "Time Express," and has also appeared on "The Incredible Hulk," "Diff'rent Strokes," "227," "Highway to Heaven," "The Dukes of Hazzard," "Keeper of the Wild," "The Magic of Lassie," and "Mr. Majestic." Outside of performing, he is the spokesperson for the National Jewish Hospital, and out of appreciation the organization has named the actor their Man of the Year five times. He is also active with the "Living the Dream Committee" and the South Pasadena Site Council. In his spare time, Reynolds, who shares his home with wife, Lissa, and son, Jed, enjoys racquetball, basketball, backpacking, reading, and coaching.

ALLYSON RICE-TAYLOR

Born: November 26, 1963 in Huntington, West Virginia
Marital Status: married to actor/cellist Andy Taylor on May 13, 1990
Height: 5' 9"   **Eyes:** green   **Hair:** brown
Education: Northwestern University, B.S. in Speech, major in theater, 1986
Interests: art, football, quilting, collecting Pez dispensers, hats and wigs in every hair color,shooting pool, good restaurants, family and friends
Awards: 1989 Drama-Logue Critics Award for Minimata

Daytime Dramas: "All My Children," the ghost of Estelle LaTour, 3 days; **"As the World Turns,"** Connor Jamison, 1990-

Since joining the cast of "As the World Turns" in October of 1990, Allyson Rice-Taylor has proven to be one of the freshest and most exciting actresses on daytime drama. A native of Huntington, West Virginia, Allyson's family moved around quite a bit, including stops in Mississippi and Connecticut, before settling down permanently in Bethesda, Maryland. Her father, Paul Rice, is an author and professor of law at American University, while her mother, Jane, is a graphic art designer. She has one younger brother, Andrew Rice. Allyson first discovered acting while at Grosevenor Elementary School when she followed the lead of a friend who was already involved in dinner theater productions. She began taking acting and dance classes, remaining with these throughout her years at North Bethesda Junior High and Walter Johnson High School. Along with appearing in school plays, Allyson also worked as an intern at the Round House Theatre in Maryland. The young actresses next stop was Northwestern University in Chicago, where she had a double major of speech and theater. On the stage at Northwestern, Allyson had roles in "Charlotte's Web," "Step on a Crack," "Little Mary Sunshine," and "West Side Story." Her other theater credits include "Motion Fixtures," "Biloxi Blues," "Brighton Beach Memoirs," and "A Chorus Line" After graduating in 1986 Allyson set out for Los Angeles, where she found work in commercials and on such television series as "Family Ties." She also won the 1989 Drama-Logue Critics Award for her work in the Los Angeles Theatre Center production of "Minimata." Although this would seem to be an extremely promising start for a young actress, Allyson decided she didn't like the pace of the west coast and returned to New York. In May of 1990 she married Andy Taylor, a cellist whom she met during the production of "Mimimata," and the couple now resides in Greenwich Village, where according to Allyson "we're deliriously happy." When not playing Connor Jamison, Allyson keeps herself busy through a myriad of activities, among them horseback riding, skydiving, quilting, painting and collage work, camping, reading, travelling, collecting Pez dispensers, hats and wigs in every color, and cheering on her favorite teams, the Washington Redskins, Chicago Bears, New York Mets and Seattle Mariners... and the list goes on.

KELLY RIPA

Born: October 2 in Stratford, New Jersey
Marital Status: single
Height: 5' 4" **Eyes:** blue **Hair:** blond
Education: Camden Community College
Interests: music, ballet

Daytime Dramas: "All My Children," Hayley Vaughan, 1990-

While finishing up high school, Kelly Ripa's future plans consisted of majoring in communications at college and then getting a job as a radio deejay. However, her performance in a school production of "The Ugly Duckling" caught the attention of talent scout, Cathy Parker, who encouraged Ripa to consider being an actress. Kelly agreed and her career has since progressed at a phenomenal rate. After appearing in several national commercials, Kelly's big break came in 1990 when she landed the role of the rebellious Hayley Vaughan on "All My Children." Since then her character has been kidnapped, injured in a street gang war, injured in a car accident, and dedicated herself to helping her alcoholic mother, and along the way Ms. Ripa has become one of daytime's brightest new faces. Born on October 2 in Stratford, New Jersey, Kelly began studying ballet at the age of three, and is the first member of her family, which includes one sister, to enter show business. Previously enrolled at Camden Community College, Kelly has put college on hold for the time being, focusing her energies on her acting career. In addition to television, she has also appeared in local productions of "H.M.S. Pinafore," "The Wizard of Oz," and "A Connecticut Yankee in King Arthur's Court." Now living on her own in New York City, Kelly relishes the city's fast pace, just as she did on her first visit at the age of eight, when her grandfather took her to Radio City Music Hall to see the Rockettes. Knowing how fortunate she has been, Kelly donates much of her time raising money for the Leukemia Society and National Scoliosis Foundation. She is looking forward to a long career as an actress, while continuing to develop her musical skills, both as a piano player and a singer.

CLINT RITCHIE

Born: August 9 in Grafton, North Dakota
Marital Status: engaged to D.J. Shepard
Height: 6' 1" **Eyes:** brown **Hair:** brown
Interests: horses

Daytime Dramas: "One Life to Live," Clint Buchanan, 1979-

A self proclaimed "North Dakota plowboy", Clint Ritchie is the perfect match for the role of Clint Buchanan, a part he has played since 1979 on "One Life to Live." Ritchie was raised on a farm in Grafton, North Dakota, where by age seven he was dreaming of being an actor and by the age of sixteen he was headed to California to study acting. Ritchie made his television debut playing, appropriately enough, a cavalry officer on horseback, on the series pilot of "Wild, Wild, West." Since then he has also appeared on episodes of "Dallas," on the children's program "Thunder," and in the mini-series "The Centennial." Ritchie broke into movies when a 20th Century Fox talent scout saw his portrayal of McMurphy in a production of "One Flew Over the Cuckoo's Nest" and immediately offered him a contract. This lead to roles in such films as "Patton," "A Force of One," and "Bandolero!" In the fall of 1979, Ritchie joined the cast of "One Life to Live," and has continued to play that role ever since. In his spare time Ritchie is still an avid horseman, owning and operating his own horse ranch in Northern California, where he trains his own horses. He is engaged to D.J. Shepard, the owner of the neighboring ranch. When he has the time he also likes to compete in 50-100 mile endurance races on horseback.

ALEXIA ROBINSON

Born: January 1 in Fort Lauderdale, Florida
Marital Status: married to David on September 9, 1989
Height: 5' 3"   **Eyes:** brown   **Hair:** dark brown
Education: Florida State University, Bachelor's Degree
Interests: exercising

Daytime Dramas: "General Hospital," Meg Lawson, 1990-

Born on January 1, in Fort Lauderdale, Florida, Alexia Robinson first appeared in commercials at the age of nine. She continued to do commercial work during her years at Nova High School where she also performed in numerous stage productions. After earning a degree in business administration from Florida State University, Robinson relocated to Los Angeles with only her car and five hundred dollars to her name; however, she quickly found work guest starring on such shows as "Fame," "Hill Street Blues," "What's Happening Now," and "Rituals," as well as a role in the pilot "Liven' Large." She made her feature film debut in the 1990 blockbuster "Total Recall." Shortly thereafter, she made her daytime debut as Meg Lawson on "General Hospital." The actress donates much of her spare time to working with the homeless. A resident of Los Angeles, Robinson shares her home with her husband an accountant, David, and her collection of thirty-five teddy bears.

WILLIAM ROERICK

Born: December 17, 1912 in Hoboken, New Jersey
Marital Status: single
Hair: white
Education: Hamilton College
Interests: gardening, carpentry, mycology
Awards: 1991 Daytime Emmy nomination, Outstanding
Supporting Actor; named Honorary Doctor of Fine Arts by
Hamilton College

Daytime Dramas: "The Clear Horizon," Col. Theodore Adams,
1960-1962; **"Guiding Light,"** Dr. Bruce Banning; **"Guiding
Light,"** Henry Chamberlain, 1980-

An actor, author, and fungi expert, William Roerick is best known to daytime fans as Henry Chamberlain on "Guiding Light," a role he has played since 1980. For his efforts he earned a Daytime Emmy nomination for Outstanding Supporting Actor in 1991. "Guiding Light" fans may also remember Roerick as Dr. Bruce Banning, a role he played back in 1974. Born on December 17, 1912 in Hoboken, New Jersey, Roerick attended Hamilton College, following which he honed his performing skills at the Berkshire Playhouse School. Throughout his career, he has consistently worked on the stage, appearing in Broadway productions of "Dear Charlie," "The Heiress," "The Importance of Being Earnest," "Tonight at 8:30," "Saint Joan," "Romeo and Juliet," "Hamlet," "The Homecoming," "Marat/Sade," and the original production of "Our Town." Roerick's additional theater credits include "Medea," "Macbeth," "Life Class," "The Trials of Oz," and "A Passage to E.M. Forster." (Forster dedicated his final collection of essays to Roerick) The actor has also remained a vital part of the Berkshire Playhouse, serving for many years on it's Board of Directors, as well as performing in scores of productions. His 1984 appearance in "Sabrina Fair" not only marked his fiftieth production, but also afforded Roerick the opportunity to play the father of a character he had played thirty years earlier. He is also influential at his alma mater, Hamilton College, where he is the Chairman of the School's Fine Arts Advisory Committee, as well as donating over 80 prints and drawings to the schools art collection. For his service, Roerick was named an Honorary Doctor of Fine Arts by the school in 1971. Not only a stage actor, he has appeared in such films as "A Separate Peace," "This is the Army," "Say of the Dolphins," "The Love Machine," and "The Other Side of the Mountain." Before "Guiding Light," he made his daytime debut as Colonel Theodore Adams on "The Clear Horizon." Clearly not a man who lacks versatility, Roerick has also written scripts for several television programs, among them "Mama," "Crime Photographer," "Claudia," and "Climax," as well as co-authoring the Broadway play, "The Happiest Years." In his spare time, William, who makes his home on a farm near Stockbridge Massachusetts, enjoys gardening, carpentry, and mycology, the study of fungi.

GIL ROGERS

Born: February 4, 1934 in Lexington, Kentucky
Marital Status: married to actress Margaret Hall,
one daughter, Amanda
Height: 6' 3" **Eyes:** hazel **Hair:** grey
Education: Harvard, A.B.; Transylvania College
Interests: horse racing and breeding, tennis, basketball,
spectator sports

Daytime Dramas: "All My Children," Ray Gardner,
1977-1979, 1982; **"The Doctors,"** Dr. Martin Brandt;
"Search for Tomorrow," Brent Kenwood; **"Guiding Light,"**
Hawk Shayne, 1987-

The multi-talented, Gil Rogers was born to John and Betty Rogers in Lexington, Kentucky on February 4, 1934 and raised there with his sister, Sally. His father was a rural appraiser and tenor. After attending Transylvania College and graduating from Harvard, Gil began a career that has taken him into every phase of acting. His credits include the Broadway productions of "The Corn is Green," "The Great White Hope," and "The Best Little Whorehouse in Texas." (he played Sheriff Ed Earl Dodd) Off-Broadway, Gil has appeared in "Frankie," directed by George Abbott; The New York Shakespeare Festival production of "Remembrance," and the Playwrights Horizons production of "Arms and the Man." He has also performed with many touring companies and starred in numerous prestigious regional productions, including three shows with the San Diego Shakespeare Festival. According to Gil, he has been in "more than 200 plays, more TV and 17 movies." His film credits include, "The Bell Jar," "Pretty Poison," "The Front," "The Children," "A Fans Note," "Eddie Macon's Run," "W.W. and the Dixie Dance Kings," "Nothing but a Man," "The Panic in Needle Park," and "The Line," to name a few. His more than 200 television credits include the NBC Afterschool Special, "Rodeo Red and the Run Away; the "Nova" episode of "The Trial of Denton Cooley;" the NET series,"Eyewitness" episode titled "Deathwish," and four shows on the NET series, "Our Story." Best known to television audiences for his daytime roles, Rogers has portrayed Brent Kenwood on "Search for Tomorrow," Dr. Martin Brandt on "The Doctors," Ray Gardner on "All My Children," and as Hawk Shayne on the "Guiding Light." Off camera, Gil is past president and treasurer, and current secretary and board member of Actors Federal Credit Union. He is also active with the Actors Equity Association. Gil, who is married to actress, Margaret Hall, has one daughter, Amanda, an actress and student. In his leisure time, Gil enjoys horse racing and breeding, as well as tennis, basketball, and spectator sports.

JANE ROGERS

Born: April 6 in Minnesota
Marital Status: single
Eyes: brown **Hair:** brown
Education: Children's Theater Company
Interests: kayaking, windsurfing, stunt driving, horseback
riding
Awards: 1990 Soap Opera Award for Outstanding Supporting
Actress; 1992 Soap Opera Award nomination for Outstanding
Villainess

Daytime Dramas: "General Hospital," Celeste Gabriel;
"Santa Barbara," Heather Donnelly; **"The Bold and the
Beautiful,"** Julie DeLorian, 1989-1991

After playing two virtuous daytime nurses on "General Hospital" and "Santa Barbara," Jane Rogers jumped at the chance to play the villainess, Julie DeLorian on "The Bold and the Beautiful." A Minnesota native, Ms. Rogers received her theatrical training at the Children's Theater Company of Minneapolis, and has since appeared in such regional productions as "I Oughta be in Pictures," "The Crucible," and "Taming of the Shrew." After being discovered on a nationwide talent search, Rogers went on to co-star in the film, "Purple Haze." On television, she played a recurring role on "Falcon Crest," as well as making guest appearances on "Knot's Landing," "9 to 5," "T. J. Hooker," "True Confessions," and "The Redd Foxx Show." Off camera, Jane can be heard doing voice overs for Nike shoes. For over four years, the actress has been romantically involved with actor/director Daniel Rojo, and recently he directed Rogers in two one act plays, presented at the Gnu Theater in North Hollywood. Away from the set and the stage, Rogers enjoys such adventurous hobbies as stunt driving, kayaking, windsurfing and horseback riding.

LYNNE ROGERS

Born: June 15 in New York, New York
Marital Status: single
Height: 5' 2"　**Eyes:** brown　**Hair:** blond
Education: Queens College; Yale Drama School
Interests: writing

Daytime Dramas: "Guiding Light," Marie Wallace, 1954-1962

After achieving success as an actress, Lynne Rogers decided to share her expertise with aspiring performers. As co-author of "How To Be A Working Actor," Ms. Rogers has created what many consider to be the definitive handbook for anyone interested in pursuing this particular career. A New York City native, Lynne was born on June 15. She began her training at the Music and Arts High School, graduating at the head of her class, following which she continued this excellence at Queens College, from which she graduated magna cum laude. Furthering her acting training, Ms. Rogers studied at the Yale Drama School, and in 1954 made her daytime debut as Marie Wallace on "Guiding Light." She stayed with the show until 1962, and has since made guest appearances on several other soap operas, including "As the World Turns," "The Doctors," "A Time For Us," and "Edge of Night," as well as appearing in scores of commercials. For several years, Lynne has been on the Board of Governors of NATAS and the local and national boards of AFTRA. In addition to her acting guide, she has also penned two other books, "A Concise Guide to Executive Etiquette" and "Love of their Lives," a backstage look at daytime television.

SUZANNE ROGERS

Born: July 9 in Colonial Heights, Virginia
Awards: Emmy Award in 1979 for Best Supporting Actress

Daytime Dramas: "Days of Our Lives," Maggie Horton, 1973-1984, 1985-

Dancing her way into the hearts of America, Suzanne Rogers began her career at seventeen when she left her home in Colonial Heights, Virginia to become one of Radio City Music Hall's legendary Rockettes. In 1973 Ms. Rogers came to Los Angeles with the musical "Follies" and later that same year Suzanne joined the cast of "Days of Our Lives." In 1979 her portrayal of Maggie Horton was honored with a Daytime Emmy Award for Best Supporting Actress. Other television credits include "Little House on the Prairie," "Kraft Music Hall," and "Quincy." Suzanne also appeared on the "Ed Sullivan Show" as one of the Peter Gennaro Dancers. Her stage credits include "Coco," "Hallelujah Baby!," "Funny Girl," "110 in the Shade," and "Lock up Your Daughter."

TRISTAN ROGERS

Born: June 3 in Melbourne, Australia
Marital Status: single
Height: 6' 1"   **Eyes:** blue   **Hair:** light brown
Interests: fishing, sailing
Awards: 1981 Soap Opera Award, Favorite Male Newcomer; 1983 Soap Opera Award, Outstanding Lead Actor; 1989 Soap Opera Update, Magazine's Reader's Poll, Best Actor on Daytime Television; Most Valuable Player on "General Hospital"

Daytime Dramas: "General Hospital," Robert Scorpio, 1980-1985, 1986, 1987-1992

Through the 1980's, Tristan Rogers was the actor behind one of daytime's great heroes, Commissioner Robert Scorpio on "General Hospital." For his efforts, the Australian born Rogers earned several awards, including a 1980 Soap Opera Award for Most Exciting New Actor, a 1983 Soap Opera Award for Outstanding Lead Actor, a Most Valuable Player Award from "General Hospital," and a Best Actor in Daytime Award from Soap Opera Update Magazine, the latter the result of a nationwide reader's poll. Born on June 3, Rogers began his career as a drummer and model in Melbourne, and began his acting career in London during the early seventies. In 1978, he moved to the United States, where he soon landed the role of suave Australian agent, Robert Scorpio, this despite the fact that Rogers had spent the preceding months perfecting his American accent. Since working on "General Hospital," he has also found success in prime time, appearing on such programs as "The Love Boat," "Hotel," "Cover-Up," "Mancuso, FBI," and the syndicated series "Superforce." Recently, Rogers could be heard on the big screen, providing one of the principle voices for the animated Disney film, "The Rescuers Down Under." In 1992, he decided to leave "General Hospital" to pursue other interests, which include more feature films, as well as writing, directing, and producing. Since 1984, Rogers has worked closely with the American Cinema Awards Foundation, and is now the organization's vice president, as well as the executive producer of it's annual gala fund raiser. In addition, he directed the 1989 and 1990 American Cinema Awards, an event honoring such show business luminaries as Bette Davis, Clint Eastwood, Elizabeth Taylor, Gregory Peck, and Michael Jackson. To relax, Rogers enjoys fishing, travelling, and sailing.

JULY RONNIE

Born: March 21, 1963 in Torrance, California
Marital Status: single
Height: 5' 5"   **Eyes:** green   **Hair:** blond
Education: Torrance High School, studied dance and movement therapy
Interests: dance, drawing, visiting museums, writing

Daytime Dramas: "Santa Barbara," Laken Lockbridge, 1984-1985

Best known to daytime audiences for her work as Laken Lockbridge on "Santa Barbara," July Ronnie began her professional acting career directly after high school. Born on March 21, July's family includes her father, a high school teacher, her mother, a real estate investor, one brother, and three sisters. July's parents divorced when she was seven and she and two of her sisters lived with her father. As a child, July was interested in art and was active on the student council, while she and her family spent their summers in the country or travelling, by car, throughout the United States. After graduating from Torrance High School, July continued her study of drama while looking for acting work. She was particularly interested in her study of intuitive counseling, and continues to pass on her expertise to this day. July regularly teaches acting, dance, and movement therapy, and believes in "exploring the different ways we relate, communicate with each other, and what keeps us from connecting." On stage, July has been seen in such productions as "Bus Stop" and "The Miracle Worker," while July's television credits include "Matlock," "Poor Little Rich Girl," "Knightrider," "Love Boat," "Dallas," "T.J. Hooker," "A Year in the Life," and a regular role on "Heartbeat." In her spare time, the actress serves as Administrative Director of the Arts for the Triple Eye Foundation, a prestigious non-profit organization. July, who is single and lives in Los Angeles, lists drawing, dance, writing, interior decorating, cooking, making collages, and visiting museums as some of her favorite hobbies. Most importantly she believes in "teaching and learning, being creative as a way of life."

NADA ROWAND

Born: November 30 in Melvin, Illinois
Marital Status: single
Height: 5' 5" **Eyes:** grayish-blue **Hair:** honey blond
Education: University of Illinois
Interests: bicycling, folk art, swimming

Daytime Dramas: "Loving," Kate Rescott, 1984-

Along with being an accomplished stage actress, Nada Rowand has enjoyed equal success on daytime television as Kate Rescott on "Loving." An only child, Nada was born in Melvin, Illinois, where from an early age her favorite activities were singing and going to the movies. After graduating high school, she enrolled at the University of Illinois as a music major, following which she moved to New York City to hone her acting skills. Over the years Rowand has amassed an impressive list of theatrical credits, among them roles on Broadway in "Richard II," with Al Pacino, "Milk and Honey," "Walking Happy," and "The Survivors," while she has additionally been seen in dozens of off-Broadway and regional productions, including "Ladies in Waiting," "Orlando," "The Rainmaker," "Hansel and Gretel," "The Marriage of Figaro," "The Iceman Cometh," as Cora (Ms. Rowand's favorite role) "The Price," "Mrs. Warren's Profession," "Bells Are Ringing," "Blithe Spirit," "The Diary of Anne Frank," "Dance of Death," "The Man Who Came To Dinner," "Richard III," and "Guys and Dolls." Nada has also worked in feature films, appearing in "Captain Nemo," "Rage," "F.I.S.T.," "Masquerade," and in the Academy Award-nominated feature short, "Double Talk." On television, in addition to numerous national commercials, Ms. Rowand was a regular on "Blind Alley," with Pat Morita and Cloris Leachman, and has made guest appearances on "Three's Company," "Bewitched," "Nancy," "Movin' Right Along," "Chris," and "Highway to Heaven." In 1970, and again in 1972, Nada joined the USO and travelled to Vietnam to entertain the troops. Away from the set of "Loving," where she has worked since 1984, the actress enjoys bicycling, swimming, and working out. She also owns her own folk art store.

VICTORIA ROWELL

Born: May 10 in Portland, Maine
Marital Status: seperated, one daughter, Maya
Height: 5' 7" **Eyes:** brown **Hair:** black
Education: Cambridge School of Ballet
Interests: hunting arrowheads in desserts, doll collecting, flea markets
Awards: 1991 "Look At Me, Ar'n't I A Woman" Award

Daytime Dramas: "One Life to Live;" "As the World Turns;" "The Young and the Restless," Drucilla Barber

Victoria Rowell the actress or Victoria Rowell the dancer no matter which one you pick, you have a winner. Add to that, Victoria Rowell the philanthropist, and you can not go wrong. Born May 10 in Portland Maine, Victoria was raised by foster parents in Maine and Boston. Her foster family, and social workers encouraged and supported her love of dance and at the age of eight, Victoria received a dance scholarship from the Ford Foundation and was accepted to the Cambridge School of Ballet. Seven years later, at age fifteen she joined the junior company of the American Ballet Theater and toured the country for two years. Although she loves dance, Victoria felt better suited to acting and the life of an actor compared to that of a dancer. Evening audiences will remember Rowell in her recurring role as Paula on "The Cosby Show," as well as guest starring on "The Fresh Prince of Bel Air," and in the film "Leonard Part VI." She has just completed filming "The Distinguished Gentleman" with Eddie Murphy. The film is due for a December 1992 release. Victoria's daytime dramas include "One Life to Live," "As the World Turns" and as Drucilla Barber on "The Young and the Restless." One that obviously has not forgotten her past, Victoria established the Rowell Children's Scholarship Fund which sponsors foster children who are studying ballet. Currently, the fund is helping five children. (ages 8 to 13; 4 in Maine, 1 in Boston) The Fund was established in 1990 with seed money that came from a "The Young and the Restless" "Family Feud" game show celebrity week. Victoria also keeps track of the student progress through the schools, social workers and visits throughout the year. If all of that isn't enough for this busy woman, she also has spoken on Capitol Hill on behalf of increased funding for child welfare programs. Victoria was a recipient of the 1991 "Look At Me, Ar'n't I A Woman" Award, presented by the Black Educational, Cultural and Historical Society fo the State of Maine. She received the award in appreciation for her cultural contribution to the state. Once a year Victoria travels back to Maine to teach ballet at the Oak Street Dance School. She also gives lectures on dance and theater in both public and private schools. Her hobbies include hunting for arrow heads in the dessert, doll collecting, and searching for forgotten treasures in flea markets. A resident of Los Angeles, Victoria, who recently separated from her husband Tom Fahey, has one daughter, Maya.

FRANK RUNYEON

Marital Status: married to Anne Runyeon, three children
Eyes: brown   **Hair:** black
Education: Princeton University, Bachelor's Degree
Interests: playing the piano, standup comedy
Awards: Four consecutive years, voted one of the "Top Three Popular Leading Men"

Daytime Dramas: "As the World Turns," Steve Andropolis, 1980-1986; **"Santa Barbara,"** Michael Donnelly; **"General Hospital,"** Simon Romero, 1992

Actor, comedian, and pianist, are just some of the successes Frank Runyeon has earned. Tall, dark, handsome, and talented, it is no wonder this soap veteran has been voted one of "The Top Three Popular Leading Men" for four consecutive years. Born in Pennsylvania, Frank earned a degree in theology from Princeton University. His stage credits include the off-Broadway production of "Sudden Death" and "The Birds" at La Mama. On television, Frank appeared in "A Table at Ciro's," a segment of the PBS "Tales from Hollywood" series, and "High Mountain Rangers." His feature film credits include "Sudden Death" and "Bolero." Frank is best known for his six years as Steve Andropolis on the daytime drama, "As the World Turns." He recently completed a stint in the recurring role of Simon Romero on "General Hospital," and has returned to his Connecticut home which he shares with his wife, Anne and their three children. When not on the set, he has be known to take the stage as a comedian at The Improvisation and Catch a Rising Star comedy clubs, as well as having been a Los Angeles disc jockey for a rock station. He is also an accomplished classical, jazz and ragtime pianist.

Michael M. Ryan

MICHAEL M. RYAN

Born: March 19, 1929 in Wichita, Kansas
Marital Status: widowed, three sons, Michael, Chris and Anthony
Height: 6' **Eyes:** brown   **Hair:** grey
Education: Georgetown University, B.S.
Interests: baseball, carpentry
Awards: three Emmy nominations

Daytime Dramas: "Ben Jerrod," Ben Jerrod, 1963; **"Another World,"** John Randolph, 1964-1979; **"Another Life,"** Vince Gardello, 1981-1984

Had it not been for a chance remark of a college roommate, Michael Ryan would most likely not have been mentioned in this book. It happens that Ryan was poised for a career in the diplomatic corps, having completed six years in Georgetown University's foreign service program, when his friend put forth the notion that the key to life was "doing" rather than "being." Well at that moment it occurred to young Mr. Ryan that he may have wanted to "be" a diplomat, but what he really wanted to "do" was act. What affect he might have had on international relations will forever remain a mystery, but Ryan certainly has made an impact on daytime television. Ryan was born on March 19 in Wichita, Kansas, where his father worked as a civil engineer. After completing his years at Georgetown, and deciding to pursue his dream, Michael moved to New York where he began life as a struggling actor. He arranged his schedule around acting classes, often working at nights so he could attend day classes with famed acting coach Stella Adler, whom Ryan credits as the person most singularly responsible for helping him with his craft. During these early years, when roles were difficult to find, he supported himself through a wide array of jobs, including bank clerk, bartender, and oil salesman.   Eventually, however, his efforts paid off, and Ryan soon embarked on a successful career which encompassed t.v., movies, and theater. Best known for his daytime work, Michael spent one year as the title character on "Ben Jerrod" before taking on the role of John Randolph on "Another World." He remained with the show for fifteen years, earning both popular and critical praise for his performance. In addition, Ryan has guest starred on such series as "Naked City," "The Lieutenant," and "Eleventh Hour." He has also appeared in an impressive list of feature films, including "Tootsie," "Body Heat," "The Strangler," "The Killing Ground," and "Small Hours," while Ryan's stage credits include roles on Broadway in "Advise and Consent" and "The Complaisant Lover," and in such off-Broadway and regional productions as "Hamlet," "Richard III," "Hedda Gabler," and "Portrait of the Artist." A long time New York City resident, Ryan has three sons, Michael, Chris, and Anthony. Sadly, the actor's wife died in 1986, after twenty seven years of marriage. Not presently on a daytime drama, Ryan lists among his hobbies baseball and carpentry and is a lector and serves on the parish council.

MICHAEL SABATINO

Born: June 25, 1955 in Venice, California
Marital Status: separated
Height: 6' 1 1/2"   **Eyes:** green   **Hair:** brown
Education: University of California at Irvine, Bachelor's Degree
Interests: hiking, skiing, theater
Awards: two time winner, Western States Accordion Festival; Solo Competition; NCAA Pole Vaulting Championship - three times; Dramalogue Award, Outstanding Performance in a Comedy ("The Strange Case of the Tenacious Suitcase")

Daytime Dramas: "Days of Our Lives," Lawrence Alamain, 1990-

A world class pole vaulter turned world class villain, Michael Sabatino has spent the past decade portraying some of television's most memorable bad guys. His first evil character was Chip Roberts on "Knots Landing," and for the past two years he has established himself as daytime's premiere villain, Lawrence Alamain on "Days of Our Lives." He was originally brought in for a brief role as a rapist and murderer, but then the unexpected happened. The audiences loved him, the fan mail poured in, and Michael Sabatino signed a two year contract. The son of Carl and Cathy Sabatino, Michael was born on June 25, 1955 in Venice, California, the oldest of four children. The majority of his childhood was spent in Brentwood, California, where Michael enjoyed hiking in the woods, watching Marx Brothers movies, and making his own home movies, usually slapstick chases, with his friends. Not wanting to start his resume on a dull note, Michael's first job, at the age of eight, called on him to feed calf hearts to the neighbors owl. A dedicated Boy Scout, Sabatino excelled both musically and athletically. On the musical front he was an accomplished accordion player, twice winning the solo competition at the Western States Accordion Festival, while his athletic talents focused primarily on pole vaulting. During his years at Notre Dame High School, along with track, water polo, and cross country, Michael became a top pole vaulter, eventually earning a scholarship to the University of California at Irvine. While at this institution, he proved himself a three time NCAA pole vaulting champion, and even qualified for the Olympic trials in 1976. His first consideration of an acting career came during college, when he lived in a trailer parked near the campus' arts center. After three years of seeing productions in the works, Sabatino auditioned for a school play, landing the lead role in "6 RMS RIV VU," a production directed by Joan McGillis (Kelly McGillis' mother). Although he thoroughly enjoyed the stage experience, Michael was still devoted to pole vaulting, and after completing the semester he travelled to Europe where he competed and trained for the next Olympic tryouts. The acting bug soon became more and more persistent, however, and Sabatino ended up returning to school, where he earned a degree in drama and appeared in a plethora of school productions. Graduating in 1979, the young actor moved to Los Angeles, where after working a series of odd jobs, he landed his first professional role in "Sweet Bird of Youth," opposite Ed Harris. This was followed by another role in "The Strange Case of the Tenacious Suitcase," for which Sabatino was awarded a Dramalogue Award for Outstanding Performance in a Comedy. Attracting the attention of television producers, he quickly landed two prominent roles, first on the late night soap opera, "Behind the Scenes," and then as Chip Roberts on "Knots Landing." Sabatino's run on this show lasted from 1982 until the following year, at which point his truly evil character met his maker by falling on a pitchfork. Over the next several years, Michael guest starred on a number of shows, including "Simon and Simon," "Hotel," and "Empty Nest," each one solidifying his reputation as an actor adept at playing the villain, an ability which soon landed him the role of Lawrence on "Days of Our Lives." In 1992 he was on of the cast members selected to be featured in a "Days" primetime special, "One Stormy Night." While he has concentrated chiefly on television, Sabatino has continued to work on stage as well, working with the Theatre West, as well as serving as a Board Member for the organization. Now living in the San Fernando Valley, the decidedly unvillainess Sabatino still enjoys hiking and exploring the wilderness, regularly taking trips to such untamed locations as Kings Canyon National Park. Recently separated from Laura Bassett, the actor has been romantically linked with "Days of Our Lives" co-star Crystal Chappell.

ELIZABETH SAVAGE

Born: November 26 in Pittsburgh, Pennsylvania
Marital Status: single
Height: 5' 8" **Eyes:** green **Hair:** red
Education: California State University; Royal Academy of
Dramatic Arts
Interests: antique collecting & finishing

Daytime Dramas: "General Hospital," Linx Henshaw;
"Loving," Gwyneth Alden, 1989-1991

Elizabeth Savage, who claims to be the only natural redhead in soap operas, is clearly as boisterous and outspoken as her character on her last show, "Loving." Born in Pittsburgh and educated at California State University, Elizabeth has also studied acting at the Royal Academy of Dramatic Arts, as well as with Lee Strasberg. Since then Elizabeth has been featured on numerous prime time series, including "Dear John," "Murphy's Law," "Murder She Wrote," "Simon and Simon," "Matlock," and "Mike Hammer," as well as the television movies "Rich Men, Single Women," and "Secret Affairs." Currently Elizabeth is the host of "The Image Workshop," which is aired on the Lifetime Network. An accomplished singer as well, Elizabeth has performed on stage in "Anything Goes" with Van Johnson, "Frankie and Johnny," "Lunch Girls," and "On a Clear Day," with Robert Goulet. Her longtime boyfriend, actor/director Robert Paisley will soon be directing Elizabeth in a cabaret act called, "The Savage Truth." Her daytime drama work includes roles on both "General Hospital" and "Loving." In her spare time Elizabeth enjoys collecting and refinishing antiques.

STEPHEN SCHNETZER

Born: June 11 in Boston, Massachusetts
Marital Status: married to actress Nancy Snyder, March 18, 1981, two sons, Max and Ben
Height: 6' **Eyes:** brown **Hair:** brown
Education: University of Massachusetts, B.A.
Interests: sports, theater
Awards: 1989 Soap Opera Award for Outstanding Comic Performance Another World"); 1992 Soap Opera Award nomination, Outstanding Lead Actor

Daytime Dramas: "Days of Our Lives," Steve Olsen, 1978-1980; **"One Life to Live,"** Marcello Salta, 1980-1982; **"Another World,"** Cass Winthrop, 1982-

A strong daytime presence for close to fifteen years, Stephen Schnetzer has portrayed Cass Winthrop on "Another World," since 1982. Born on June 11 in Boston, Massachusetts, Schnetzer was raised in nearby Canton, where he attended an all boys Catholic High School. After receiving his B.A. degree in French from the University of Massachusetts, Stephen studied drama at the Julliard School in New York City, as well as training at Alvin Ailey's American Dance Center. An accomplished stage actor, Schnetzer made his Broadway debut in "A Talent for Murder," with Claudette Colbert, as well as appearing in a production of "Filumena," directed by the legendary Laurence Olivier. His additional theater credits include a national tour of "Shakespeare's People," with Sir Michael Redgrave, "Romeo and Juliet," a PBS presentation of "The Taming of the Shrew," and numerous other productions with the American Conservatory Theater in San Francisco, with whom Schnetzer spent four seasons as a company player. Since 1982, his work as Cass Winthrop on "Another World" has made the character one of daytime fan's favorite leading men. In 1986, Schnetzer left the show briefly to travel to Los Angeles and explore other acting avenues, but happily returned a short time later. In addition to "Another World," Stephen has been featured on "One Life to Live" and "Days of Our Lives," as well as making guest appearances on "Fantasy Island," "The Love Boat," and "Hawaii Five-0." Married once before, the actor has been happily married for over ten years to his second wife, actress Nancy Snyder (ex Katrina Karr, "One Life To Live"), whom he met when both were appearing on "One Life to Live." The couple now have two sons, Benjamin and Max, and divide their time between their New York City apartment and their Massachusetts country house. An avid sports fan, Stephen's favorite team is the New York Giants, but aside from football he always roots for Boston teams.

MELODY THOMAS SCOTT

Born: April 18
Marital Status: married to Edward Scott
Height: 5' 5" **Eyes:** blue **Hair:** blond
Education: University of Southern California
Interests: environmental causes

Daytime Dramas: "The Young and the Restless,"
Nikki Abbott, 1978-

Since beginning her career at the age of three, Melody Thomas Scott has found success in film, television, and on the stage. She is beloved by millions of daytime fans as Nikki Abbott on "The Young and the Restless," a character she began playing in 1978. Born on April 18, Scott, who was raised by her grandmother, began her professional career at the age of three, when she was discovered by Ethel Meglin, an acting coach who had previously guided the career of Shirley Temple. A student of voice and dance, Scott showcased these skills throughout her childhood, performing in U.S.O. shows around southern California. Moving towards television, the young actress began working in commercials, (including one for Rice Krispies, which afforded Melody the opportunity to work with renowned cereal celebrities, Snap!, Crackle!, and Pop!) and making guest appearances on such shows as "Ironside" and "My Three Sons." Quickly becoming one of Hollywood's top young actresses, Scott began working in feature films at the age of eight, making her film debut in Alfred Hitchcock's, "Marnie," in which she portrayed the title character as a child. Her other films include, "The Beguiled" and "Dirty Harry," both with Clint Eastwood. Melody read in the trade papers that the director of "The Beguiled" was looking for a "chubby little girl." So badly did she want this part, that Melody ate nonstop, rented a Civil War costume and went to her audition. She got the part. Other films include "Posse," "The Shootist" which was John Wayne's last film, "The Fury," "Studs Lonigan," and "Movieola." While establishing herself on the big screen, Scott also found time to attend USC as a music major. Prior to taking on the role of Nikki on "The Young and the Restless," she was seen in a recurring role on "The Waltons," and in the mini-series, "Secrets." Actually, the week that Melody was offered the soap role, she also received offers for three pilots. She chose the soap and has had the privilege of accidently killing her father who was trying to rape her, joining a cult, becoming a stripper, accidents, addictions and more. It's been an exciting time. Away from the set, Ms. Scott has taken advantage of her celebrity status as a means of helping the environment, and she is now the national spokesperson for the Save the Earth Foundation, an organization that funds grants for environmental research. Since 1985, Melody has been married to Edward Scott, executive producer of "The Young and the Restless," and together they are raising three children, her daughter Alexandra, his daughter Jennifer, and their daughter Elizabeth.

CHARLES SHAUGHNESSY

Born: February 9 in London, England
Marital Status: married to Susan Fallender, one daughter, Jenny
Height: 5' 11 1/2" **Eyes:** green **Hair:** brown
Education: Eton College; Cambridge University
Interests: theater
Awards: 1985 Soap Opera Award, Outstanding Male Newcomer; 1986, 1988 Soap Opera Award for Favorite Super Couple (w/Patsy Pease); 1992 Soap Opera Award nomination, Outstanding Lead Actor

Daytime Dramas: "General Hospital," Allistair, 1984;
"Days of Our Lives," Shane Donovan, 1984-1992

Since debuting as Shane Donovan on "Days of Our Lives," in 1984 Charles Shaughnessy has established himself as one of the premiere actors of daytime drama. For his work he has received three Soap Opera Digest Awards as well as consistently placing among the favorites in numerous reader polls. Born in London England, Shaughnessy was surrounded by the entertainment business throughout his childhood. His mother was a well known actress in their native Britain during the 1950's and 60's, while his father, Alfred, is best known as the principal writer and script editor on the PBS series "Upstairs Downstairs." Sharing in the families artistic endeavors is Charles' brother, David, an actor\director currently working as a producer on "The Young and the Restless." Charles' first experience on stage came at the age of seven in a fourth grade production of "The Wicked Wizard," a theatrical triumph made sweeter by the fact that young Charles had lost out the title role in the schools third grade presentation of "Peter Rabbit." Although acting was always his true ambition, Shaughnessy nonetheless excelled in academics, graduating from Eton College and enrolling as a law student at Cambridge University. While at this venerable institution, Charles joined the famous theatrical group, Footlights Revue following which he continued to work onstage at the Edinburgh Festival. It soon became clear to him that his heart belonged to acting and he left Cambridge to study at the London Central School of Speech and Drama. While there he met his future wife, Susan Fallender, an American exchange student. After completing their course of study, Shaughnessy remained in London to work in the theater, while Fallender returned to Los Angeles. Their romance survived the transatlantic gap and they were later married in Los Angeles. During his years in London, Shaughnessy appeared in a wide range of theatrical productions from "Death of a Salesmen," to "A Christmas Pantomime Show," in which he played the back of a cow. The actor then landed roles in two popular British television series, Agatha Christie's "Partners in Crime" and the BBC drama, "Jury." In 1983, he moved to Los Angeles to wed Ms. Fallender and began to cultivate his American acting career. Initially acting roles were scarce, and Shaughnessy found himself working such jobs as a salesman for an adult video company, and as a private investigator. His first break came with a role on stage in the American premiere of "The Genius," which was followed by another stage performance, opposite Alan Bates, in "A Patriot For Me." Most recently, Charles was seen in a production of "Loot." His first daytime role was a four day run as Holly Scorpio's brother on "General Hospital," and this was immediately succeeded with the part of Shane on "Days of Our Lives." Originally slated to be temporary, Shaughnessy made such an instant impression that he was soon offered a long term contract. While working on "Days of Our Lives," he has branched out into other areas of television, appearing in the t.v. film, "Day-O," with Delta Burke, and as Armand Sadowski in the mini-series "Till We Meet Again." Recently, Shaughnessy landed the starring role in an upcoming pilot, "McBride and Groom," and also stepped out of character to try his hand at stand up comedy as guest host of "An Evening at the Improv." Now living in Los Angeles, Charles and Susan, who have one daughter, Jenny Johanna, are approaching their ten year anniversary.

SLOANE SHELTON

Born: March 17, 1934 in Hahira, Georgia
Marital Status: single
Height: 5' 5"   **Eyes:** brown   **Hair:** brown
Education: Berea College; Royal Academy of Dramatic Arts
Interests: cooking, gardening, tennis, chess, fishing, poker
Awards: Emil Littler Award

Daytime Dramas: "As the World Turns," Harriet Corbman, 1985-1990

A daytime favorite, equally at home on stage and in feature films, Sloane Shelton has thus far enjoyed a richly diverse career. Born on March 17, 1934 in Hahira, Georgia, where her father worked as a salesman, Sloane attended Berea College, following which she continued her acting training at London's Royal Academy of Dramatic Arts. After graduating with honors from this prestigious institution, she returned to the United States, where she soon found work in the theater. Ms. Shelton's Broadway credits include "Orpheus Descending," "Open Admissions," "Passione," "The Shadow Box," "The Runner Stumbles," "Sticks and Bones," and "I Never Sang for My Father," while she has been seen off-Broadway and regionally in "April Snow," "Blood Relations," "Play & Other Plays," "Nightingale," "Other People's Money," "Laughing Stock," "'Night Mother," and with fellow daytime stars, Jill Larson and Linda Cook in "Dearly Departed." On the big screen, Ms. Shelton has co-starred in several critically acclaimed films, among them "Jackknife," "Lean On Me," "All That Jazz," "Running On Empty," "All the President's Men," and "Tiger Warsaw," while she has appeared on the small screen in "Keeping On," "FDR-The Last Year," "Summer Switch," "Concealed Enemies," "Murder: By Reason of Insanity," and a TNT production of "Orpheus Descending." Active behind the scenes as well, Ms. Shelton served as co-producer on the documentary "Millay at Steepletown." Daytime fans know Sloane best as Harriet Corbman on "As the World Turns," a role she played from 1985 to 1990. She additionally appeared briefly on "Another World." Now living in New York City, Sloane, who is single, has been a member of the New York State Council of the Arts Theatre Panel for three years. She additionally donates her time to St. Vincent's Hospital, the reading for the blind program sponsored by the New York Public Library, the 52nd Street Project for Children, and as a hospice volunteer. In her spare time, she enjoys cooking, gardening, tennis, fishing, poker, backgammon, and chess.

RICHARD SHOBERG

Born: March 1 in Grand Rapids, Michigan
Marital Status: married, two children
Height: 6'   **Eyes:** blue   **Hair:** brown
Education: Albion College
Interests: music, karate
Awards: nominated for 1982 Daytime Emmy, Outstanding Lead Actor; nominated for 1992 Soap Opera Award, Outstanding Supporting Actor

Daytime Dramas: "Somerset," Mitch Farmer, 1971-1972; **"Edge of Night,"** Kevin Jamison, 1972-1975; **"All My Children,"** Tom Cudahy, 1977-

A daytime veteran for over twenty years, Richard Shoberg has portrayed Tom Cudahy on "All My Children" since 1977, a role which earned him a Daytime Emmy nomination for Best Actor in 1982 and Soap Opera Award nomination in 1992. Born in Grand Rapids, Michigan, Richard grew up in the Les Cheneaux Islands in the upper peninsula of Michigan. After graduating high school, Shoberg remained in his home state and attended Albion College, where he divided his time between football and theater. In 1970, he moved to New York City to pursue a professional acting career, landing his first role as Mitch Farmer on "Somerset," which was immediately followed by another daytime character, Kevin Jamison on "Edge of Night." Shoberg has additionally been seen in the television film "The Silence," which also starred Richard Thomas. In his spare time, the actor who is happily married with two children is an accomplished singer/guitarist/songwriter, and can also be found demonstrating his karate skills on instructional videos.

KIN SHRINER

Born: December 6, 1953 in New York, New York
Marital Status: single
Height: 5' 11" **Eyes:** blue **Hair:** blond
Education: Richland College/UCLA, B.A.
Interests: water skiing, scuba diving, motorcycles
Awards: nominated for Outstanding Supporting Actor for Daytime Emmy, 1990; 1982 Soap Opera Award for Favorite Villain; 1991 Soap Opera Award, Outstanding Villain; 1992 Soap Opera Award nomination, Outstanding Comic Performance ("General Hospital")

Daytime Dramas: "General Hospital," Scott Baldwin, 1977-1979, 1981-1982; **"Texas,"** Jeb Hampton, 1980-1981; **"General Hospital,"** Scott Baldwin, 1987-

Known to millions as Scott Baldwin on "General Hospital," Kin Shriner first debuted the character in 1977. Along the way the character has undergone many changes, evident by the fact that Shriner has received Soap Opera Award nominations for both outstanding villain and outstanding comic performance. In addition, the actor was nominated for a 1990 daytime Emmy for outstanding supporting actor. Born on December 6, 1953, in New York City, Kin is the son of the late Herb Shriner, a popular comedian and t.v. personality of the 1950's and 60's. In fact, Kin and his twin brother Will, a successful comedian in his own right, were each named after performer-friends of their father. Will after Will Rogers and Kin after the far less famous Kin Hubbard. After spending his childhood in various parts of the United States, including Florida, Texas, and Los Angeles, Kin eventually graduated from a Richardson, Texas high school, following which he went on to attend Richland College. His first foray onto the stage came when he transferred to UCLA and enrolled in the drama program, and since then he has enjoyed a successful career in television and film. Along with his role on "General Hospital," Shriner has also been seen on the daytime drama, "Texas," and on such prime time shows as "Rituals," "Full House," "The Six Million Dollar Man," "Baa Baa Black Sheep," "The Waltons," and "Eight Is Enough." He has furthermore appeared in the television films, "Once an Eagle," "Little Vic," "Deadly Medicine," and "MacNamara's Band," as well as in two popular mini-series, "Rich Man, Poor Man, Book Two" and "War and Remembrance". Shriner made his feature film debut in "MacArthur," and has co-starred in "Young Doctors in Love," "Manhunter," "Nowhere to Hide," and "Angel III." A resident of Los Angeles, Shriner, who is single, lists amongst his hobbies, water skiing, scuba diving and riding his motorcycle.

KIMBERLY SIMMS

Born: July 27 in Toledo, Ohio
Marital Status: single
Height: 5' 3"   **Eyes:** green   **Hair:** blond
Education: University of California at Los Angeles, B.A.
Interests: painting, water sports, movies, working out
Awards: 1991 Soap Opera Award for Outstanding Female Newcomer

Daytime Dramas: "Guiding Light," Mindy Lewis, 1989-1992

A popular young actress, Kimberly Simms ended her three year run as Mindy Lewis on "Guiding Light" in 1992. During those three years, Simms established herself as a daytime favorite, taking home the Soap Opera Award for Outstanding Female Newcomer in 1991. Born on July 27 in Toledo, Ohio, one of five children, Simms and her siblings were raised by father, Donald, a land developer, and mother, Patricia, a creative designer. From an early age, Kimberly studied dance and gymnastics, and in addition worked as a model and performed in community theater throughout her high school years. The family moved to Melbourne, Florida when the young actress was 15, and after graduating from Eau Gallic High School, Simms moved to California, where she received her B.A. in theater arts from UCLA. Among the numerous school and regional productions in which she has performed: "Loose Ends," "Crimes of the Heart," "Spoon River Anthology," "Misalliance," "Grease," and "Bus Stop." Prior to joining the cast of "Guiding Light," Simms appeared briefly on "Capitol," as well as on the show, "Kids are People Too." She also co-starred in the feature film, "Caught." Other feature films include "Buster's First Date" and "Freedom From Fury." Now living in New York City, Simms is considering future projects, and in her spare time enjoys painting, water sports, working out, and going to the movies.

PETER SIMON

Born: September 27 in New York, New York
Marital Status: married to Courtney Sherman in 1975
Height: 5' 11"   **Eyes:** hazel   **Hair:** brown
Education: Williams College, Bachelor's Degree
Interests: theater, writing

Daytime Dramas: "Search for Tomorrow," Scott Phillips, 1969-1977; **"As the World Turns,"** Ian McFarland, 1979-1980; **"Guiding Light,"** Dr. Ed Bauer, 1981-1984, 1986-

An actor and playwright, Peter Simon has portrayed three popular daytime characters over the past twenty years. He was first seen by daytime audiences as Scott Phillips on "Search for Tomorrow," following which he took on the role of Ian McFarland on "As the World Turns." Presently, Simon is the man behind Dr. Ed Bauer on "Guiding Light," a character he has played since 1981. Born on September 27 in New York City, Peter attended Exeter Academy, after which he went on to earn a degree in French literature from Williams College. Following graduation, he got his professional start as part of a repertory theater company at Purdue University, and has since gone on to appear in numerous off-Broadway and regional productions, including a season at the Barn Theatre in Michigan and frequent work with the New York Shakespeare Festival. Among his theater credits are roles in "Romeo and Juliet," "The Homecoming," "Night Must Fall," "Kicking the Castle Down," "P.S., Your Cat is Dead," "The Happiness Cage," "The Cathedral of Chartres," and a Central Park production of "Twelfth Night." A playwright as well, Simon's "In Case of Accident" was presented off-Broadway, and some of his other works can currently be seen in regional theaters. On television, he has concentrated chiefly on daytime dramas, even bringing his "Guiding Light" character to prime time, in the television film, "The Cradle Will Fall." Along with acting and writing, Simon was also the co-owner of a popular downtown restaurant during the early seventies. Unfortunately, neither he nor his partner had the necessary restaurant business sense, and the venture went under a few years later. Since 1975, Simon has been married to actress/writer Courtney Sherman, who currently works on the writing staff of "As the World Turns," as well as playing the recurring role of Dr. Lynn Michaels on the program. In addition she also plays Dr. Anna Tolan on "All My Children." The two met when they portrayed husband and wife on "Search for Tomorrow." Between them they are raising five children, and the family lives north of New York City, where Simon happily enjoys the life of a family man.

LAURA SISK

Born: September 11 in Washington, D.C.
Marital Status: single
Eyes: blue **Hair:** blond
Education: one semester of college
Interests: movies

Daytime Dramas: "Loving," Allison Rescott, 1991-

A small town girl who works at her father's gas station goes from being a die hard soap opera fan to landing a role on one of her favorite shows. While this may sound like a movie of the week, it just so happens to be the real life story of Laura Sisk. Born in Washington D.C., Laura was raised in Clinton, Maryland, where her acting assignments were limited to some high school productions, a music video and commercial on local television, and an occasional fashion show. Although she had dreamed of being an actress, Laura never gave the option serious consideration, assuming that she would follow in her father's footsteps and own a gas station. When she was invited up to New York to audition for the role of Allison Rescott on "Loving," Ms. Sisk took along her camera and autograph book, figuring that if she wasn't going to land the part, she would at least take home some souvenirs. Well as it happens she struck a chord with the producers, and joined the cast in 1991. Now living in New York, Laura is adjusting to big city life with the help of such friends as Kelly Ripa and Joey Thrower. One of Laura's favorite hobbies is collecting dolls from her favorite movie, "The Wizard of Oz."

JEREMY SLATE

Born: February 17, 1926 in Margate, New Jersey
Marital Status: single, five children, Jef, Jamesen, Jeremy, Jason and Rebecca
Height: 6' **Eyes:** blue **Hair:** grey
Education: St. Lawrence University, B.A.
Interests: swimming, writing, theatre directing
Awards: Tiahuanaco Award for "The Rainmaker"

Daytime Dramas; "One Life to Live," Chuck Wilson, 1980-1985, 1988; **"Guiding Light,"** Locke Walls, 1985

An actor, writer, and director, Jeremy Slate has successfully divided his career between film, television, and theater. He is best known to daytime audiences as Chuck Wilson on "One Life to Live," a role he originated in 1980. Born on February 17, 1926 in Margate, New Jersey, Slate received his B.A. degree from St. Lawrence University, and began his theater career in a Lima, Peru production of "The Rainmaker." After winning the prestigious Tiahuanaco Award for this performance, Jeremy returned to the United States, where he landed his first Broadway role in "Look Homeward Angel." A prolific stage actor, his additional credits include "An Enemy of the People," "Sweet Bird of Youth," "Medea," and "The Further Inquiry," while he has directed such productions as "Glengary Glen Ross" and "1959 Pink Thunderbird." On the big screen, Slate has been seen in such feature films as "G.I. Blues" and "Girls, Girls, Girls," both with Elvis Presley. He also appeared in "The Sons of Katie Elder," and "True Grit," both with John Wayne, "The Born Losers," "I'll Take Sweden," "The Devil's Brigade," "Hell's Angels '69," (as a writer and co-star) "Goodnight, Sweet Marilyn," "Deadlock," "Steelhead," "The Dead Pit," "Maddalena Z," "Dream Machine," and most recently, "The Lawnmower Man." In addition to his role on "One Life to Live," the actor has also played recurring roles on "Guiding Light," "As the World Turns," and "In Your Backyard." He starred in his own series, "The Aquanauts/Malibu Run," while he has guest starred on such shows as "Gunsmoke," "Run for Your Life," "Alfred Hitchcock," "Perry Mason," "Bonanza," "The Virginian," "One Step Beyond," "Starman," "Naked City," "The Defenders," "Dr. Kildare," "Bat Masterson," "Man from UNCLE," "Mission Impossible," "Tales from the Darkside," "Empire," and "Bewitched," among others. Slate has additionally been seen in the made for television films "Wings of Fire," "The Cable Car Murders," "The Year of the Big Cat," "Stowaway to the Moon," "Mr. Horn," "Stranger in Our House," "A Whisper Kills," and "Trenchcoat in Paradise." Presently living in Pacific Grove, California, Jeremy, who is single, is the father of five, Jef, Jamesen, Jeremy, Jason, and Rebecca. In his spare time, he enjoys writing, going to the theater, and "swimming in warm, clear water."

ERIKA SLEZAK

Born: August 5 in Los Angeles, California
Marital Status: married to actor Brain Davies, two children, Michael and Amanda
Height: 5' 5"   **Eyes:** blue   **Hair:** blond
Education: Royal Academy of Dramatic Arts
Interests: reading, skiing, tennis, riding, cooking, needlepoint, loafing
Awards: nominated for Daytime Emmy for Outstanding Lead Actress, 1983; Daytime Emmy for Outstanding Lead Actress, 1984, 1986, 1992

Daytime Dramas: "One Life to Live," Victoria Lord Buchanan, 1971-

Since 1971, when she she first created the role of Victoria Lord on "One Life to Live," Erika Slezak has become one of the most beloved actresses in the history of daytime drama. As Viki, Erika has had the opportunity to live through every conceivable daytime calamity, from amnesia and an evil twin,(who even gave birth to a child Viki never knew existed) to brain surgery and a near death experience. Yet throughout it all, Erika has brought to the role a freshness and vitality which has only increased over the years. This was proven when she won her third Emmy as Outstanding Lead Actress, making her the most honored actress by the Emmys. Coming from a family rich in artistic history, it seems only appropriate that Erika should pursue a career in the arts. Her siblings, Ingred and Leo, however, chose not to enter the arts professionally, being a lawyer and pilot respectively. Her grandfather, Leo Slezak was a world famous tenor with the Metropolitan Opera House in New York City; while her father, Walter Slezak, was a star of stage and screen, winning a Tony award for his work in the musical, "Fanny." Her mother was singer, Johanna Van Rign. Erika was born in Los Angeles, California growing up in a bilingual household speaking both German and English. Her education ranged from convent boarding schools in Connecticut and Philadelphia, to the Royal Academy of Dramatic Arts in London, where she was admitted at the age of seventeen. From the start Erika wanted to become an actress, and began to consider this as a full time career when she was a sophomore in high school. Her father was very supportive of her decision, but made certain she understood that as a daughter of a well known actor, she would have to work twice as hard to prove her own worth. Erika took this advice to heart, and after finishing her education, she began to establish herself as a theatrical actress. During this period she was a member of the Milwaukee Repertory Company, where she performed in a widely divergent range of productions. From Milwaukee she moved to Houston where she appeared for a season at the Alley Theater. In 1971 Erika decided to look into work on daytime drama, and in March of that year she was offered her first job on tv., playing Victoria Lord on "One Life to Live," a character which she has relished playing for the last two decades. Erika has no desire to leave daytime drama for prime time or feature films, mediums she feels would take too much of her time away from her family. Presently Erika lives in in a suburb of New York with her husband, actor Brian Davies (Pine Valley DA, Dick Hamilton, "All My Children"), and their two children, Michael, born on November 23, 1980 and Amanda, born October 29, 1981. Away from the set, Erika enjoys reading, skiing, tennis, riding, cooking, needlepoint, and hard to believe, but - loafing.

TINA SLOAN

Born: February 1, 1943 in Bronxville, New York
Marital Status: married to Steve McPherson in 1975, one son, Renny
Height: 5' 6"   **Eyes:** green   **Hair:** blond
Education: Manhattanville College, B.A.
Interests: Renny's school, mountain climbing, books, movies, theatre, tennis, skiing, travel, aerobics, marathons

Daytime Dramas: "Somerset," Kate Cannell, 1974-1976; **"Search for Tomorrow,"** Patti Baron, 1976-1977; **"Another World,"** Dr. Olivia Delaney, 1980-1981; **"Guiding Light,"** Lillian Raines, 1983-

A veteran of no less than four daytime dramas, Tina Sloan has carried into her real life an adventuresome spirit which would be the envy of any globe trotting soap opera heroine. Born on February 1, 1943 and raised in Bronxville, New York, with her brother, John and sister, Margo, Tina's father, Walter, is a Harvard educated lawyer and her mother Peggy, a homemaker. Away from the set, one can find this New York native scaling such formidable peaks as Mount Kilimanjaro, or making her way through the Lamjung region of Nepal, or perhaps competing in marathons around the world, including those in New York, Los Angeles, London and Honolulu. To date, she has run in 8 marathons. With all this activity, it is no surprise that she is on the board of advisors of Outward Bound. While Tina does enjoy the challenge of these expeditions, her true love has always been acting. Her study of the craft began at Manhattanville College and continued in London at the Royal Academy of Dramatic Arts. She has also studied with acting coaches, Bob McAndrew and Warren Robertson. On stage she has appeared off-Broadway in "Blithe Spirit," "The Labor Party," "What are You Doing for Lunch Today?," and "The Song of Bernadette." Tina also created the lead role in the musical, "The Fine Art of Falling." Her feature film work includes a role in the 1989 film, "She-Devil." On the small screen, Tina has appeared on four daytime dramas, "Somerset," "Search for Tomorrow," "Another World," and "Guiding Light." She was also in the TV movie, "Too Easy to Kill." Away from the set, and when not testing her limitation, Tina lives in New York City with her husband Steve McPherson, and their son Renny, born in 1979.

HILARY BAILEY SMITH

Born: May 25, 1957 in Boston, Massachusetts
Marital Status: married to Philip Smith, two children, Courtney and "Phips"
Height: 5' 7 1/2"   **Eyes:** brown   **Hair:** brown
Education: Sarah Lawrence College, B.A.
Interests: tennis, golf

Daytime Dramas: "The Doctors," Kit McCormick, 1981; **"As the World Turns,"** Margo Montgomery,1983-1989; **"One Life to Live,"** Nora Gannon, 1992-

An accomplished theater actress, Hilary Bailey Smith has additionally starred on three popular daytime dramas, "The Doctors," "As the World Turns," and most recently on "One Life to Live." Born on May 25, 1957, in Boston, Massachusetts, Hilary was the youngest of four girls. After graduating from the Dana Hall School and Sarah Lawrence

College, Ms. Smith began her professional career, which has focused largely on stage work. Her theater credits include roles on Broadway in "The Heidi Chronicles" and "Reel American Hero," while she has appeared in numerous off-Broadway and regional productions, among them "Lips Together, Teeth Apart," "World of Black and White," "Song Night In The City," "Don Juan," "Serial," "Phantom Tollbooth," "Our Town," "Miracle Worker," and "The Boyfriend." Ms. Smith has been seen on the big screen in "Love Potion #9" and "Purple Hearts," while she has co-starred in the television film, "Sharing Richard." Along with her daytime work, Hilary has been a regular on such prime time series as "Acting Sheriff," "Family Business," and "No Soap Radio," as well as guest starring on "Baby Makes Five," "Baker's Dozen," and "Nurse." Most recently the television show based on the award winning movie, "Driving Miss Daisy." Now living in New Jersey, Hilary is married to Philip Smith, with whom she has two children, daughter, Courtney, and son, Phips.

REX SMITH

Born: September 19 in Jacksonville, Florida
Marital Status: married to Jamie Smith on February 28, 1987, two daughters, Meagan and Madison
Height: 6' **Eyes:** blue **Hair:** light brown
Interests: music
Awards: Best Actor, Theatre Award; nominated for Tony Award, both for "Pirates of Penzance;" nominated for 1992 Soap Opera Award, Outstanding Male Newcomer

Daytime Dramas: "As the World Turns," Darryl Crawford, 1990-

Only in his thirties, Rex Smith's phenomenal career has proven him to be a best selling singer, actor, and Broadway star. Born on September 19 in Jacksonville, Florida, Rex and his family frequently relocated, living in Atlanta, Chicago, Greenville, South Carolina, and Birmingham, Alabama. An illustrious family steeped in history, (Rex's great Uncle fired the first shot of the U.S. Civil War) Rex's father worked as an advertising executive for a large insurance company. He began his ascent to stardom at the age of twenty, thanks largely to his mother, whom he credits as the driving force behind his career, when he moved to New York City looking for work as a singer. His two brothers also pursued music careers, one as a concert pianist, the other as a songwriter. Another musically inclined relative is his uncle Robert Giles, a concert pianist. By the late 70's he was working steadily, often as an opening act for such hard rock bands as Aerosmith, Ted Nugent, and Lynyrd Skynrd. Smith was signed to a record contract with Columbia Records, with whom he released six albums, including the 1979 platinum smash "Sooner or Later." His biggest selling single was the love song "You Take My Breath Away," which to this day fans continually ask him to perform. While his records made him a star, it was the t.v. movie "Sooner or Later" that catapulted Rex into the ranks of superstar. This proved to be for the young actor/singer the start of a hectic period as one of America's leading teen heartthrobs. When this phase seemed to be winding down, Smith realized that he would have to move his career in another direction, and thus decided to look for work on the Broadway stage. His first job came as an understudy in the musical "Grease," which Smith eventually parlayed into a starring role. Following this he made his leap into the ranks of the Broadway elite when he landed a leading role in Joseph Papp's production of "Pirates of Penzance." For his efforts Smith was awarded the Theatre Award for Best Actor, and was nominated for a Tony award as well. Smith played opposite Kevin Kline and Linda Ronstadt. His other Broadway roles include the Tony winning "Grand Hotel" and the New York Shakespeare Festival production of "The Human Comedy." In addition Smith has appeared off-Broadway in "Brownstone," and as Tony in the Kennedy Center revival of "West Side Story," as well as in national tours of "Oklahoma," "Anything Goes," and "Carousel." While Smith has concentrated chiefly on theater, he has appeared in the films "Pirates of Penzance" and "Headin' for Broadway." On the small screen he served as host of "Solid Gold," and played the title character in the series "Streethawk," and has also guest starred on "Cagney & Lacey," "Murder, She Wrote," "Faeretale Theatre," and "Houston Knights." Along with "Sooner or Later," Smith also starred in the television motion picture "Daredevil." In October of 1990 he returned to t.v. as Darryl Crawford on "As the World Turns." Smith and his wife Jamie, a former L.A. Laker girl, met on the set of "Streethawk" and were married February 28, 1987. The couple currently live in a suburb of New York City, with their two daughters, Meagan and Madison. One of Smith's favorite hobbies is collecting 78's from the 1920's to 1940's. He is also involved in a band with co-stars Mary Ellen Stuart and Scott Holmes. In addition, the actor stretched his vocal talents recently, singing the National Anthem, along with Scott Holmes, at a Nets basketball game.

LOUISE SOREL

Born: August 6 in Hollywood, California
Marital Status: single
Eyes: brown   **Hair:** brown
Education: Neighborhood Playhouse
Interests: theater, travelling

Daytime Dramas: **"Santa Barbara,"** Augusta Lockridge, 1984-1986; 1988-1991; **"One Life to Live,"** Judith Sanders, 1986-1987; **"Days of Our Lives,"** Vivian, 1992-

An accomplished actress of television, stage, and film, Louise Sorel recently joined the cast of "Days of Our Lives." Prior to this, the actress had enjoyed a seven year run as Augusta Lockridge on "Santa Barbara." Born in Hollywood, Sorel studied acting at the Neighborhood Playhouse in New York City, making her Broadway debut at the age of twenty in "Take Her, She's Mine." During this time, she was also featured in a pilot for a proposed Woody Allen television series. Continuing to work on Broadway, Sorel has since appeared in such productions as "Lorenzo," "The Dragon," "The Sign in Sidney Brustein's Window," "Philadelphia, Here I Come," "Man and Boy," with Charles Boyer, and opposite George C. Scott and Colleen Dewherst in "A Lion in Winter." On the big screen, she has been seen in, "The Party's Over," "Plaza Suite," "Cocky," "Airplane II," "Where the Boys Are '84," and "Crimes of Passion," while Sorel has also starred on two television series, "Ladies Man" and "The Survivors." A much sought after prime time guest star, she has appeared on over eighty shows, including "Matt Houston," "Simon & Simon," "Star Trek," (a role she is still recognized for, by "Trekkies") and "Knots Landing." On daytime, she took eighteen months away from "Santa Barbara" to portray Judith Sanders on "One Life to Live." Now living in Los Angeles, Louise, who is single, enjoys travelling, and additionally donates much of her time to helping the homeless and environmental causes.

KRISTOFF ST. JOHN

Born: July 15, 1966 in New York, New York
Marital Status: separated, two children, Julian and Paris
Height: 6' 1" **Eyes:** brown **Hair:** brown
Education: Calabasas High School; Nordoff High School;
The Actors Studio
Interests: guitar, movies, television, reading
Awards: nominated for 1990 Daytime Emmy for Best
Supporting Actor for "Generations;" 1992 Daytime Emmy Award
for Outstanding Younger Actor for "The Young and the Restless"

Daytime Dramas: "Generations," Adam Marshall, 1989-1991;
"The Young and the Restless," Neil Winters, 1991-

One of the most popular and well respected actors in daytime drama, Kristoff St. John has received two Daytime Emmy nominations for his work on both "The Young and the Restless" and "Generations." In 1992, he earned the award for Outstanding Younger Actor. Born on July 15, 1966 in New York City, St. John was raised in Bridgeport, Connecticut and Los Angeles. Interested in acting from an early age, he got his initial training from his father, actor Charles St. John, best known for his work in the film "Shaft." His stepmother, Marie, was a British actress who gave up her career to raise her family. The younger St. John divided his childhood between school (he attended Calabasas High School and Nordoff High School) and a myriad of television and film roles. He also trained at the Actor's Studio in Los Angeles, The Virgil Frye Workshop, and the Tony Morina Workshop. His first big break came at the age of seven when he guest starred on the t.v. series, "That's My Mama," and subseqently went on to appear on such shows as "Happy Days," "Wonder Woman," "The Cosby Show," "A Different World," "You Again," "What's Happening Now," "Foul Play," and "Me and Mrs. C." In addition, the young actor was a regular performer on several series, including "Big John, Little John," "San Pedro Beach Bums," "The Bad News Bears," and "Charlie & Company," while he appeared in the television movies "An Innocent Love," "Sister, Sister," and "Finish Line." St. John also took on roles in the mini-series, "Roots II: The Next Generation," in which he played a young Alex Haley, "Beulah Land," and "The Atlanta Child Murders." His feature film credits include "Avatar," "Top of the Heap," and "The Champ." Recently separated from actress Mia Richardson, St. John has two children, Julian and Paris Nicole, born on April 30, 1992, the first day of the Los Angeles riots. Away from the set, the popular actor makes frequent guest appearances on behalf of the L.I.F.E. Organization and the Adam Walsh Foundation. In his spare time, St. John enjoys playing the guitar, going to movies, watching television, and reading.

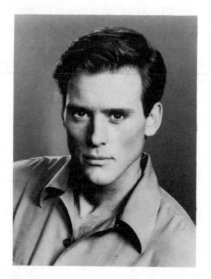

LEONARD STABB

Born: July 15 in Woodside, California
Marital Status: single
Height: 6' 2" **Eyes:** blue **Hair:** blond
Education: William Esper Studios
Interests: hang gliding, carpentry, painting

Daytime Dramas: "One Life to Live," Hunter Guthrie

Originally a model, Leonard Stabb has only recently begun to pursue an acting career, making his professional debut as Hunter Guthrie on "One Life to Live." Stabb hails from Woodside, California, where from an early age he dreamed of becoming an actor, even going so far as to perform for family and friends in his backyard. His first professional assignments came as a model, an occupation which enabled him to travel throughout the United States, Europe, Japan, and Australia. While Stabb enjoyed the excitement of this lifestyle, he still longed to become an actor, and thus decided to move to New York where he began to study acting with William Esper. It was a short time later that Stabb appeared on "One Life to Live." During his spare time Stabb is an avid hang glider, which he tries to do every weekend. He also enjoys football and basketball, as well as exercising the carpentry skills he picked up from his father. While Stabb does not have a family of his own yet, he does spend a lot of time with his Girl - a dog, he found abandoned several years back in a New York subway station.

JACK STAUFFER

Born: December 3, 1945 in New York, New York
Marital Status: married to Katy Stauffer, three children, Drew, Chris and Samantha
Height: 5' 11" **Eyes:** blue **Hair:** brown
Education: Northwestern University, B.A.
Interests: tennis, theater

Daytime Dramas: "All My Children," Chuck Tyler, 1970-1974; **"The Young and the Restless,"** Dr. Scott Adams, 1978-1979; Sherm Madsen, 1987; **"General Hospital,"** Phil Kennicott

A familiar face on daytime drama, Jack Stauffer is perhaps best known for creating the role of Dr. Chuck Tyler on "All My Children," on primetime, many know him as Bojay on the popular series "Battlestar Galactica." His daytime credits include starring roles on "All My Children," "The Young and the Restless," and "General Hospital," while he has additionally made cameo appearances on "Days of Our Lives" and "Santa Barbara." Born on December 3, 1945 in New York City, where his father worked as a television executive, his mother a radio producer, Stauffer was interested in performing from an early age. After receiving his B.A. degree from Northwestern University, he began to work on stage, television, and in feature films. Jack has starred in several t.v. pilots, including "Downtown," "Alex and the Doberman Gang," "Mobile Medics," and "Fantastic Journey," as well as guest starring on such prime series as "Perfect Strangers," "Knots Landing," "Growing Pains," "Jake and the Fatman," "The Bradys," "Dragnet," "Scarecrow and Mrs. King," "Dynasty," "The Fall Guy," "Highway to Heaven," "Hotel," "How the West Was Won," "Hawaii Five-0," "Superior Court," "Barnaby Jones," "Bionic Woman," "Family," "Streets of San Francisco," "Rockford Files," "Divorce Court," and "The Partridge Family," among others. Along with a co-starring role in the feature film "Chattanooga Choo Choo," Stauffer has appeared in such television motion pictures as "Go Towards the Light," "If Tomorrow Comes," "Intimate Strangers," "Police Story," "Sgt. Matlovitch vs. The Air Force," "Eleanor and Franklin,: and in the ABC Playbreak "I Never Said Good Bye." On stage, the actor starred in "The Hazing of Mr. Barrow," and also co-founded the APTA Theater in North Hollywood, which recently staged such productions as "Play it Again, Sam," "Mr. Roberts," and "Chapter Two." Throughout his career, Stauffer has additionally appeared in over 250 commercials. Now living in Sherman Oaks, California, with his wife Katy, and three children, Drew, Chris, and Samantha, Jack enjoys playing tennis, a sport he has also taught for over fifteen years.

PERRY STEPHENS

Born: February 14 in Frankfurt, Germany
Marital Status: engaged to former Miss Alabama,
Jenny Jackson
Height: 6' 2" **Eyes:** blue **Hair:** brown
Education: Samford University
Interests: music, weight lifting, bicycling

Daytime Dramas: "Loving," Jack Forbes, 1984-1990

While Perry Stephens may claim that singing is his first love, he has nonetheless enjoyed great success as an actor on "Loving" for six years. Born in Frankfurt, Germany, Stephens was raised in Decatur, Alabama. From an early age he was passionate about singing, performing with the church choir, and later serving as the student director of his high school choir. In his senior year, Stephens played Curly, the lead male in "Oklahoma," and from the moment he heard the applause he knew he had found his calling. He continued his voice training at Samford University, in Birmingham, where he sang everything from opera to musical theater, spending his summer applying this knowledge at Opryland in Nashville, Tennessee. It was there that he appeared in the Dick Clark special "Night of the Stars and Future Stars," where he appeared with such luminaries as Ben Vereen and Gene Kelly. When the opportunity to play the lead role in the national touring company of "Li'l Abner" presented itself, Stephens left school to join the cast. The ill-fated tour got as far as the Northwest before going bankrupt, but despite this auspicious start, Stephens decided that it was time for him to move to New York to further pursue his acting career. He arrived in the city with no money and a lot of hope, but Stephens' talent and persistence eventually landed him the role of Jack Forbes on "Loving." Stephens' has not, however, turned his back on his singing career. He has sung with the Nitty Gritty Dirt Band at the Blue Grass Country Music Festival, and has performed on the cabaret stage, where he presents a wide variety of musical styles. His other stage work includes a stint in "Dr. Bartolo," a musical recital at Carnegie Hall, and a starring role in the Pittsburgh Civic Light Opera Company production of "Annie Get Your Gun." In his spare time Stephens enjoys weight lifting, racquetball, and bicycling. He still finds time for his music, frequently performing his cabaret act with Bill Timoney (ex Alfred Vanderpool, All My Children) in New York City clubs and as far away as Geneva, Switzerland.

JIM STORM

Born: October 12 in Highland Park, Illinois
Marital Status: married to Jackie Storm, three children
Hair: brown
Interests: music, travel, theater

Daytime Dramas: "One Life to Live," Larry Wolek, 1968-1969;
"Dark Shadows," Gerard Stiles; **"Secret Storm,"** Sean
Childers, 1971; **"The Doctors,"** Mike Powers, 1979-1981;
"The Young and the Restless," Neil Fenmore, 1983-1986;
"The Bold and the Beautiful," Bill Spencer, 1987-

A soap opera veteran, Jim Storm's first daytime character was Larry Wolek on "One Life to Live," a role he originated in 1968. However, a year later, the character suffered a car accident when Jim decided to leave the show, and when the bandages were removed, the actor behind Larry Wolek was none other than Jim's brother, Michael Storm (the 1st time a different actor took over a role). Jim, however, went on to appear in several other daytime dramas, and since 1987 he has been seen as Bill Spencer on "The Bold and the Beautiful." Born in Highland Park, Illinois, Jim was raised in California and England. Always interested in acting, Storm got off to an early start when he formed his own theater company in San Diego at the age of eighteen, following which he performed in "Henry VIII" at the San Diego Shakespeare Festival. After a brief stint with a Milwaukee repertory theater company, the actor relocated to New York, where he was accepted into the prestigious APA Repertory Theater. With this company he performed, opposite Christopher Walken and Brian Bedford, in "Arms and the Man." Some of Storm's additional theater credits include a national tour of "The Lion in Winter" and a recent Los Angeles production of "Secret of Body Language." On the big screen he has been seen in "The Trial of Billy Jack" and "House of Dark Shadows," while he has also appeared in the t.v. film "Blacke's Magic," with Hal Linden. Daytime fans have come to know Jim in several roles, as Gerard Stiles on "Dark Shadows, "Mike Powers on "The Doctors," Sean Childers on "Secret Storm," and as Neil Fenmore on "The Young and the Restless." Among his many prime time appearances are guest starring roles on "Hotel," "Hardcastle and McCormick," "St. Elsewhere," "Automan," "The Rockford Files," and in the premiere episode of "Kung Fu." Throughout his career, Storm has frequently used his time away from television work to travel around the world. In his spare time the actor is an accomplished guitar player, and recently released an album of country western songs entitled "Dust Bowl." Storm also used a recent hiatus to publish his own newspaper, "The Garment Trader." Storm and his wife, Jackie, have three children.

MICHAEL STORM

Born: August 9 in Chicago, Illinois
Marital Status: married to Sally Storm, two children, Maggie and Jason
Height: 6' 1" **Eyes:** hazel **Hair:** blond
Education: Bachelor's Degree in Art
Interests: fencing, orchids, golf, fishing
Awards: nominated 1978 Emmy for Best Actor

Daytime Dramas: "One Life to Live," Dr. Larry Wolek, 1969-

Born in Chicago, Michael Storm has portrayed Dr. Larry Wolek on "One Life to Live," since 1969; making him the shows longest performer. Aside from the two years he lived in England, Storm spent most of his youth in La Jolla, California. He received his B.A. in fine arts painting before making his professional debut as a singer on "The Andy William's Show." An accomplished musician and singer, as well as actor, Storm has appeared in such stage productions as "Summer and Smoke," "Serenading St. Louis," and "Just the Immediate Family." He took over the role of Larry Wolek from his brother, James, in 1969, and has played the part ever since, receiving a daytime Emmy nomination for Best Actor in 1978. The change in actors was explained in what is today a common soap opera ploy - a terrible accident and a lot of plastic surgery. The first time this ploy was used was in the case of Jim and Michael Storm. It remains the only time a role was taken over by a brother. Storm lives in Westchester County with his wife Sally and their two children, Maggie and Jason. Away from work, Storm serves as the Daytime Celebrity Chairman of the National

Foundation for Ileitis and Colitis, as well as being active with the Special Olympics. To relax Storm enjoys tennis, golf, fishing, and fencing, and growing orchids. In his greenhouse, Storm has raised over two hundred kinds of orchid plants, including an award winning pale pink miltoniopsis, and currently serves on the Board of Trustees of the Greater New York Orchid Society.

COUNT STOVALL

Born: January 15 in Los Angeles, California
Marital Status: single, one son, Count-Paul
Height: 5'10" **Eyes:** brown **Hair:** brown
Education: Merritt College; University of California at Berkeley; Defense Language Institute; American Conservatory Theater
Interests: poetry, tennis
Awards: Audelco Recognition Award for Best Actor for "Shade of Brown;" Recognition Award from the National Urban League; two time winner of Lee Elder Invitational Tennis Tournament

Daytime Dramas: "The Doctors," Hank Chambers;
"As the World Turns," Roy Franklin, 1985-1989;
"All My Children," Cal Cummings, 1989-1991

An actor, poet, and public speaker, Count Stovall has brought to daytime drama some of the most memorable characters of recent years. Most recently he portrayed Cal Cummings on "All My Children," and prior to that was seen on "As the World Turns," "The Doctors," "Generations," and "Love of Life." Born on January 15 in Los Angeles, California, Stovall, who's first name is taken from his grandfather's last name, was raised in Oakland. After graduating from Salesian High School in 1964, he went on to study at Merritt College and the University of California at Berkeley, as well as earning a degree in Hungarian from the Defense Language Institute. Along with this, Stovall also spent three years in the Army, following which he continued to hone his acting skills at the American Conservatory Theater in San Francisco. Since then he has appeared on Broadway in the Pulitzer Prize winning drama, "No Place to Be Somebody," "The Philadelphia Story," "Inacent Black," while his off-Broadway credits include "Rashomon," "Split Second," and "Shades of Brown," for which Stovall earned the Audelco Recognition Award for Best Actor. Along with daytime, he has also appeared on such television programs as "Zora Is My Name," "Gimme a Break," (in the recurring role of Nell Carters ex husband) "Melba," "Kojak," the television movie, "A Doctor's Story," and the PBS series, "Booker T. Washington: The Educator." He was also in the Robert Townsend movie, "The Five Heartbeats." A published poet and playwright, Stovall is also a much sought after guest speaker. Originally he had intended on lecturing on nutrition and health, (Stovall used to be an overweight smoker) but soon this developed into a seminar on the importance of self image, black unity, and the hazards of drug abuse. Touring the country, Stovall has travelled as much as ten thousand miles in one year, and has also worked extensively at many federal prisons. He established a prison arts program at Vacaville Medical Facility, and has also helped inmates at San Quentin, Cook County Jail, and the Federal Correctional Center of New York. For all his efforts, Stovall was honored with a Recognition Award from the National Urban League for his work with young people and his lifetime of artistic achievements. Today, Count, who has one teenage son, Count-Paul, lives in New Jersey. In his spare time he enjoys playing tennis, and has twice won the Lee Elder Invitational Tennis Tournament.

SHERRY STRINGFIELD

Born: June 24 in Colorado Springs, Colorado
Marital Status: single
Height: 5' 7" **Eyes:** green **Hair:** auburn
Education: State University of New York at Purchase, B.F.A.
Interests: sports, theater, skiing, jogging
Awards: 1991 Soap Opera Award nomination for Outstanding Villainess

Daytime Dramas: "Guiding Light," Blake Lindsay, 1989-1992

Bypassing the whole struggling actor thing, Sherry Stringfield's first professional audition resulted in her first professional job, the role of Blake Lindsay on "Guiding Light." Born on June 24th in Colorado Springs, Colorado, Sherry was raised, along with her two brothers, in Spring, Texas. Always interested in theater, she first appeared on stage in a high school production of "Blood Wedding," and upon graduation was accepted into the Acting Conservatory at the State University of New York at Purchase. During her college years Ms. Stringfield continued to explore stage roles, starring in such productions as "Hurly Burly," "Hot L Baltimore," "Devil's Discipline," and "Goose & Tom Tom." She landed the role of Blake Lindsay in 1989, just two months after graduation. In 1992, she decided to leave daytime in search of other acting challenges. Sherry, who is single, lives in New York City, and lists amongst her hobbies skiing, jogging, and hiking.

MARY ELLEN STUART

Born: October 4 in Little Rock, Arkansas
Marital Status: married to actor Mark Lewis
Height: 5' 7" **Eyes:** green **Hair:** blond
Education: Oklahoma City University
Interests: ice skating, acrobatics
Awards: Miss Little Rock; First Runner up, Miss Arkansas

Daytime Dramas: "Guiding Light," Jenny Holmes;
"As the World Turns," Frannie Hughes, 1989-

Born in Little Rock, Arkansas, Mary Ellen Stuart came upon her love of performing while she was still in high school. Her mother, who works as a nurse, offered her daughter ten dollars to audition for the school play, and Mary Ellen, obviously a little low on funds, agreed. Well as fate would have it the experience turned out to be a crossroads, and Ms. Stuart decided then, that her future was in performing. Born on October 4, the fourth of five children, Ms. Stuart, whose father is a post office employee, joined a small Arkansas theater group at the age of seventeen, and travelled to New York and Los Angeles. After her visit to L.A. Ms. Stuart decided that she would stay and pursue her acting career full time, but her parents convinced her to wait a few years before making that move. She returned to Arkansas and enrolled as a musical theater major at Oklahoma City University. During her time in college, Ms. Stuart was crowned Miss Little Rock and was first runner up the following year in the Miss Arkansas pageant. Her next move was to New York City, where Ms. Stuart continued to study acting while working as an understudy and featured dancer in many Broadway shows. Among her theater credits are roles in "Jerome Robbins' Broadway," "Song and Dance," and "Alone Together," as well as in regional productions of "Big Time" and "Papa Bear, Mama Bear." On the big screen Ms. Stuart has been seen as a principal dancer in the film "A Chorus Line." In addition to roles on "As the World Turns" and "Guiding Light," she also appeared as Holly Hathaway on "Greatest American Heroine." During her spare time, Ms. Stuart, who is married to actor Mark Lewis (ex-Kurt Corday, "Guiding Light"), whom she met on the set of "Guiding Light," enjoys ice skating, horseback riding, and acrobatics. She can also be seen singing in the New York clubs with fellow co stars, Rex Smith and Scott Holmes.

PATRICK STUART

Born: June 16 in Encino, California
Marital Status: single
Height: 6' **Eyes:** hazel **Hair:** brown
Education: San Francisco State College, two years; Stella Adler Training
Interests: music, sky diving, tennis
Awards: nominated for 1992 Daytime Emmy for Outstanding Younger Actor

Daytime Dramas: "All My Children," Will Cortlandt, 1990-1992

Confident and charismatic, Patrick Stuart has quickly established himself as one of daytime's leading villains and brightest stars. How quickly? Well, after being on "All My Children" a mere seven months Stuart, along with then co-star Michael Knight, attended the annual White House Christmas party at the request of First Lady, Barbara Bush, a devoted fan. No stranger to the world of celebrities, Patrick is the son of Chad Stuart, one half of the popular sixties rock group Chad and Jeremy. (A Summer Song, Yesterday's Gone) Born and raised in Encino, California, the eldest of six children, (one full sibling, two half siblings & four step) Patrick grew up immersed in a show business lifestyle, with family friends running the gamut from Roger Daltrey to George Hamilton. The environment around the Stuart house was creative and free thinking, and this contributed immeasurably to Patrick's artistic sensibilities. His parents divorced after 13 years of marriage, and both have happily re-married. Stuart's mother, Jill, currently lives in San Diego, while his father is living in Idaho. The elder Stuart spent several years writing commercial jingles, and is now at work on a musical. Long before joining the good people of Pine Valley, Patrick spent much of his childhood working as a model and in commercials. At the age of twelve he was cast as Dr. Zee on the series "Galactica 80," with Lorne Green. Once this series had run it's course, Stuart concentrated on life at Laguna Beach High School, and upon graduation he moved to London with his father. The trip proved to be a great learning experience, and after performing at the Westminster Theatre, Patrick returned to the United States and enrolled in San Francisco State College. He stayed there for two years but the acting bug never left him, and so he relocated to Los Angeles, where he began studying with Stella Adler. It seemed that nothing was going to keep Patrick from the role of Will - not even the earthquake that shook California (and the casting director) during his audition. Among his other recent work was a role in the mega-blockbuster "Pretty Woman." (Most of Patrick was edited out) Although he has achieved great acting success, Stuart also seriously considered a career in music. Inspired by another daytime star, Rick Springfield, he plays the guitar, the drums, and keyboards. Playing with professional musicians made him realize that he did not have the necessary devotion to music to be a truly great artist and since then music has taken a backseat to acting. However Patrick continues to write songs and perform with a band. Since joining the cast of "All My Children," the young actor, who enjoys sky diving, scuba diving, and tennis, has become good friends with many of his co-stars. Stuart presently lives in Manhattan's upper west side. His character was murdered in 1992, but judging from his outstanding performance as the ambitious turned evil man, audiences will be seeing a lot more of Patrick Stuart in the future.

MICHAEL SWAN

Born: June 11 in San Jose, California
Marital Status: divorced, two children
Education: Foothill College
Interests: poetry, music, writing, gambling, traveling

Daytime Dramas: "As the World Turns," Duncan McKechnie, 1986-

An accomplished actor of stage and screen, Michael Swan is also a singer, composer and writer. Born in San Jose, California, Swan grew up in Palo Alto and San Francisco. His father works as a printer in Hawaii, while his mother resides in Los Angeles where she is an actress, as well as a professional development consultant. Before deciding on a career in acting, Swan considered life as a winemaker, after learning the business from his cousin Joseph, owner of the Joseph Swan Vineyards in Sonoma County, California. Michael decided to stick with acting, enrolling in Foothill College to study theater. While still in college he worked with an improvisational group known as "The Illegitimate Theatre," which lead to more regional theater and a role in the 1970 film, "The Strawberry Statement." In addition to his work on the stage, Swan has also served as a member of the board at two theater companies, The Marriott Theatre Foundation and The Will Geer Theatricum Botanicum, where he has starred in five Shakespeare productions. On television, along with his work on "As the World Turns," Swan has appeared in over 130 prime time series. Among them recurring roles in "Bronk" and "Medical Center," as well as guest spots on the last regular episode of "M*A*S*H*," "Murder, She Wrote," "Magnum P.I.," "The Rockford Files," and the original pilot of "Falcon Crest." In his spare time Swan keeps busy working out, writing short stories and poems, and performing his own cabaret act twice a year in New York City.

WILLIAM SWAN

Born: February 6, 1932 in Buffalo, New York
Marital Status: single
Height: 6' 1"   **Eyes:** blue   **Hair:** salt/pepper
Education: Amherst Central High School; Geller Theatre Workshop
Interests: tennis

Daytime Dramas: "As the World Turns," Rex Witmore; **"The Young and the Restless,"** Dr. Ralph Jennings; **"All My Children,"** Walter Hines, 1982-

A true Hollywood veteran, William Swan has been a popular performer for over a quarter of a century. During his distinguished career he has appeared on over 200 prime time series, and in more than 100 stage productions. Born in Buffalo, New York, on February 6, Swan's family included his father Earl, a businessman, his mother, Irene, a housewife, and his sister, Barbara. Before embarking on his career, Swan attended Amherst Central High School, as well as honing his acting skills at the Geller Theatre Workshop, in Los Angeles. Known to daytime audiences for his role as Walter Hines on "All My Children," which he has played recurringly for over eleven years, Swan also appeared on "As the World Turns" and "The Young and the Restless." As stated earlier, Swan is one of the most sought after actors for prime time guest appearances, and among his hundred's of credits are roles on PBS's, "Stained Glass," "Quincy," "Streets of San Francisco," "Matinee Theatre," "Studio One," "Kraft Theatre," "Rockford Files," "Barnaby Jones," "Cannon," "Have Gun, Will Travel," "Father Knows Best," "Mike Hammer," and "12 O'Clock High." In addition, Swan appeared on the big screen in "Lady In A Cage," with Olivia de Havilland and James Caan, "The Parallax View," with Warren Beatty, "Hotel," "Bombers B-52," and "The Horizontal Lieutenant." While it would seem that he has no time for other work, Swan is primarily known as a stage actor. His list of credits include roles off-Broadway in "Night Fishing In Beverly Hills" and "Anne Of A Thousand Days," and leading roles in such regional productions as "Stained Glass," "The Price," "A Delicate Balance," "What The Butler Saw," "Teahouse Of The August Moon," "California Suite," "Dial M For Murder," "Blithe Spirit," "Pygmalion," "Macbeth," and "The Matchmaker." A member of the Player's Club, Swan lives both in New York and Massachusets, where he plays tennis and serves on the Board of Trustees of the Berkshire Theatre Festival.

ANNE SWARD

Born: December 9, 1949 in Bronxville, New York
Marital Status: married to Robert Hansen, one daughter, Cori Anne
Education: Emerson College, B.S. in Theatre Arts; University of Miami, M.A., Theatre Arts
Interests: singing, going to pow wows, hiking on her land in Vermont
Awards: Irene Ryan Award for college acting skills

Daytime Dramas: "As the World Turns," Lyla Perretti, 1980-

An actress, singer, and songwriter, Anne Sward's role on "As the World Turns" has afforded her the opportunity to display all of these gifts. Born in Bronxville, New York, the youngest of four children, Anne's family consisted of her father, a chemical engineer for Union Carbide, her mother, who Anne describes as a "Creative Housewife," and three older brothers. The youngest Sward graduated from Boston's Emerson College with a B.S. degree in theater arts, following which she went on to receive her masters from the University of Miami. Anne continued her acting studies in New York City with Herbert Berghof, before becoming a teacher herself, instructing students at the University of Miami, Cypress Community College, and the Robert Collier Acting School. A popular stage actress, Ms. Sward has appeared in "The Lark," "Jacques Brel Is Alive and Well and Living in Paris," "The Cherry Orchard," "School for Scandal," "The Gingerbread Lady," "Of Mice and Men," "The Seagull," and "Oliver." For her college acting, she was awarded the prestigious Irene Ryan Award, (an award presented to a senior i college for outstanding acting) presented at the Kennedy Center in Washington D.C. On television, Anne has co-starred on several prime time series, movies of the week, and PBS productions, but is best known as Lyla on "As the World Turns," a role she has played for over twelve years. Sward was originally slated to play the role of Maggie, Lyla's sister, but when the actress showed up for work she found she had been recast as Lyla. When the storyline called for a singer, Sward answered the call and has since performed on the show many times. Flexing her skills as a songwriter as well, she wrote Lyla and Cal's theme song, "Till I Found You," which she debuted September 1991. Always interested in music, Anne first sang in church, and was introduced to the guitar by high school friend Steven Tellericho, now better known as Steven Tyler of Aerosmith. During her college years, Sward also sang both folk and jazz, and currently performs in her own nightclub act. Away from the set, Anne is devoted to the cause of Native Americans, and is the founding chairman of the American Indian College Fund. She has travelled extensively to reservations throughout the United States, and lists going to pow wows as one of her favorite hobbies. In the hopes of educating daytime fans, Anne recently proposed to the "As the World Turns" writers a storyline centering on the protection of land belonging to Native Americans. Sward currently lives in Greenwich, Connecticut with her husband, Robert Hansen, and their child, Cori Anne, who can also be seen reprising this role as Lyla's daughter, Katie, on "As the World Turns." In her spare time the actress likes to travel to Vermont, where she hikes on her fifty acres of land.

BRIAN TARANTINA

Born: March 27 in New York, New York
Marital Status: single
Height: 5' 10" **Eyes:** hazel **Hair:** brown
Education: High School of Performing Arts; Stella Adler Training
Interests: theater, baseball, pool

Daytime Dramas: "One Life to Live," Lucky Lippman

Born and raised in New York City, Brian Tarantina made his daytime debut on "One Life to Live," playing the offbeat Lucky Lippman. Always certain that acting was his calling, Tarantina attended the High School of Performing Arts in New York City, following which he continued his study of acting with such renowned acting coaches as Stella Adler and Clyde Vinson. Tarantina has since become a member of the Circle Repertory Acting Company, and has appeared onstage in such Circle Rep productions as "Third Street," Innocent Thoughts and Harmless Intentions," "Out Post" and "Balm in Gilead." Brian's Broadway credits include "Biloxi Blues," "The Boys of Winter" and "Angels Fall." On the big screen, Tarantina has worked with some of the world's premiere directors, appearing in Oliver Stone's "Born on the

Fourth of July," Adrian Lyne's "Jacob's Ladder," and two upcoming Woody Allen projects. In addition, Tarantina has co-starred in "Uncle Buck," "Critical Condition," and "The January Man." Along with his work on "One Life to Live," Tarantina has made guest appearances on "Miami Vice" and "The Equalizer." Currently residing in Manhattan, Tarantina is an avid theater goer, and also enjoys baseball, shooting pool and, like most New York City residents, having takeout food delivered to his home.

BILL TATUM

Born: May 5, 1947 in Philadelphia, Pennsylvania
Marital Status: married to Karen Ziemba, one son, Will
Height: 5' 11" **Eyes:** blue   **Hair:** light brown
Education: Catawba College
Interests: golf, theater
Awards: Best Actor Award at Catawba College

Daytime Dramas: "One Life to Live," Warren Baker;
"Edge of Night," Dave Grace; **"As the World Turns,"**
Arthur Claiborne, 1991-

Primarily a theater actor, Bill Tatum has appeared briefly on "One Life to Live," as Warren Baker, "Edge of Night," as Dave Grace, and most recently as Arthur Claiborne on "As the World Turns." Born on May 5, 1947 in Philadelphia, where his father was a food broker, Bill describes his younger self as a "bad ball player but a great boy scout." After attending North Carolina's Catawba College, where he earned best actor awards for his stage performances, Tatum moved to New York City to begin his professional career. Along the way he has appeared in commercials, and in off-Broadway and regional productions, including such shows as "Promises, Promises," "Seesaw," and "And the World Goes Round." Bill relishes the diversity of his career, stating that "it's always something new and different." Still a New York City resident, Tatum is married to actress Karen Ziemba, whom he met while both were appearing in "Seesaw." The couple have one son, Will, presently a college student. In his spare time, Bill is a little league coach, and serves on the board of directors of his co-op. He also tells us that, "I do as much theatre work as I can afford to do, whatever, wherever, otherwise I play golf."

LAUREN-MARIE TAYLOR

Born: November 1 in Bronx, New York
Marital Status: married to John Didrichsen on April 23, 1983, three children, Katherine Elizabeth, Wesley John and Olivia Anne
Height: 5' 6" **Eyes:** hazel   **Hair:** brown
Education: New York University; Circle in the Square Theatre School
Interests: running, skiing, tennis, mountain climbing
Awards: Best Female Runner (in her age group) at Prospect Park Track Club; finished #1 in Media Challenge Race

Daytime Dramas: "Loving," Stacey Donovan, 1983-

Since the 1983 debut of "Loving," Lauren-Marie Taylor has taken the role of Stacey Donovan and made it uniquely her own, and in the process, created one of the most enduring characters in daytime drama. The actress behind the character was born in the south Bronx and educated at Loyola School in Manhattan, during which time she managed to make several appearances in television commercials. From there Lauren-Marie attended Wagner College, as well as studying at New York University and the Circle in the Square Theatre School. After completing her education, Lauren-Marie found work in several productions, including a featured role in the film "Neighbors," starring the late John Belushi. She also did a pilot film for WCVB-TV in Boston, and performed in the New York and Chicago productions of "Album," before landing the role of Stacey on "Loving." These days if she not on the set of "Loving," it is a safe bet that Lauren-Marie is out pursuing her other great passion: running. An accomplished long distance runner, she covers at least fifty miles each week, as well as competing in such long distance races as the Corporate and Media Challenge series, held each year in New York City. Representing Capital Cities/ABC, Lauren-Marie has consistently placed among the top women in the Corporate Challenge event, while often finishing number one in the Media Challenge race. Along with these accolades Lauren-Marie was also named Best Female Runner in her age group at the Prospect Park Track Club in Brooklyn. Currently Lauren-Marie lives in the suburbs of New York City with her husband, songwriter John Didrichsen, and their three children, Katherine Elizabeth, Wesley John and Olivia Anne. All of Lauren-Marie's pregnancies have been incorporated into the Loving scripts. Together, they share their English-style stone house with their dauschand, Max. In her spare time Lauren-Marie enjoys mountain climbing, tennis, running, and skiing.

RICK TELLES

Born: November 10 in Hayward, California
Marital Status: single
Height: 5' 11 1/2"   **Eyes:** brown   **Hair:** black
Education: UCLA, Bachelor's Degree; London Academy of Music and Dramatic Arts
Interests: baseball, basketball

Daytime Dramas: "Loving," Rio Domecq

Born and raised in Hayward, California, Rick Telles' first exposure to the world of professional actors came when he worked as an extra on "General Hospital." The impact was profound, and he immediately decided that he would pursue an acting career. Telles, who received his degree in economics from UCLA, spent his summers working with repertory theater companies, and upon graduation enrolled in the London Academy of Music and Dramatic Arts. Since then Telles career has been advancing steadily, with guest appearances on such shows as "Knots Landing," Arthur Hailey's Hotel," "Divorce Court," and "Jake and the Fatman," as well as roles in the feature films "Fatal Beauty," and "Colors." Prior to landing the role of Rio Domecq on "Loving," Telles put his economic degree to work, managing an Italian restaurant in Los Angeles, as well as working as a substitute teacher in East L.A. He continues to support educational causes. To keep in shape, Telles goes to the gym every day, and plays baseball and basketball on the weekends.

CHRISTOPHER TEMPLETON

Born: February 26, 1952 in Chicago, Illinois
Marital Status: single
Height: 5' 4"   **Eyes:** brown   **Hair:** reddish-brown
Education: Texas Christian University, one year
Interests: rodeo, needlepoint
Awards: 1991 Outstanding Contribution Award, California
Governor's Committee; 1990 Public Awareness Award, The Dole
Foundation; 1989 A Project with Industry Award; 1986 Public
Service Achievement Award, National Legislation Council for
Handicapped; 1984 Individual Achievement Award, California
Governor's Committee

Daytime Dramas: "The Young and the Restless," Carol
Robbins Evans, 1982-

Approaching her ten year anniversary as Carol Robbins Evans on "The Young and the Restless," Christopher Templeton has established herself as one of daytime's top performers. Born on February 26, 1952, one of five children, Christopher was named for the lead character, Christopher Robbins, from "Winnie the Pooh." After attending New Trier East High School, she went on to major in art at Texas Christian University, and although she was involved in theater all along, she never gave acting serious career consideration. This changed when Templeton visited Los Angeles in her early twenties. Although she had been working at the Plaza B Modelling and Talent Agency in Phoenix, her trip to L.A. convinced her that acting was her true ambition, and once this realization occurred, she relocated to California immediately. Her first big break came with a guest starring role on "Kojak," and since then she has appeared on dozens of other series, among them "In The Heat Of The Night," "Knots Landing," "Duet," "Jake And The Fatman," "Charles in Charge," "9 to 5," "Brothers," "T.J. Hooker," "The Fall Guy," and recurring roles on "Hill Street Blues," "Trapper John M.D.," and "Ryan's Four." In addition, Ms. Templeton has been seen in the feature films "Why Me?" and "Night Kill." A writer as well as an actress, she has scripted an episode of "Simon and Simon," and is presently at work with a partner on a television movie. A long time advocate for the fair treatment of the disabled, Christopher, who's childhood bout with polio left one of her leg's paralyzed, is recognized as a leader in promoting the rights of the disabled. Over the years, the actress has received tremendous recognition for her crusade, including the 1984 "Individual Achievement Award," the 1986 "Exceptional Merit Award," bestowed by the Governors Committee for Employment of the Handicapped, "The Public Service Achievement Award," from the National Council of the Handicapped, and in 1987 the "Award of Excellence," from the Media Access Office. The most recent honors given Ms. Templeton were the 1990 Dole Foundation "Media Award," in recognition of her contribution to the understanding of the disabled in the media, and the 1991 Outstanding Contribution Award, given by the California Governor's Committee. For the past five years, Christopher has been the vice-president of The Media Access Office, as well as serving on the board, and as a special public relations advisor, for the President's Committee of Employment for Persons with Disabilities. The tireless Templeton is additionally the National Spokesperson for two organizations, Rotary International's Polio Plus Program and Fulfillment, an organization which brings together high school students with successful disabled adults. Recognizing that there is still a long way to go in her quest, Christopher also recently participated in a demonstration in Washington D.C., hoping to encourage Congress to the pass "The Americans With Disabilities Act." Since being on "The Young and the Restless," the actress has also found the time to start, along with her brother Bill, a mail-order t-shirt business, known as "The T's," which deals in "The Young and the Restless" and "The Bold and the Beautiful" products. Away from her hectic life, Christopher enjoys rodeo events and needlepoint.

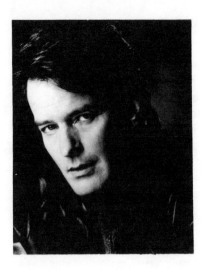

GORDON THOMSON

Born: March 2 in Ottawa, Canada
Marital Status: divorced
Hair: brown
Education: McGill University
Interests: reading, travelling
Awards: 1987 Golden Globe Award for Dynasty

Daytime Dramas: "Ryan's Hope," Aristotle Benedict-White, 1981-1982; "Santa Barbara," Mason Capwell, 1991-

While most actors discover their love of performing in a grade school play, Gordon Thomson never even considered becoming an actor until he was eighteen years old. Born in Ottawa, Canada, and raised in Montreal, Thomson describes himself as a shy and well mannered child. A voracious reader, his exposure to t.v. and movies was limited, and it was not until he enrolled at McGill University that the notion of an acting career occurred to him. However, a short year later found Thomson making his professional debut on a Canadian television show called "Let Man Live." Following this he intensified his acting studies when he apprenticed at Ontario's Stratford Shakespeare Festival. After graduating with honors from McGill, Thomson embarked on a successful run of stage roles, appearing in such productions as "A Month in the Country," "The Imaginary Invalid," "Love's Labour Lost," "A Dolls House," "The Fantasticks," and "Godspell," a Stratford production which also starred such notable talents as Martin Short, Gilda Radner, and Eugene Levy. More recently Thomson has appeared on stage in Los Angeles in "Dick Whitingham" and "Eastern Standard." In 1982 Gordon moved to Los Angeles, and was soon accepted into the ABC T.V. Talent Development Program. It was through this that he received his most well known role to date, Adam Carrington on "Dynasty." He stayed with the show for seven years, earning a Golden Globe nomination for his work in 1987. After "Dynasty" went off the air, Thomson would occasionally revive the character of Adam for guest appearances on "The Colbys." He recently sued the producers of "Dynasty" for breach of contract when he was unable to participate in "Dynasty: The Reunion." Thomson claims that negligent communication by the Dynasty producers made it impossible for him to be released from "Santa Barbara" for the filming. The case is still pending. He has also been seen on the Canadian series "Street Legal," and as the North American celebrity correspondent for the British morning program "Good Morning London." In addition, Thomson has guest starred on "Ray Bradbury Theater" and on two episodes of "Murder, She Wrote." These episodes, which were filmed in Rome, gave the actor the opportunity to combine two of his favorite things, travel and work. For his daytime debut, Thomson faced the considerable task of playing Mason Capwell on "Santa Barbara;" no small feat considering the talented actors who preceded him in the role. Yet Gordon has managed to take the character and make it his own, bringing to Mason much of the dark charisma which made Adam Carrington so compelling. When not working, Thomson devotes much of his time to AIDS related charities and has participated in the annual San Diego fund raising walk for the past six years. He is also active with the Project Angel Food organization. Previously married, Thomson now lives alone in Los Angeles. He enjoys working out, reading, and travelling, particularly to Scotland which he lists as his favorite vacation spot.

LINDA THORSON

Born: June 19 in Toronto, Canada
Marital Status: single
Height: 5' 8"   **Eyes:** green   **Hair:** red-brown
Education: Royal Academy of Dramatic Arts
Interests: theater, dancing, biking
Awards: Drama Desk Award for "Noises Off," Theater World Award for "Steaming"

Daytime Dramas: "One Life to Live," Julia Medina

Born in Canada, Linda Thorson has appeared on stage and screen throughout the world. She received her formal training in London at the Royal Academy of Dramatic Arts, and has appeared in numerous productions, both on the London stage and in the United States. Linda won the Drama Desk Award for her performance in the Broadway production of "Noise Off," and also appeared in the Los Angeles production of "Steaming," for which she was awarded the Theater World Award. Most recently Linda completed a run in the Broadway production of "Getting Married" and moved a few theaters away to the hit play, "City of Angels." Her feature films include "Sweet Liberty," The Greek Tycoon," "Valentino," and "Curtains." Moving to the small screen, Linda has appeared on television on a wide variety of shows, including "Dynasty," "St. Elsewhere," "The Bronx Zoo," "Empty Nest and most recently, "Marblehead Manor." She is perhaps best known for her work on the classic television series "The Avengers." As a recent drama school graduate, Linda won the role of Tara King, Steed's new partner, replacing the departing Diana Rigg. Still wet behind the ears, Linda performed all her own stunts on the highly rated show - a feat made easy by her own athletic abilities, Linda is a figure skating champion. The show ran in the United States till 1969 and can be seen today in syndication, Along with the television reruns is a new comic book that begins where the series ended, and Linda wrote the forward to a coffee table book based on the show. In her spare time Linda enjoys going to the theater, as well as keeping in shape through aerobics, dancing, biking and jogging. Her son, Trevor, was born in 1985.

JOEY THROWER

Born: April 30, 1968 in Jacksonville, Alabama
Marital Status: single
Height: 5' 9"   **Eyes:** green   **Hair:** brown
Education: Jacksonville State University; Mercer University
Interests: music, skiing

Daytime Dramas: "One Life to Live," Kevin Buchanan, 1991-1992

A native of Jacksonville, Alabama, Joey Thrower made his television debut as Kevin Buchanan on "One Life to Live." Thrower first studied acting at Jacksonville State University, where his mother, Linda Rainwater, is a literature professor. (she recently completed her first novel, "A Dream Changed") Moving to New York City at the age of seventeen, Joey continued his theatrical training at the Circle in the Square Theater, and spent the subsequent few years waiting tables, tending bar, and searching for acting roles. He took a brief hiatus from this life to study communications at Mercer University. Returning to New York, Thrower soon found work in regional theater, and in addition landed small roles in the acclaimed feature films, "Running on Empty" and "Working Girl." First seen by television viewers on national commercials for such products as Nintendo and Bubble Yum, the young actor has since included an episode of "In the Heat of the Night" to his list of t.v. credits. Away from the set, Thrower, who lives in New York City, enjoys music, (he is learning to play guitar) skiing, and softball.

RUSSELL TODD

Born: March 14, 1958 in Troy, New York
Marital Status: married to Kim Todd
Height: 6' **Eyes:** blue **Hair:** brown
Education: Syracuse University, Bachelor's Degree
Interests: movies, theater, skiing, writing, tennis
Awards: Kodak Young Filmmakers Award

Daytime Dramas: "Capitol," Jordy Clegg; **"Another World,"** Dr. Jamie Frame, 1990-

A familiar face to film and television, Russell Todd currently portrays Dr. Jamie Frame on "Another World," a role he has played since 1990. Previously, the actor was seen as Jordy Clegg on "Capitol." A native of Troy, New York, Todd was born Russell Todd Goldberg on March 14, 1958. After graduating from Syracuse University, where he majored in film and acting, he moved out west, where he has since appeared in several films. Among Todd's big screen credits, "Where the Boys Are '84," "Friday the 13th Part II," "He Knows You're Alone," "Chopping Mall," "Border Shootout," and "Sweet Murder," while he has also guest starred on such television shows as "Jake and the Fatman," and "Riptide." In addition to his daytime work, Todd was also a series regular, playing ranger Jim Cutler, on "High Mountain Rangers," with Robert Conrad. Aside from acting, Todd, who was the recipient of the Kodak Young Filmmakers Award, lists amongst his interests, movies, theater, skiing, tennis, and writing, as well as donating his time to a number of local charities dealing with children and animals. Although "Another World" is filmed in New York, Russell considers Van Nuys, California his home and lives there with his wife, Kim.

HEATHER TOM

Born: November 4, 1975 in Hinsdale, Illinois
Marital Status: single
Height: 5' 7"   **Eyes:** blue   **Hair:** brown
Education: currently attending South Pasadena High School
Interests: theater, horseback riding, water skiing

Daytime Dramas: "The Young and the Restless,"
Victoria Newman, 1991-

Few daytime characters have undergone a more radical transformation than Victoria Newman on "The Young and the Restless." When she left for boarding school she was an angelic five year old, but returning several months later, she had become a rebellious teenager, much to the chagrin of her parents, Victor and Nikki. While fans of the show may have initially found this plot twist somewhat hard to swallow, the stunning performance of Heather Tom, as the teenage Victoria, quickly quelled all doubts, and she has since become one of daytime's brightest new stars. An actress, dancer, and model, Ms. Tom was born on November 4, 1975 in Hinsdale, Illinois, and has been involved in show business from an early age. (Heather's younger twin siblings, David and Nicole, are also forging acting careers) Her career has thus far included modelling, television, film, and theater, and along the way she has honed her skills with such acting coaches as Margrit Pollak at the Strasberg Institute, and Diane Hardin at the Young Actors Space. Additionally, Heather has worked with the Seattle Children's Theater and the Pacific Northwest Ballet. Also a pianist, she studied at the Academy of Music and Dance. Moving to Seattle when Heather was ten years old, the Tom family spent three years in the city before relocating to Hollywood, where Heather quickly found television and film work. She has guest starred on such shows as "Who's the Boss?," (she gave Danny Pintauro his first onscreen kiss) "Trial by Jury," "Kids Inc.," and "Divorce Court," while she additionally co-starred with Linda Evans in the television film, "I'll Take Romance." On the big screen, Ms. Tom was featured in "Lookin' Good" and "Lessie Rainbow." Equally at home on stage, she toured the country in the Center Stage USA production of "Pinnocchio II," and has also been seen in, "The Nutcracker," and "The Greatest Story Ever Told." Continuing her studies, Heather is an honors student at South Pasadena High School, and plans on studying entertainment law in college. When she's not juggling school and work responsibilities, Ms. Tom, who continues to attend acting classes, enjoys horseback riding and water skiing.

JEFF TRACHTA

Born: October 6 in Staten Island, New York
Marital Status: single
Height: 6' 2"   **Eyes:** green   **Hair:** blond
Education: St. John's University, B.A.; American Academy of Dramatic Arts
Interests: tennis, water and snow skiing

Daytime Dramas: "One Life to Live," Boyce McDonald;
"Loving," Hunter Belden; **"The Bold and the Beautiful,"**
Thorne Forrester, 1989-

Currently seen as Thorne Forrester on "The Bold and the Beautiful," Jeff Trachta has previously appeared on daytime television as Hunter Belden on "Loving" and Boyce McDonald on "One Life to Live." Born on October 6, a native of Staten Island, New York, Trachta attended St. John's University, where he majored in psychology. Following graduation he honed his acting skills at the American Academy of Dramatic Arts, from which he quickly found work on stage, appearing in such productions as "Prince in Cinderella," "Love Letters," "Little Shop of Horrors," "Cabaret," "Africanus Instructus," "Grease," "Equus," and "Bleacher Bums." His feature film credits include "Do It Up" and "Catch Your Future," while he has additionally been seen on television in the HBO special "Robert Klein on Broadway," and the syndicated show, "Star Search." Jeff, who is single, recently relocated to Los Angeles, where in addition to acting he plans to pursue a singing career. In his spare time, he enjoys skiing, tennis, and spending time with his two dogs, Lucy and Ricky.

JESSICA TUCK

Born: February 19 in New York, New York
Marital Status: single
Height: 5' 7" **Eyes:** blue **Hair:** blond
Education: Yale University, Bachelor's Degree
Interests: skiing, softball, mountain climbing, horseback riding
Awards: nominated for a 1992 Daytime Emmy for Outstanding Lead Actress

Daytime Dramas: "One Life to Live," Megan Gordon, 1988-1992

Jessica Tuck has translated her own passion and flamboyancy onto the screen through her role as Megan Gordon on "One Life to Live." Jessica was born in New York City, where she was raised with her five brothers and stepbrothers. Being the only girl in a large family helped nurture her flair for the dramatic, which from an early age was the best way to get attention and keep up with her brothers. Jessica attended Yale University where she received her degree in psychology. It was at Yale that Jessica first began to seriously consider a career as an actress when she starred in a student written play called "Parkington and Me." After graduation Jessica traveled extensively before returning to New York to begin her acting and voice training at H.B. Studio, Julliard and the Michael Howard Studio. She made money during this time by working as a waitress for a catering company, a job she says afforded her the opportunity to see the best and beautiful of New York and at the same time, by Jessica's admission, spill a lot of drinks on alot of famous people. Aside from soiling the rich and famous, Jessica also used this time to establish her acting credentials. She appeared in a number of low budget and student films, such as "The Dating Game," "Gravitational Attraction," "Who Shot Patakango?," and "Bloodscape." Along with these she continued her stage training, playing a wide variety of roles. On August 4, 1988 Jessica made her daytime debut on "One Life to Live." Aside from her work on this popular daytime drama, Jessica has also starred in a comedy short which aired on VH-1, as well as creating a one woman show which she hopes she can bring to the New York stage. She also has starred, with fellow soap actor, Ricky Paull Goldin, in the off-Broadway play, "Welcome to My Life." Away from her professional life Jessica is an avid environmentalist, and has recently started the New York chapter of ECO, a California based organization devoted to saving the environment. When she left "One Life to Live", Jessica hosted a farewell luncheon to benefit the Student Environmental Action Coalition (SEAC) and had Capital Cities/ABC donate her last paycheck to the cause. Since leaving the show, Jessica has been working on the feature film "Ain't Love Grand" (a working title). Jessica also enjoys skiing, horseback riding, mountain climbing, and softball.

TAMARA TUNIE

Born: March 14 in Pittsburgh, Pennsylvania
Marital Status: single
Height: 5' 9" **Eyes:** brown **Hair:** black
Education: Carnegie Mellon University, B.F.A. in Musical
Theatre
Interests: dance, music

Daytime Dramas: "As the World Turns," Dana, 1983;
Jessica Griffin, 1987-

Born on March 14 in Pittsburgh, Pennsylvania, Tamara Tunie has accomplished a tremendous amount during her first ten years as a professional actress and dancer. The fourth of five children, Tamara discovered the stage in the third grade when she appeared in the Barett Elementary School production of "Rumplestiltskin," and continued to cultivate her singing, dancing, and acting for the next several years. As a student at Steel Valley High School, Tamara focused on sports and academics, planning on a future as a pediatrician. However, her love of acting proved too powerful to ignore, and Tamara wound up majoring in musical theater at Carnegie Mellon University. After graduating the young actress moved to New York City, landing her first professional job in a Connecticut dinner theater production. Since then Tamara has appeared on Broadway in "Lena Horne: The Lady and Her Music," as well as in such off-Broadway and regional productions as "Basin Street" "The Storyville Musical," "To Whom it May Concern," "The Fantasticks," "The Sound of Music," "Sweet Charity," "Lost in the Stars," and "Don't Bother Me, I Can't Cope." In addition, Tamara has travelled to Munich and Frankfurt to perform in "Bubblin' Brown Sugar." Her feature film credits are equally impressive, including such films as "Wall Street," "Sweet Lorraine," "Ishtar," "Hannah and Her Sisters," F/X," and "Desperately Seeking Susan." Along with her work on daytime drama, Tamara has also appeared on "Spencer: For Hire," the pilot, "FM-TV," the television movie "Fighting Back!," and as a dancer in numerous music videos. While fans of "As the World Turns" know her today as Jessica Griffin, some may remember her as Dana, a character she played briefly in 1983. Tamara presently lives in New York City.

PAIGE TURCO

Born: May 17 in Boston, Massachusetts
Marital Status: single
Height: 5' 5" **Eyes:** brown **Hair:** brown
Education: University of Connecticut, B.F.A.
Interests: dance, theater

Daytime Dramas: "Guiding Light," Dinah Morgan, 1987-1988;
"All My Children," Melanie Cortlandt, 1989-1991, 1992

Formerly seen as Dinah Morgan on "Guiding Light," and then as Melanie Cortlandt on "All My Children," Paige Turco is finding success on the big screen, having appeared in "Teenage Mutant Ninja Turtles II," as well as being slated to reprise the role in the upcoming third installment. Born in Boston, Massachusetts on May 17, Turco was raised in Springfield, where her childhood ambition was to be a ballerina. Following this dream, she studied ballet at the Walnut Hill School of Performing Arts, and performed as a soloist with the New England Dance Conservatory, the Amherst Ballet Theater Company, and the Western Massachusetts Ballet Company. Unfortunately, Turco's ballet career was cut short by an ankle injury, and during her years at the University of Connecticut, she began to concentrate on acting, particularly musical theater. In addition to performing with the Miss America USO troupe, the actress has also performed on stage in such productions as "A Chorus Line," "Alice in Wonderland," "A Little Night Music," "George M.," and "Carnival." Now living in New York, Ms. Turco can also be seen on television in Nike shoe commercials

---

JANINE TURNER

Born: December 6 in Lincoln, Nebraska
Marital Status: single
Height: 5' 6" **Eyes:** green **Hair:** brown
Education: Actors Studio
Interests: poetry, theater

Daytime Dramas: "General Hospital," Laura Templeton, 1982-1983

With her portrayal of Maggie on the popular series "Northern Exposure," Janine Turner has successfully made the often difficult leap from daytime to primetime stardom. Her prime time character, a feisty pilot from the mid west, seems perfectly suited to Janine who was born in Lincoln, Nebraska, and who's father was one of the few pilots to achieve a speed of Mach II. At the age of three, Janine, her father, and her mother, a homemaker and realtor, moved to Euless, Texas, where the younger Turner began her study of dance. By the time she was in junior high, Janine was an apprentice with the Fort Worth Ballet, and had also developed an interest in acting as well. Her first stage role was in a local summer production of "Charlotte's Web." At the age of fifteen another facet of Janine's career began when her mother submitted photos of her daughter to the Wilhelmina modelling agency. Two weeks later she was signed on as the agency's youngest client and embarked on a prosperous modelling career. She spent two years attending the Professional Children's School, but at her parents insistence Janine returned to Texas to finish high school. Ambitious as always she graduated a year early, and at the recommendation of Leonard Katzman, the producer of "Dallas" who cast her as Lucy Ewing's friend Susan, Janine packed up her Buick Regal and headed off to Hollywood. Her first show was another nighttime soap, a late night program called "Behind the Screen," which ran opposite "The Tonight Show" for thirteen weeks. After this show ran it's course Janine's search for a new role ended with the part of Laura Templeton on "General Hospital." This lead to more acting assignments, including a cameo in the film "Young Doctors in Love," a co-starring role in "Knights of the City," and the part of Shevan Tillman in Dino De Laurentiis' "Tai Pan." For this last production Janine spent ten weeks travelling through China, and this proved to be a life changing experience. She decided that, although she was achieving a certain amount of success, she was not living up to her potential as an actress. With new found drive, and the vehement objections of her agent, Janine packed her bags and moved to New York City to study her craft. Years earlier she had visited this metropolis with her theater group and had been immediately struck by it's energy and excitement. Moving into a fifth floor walk up on 38th Street, Janine began studying with acting coach Marcia Haufreicht, a member of Lee Stasberg's renowned Actors Studio. Turner spent the next three years studying drama and sharpening her skills in various off-Broadway productions. She appeared as Susan in "Full Moon and High Tide in the Ladies Room," as well as becoming a member of an avant-garde theatre group known as "The Common Ground Theatre." This allowed her to develop not only as an actress, but as a playwright and a poet as well. During this time Janine also appeared on the big screen in "Monkey Shines," "The Ambulance," with Eric Roberts, and as Olympia Dukakis' niece in "Steel Magnolias." With her star making performance on "Northern Exposure" fans can be certain that this talented actress will be around for a long time.

ROBERT TYLER

Born: April 19 in Stockton, California
Marital Status: single
Height: 6' **Eyes:** brown **Hair:** brown
Education: one year of college
Interests: music

Daytime Dramas: "As the World Turns," Spence Davies, 1988; **"Loving,"** Trucker McKenzie, 1989-

Through his roles on "Loving" and "As the World Turns," Robert Tyler has established his reputation as an actor of great intensity and passion. Born in Stockton, California, Tyler's first love was music, and although he would eventually opt for an acting career, he remains to this day a die hard rock and roll fan. Tyler attended college for a year before moving to New York to look for work in the theater. He began taking acting lessons, supporting himself through a wide array of jobs, from waiter, to messenger, to backstage gofer at Radio City Music Hall. This job involved any number of duties, from selling t-shirts at Grateful Dead concerts to operating the elevator which would take the Rockettes to the stage. Eventually Tyler began to find work as an actor, appearing off-Broadway in the comedy "Almost Romance" with Helen Slater, and in the Vietnam drama, "Sorrows and Sons." Tyler first appeared on daytime drama in the role of Spence Davies on "As the World Turns," which was quickly followed by the role of rebellious Trucker McKenzie on "Loving." He even auditioned for the role of Trucker during a rehearsal break from "As the World Turns."

HUNTER TYLO

Born: July 3, 1962 in Fort Worth, Texas
Marital Status: married to Michael Tylo, July 7, 1987
Height: 5' 6 1/2" **Eyes:** blue **Hair:** brown
Education: Fordham University
Interests: medicine, horseback riding

Daytime Dramas: "All My Children," Robin McCall, 1985-1987; **"Days of Our Lives,"** Marina Toscono **"The Bold and the Beautiful,"** Dr. Taylor Hayes, 1990-

Now seen as Dr. Taylor Hayes on "The Bold and the Beautiful," Hunter Tylo has additionally co-starred on "All My Children" and "Another World." However, fans of "All My Children," may have trouble recognizing the actress in her new role, since during her stint in Pine Valley she had blond hair and went by her professional name of Deborah Morehart. Her real name is in fact Deborah Hunter, her hair naturally dark, and after several years of playing a blond bimbo on "All My Children," she decided it was time to change her image. Once she had married Michael Tylo, with whom she co-starred on "All My Children," she started anew, letting her hair return to it's natural color and changing her professional name to Hunter Tylo. Today that change is evident to anyone who has seen her as the straight laced Taylor Hayes. Born on July 3, 1962 in Fort Worth, Texas, one of two girls and two boys, Hunter was a mischievous child and was particularly fond of reptiles, keeping such pets as boa constrictors and alligators. Her professional acting career has included film, t.v., and theater. She has appeared on stage in "The Star Spangled Girl," "Last of the Red Hot Lovers," and "I Ought to be in Pictures," while she was seen in the feature film, "Zorro." Along with her daytime work, which also included a stint as Marina Toscono on "Days of Our Lives," Tylo regularly works in commercials for such products as Clairol, Clarion Cosmetics, Ban Deodorant, and Cover Girl. During her time away from television, the actress decided to pursue another dream, enrolling in the pre-med program at Fordham University. Although she has not yet completed the course of study, she continues to take classes when time allows. Now living in California, Hunter and Michael are raising two sons, Christopher, her's from a previous marriage, and Mickey, born April 24, 1988. In her spare time, she is an accomplished equestrian bareback rider.

MICHAEL TYLO

Born: October 16 in Michigan
Marital Status: married to Hunter Tylo, July 7, 1987
Height: 6' **Eyes:** blue **Hair:** brown
Education: Wayne State University; University of Detroit, M.B.A.
Interests: theater, golf, gardening, reading

Daytime Dramas: "Another World," Peter Belton; **"Guiding Light,"** Quint Chamberlin, 1981-1985; **"All My Children,"** Matt Conelly, 1986-1988; **"General Hospital,"** Charlie Prince; **"The Young and the Restless,"** Blade, 1992-

Presently seen as Blade on "The Young and the Restless," Michael Tylo has worked steadily in daytime drama for the past ten years, appearing on "Another World," "Guiding Light," "All My Children," and "General Hospital." Born on October 16 in Michigan, Tylo grew up in the suburbs of Detroit, following which he enrolled as a pre-law student at Wayne State University. He eventually changed to a double major of political science and theater, and after graduating he continued his education at the University of Detroit, receiving his M.B.A. from this institution. Deciding on an acting career, Tylo moved to New York City in search of stage work, eventually landing his first theater role in "The Misanthrope," which was followed by another role in "The Winslow Boy," a production that began at the Kennedy Center before touring the country. Tylo's additional theater credits include "Cyrano De Bergerac," "The Shadowbox," and "Ring Around the Moon," and he presently serves on the Board of Directors of the Pennsylvania Theater Group. The actor also produced a play, "Vikings," which was presented at the Manhattan Theatre Club. On the big screen, Michael has been seen in the futuristic drama "Detroit 9000." In 1987, he moved to Los Angeles, where in addition to his daytime work, he was a regular on "Hawk," as well as making appearances on "The Insiders," and in the mini-series "Lonesome Dove." After spending two years in Madrid (1988-1990), where he starred in the t.v. series "Zorro," Tylo returned to the U.S. to continue his work, guest starring on "Tequilla and Bonetti" and "Gabriel's Fire." Michael met his wife Hunter, now seen on "The Bold and the Beautiful," when both starred on "All My Children." The couple was married in 1987, and are now raising two children, Chris and Mickey. In his spare time, Michael is a passionate golfer, and also enjoys reading and gardening.

PAUL MICHAEL VALLEY

Born: September 24 in Whitefish Bay, Wisconsin
Marital Status: single
Height: 6' 2" **Hair:** brown
Education: Julliard; American University
Interests: sports, theater
Awards: 1992 Soap Opera Award for Outstanding Newcomer

Daytime Dramas: "Another World," Ryan Harrison

The youngest of four children, Paul Michael Valley was born on September 24 in Whitefish Bay, Wisconsin. His father's job as an IBM executive called for frequent relocations, and as a result the Valley's resided in Minneapolis, Minnesota, Fargo, North Dakota, and Lake Forest, Illinois, before eventually settling in Greenwich, Connecticut. As a student, Paul excelled in both athletics and the arts, lettering in high school soccer as well as performing in school plays and singing with the glee club. He continued this during his years at American University, where he played rugby and honed his acting skills at the Maryland Shakespeare Festival. Valley eventually decided to leave college to work at the Shakespeare Theatre at the Folger, and has since appeared in such productions as "Macbeth," "Winter's Tale," "The Tempest," "Scapino!," "As You Like It," "Love Labours Lost," and "Romeo and Juliet." Returning to school, Paul attended Julliard for three years before landing the role of Ryan Harrison on "Another World" - a role he never knew could be so dangerous. In a scene that called for him to faint, Paul missed his mark and ended up suffering a concussion when he hit his head on the mantelpiece. Today, Valley, who is completely recovered, and single, lives in New York City, and when not on the set he enjoys all sports (especially watching them).

RAWLEY VALVERDE

Born: in California
Marital Status: single
Eyes: brown   **Hair:** brown
Education: University of California at Irvine; UCLA
Interests: softball, theater

Daytime Dramas: "Santa Barbara," Amado Alvarez,
1991-1992

A California native, Rawley Valverde is known as Amado Alvarez on "Santa Barbara." Raised in Ontario, California, Valverde attended both the University of California at Irvine and UCLA, where he worked his way through school as a mobile disc jockey. During his years as a d.j. he established an excellent reputation, and when the UCLA campus served as the athlete's village during the 1984 summer Olympics, the U.S. Olympic Committee recruited Valverde to be the official village disc jockey. Although he certainly excelled in this field, his heart belonged to acting, which he pursued rigorously, attending acting classes and appearing in numerous summer stock productions. On stage, Valverde has been seen in "Asylum," "G.R. Point," "Bleacher Bums," and "Kennedy's Children," while his t.v. credits include guest roles on "Married with Children," "Just the Ten of Us," and "Paradise." Recently, the actor was seen on the big screen in the horror film, "Welcome to Spring Break." Now enjoying new found success on "Santa Barbara," Valverde frequently participates in charity sporting events, and on his own enjoys, theater, playing softball and going to the beach.

RICHARD VAN VLEET

Born: January 19 in Denver, Colorado
Marital Status: married to Kristine Van Vleet, two daughters, Heather and Shannon
Height: 6' **Eyes:** blue **Hair:** sandy
Education: Western State College; American Academy of Dramatic Arts
Interests: writing, flying, art

Dramas: "All My Children," Dr. Chuck Tyler, 1975-1984, 1986, 1989-1992; **"Guiding Light,"** Dr. Ed Bauer, 1984-1986

An actor/writer/stuntman/teacher/pilot/artist, Richard Van Vleet (Van to his friends) is best known to daytime audiences as Dr. Chuck Tyler on "All My Children," a role he first began in 1975. A native of Denver, Colorado, Van Vleet graduated from Western State College following a four year stint in the Marines. At school he appeared in such productions as "The Merchant of Venice" and "A Marriage Proposal," while he also took the time to tour with the USO in "Gigi." Moving east, he continued his acting training in New York, at the American Academy of Dramatic Arts, following which he headed towards Hollywood, where he was placed under contract by Universal. Over the course of his career, Van Vleet has appeared in over sixty prime time productions, among them, "Mannix," "Mission Impossible," "Name of the Game," "The Bold Ones," "Cannon," and "McCloud." His appearances on "Dan August," "To Catch a Thief," and "Ironside," afforded Van Vleet the opportunity to perform his own stunts, showcasing his abilities not only as an actor but as a stuntman. Although the lion share of his daytime work has been on "All My Children," he additionally spent two years as Dr. Ed Bauer on "Guiding Light." Along with acting, Van Vleet has written a screenplay, "Citizen Ride," a semi-documentary which aired on NEA-TV, and is currently at work on a novel, "Got Some." Just as comfortable in front of a classroom as he is in front of the camera (or at the typewriter), he has taught grade school for American dependents in Japan, speech and drama at both a Colorado high school and Western State College, his alma mater, and headed the drama department, taught cinematography, and produced two films at Central Arizona College. Moving upward, Van Vleet is also a licensed pilot, (he once worked as a crop duster) and is now building his own plane in the basement of his Connecticut home. He shares this home with wife, Kristine, with whom he has two daughters, Heather and Shannon. He recently became a grandfather when Shannon gave birth to a son. To relax, Van Vleet enjoys painting and sculpting.

LIZ VASSEY

Born: August 9 in Raleigh, North Carolina
Marital Status: single
Height: 5' 8"   **Eyes:** brown   **Hair:** dark brown
Interests: theater, music
Awards: 1991 Emmy nomination for Outstanding Younger Actress Daytime Emmy

Daytime Dramas: "All My Children," Emily Ann Sago

Having made a formidable daytime debut, with her Emmy nominated portrayal of Emily Ann Sago on "All My Children," Liz Vassey has since moved on to similar prime time success. Born on August 9, in North Carolina, the youngest of three girls, Vassey was raised in Florida. Although she was eleven years old when she first started studying acting, voice, and dance, her performing career began two years earlier when she landed the title role in "Oliver." Since then, Ms. Vassey has gone on to appear in over forty regional productions, among them "A Chorus Line," "George M.," "Two Gentlemen of Verona," "The Crucible," and in the national tour of "Evita." She also performed in a cabaret act, "Bubbles," presented at New York's Whaler Bar. In addition to daytime, she has been seen in the television films, "Futureprobe" and "FBI Murders," as well as on such programs as "The New Leave it to Beaver," "Superboy," "Jake and the Fatman," "Star Trek: The Next Generation," "Quantum Leap," "Beverly Hills 90210," "Grapevine," and as Brian Keith's daughter in "Walter and Emily." Her appearance on "Jake and the Fatman" as a rock and roll singer, gave Vassey the opportunity to sing three original songs, showcasing her abilities as a vocalist and lyricist. Additionally her voice has been heard on two songs written by Gladys Shelley, "Only You Can Do It" and "Some Rainy Day," as well as on a Christmas Album featuring daytime actors, which benefited the Save the Children Foundation. Future plays for Vassey include working with Jason Priestley of Beverly Hills 90210, in the movie, "Monroe and Me." Vassey, who is single, now resides in Los Angeles.

JERRY verDORN

Born: November 23, 1949 in Sioux City, Iowa
Marital Status: married to Beth verDorn, two sons, Jake and Peter
Height: 5' 11"   **Eyes:** blue   **Hair:** brown
Education: Moorehead State University, B.A.; Studio of the Performing Arts
Interests: cycling, reading, being a father
Awards: nominated for three Daytime Emmys for Outstanding Supporting Actor 1990, 1991, 1992 ("Guiding Light")

Daytime Dramas: "Guiding Light," Ross Marler, 1979-

Nominated for three daytime Emmys, Jerry verDorn has portrayed Ross Marler on "Guiding Light" since 1979. One of daytime's most popular characters, verDorn recreated the role for a prime time television movie, "The Cradle Will Fall." Jerry was born on November 23, 1949, in Sioux City, Iowa, where his father worked as a salesman, an occupation which called for frequent relocation. For that reason, Jerry, along with the rest of his family, which included three siblings, spent much of his youth travelling throughout North Dakota, South Dakota, and Minnesota, where he says he had a "lovely Minnesota childhood." The verDorn family is now settled in the city of Fargo. Originally intent on being an English teacher, Jerry's plans changed when he got involved with the theater department at Moorehead State University. Over the next few years he appeared in several school productions, as well as travelling to London to study at Studio of the Performing Arts, an acting school founded by Sean Connery. After graduation, verDorn landed his first role in a New Jersey production of "Black Elk Speaks," a play which soon found it's way to Washington D.C., where the young actor was discovered by a New York theater producer. Before heading to Manhattan, however, Jerry returned home for the summer, where he appeared in a local production and married his college sweetheart, Beth. After moving to New York in 1977, Jerry appeared on stage in "Are You Now or Have You Ever Been?," a play which premiered at Rutgers University, but eventually found it's way to the Broadway stage. At the same time, verDorn starred in another play, "Man and Superman," at the Circle in the Square Theater. It was his work in this production that caught the eye of "Guiding Light" producers, and in 1979, Jerry took on the role of Ross Marler. He originally planned to stay just eighteen months, but over a decade later he is still going strong. As for his other credits, verDorn tells us there are "too many to list." Continuing to work on stage as well, his additional theater credits include, "Star Spangled Girl" and "A Phoenix Too Frequent," which was seen as part of the George Bernard Shaw Festival. In 1982, Jerry and his wife re-organized the Playhouse on the Mall in Paramus, New Jersey, where they presented a season of plays through their company, Fourstar Productions. The couple presently live in the suburbs of New York City, where they are raising their two sons, Jacob (born 12/83) and Peter (born 12/85). Jerry donates much of his spare time to literacy programs, as well as working with the Methodist church. He lists amongst his interests: cycling, reading, and fatherhood.

JOHN VISCARDI

Born: August 19 in New York, New York
Marital Status: single
Height: 6' 1"   **Eyes:** brown   **Hair:** brown
Education: Columbia University, B.A.
Interests: writing, theater

Daytime Dramas: "One Life to Live," Father Tony Vallone

A native of New York City, John Viscardi received his B.A. in literature from Columbia University. For his acting training he studied with Aaron Frankel, before becoming a member of the Circle Repertory Actor's Lab, where Viscardi has starred in productions of "Borderlines," "Amulets Against the Dragon Forces," and "Cave Life." He has also performed with New York's American Shakespeare Repertory in such works as "Hamlet" and "Romeo and Juliet." Viscardi's role as Father Tony Vallone on "One Life to Live," was originally intended to be a limited one, however the producers and writers were so impressed that he was shortly hired as a contract player. Prior to his daytime debut, John had appeared in the TV specials, "The Julie Brown Show, "Heart" and "Streets of Gold." Viscardi is now concentrating on his writing, having just completed a screenplay, as well as an a series of one act plays which he would like to bring to the stage. Although not married, he has been romantically linked with former "One Life to Live" co-star, Fiona Hutchison.

LESLEY VOGEL

Born: April 11, 1958 in Louisville, Kentucky
Marital Status: married to Alan Panettiere, one daughter, Hayden
Height: 5' 5" **Eyes:** hazel **Hair:** brown
Education: Stephens College, B.F.A.; University of Washington, M.F.A.
Interests: theater, skiing, tennis, antiques, sewing, gardening

Daytime Dramas: "Loving," Edy Lester Donovan, 1984; **"All My Children,"** Pauline Blake; **"Guiding Light,"** Tina Birkel

Over the past several years, Lesley Vogel has appeared on three daytime dramas, "All My Children," "Loving," and "Guiding Light." Vogel was born on April 11, 1958, in Louisville, Kentucky, where her father worked as a heart specialist, while her mother was a teacher. The Vogel family also includes Lesley's sister, Jane, currently the owner of a Florida health studio. After graduating from Stephens College with a B.F.A., Lesley went on to receive her M.F.A. from the Professional Actor Training Program at the University of Washington. Along with daytime, Vogel has concentrated chiefly on stage roles, appearing on Broadway in "Breakfast, Lunch, and Dinner," and in such off-Broadway and regional productions as "Review, Review," "Laundry and Bourbon," "Bus Stop," "Julius Caesar," "Love's Labours Lost," "Coal Diamond," "The Miser," "Vanities," "Steambath," "Blithe Spirit," and "A Midsummer's Night Dream." Presently, Vogel works as the producer of the "Hit and Run" Theater Company, which has an off-Broadway production slated for a fall 1992 opening. On television, in addition to daytime, the actress has been seen on "Cheers," "Murder Ink.," and in a recurring role on "In the Heat of the Night." Her film credits include a role in Woody Allen's "The Purple Rose of Cairo." Lesley now lives in a New York suburb, with her husband, Alan Panettiere, and their daughter, Hayden. In her spare time, she lends her expertise to productions at the Grace Episcopal Church, and Vogel lists amongst her other interests, skiing, sailing, antiques, gardening, golfing, tennis, interior design, and sewing.

HELEN WAGNER

Born: September 13, 1918 in Lubbock, Texas
Marital Status: married to Broadway producer Robert Willey since 1954
Education: Monmouth College, Bachelor's degrees in dramatics and music
Interests: theater
Awards: Honorary Degree of Doctor of Humane Letters, Monmouth College

Daytime Dramas: "Guiding Light," Trudy Bauer, 1952; **"As the World Turns,"** Nancy Hughes McClosky, 1956-

Not many performers can say they were at the forefront of the television revolution, but after thirty five years Helen Wagner has certainly earned the right. On April 2, 1956, "As the World Turns" premiered, and the first line spoken, "Good Morning, dear," was delivered by Ms. Wagner herself. Over three decades later, she is still warming viewers hearts as Nancy Hughes McClosky. Born on September 13 in Lubbock, Texas, Helen discovered her love of performing at an early age, inspired greatly by her aunt, who sang on the Redpath-Horner Chautauqua circuit. After studying music and drama at Monmouth College in Illinois, Helen headed for New York City, where she continued her acting training, as well as her study of piano. She was able to display her vocal skills as a soloist in church choirs, and soon began landing professional roles. Among the many Broadway productions which Helen has been involved with include: "Winter's Tale," "Oklahoma," "Eastward in Eden" and "The Bad Seed." In addition she starred as Blanche Du Bois in the touring production of "A Streetcar Named Desire," with Lee Marvin, and played all the female roles in a production of "Lovers and Other Strangers." As accomplished a singer as she is an actress, she also flexed her vocal skills with the St. Louis Municipal Opera. Helen made her television debut playing the queen on a G.E. produced fairy tale, which she followed in 1951 to 1955, with the role of Charlie Ruggles daughter on the popular series "The World of Mr. Sweeney." Before "As the World Turns" Ms. Wagner also appeared for one year as Trudy Bauer on "Guiding Light," but it is safe to say that more people know her as Nancy Hughes. However, she almost didn't make it past the first year, let alone the thirty fifth. Amazingly enough the producers of "As the World Turns" released her from her contract nine weeks after the show premiered, but a search yielded no worthy replacements and she was rehired. Presently daytime dramas longest running performer, Helen appeared only sporadically in the early eighties, showing up on wedding episodes in 1982 and 1984, and not at all in 1983. However, Helen has remained a favorite with the viewers, and continues to be the glue that holds Oakdale together. Since 1956 there have been many changes, most notably the fact that up until 1975 the show was filmed live. While the show is now taped in advance, Helen still enjoys the exhilaration of a live performance, and her flexible daytime schedule gives her the opportunity to pursue stage work. One of her most recent performances was in "The Lion of the Winter" at her alma mater, Monmouth College. The production was produced by her husband of thirty eight years, Robert Willey, a successful Broadway producer. In 1988, Ms. Wagner was a recipient of an Honorary Degree of Doctor Humane Letters from her Alma Mater, Monmouth College.

JACK P. WAGNER

Born: October 3 in Washington, Missouri
Marital Status: single, one son, Peter John
Height: 5' 11" **Eyes:** blue-green **Hair:** brown
Education: University of Arizona, Bachelor of Fine Arts
Interests: tennis, golf, racquetball, weight lifting, softball
Awards: 1985 Daytime Emmy nomination for Outstanding Younger Man

Daytime Dramas: "A New Day in Eden," Clint Masterson, 1982-1983; "General Hospital," Frisco Jones, 1983-1987; 1989-1991; "Santa Barbara," Warren Lockridge, 1991-

A talented performing artist, Jack Wagner is not only a gifted musician but a fine actor as well. Born on October 3 in Washington, Missouri, Wagner began acting in high school productions. A self taught guitar player, it was also during this time that he began performing in local clubs. Along with this, Wagner found the time to letter all four years in football and basketball. Upon graduation, he enrolled in the University of Missouri from which he transferred to East Central College, where he won the Missouri State Junior College Golf Championship. Today, Wagner is a pro-level golfer, the current Club Champion at Bel Air Country Club, and winner of the AT & T Pro-Am Tournament at Pebble Beach. In 1981 Wagner transferred once again, this time to the University of Arizona on a drama scholarship. (he applied for a golf scholarship) After graduating with a Fine Arts degree in 1982, he moved to Los Angeles. During college, Wagner appeared in numerous stage productions and still continues his work in theater. He has performed in over thirty major stage productions and has appeared in the national touring companies of "Grease" and "West Side Story," playing the lead role in each production. He has also performed in "Butterfly" at the Goodspeed Opera House in Connecticut. Wagner also starred in, and produced, Michael Weller's "Split" at the Beverly Hills Playhouse. In 1984 Wagner achieved great success in his musical career when his single, "All I Need" became a gold record. His other records include the 1985 release of "Lighting up the Night," and "Don't Give up Your Day Job." Before going to "General Hospital" Wagner made appearances on "Knots Landing" and on the cable soap opera, "A New Day in Eden." He has also been seen in the television movie "Moving Target," along with the theatrical motion picture "Play Murder For Me." Off screen, Wagner has been involved, for many years, with former "GH" co-star, Kristina Malandro. Together they have one son, Peter John. In his leisure time, Wagner enjoys all sports including tennis, racquetball, weight lifting, softball, and golf.

MARCY WALKER

Born: November 26 in Paducah, Kentucky
Marital Status: divorced
Eyes: blue   **Hair:** blond
Education: Southern Illinois University
Awards: 1983 and 1984 Daytime Emmy nominations for Best Supporting Actress ("All My Children"); 1987 Daytime Emmy nomination for Best Actress; 1989 Daytime Emmy for Best Actress Award ("Santa Barbara"); 1989 Soap Opera Award for Outstanding Heroine; 1990 Soap Opera Award for Outstanding Lead Actress; 1990 Soap Opera Award for Outstanding Super Couple (with A Martinez)

Daytime Dramas: "All My Children," Liza Colby, 1981-1984; **"Santa Barbara,"** Eden Capwell Castillo, 1984-1990

Emmy winning actress Marcy Walker has portrayed two of daytime's most popular characters of the past decade, the manipulating Liza Colby on "All My Children," and the captivating Eden Capwell Castillo on "Santa Barbara." Twice nominated for Best Supporting Actress Daytime Emmys for her work on "All My Children," Walker switched soaps in 1984, taking on the role of Eden on "Santa Barbara." Since then, she has been called on to play four different personalities, and for her efforts earned a Daytime Emmy as Best Actress. Walker was born on November 26 in Paducah, Kentucky, where her father worked as a field service engineer, a job which required frequent relocations. As a result, Marcy's family resided throughout the United States, and even spent time in Iran and Switzerland. Eventually graduating from a Troy, Illinois high school, Walker enrolled at Southern Illinois University. However, her college career was shortened when she overheard, during enrollment, that Jane Ireland was looking for an actress for a role in the PBS production of "Life on the Mississippi." Walker ended up landing the role, beating out two thousand applicants, and soon found herself living in New York City with Jane Ireland as her manager. Since then she has gone on to appear in scores of television projects, including, "Christian and Katherine," "The Sister's Room," "Babies," "Case of the Paris Paradox," and "Desperado: A Town Called Beauty." In 1991, Ms. Walker left "Santa Barbara" to star in the prime time series, "Palace Guard." She also starred in the 1992 Lifetime movie, "Au Pair." Marcy has also been seen in many commercials and on the big screen in "Hot Resorts." Walker is currently separated from her third husband, Stephen Collins. They have one son, Taylor. Previously she has been married to actor Billy Warlock and Stephen Ferris.

NICHOLAS WALKER

Born: July 26 in Bogota, Columbia
Marital Status: married to Wendy Walker, two children,
Ian and Olivia
Height: 6' **Eyes:** hazel **Hair:** light brown
Education: Providence College, B.A. in theater and humanities;
University of California, Irvine, M.A. in theater
Interests: cooking, theater, camping, hiking, canoeing,
landscaping

Daytime Dramas: "The Doctors," Brad Huntington, 1980-1981;
"Capitol," Sam Clegg III, 1982-1987; **"General Hospital,"**
Jimmy O'Herleihy; **"One Life to Live,"** Max Holden, 1990-1991;
"Santa Barbara," Frank, 1992-

A true veteran of daytime drama, Nicholas Walker has had starring roles in several daytime dramas, including "General Hospital," "Capitol," "The Young and the Restless," "One Life to Live" and most recently "Santa Barbara." Born in Bogota, Columbia, Walker received his B.A. in theater and humanities from Providence College, as well as his M.F.A. from the University of California at Irvine. Along with his extensive work on daytime drama, Walker has also appeared as the guest star on such series as "Jake and the Fatman," and "Matlock," as well as starring in the television movies "For Ladies Only" and "Addicted to His Love." His theater credits include performances in the Broadway production of "Major Barbara," and off-Broadway in "Saint Joan" and "Godspell." In addition, Walker has appeared in numerous regional productions. Over the years Walker has lived in several European countries and is fluent in both French and Spanish; English is his third language. Since living in California, Walker volunteers at the L.A. Grief Recovery Institute founded by grief expert John James (Jess Walton's husband) In his spare time Walker feels equally at home in the kitchen or outdoors -he enjoys going to the theater, as well as landscaping, camping, hiking, cooking, and white water canoeing. He is married with two young children, Ian and Olivia.

TONJA WALKER

Born: September 19 in Huntington, West Virginia
Marital Status: single
Height: 5' 6" **Eyes:** blue **Hair:** blond
Education: Peabody Conservatory of Music
Interests: gardening, football, decorating
Awards: 1979 Miss Teen All American; 1980 Miss Maryland in
the Miss USA pageant

Daytime Dramas: "Capitol," Lizbeth Bachman, 1982-1986;
"General Hospital," Olivia Jerome; **"One Life to Live,"**
Alex Olanov

Deciding at three years old that she would be an actress, Tonja Walker first came into the public eye when she won the Miss Teen All-American pageant for her home state of Maryland. Her next step was the Miss U.S.A. pageant, where she was named one of the ten finalists. As serious about music as she is about acting, Tonja also studied at the Peabody Conservatory of Music in Baltimore and has become an accomplished songwriter as well as singer. At the age of nineteen Tonja left home for California to pursue her acting career, and within four months she found work in several national commercials, the feature film "Liars Moon," starring Matt Dillon, a mini series, and two television pilots. She eventually decided to join the cast of "The Hoyt Axton Show," which took her on the road and afforded her the opportunity to display her vocal skills nightly in front of an audience. This proved to be short lived as the show was cancelled after a few months. Returning to California Tonja decided that she was in the need for a change, and against her agent's wishes began auditioning for daytime dramas. Her first big role came as Lizbeth Bachman on "Capitol," after which she played the much hated Olivia Jerome on "General Hospital." When this character had run its course Tonja began shopping around for a new part, and eventually ended up as Alex Olanov on "One Life to Live," a role created especially for her. Originally she auditioned for the role of Tina, a part that went to Karen Witter. She can currently be seen hosting an infomercial for a hair removal technique. Away from work Tonja enjoys decorating, gardening and working out.

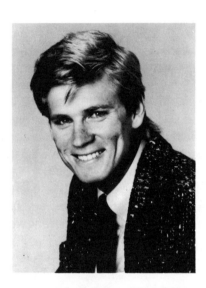

DAVID WALLACE

Born: November 23 in Miami, Florida
Marital Status: married to Lisa Trusel on November 1, 1986, two children, Ryan and Benjamin
Height: 6' 2"   **Eyes:** blue   **Hair:** blond
Education: Long Beach State College
Interests: fixing cars, surfing, motorcycling, volleyball

Daytime Dramas: "Days of Our Lives," Todd Chandler, 1985-1986; **"General Hospital,"** Dr. Tom Hardy, 1987-

Formerly seen as Todd Chandler on "Days of Our Lives," David Wallace has portrayed Dr. Tom Hardy on "General Hospital" since 1987. Born on November 23 in Miami, Florida, Wallace moved to Long Beach, California at the age of five. After graduating from Millikan High School, he studied drama at Long Beach State College, and then went into the Air Force Academy (today he is a licensed private pilot), and soon began working in commercials, as well as appearing on stage at the Long Beach Community theater in such works as "Butterflies are Free" and "Our Town." Wallace made his television debut on the series "Operation Runaway," and has additionally been seen on prime time television in "Facts of Life," "Hart to Hart," "Trauma Center," "Vegas," and as a recurring character on "Hotel." His film credits include the television movies, "Mazes and Monsters," "Miracle on Ice," and "The Baby Sitter," while he has also starred on the big screen in "Humungous" and "Mortuary." Since 1986, Wallace has been married to actress Lisa Trusel, whom he met while both were starring on "Days of Our Lives." Today the couple live by the beach in California with their two children, daughter, Ryan Elizabeth, born December 10, 1989, and son, Benjamin David, born May 12, 1992. A deeply religious man, David enjoys life by the water and lists amongst his hobbies, surfing, swimming, volley ball, motorcycling, bicycling, and fixing cars.

JESS WALTON

Born: February 18 in Grand Rapids, Michigan
Marital Status: married to John W. James, one son, Colt
Height: 5' 7" **Eyes:** brown **Hair:** brown
Education: Loretto Abbey High School
Interests: landscaping, travelling, bowling, fine arts
Awards: nominated for 1990 Daytime Emmy for Outstanding Supporting Actress; Daytime Emmy for Outstanding Supporting Actress,1991

Daytime Dramas: "Capitol," Kelly Harper, 1984-1987;
"The Young and the Restless," Jill Foster Abbott, 1987-

Since 1987, Jess Walton has portrayed the manipulative and pragmatic Jill Foster Abbott on "The Young and the Restless." Over the course of her years on the show the talented actress has twice been nominated for a Daytime Emmy as Outstanding Supporting Actress, a prize she took home in 1991. Born on February 18 in Grand Rapids, Michigan, Jess spent most of her childhood in Toronto, Canada, where she attended high school at the Loretto Abbey. After graduating, she embarked immediately on a professional acting career, working for three years with the Toronto Workshop Production's Repertory Theatre. While there she appeared on stage in numerous productions, among them "Uncle Vanya" and "The Right Honorable Gentleman." Relocating to Los Angeles in 1969, Ms. Walton soon became a much sought after television guest star, appearing on such shows as "The Rockford Files," "Cannon," "Marcus Welby M.D.," "The Six Million Dollar Man," "The Streets of San Francisco," "Barnaby Jones," "Ironside," "Starsky and Hutch," and "Kojak." The actress has also appeared in the television films "Monserrat," "You'll Never See Me Again," "The Storm," "Diary of a Madman," "Noises in Paradise," and "Mod Squad II." She has been seen on the big screen in "Monkeys in the Attic." Before beginning her work on "The Young and the Restless," Jess spent three years as Kelly Harper on "Capitol." Away from the set, she donates her time to two charitable organizations, The Clare Foundation, which helps recovering alcoholics, and The Adam Walsh Child Resource Center. Walton also works closely with her husband, John W. James, a renowned grief recovery authority and founder of the Grief Recovery Institute in Los Angeles. Their national help line is (800) 445-4808 and is open M-F, 9-5 (pacific time). John founded the institute in 1978 following the death of his three year old son. He also co-authored "The Grief Recovery Handbook." The couple, who have one son, Colt, currently reside in Los Angeles. In her spare time, Jess lists amongst her interests, the fine arts, landscaping, redecorating, travelling, bowling, and working out in her home gym.

STUART WARD

Born: November 19, 1962 in Quantico, Virginia
Marital Status: married to Allison Kurki Ward
Height: 6' 2" **Eyes:** hazel **Hair:** brown
Education: East Carolina University, B.S.
Interests: golf, cooking

Daytime Dramas: "Guiding Light," Levy, 1990-

An up and coming actor, Stuart Ward landed his first daytime role, Levy on "Guiding Light," in 1990. Born on November 19, 1962, in Quantico, Virginia, where his parents, Charles and Beth, worked as educators, Stuart was one of three children. After attending East Carolina University, he studied acting technique with David Zittel, and has since appeared on stage in "Loyalties" and "The Foreigner," while he has been seen on the big screen in "Goatfeathers," "Perfect Moment," and "Fighting Light." Ward also serves as the artistic director for the Dynamic Theater Company. Now living in Queens, New York, the actor enjoys golf, cooking, and spending time with his wife, Allison Kurki.

RUTH WARRICK

Born: June 29, 1916 in St. Joseph, Missouri
Marital Status: single, three children, Karen, Jon Erik and Robert Timothy
Height: 5' 6 1/2" **Eyes:** blue **Hair:** auburn
Education: University of Kansas City, two years; Unity School of Practical Christianity, Bachelor's Degree
Interests: theater, civil rights, the environment, writing
Awards: nominated for two Best Actress Daytime Emmys, 1975, 1977 ("All My Children"); 1980 and 1981 Soap Opera Award, Favorite Mature Actress; Emmy Award nomination for "Peyton Place;" Humanitarian Award from Midland Empire Arthritis Association; National Arts in Education Award; Regent of Cathedral of St. John the Divine; Entitled Dame Ruth Warrick, D.M., O.S.J., Dame of Honour and Merit by the Imperial Russian Order of Saint John of Jerusalem Ecumenical Foundation

Daytime Dramas: "Guiding Light," Janet Johnson, 1953-1954; **"As the World Turns,"** Edith Hughes, 1956-1960; **"All My Children,"** Phoebe Tyler Wallingford, 1970-

A woman of tremendous accomplishments, Ruth Warrick made her feature film debut in 1941 as Emily Norton Kane in "Citizen Kane," a movie considered by many to be the greatest of all time. For the past twenty two years, Ruth has earned a new generation of fans, with her portrayal of Phoebe Tyler Wallingford on "All My Children." Along the way she has received two Best Actress daytime Emmy nominations, as well as winning the 1980 and 1981 Soap Opera Award for Favorite Mature Actress. Born on June 29, 1916, in St. Joseph, Missouri, Ruth moved to Kansas City while still in high school. She describes her family, which included her mother, a singer, her father, a sales manager, and one sister, as a "Middle West family where music, church, education, arts, were main concerns." Interested in theater from an early age, Ms. Warrick first appeared on stage at the University of Kansas City, where she also was named Miss Jubilesta. After college, she headed east, to New York City, where her first roles were on radio, including a stint on the soap opera "Joyce Jordan, Girl Interne." Also concentrating on stage work, Ruth performed at the Mercury Theater, an institution headed by Orson Welles, who would later bring the young actress to Hollywood to appear in "Citizen Kane." Over the course of her career, Ruth has never strayed far from the stage, and her theater credits include roles on Broadway in "Take Me Along," with Jackie Gleason, "Irene," with Debbie Reynolds and "Pal Joey," while she has performed regionally in scores of productions, among them, "Butterflies are Free," "Legends," "Miss Lonelyhearts," and "Long Day's Journey Into Night." Moving to Hollywood, Ruth became an immediate sensation with "Citizen Kane," which she followed up with over thirty major motion pictures, including "The Great Bank Robbery," "Perilous Holiday," "China Sky," "Let's Dance," with Fred Astaire, "Guest in the House," "Daisy Kenyon," "The Corsican Brothers," and "Song of the South." On daytime television, before beginning her run on "All My Children," Ruth also starred as Edith Hughes on "As the World Turns," Janet Johnson on "Guiding Light." She also portrayed Hannah Cord on the night time soap,"Peyton Place," earning an Emmy nomination for her work Ms. Warrick reprised this role in 1985 in the television film, "Return to Peyton Place." In addition, she co-starred on the t.v. series "Father of the Bride," and guest starred on "Studio One," "Robert Montgomery Presents," "The Love Boat," and in the ABC Afterschool Special, "Sometimes I Don't Love My Mother." Ms. Warrick wrote of her phenomenal life and career in her 1980 bestselling autobiography, "The Confessions of Phoebe Tyler," and is currently at work on her second book, a study of Orson Welles. While she is chiefly known as an actress, Ms. Warrick's accomplishments extend far beyond the realm of entertainment. She has focused much of her energies on promoting arts in education, particularly within inner city schools. In 1983, she received the first national Arts in Education Award from the Board of Directors of Business and Industry for Arts in Education Inc., a prize since renamed the Ruth Warrick Award, now presented annually. Extending her influence to an international level, Ms. Warrick recently travelled to Moscow as part of "The Global Forum," a group that met with Mikail Gorbachev to discuss the world's environmental concerns. The trip proved to be a double success for Ruth, who after meeting Russian playwright Vladmir Gubaryev, offered to produce his play dealing with the romance between his country's top physicist, Roald Sagdeyev, and Susan Eisenhower, an American businesswoman. Back at home, Warrick has been involved with a myriad of community activities: she co-founded Operation Bootstrap in Watts, served as a consultant under Presidents Kennedy and Johnson on Drop out Prevention for the Department of Labor and the Job Training Corps, and taught in both the "City in Schools" and "Learning to Read Through the Arts" programs. An ardent environmentalist, Warrick is a member of the Office of Environmental Concerns as well as donating her time to Green Seal. She is also a licensed teacher of Metaphysics for the Unity School. For her numerous contributions, Ms. Warrick has received such honors as the Humanitarian Award from Midland Empire Arthritis Association, and earned such titles as Dame Ruth Warrick, D.M, O.S.J., Regent of Cathedral of St. John the Divine, and Dame of Honour and Merit by the Imperial Russian Order of Saint John of Jerusalem Ecumenical Foundation. Ruth, who has been married, divorced, and widowed, is now single, and has three children, Karen, Jon, and Robert. She lives in New York City, and lists amongst her interests: theater, writing, civil rights, and the environment.

PATTY WEAVER

Born: September 23 in Clarksburg, West Virginia
Marital Status: single
Height: 5' **Eyes:** blue **Hair:** blond
Interests: songwriting, scuba diving, cooking, hiking

Daytime Dramas: "Days of Our Lives," Trish Clayton Banning, 1973-1982; **"The Young and the Restless,"** Gina Roma, 1982-

A singer and an actress, Patty Weaver has divided the past two decades between prominent daytime roles and a successful recording career. Since 1982 she has portrayed Gina Roma on "The Young and the Restless," and prior to that she enjoyed tremendous popularity as Trish Clayton Banning on "Days of Our Lives." Born in Clarksburg, West Virginia, on September 23, Weaver first performed on stage with her family's Pentecostal singing group. After graduating from high school, she continued the touring life, singing with the rock group, "The Lov'd Ones," with whom she recorded an album for Atlantic Records. After another stint with the band, "Easy," best known for their album, "Goin' Down," Weaver moved to Hollywood, working as a Beverly Hills shoeshine girl to pay for acting classes. She soon landed a job as a production assistant on a local news program, and eventually got the opportunity to display her acting talents, guest starring on such shows as "Maude," "All in the Family," and "Insight." From 1973 until 1982, Weaver became a daytime favorite for her work on "Days of Our Lives," and shortly after leaving this show, found a new home on "The Young and the Restless." Along with her acting career, she has continued to sing, recording four albums, including a self titled 1982 Warner Bros. release. A much sought after performer, Weaver has opened for such notables as George Burns, Jerry Lewis, and Don Rickles. She currently works with Variety Clubs International, as well as donating her time to the National Coalition for Battered Women. In her spare time, Weaver enjoys writing music, scuba diving, cooking Italian foods, and hiking through the mountains of Yosemite.

KASSIE WESLEY

Born: March 21, 1961 in Morganfield, Kentucky
Marital Status: married to Richard Hankins
Height: 5' 9" **Eyes:** green **Hair:** brown
Education: UCLA, Indiana University
Interests: singing, golf, songwriting, gardening, cooking

Daytime Dramas: "Guiding Light," Chelsea Reardon, 1986-1991

An accomplished singer and actress, Kassie Wesley portrayed Chelsea Reardon on "Guiding Light" from 1986 to 1991. Today, she is concentrating largely on her singing career, which recently resulted in the single, "Hand out of Heart." Ms. Wesley, who performs as a soloist at the Grand Ole Opry, hopes to have an album out sometime in the near future. A native of Morganfield, Kentucky, she was born on March 21, 1961. The rest of Kassie's family, whom she describes as a "happy and fun family," includes parents, Quentin and Hildegarde, brothers, Jeff and John, and sister, Sara. After attending college at UCLA and Indiana University, Wesley began acting professionally, appearing on daytime and in the feature film, "Evil Dead II." Today, she is married to Richard Hankins, an Emmy winning art director whom she met while both worked on "Guiding Light." The couple now divide their time between New York and Los Angeles. An avid golfer, Kassie also enjoys songwriting, cooking, and gardening.

DONDRE WHITFIELD

Born: May 27, 1969 in Brooklyn, New York
Marital Status: single
Height: 6' **Eyes:** brown **Hair:** black
Education: High School of the Performing Arts
Interests: boxing, softball
Awards: 1992 Emmy nomination for Outstanding Younger Actor

Daytime Dramas: "Another World," Jesse Lawrence;
"All My Children," Terrence Frye, 1991-

A native of Brooklyn, New York, Dondre Whitfield (initially his mother was going to name him Andre, but decided it sounded too common, and thus came up with this variation) is probably best known for his recurring role of Robert, would be boyfriend of Vanessa, on "The Cosby Show." He made his daytime debut as Jesse Lawrence on "Another World," and in 1991 joined the cast of "All My Children," as Terrence Frye. Like his character, Terrence, Dondre was born to a teenage, single mother who struggled to put herself through school. Dondre has not seen his father since he was nine years old - his father is in prison. Whitfield grew up in the troubled Bushwick area of Brooklyn, but his mother, who has since remarried, and had two more sons, relocated her family to South Carolina. Dondre began acting in elementary school and was working professionally by the time he graduated high school. In addition to his television series work, Whitfield has also appeared on many national commercials, as well as co-starring in an ABC Afterschool Special, "All That Glitters." Presently single, Dondre lives in New Jersey, with his girlfriend Lisa. In his spare time the young actor plays softball and studies boxing with world welter weight champion, James "Buddy" McGirt.

KATHLEEN WIDDOES

Born: March 21 in Wilmington, Delaware
Marital Status: married to Jerry Senter, one daughter
Eyes: brown **Hair:** brown
Education: Sorbonne
Interests: gardening, weaving
Awards: Two Obie Awards for "Beggar's Opera" and "Tower of Evil;" 1990 Daytime Emmy: Best Supporting Actress ("As the World Turns"); 1986, 1987, 1990 Daytime Emmy nominations for Best Supporting Actress ("As The World Turns"); Tony nomination for "Much Ado About Nothing"

Daytime Dramas: "Young Dr. Malone," Jill Malone, 1958-1959; **"Another World,"** Rose Perrini, 1978-1980; **"Ryan's Hope,"** Una MacCurtain,1983; **"As the World Turns"** Emma Snyder, 1985-

An award winning actress of both stage and screen, Kathleen Widdoes has been involved with daytime drama for over three decades. A native of Wilmington, Delaware, Kathleen relocated to New York City after completing her education. Once in Manhattan she continued to study acting, including a year in Paris spent at the prestigious Sorbonne, on a Fulbright Scholarship. Since then Kathleen has amassed an impressive list of stage credits, among them "A View From the Bridge," her first stage role, and on Broadway in "The Importance of Being Earnest," "Brighton Beach Memoirs," "You Can't Take It With You," and a Joseph Papp production of "Much Ado About Nothing," for which she earned a Tony Award nomination. Not one to shy away from the classics, she has been involved with a number of Papp's Shakespeare productions, including "Hamlet," "A Midsummer Night's Dream," "As You Like It," "Henry V," and "Richard III." Among Kathleen's other off-Broadway credits: "Castaways," and two Obie award winning performances in "The Beggar's Opera" and "Tower of Evil." The actress has also starred in such films as "The Group," "Petulia," "The Mephisto Waltz," "Without a Trace," "I'm Dancing as Fast as I Can," "The Sea Gull," and "The End of August." In addition to her work on such daytime dramas as "Another World," "Young Dr. Malone," and "Ryan's Hope," Kathleen has guest starred on "Kojak," "Nurse," "Toma," "The Secrets of Midland Heights," and portrayed the title role of the PBS production, "Edith Wharton." She has also co-starred with Tony Curtis and Susan Lucci in the television movie, "Mafia Princess." Since joining the cast of "As the World Turns" in 1985, she has been nominated for three daytime Emmys as Best Supporting Actress, taking home the award in 1990. Kathleen is married to Jerry Senter, and together they have one daughter. Kathleen and her husband opened the restaurant The Blue Hen, which closed after two years. When not on stage or in front of a camera, Kathleen enjoys gardening and weaving. She and her family live in a suburb of New York City.

TOM WIGGIN

Born: July 6 in New York, New York
Marital Status: married to Amy Forte, one daughter
Height: 6' **Eyes:** blue **Hair:** light brown
Education: Columbia University; Royal Academy of
Dramatic Art
Interests: writing, music, softball, tennis

Daytime Dramas: "Texas," Joe Foster, 1981; **"Another World,"** Gil Fenton, 1983-1984; **"As the World Turns,"** Kirk Anderson, 1988-

Previously seen on "Texas" and "Another World," Tom Wiggin has portrayed Kirk Anderson on "As the World Turns" since May of 1988. A New York City native, Wiggin was raised in Alexandria, Virginia, where he began acting in community theater at a young age, continuing this trend during his years at St. Paul's Prep School in Concord, New Hampshire. After enrolling at Columbia University, Wiggin decided to put aside his dream of playing professional baseball and concentrate fully on acting. He then studied with such teachers as Aaron Frankel and Harold Clurman, as well as training at the Royal Academy of Dramatic Arts in London. Wiggin's first big break came when he won the role of Danny in the national touring company of "Grease" in 1978, following which he continued with the role for ten months on Broadway. His additional theater credits include, "Class Enemy," "The Foreigner," "Breakfast With Less and Bess," "Livin' Dolls," and as a chorus member in a production of "Oedipus Rex," starring James Earl Jones, presented at the St. John the Divine Cathedral in New York. On television, Wiggin was a regular on the series, "Breaking Away," and was additionally seen on "Hotel" and in the television movie, "Izzy and Moe," with Art Carney and Jackie Gleason. A resident of New York City, Wiggin is married to Amy Forte, a psychologist, with whom he has one daughter. In his spare time he enjoys writing, softball, tennis, and live music.

KATE WILKINSON

Born: October 25 in San Francisco, California
Marital Status: widowed, three sons, John, Michael and
Jeffrey
Height: 5' 4" **Eyes:** hazel **Hair:** gray
Education: San Jose State College
Interests: theater, museums, piano

Daytime Dramas: "Love of Life," 1959; **"Love is a Many Splendored Thing,"** Mother Irene, 1971; **"Guiding Light,"** Viola Stapleton, 1976-1980; **"Another World,"** Clara Hudson, 1987-1988; **"One Life to Live,"** 1988

A daytime veteran, Kate Wilkinson has managed to successfully divide her career between television and the stage. Her first soap opera role was on "Love of Life," in 1959, and since then she has gone on to star on "Love is a Many Splendored Thing," "Guiding Light," "Another World," and "One Life to Live." Born on October 25, in San Francisco, California, Wilkinson's family also includes her brother John, a doctor, and her sister, Beverly Campbell, an opera singer with the San Francisco Opera. After attending San Jose State College, Wilkinson moved to New York City to continue her acting training, eventually landing stage roles. Over the years she has since appeared on Broadway in "The Man Who Came to Dinner," "Man and Superman," "The Last of Mrs. Lincoln," "Hedda Gabler," "A Doll's House," "Frankenstein," and "Over Here." In addition, Ms. Wilkinson has performed in countless off-Broadway and regional productions, among them "Much Ado About Nothing," "Steel Magnolias," "Close of Play," "The Contractor," "The Real Inspector Hound," "Ernest in Love," "Lumiere," "Suddenly Last Summer," "Major Barbara," "Three Sisters," "The Importance of Being Earnest," "Joe Egg," "Our Town," "The Heiress," "The Whales of August," "The Glass Menagerie," and "Romeo and Juliet." Becoming active behind the scenes, Kate is now at work co-producing a new play. She recently co-starred in the feature film "See You in the Morning," and has appeared on television on "Kate and Allie," "Law and Order," "Beyond the Horizon," "The Adams Chronicles," and "A Mistaken Charity," a PBS American Playhouse presentation. A New York City resident, Kate was married for forty eight years to the late Bruce Wilkinson, with whom she had three sons, John, Michael, and Jeffrey. The actress, donates her time and efforts to the Unitarian Church program which brings food to the homebound, and in the past has worked for the Actors Federal Credit Union. In her spare time Kate enjoys museums, playing the piano, and going to the theater.

WALT WILLEY

Born: January 26, 1951 in Ottawa, Illinois
Marital Status: divorced
Height: 6' 3"   **Eyes:** blue   **Hair:** blond
Education: Southern Illinois University
Interests: art, computerized cartoons, scuba diving, snorkeling
Awards: 1992 People's Choice Award nomination for Favorite Daytime Male Performer

Daytime Dramas: "Ryan's Hope," Jack Novak, 1986-1987; **"Another World,"** James LaRusso; **"All My Children,"** Jackson Montgomery, 1988-

An artist in every sense of the word, Walt Willey has enjoyed success as an actor, sculptor, comedian, and cartoonist. Born January 26 in Ottowa, Illinois, Walt remains very close to his parents. His father was a pitcher for the St. Louis Cardinal's farm team, until an injury ended his chances for a professional career. Willey attended Southern Illinois University majoring in art. Although he loved the theater, after graduating college, Willey chose to enter the business world. While working as the director of sales for a men's clothing line, he heard about auditions for a show at his alma mater. He auditioned, won the part and eight shows later, at 30 years old, Willey moved to New York to pursue a career as an actor. His first role in fact, was as an extra at Foxy's Bar on "All My Children." Since then he has continued his work on daytime drama in more prominent roles, as well as working in theater. His theater credits include the off-Broadway production of "Frankenstein," "Cyrano de Bergerac," "Five Finger Exercise," and most recently, in the 1992 Valley Forge and Westbury Music Fair productions of "Barefoot in the Park." Willey can also be seen across the country in comedy clubs where he performs his stand up routine. He has also designed a tee shirt line with five of his cartoons, that are sold in the comedy clubs where he performs as well as selected department stores. Willey maintains his interests in art, working on line drawings for greeting cards and computerized cartoons. He also enjoys scuba diving and snorkeling.

STEPHANIE WILLIAMS

Born: February 4 in St. Louis, Missouri
Marital Status: single
Height: 5' 6" **Eyes:** brown **Hair:** brown
Education: Webster College; University of Missouri-Kansas City
Interests: dance, tennis, writing songs, script and educational programs

Daytime Dramas: "The Young and the Restless," Amy Lewis, 1982-1988, 1990; **"General Hospital,"** Dr. Simone Hardy, 1989-

An actress/singer/dancer/choreographer/writer, Stephanie Williams is a performer who believes in combining entertainment with education. Best known to daytime audiences for two popular roles, Amy Lewis on "Young and the Restless," and Dr. Simone Hardy on "General Hospital," Ms. Williams has also flexed her talents in feature films and on stage. Born and raised in St. Louis, Missouri the only girl of four children, today Stephanie's father is retired, her mother is a Brachy therapy technologist in Radiation Oncology. Stephanie attended University City High School, where she appeared in many school productions and was voted homecoming queen. After graduation she received subsequent dance scholarships to Webster College and the University of Missouri-Kansas City, continuing her drama, dance, and voice training. She made her professional debut with the St.Louis Municipal Opera, and this was followed by additional performances at Kansas City's Starlight Theatre. Her big break came during a trip to New York City, where she not only earned a place with the Alvin Ailey American Dance Theatre, but also landed a role in the off-Broadway production of "Take it from the Top," written by Ossie Davis and Ruby Dee. Although she originally intended to visit New York for two weeks, Stephanie ended up living in Manhattan full time, eventually landing her first role on Broadway in "West Side Story." An immensely popular production, Williams and the rest of the cast performed at The White House and at the 1980 Tony Awards. No stranger to award shows, Stephanie has additionally been seen dancing on such telecasts as "The Grammys," "The American Music Awards," and "The Black Achievement Awards." After landing her first film role in "The Fan," with Lauren Bacall, Stephanie relocated to Hollywood, where she soon became a regular dancer, and co-choreographer on the t.v. series "Fame." Eventually she worked her way up to a dramatic role, playing Stephanie Harrison an aspiring ballerina and girlfriend of Leroy. Since then she has appeared on several television programs, including "Midnight Caller," "A Different World," "Dynasty," "Diff'rent Strokes," "The Edge of Night," and "Robert Townsend and His Partners in Crime," for which she also served as choreographer. She has taken on similar duties for the Jamaica Boys' video "It's That Lovin' Feeling," while her other music video credits include James Ingram's "I Wanna Come Back," "Lionel Ritchie's "Running with the Night," and O'Bryan's "Love Light." Along with "The Fan," Ms. Williams has co-starred in the feature films "Back to the Future 2" and "Times Square." She has continued to work in the theater as well, appearing in such productions as "Ceremonies In Dark Old Men," "A Woman's Choice," "American Tap Show," "Carousel," "Oklahoma," "Damn Yankees," and "The Choice is Yours." In addition, she is in pre-production on "Images," a musical love story she has written. Equally active behind the scenes, Stephanie has her own production company, Sweet Productions, Inc., for which she has very specific goals, namely to entertain as well as educate. (thus the name of the company which is an anagram for Stephanie Williams Educational & Entertainment Theatrics) As part of this objective, she works with a youth support group at the Los Angeles Challengers Boys and Girls Club. The actress, along with several of her former "Young and the Restless" cast mates, is also part of "Stars Behind Bars," an outreach program at the Chino Penitentiary. Hoping to help others, the actress frequently conducts workshops and lectures on self-esteem, self awareness, and the power of self control. In her spare time, Stephanie, who is single, enjoys golf, tennis, and writing.

TONYA LEE WILLIAMS

Born: July 12 in England
Marital Status: single
Eyes: brown   **Hair:** brown
Education: Ryerson Theatre School
Interests: restoring homes, swimming, hiking, reading, tennis

Daytime Dramas: "Generations," Linda;
"The Young and the Restless," Dr. Olivia Barber

Born on July 12 in England, Tonya Maxine Williams grew up in England, Kingston, Jamaica, and Oshawa, Canada. As a result, today she is a dual citizen of Canada and Great Britain. The name change came as a result of the Screen Actors Guild union which lists a member named Tanya Williams. SAG told Tonya that her name was too similar to Tanya's and she should change hers to avoid confusion. Tonya Maxine Williams was too long for a professional name, hence Lee. Always interested in performing, and encouraged by her mother, a nurse, Williams began taking ballet lessons at the age of three, followed by piano lessons two years later, and soon after, she studied voice, violin, and tenor saxophone. By the time she was in high school, she was working as a model, but she began to concentrate on acting after she enrolled in Ryerson, a leading Canadian theater school. Williams made her television debut as the host of "Polka Dot Door," the Canadian equivalent of "Sesame Street," and following this she worked as a reporter on the show, "Welcome to My World." Today, American t.v. fans know her best as Dr. Olivia Barber on "The Young and the Restless," though she originally auditioned for the part of Drucilla. She has additionally been seen on daytime as Linda on "Generations." Williams' other t.v. credits include recurring roles on "Time of Your Life" and "Check it Out," and guest roles on "Falcon Crest," "Hill Street Blues," "T&T," "Matlock," "A Peaceable Kingdom," and the television films, "The Liberators" and "A Very Brady Christmas." On the big screen, the actress has co-starred in "Easy Prey," "Spaced Invaders," "Hearts of Fire," and "Separate Vacations." While living in Toronto, Ms. Williams donates her time as the spokesperson for the Cystic Fibrosis Foundation, and recently took a position on the Board of Directors of the International Medical and Educational Foundation, an organization that strives to bring medical care to underprivileged people throughout the world. Now living in Los Angeles, Williams, who is single, lists amongst her interests, dinner parties, tennis, swimming, hiking, horseback riding, walking, reading (particularly Agatha Christie novels), and playing with her dog, Berkeley. However, her most lucrative hobby is buying and restoring real estate. At present, she is the proud owner of three houses and a condo.

VINCE WILLIAMS

Born: July 11 in Natchitoches, Louisiana
Marital Status: married to Kathryn Williams, one son, Heru, born May 1988
Height: 6' 5 **Eyes:** hazel **Hair:** brown
Education: Northwestern University of Louisiana, B.A.; Florida State University, M.F.A.
Interests: music, writing
Awards: Irene Ryan Award for "Home"

Daytime Dramas: "Loving," Joe Mason; **"As the World Turns,"** Lemar Griffin; **"Guiding Light,"** Hampton Speakes, 1989-

Daytime star, Shakespearean actor, jazz musician, and budding playwright, Vince Williams is clearly not a man of limited talent. Born and raised in Natchitoches, Louisiana, Williams was a child musical prodigy, playing several instruments and earning state honors for his abilities in both jazz and classical music. He made his professional debut while only a freshman in high school. In addition Williams also excelled as a runner, earning All American status in the quarter mile. Not surprisingly he was offered both music and athletic scholarships, eventually deciding on Northwestern State University of Louisiana. After graduation Williams studied with Alvin Baptist at the Southern Jazz Institute, but soon returned to Northwestern where, following the advice of his mother and teachers, he enrolled as a drama student. After winning the prestigious Irene Ryan Award (given annually to a college student for excellence in acting) for his debut stage performance as Cephus in "Home," Williams transferred to the Florida State University Conservatory of Professional Actor Training. There his work attracted the attention of Joseph Papp, and after successfully auditioning he was hired by Estelle Parsons as a member of the New York Shakespeare Festival Company. Among the plays in which Williams performed: "As You Like It" and "Romeo and Juliet." His other stage work includes roles in both the San Francisco and Broadway productions of "Fences," with James Earl Jones and Billy Dee Williams. Williams has also performed in "Playboy of the West Indies," and helped director Josh Logan develop the musical "Huck and Jim," in which Williams played the latter role. Williams is the first African-American performer in Guiding Light's 30 year history to become a contract player. Along with his work on "Guiding Light," Williams daytime drama credits include "As the World Turns," as Lemar Griffin, and "Loving," as Joe Mason. Other credits include the television film "Gideon Oliver," with Louis Gossett Jr., as well as numerous national commercials. Apart from his acting, he has written a play about jazz legend John Coltrane called, "Silent Prophet." Currently Williams and his band, The Company of One, is working on an album. The band has developed a musical form, "Afrazz," a combination of Latin, Haitian, and African rhythms with jazz overtones. Williams and his wife, Kathryn, have one son, Heru Hampdyn Behm-Leon Williams IV born in May of 1988. Although it would seem that the Hampdyn in his son's name was a reference to Williams "Guiding Light" character, it is in fact a tribute to Kathryn's father, also named Hampton.

WILLIAM WINTERSOLE

Hair: grey
Education: University of California at Los Angeles, M.A.;
University of Southern California, post graduate studies
Interests: theatre, writing
Awards: Best Actor Awards from USC and UCLA

Daytime Dramas: "The Young and the Restless,"
Mitchell Sherman

Over the course of his many decades in show business, William Wintersole has proven himself the consummate character actor, tackling widely divergent roles on stage, film, and on over two hundred prime time television programs. To daytime fans, however, he is sure to be recognized as Mitchell Sherman on "The Young and the Restless," one of the finest legal minds in Genoa City. The actor has been playing the role for close to fifteen years. Wintersole got his start after receiving his M.A. in theater form UCLA, following which he did post graduate work in communications at USC. Among the hundreds of television programs on which he has appeared: "Star Trek," "Mission Impossible," "Gunsmoke," and "Sara," while his film credits include a variety of roles in such films as "Leadbelly," "Valley of the Dolls," and "Coma." On stage he has performed in the debut production of "The Deputy," "What the Wine Sellers Buy," and in several Chekhov plays. He also earned Best Actor Awards at UCLA and USC for his work in "Cyrano " and "Petruchio." Branching out from acting, Wintersole spent two years on the faculty on the Board fo Directors for the Screen Actors Guild

KAREN WITTER

Born: December 13 in Long Beach, California
Marital Status: single
Height: 5' 6" **Eyes:** blue **Hair:** blond
Education: University of California at Irvine; University of Hawaii
Interests: sailing, painting

Daytime Dramas: "One Life to Live," Tina Lord Roberts, 1990-

Karen Witter accomplished the near impossible when she successfully took over the role of Tina Roberts from former daytime star Andrea Evans. Yet in a short time Karen managed to bring her unique qualities to the part, and in doing so she made it her own. Karen grew up in Long Beach, California, where her father is a school administrator, and her mother a substitute teacher. From an early age she had an adventurous spirit that could not be quelled. In fact, this is one actress whose real life seems to be just as exciting as the life of any soap opera character. Granted, Karen has never had an evil twin, been abducted by aliens, or had a nagging case of amnesia, at least not as far as she can recall, but at 15 she spent the summer building a school house in Mexico, and another summer she lived and worked on a ranch in Montana. To overcome her fear of water, she spent two weeks sailing to Hawaii (and ended up living on the boat for two years while attending college). She has been on safari in Africa, and she has worked as a champagne serving stewardess on a hot air balloon (a job to help offset her college tuition), as well as an interpreter for three deaf physic students. Along with all of these, Karen still managed to attend school, first at the University of California at Irvine, and then at the University of Hawaii, where she majored in premed and psychophysiology. After college she found work as a model, but quickly made the switch to acting, guest starring on such shows as "Cheers," "Matt Houston," "Trapper John M.D.," and "Mike Hammer." Karen's feature films include "The Vineyard," "The Perfect Match," "Dangerously Close," "Midnight" and the soon to be released, "Popcorn," starring Tony Roberts. In 1992 Karen took a vacation in France to pursue a dream, and enrolled in a trapeze school outside of Paris. After her two week class, she returned to New York, and asked the international troupe, Cirque du Soleil if she could fly with them for one night; they said yes and for one performance Karen Witter became a trapeze artist. In her spare time Karen enjoys gymnastics, sailing, painting and reading.

SHERILYN WOLTER

Born: November 30 in Clarksburg, West Virginia
Marital Status: single
Height: 5' 7"   **Eyes:** blue   **Hair:** brown
Education: three years of college
Interests: theater, mountain climbing, writing, swimming, tennis
Awards: 1983 Soap Opera Digest, Exciting New Actress Award; 1982 Best Actress of the Year, Glendale Center Theatre

Daytime Dramas: "General Hospital," Celia Quartermaine, 1983-1987; **"Santa Barbara,"** Elena Nikolas, 1988-1989

A popular daytime actress, Sherilyn Wolter made her soap opera debut in 1983 as Celia Quartermaine on "General Hospital." Named the Most Exciting New Actress of that year by Soap Opera Digest, she remained with the role for the next four years, following which she began a two year stint portraying Elena Nickolas on "Santa Barbara." Born on November 30, in Clarksburg, West Virginia, where her father was a psychologist, her mother a teacher, Sherilyn attended college for three years before beginning her professional acting career. Along with daytime, Ms. Wolter co-starred on the prime time series "B.J. and the Bear," as well as making guest appearances on such shows as "My Sister Sam," "Matlock," "The Devlin Connection," "Who's the Boss?," "Father Dowling Mysteries," and "Baywatch." She is presently at work on the mini-series, "Secrets." On the big screen Sherilyn has been seen in "Eyewitness to Murder." All the while she has continued to work steadily on stage, including roles in "King Lear," "Three Sisters," "Taming of the Shrew," and "Romantic Comedy." In 1982 she received the Best Actress of the Year Award from the Glendale Center Theatre. A resident of Los Angeles, Sherilyn, who is single, donates her time to the Special Olympics, and in addition, is a volunteer at a residential home for the psychologically handicapped. In her spare time, she enjoys mountain climbing, going to the theater, hiking, tennis, swimming, volleyball, reading, and writing short stories and poetry.

ERIC WOODALL

Born: September 3 in Raleigh, North Carolina
Marital Status: single
Height: 6' 2" **Eyes:** hazel **Hair:** light brown
Education: Carnegie Mellon University, Bachelor's Degree
Interests: movies, reading

Daytime Dramas: "Loving," Matthew Ford, 1991-1992;
"As the World Turns," 1992-

Now on "As the World Turns," Eric Woodall landed his first television role, as Matthew Ford on "Loving," less than two weeks after graduating with honors from Carnegie Mellon University. Born on September 3 in Raleigh, North Carolina, Woodall was raised in the towns of Raleigh and Benson. He began acting at the age of nine, making his first stage performance as one of the Von Trapp children in a local production of "The Sound of Music." Before studying drama at college, he spent summers at the North Carolina School for the Arts, and has over the years appeared in such stage productions as "Our Town," "Camelot," "Dreamgirls," "The Mystery of Edwin Drood," "Jesus Christ Superstar," "As Is," and "Romeo and Juliet." In his spare time, the actor enjoys reading, going to the movies, running, and lifting weights.

ROBERT S. WOODS

Born: March 13 in Maywood, California
Marital Status: married to Loyita Chapel Woods in 1985, one son, Tanner, born November 1990
Height: 5' 11" **Eyes:** blue **Hair:** brown
Education: California State College at Long Beach, Bachelor's Degree
Interests: his family
Awards: 1993 Daytime Emmy Award for Best Actor; nominated for Daytime Emmy for Best Actor, 1985 (both for "One Life to Live")

Daytime Dramas: "One Life to Live," Bo Buchanan, 1979-1985; **"Days of Our Lives,"** Paul Stewart, 1986-1987; **"One Life to Live,"** Bo Buchanan, 1988-

As Bo Buchanan on "One Life to Live, Robert S. Woods brings to the role a diversity which is uniquely his own. Woods has starred on two popular daytime dramas, "Days of Our Lives," and as Bo Buchanan on "One Life to Live." For the latter, Woods was awarded an Emmy in 1983, and nominated again in 1985. Born the youngest of six children in Maywood, California, and raised in the Long Beach area, Woods always knew that he would become an actor. However before his career could start, Bob dropped out of college and was drafted, serving fifteen months as a Green Beret in Vietnam. (His Vietnam experience served as the inspiration for his character's own war stories) He remains an active member of the New York's Vietnam Veterans Commission, which sponsors programs to benefit those who served. After leaving the army, Woods' next stop was California State College at Long Beach, where he majored in broadcasting. In July 1973 Bob married longtime girlfriend Loyita Chapel. Loyita appeared briefly in "One Life to Live" during the Old West storyline, portraying Blaize Buchanan, Bo's great great grandmother. Upon graduation he followed his wife, who was singing at Disneyland, and took a parttime job there. Bob took up his acting training, studying at the Film Actors Workshop, The James Best Theater Center, and the Director Lab. After this training, Woods appeared in numerous television productions, among these were the recurring roles as Dr. David Spencer in "The Waltons" and Lt. Bob King in "Project UFO." He also guest starred in "Newhart," and "Family," as well as appearing in the television films "Just a Little Inconvenience," "Fantasies," "Police Story," "The Night They Took Miss Beautiful," and "Chase." In 1979, Bob won the role of Bo Buchanan and moved to New York. His marriage suffered from the bi-coastal separation and he and Loyita divorced in 1981. But, as if their real life paralleled that of a soap opera, after two years of not speaking they realized their love had never died and in 1985 they remarried. Bob left "One Life to Live" in 1985 , and returned to the west coast to further his career. During his hiatus from daytime, (until 1988) Bob appeared in Herman Wouk's "War and Remembrance," in which he portrayed Commander Eugene Lindsey as well as the television movie, "Carly's Web." He also appeared on stage in "Stitch and Eubie," which won the Drama-Louge Critics' Award and was in the tv pilot, "Changing Patterns." On the big screen, Woods has co-starred in "The China Syndrome," and "Big Wednesday." Back in New York, Bob and his wife were expecting twins in February 1990. Ten weeks early, Loyita went into premature labor and delivered twins, Dylan and Tanner. Dylan, suffering severe birth defects, survived only one month. Tanner grew stronger and after two months in the hospital, he went home with his parents. Bob, like many other daytime actors finds soap operas a perfect medium to satisfy his career goals, as well as give him what's most important - time for his family.

SHARON WYATT

Born: February 13 in Lebanon, Tennessee
Marital Status: single
Height: 5' 9" **Eyes:** blue **Hair:** blond
Education: University of Tennessee
Interests: tennis, skiing, cooking, reading, rollerskating, dancing, horseback riding
Awards: 1983 Soap Opera Award, Favorite Supporting Actress

Daytime Dramas: "General Hospital," Tiffany Hill Donely, 1981-1983; 1986-

As Tiffany on "General Hospital," Sharon Wyatt has created one of daytime drama's most memorable characters. Sharon was born in Lebanon, Tennessee, and grew up in nearby Carthage. From an early age she knew that she wanted to be an actress and wasted no time getting started. She began dancing lessons at the age of two, which were shortly followed by piano lessons, and even performances on her front porch. She maintained this enthusiasm through her years at Smith County High School and on to the University of Tennessee in Knoxville, where she not only was active in the drama department, but played alto saxophone in the school band as well. (she also plays the piano, guitar and organ) After leaving school she continued her study of acting with some of the world's premier teachers, among them Lee Strasberg, Kenneth McMillan, and Jose Quintero. Along with her training, Sharon had an assortment of jobs, including nightclub singer, but eventually her big break came with a role in "A Funny Thing Happened on the Way to the Forum." Since then she has appeared in such stage productions as "Triplet Collection," "The Sound of Music,"

"The Contrast," "Sweet Charity," and most recently "Women of Manhattan." On television, since her debut as a prostitute on the show "Nashville 99," Sharon has been guest starred on "Hotel," and "Three's A Crowd," and in the television movies "Final Jeopardy" and "Roses Are For the Rich." Her feature films include "Commando," with Arnold Schwarzenegger, "Armed and Dangerous," "Class of 1999," and the lead in "Perfection," the film adaptation of the Tom Robbins novel, "Even Cowgirls Get the Blues." Sharon introduced the character of Tiffany Wells to "General Hospital" fans in 1981, and continued to play the role for the next two years. She then took a hiatus, but returned to the show in 1986. In her spare time Sharon, who now resides in the San Fernando Valley area of Los Angeles, enjoys dancing, skiing, tennis, reading, horseback riding, and cooking.

VICTORIA WYNDHAM

Born: May 22 in Chicago, Illinois
Eyes: brown   **Hair**: brown
Education: Bennett College
Interests: art, music
Awards: 1978 Soap Opera Award for Favorite Actress; nominated for Best Actress Daytime Emmys, 1978, 1979

Daytime Dramas: "Guiding Light," Charlotte Waring Bauer, 1967-1970; **"Another World,"** Rachel Davis Cory, 1972-

Since the 1972 debut of "Another World," Victoria Wyndham has faithfully portrayed Rachel Davis Cory, a role that has earned the actress two daytime Emmy nominations for Best Actress. Born in Chicago on May 22nd, and raised in Westport, Connecticut, Wyndham is the daughter of actor Ralph Camargo, who at one time co-starred with Victoria's mother, also an actress, on the radio version of "Guiding Light." Over the course of her career, Wyndham has proven herself to be an accomplished stage actress, as well as a writer and director. On Broadway, she has co-starred in "Fiddler on the Roof," with Bette Midler, and also teamed with Lily Tomlin in a satirical improvisational revue, presented at the New York club, Upstairs at the Downstairs. Prior to joining the cast of "Another World," Wyndham spent three years as Charlotte Waring Bauer on "Guiding Light." While she has spent the last twenty years as Rachel Davis Cory, the actress has also found the time to manage several rock and roll bands, direct a video for a punk rock dance troupe, write for television and film, and co-write a libretto for a story entitled "Winter Dreams," which was performed by the Pennsylvania Ballet. In addition, Ms. Wyndham is an accomplished artist and sculptor.

JOHN J. YORK

Born: December 10 in Chicago, Illinois
Marital Status: married to Vicki York in August 1986,
one daughter, Schyler
Height: 5' 11"   **Eyes:** green   **Hair:** light brown
Education: University of Whitewater, two years; training with
Edward Kaye Martin
Interests: gardening, biking
Awards: 1992 Soap Opera Award nomination for Outstanding
Male Newcomer

Daytime Dramas: **"General Hospital, "** Mac Scorpio, 1990-

"It's always darkest before the dawn" is a phrase perfectly suited to the career of John J. York. After starring in the series "Werewolf," York seemed to be poised for greater success; yet inexplicably the handsome young actor found himself in a two year professional drought. During this difficult period the only acting role York was able to land was in an educational film on door-to-door salesmanship. With his wife pregnant, bills mounting, and his career at a virtual standstill, York seemed to be heading into dangerous waters. Then out of nowhere came the role of Malcolm "Mac" Scorpio on "General Hospital." York was working at a restaurant called The Cheesecake Factory when he heard that an actor was needed for the pivotal role of Robert Scorpio's brother. Determined to get the job, York immediately began working on an Australian accent, listening to language tapes and even renting "Crocodile Dundee." His dedication paid off and shortly before the birth of his daughter he made his first appearance on "General Hospital." He beat out Paul Satterfield, Jr. for the role, but the producers were so impressed with Paul that they created the role of Paul Hornsby specifically for him. Far from Australia, York was born to Thomas and Donna on December 10, the fourth out of six children. He was raised on the south side of Chicago, where he attended St. Rita's Grammar School and Brother Rice High School. While a student, York excelled in both football and baseball, as well as developing an interest in film. He was particularly partial to war movies and initially considered a career behind the camera. After graduation he enrolled as a marketing major at the University of Whitewater in Wisconsin, but after two years at college, York decided that it was time to give all he had to acting. He returned to Chicago where he began studying with Edward Kaye-Martin, making his professional debut at the Wisdom Bridge Theatre in "Picnic." His other stage credits include: "Loss of Roses," "Career," and "The Golden Boy." In 1983, John moved to Los Angeles with only $120 in his pocket, however, he quickly found work in both television and movies. Along with his role on "Werewolf" he made guest appearances on "Family Ties," "21 Jump Street," "Murder, She Wrote," "Hunter," and "Newhart." He has been seen on the big screen in such films as "Steel and Lace," "House of the Rising Sun," "The Bear," a film about legendary football coach Bear Bryant, and "Chattanooga Choo Choo." It was on the set of this last film that York met his future wife, Vicki, a casting director on the film. The couple were married in 1986 and now have one daughter, Schyler Nicole born on February 9, 1991. York is a devoted family man and enjoys bicycling and gardening. He is also the proud owner of two purebred Himalayan cats, Smokey and Alex.

COREY YOUNG

Born: March 27 in Long Beach, California
Marital Status: married to actress Roberta Leighton on
August 20, 1988
Height: 5' 11" **Eyes:** green **Hair:** brown
Education: Orange Coast College, Lee Strasberg Institute
Interests: dirt biking, scuba diving, golf, football, softball

Daytime Dramas: "General Hospital," Dr. Walt Benson

Originally hired for only a recurring role, Corey Young made such an impression on the "General Hospital" fans, that the actor was offered a full time contract only a brief time later. Born in Long Beach, California, on March 27, Young was raised by his father, Robert (not the actor) and his mother, Janys, a former Rockette. During his years in Long Beach, Corey lived on the same street as his future "General Hospital" castmate David Wallace, although the two did not know each other. After moving to Anaheim, Young attended Katella High School, where he played football and was the co-captain of the wrestling team. He first became interested in acting while at Orange Coast College, where he appeared in scores of school and regional productions, some of which he directed. After moving to New York and studying with Stella Adler and at the Lee Strasberg Institute, Young toured the country in "They Went Thataway," before settling in Hollywood. He appeared in several commercials which were seen in Europe before landing roles on such programs as "Capitol," "Dynasty," and "Knots Landing." Also a writer, Young has scripted a television pilot and several romance novels. He and his wife, actress Roberta Leighton, are co-writing a movie of the week and together, have written for network series. Away from acting and writing, the actor enjoys scuba diving, dirt biking, golf, football, and softball.

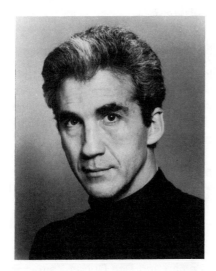

MICHAEL ZASLOW

Born: November 1, 1942 in Inglewood, California
Marital Status: married to writer Susan Hufford, two
daughters, Marika and Helena
Eyes: brown **Hair:** salt & pepper
Education: UCLA, Phi Beta Kappa
Interests: music, theater
Awards: nominated for Daytime Emmy, Outstanding Leading
 Actor, 1991; 1992 Soap Opera Award, Outstanding Villain

Daytime Dramas: "Love is a Many Splendored Thing,"
Dr. Peter Chernak, 1970; **"Search for Tomorrow,"** Dick Hart,
1970-1971; **"Guiding Light,"** Roger Thorpe, 1971-1980;
"One Life to Live," David Renaldi, 1983-1986; **"Guiding
Light,"** 1989-

Through the 1970's, and now again in the nineties, Michael Zaslow has been the driving force behind one of daytime's great villains, Roger Thorpe on "Guiding Light." During his run, the actor has been recognized with a Soap Opera Award for Outstanding Villain and a Daytime Emmy nomination for Outstanding Lead Actor. Born on November 1, 1942, in Inglewood, California, Zaslow grew up in Chicago, New York, and Los Angeles, eventually enrolling at UCLA as a political science major. During college, Michael was also active in the school theater, and even took some time off to tour the Orient in a USO production of "Carousel," in which he appeared as Billy Bigelow. After graduating Phi Beta Kappa, Michael continued his theatrical training in both New York and Los Angeles. His first professional role found him displaying his baritone voice with the Los Angeles Civic Light Opera Company. This was soon followed by a string of television appearances on such shows as "Star Trek," "Slattery's People," "Custer," "Long, Hot Summer," and "Barnaby Jones." To this day the actor is recognized by "trekkies" for his guest role on "Star Trek." From 1971 to 1980, Zaslow inhabited the role of Roger Thorpe, but after nine years decided to leave the show to pursue theater work. He made his Broadway debut in "There's a Girl in My Soup,"a production he remained with during the national tour. Zaslow's additional theater credits include the Broadway production of "Fiddler on the Roof," "Cat on a Hot Tin Roof," "Boccaccio," and "Onward Victoria," while he has also been seen in "Henry IV Part One ," "Men in the Kitchen," "Taking Steps," "D," "Master Class," "Macbeth," "The Petrified Forest," "Sarah and Abraham," and "She Loves Me." On the big screen, the actor has co-starred in two films, "You Light Up My Life" and "Meteor." Along with "Guiding Light," Michael has also been featured on "King's Crossing," "One Life to Live," "Love is a Many Splendored Thing," and "Search for Tomorrow," and has flexed his writing talents behind the scenes for "Another World." In 1989, the actor made his triumphant return to "Guiding Light." Zaslow has been married to actress/writer Susan Hufford for more than fifteen years, and the couple live in New York City with their two adopted Korean daughters, Marika (9/24/82) and Helena (10/23/85). In his spare time, Michael enjoys writing songs and playing the piano, often accompanying his two daughters, both of whom are accomplished violinists.

JACKLYN ZEMAN

Born: March 6 in Englewood, New Jersey
Marital Status: married to Glenn Gorden, February 14, 1988, two daughters, Cassidy Zee, 1990, and Lacey Rose, July 1992
Height: 5' 4" **Eyes:** brown **Hair:** red
Education: New York University
Interests: family, children, animal rights, cooking, exercising, swimming, water skiing
Awards: 1979 Soap Opera Award, Favorite Villainess; 1985 Hollywood Tribute to Soaps Favorite Actress Award; 1985 American Heart Association Les Etoiles de Coeur Award; 1987 National Ambassador - Where are the Children; Hollywood International Actress Award; nominated for 1981 Daytime Emmy as Best Supporting Actress

Daytime Dramas: "One Life to Live," Lana McClain, 1975-1977; **"General Hospital,"** Bobbie Spencer, 1977-1981, 1982-

A sixteen year daytime veteran, Jacklyn Zeman has also enjoyed success as an author, producer, and radio personality. Born in Englewood, New Jersey to IBM executive Richard Zeman and Rita Duhart Zeman Ruhlman, Jacklyn began studying classical ballet at the age of five, and entered the ranks of professionals at the age of thirteen when she became a member of the New Jersey Dance Company. Clearly no stranger to the fast track, she completed high school at fifteen and enrolled at New York University on a dance scholarship. While in college, Jacklyn supported herself through dancing and modelling assignments, before deciding that her future was as a daytime actress. With her usual determination she enrolled in a drama school specializing in television acting, and three months later Jacklyn landed the role of Lana McClain on "One Life to Live." She remained with the show for just one year before moving to Los Angeles to create the role of Bobbie Spencer on "General Hospital." While a constant daytime force for the past sixteen years, Jacklyn has also appeared on stage in "Come Blow Your Horn," "Barefoot in the Park," and "The Boyfriend," and has been featured in such films as "Young Doctors in Love," "National Lampoon's Class Reunion," "The Groove Tube," and "The Day the Music Died." When not portraying Port Charles' favorite nurse, Jacklyn's work has been seen on television in many different capacities. She most recently co-starred in the television movie, "Jury Duty: The Comedy," with Alan Thicke and Bronson Pinchot, as well as being a popular guest on talk and game shows. Jacklyn has also served as co-host of "The Home Show," on which she frequently appears with beauty and fitness advice. In addition, she has been featured in several segments of "Runaway" "Lifestyles of the Rich and Famous," and in 1989, co-hosted the Easter Seals Telethon in California. Another charity for which Jacklyn has devoted her time is the American Heart Association, who awarded her efforts with the Les Etoiles de Coeur Award. Jacklyn's first radio assignment was in 1984 as the host of the nationwide program "Soap Talk," an ABC Radio production, and has also been heard as a regular guest on Jamie Jamison's "Home Tips," advising listeners on beauty and fitness. Jacklyn synthesized much of this expertise into her 1986 book, "Beauty on the Go." Now establishing a career behind the camera as well, the busy Ms. Zeman recently formed her own production company, who's first endeavor was the 1988 play "Seacliff, California", which she not only produced but starred in. Her future plans include producing television shows as well as regional theater. Jacklyn, who resides in Studio City, was married on Valentine's Day in 1988, to real estate developer Glenn Gorden. The couple's first child, Cassidy Zee, was born in 1990, and their second daughter, Lacey Rose was born July 15, 1992.

RECEIVED TOO LATE FOR CLASSIFICATION

RICHARD COX

Born: in New York City
Marital Status: single
Height: 6' 1"   **Eyes:** brown   **Hair:** brown
Education: Yale University, B.A. in anthropology
Awards: Clarence Derwent Award for "Platinum;"
Tony and Drama Desk nominations for "Platinum;"
Los Angeles Critics Award for "Savage in Limbo"

Daytime Dramas: "Love of Life," Bobby Mackey;
"Loving," Giff Bowman, 1991-

An award winning actor, Richard Cox has brought his talents back to daytime as Giff Bowman on "Loving." A fifth generation New Yorker, Cox is also the fifth generation to live in the family Greenwich Village brownstone where he describes his childhood as "very happy." Raised an only child, Cox's mother is an actress and psychotherapist while his father is involved in real estate and community work. Beginning his acting career at the age of 8, Richard's career has spanned from Broadway to feature films to television and more. His theatre credits include the Broadway productions of "Richard II" with William Hurt, "Captain Brassbound's Conversation" with Ingrid Bergman, "The Sign in Sidney Brustein's Window" with Hal Linden, "Grease," and his award winning performance in "Platinum." Off-Broadway productions include: "Alice in Concert" with Meryl Streep, "Saved" with James Woods, and the Obie Award winning play, "Moonchildren." No stranger to prime time, Cox's television credits include guest starring roles on "Designing Women," "Star Trek: The Next Generation," "Murder She Wrote," "LA Law" and the acclaimed PBS miniseries, "The Adams Chronicles." His movie of the week credits include "Unholy Matrimony," "Shattered Innocence," and Showtime's, "Slow Burn."

SHARON GABET

Born: January 13, 1952 in Fort Wayne, Indiana
Marital Status: married to Larry Joshua, three children,
Jasmine, Maxwell, and Johanna
Height: 5' 5"   **Eyes:** hazel   **Hair:** red
Education: Purdue University, B.S.; Cornell University, M.F.A.
Interests: astrology, her children, metaphysics, travelling,
antiques
Awards: nominated for Outstanding Actress, 1981, 1983 for
"Edge of Night"

Daytime Dramas: "Edge of Night," Raven Alexander,
1977-1984; **"Another World,"** Brittany Ewing, 1985-1987;
"One Life to Live," Melinda Kramer, 1987-1989

Although not presently on a daytime drama, Sharon Gabet remains a favorite among soap opera fans. For seven years she starred as Raven of "The Edge of Night," and for her efforts was twice nominated for Outstanding Actress Emmys. Born on January 13 in Fort Wayne, Indiana, Sharon was one of nine children, which included five boys and four girls. Her father worked as the senior cost estimator for Magnavox, while Sharon's mother held various positions in the banking industry. Clearly a happy child, Gabet describes her early years as a "very simple secure childhood in a very small but sweet farm town-New Haven, Indiana. A dozen children on every corner with plenty of alleys to hide in and trees to climb." After receiving her B.S. from Purdue University, (Sharon is a registered nurse) she went on to study acting at Cornell University, from which she was awarded a Masters degree. Since starting her professional career, Sharon has enjoyed great success. Along with "Edge of Night," she has also had co-starring roles on "Another World" and "One Life to Live," as well as making guest appearances on "The Love Boat," starring in off-Broadway productions, and performing her own cabaret act. Sharon is now taking the time to raise her own family. She and her husband, Larry Joshua, have three children, Jasmine, Maxwell, and Johanna. She lists among her other interests, astrology, new age healing techniques, travel, antiques, and dance. For her fans who no doubt miss seeing her everyday on their favorite soap opera, they can take comfort in the fact that Sharon is planning on returning to television in the near future.

FINOLA HUGHES

Born: October 29 in London, England

Marital Status: married on July 4, 1992 to photographer/music video director, Russell Young

Height: 5' 5" **Eyes:** brown **Hair:** brown

Education: Norland Place; Art's Educational

Interests: ballet, swimming, aerobics, reading, movies

Awards: 1989 Soap Opera Update Most Valuable Player and 1989 Best of the Best, Daytime Actress Awards; 1990 Soap Opera Award for Outstanding Daytime Heroine; 1991 Daytime Emmy for Outstanding Lead Actress; 1991 Soap Opera Award for Outstanding Lead Actress; 1992 People's Choice Award nomination for Favorite Daytime Female Performer; 1992 Daytime Emmy nomination for Outstanding Lead Actress

Daytime Dramas: "General Hospital," Anna Devane Lavery Scorpio, 1985-1992

An accomplished dancer as well as actress, Finola Hughes has succeeded on the London stage, foreign films, American films, daytime, and now, prime time television. Born October 29 in London, England, Finola and her younger brother Sean, were raised in London and Cork, Ireland. As a child she attended Norland Place, an English private school. At the age of ten she began studying ballet at Art's Educational, a theatrical school, and by eleven was dancing at the Royal Opera House in Covent Garden. Finola continued to study ballet for the next seven years, after which she toured with the Northern Ballet Company. After finishing school she continued dancing, as well as appearing in films. In 1980 she created the role of Victoria, the white cat, in the original London production of "Cats." Finola remained with this role for a year, after which she performed in "Song and Dance," as well as appearing in the British film "The Nutcracker," with Joan Collins. Her performances in "Cats" and "Song and Dance" inspired Sylvester Stallone to cast Finola in her first American film, "Stayin' Alive," co-starring John Travolta. After this film she returned to London and starred in the BBC television series "The Hot Shoe Show." Finola's other television credits include roles in several mini-series, including "The Masters of Ballantrae," "The Prime of Miss Jean Brodie," "Grace Kennedy," and "The Monte Carlo Show." She was also featured in the Berlin based film "The Apple." Her second American feature film was

"Soapdish." Finola was only on for a cameo appearance and chose not to have her name in the credits. She has co-starred with Susan Lucci in two movies for television, "The Bride in Black," and "Secret Passions," as well as making three guest appearances on "L.A. Law." Since leaving "General Hospital," Finola can be seen in the prime time series, "Jack's Place," starring Hal Linden. On the personal side, Finola wed photographer/music video director, Russell Young on July 4, 1992. The two met at a party given by mutual friend, Ian Buchanan, (ex Duke Lavery, "General Hospital") and they married in London.

VERONICA REDD-FORREST

Born: August 8 in Washington, D.C.
Marital Status: married, one daughter, Marina from a previous marriage
Eyes: brown   **Hair:** black
Education: Interlochen Arts Academy; Julliard School
Interests: cooking, travelling, movies
Awards: New York Drama Desk Award for "Sirens"

Daytime Dramas: "The Young and the Restless,"
Mamie Johnson

Veronica Redd-Forrest was born on August 8 and raised in Washington, D.C. She attended the Washington Theater Club, the Interlochen Art Academy and the Julliard School. Veronica's professional debut was in the Manhattan Theatre Club production of "Sirens." For her performance she was honored with the Drama Desk Award. Her acting credits also includes the off-Broadway production of "The Believers" as well as stage productions of "Anthony and Cleopatra," "Sweet Charity," and "Ma Rainey's Black Bottom." She also starred in the Dramalogue Critics Award Winner, "The Trojan Woman" at the Los Angeles Actor's Theater. Veronica's feature films include roles in "The Five Heartbeats" and "Clean and Sober." Her television credits are many and range from t.v. movies to daytime drama. Veronica had a featured role in the made for t.v. movie "The Women of Brewster Place," and also in the miniseries "The Blue and the Gray." Her television appearances include, "Small Wonder," "Berengers," "What's Happening Now," "Johnnie Mae Gibson: FBI," "227," and "The Scarecrow and Mrs. King." On daytime, she portrays Mamie Johnson housekeeper for the Abbott family. Veronica recently remarried, and has a daughter, Marina, a filmmaker, from a previous marriage. Veronica enjoys the movies, cooking, travelling and meeting new people.

NETWORK ADDRESSES

All My Children
c/o ABC-TV
Audience Information
77 West 66th St.
New York, NY 10023

Another World
c/o NBC-TV
30 Rockefeller Plaza
New York, NY 10112

As The World Turns
c/o CBS-TV
51 West 52nd St.
New York, NY 10019

The Bold And The Beautiful
c/o CBS-TV
7800 Beverly Blvd.
Los Angeles, CA 90036

Days Of Our Lives
c/o NBC-TV
3000 West Alameda Ave.
Burbank, CA 91523

General Hospital
c/o ABC-TV
4151 Prospect Ave.
Hollywood, CA 90067

Guiding Light
c/o 51 West 52nd St.
New York, NY 10019

Loving
c/o ABC-TV
Audience Information
77 West 66th St.
New York, NY 10023

One Life To Live
c/o ABC-TV
77 West 66th St.
New York, NY 10023

Santa Barbara
c/o NBC-TV
3000 West Alameda Ave.
Burbank, CA 91523

The Young And The Restless
c/o CBS-TV
7800 Beverly Blvd.
Los Angeles, CA 90036

FAN CLUBS

Friends of All My Children
c/o Kathy Hudson
132 Ragsdale St.
Kingsport, TN 15205

Terry Alexander
c/o 56 West 66th St.
New York, NY 10023

Jed Allen Fan Club
c/o Nancy Parr
P.O. Box 4662
Anaheim, CA 92803

Another World Viewer Alliance
71 Berry St.
Pittsburgh, PA 15202

As the World Turns Fan Club
c/o Deanne Turco
212 Oriole Dr.
Montgomery, NY 12549

Jane Badler Society
c/o Brian Tosko
P.O. Box 1407
Tempe, AZ 85280-1407

Julia Barr
c/o Michelle Saint-Laurent
1410 York Ave., Apt. 4D
New York, NY 10021

Anthony Call
c/o Michele Saint-Laurent
1410 York Ave., Apt. 4D
New York, NY 10021

Leslie Charleson Fan Club
c/o Judy Chrismen
874 S. Orange St.
West Covina, CA 91790

Thom Christopher Fan Club
4307 N. Second Rd., Apt. 1
Arlington, VA 22203

Darlene Conley/Sally Spectra Gang
c/o Jodie Rizzuto
9 Metcalf St.
Medford, MA 02155

Colleen Dion Fan Club
P.O. Box 46609
Los Angeles, CA 90046

Nicolas Coster
Coster's Crew
3000 West Alameda Ave.
Burbank, CA 91523

Terry Davis
c/o OTML
500 S. Sepulveda, Ste. 500
Los Angeles, CA 90049

Ellen Dolan Fan Club
c/o Chip Capelli
P.O. Box 1162
Absecon, NJ 08201

Bobby Eakes Fan Club
c/o Jean Smith
7800 Beverly Blvd., Ste. 3371
Los Angeles, CA 90036

Patricia Elliott
c/o Michele Saint-Laurent
1410 York Ave., Apt. 4D
New York, NY 10021

Tom Eplin Fan Club
c/o Mindi Schulman
1500 Hornell Loop, Apt. 10E
Brooklyn, NY 11239

Alan Feinstein Fan Club
c/o Darlene Harff
3401 Knox Ave. North
Minneapolis, MN 55412

Michael Fox Fan Club
c/o Tommy Garrett
P.O. Box 215
New Canton, VA 23123

GH Questionnaire Club
656 Westbury Ave.
Westbury, NY 11590

Fans of General Hospital
c/o Barb Williams
390 Blairwood Circle South
Lake Worth, FL 33467

Ricky Paull Goldin Fan Club
c/o Carol Dickson Entertainment
1218 North Main St.
Glassboro, NJ 08028

Guiding Light Fan Club
c/o Sharon Kearns
104 St. George Dr.
Camillus, NY 13031-2147

Deidre Hall Fan Club
c/o Evelyn Reynolds
9570 Apricot
Alta Loma, CA 91701

Bob Hastings Fan Club
2212 Parkhaven Dr.
Plano, TX 75075

Rick Hearst Fan Club
c/o Debra Holdbrook
P.O. Box 93921
Hollywood, CA 90093

Finola Hughes Fan Club
c/o Michelle Saint- Laurent
1014 York Ave., Apt. 4D
New York, NY 10021

Fiona Hutchison
c/o Hutchison Ent. Ltd.
126 Hall Rd.
Aliquippa, PA 15001

Wallace Kurth & Judi Evans Support Group
c/o Ann Whitesell & Jerry D. Swink
5028 NW 60th St.
Oklahoma City, OK 73122

**The Lakeside Association
An Organization of Supporters for Mary Beth Evans, Stephen Nichols and Days**
37663 Charter Oaks Blvd.
Mt. Clemens, MI 48043

Katherine Kelly Lang Fan Club
c/o Amy Farina
109 Hughes St.
East Haven, CT 06512

Jill Larson
c/o Michelle Saint-Laurent
1410 York Ave., Apt. 4D
New York, NY 10021

Jean LeClerc
c/o Carol Dickson Entertainment
1218 N. Main St.
Glassboro, NJ 08028

Carol Lawrence National Fan Club
3886 Shattuck Ave.
Columbus, OH 43220

Terry Lester
c/o 11288 Ventura Blvd., Ste. B315
Studio City, CA 91604

Robert Lupone
Manhatten Class Co.
12 West 28th St.
New York, NY 10001

John McCook Fan Club
c/o Mackie Mann
7800 Beverly Blvd., Ste. 3371
Los Angeles, CA 90036

Daniel McVicar Fan Club
c/o Tommy Grant
P.O. Box 215
New Canton, VA 23123

Shelly Taylor Morgan
c/o The Home Show
4151 Prospect Ave.
Los Angeles, CA 90027

Ron Moss Fan Club
c/o Mackie Mann
7800 Beverly Blvd., Ste. 3371
Los Angeles, CA 90036

One Life to Live Fan Club
c/o Carol Dickson Entertainment
1218 N. Main St.
Glassboro, NJ 08028

Janis Paige
c/o Sandy Lane
5619 1/2 Willowcrest
N. Hollywood, CA 91601

J. Eddie Peck
P.O. Box 10835
Burbank, CA 91510-10835

Ashley Peldon
c/o Leslie Penny
c/o Rita Anne Salk Public Relations
250 West 57th St.
New York, NY 10019

Lisa Peluso Fan Club
c/o Shauna Sickinger
103 W. 80th St., Apt. 4C
New York, NY 10024

Elaine Princi Fan Club
c/o Scott Carson
496 Hudson St., Ste. K64
New York, NY 10014

National Days Fan Club
c/o Polly Hazen
424 A Johnson St.
Sausalito, CA 94965

John Rielly Fan Club
c/o Debbie Morris
13518 Louisville St.
Houston, TX 77015

Sandi Reinhardt Fan Club
c/o Patricia Weaver
660 Nereid Ave., Apt. 6E
Bronx, NY 10470

Clint Ritchie Official Fan Club
c/o Nadine Shanfeld
140 Alexander Ave.
Staten Island, NY 10312

Santa Barbara Fan Club
c/o Kim Jalet
P.O. Box 9080
Albany, NY 12209

Erika Slezak Official Fan Club
c/o Walter Miller, Jr.
2375 Hudson Terrace Apt. 2E
Fort Lee, NJ 07024

Lauren-Marie Taylor
c/o Michele Saint-Laurent
1410 York Avenue, Apt. 4D
New York, NY 10021

Jeff Trachta Fan Club
c/o Jean Smith
7800 Beverly Blvd., Ste. 3371
Los Angeles, CA 90036

Jessica Tuck Fan Club
c/o Debbie Morris
13518 Louisville St.
Houston, TX 77015

Robert Tyler Fan Club
c/o Carol Dickson Entertainment
1218 N. Main St.
Glassboro, NJ 08028

Hunter Tylo Fan Club
c/o Pat Freeman
P.O. Box 214
Lafayette, AL 36882

Jack Wagner Fan Club
P.O. Box 1608
St. Louis, MO 63188

Karen Witter Fan Club
c/o Funky Fan Clubs
P.O. Box 9624
New Haven, CT 06535

Sharon Wyatt Fan Club
c/o Allison Hood
8949 Falling Creek Ct.
Annandale, VA 22003

John J. York Fan Club
c/o Claire Weisberg
13043-3 Hubbard St.
Sylmar, CA 91342

ACTORS INDEX

Adams, Marla, *The Secret Storm; Capital; The Young and the Restless*
Addy, Wesley, *Edge of Night; Ryan's Hope; Loving*
Aleksander, Grant, *Guiding Light; Capital; Guiding Light*
Alex, Marilyn, *General Hospital; As the World Turns; The Young and the Restless*
Alexander, Terry, *Another World; One Life to Live*
Allan, Jed, *Love of Life; The Secret Storm; Days of Our Lives; Santa Barbara*
Ames, Rachel, *General Hospital*
Aniston, John, *Days of Our Lives; Love of Life; Search for Tomorrow; Days of Our Lives*
Anthony, Terrell, *Another World; Guiding Light; All My Children*
Aprea, John, *Days of Our Lives*
Arnold, Tichina, *Ryan's Hope; All My Children*
Arveson, Nina, *The Young and the Restless; Santa Barbara*
Ashford, Matthew, *One Life to Live; Search for Tomorrow; Days of Our Lives*
Backus, Richard, *Lovers and Friends; For Richer, For Poorer; Another World; Ryan's Hope; As the World Turns*
Badler, Jane, *One Life to Live; The Doctors*
Baker, Scott Thompson, *General Hospital; All My Children*
Baler, Laura, *As the World Turns*
Bannon, Jack, *Santa Barbara*
Barr, Hayley, *As the World Turns*
Barr, Julia, *Ryan's Hope; All My Children*
Barrow, Bernard, *Where the Heart Is; Secret Storm; Ryan's Hope; Loving*
Barton, Peter, *The Young and the Restless*
Batten, Susan, *All My Children; One Life to Live*
Beck, John, *Santa Barbara*
Beck, Noelle, *Loving*
Bell, Lauralee, *The Young and the Restless*
Bennett, Meg, *Search for Tomorrow; The Young and the Restless; Santa Barbara*
Beradino, John, *General Hospital*
Bergman, Peter, *All My Children; The Young and the Restless*
Bernard, Robyn, *General Hospital*
Best, Kevin, *General Hospital*
Birn, Laura Bryan, *The Young and the Restless*
Blake, Theresa, *All My Children*
Bleeth, Yasmine, *Ryan's Hope; One Life to Live*
Bonarrigo, Laura, *Another World; One Life to Live*
Bond, Steve, *General Hospital; Santa Barbara*
Bonifant, Evan, *Guiding Light; One Life to Live*
Booth, Bronwen, *One Life to Live*
Borlenghi, Matt, *All My Children*
Borne, Roscoe, *Ryan's Hope; One Life to Live; Santa Barbara*
Boynton, Peter, *One Life to Live; The Catlins; As the World Turns*
Braeden, Eric, *The Young and the Restless*
Brainard, Michael, *All My Children; Santa Barbara*
Breen Joseph, *Guiding Light; Loving; As the World Turns*

Bregman-Recht, Tracey, *Days of Our Lives; The Young and the Restless*
Brettschneider, Mark, *One Life to Live*
Brock, Brenda, *One Life to Live*
Brooks, Randy, *Generations; The Young and the Restless*
Brown, Kimberlin, *Santa Barbara; The Young and the Restless; The Bold and the Beautiful*
Brown, Lisa, *Guiding Light; As the World Turns*
Brown Peter, *Days of Our Lives; The Young and the Restless; Loving; One Life to Live; The Bold and the Beautiful*
Bruder, Patricia, *As the World Turns*
Bryant, Lee, *Another World; As the World Turns*
Byrggman, Larry, *Love is a Many Splendored Thing; As the World Turns*
Buchanan, Ian, *General Hospital*
Buchanan, Jensen, *All My Children; One Life to Live; Another World*
Buffinton, Brian, *Guiding Light*
Burke, Gregory, *Guiding Light*
Burke, Maggie, *Edge of Night; Guiding Light; Another World; One Life to Live; As the World Turns*
Call, Anthony, *Edge of Night; Guiding Light; One Life to Live*
Callahan, John, *General Hospital; Santa Barbara; All My Children*
Canary, David, *Another World; All My Children*
Carey, MacDonald, *Days of Our Lives*
Carey, Philip, *One Life to Live*
Carol, Jean, *Guiding Light*
Carson, Crystal, *General Hospital*
Cass, Christopher, *Loving*
Cast, Tricia, *Santa Barbara; The Young and the Restless*
Castellanos, John, *The Bold and the Beautiful; The Young and the Restless*
Chamberlin, Beth, *Guiding Light*
Chappall, Crystal, *Days of Our Lives*
Charleson, Leslie, *A Flame in the Wind; As the World Turns; Love is a Many Splendored Thing; General Hospital*
Cheatham, Maree, *Days of Our Lives; Search for Tomorrow; General Hospital*
Chris, Marilyn, *One Life to Live*
Christian, William, *Another World; All My Children*
Christopher, Thom, *Edge of Night; Love of Life; One Life to Live*
Clarke, Brian Patrick, *General Hospital; The Bold and the Beautiful*
Clarke, Jordon, *Guiding Light*
Clary, Robert, *Days of Our Lives; The Young and the Restless; The Bold and the Beautiful*
Collins, Jessica, *Loving*
Collins, Kate, *One Life to Live; Guiding Light; Search for Tomorrow; Another World; All My Children*
Conley, Darlene, *The Young and the Restless; Days of Our Lives; Capitol; General Hospital; The Bold and the Beautiful*
Connolly, Norma, *The Young and the Restless; General Hospital*

Considine, John, *Bright Promise; The Young and the Restless; Another World*

Cook, Linda, *Edge of Night; All My Children; Loving*

Cooper, Jeanne, *The Young and the Restless*

Corbett, Michael, *Ryan's Hope; Search for Tomorrow; The Young and the Restless*

Cordell, Melinda, *The Young and the Restless; General Hospital; The Young and the Restless*

Cordova, Margarita, *Days of Our Lives; General Hospital; Santa Barbara*

Coster, Nicholas, *Young Doctor Malone; Secret Storm; Our Private World; As the World Turns; Somerset; One Life to Live; All My Children; Santa Barbara*

Cote, Suzy, *Guiding Light*

Courtney, Jacqueline, *Edge of Night; Our Five Daughters; Another World; One Life to Live; Loving*

Cousins, Christopher, *Another World; As the World Turns; One Life to Live*

Cox, Richard, *Love of Life; Loving*

Crampton, Barbara, *Days of Our Lives; The Young and the Restless*

Crane, Dagne, *Guiding Light; One Life to Live; As the World Turns*

Crane, Matt, *Another World*

Dabney, Augusta, *Young Doctor Malone; Another World; As the World Turns; A World Apart; Guiding Light; General Hospital; The Doctors; Loving*

Dailey, Irene, *Edge of Night; Another World*

Damian, Michael, *The Young and the Restless*

Damon, Stuart, *General Hospital*

Danielson, Shell, *Santa Barbara; General Hospital*

Dano, Linda, *One Life to Live; As the World Turns; Another World*

Darrow, Henry, *Santa Barbara*

Davidson, Doug, *The Young and the Restless*

Davidson, Eileen, *The Young and the Restless; Santa Barbara*

Davis, Terry, *Edge of Night; Another World; Santa Barbara*

DeFreitas, Scott, *As the World Turns*

DeJesus, Wanda, *Another World; Santa Barbara*

DePaiva, James, *General Hospital; One Life to Live*

Derwin, Mark, *The Young and the Restless; Guiding Light*

Diamont, Don, *Days of Our Lives; The Young and the Restless*

Dicopoulos, Frank, *Guiding Light*

Dion, Colleen, *Search for Tomorrow; Loving; The Bold and the Beautiful*

Dolan, Ellen, *Guiding Light; As the World Turns*

Dolenz, Ami, *General Hospital*

Donaldson, Norma, *General Hospital; The Young and the Restless*

Douglas, Jerry, *The Young and the Restless*

Dubac, Robert, *Loving*

Duncan, Carmen, *Another World*

Eakes, Bobbie, *The Bold and the Beautiful*

Earley, Candice, *All My Children*

Easton, Michael, *Days of Our Lives*

Edmonds, Louis, *Young Doctor Malone; Dark Shadows; All My Children*

Ehlers, Beth, *Guiding Light*

Ellingsen, Maria, *Santa Barbara*

Elliot, Jane, *A Flame in the Wind; General Hospital; Guiding Light; All My Children; Days of Our Lives; General Hospital*

Elliott, Patricia, *One Life to Live*

Englund, Morgan, *Guiding Light*

Eplin, Tom, *Another World*

Epperson, Brenda, *The Bold and the Beautiful; The Young and the Restless*

Evans, Judi, *Guiding Light; Days of Our Lives; Another World*

Evans, Michael, *The Young and the Restless; Capitol; The Young and the Restless*

Farrell, Sharon, *The Young and the Restless*

Feinstein, Alan, *Love of Life; Edge of Night; General Hospital; Santa Barbara*

Flannery, Susan, *Days of Our Lives; The Bold and the Beautiful*

Fontaine, Robert, *General Hospital; Santa Barbara*

Ford, Steven, *The Young and the Restless*

Forsyth, David, *Texas; As the World Turns; Search for Tomorrow; Another World*

Fox, Michael, *Clear Horizons; The Bold and the Beautiful*

Frabotta, Don, *Days of Our Lives*

Francis, Genie, *General Hospital; Days of Our Lives; All My Children*

Fry, Ed, *Another World; As the World Turns*

Fulton, Eileen, *As the World Turns*

Gabet, Sharon, *Edge of Night; Another World; One Life to Live*

Galloway, Don, *The Secret Storm; General Hospital*

Garber, Terri, *Texas; Santa Barbara*

Garland, Carrington, *Santa Barbara*

Garrett, Joy, *The Young and the Restless; Days of Our Lives*

Garrett, Maureen, *Guiding Light; Ryan's Hope; Guiding Light*

Gates, Larry, *Guiding Light*

Geary, Anthony, *Bright Promise; The Young and the Restless; General Hospital*

Gibbs, Timothy, *Santa Barbara*

Goldin, Ricky Paull, *Another World*

Grahn, Nancy, *One Life to Live; Santa Barbara*

Grant, Bernard, *Guiding Light; One Life to Live*

Greason, Staci, *Days of Our Lives*

Green, Brian, *Days of Our Lives; Another World*

Gregary, James Michael, *The Young and the Restless*

Gregory, Stephen, *As the World Turns; The Young and the Restless*

Guido, Michael, *All My Children*

Hall, Deidre, *The Young and the Restless; Days of Our Lives*

Hallick, Tom, *The Young and the Restless; Days of Our Lives*

Hallock, Bradley, *Days of Our Lives*

Hammer, Charles Jay, *Texas; Guiding Light*

Harrison, Shae, *General Hospital; The Bold and the Beautiful*

Haskell, Susan, *One Life to Live*

Hastings, Don, *Edge of Night; As the World Turns*
Hayes, Susan Seaforth, *General Hospital; The Young Marrieds; Days of Our Lives; The Young and the Restless; Days of Our Lives*
Hays, Kathryn, *Guiding Light; As the World Turns*
Headley, Shari, *All My Children*
Hearst, Rick, *Days of Our Lives; Guiding Light*
Hedison, David, *Another World*
Heffley, Wayne, *Days of Our Lives*
Hensley, Jon, *One Life to Live; As the World Turns*
Herrera Anthony, *The Young and the Restless; As the World Turns; Loving*
Herring, Laura, *General Hospital*
Herring, Lynn, *General Hospital; Days of Our Lives*
Hertford, Brighton, *General Hospital*
Hogestyn, Drake, *Days of Our Lives*
Holbrook, Anna, *Another World*
Holmes, Scott, *Ryan's Hope; As the World Turns*
Hooyman, Babs, *All My Children*
Hopkins, Kaitlin, *One Life to Live; Another World*
Horan, James, *Another World; Edge of Night; General Hospital; All My Children; Loving*
Hossack, Allison, *Another World*
Hoty, Dee, *Guiding Light; Capitol; As the World Turns*
Hubbard, Elizabeth, *Guiding Light; Edge of Night; The Doctors; As the World Turns*
Huges, Finola, *General Hospital*
Hutchison, Fiona, *As the World Turns; Guiding Light; One Life to Live; Guiding Light*
Irizarry, Vincent, *Guiding Light; Santa Barbara; Guiding Light*
Irvine, Paula, *Santa Barbara*
Jackson, Andrew, *All My Children*
Johnson, Johanna, *The Bold and the Beautiful*
Kanakaredes, Melina, *Guiding Light*
Kasdorf, Lenore, *Guiding Light; Days of Our Lives; Santa Barbara*
Kayzer, Beau, *The Young and the Restless*
Keith, Susan, *One Life to Live; Another World; Loving*
Kelleghan, Peter, *General Hospital*
Kiberd, James, *Loving; All My Children*
Kinkade, Amelia, *The Young and the Restless*
Kinkead, Maeve, *Another World; Guiding Light*
Knight, Michael E., *All My Children*
Korf, Mia, *Another World; Loving; One Life to Live*
Korot, Alla, *Another World*
Koslow, Lauren, *The Young and the Restless; The Bold and the Beautiful*
Krimmer, Wortham, *Days of Our Lives; One Life to Live*
Kristen, Ilene, *Ryan's Hope; One Life to Live; Loving*
Lando, Joe, *One Life to Live*
Lang, Charlie, *Days of Our Lives*
Lang, Katherine Kelly, *The Young and the Restless; The Bold and the Beautiful*
Larson, Jill, *As the World Turns; One Life to Live; All My Children*
Lawrence, Carol, *General Hospital*
Lawrence, Elizabeth, *The Road of Life; Edge of Night; A World Apart; The Doctors; All My Children*
Lawson, Lee, *Love of Life; One Life to Live; Guiding Light*

LeBlanc, Christian, *As the World Turns; The Young and the Restless*
LeClerc, Jean, *The Doctors; One Life to Live; All My Children; Loving*
Lee, Anna, *General Hospital*
Lehman, Edie, *General Hospital*
Leighton, Roberta, *The Young and the Restless; General Hospital; Days of Our Lives*
Lester, Terry, *The Young and the Restless; Santa Barbara*
Lewis, David, *Bright Promise; General Hospital*
Lien, Jennifer, *Another World*
Linder, Kate, *The Young and the Restless*
Linn, Terri Ann, *The Bold and the Beautiful*
Lockerman, Brad, *Capitol; General Hospital*
Long, Nia, *Guiding Light*
Loprieno, John, *Search for Tomorrow; One Life to Live*
Lucci, Susan, *All My Children*
LuPone, Robert, *Ryan's Hope; Search for Tomorrow; All My Children; As the World Turns; Loving; Another World; Guiding Light*
Lupton, John, *Never Too Young; Days of Our Lives*
Lyons, Phyllis, *All My Children*
Mailhouse, Robert, *Days of Our Lives*
Maitland, Beth, *The Young and the Restless*
Malandro, Kristina, *General Hospital*
Mallory, Edward, *Morning Star; Days of Our Lives*
Malloy, Larkin, *Edge of Night; Guiding Light; All My Children; Loving*
Marshall, Amelia, *One Life to Live; Guiding Light*
Martinez, A, *Santa Barbara*
Massey, Marisol, *Loving*
Masters, Marie, *Love of Life; As the World Turns; One Life to Live; As the World Turns*
Mattson, Robin, *Guiding Light; General Hospital; Ryan's Hope; Santa Barbara*
Maule, Brad, *General Hospital*
McCay, Peggy, *Love of Life; For Better or Worse; The Young Marrieds; General Hospital; Days of Our Lives*
McClain, Cady, *All My Children*
McConnell, Judith, *General Hospital; As the World Turns; Another World; One Life to Live; Santa Barbara*
McCook, John, *The Young and the Restless; The Bold and the Beautiful*
McCullough, Kimberly, *General Hospital*
McKee, Todd, *Santa Barbara; The Bold and the Beautiful*
McKenna, Chris, *One Life to Live*
McKinney, Kurt Robin, *Days of Our Lives; General Hospital*
McKinsey, Beverlee, *Love is a Many Splendored Thing; Another World; Texas; Guiding Light*
McVicar, Daniel, *The Bold and the Beautiful*
Meeker, Ken, *One Life to Live*
Michaels, Tommy, *As the World Turns; All My Children*
Middendorf, Tracey, *Days of Our Lives*
Mills, Judson, *As the World Turns*
Miner, Rachel, *Guiding Light*
Mitchell, Ann, *As the World Turns*
Mitchell, James, *Edge of Night; Where the Heart Is; All My Children*
Mitchum, Carrie, *The Bold and the Beautiful*

Moncrieff, Karen, *Guiding Light; Days of Our Lives; The Bold and the Beautiful; Santa Barbara*

Mooney, William, *All My Children; One Life to Live; All My Children*

Moore, Allan Dean, *One Life to Live*

Morgan, Shelley Taylor, *General Hospital; Days of Our Lives*

Moss, Ronn, *The Bold and the Beautiful*

Nadar, Michael, *As the World Turns; All My Children*

Newman, Christine Tudor, *Loving*

Nichols, David, *As the World Turns*

Paige, Janis, *General Hospital; Capitol; Santa Barbara*

Palance, Michael, *Guiding Light; Ryan's Hope; One Life to Live*

Parker, Ellen, *Guiding Light*

Pavia, Ria, *Santa Barbara*

Pease, Patsy, *Search for Tomorrow; Days of Our Lives*

Peck, J. Eddie, *Days of Our Lives*

Peldon, Ashley, *Guiding Light*

Peluso, Lisa, *Search for Tomorrow; One Life to Live; Loving*

Pena, Anthony, *The Young and the Restless; General Hospital; The Young and the Restless*

Pettiford, Valerie, *Another World; One Life to Live*

Phillips, Grace, *One Life to Live*

Phillips, Jeff, *As the World Turns; Guiding Light*

Pierce, Devon, *Santa Barbara; The Young and the Restless*

Pilon, Daniel, *Ryan's Hope; Guiding Light; Days of Our Lives*

Pinkins, Tonya, *As the World Turns; All My Children*

Pinter, Colleen Zenk, *As the World Turns*

Pinter, Mark, *Love of Life; Guiding Light; As the World Turns; Loving; Another World*

Posey, Parker, *As the World Turns*

Pratt, Susan, *General Hospital; Guiding Light; All My Children*

Preston, John, *General Hospital*

Price, Lindsay, *All My Children*

Prince, Clayton, *Ryan's Hope; Another World*

Princi, Elaine, *As the World Turns; Days of Our Lives; One Life to Live*

Prinz, Rosemary, *First Love; As the World Turns; All My Children; How to Survive a Marriage*

Props, Renee, *As the World Turns*

Pruitt, Keith Douglas, *As the World Turns; Loving*

Purdee, Nathan, *General Hospital; The Young and the Restless; Santa Barbara; One Life to Live*

Quinn, Colleen, *Loving*

Rambo, Dack, *Never Too Young; All My Children; Another World*

Ramsey, Gail, *General Hospital; Generations*

Rattray, Heather, *Guiding Light; As the World Turns*

Reckell, Peter, *As the World Turns; Days of Our Lives*

Redd-Forrest, Veronica, *The Young and the Restless*

Redecker, Quinn, *The Young and the Restless; Days of Our Lives; The Young and the Restless*

Reeves, Melissa Brennan, *Santa Barbara; Days of Our Lives*

Reeves, Scott, *Days of Our Lives; The Young and the Restless*

Reilly, John, *As the World Turns; General Hospital*

Reinhardt, Sandra, *Another World*

Reynolds, James, *Days of Our Lives; Generations; Days of Our Lives*

Rice-Taylor, Allison, *All My Children; As the World Turns*

Ripa, Kelly, *All My Children*

Ritchie, Clint, *One Life to Live*

Robinson, Alexia, *General Hospital*

Roerick, William, *The Clear Horizon; Guiding Light*

Rogers, Gil, *All My Children; The Doctors; Search for Tomorrow; Guiding Light*

Rogers, Jane, *General Hospital; Santa Barbara; The Bold and the Beautiful*

Rogers, Lynn, *Guiding Light*

Rogers, Suzanne, *Days of Our Lives*

Rogers, Tristian, *General Hospital*

Ronnie, July, *Santa Barbara*

Rowand, Nada, *Loving*

Rowell, Victoria, *One Life to Live; As the World Turns; The Young and the Restless*

Runyeon, Frank, *As the World Turns; Santa Barbara; General Hospital*

Ryan, Michael, *Ben Jerrod; Another World; Another Life*

Sabatino, Michael, *Days of Our Lives*

Savage, Elizabeth, *General Hospital; Loving*

Schnetzer, Stephen, *Days of Our Lives; One Life to Live; Another World*

Scott, Melody Thomas, *The Young and the Restless*

Shaugnessy, Charles, *General Hospital; Days of Our Lives*

Shelton, Sloane, *As the World Turns*

Shoberg, Richard, *Somerset; Edge of Night; All My Children*

Shriner, Kin, *General Hospital; Texas; General Hospital*

Simms, Kimberly, *Guiding Light*

Simon, Peter, *Search for Tomorrow; As the World Turns; Guiding Light*

Sisk, Laura, *Loving*

Slate, Jeremy, *One Life to Live; Guiding Light*

Slezak, Erika, *One Life to Live*

Sloan, Tina, *Somerset; Search for Tomorrow; Another World; Guiding Light*

Smith, Hilary Bailey, *The Doctors; As the World Turns; One Life to Live*

Smith, Rex, *As the World Turns*

Sorel, Louise, *Santa Barbara; One Life to Live; Days of Our Lives*

St. John, Kristoff, *Generations; The Young and the Restless*

Stabb, Leonard, *One Life to Live*

Stauffer, Jack, *All My Children; The Young and the Restless; General Hospital*

Stephens, Perry, *Loving*

Storm, Jim, *One Life to Live; Dark Shadows; Secret Storm; The Doctors; The Young and the Restless; The Bold and the Beautiful*

Storm, Michael, *One Life to Live*

Stovall, Count, *The Doctors; As the World Turns; All My Children*

Stringfield, Sherry, *Guiding Light*

Stuart, Mary Ellen, *Guiding Light; As the World Turns*
Stuart, Patrick, *All My Children*
Swan, Michael, *As the World Turns*
Swan, William, *As the World Turns; The Young and the Restless; All My Children*
Sward, Anne, *As the World Turns*
Tarantina, Brian, *One Life to Live*
Tatum, Bill, *One Life to Live; Edge of Night; As the World Turns*
Taylor, Lauren Marie, *Loving*
Telles, Rick, *Loving*
Templeton, Christopher, *The Young and the Restless*
Thomson, Gordon, *Ryan's Hope; Santa Barbara*
Thorson, Linda, *One Life to Live*
Thrower, Joey, *One Life to Live*
Todd, Russell, *Capitol; Another World*
Tom, Heather, *The Young and the Restless*
Trachta, Jeff, *One Life to Live; Loving; The Bold and the Beautiful*
Tuck, Jessica, *One Life to Live*
Tunie, Tamara, *As the World Turns*
Turco, Paige, *Guiding Light; All My Children*
Turner, Janine, *General Hospital*
Tyler, Robert, *As the World Turns; Loving*
Tylo, Hunter, *All My Children; Days of Our Lives; The Bold and the Beautiful*
Tylo, Michael, *Another World; Guiding Light; All My Children; General Hospital; The Young and the Restless*
Valley, Paul Michael, *Another World*
Valverde, Rawley, *Santa Barbara*
Van Vleet, Richard, *All My Children, Guiding Light, All My Children*
Vassey, Liz, *All My Children*
verDorn, Jerry, *Guiding Light*
Viscardi, John, *One Life to Live*
Vogel, Leslie, *Loving; All My Children; Guiding Light*
Wagner, Helen, *Guiding Light; As the World Turns*
Wagner, Jack, *A New Day in Eden; General Hospital; Santa Barbara*

Walker, Marcy, *All My Children; Santa Barbara*
Walker, Nicholas, *The Doctors, Capitol; General Hospital; One Life to Live; Santa Barbara*
Walker, Tonja, *Capitol; General Hospital; One Life to Live*
Wallace, David, *Days of Our Lives; General Hospital*
Walton, Jess, *Capitol; The Young and the Restless*
Ward, Stuart, *Guiding Light*
Warrick, Ruth, *Guiding Light; As the World Turns; All My Children*
Weaver, Patti, *Days of Our Lives; The Young and the Restless*
Wesley, Cassie, *Guiding Light*
Whitfield, Dondre, *Another World; All My Children*
Widdoes, Kathleen, *Young Doctor Malone; Another World; Ryan's Hope; As the World Turns*
Wiggin, Tom, *Another World; As the World Turns*
Wilkinson, Kate, *Love of Life; Love is a Many Splendored Thing; Guiding Light; Another World; One Life to Live*
Willey, Walt, *Ryan's Hope; Another World; All My Children*
Williams, Stephanie, *The Young and the Restless; General Hospital*
Williams, Tonya Lee, *Generations; The Young and the Restless*
Williams, Vince, *Loving; As the World Turns; Guiding Light*
Wintersole, William, *The Young and the Restless*
Witter, Karen, *One Life to Live*
Wolter, Sherilyn, *General Hospital; Santa Barbara*
Woodall, Eric, *Loving; As the World Turns*
Woods, Robert S., *One Life to Live; Days of Our Lives; One Life to Live*
Wyatt, Sharon, *General Hospital*
Wyndham, Victoria, *Guiding Light; Another World*
York, John J., *General Hospital*
Young, Corey, *General Hospital*
Zaslow, Michael, *Love is a Many Splendored Thing; Search for Tomorrow; Guiding Light; One Life to Live; Guiding Light*
Zeman, Jacklyn, *One Life to Live; General Hospital*

PHOTO CREDITS